# Children's Literature

## Discovery for a Lifetime

Barbara D. Stoodt
*Northern Kentucky University*

Linda B. Amspaugh
*University of Cincinnati*

Jane Hunt
*Guilford County School*

**GORSUCH SCARISBRICK, PUBLISHERS**
An imprint of PRENTICE HALL
Upper Saddle River, New Jersey 07458

To Sarah Price, Kyle Neu, and
Matthew Price, with love,
*Grandma Barbara*

Library of Congress Cataloguing-in-Publication Data
Stoodt, Barbara D.
    Children's literature : discovery for a lifetime / by Barbara D.
Stoodt, Linda B. Amspaugh, Jane Hunt.
        p.    cm.
    Includes bibliographical references and index.
    ISBN 0–89787–540–0 (alk. paper)
    1. Children's literature—Study and teaching (Elementary)
2. Children—Books and reading.    I. Amspaugh, Linda B.    II. Hunt,
Jane, 1958–    . III. Title.
LB1575.S86    1996
372.64 ' 044—dc20                                    96–400

| | |
|---|---|
| *Publisher* | Gay L. Pauley |
| *Editor* | A. Colette Kelly |
| *Developmental Editor* | Katie Bradford |
| *Production Editor* | Patricia Shelton |
| *Cover Design* | Don Giannatti |
| *Interior Design* | Mary B. Cullen |
| *Typesetting* | John and Rhonda Wincek, Aerocraft Charter Art Service |

Credits are listed beginning on page 485, constituting an extension of the copyright page.

10  9  8  7  6  5  4  3

ISBN 0-13-777806-6

Prentice-Hall International (UK) Limited, *London*
Prentice-Hall of Australia Pty. Limited, *Sydney*
Prentice-Hall of Canada, Inc., *Toronto*
Prentice-Hall Hispanoamericana, S. A., *Mexico*
Prentice-Hall of India Private Limited, *New Delhi*
Prentice-Hall of Japan, Inc., *Tokyo*
Pearson Education Asia Pte. Ltd., *Singapore*
Editora Prentice-Hall do Brasil, Ltda., *Rio de Janeiro*

# Abbreviated Contents

# Contents

# Preface

These are exciting times for everyone interested in children's literature. More and more people recognize the significance of children's reading. The rich array of books available to readers includes classics like *Where the Wild Things Are*, *Charlotte's Web*, and *Alexander and the Terrible, Horrible, No Good, Very Bad Day* and wonderful newer books such as the *True Story of the Three Little Pigs*, *Nuts to You*, and *Lyddie*. Children's bookstores are flourishing due to parents' and teachers' growing awareness of the influence of children's books.

While the profusion of books and the widespread interest in literature are welcome, they create an even greater need to educate parents, teachers, and librarians to select books and plan literary experiences. Because children's pleasure in literature can be stymied by the dull, the difficult, and the obscure, it is crucial for adults to optimize children's interactions with literature. Moreover, the curriculum and the textbooks used in elementary classrooms cry out for the richness of literature.

We created this book to help teachers, parents, and librarians bring literature into children's lives very early and to promote a continuing interest in books throughout their lives. The theme of this text is *literature for a lifetime*. In addition, this book seeks to prepare educators to:

- Know which books children will respond to
- Share literature with children in authentic ways that encourage their responses
- Infuse literature into the elementary curriculum, including literature for multicultural education
- Identify books for children with special needs and encourage their responses to literature

Chapters One through Four provide an overview of children' literature, including evaluating and selecting literature and encouraging children's response. Chapters Five through Nine explore the content of children's literature in picture books, poetry, traditional literature, modern fantasy, realistic fiction, and nonfiction. Chapters Ten through Twelve prepare adults to nurture children's response to literature by showing how creating a literary community of readers, authors, and illustrators can enhance experiences with literature and by providing an understanding of oral and silent approaches to literature as well as emergent literacy. Chapter Thirteen explores ways of using real-life literature with children who have special needs, while Chapter Fourteen presents ways of using literature to foster multicultural understanding. The final chapter, Chapter Fifteen, synthesizes and organizes material from the preceding chapters and presents sample guides and units that teachers have used in developing a literature-based curriculum.

Each chapter opens with a list of key terms, guiding questions, and an overview that previews the content of the chapter. Each chapter also includes a vignette that gives examples of teachers and children involved with literature—examples that can be used to model good teaching for the reader. Chapter introductions provide explanations of the accompanying vignettes and relate them to the chapter content. Throughout the book, activities and unit suggestions develop deeper cognitive and affective understandings and critical aesthetic awareness. In addition, each chapter includes thought questions and enrichment activities that recommend both field and literary experiences. Some activities involve students working with children, while others are designed for students who do not have access to children. Finally, each chapter ends with an annotated bibliography of the recommended children's books mentioned in that chapter.

In writing this book, we hope to stimulate parents, teachers, librarians, and caregivers to build children's response to literature. All children can benefit from the enthusiasm, interest, and expertise of adults who know children and their books. By heightening children's understanding and response to literature, we can acquaint them with the joy of literature, thus providing pleasure that will last throughout a lifetime.

## ACKNOWLEDGMENTS

We would like to thank the following reviewers for their pointed and meaningful comments: Susan M. Tancock, Ball State University; Jim Jacobs, Brigham Young University; Norma Sadler, Boise State University; and Leona J. Manke, Albertson College. A special thanks to Albert Spencer, Rice University, whose many constructive suggestions helped shape the final manuscript.

# Children's Literature

## Discovery for a Lifetime

# One

## KEY TERMS

authentic literary
  experiences
basal readers
characters
community of readers
integrated instruction
integration
learner-centered
  literary experiences
literature

literature-based instruction
plot
reader response
setting
story grammar
textbooks
themes
touchstone
trade books
whole language

## GUIDING QUESTIONS

Think about a book that you enjoyed as a child. Can you remember the title or the main character's name? What did you like about this book? What children's books have you read in the last year?

1. What is children's literature?

2. What value does children's literature have in children's lives?

3. What do teachers need to know about children's literature?

4. What constitutes an authentic experience with children's literature?

## OVERVIEW

Do you remember favorite books from childhood days? If so, you were a fortunate child whose response to pleasurable experiences with literature helped create a lifelong love of reading. Stories are a powerful factor in all of our lives; they influence us in untold ways. Children who have a rich variety of literary experiences become literate, caring, cultured, humanized, and informed people (Livingston, 1988). Moreover, contemporary educational thought accentuates the significance of literature in educational processes. The educational processes focus on building children's ability to develop and ponder their own and others' meanings and to respond to these meanings; therefore, literature and building this meaning-making process are central to education.

As the educational influence of children's books has increased, they have become more and more plentiful, more than doubling in number in recent years. This gives teachers, librarians, and parents a large number of books from which to choose as they create inviting literary encounters, but it also makes book selection more crucial than before in finding literature that children will appreciate.

In this chapter, we create a foundation for adults who are concerned with fostering children's literary experiences. We explore the nature of children's literature and its value in children's lives and identify the types of literary backgrounds that facilitate their development of the meaning-making process.

# Introduction to Children's Literature

In the opening vignette, Susan Stanley, a first-grade teacher, selects a trade book rather than a textbook to present to her class. **Trade books** are *books of general interest,* whereas **textbooks** are *books written for specific instructional purposes.* Authors of trade books frequently use vivid language to express thoughts and feelings. Ms. Stanley selects *The Napping House* because of its repetitive, rhythmic language and interesting illustrations. She recognizes that young children love the sounds of words for words' sake and anticipates that first graders will respond to the poetic cadence of language in this story. She consistently encourages her pupils to talk about the authors' language and the artists' illustrations, making it a point to acquaint students with the idea that writers and illustrators communicate through books.

Ms. Stanley also relates *The Napping House* to the children's experiences, establishing a connection that enriches both their understanding and their response. After listening to the story, the children discuss their thoughts and feelings in response to the book, after which the teacher rereads the story so they can build deeper appreciation of it.

This teacher brings children and books together in meaningful ways. Her own enthusiasm for literature sparks her students' interests. She talks about favorite books, authors, and illustrators, so they learn how important literature is in her life. Other teachers, as well as librarians and parents, can likewise build children's enthusiasm for literature with exposure to good books.

Stimulating literary experiences motivate readers to share their thoughts with others and to create **communities of readers,** *informal groups of readers who stimulate, encourage, motivate, and sustain one another's reading activities.* These reading communities give students opportunities to explore exciting literature, to find connections among books, and to relate books to their own lives.

One Tuesday morning in late February, Susan Stanley greeted her students: "I'm so glad you're here! I have a new book to read."

The children stowed their coats and settled on the story rug. Ms. Stanley sat on a low chair and held up *The Napping House.*

"Don and Audrey Wood wrote this funny story and illustrated it with beautiful pictures. They have written many books that we'll enjoy on other days. This one is about a nap. Who can tell us what a nap is?"

Christopher volunteered, "It's when you sleep, but it isn't night."

Then Sarah said, "It's when you sleep in the afternoon." Several children nodded in agreement.

"What words do you think the Woods used to write about a nap?" Ms. Stanley asked.

The children volunteered words and the teacher wrote them on the chalkboard. When they finished brainstorming, the list included *sleeping, napping, snoring, eyes closed, dreaming, nightmares, sleepwalking,* and *wake up.*

Ms. Stanley said, "Close your eyes and think about the place where you take naps and imagine how it looks." She paused for a moment, then continued, "Open your eyes and look at the first illustration. As you listen to the story think about the way you imagined it and the way Don Wood drew it."

She then began to read: "There is a house, a napping house, where everyone is

*(continued)*

sleeping…" As she read, the children joined in on the repetitive lines.

After finishing the story, Ms. Stanley asked, "What surprise was in this story, boys and girls?"

Matt laughed and said, "When the flea bit the mouse and everyone waked up."

"I think it was when the rainbow came out," Jenny said.

"Good thinking," said Ms. Stanley.

"I think it was when the bed broke," said Christy.

"That's a thoughtful answer too," the teacher replied. "Many times we have different ideas about stories because each person thinks differently." Then she asked, "What special things did you notice in this story?"

"The parts where they said the things that happened over and over," said Jeremy.

"Why do you think the writer repeated those parts?" Ms. Stanley asked.

Jimmy said, "Because she wanted us to remember those parts."

"I think it's because the words go together, kind of like a song," Mary said.

After some discussion, Ms. Stanley asked, "What words did Audrey Wood use to talk about napping in this story?" After the children identified *snoozing, dozing, dreaming, snoring,* and *sleeping,* she asked, "Why do you think she used these words?"

Richie said, "Because they tell about sleeping and napping and the story is about the napping house." Many of the children agreed with him.

Then Mark said, "Read it again." So she did.

## WHAT IS LITERATURE?

**Literature** is *thought, experience, and imagination shaped into oral or written language that may include visual images.* There are different forms of literature, such as stories, ballads, family narratives, jokes, jump-rope jingles, street rhymes, videos, paintings, drawings, film, recorded books, and computer programs. Literature entertains listeners and readers, at the same time giving them access to the accumulated experience and wisdom of the ages. "Offering stories to children is the way our print-dominated society carries on a habit even older than writing and as common as bread—telling stories and listening to them" (Meek, 1977). Literature is central to education in that it contributes to readers' growing experiences—extending and enriching knowledge while stimulating reflection.

Stories are a natural part of life. Constructing stories in the mind is a fundamental way of making meaning (Wells, 1986). Through literature and language, humans record, explain, understand, and control their experience. Authors reflect about experiences and events, organizing the significant episodes into a coherent sequence. The order and form thus created shows life's unity and meaning (Lukens, 1986). Reading what others have written about their experiences gives us insight about ourselves and helps put our own experiences in perspective. Clarissa Estes (1992) claims, "Stories are medicine. I have been taken with stories since I heard my first. They have such power; they do not require that we do, be, act anything—we need only listen" (p. 5).

Stories are behind the nightly news, the comics, and the eleven o'clock sports report. When you ask a friend about her experiences in a hurricane, she creates a narrative to tell what happened, helping both of you understand her experience. Victims of shocking experiences such as automobile accidents often need to talk about their experiences in order to comprehend what occurred. Through telling, retelling, believing, and disbelieving stories about each other's pasts, futures, and identities, we come to know one another better.

## What Is Children's Literature?

Children's literature is a part of the mainstream of all literature. It explores, orders, evaluates, and illuminates the human experience—its heights and depths, its pains and pleasures (Saxby and Winch, 1987). Like adults, children learn about the breadth and depth of life from literature. Memorable children's authors skillfully engage readers with the

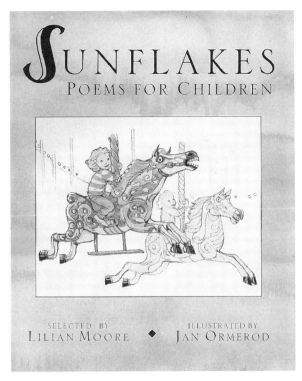

*Fortunate children have a variety of literary experiences. Sunflakes: Poems for Children contains verses by some of America's best poets who write for children.*

information, language, unique plots, and many-faceted characters they create. "By allowing our readers into the soul of a character we are letting them know more than life will ever divulge about another human being" (Paterson, 1981a, p. 35).

Children's literature is literature to which children respond; it relates to their range of experience and is told in language they understand. The primary contrast between children's literature and adult literature takes into account the more limited life experience of the audience, which is significant since readers use experience to understand text. Katherine Paterson (1981a), a noted children's author, says that adult literature is analogous to a symphony orchestra: the themes, characters, plots, and subplots create harmonies like those found among the elements of a great orchestra. On the other hand, fine children's literature has the qualities of the clear, true notes of a flute solo: its beauty and truth are not complicated by experiences that go beyond the readers' ability to understand. Reading and listening to stories, children expand their background and generate meanings that are the foundation for their response to literature, permitting them to comprehend more complex literature as they mature.

## Response to Literature

Readers make books come alive. What they bring to literature is as important as the literary work itself. Readers relate the text they read to life as they know it in order to construct meaning within the text, using the author's words as meaning cues and constructing meaning for the words based on their personal knowledge, associations, and feelings. In this way, readers construct and confer meaning on the text rather than extracting a single, given meaning from it (Smith, 1985; Bleich, 1978; Rosenblatt, 1978). Because each reader brings a different set of experiences to the text, different readers may create different meanings for the same text (Rosenblatt, 1978). In addition, because the meaning of a text depends on the reader's experience, the same reader may construct different meanings for the same text in separate readings of that text. "Each time we talk about a book we discover our sense of it, our ideas about it, our understanding of what it is and means, even the details we remember have changed and shifted and come to us in different arrangements, different patterns" (Chambers, 1983, p. 167).

Responses to literature fall on a broad continuum as shown in Figure 1.1. One kind of response is total absorption in reading; this occurs when a reader enjoys the sense of being a character who is engaged in story events. The reader feels that she is inside the book and does not want it to end (Chambers, 1983). A story may be so delightful that it prompts the reader to hunt for another book by the same author. The reader may want to compare responses with a friend who has read the book. Literature can be so moving that a reader cries, laughs aloud, or hurls the book across the room. At the other end of the continuum, the reader may simply close the book with satisfied feelings, or at times close it before even finishing it.

## FIGURE 1.1

Literary response continuum.

......................................................................................

## BOOK READER

| Uninterested, does not finish book | Somewhat interested | Enjoys book, finds it satisfying | Excited, wants to share feeling about book | Finds book totally absorbing |

......................................................................................

Because understanding the nature of reader response is significant to guiding children's literary experiences, this text is anchored in a response-centered philosophy. Throughout the book we focus on **learner-centered literary experiences** *in which readers' personal responses to literature are the basis of literature explorations.* The general characteristics of **reader response** are:

1. Response implies active involvement of the reader.

2. Response includes both immediate reactions and later effects.

3. Overt responses such as verbal expressions may indicate very little of the reader's inner response. (Harding, 1963)

Giving students occasion to read, discuss, discover, consider, represent, and reread—to make their own meanings—cultivates their response to literature (Hickman and Cullinan, 1989). The activities suggested throughout this book will help adults as they plan ways to foster children's response to literature, a topic explored in detail in Chapter Four.

## THE POWER OF LITERATURE

Books enrich, broaden, and bring joy to children's lives (Paterson, 1981a). However, isolating and identifying the values of children's literature is a daunting task because literature affects our lives so deeply. Literature motivates readers to think, enhances language and cognitive development, and stimulates thinking. It takes them beyond everyday experiences, broadening their background, developing their imagination and sense of humor, enabling them to grow in humanity and understanding (Viguers, 1964). Literature can provide pleasure, relaxation, and opportunities for aesthetic responses. It expands knowledge and experience, helps readers solve problems, and plays a significant role in children's developmental journey. Literature permits readers to walk in someone else's shoes for a time, thus giving them a better understanding of another's feelings. From this beginning, we can formulate some of the major values of children's literature: enjoyment, aesthetics, understanding, imagination, information and knowledge, cognition, and language. These values are examined in this section.

### Providing Enjoyment

Good books give readers pleasure. Some readers respond to an enjoyable book through total immersion, concentrating to the exclusion of all else, laughing or crying as the mood of the story shifts. Others find literary enjoyment from acquiring new, fascinating information from nonfiction. A well-written informational book piques interest in new topics and whets the appetite for more knowledge. For instance, the book *From Hand to Mouth* by James Giblin tells how knives, forks, spoons, chopsticks, and table manners were invented and explains why Americans hold their forks differently than Europeans.

Children respond emotionally to a good book. They enjoy a good laugh with Beverly Cleary's *Ramona Quimby Age 8* (Ramona cracks a raw egg on her head, thinking the egg was boiled) or Jack Prelutsky's poem *Rolling Harvey Down the Hill.* Books such as *The Lottery Rose* by Irene Hunt move readers to tears as they learn about the pain of an abused child's treatment at the hands of his mother and her boyfriend. Their sympathy grows as they learn about Georgie's experiences and their spirits soar as he works through his problems.

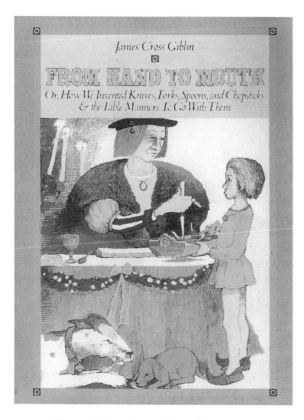

James Cross Giblin

# FROM HAND TO MOUTH

Or, How We Invented Knives, Forks, Spoons, and Chopsticks & the Table Manners To Go With Them

*The goal has always been the same, so this story goes—to get food to the mouth as quickly and gracefully as possible.*

Poetry is a favorite literary form; many readers appreciate poets' efforts to capture the essence of experiences and ideas in language. Poets use everything about language to convey meaning: rhythm, image, metaphor, sound effect, tone, word choice, and line length. In poetry, what is unsaid is as important as what is said because readers use their own experiences to interpret these silences and construct meaning from the poem.

Readers who experience pleasure in literature read more and more. The best literature is so enjoyable that they are oblivious to any value other than enjoyment. Books that obviously preach or teach are often too didactic to invite enjoyment. Unless children can relate to the ideas and experiences expressed, they will not listen to the voice of a work, and often they will not even finish reading it.

Superb writers first and foremost share their stories with readers, who find these stories fascinating and come back for more.

## Perceiving Aesthetics

Aesthetics pertain to the beauty readers perceive in a literary work. Literature is verbal art that leads readers to appreciate the beauty of language. It adds aesthetic dimensions to readers' lives, leading them to view their personal experiences in different ways. Fiction, nonfiction, and poetry are artistic interpretations of experiences, events, and people. Picture books add the dimension of visual art, which interacts with language to tell a story, create a poem, or impart information.

Readers have personal concepts of beauty that evolve from individual experiences and therefore exhibit considerable variation in literary appreciation. A book that transforms one person may not affect someone else. Of literature he considered second-rate, author W. H. Auden said, "That's just the way I always felt." But his response to first-rate literature was quite different: "Until now, I never knew how I felt. Thanks to this experience, I shall never feel the same way again" (Auden, 1956). Books that project beauty and truth to many different people become classics. In the United States, E. B. White's *Charlotte's Web* and Madeleine L'Engle's *A Wrinkle in Time* are considered classics because they have given so much to so many people for so many years.

## Enhancing Understanding

### Understanding self and others

Books stimulate readers' emotional responses. Readers chuckle over the antics of children on a class trip in *The Day Jimmy's Boa Ate the Wash* by Trinka Hakes Noble and identify with Alexander's feelings in *Alexander and the Terrible, Horrible, No Good, Very Bad Day* by Judith Viorst. They gain insights into different roles in life from *Amazing Grace* by Mary Hoffman. In *The Facts and Fictions of Minna Pratt* by Patricia MacLachan, readers learn about the feelings associated with the precarious journey of growing up.

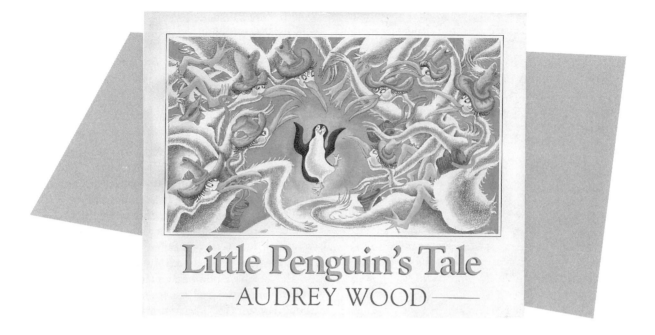

## Little Penguin's Tale
### —AUDREY WOOD—

*Audrey and Don Wood have written and illustrated many books. Readers return again and again to Little Penguin's Tale, only to discover that some of us can just hear a story—and others have to experience it.*

Children acquire compassion for others and insight into their own behavior and feelings from reading. As they read, children begin to realize that others have basically the same feelings as they do, that people around the world share their hopes, dreams, and fears. Through stories children learn about happiness, sadness, warm family relationships, death, and loneliness. Indeed, they learn that many life experiences are universal. They empathize with the title character in Lucille Clifton's *Amifika*, who fears that the father he cannot remember will replace him in his mother's affections. Children also understand the fears of the youngster in Mercer Mayer's *There's a Nightmare in My Closet.*

Reading about story characters' feelings and actions develops children's ability to understand and appreciate others' feelings (Aaron, 1987). Identifying with characters gives readers a deeper involvement with the story, making reading a meaningful experience. In the book *Ramona and Her Mother*, Beverly Cleary depicts Ramona's negative feelings about her working mother, feelings that are familiar to many children in similar situations. Paula Fox helps readers understand Ned's guilt about injuring the cat in *One-Eyed Cat*. In the book *I Have a Sister, My Sister Is Deaf* by Jeanne Whitehouse Peterson, readers learn about the lives of children who have physical impairments. Each of these books addresses the realistic problems and struggles that individuals encounter in life. (Chapters Eight and Fourteen explore this literature in greater depth.)

Today's authors discuss death, birth, anger, mental illness, alcoholism, and brutality more explicitly than was acceptable in earlier times. Adults who have not read recently published children's books may find the realism shocking, but contemporary realism contributes to children's self-understanding. In *Homecoming*, Cynthia Voigt writes about the harsh realities of life. The mother, who is mentally ill, abandons her children. The protagonist, Dicey, takes the responsibility for feeding and sheltering the younger children as she and her siblings set out on foot to find a home. (Chapter Eight addresses understanding and appraising realistic fiction.)

### Understanding cultures

Through identifying with children in other cultures, readers learn about the ties that unite people everywhere. Children who come to understand and appreciate various cultures are more likely to realize that people throughout the world share the same emotions, experiences, and problems. Understanding the shared aspects of life fosters children's appreciation of the cultures that comprise the United States and the world at large.

Traditional literature, often called folktales, acculturates children to the values of their own and others' culture. Such tales help children learn the taboos of cultures, identifying the behavior, attitudes, values, and beliefs that are acceptable and unacceptable. They teach that good is rewarded and evil is punished. Many of the plots and characters appearing in folktales are similar from culture to culture, and reading traditional stories from other cultures helps children realize the similarity of human qualities that exists in all cultures. (Chapter Fourteen explores multicultural literature in greater depth.)

Realistic fiction also develops cultural understanding. In *Zeely*, by Virginia Hamilton, 11-year-old Geeder makes up a story about Zeely, a tall, beautiful, black woman whom she imagines to be like a Watusi queen. In direct contrast to her queenly bearing, Zeely takes care of pigs. Through the contrast, Zeely helps Geeder discover the beauty of living in the present and walking tall.

In Doris Buchanan Smith's *Return to Bitter Creek*, readers meet another strong female character, Lacey, who was born to an unmarried mother in Appalachia. Lacey has never met any of her relatives since her mother ran away from the family who judged her so harshly. The story opens with Lacey, her mother, and her mother's boyfriend traveling to meet the unknown family that rejected her so long ago. When tragedy strikes, they realize the importance of their close-knit family.

## Developing Imagination

Imagination is a creative, constructive power. Every aspect of daily life involves imagination. People imagine as they talk and interact with others, make choices and decisions, analyze news reports, or assess advertising and entertainment (Sloan, 1984). Creative thought and imagination are intimately related to higher-order thinking skills. Creative thinkers strive to develop or invent novel, aesthetic, constructive ideas (Presseisen, 1986; Perkins, 1986; Mansfield and Busse, 1981).

Literature is essential to educating the imagination, as it illustrates the unlimited range of the human imagination and extends readers' personal visions of possibilities (Frye, 1967). Literature nourishes readers' creative processes by stirring and stretching the imagination, providing new information, ideas, and perspectives so that readers can imagine possibilities and elaborate on original ideas. In this way, it expands readers' ability to express imagination in words and images.

Many children's books inspire creative thought. The imaginary worlds that writers create help readers understand the real world. For instance, in *Conrad's Castle*, Ben Shecter writes about a young boy who builds a magnificent castle in the air, which crumbles when a bird says, "That's impossible." A determined Conrad, however, rebuilds his castle in the air. Books such as this one connect real and make-believe worlds, making it clear to children that imagining is a valuable activity.

Older children respond to William Steig's flights of imagination and rich prose in *Abel's Island*. In this story, Abel, who is something of a dandy, finds himself marooned on an island after venturing into a violent rainstorm to retrieve his wife's scarf. While on the uninhabited island, Abel has time to contemplate nature and create many sculptures.

After a year on the island, he is able to return home to his wife and resume their life together.

Literature set in the contemporary world also enriches children's imagination. For example, Stephen Manes's popular books *Be a Perfect Person in Just Three Days!* and *Make Four Million Dollars by Next Thursday* appeal to the imaginative energies of middle-grade students through the adventures of Jason Nozzle, who uses Dr. K. Pinkerton Silverfish's rules for becoming a perfect person in just three days. In the sequel, he applies Dr. Silverfish's rules for making four million dollars.

## Increasing Information and Knowledge

Children find the real world and real events fascinating. Reading enables them to participate in experiences that go far beyond mere facts. Trade books often give readers a sense of people, times,

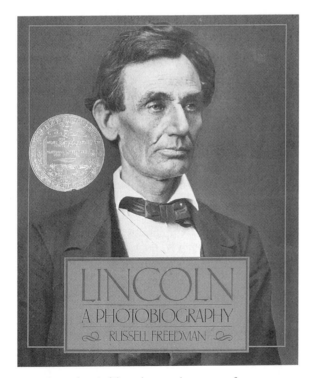

*Lincoln: A Photobiography is an informational book that concludes with a sampling of Lincoln's writings and a detailed list of Lincoln historical sites.*

and places that textbooks do not, because they draw from all types of subjects to expand children's background experiences. For instance, Russell Freedman's photobiography, *Lincoln*, is a trade book concerning a topic addressed in many textbooks, but Freedman's vivid, interesting style appeals to readers, providing a different perspective. "Abraham Lincoln wasn't the sort of man who could lose himself in a crowd. After all, he stood six feet four inches tall, and to top it off, he wore a high silk hat" (p. 1). This superb introduction gives readers a greater sense of Lincoln's physical presence than a mere statement of his height. Freedman uses photos and text to reveal the complexity of Lincoln's character and achievements.

Fine nonfiction writers not only increase their readers' store of knowledge, they also stimulate readers to think about the many dimensions of the concepts explored in their books, encouraging questioning and critical thinking. Often their readers discover new interests as well, continuing to explore the topic that has been opened to them. James Giblin arouses interest in an unlikely topic in his book *Let There Be Light* by exploring the function, history, beauty, and significance of windows.

Nonfiction and informational books can also give children an awareness of things they have not yet experienced for themselves. In *Planting a Rainbow* by Lois Ehlert, readers share a young child's experiences planting flowers, enabling them to experience the brilliant rainbow colors of summer and the flowers that produce these colors. The illustrator's clear, simple pictures expand readers' awareness of nature.

## Stimulating Cognition

Literature is a way of thinking. It serves as a source of knowledge and a sounding board for children's reasoning. All literature, stories and poems as well as nonfiction, stimulates thinking by giving readers substance for reflection; this facilitates cognitive development (Ennis, 1989). Authorities such as Barbara Hardy (1977) believe we tell ourselves stories about the way the world works, and such stories help us think about and understand our world. For instance, in the fictional *Alexander and the Terrible, Horrible, No Good, Very Bad Day*, Judith

Viorst recounts the events in a day when everything went wrong for Alexander. Children identify with the ups and downs of Alexander's life, connecting his day to their own "terrible, horrible, no good, very bad" days. On the other hand, the nonfiction *The Complete Frog* by Elizabeth Lacey introduces interesting facts about ordinary and exotic frogs, prompting readers to think about frogs they have seen and to seek more information.

Literature is a forum that can offer readers diverse perspectives on familiar topics by giving readers a safe medium for trying different roles, imagining new settings, and puzzling out unique solutions to problems. Many books model thinking processes such as problem solving, inferencing, evaluative thinking, relational thinking, and imagining. Consider Russell Erickson's *A Toad for Tuesday*, in which George the owl plans to eat his captive toad, Morton, on Tuesday. Faced with this life-threatening problem, Morton generates several life-saving alternatives. (Chapters Four, Eight, and Fifteen explore these ideas further.)

### Providing a Language Model

Language and thinking are so closely interrelated that "the ability to think for one's self depends upon one's mastery of the language" (Didion, 1968). Exposure to language as an interactive process is a critical factor in acquiring higher-order thinking (Healy, 1991). Literature assumes greater importance when considered as a model of language and the interactive language process.

Children acquire language through such social activities as conversations, hearing and telling stories, and discussions. Literature, however, often furnishes a richer model for language than conversation, as authors frequently use elaborate sentences and sumptuous words, while speakers tend to employ the same few words over and over in conversation. Children learn language from literature when the stories are associated with their experiences so that they can relate to the text and build meaning from it. Children appreciate authors' artistry with language in books and will repeat phrases and sentences they like over and over. In *Swimmy*, Leo Lionni provides a rich language model, with a lobster that walks like a "water-moving machine" and an "eel with a tail that is too long to remember." Such literature expands children's range of experience and enriches their language; from this store of language they develop a greater facility in thinking, imagining, reading, and writing. Thus literature has a major impact on language and thought because children incorporate literary language and use it to express their ideas. Teachers, parents, and librarians often hear children use language acquired from their favorite stories.

Literary experiences are necessary throughout the life span but are most important in the early years when children are establishing foundations for future development. "Literature is a continuous process from childhood onward, not a body of work sprung full-blown from the heads of adults who never read or were read to as children" (Yolen, 1981b, p. 9). Furthermore, researchers tell us that "the single most important activity for building the knowledge required for eventual success in reading is reading aloud to children" (Anderson, Hiebert, Scott, and Wilkinson, 1985, p. 23). In the same vein, Adrian Chambers (1983) writes that "a child who comes to school at the age of 5 without certain kinds of literary experience is a deprived child" (p. 13). (Chapters Three and Thirteen explore these important concepts further.)

## LITERATURE AND THE CURRICULUM

Literature is central to the elementary curriculum because it gives students access to the accumulated experience and wisdom of the past. Integrating literature in the curriculum can enhance learning in all subject areas and is possible regardless of the prevailing philosophy of learning. In schools with more traditional philosophies, literature enhances textbook-based lessons. More contemporary teaching philosophies—often called literature-based instruction, integrated instruction, or whole language—tend to be based on literature, although teachers tend to vary widely in their implementation of these approaches to instruction (Pahl and Monson, 1992). This section explores the use of literature throughout the curriculum.

## Traditional Teaching Philosophies

Traditional reading instruction is a part-to-whole process with initial instruction focusing on words or sounds, then moving to wholes such as stories, poems, and nonfiction. Sequenced sets of reading skills are central to traditional teaching. Instruction helps children learn to recognize words in print. They also learn to unlock new words. Children practice their reading skills with materials in a **basal reader** *comprised of short stories and rewritten children's literature.* Basal reading programs include guidebooks that give teachers background, discussion questions, and exercises to develop children's reading skills. Students practice their reading skills in the workbooks that accompany basal readers. Teachers assess children's progress with the tests included in the basal program.

## Contemporary Teaching Philosophies

Contemporary views of literacy are based on the philosophy that children learn best when they read real texts for reasons that make sense to them, and this is the basis for **literature-based instruction.** Just as they learn to write through communicating ideas and information for reasons that make sense to them, *they learn to read through meaningful interactions with text that has meaningful content.* Moreover, there is a growing realization that literacy develops best in classrooms in which the guiding philosophy is **integration** across the instructional areas—which means that language arts, social studies, science, and math are *connected rather than separated in teaching and learning.* Integration may involve connecting all of these subjects or only some of them, depending on the topic and instructional goals.

### Whole language

*Integrated instruction and literature-based instruction are components of the* **whole language** approach, which is a philosophy and a set of beliefs that can be interpreted and applied in many different ways rather than a single teaching approach or method (Weaver, 1994). Teachers vary widely in their individual interpretations of whole language and literature-based instruction; however, whole language philosophies vary significantly from country to country. In Australia and New Zealand, the whole language philosophy emphasizes more direct instruction than is usual in the United States (Weaver, 1994).

Most whole language programs in the United States concentrate on helping children learn to read with literature rather than basal readers. Most instructors (although not all) who use whole language plan child-centered literary experiences, seeking to provide children with *whole* literature to experience rather than spending weeks on each story, concentrating on it piece by piece, answering many questions about each segment or chapter, and completing workbooks or duplicated worksheets that accompany the story. They feel that this approach to reading and responding to literature guarantees that children will not have opportunities to construct meaning or to develop their own response to and appreciation for a given work. In general, proponents of whole language promote authentic literary experiences that will preserve the integrity of literature.

### Integrated instruction

**Integrated instruction,** or interdisciplinary instruction, enables students to see the connectedness of separate subjects. An integrated curriculum is one in which teachers plan for *students to learn language at the same time they are learning something else,* which may be science, social studies, math, or art, or even a project such as planning a program for an assembly. New knowledge more often than not is created interdisciplinarily (Harste, 1993). For example, new scientific knowledge is generally interrelated with social and cultural aspects of life. In the same way, language learning does not occur in a vacuum but is always context bound (Wilson, Malmgren, Ramage, and Schulz, 1993). These contexts anchor students' language learning so that it is meaningful to them and not simply arbitrary instruction by the teacher.

Integrated instruction enables learners to make connections and find patterns throughout their daily lives, carrying ideas from one subject to another. Learning is a process of making connections and finding patterns (Vygotsky, 1978; Short, 1993), and the most productive learning experiences occur when students connect their old knowledge with new experiences (Short, 1993). Students who have opportunities to make connections and find patterns in their experiences are developing a zone of optimal learning (Vygotsky, 1978). When students cannot make connections, they cannot learn. This is why integrated instruction, thematic units, and literature-based instruction support optimal learning.

### Literature-based instruction

Many educators recognize that children's literature is an important aspect of developing literacy and is not restricted to whole language. Children who learn to read in traditional classrooms, which tend to separate language arts from other subjects, may develop a foundation for reading, but they need a quality literature program so they can apply their reading skills in context, using "real" books. Canavan and Sanborn (1992) identify children's literature that can be used with a traditional basal program effectively. They also identify the particular skills that the books emphasize, focusing on these skills:

1. letter recognition
2. letter-sound association
3. decoding skills—context clues, syntax clues, word structure clues
4. sight vocabulary

## Literature and Language Arts

Children's literature is essential to teaching and learning the language arts, which encompass speaking, listening, reading, and writing. Much of the content for teaching speaking, listening, reading, and writing is taken from children's books. Reading to children builds their sense of story and enhances their understanding of the ways authors structure and organize text (Meyer and Rice, 1984). For example, children who hear and read many stories

# Planting a Rainbow by Lois Ehlert

*This informational book illustrates and identifies by name more than 20 different flowers and plants.*

can adjust their expectations to new stories and even predict how the stories will progress. Different types of literature have unique structures (discussed more fully in Chapters Two through Seven).

The power of language is extended as children read and listen to stories and poems. Elkind (1978) observed that children "who from an early age are exposed to good literature begin to get a sense of the power and beauty of language." Children can learn about language and literature through finger rhymes like "John Brown's Baby Had a Cold Upon Its Chest" and other interactive rhymes in Marc Brown's *Finger Rhymes*. They also enjoy chanting the repeated phrases and rhythmic language found in some books. They savor the language in books such as *Goodnight Moon*, *Elbert's Bad Word*, and *One Monday Morning* by Margaret Wise Brown, Audrey and Don Wood, and Uri Shulevitz, respectively. After reading these books, parents and teachers often hear children repeating words, phrases, and sounds they have learned.

### Literature and writing

Most writers are also avid readers (Stotsky, 1984). When prominent authors were asked to advise young writers about ways to improve their writing, they consistently stated that reading was indispensable for learning to write (Gallo, 1977). Literature provides young writers with a source of ideas and inspiration as well as structural models for organizing ideas in text. Graves (1983) recommends "surrounding children with literature" to prepare them for writing.

Reading cultivates writing abilities because it enlarges children's sensitivity to and understanding of language, thus enabling them to choose the words and create the syntax that best express their thoughts. Fiction, exposition, and poetry help children remember what they have read, promote their sense of the ways in which discourse may be structured, and give them patterns for structuring their own writing. Research reveals that the stories children write reflect the characteristics of their reading materials (Eckhoff, 1983; DeFord, 1981; Bissex, 1980). Children whose reading reflects a wide range of writing structures, complex sentence patterns, and rich vocabulary exhibit these characteristics in their own writing; whereas those who read simple, repetitious stories also write in a simple, repetitive style. Reading and discussing a wide variety of stories seem to help students discover the ways authors create meaning in written language, as these children are more sensitive to plot, character, setting, and writing style than their less well-read peers (Calkins, 1986; Graves, 1983; Smith, 1982).

### Literature and fine arts

Writers are verbal artists who use language as their medium, but other artists search for truth in visual art, music, and drama. Literature is an excellent medium for cultivating children's appreciation of the fine arts. They can learn about music from books such as *A Very Young Musician*, a photo essay by Jill Kremetz based on the experiences of a young trumpet player. In *Picture This: A First Introduction to Paintings*, Felicity Woolf introduces 24 paintings to illustrate styles of art and the changes in artistic style that have occurred over time.

Art, music, and drama provide children with the means to express their responses to literature. Students can choose the medium that reflects their own individual interests and talents for interpreting and extending the books they read. One child may create a mural to express appreciation of a book. Another may paint or draw a picture to illustrate feelings about a story or poem. Still others may use music to recreate the mood of a story or poem.

### Literature and Other Content Areas

Literature supports learning in other content areas as well; it can make a topic memorable and understandable by widening the reader's world beyond the immediate time and place. Reading is an instrument for accessing ideas and information. Moreover, it gives students opportunities to interact with one another and to understand the ways that others think and respond. For example, students who read Kurusa's true story *The Streets Are Free* for a social studies unit learn that Venezuelan children became community activists to get a playground. They learn that Venezuelan children have some of the same concerns as children in the United States.

Literature also enables students to generate hypotheses and cultivate multiple perspectives, ways of thinking that are used in all subject areas (Bruner, 1986). For instance, scientists generate hypotheses and test these hypotheses through experiments. Social scientists examine various cultures using multiple perspectives to help them understand the differences within cultures. Reading literature gives students the content to generate hypotheses and to understand different perspectives.

Literature is an excellent vehicle for interrelating and integrating science and social science. Consider the book *Water Sky*, which portrays cultural change through an Inuit youngster's search for his cultural heritage. Jean Craighead George carefully researched cultural change and scientific information to create an accurate portrayal that goes beyond mere facts and descriptions. For example, the scientific information revealed how sled dogs were trained and managed, as well as how to drive them on different types of snow. Moreover, the author expressed the feelings and sensory experiences of a driver who communes with the dogs as they fly over the snow. Readers can identify with the main character and experience the story through his eyes, giving them a

*Each time the doorbell rings, readers of this book get another exercise in the mathematical skill of division.*

greater understanding of another culture. Students who read and write about science thoughtfully get a picture of how scientists think and communicate (Shanahan, Robinson, and Schneider, 1993).

The role of literature in science and social science is clear, but literature as a means of enriching mathematics understandings and concepts may appear less useful. Nevertheless, literature can indeed contribute to the subject of mathematics. In *The Doorbell Rang* by Pat Hutchins, children learn about one-to-one correspondence when the people in the story try to bake enough cookies for all their guests. Both novels and informational books can be used to develop logic, problem solving, and mathematics concepts. In *The King's Chessboard*, based on a folktale from ancient India, David Birch demonstrates the squaring of numbers.

Literature enhances understandings across the curriculum at all grade levels. Preschool students acquire concepts about street signs from books like Tana Hoban's *I Read Signs* and learn about different occupations from Margaret Miller's marvelous photographs in *Guess Who?*, while primary-grade children acquire concepts of biology from books such as Carol and David Carrick's *The Blue Lobster, A Life Cycle*. Children learn ways of helping adults in the yard, around the house, on the farm and at

school in George Ancona's photo essay *Helping Out*. These and other informational books enhance children's subject matter knowledge.

## EXPERIENCING LITERATURE

Reading is a demanding activity that requires a significant expenditure of energy. Interesting literature can increase students' willingness to put forth this energy and cultivate their desire to read. For instance, discovering the heartfelt friendship between a mouse and a whale in a book like William Steig's *Amos and Boris* motivates many children to read, and reading such stories aloud is a good means of initially engaging children's interest. "Although being read to is not reading for oneself, it is unquestionably the prerequisite for developing a desire to do so" (Sloan, 1984, p. 2).

Clearly, literature is a major asset in creating within students the desire to read, an unquestionably crucial skill in education. Children need a host of reading experiences to build interest and motivation. These experiences should include all types of literature. As students read more and more books they establish a basis for comparison that in time will lead them to recognize the qualities of fine writing. Moreover, offering children extensive opportunities to discuss books encourages students to weigh their own responses against those of others in their community of readers. This section explores ways of offering children opportunities to explore literature as well as ways of structuring and nurturing these experiences.

### Creating Effective Literary Experiences

The major approaches to creating effective literary experiences are the story approach, the great books or classics approach, the author approach, and the unit approach.

#### The story approach

The story approach focuses on literary genre and the elements of literature. The genre of literature commonly included in children's literature are picture books, traditional literature, fantasy, poetry, contemporary realistic fiction, historical fiction, biography, and informational books. Literary genre and the elements of literature as aspects of children's literature are discussed in detail in Chapters Two, Five, Six, Seven, Eight, and Nine.

### The great books or classics approach

A great books approach to literature focuses on works of established literary value. These books become models of quality for readers and writers. There are many lists, reviews, and evaluations of children's books that teachers and librarians can consult for information and guidance in choosing great books. Chapter Three examines great books, sources of information about them, and their relationship to children's reading interests.

### The author approach

The author approach focuses on in-depth studies of authors and their writings. In studying an author, students often read all or many of the books the author has written, which gives them a sense of the author's body of work. As readers explore the various writings by an author, they scrutinize writing styles, techniques, and subjects and usually research the author's background and experiences and relate these to the body of work. These studies develop children's understanding of the relationship between reading and writing. More and more books and biographies of children's writers are being published, most of which provide photographs, interviews, and author explanations of their work. Videos featuring current children's authors also enrich these studies. This approach is examined in depth in Chapter Ten.

### The unit approach

In developing literature units, teachers may choose a diverse collection of literary and artistic styles to build students' in-depth understandings of a concept. For instance, a thematic unit focusing on courage amplifies children's understanding of ideas such as moral courage, physical courage, integrity, and responsibility. The theme of courage could be developed through poetry, fiction, nonfiction, and fine arts.

**Themes** are *important ideas or universal understandings* that evolve from reading a work or works of literature. One of several themes emerging from Maurice Sendak's *Where the Wild Things Are* is children's anger with parents when they are punished, although they continue to need the reassurance of parental love. Thematic understanding emerges gradually from reading a variety of related materials; therefore, thematic units are organized around all types of literature, including fiction, nonfiction, and poetry.

Subject-matter units address topics, such as farm life, problem solving, or the circus, rather than themes. In developing these units, teachers select a variety of materials that enrich students' understanding of the focus topic. Chapter Fifteen explores various kinds of units.

## The Teacher and Children's Literature

Teachers who share their own pleasure in literature help children recognize the meaning and value that books can have in their lives. Enthusiastic teachers create classrooms where children read books, talk about them, experience them, and learn to love them. Teachers who share their favorite books and who read aloud to children create warm, literate environments and a community of readers within their classrooms. This section identifies and discusses the knowledge, skills, and attitudes that enable teachers, librarians, and other concerned adults to create exciting literary experiences for children.

*Know a wide variety of books written for children.* This is a formidable task, since more than 6,000 children's books are published each year. Obviously, teachers cannot read every available book. They can, however, use reviews of children's books to identify a sampling from different genre as a basis for selecting books to read aloud and for developing units of study. Knowledgeable teachers can help children find appealing books and suggest ones related to their interests.

In the early stages of learning about children's books, teachers and students read widely, voraciously, and indiscriminately. They read entertaining books that engage their attention. This reading style enables them to compare books and authors and eventually identify touchstone

## FIGURE 1.2

Front and back of card-file card.

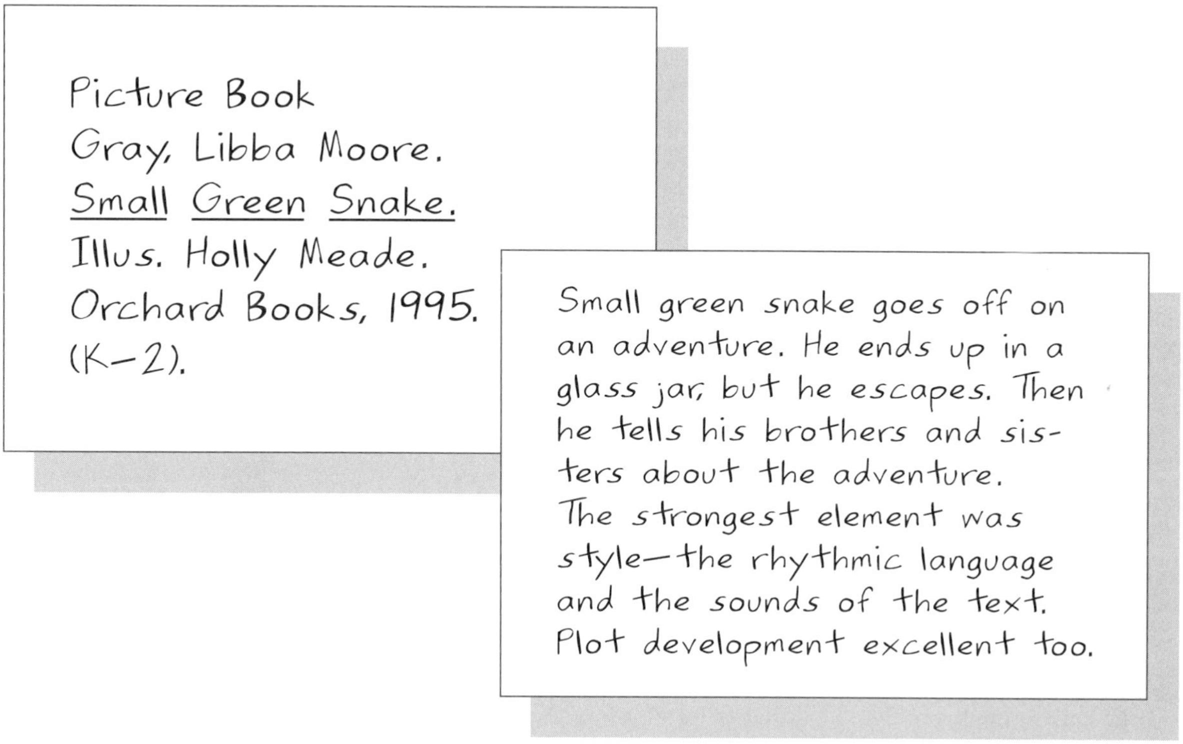

Picture Book
Gray, Libba Moore.
Small Green Snake.
Illus. Holly Meade.
Orchard Books, 1995.
(K—2).

Small green snake goes off on an adventure. He ends up in a glass jar, but he escapes. Then he tells his brothers and sisters about the adventure.
The strongest element was style—the rhythmic language and the sounds of the text.
Plot development excellent too.

books that represent standards of literary quality against which they can compare subsequent reading. According to Holman, Hugh, and Harmon (1986) a touchstone is a hard black stone used to test the quality of gold or silver. The term **touchstone** was used by Matthew Arnold as a metaphor for *literary work that meets a critical standard:* "lines and expressions of the great masters" that the critic should hold always in mind when reading (Holman et al., 1986). In this book, the term denotes literature of recognized quality against which to compare other works. For instance, E. B. White's *Charlotte's Web* is a touchstone in fantasy with which we compare other fantasies.

Touchstone books help adults learn about literary quality in children's books. Their knowledge of literary quality helps them select children's books. Children identify their own touchstone books through reading widely and use these books as measures of quality in later reading. Touchstone books are identified in each chapter of this book.

*Identify and read exemplary books in each genre of literature.* Teachers and prospective teachers often keep card files for future reference of the books they read. The first step in creating a file is choosing an organizational structure, such as genre, author, theme, or grade level. Whatever the organizational structure, the file cards should contain basic information such as author's name, title, publisher, year of publication, and appropriate grade levels on one side of the card. The reverse should contain a brief synopsis and identify the outstanding elements in the book (plot, characterization, setting, theme, style). Figure 1.2 shows what a file card might look like.

*Read widely in order to be able to select appropriate books.* Book knowledge enables teachers and other concerned adults to make informed judgments when selecting appropriate books for children. In addition to reading widely, they supplement this knowledge by using book selection tools such as *The Elementary School Library Collection, Bookfinder,* and *Media Yearbook.* They combine book knowledge with understanding of children's development, interests, and reading abilities. Teachers who create a literature-based reading program or a literature-based curriculum choose books that enhance the classroom program. For instance, they identify books that relate to specific themes or topics to generate teaching units. Chapter Fifteen and the appendix will help teachers learn more about these guides.

*Know about children's authors.* As children (and adults) learn about an author they come to feel the person is a friend and a member of their community of readers and writers, so teachers should be prepared to help children find information about authors. Students become very excited when given opportunities to actually meet authors, including children as young as five and six. Teachers and children can learn about authors through reading their works and through profiles published in professional journals, biographies, interviews, and personal appearances.

*Create a warm, literate environment.* In a warm, literate environment, children have time to read each day. Many children in our hectic modern world have limited opportunities to read outside school because they attend after-school programs outside their homes or are involved in a variety of activities. Thus schools play a pivotal role in providing books and creating time to read. A warm, literate environment should include an inviting physical setting in addition to a teacher's positive attitudes toward literacy. The physical environment may feature an attractive book-browsing center, book displays, and bulletin boards for authors' pictures and book jackets. Children are more likely to read when surrounded by inviting reading materials, which teachers can provide through school materials or long-term book loans from public libraries. Many teachers purchase second-hand books and paperbacks for their classroom book collections. All of these materials should be displayed in ways that invite children to pick them up.

*Encourage children's response to literature.* Teachers who understand response theory are better able to provide experiences that build children's response to literature and nurture their growth. As discussed earlier in this chapter, response to literature varies widely, as does readers' expression of their responses. However, realizing that each reader interacts with books and reading situations to create individual responses to a book is a recognition of the importance of stimulating readers to respond in unique ways. Perhaps the most important stimulus of all is a teacher who respects each varying response.

*Understand the genre and elements of literature and story structures.* One way of organizing literature experiences is through the structures that characterize the various genre of children's literature. These include picture books, traditional literature, fantasy, poetry, realistic fiction, historical fiction, biography, and nonfiction. (Chapters Two, Five, Six, Seven, and Eight explore these genre in more detail.)

Studying story **elements** is another approach to understanding literature. Elements include *plot, character, setting, theme,* and *style.* **Plot** is *the sequence of events in a story.* The **characters** are *the people or personified animals or objects who are responsible for the action in the story.* Characters and story events occur in a **setting,** *the place and time of the story.* As the story unfolds a central meaning or theme emerges; this central meaning is usually a universal idea or truth. For example, one of the lasting truths expressed in *Charlotte's Web* is the concept of loyalty in friendship; like many books, this one has several layers of meaning, so that readers may identify other themes that are meaningful to them. (The elements of literature are explained in Chapter Two.)

A story's elements can also be studied through **story grammars,** literary structures organized around *setting, story problem, attempts to solve the problem, and problem resolution.* Figure 1.3 illustrates a story grammar.

*Know storytelling and reading aloud techniques.* Storytelling is a natural activity for children, and oral stories often provide children's first encounter with literature. Stories are so important in children's lives, they should hear stories every day. Reading and telling stories builds teachers' confidence in their ability to entertain and motivate their students. Children also enjoy telling stories and should have occasions to do so. Chapter Eleven explores storytelling and other oral strategies for presenting literature.

*Know strategies for guiding children's literature experiences.* Teachers and other adults concerned about children's response to literature should prepare to introduce books to children. Sharing their own favorite books and authors, guiding discussions, and creating a community of readers and writers in their classrooms are all ways of providing literature experiences. Teachers should give children many opportunities to respond to literature through speaking, listening, reading, writing, and the fine arts.

*Develop authentic literary experiences.* **"Authentic" literary experiences** are those that *preserve the integrity of the literature, that grow out of children's responses* to the books they read. In some instances, their responses will be expressed in thoughts and feelings rather than a concrete project or product. Authentic experiences are those that are founded on the reader's response to the entirety of the piece, to the overall theme, plot, characters, setting, and author style. Fragmenting literature to examine it word by word, line by line, or chapter by chapter reduces the impact of the author's work and can evolve into requiring that children learn the teacher's interpretation and response to a piece rather than encouraging them to construct their own understanding. Authentic literature-based approaches are child-centered and focus on a seamless literary experience.

*Incorporate children's literature throughout the curriculum.* Literature can easily be used to build children's interest in a particular subject area, as discussed earlier in this chapter. Trade books can also be used to provide more current sources of information than textbooks, which are in print longer and may become dated. As more parents, teachers, and school administrators learn the value of literature in the curriculum, teachers have been encouraged to enrich instruction with related literature. Some schools encourage teachers to develop

## FIGURE 1.3

Story grammar.

Title:
Author:

Setting (who, where, when):

 time

 character

 place

Problem:

Efforts to solve the problem (also called events):

 1.

 2.

 3.

 4. (number of events vary)

The resolution:

literature-based programs throughout the curriculum. Literature and content are usually integrated in these programs and the curriculum is built around the various genres of literature.

## SUMMARY

This chapter introduced various concepts of children's literature—literature that children understand and enjoy—and established its importance in the elementary classroom as a means of exploring and seeking meaning in human experience. Successful teachers involve their students with literature on a daily basis by reading aloud and providing time for students to read on their own.

Children's literature includes all types of books that entertain and inform children, including picture books, traditional literature, realistic fiction, historical fiction, biography, fantasy, poetry, and nonfiction, among other media such as narratives, videos, verbal stories, and the fine arts. The content of children's literature is limited only by the experience and understanding of the reader. Teachers should remember that many children's books were intended for children to hear rather than for them to read independently.

Literature has many personal values for children. Foremost among these are entertainment, aesthetics, thinking, and imagination. Learning is an important value of literature in elementary classrooms. Fine books can contribute to learning in language arts, social sciences, science, mathematics, and fine arts.

A knowledge of literature will enable teachers and other adults to select appropriate literature and to guide literature experiences. These experiences can be organized around stories (genre), great books, authors, and units. Many programs utilize all of these approaches.

## THOUGHT QUESTIONS

1. Write your own definition of children's literature.

2. How does literature develop children's imagination?

3. Which values of literature are most important, in your opinion?

4. How is a good children's book like a good adult book? How is it different from an adult book?

5. What do you think you need to learn in order to teach children's literature?

6. Could the same criteria be used to evaluate both adult and children's literature? Why or why not?

## ENRICHMENT ACTIVITIES

1. Interview three of your friends to determine their favorite books from childhood, then interview three children. Compare their responses. What do the responses tell you about children's reading interests?

2. Read three new children's books (published within the last five years). How are they like the ones you read as a child? How are they different? Make file cards for each of these books to start your children's literature file.

3. Interview three teachers. Ask them how often they read aloud and what books they choose to read aloud.

4. Read several books by the same author to help you become acquainted with a children's author. What did you learn about the author from his or her writing? Add these books to your children's literature file.

5. If you are participating in an internship experience accompanying this course, observe the following in your classroom:
   a. How often does the teacher read aloud?
   b. What does the teacher read aloud?
   c. How often do the children independently read trade books?

6. Read one of the children's books mentioned in this chapter and compare your response to the book with this author's comments about it.

# RECOMMENDED CHILDREN'S BOOKS

Ancona, George. (1985). *Helping Out.* New York: Clarion. (preschool–3)

The black and white photographs and the text show many of the ways young children from diverse backgrounds can help adults.

Baylor, Byrd. (1978). *The Other Way to Listen.* Illustrated by Peter Parnall. New York: Scribner's. (2–adult)

This is a book-length poem that explores ways of listening and knowing. The theme is respect for all things.

Birch, David. (1988). *The King's Chessboard.* Illustrated by Devis Greby. New York: Dial. (2–4)

The wiseman asks for an unusual reward, a grain of rice for the first square on his chessboard, and double for the second and so on.

Brown, Marc. (1980). *Finger Rhymes.* New York: Dutton. (preschool)

This is a collection of traditional finger rhymes for young children.

Brown, Margaret Wise. (1947). *Goodnight Moon.* New York: Harper & Row. (3–6)

The main character in this book says goodnight to each of the things in his bedroom.

Carrick, Carol and Donald Carrick. (1975). *The Blue Lobster, A Life Cycle.* New York: Dial. (2–6)

This informational book shows the life cycle of a lobster from birth through adulthood.

Cleary, Beverly. (1988). *A Girl from Yamhill.* New York: Morrow. (4–8)

This is an autobiography of Beverly Cleary, the esteemed author of many children's books. It gives children an understanding of her reasons for writing.

_____ . (1981). *Ramona Quimby Age 8.* New York: Morrow. (3–5)

Ramona has a working mother and a father who has left his job to return to college.

_____ . (1979). *Ramona and Her Mother.* New York: Morrow. (3–5)

Ramona's mother gets a job and Ramona finds her life is changed: she has to take greater responsibility for herself and share chores with her sister, Beezus.

Clifton, Lucille. (1977). *Amifika.* New York: Dutton. (K–2)

Amifika's father is in the army and he is coming home. Amifika is afraid that there will be no room in the apartment for him when his dad returns and that he won't know his father.

Ehlert, Lois. (1988). *Planting a Rainbow.* New York: Harcourt Brace Jovanovich. (K–2)

In simple language, the author discusses planting a flower garden that has all the colors of the rainbow.

Erickson, Russell. (1974). *A Toad for Tuesday.* New York: Lothrop, Lee, and Shepard. (2–4)

A toad is captured by an owl who plans to eat him on Tuesday. The toad tries various ingenious strategies for escaping.

Fox, Paula. (1988). *The Village by the Sea.* New York: Orchard Books. (4–7)

Ten-year-old Emma must stay with her alcoholic aunt and her understanding uncle while her father has surgery. She builds a village by the sea as an escape.

_____ . (1985). *One-Eyed Cat.* New York: Orchard Books. (4–7)

The protagonist must deal with his guilt after seeing a cat that has been shot with an air gun.

Freedman, Russell. (1988). *Lincoln: A Photobiography.* New York: Clarion (4–8)

This well-written photographic essay portrays Lincoln in ways that children can understand.

Friedman, Ina. (1984). *How My Parents Learned to Eat.* Boston: Houghton Mifflin. (2–4)

This humorous story tells how the main character's parents each learned to eat in the traditional ways of the other's culture.

George, Jean Craighead. (1987). *Water Sky.* New York: Harper & Row. (4–8)

An Eskimo boy learns about the importance to his culture of whaling after joining the crew of an Eskimo whaling ship.

Giblin, James. (1987). *From Hand To Mouth: Or How We Invented Knives, Forks, Spoons, and Chopsticks and the Table Manners To Go with Them.* New York: Crowell. (3–8)

The title is actually a survey of the content of this book, which examines history related to eating utensils and manners.

————. (1989). *Let There Be Light.* New York: Crowell. (4–8)

This informational book uses text and photographs to examine the function and beauty of windows.

Hamilton, Virginia. (1967). *Zeely.* New York: Macmillan. (4–8)

Geeder meets Zeely, who Geeder thinks may have been a Watusi queen, and fantasizes about her life.

Hoban, Tana. (1983). *I Read Signs.* New York: Greenwillow. (K–1)

This picture book is based on the signs in our everyday environment.

Hoffman, Mary. (1991). *Amazing Grace.* Illustrated by Caroline Binch. New York: Dial. (3–6)

Amazing Grace loves stories and acting. She hopes to play Peter Pan, but her classmates point out that because she is black and a girl, she cannot be Peter Pan.

Hutchins, Pat. (1986). *The Doorbell Rang.* New York: Greenwillow. (K–2)

Through dividing cookies among friends to give everyone an equal number, children learn about one-to-one correspondence and problem solving.

Hunt, Irene. (1976). *The Lottery Rose.* New York: Scribner's. (4–8)

Georgie, an abused child, is sent to a private school where he begins to heal and build some permanent relationships.

Kremetz, Jill. (1991). *A Very Young Musician.* New York: Simon & Schuster. (3–6)

This photoessay is based on the experiences of a ten-year-old trumpet player.

Kurusa. (1985). *The Streets Are Free.* Illustrated by Monika Doppert. Translated from Spanish by Karen Englander. Toronto: Annick Press. (3–6)

This true story set in Caracas, Venezuela, tells about a group of children who ask the mayor for a playground.

Lacey, Elizabeth. (1989). *The Complete Frog: A Guide for the Very Young Naturalist.* Illustrated by Christopher Santaro. New York: Lothrop. (2–5)

The topflight science writing in this book explores the anatomy, characteristics, and habitat of frogs.

Lauber, Patricia. (1982). *Journey to the Planets.* New York: Crown. (4–6)

This book explores the planets of our solar system. The author–illustrator shows the Earth as it is seen from space, which helps readers conceptualize the solar system.

L'Engle, Madeleine. (1962). *A Wrinkle in Time.* New York: Farrar, Straus & Giroux. (5–8)

Meg and her brother, Charles Wallace, set out to find their missing father. Their search leads to many interesting adventures.

Lionni, Leo. (1963). *Swimmy.* New York: Pantheon. (K–2)

In this picture book about a little fish whose family is eaten by a fierce tuna, the little fish teaches other little fish to swim together like a big fish so they will not be eaten by the tuna or other big fish.

Lord, Bette Bao. (1984). *In the Year of the Boar and Jackie Robinson.* Illustrated by Marc Simont. New York: Harper & Row. (4–6)

A young Chinese girl, Shirley Temple Wong, moves to Brooklyn. As she learns about her new home, she discovers baseball and becomes a Jackie Robinson fan.

MacLachlan, Patricia. (1988). *The Facts and Fictions of Minna Pratt.* New York: Harper & Row. (4–6)

Minna is a musician who meets a boy musician and is very worried about her less than ideal family.

Manes, Stephen. (1991). *Make Four Million Dollars by Next Thursday.* New York: Bantam. (4–6)

Jason Nozzle discovers a book by Dr. K. Pinkerton Silverfish that gives the rules for making four million dollars by next Thursday. He follows the rules.

————. (1989). *Be a Perfect Person in Just Three Days!* New York: Bantam. (4–6)

Jason Nozzle decides to become a perfect person in three days by following Dr. K. Pinkerton Silverfish's rules.

Mayer, Mercer. (1968). *There's a Nightmare in My Closet.* New York: Dial. (K–2)

A boy imagines that there is a nightmare in his bedroom closet. Finally, the nightmare comes out, and the boy discovers that the nightmare is afraid, too.

McPhail, David. (1972). *The Bear's Toothache.* New York: Little, Brown. (5–7)

This imaginative picture book story tells how a boy assists a bear in pulling his painful tooth.

Miller, Margaret. (1994). *Guess Who?* New York: Greenwillow. (4–7)

The photographs in this book introduce people in a variety of occupations.

Noble, Trinka Hakes. (1980). *The Day Jimmy's Boa Ate the Wash.* New York: Dutton. (K–2)

When the class goes to the farm on a field trip, Jimmy takes his boa along. The boa creates havoc on the farm and Jimmy comes home with a pig instead.

Numeroff, Laura. (1985). *If You Give a Mouse a Cookie.* New York: Harper & Row. (K–2).

When the hero of this story offers a mouse a cookie, he has no idea that the mouse will ask for so many other things.

Paterson, Katherine. (1978). *The Great Gilly Hopkins.* New York: Crowell. (4–6)

Gilly is a foster child who resents her placement with Trotter and hopes her mother will rescue her.

————. (1977). *Bridge to Terabithia.* New York: Crowell. (4–7)

Jess makes friends with the new girl in school, who outruns him. Their friendship evolves and they create an imaginary land, but Jess loses his friend.

Peterson, Jeanne Whitehouse. (1977). *I Have a Sister, My Sister Is Deaf.* New York: Harper & Row. (3–5)

This story is about a real person, the author's sister, who happens to be deaf.

Prelutsky, Jack. (1980). *Rolling Harvey Down the Hill.* New York: Greenwillow. (1–6)

A collection of poetry. The title poem is a special favorite of primary-grade children.

Reid, Alastair. (1958). *Ounce Dice Trice.* New York: Little, Brown. (1–6)

This is a book of words. Some are funny, some are serious, some are beautiful, some are rude, and some are just plain odd.

Rey, Hans. (1941). *Curious George*. Boston: Houghton Mifflin. (K–2)

Curious George the monkey, who belongs to the man in the big yellow hat, manages to get into lots of trouble.

Rylant, Cynthia. (1983). *Miss Maggie*. New York: Dutton. (2–4)

Miss Maggie is rumored to have a snake in her house, but during one cold winter Nat learns otherwise. He saves Miss Maggie from freezing and they become friends.

_____ . *When I Was Young in the Mountains*. New York: Dutton. (1–3)

A woman remembers what life in the mountains was like when she was young and lived with her grandparents.

Sendak, Maurice. (1963). *Where the Wild Things Are*. New York: Harper & Row. (all ages)

Max is so wild that his mother sends him to bed without his dinner. Max escapes to where the wild things are, but grows tired of the wild things and returns to where he is loved best of all and finds his dinner waiting.

Shecter, Ben. (1967). *Conrad's Castle*. New York: Harper & Row. (all ages)

Conrad builds a wonderful castle in his imagination until a bird says "that's impossible."

Shulevitz, Uri. (1967). *One Monday Morning*. New York: Scribner's. (1–3)

The size of the imaginary characters who come to visit a little boy increases each day they visit.

Smith, Doris Buchanan. (1986). *Return to Bitter Creek*. New York: Viking. (4–6)

The protagonist meets her grandmother, aunts, and uncles when she returns with her mother to the home that her mother ran away from.

Steig, William. (1976). *Abel's Island*. New York: HarperCollins. (2–4)

Abel, a mouse, is trying to rescue his wife's scarf when he is washed away to an island. He learns to appreciate nature and populates the island with statues.

_____ . (1971). *Amos and Boris*. New York: Farrar, Straus & Giroux. (1–3)

An unexpected friendship blossoms between a mouse and a whale when they help each other.

Van Allsburg, Chris. (1989). *Two Bad Ants*. Boston: Houghton Mifflin. (1–4)

Two ants travel into the jungle of a modern home to obtain sugar crystals. Once there they decide to stay close to the source of the wonder crystals, but they experience the hazards of a kitchen.

Viorst, Judith. (1972). *Alexander and the Terrible, Horrible, No Good, Very Bad Day*. New York: Atheneum. (all ages)

Alexander decides he wants to be in Australia when he encounters all of his pet peeves in one day.

Voigt, Cynthia. (1981). *Homecoming*. New York: Atheneum. (4–6)

Thirteen-year-old Dicey and her brothers and sister have been abandoned by their mother. As the oldest Dicey is responsible for taking her siblings to their grandmother.

Weil, Lisl. (1991). *The First Six Years in the Life of Wolfgang Amadeus Mozart*. Illustrated by Lisl Weil. New York: Holiday House. (K–3)

This picture book concentrates on the early life of the composer. The ink and watercolor illustrations convey some of the exuberance of the Mozart family life.

White, E. B. (1952). *Charlotte's Web*. New York: Harper & Row. (3–6)

Charlotte the spider saves the life of Wilbur the pig. The characters are well drawn and the problem very real in this story. The solution to saving Wilbur's life is unique.

Wood, Audrey and Don Wood. (1984). *The Napping House*. New York: Harcourt Brace Jovanovich. (K–2)

When a child and a series of animals fall to sleep on Granny's bed, they nap until a flea bites a mouse, then they break the bed.

————. (1988). *Elbert's Bad Word*. New York: Harcourt Brace Jovanovich. (K–3)

In this picture book fantasy, Elbert catches a bad word and uses it at an elegant garden party. Elbert learns to control his problem with the help of a wizard.

Woolf, Felicity. (1990). *Picture This: A First Introduction to Paintings*. New York: Doubleday. (4–8)

This book surveys Western art between 1400 and 1950 through 24 paintings chosen to help readers see styles of art and the ways they have changed over time.

# Two

## KEY TERMS

| | |
|---|---|
| antagonist | literary genre |
| cause | nonfiction |
| character | picture book |
| climax | plot |
| conflict | poetry |
| denouement | problem resolution |
| effect | protagonist |
| elements of literature | realistic fiction |
| episode | schemata |
| fantasy | setting |
| figurative language | story grammar |
| foreshadowing | style |
| historical fiction | theme |
| literary convention | traditional literature |

## GUIDING QUESTIONS

Think about the types of books that were your favorites as a child, and classify them according to the genre of children's literature. Do you continue to enjoy the same genre that you enjoyed as a child? How has your taste changed? Understanding how your own literary tastes have developed and changed will help you to understand how children's literary tastes also develop and change. Keep in mind these guiding questions as you read the chapter.

1. Think about the plot and characters in the last book you read. How would you describe the plot? Who was the principal character? How was the character revealed?

2. How do the plots and characters in adult books differ from those in children's books?

3. Why do teachers and librarians need to understand the elements of literature?

## OVERVIEW

Authors express meaning through literary elements and story structures. Children who are read to and who read gradually learn that stories have recurring structural patterns (Applebee, 1978) or conventions that occur again and again in literature for all ages (Sloan, 1984). Thoughtful readers learn through the experience of reading, how authors select, arrange, and structure language to tell stories and poems and give information (Alexander, 1981). Readers who can anticipate the patterns of organization in literature can understand and respond more fully to it, which is not only desirable for the reader, but for the author as well. Speaking for many writers, the author of *The Little Prince* says, "I do not want anyone to read my story carelessly. I have suffered too much grief in setting down these memories" (Saint-Exupéry, 1943).

One way of anticipating the pattern of organization within a particular work is recognizing the genre to which it belongs. Genre are literary classifications or patterns of fiction, according to Van Vliet (1992); however, we also include nonfiction genre patterns. These are found in Chapter Eight. Books classified as belonging to a specific genre share common characteristics, which follow the rules of that genre for the plot, characters, settings, tone, mood, and theme (Van Vliet, 1992). For example, the fantasy genre includes literature that has an element of make-believe: perhaps a place where magical things happen, a futuristic time setting, or any other fantastic element the author chooses to invent.

# Understanding Literature

An understanding of these common elements of literature helps readers in anticipating the patterns of the story, adding to their understanding and response. This understanding comes about as a result of extensive reading—both being read to and reading independently. Reading also enables readers to focus on the ways authors design stories, poems, and information. Readers build implicit understandings about the structural elements of story—plot, character, setting, theme, and style—which they use to construct meaning (Holman et al., 1986). This knowledge of literary elements and story structures is used in conjunction with prior experience to understand books.

This chapter explores the genre classifications, literary elements, and story structures (also called story grammars) commonly found in children's books. As you read, refer to the touchstone books mentioned throughout the chapter as models of excellent literature. Reading exemplary books helps you develop insights regarding literary structures.

## INTRODUCTION

"What is it about?" is the first question children usually ask about a book. Even before they know what genre is, they understand enough of the concept of genre to have some notions about a book before reading or hearing it. The children in the opening vignette listen to a story and discuss their concepts of *real* and *make-believe,* concepts that further contribute to their understanding of fantasy. After experiencing a certain type of genre, readers construct understandings that can be used when reading other books. The vignette illustrates how teachers can develop genre understanding—in this case, fantasy—with primary-grade children.

## VIGNETTE

Christopher wiggled with anticipation as Kathy Lee finished reading *The Porcupine Mouse.*

"Is it real?" he quickly asked.

"Do you mean, did the story really happen?" Ms. Lee asked.

"Yes."

Nora said, "I know, it didn't really happen. The mice had clothes on in the pictures. Mice don't really wear clothes, do they Ms. Lee?"

Then several other first graders chimed in, "Mice don't really wear clothes."

"How can we tell whether a story really happened?" Ms. Lee asked.

"When things happen that we know aren't real." Sarah answered.

"Can you think of any other things in this story that we know couldn't happen in real life?"

"They don't carry luggage," Wong Sun answered.

"They don't buy things to eat at a grocery store," Keesha said.

"I don't think they can bake cookies," Anthony added.

"While I write the things you've said on the chalkboard, think of some things real mice can do," Ms. Lee said.

The resulting chart follows.

*(continued)*

| Make-Believe Mice | Real Mice |
|---|---|
| wear clothes | chew things up |
| bake cookies | run around the house |
| buy food at a grocery | get into food and eat it |
| talk to cats | do not have furniture |
| wear sneakers | do not wear clothes |

After completing the chalkboard comparisons, Kathy read the poem "I Think Mice Are Rather Nice" by Rose Fyleman, which describes real mice. The children compared the poem to their chart. This experience helped them understand some of the characteristics of the fantasy genre.

# GENRE IN CHILDREN'S LITERATURE

*Genre* is a French word that means *kind* or *type*. **Literary genre** are *classifications of literature based on literary form and theme*, works that share common characteristics or conventions. A **literary convention** is *an element of form, style, or content that is universal throughout the genre* (Morner and Rausch, 1991). Each genre of literature has such conventions or universals associated with its literary form. For instance, a convention of **picture books** is the *interaction between illustrations and text*. It is these universal characteristics that permit readers and reviewers to analyze and identify individual books as belonging to a particular genre, a basic step in critically analyzing a book (Frye, 1968). Once readers know that James Howe's

## TABLE 2.1

Distinguishing characteristics of various genre.

| GENRE | DISTINGUISHING CHARACTERISTICS |
|---|---|
| Picture Books | combine pictures and language or depend entirely on pictures |
| Realistic Fiction | could happen in the contemporary world |
| Historical Fiction | set in the past |
| Fantasy | could not happen in the real world; science fiction is fantasy set in the future |
| Traditional Literature | based on the oral tradition, the stories are spread through word of mouth rather than print |
| Poetry | intense, imaginative writing in rhythmic language structured in shorter lines and verses |
| Biography | based on the life of a person who has made a significant contribution to a culture |
| Nonfiction | presents information, explains |

*Bunnicula* is classified as modern fantasy, they expect to find the literary conventions for a fantasy within the book: fantastic elements in the plot, theme, characterization, setting, and style.

## Genre Classifications in Children's Literature

The fundamental patterns, conventions, or universals of literature occur repeatedly in all literature, including children's literature. Children's literature is usually classified into one of these genre: picture book, contemporary realistic fiction, historical fiction, modern fantasy, traditional literature, poetry, biography, and nonfiction (informational). Table 2.1 summarizes the basic distinguishing characteristics of each genre.

- **Realistic fiction** *contains characters that could be real, settings that could exist, and plots that could happen*, although they are products of an author's imagination rather than actual history or fact (Morner and Rausch, 1991). Phyllis Reynolds Naylor's *Shiloh* is realistic fiction about Marty, who likes to practice shooting his rifle in the West Virginia hills. Then he encounters a dog that appears to have been abused and discovers that he would do almost anything to save the dog. Most readers recognize this story could actually happen. Chapter Eight examines realistic fiction in greater detail.

- In **historical fiction** the author tells *a story associated with historical events, characters, incidents, or time periods*. But historical setting alone is not enough to make the book worthwhile; it has to be a good story as well. Avi's book *The Barn* is set in the Oregon Territory in the year 1855. The authentic historical setting is a backdrop for this rich story about understanding the various members of the family as well as the protagonist's developing maturity. Historical fiction is discussed in Chapter Eight.

- Authors of well-written fantasy convince readers to suspend disbelief, so they can believe in the unbelievable for the duration of a story. **Fantasy** is characterized by *one or more imaginary elements*, such as a make-believe world, characters who have magic powers, or imaginary events. Science fiction belongs to the fantasy genre. Writers of science fiction often employ principles of science and physics as yet undiscovered (Morner and Rausch, 1991). Fantasy is examined more fully in Chapter Seven.

- **Traditional literature** is *based on oral tradition:* stories such as *Little Red Riding Hood* have been passed from one generation to the next by word of mouth and not written down until scholars collected them (Morner and Rausch, 1991). Among the oral conventions traditional stories share are formulaic beginnings and endings: *once upon a time* and *they lived happily ever after.* The settings are created in a sentence or two and the characters are stereotypes. Traditional literature is covered in detail in Chapter Seven.

- The poetry genre includes intense and imaginative literature. **Poetry** strives to *capture the essence of an experience in imaginative language*, as Jack Prelutsky captures the essence of zoo animals in his book *Zoo Doings*. Poetry's rich imagery results in a greater concentration of meaning than is found in prose (Morner and Rausch, 1991). Poetry differs visually from other types of literature in that it generally has short lines and is in verse form, often rhyming. Chapter Six discusses poetry in greater detail.

- **Nonfiction** literature is organized and structured around main ideas and supporting details that *present information and explain* in several different styles, such as description, cause and effect, sequential order, comparison, and enumeration. Authors of informational books identify key ideas and themes to grab readers' attention and motivate them to learn more. As nonfiction focuses on actual events, places, people, and facts, authors and illustrators often use photographs and realistic drawings to illustrate these materials. Steve Parker used photographs and drawings to inform readers in *Whales and Dolphins*. Chapter Nine explores nonfiction in depth.

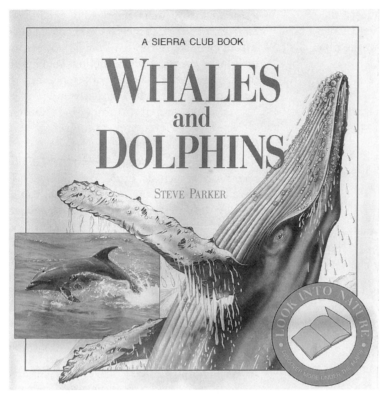

*Special fold-out pages in this book feature the drama of a baleen whale swallowing hundreds of krill in one gulp and an Irrawaddy dolphin giving birth.*

## Genre as a Teaching Tool

Although books within a genre share common characteristics, each piece of literature represents a unique experience. Readers return again and again to books that are unique. For example, both *Little Red Riding Hood* and *Goldilocks and the Three Bears* are traditional literature, but each story has distinct qualities. There are literally hundreds of versions of these tales, and each version has distinctive characteristics. Usually the variants reflect the culture in which the story originated.

The genre approach to organizing literature emphasizes the patterns and structures found in literature. This valid, time-honored approach to structuring children's experiences with literature is commonly used in literature textbooks and children's literature programs (Van Vliet, 1992; Cullinan, 1989; Stewig, 1988; Huck, Hepler, and Hickman, 1987; Norton, 1995). In a genre approach to teaching literature, students learn to understand form and content in books through listening to and reading from the various genre. Gradually, they learn to expect different things in different genre: a story that actually happened will not share many of the elements of a fantasy. In time they learn to recognize the strategies authors use to give credibility to their particular book, identifying the way in which E. B. White grounds the beginning of *Charlotte's Web* in reality to prepare readers for the fantastic elements introduced later in the story.

As they learn to recognize authors' strategies through their many experiences with literature, readers develop a frame of reference or schemata for literature that increases their comprehension of it (Rumelhart and Ortony, 1977; Spiro, 1977). **Schemata** are *clusters of memories based on experience and knowledge about a given topic* (Pearson and Johnson, 1977). These cognitive structures encompass readers' concepts, beliefs, expectations, and processes; virtually everything from a reader's past experience goes into constructing schemata to make sense of things and actions (Anderson and Pearson, 1984). Readers use the schemata of story in conjunction with information provided in the text to comprehend (Adams and Collins, 1986; Stein and Glenn, 1979).

The vignette in the box shows Jeremy, a fifth-grade student, demonstrating how his knowledge of literary elements functions when reading a novel. Jeremy expected to understand the story; his understanding of the language of narrative and narrative structure gave him this confidence (Meyer and Rice, 1984). He anticipated the story elements that appeared in the book because he had read and heard many other stories (Dias, 1987). From his many experiences with books, he had developed a frame of reference for literature.

Like other experienced readers, he anticipated that the story and the story conflict would make sense, and he expected the author to say something of consequence, which increased his comprehension (Adams and Collins, 1986; Culler, 1975).

Teachers use their explicit understanding of literary elements to guide students' experiences with literature as they explore the elements of fiction and nonfiction. The teacher in the vignette encouraged Jeremy to compare *Shades of Gray* with a story of recognized quality to enlarge his understanding. Comparing and contrasting how ideas are expressed in various literary forms and the characters, plots, settings, styles, and themes in a variety of books cultivates students' understanding of the elements of literature and enhances their understanding of how the literary experience operates (Sebesta and Iverson, 1975). Jeremy's teacher could have suggested that he compare this historical fiction with other historical fiction, nonfiction, biographies, or poetry on the same topic to enrich his understanding.

Jeremy Hamilton closed his copy of Carolyn Reeder's *Shades of Gray* and immediately thrust his hand in the air. His fifth-grade teacher, Robert Morse, asked, "What is it, Jeremy?"

"I think there's more than one conflict in this story."

"How many were there?" asked Mr. Morse.

"Well, there's a conflict between Will and his Uncle Jed, and there's the conflict between North and South. Uncle Jed had a conflict with the neighbors, and Will had a conflict with a neighbor boy. How do I know which one is *the* conflict?" Jeremy asked.

"Do you think *Shades of Gray* has more conflicts than other books you have read?" Mr. Morse responded.

"Well, I just read *The Great Gilly Hopkins*," Jeremy said. "I guess it had several conflicts, too."

"What were the conflicts in that book?" Mr. Morse asked.

"Well, Gilly had conflicts with Mrs. Trotter, Agnes, her teacher, and the social worker. Her mother and grandmother had conflicts. That's a lot of conflicts, too. Oh! I just remembered. Gilly had conflicts within herself, too," he answered. "Does that mean that all books have more than one conflict?"

"Many books do," Mr. Morse answered. "Which conflict do you think is the most important one in this story?"

Jeremy responded, "Probably the conflict between Will and Uncle Jed."

After discussing which conflicts were more important, Jeremy said, "I have another problem with this story grammar."

"What's that?" Mr. Morse asked.

"The characters didn't do anything specific to resolve the problem or conflict."

"Then how was it resolved?" Mr. Morse asked.

"Will gradually began to respect his uncle. Especially after the traveling Yankee came to the farm," Jeremy answered.

## LITERARY ELEMENTS

Narrative style is a basic way of organizing human experience employed by authors to help readers see their stories (Hardy, 1977). Joseph Conrad tells us that the novelist's aim is "to make you hear, to make you feel—it is, before all, to make you see" (1922). In much the same way that readers use their own lives as a basis for understanding literature, writers create plot, character, setting, and theme out of their own experiences. A plot is a chain of interacting events, just as life is. Each of us is involved in many plots as our lives unfold: many of you are students, all of you are children, and some of you are parents of your own children. The beginning of a semester or a quarter is similar to the beginning of a story and the final exam is a climax. These various plots are the raw material for stories. Each story leads to another because life happens that way.

Authors build events into coherent sequences that highlight dramatic events to tell an exciting story. Even when telling true or nonfiction stories, writers organize the events, which would otherwise be too chaotic to form a coherent story. In the process, authors take liberties with reality, just as memories do when reflecting on experiences. We remember the high points in life—the dramatic

This tall tale about a hungry grizzly and a
clever squirrel was first told to Ken Kesey
by his grandmother.

events, as Jean Fritz explains in the introduction to
her autobiography, *Homesick: My Own Story.*

## Plot

The plot holds the story together, making it a critical element in literature. **Plot** is *the plan of action*,
the events in the story that are linked by cause and
effect. Wyndham and Madison (1988) describe plot
as "a plan of action devised to achieve a definite and
much desired end—through cause and effect" (p.
81). Their definition is similar to Giblin's (1990),
who calls plot the blueprint of the story, or the path
it will follow from beginning to end. In developing
plot, the author weaves a logical series of events
explaining why events occur. In *Where the Wild
Things Are*, Maurice Sendak tells readers that Max
was sent to bed without his supper because he acted
like a "wild thing," which initiates the cause-and-

effect chain in this adroitly woven plot. "A well-
crafted plot, like some remarkable clockwork, can
fascinate us by its sheer ingenuity" (Alexander,
1981, p. 5).

Credible plots unfold gradually, building a
logical cause-and-effect sequence for story incidents. Story events inserted without adequate
preparation make a contrived and uninteresting
plot. Story characters act out the causes and
effects of story incidents. **Cause** *establishes the
main character's line of action* to solve a problem,
get out of a situation, or reach a certain goal;
**effect** is *what happens to the character as a result of
the action taken.*

Storytellers can make all sorts of imaginary
events credible by laying the groundwork for them
(Alexander, 1981). **Foreshadowing** is *the groundwork that prepares for future story events*, the planted
clues in situations, events, characters, and conflicts.

In Ken Kesey's *Little Tricker the Squirrel Meets Big Double the Bear*, the first two instances of foreshadowing occur in the book's title. First, the squirrel is named "Little Tricker" and he is tricky in this story. Second, the mention of Big Double the Bear identifies the antagonist.

Interesting plots usually have unique characteristics, since children enjoy stories that grab their attention. *Where the Wild Things Are* begins with a common incident, a child who misbehaves and consequently must go to bed without supper. The uniqueness of the story is introduced when Max escapes this punishment through his imagination. He goes to where the wild things are, where he can be as wild as he likes. He has fun for a while, but discovers he prefers to be "where someone loves him best." The illustrations also lend a unique quality to the story: as Max sails off in an imaginary boat, his surroundings grow larger and larger, and when he leaves the wild things to return to his own bedroom, they grow smaller again to show that he is leaving the land of the wild things.

Some enjoyable books begin more slowly. In *The Secret Garden* by Frances Hodgson Burnett the protagonist waits until nearly halfway through the book to enter the garden. Nevertheless, the book is so popular that it became a very successful Broadway play and motion picture. Although children's likes and dislikes are not entirely predictable, interesting, well-structured plots are important to fine literature. The elements that make up interesting plots include conflict, climax, and denouement.

## Conflict

Story conflicts create tension that arouse readers' suspense (Giblin, 1990). The characters in stories with interesting plots have difficulties to overcome, problems to solve, and goals to achieve. Believable conflicts and problems provide the shape, drama, tension, and movement in a story (Bond, 1984). **Conflict** is *"the struggle that grows out of the interplay of two opposing forces in a plot"* (Holman et al., 1986, p. 107). One of these opposing forces is usually the main character in the story, who struggles to get what he or she wants and is opposed vigorously, either by someone who wants the same thing or by circumstances that stand in the way of the goal (Wyndham and Madison, 1988).

A conflict implies struggle, but it also implies that there is a motivation behind the conflict or a goal that will be achieved through the conflict. The central problem or conflict must remain out of the main character's reach until near the end of the story. Nevertheless, readers are aware that a fateful decision is at hand that will precipitate a crisis in the principal character's affairs, but the outcome of this struggle is never certain.

Chris Van Allsburg creates an unusual and suspenseful conflict in *Jumanji*. Tension is introduced early in the story through a note warning the principal characters that once they begin playing a jungle-adventure board game they cannot stop until the game is completed. Heedless of the warning, the children begin playing the game, which rapidly gets out of hand as a python appears on the mantle and a rhinoceros crashes through the living room. They desperately need to stop the game— their parents are returning and the house is in chaos! Readers do not find out until the very end what happens to the children.

*Types of conflict.* Writers commonly involve characters in four major types of conflict:

1. a struggle against nature
2. a struggle against another person, usually the antagonist
3. a struggle against society
4. a struggle for mastery by two elements within the person (Holman et al., 1986)

Although the four types of conflict are distinct in literature, most stories have more than one type of conflict. For example, Jean Craighead George's *My Side of the Mountain* illustrates conflict with nature when the main character struggles to prove he can survive life in a wilderness, but he is also struggling to master elements within himself. Similarly, in *Hatchet* Gary Paulsen tells the story of a boy fighting to obtain food and shelter to survive (struggle with nature), but he also has internal conflicts about his parents' divorce.

As shown in these two examples, story characters often have conflicts within themselves, which may or may not be the only or the most obvious conflict. In Walter Dean Myers's *Scorpions*, Jamal has a number of conflicts, but the principal struggles are those within himself concerning a gun and

THE VILLAGE BY THE SEA

Paula Fox

*Emma's conflict in this story is not only with her Aunt Bea, whose voice is "like a razor blade hidden in cotton," but within herself as well.*

## Climax

The main character's most intense struggle occurs at the **climax,** which is *the highest point of interest* in the story, the point at which readers learn how the conflict is resolved. A strong conflict keeps readers turning pages until the climax because they want to know whether the protagonist makes the right decision.

*The Village by the Sea* contains an excellent example of conflict and climax. Emma's father must undergo surgery, making it necessary for Emma to spend two weeks with an aunt and uncle whom she barely knows. Before leaving for the hospital, Emma's father warns her that her Aunt Bea "can be a terror" and "make your life a misery" (p. 5), thus preparing readers for the conflict with Aunt Bea. He also tells her that Uncle Crispin won't permit Aunt Bea to make Emma's life entirely miserable. Emma hears Aunt Bea and Uncle Crispin quarreling constantly and encounters Aunt Bea's acerbic tongue herself on several occasions. These incidents heighten the conflict between Emma and her aunt. Eventually, Emma escapes to the nearby seashore to alleviate her tension and finds a friend. Together they build a village from shells, bits of driftwood, beach glass, bottles, sprigs of pine, and sea lavender. When Aunt Bea destroys the village, Emma experiences internal conflicts: she cannot decide whether to confront her aunt and uncle about the destruction or to tell her parents what happened. The conflicts reach a climax when Emma reads Aunt Bea's diary and discovers that Aunt Bea's entry reveals her awareness of her unacceptable behavior.

## Denouement

**Denouement** is *the falling action that occurs during the unwinding of the story problem after the climax.* This part of the story ties up the various threads of the plot into a satisfying, logical ending, but not necessarily a "happily ever after" ending. In *The Village by the Sea,* Aunt Bea was an unhappy person throughout her life and an alcoholic for many years. Serious problems like alcoholism are not solved in two weeks, the time frame of this story. Emma grew and developed through her experiences and achieved closure regarding Aunt Bea's

with his brother's gang, who wants him to use the gun and take over the leadership of the gang. Jamal also struggles with society when the teachers and principal in his school reject the way Jamal and his family are forced to live. In books, as in real life, people struggle with other people: conflicts occur between two children, a child and an adult, or a child and a gang or group. In Brock Cole's *The Goats,* two children struggle with different groups of children when their respective camping groups make them "the goats" and maroon them on an island. In Paula Fox's *The Village by the Sea,* Emma struggles with the insults and anger of her alcoholic aunt. The protagonist in Katherine Paterson's *Come Sing, Jimmy Joe* is in conflict with his parents, who want him to have a singing career in spite of his shyness.

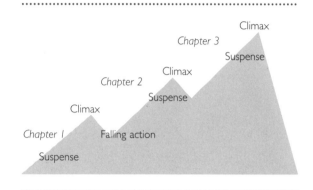

FIGURE 2.1

Dramatic plot.

Climax

Incident

Incident

Action picks up with incidents
that build suspense

Story beginning

FIGURE 2.2

Episodic plot.

Climax

Chapter 3

Suspense

Climax

Chapter 2

Suspense

Climax

Chapter 1

Falling action

Suspense

actions, thus creating a satisfying ending. The conflict resolution is revealed when her lump of hate dissolves and she is able to tell her parents about building the village by the sea.

### Types of plot

Dramatic and episodic plots are the most common types of plot structure, but several others appear in children's books, such as parallel plot and cumulative plot, which appear often in traditional literature and picture books.

*Dramatic plot.* Dramatic plots establish setting, characters, and conflicts with fast-moving action that grabs children's attention and creates enough tension to hold their interest until the exciting climax. (Figure 2.1 illustrates a dramatic plot line.) Jill Paton Walsh creates a good dramatic plot in the science fiction (fantasy) *The Green Book.* She quickly establishes the setting: planet Earth is dying and the last few people living in a very poor country must escape to a different planet. They are assigned a very old spaceship that lacks the power to transport the livestock and equipment necessary to establish a new colony. Conflict and tension build as the colonists explore their inhospitable environment: they encounter strange-looking moths and wood they cannot cut. Their seeds produce unusual wheat, forcing them to confront the specter of starvation. Gradually, the tension builds:

Will they have food or will they starve? The story builds to a climax in which the wheat is harvested and made into edible bread. Then the action falls and the protagonist ties up the loose ends through entries in her journal.

*Episodic plot.* Episodic plots are quite similar to dramatic plot. The major difference is that in an episodic plot each chapter or part has its own "miniplot," a story within the main story. Each episode or incident is at least loosely linked to the same main character or characters, has a problem relating to the total book, and is unified by the common theme of the main story. (Figure 2.2 illustrates an episodic plot.) Beverly Cleary's overall theme in *Ramona Quimby Age Eight* is Ramona's adjustment to the changes in her life when her mother gets a job and her father goes to college, and each chapter explores a conflict related to this theme. One episode revolves around Ramona's desire to have a boiled egg in her lunch box so that she can crack it on her head, a fad in Ramona's third-grade class. Unfortunately, her hurried mother puts an unboiled egg in Ramona's lunch, with disastrous results.

*Parallel plot.* In parallel plots, which appear only rarely in children's literature, two plots unfold side by side and are intertwined into a single story. In Robert McCloskey's picture book *Blueberries for Sal,* Sal and her mother go to Blueberry Hill to pick berries for canning; Little Bear and her mother go

*The author's lyric text with its repetitive style conveys the merry mood of King Bidgood's court. Together the author and illustrator have created an unforgettable bathtime story.*

to Blueberry Hill to eat berries for their winter nap. The story line moves back and forth between Sal and Little Bear, who have similar adventures on Blueberry Hill. The mothers become separated from the children, then the children join up with the wrong mothers, and the stories move toward a double climax and a denouement in which each mother finds her child and goes home safely.

*Cumulative plot.* Cumulative plots unfold through a pattern of repetition in which characters or events are added to each other, with each new character or event paralleling a previous character or event, building toward a climax that solves the problem. Cumulative plot stories, which usually appear in traditional literature or picture books, often contain repeated refrains. *King Bidgood's in the Bathtub*, a picture book written and illustrated by Audrey Wood, tells about a fun-loving king who refuses to

get out of his bathtub to rule his kingdom, despite the pleas of his court. This problem makes sense to children, who often feel the same way. Each character tries to lure the king out of the bathtub with a different ploy but is met with the same refrain: the king will deal with that problem "in the tub." When the knight announces that it is time to battle, the king counters with "today we battle in the tub." Finally, after the king rejects the efforts of all of the adults to get him out of the bathtub, a little pageboy pulls the plug and solves the problem. The plot conclusion is satisfying because children enjoy solving problems that baffle adults.

## Characters

Good authors have the ability to create believable, memorable characters (Holman et al., 1986). These characters must seem real, even though they are imaginary and different from real people, so that readers want to know them very well (Silvey, 1988). Readers care about believable characters with whom they can identify and feel truly involved. Authors use a variety of strategies to make characters live and breathe in readers' minds. One is telling the details of a character's thoughts, feelings, motivations, and attitudes. Another is depicting characters in ways consistent with their social background, educational level, and age. Portraying the human qualities, emotions, desires, hopes, dreams, and motivations that distinguish characters as individuals creates memorable characters.

**Characters** are essential to stories because they propel the plot. They are *the driving force behind the story that make things happen* (Stewig, 1988) and *the actors who direct and act out the plot.* In *Shades of Gray* Will has lost his immediate family in the Civil War and is resentful when he is forced to live with his Uncle Jed, a pacifist who refused to fight. Readers learn how Will thinks and feels about being thrust into a situation that challenges his basic beliefs; they become acquainted with Uncle Jed through Will's thoughts and Uncle Jed's actions. The drama is drawn from the series of conflicts between a man who believes in peace and a boy who believes that fighting solves disagreements. Gradually, Will begins to respect his uncle's values.

### Developing character

*Main characters.* Like many chapter books, *Shades of Gray* includes several characters, but the **protagonist** is *the principal or central character, idea, or concept that is the focus of the plot.* The central character is presented in greater detail than other characters. The **antagonist** is *a character who is in conflict with the protagonist.* The antagonist is sometimes a villain and sometimes a *foil character* (Russell, 1991), one whose traits provide a complete contrast to those of the protagonist. An antagonist lends excitement and suspense to a story but is developed with less detail than a protagonist.

The detailed information given about the protagonist usually leads readers to identify with and follow this character throughout the story. In *The Burning Questions of Bingo Brown* by Betsy Byars, many readers identify with Bingo's worries about the proper way to hold a girl's hand. His fears and embarrassments as he struggles toward maturity reveal his character, and his unexpectedly antagonistic relationship with his favorite teacher shows the dimensionality of his character, convincing the reader that Bingo will survive his problems.

Bingo Brown is a well-developed protagonist with three-dimensional or *round* characteristics. Well-rounded characters have complex, multifaceted personalities that readers come to know as they learn about their individual traits, revealed through the trouble in their lives, which never run smoothly. If there were no trouble, there would be no story (Wyndham and Madison, 1988). Well-rounded characters make readers care and want to know how the characters will resolve their predicaments. Katherine Paterson, in *Bridge to Terabithia*, acquaints her readers with the character of Jess so well that they can anticipate his actions, reactions, and feelings. They know that he is unhappy in his family and that he has no close friends. They are happy for him when Leslie moves next door and together they create the magic kingdom of Terabithia, where Jess's world changes into a happier place. They mourn with him when Leslie drowns.

*Supporting characters.* All the characters are not developed with the same depth as the protagonist. Supporting characters are *flat* or less round because they lack the depth and complexity of a real person. These characters are built around a single dominant trait or quality representing a personality type (Morner and Rausch, 1991). Flat characters are needed as part of the interactive background; their primary function is to advance the protagonist's development. Fully portraying these characters would make the story too complex for children. Supporting characters often include the protagonist's best friend, a teacher, or parents. In *The Village by the Sea*, all of the characters were flat except the protagonist, Emma. Aunt Bea is a flat character whose primary trait is unhappiness caused by alcoholism. Emma's parents are depicted as understanding, but they are flat characters as well.

Some flat characters are *stereotypes* who lack individualizing characteristics and instead represent traits generally attributed to a social group as a whole (Morner and Rausch, 1991). They exhibit a few traits representative of conventional mothers, fathers, friends, or teachers and are developed quickly with brief bits of information so that drawing their characters does not interrupt the story flow. In traditional literature, all characters are stereotypes representing traits such as good, evil, innocence, and wisdom. (Stereotypes are discussed in greater detail in Chapter Five.)

*Dynamic characters.* Dynamic or developed characters change significantly during the course of a story as incidents cause their personalities to emerge and expand. In *Bridge to Terabithia*, Jess is forever changed through his friendship with Leslie and her death. Emma, in *The Village by the Sea*, knows herself better and has a greater understanding of the people around her as a result of her encounters with Aunt Bea.

Katherine Paterson's Gilly is a well-developed dynamic character in *The Great Gilly Hopkins*. Gilly begins as a rebellious, unmanageable foster child who gradually comes to understand her foster mother, Mrs. Trotter. Later Gilly meets and grows to understand her grandmother. Readers see Gilly develop into a sensitive girl who is able to tell Mrs. Trotter she loves her. Many readers do not like Gilly at the outset but view her more sympathetically as she develops, hoping that she will find that her real mother is the mother of her dreams. By the time of the long-awaited meeting with her mother, who falls far short of her expectations, Gilly has matured enough to cope with her disappointment.

*Static characters.* Static or delineated story characters are the opposite of developed characters. They seem impervious to experience and remain essentially the same throughout the story. These are the "Peter Pan" characters who never grow up. The principal character in Astrid Lindgren's *Pippi Longstocking* is static. Pippi, a nine-year-old Swedish girl, is well rounded and fully described. She lives alone with a monkey and a horse and manages to have many hilarious adventures. Although her adventures are novel, she does not change; she is always irrepressible. Not all static characters are juvenile Peter Pan types, however. Charlotte, in *Charlotte's Web*, solves Wilbur's problem and is helpful to animals in the barnyard, but her character remains the same throughout the story.

*Character interaction.* Authors use any number of different characterizations in writing, which work together to create vivid and interesting stories. For instance, the animal fantasy *Redwall* has a variety of characters: the mouse Matthias is a clumsy, inept youth and an unlikely hero who lives peacefully in Redwall Abbey until that scourge Cluny, the terrible one-eyed rat, threatens to conquer the Abbey. Matthias's well-rounded, dynamic character grows from a bumbling youth to a fierce warrior when challenged by Cluny and his battle-seasoned horde. His development is credible because he is pushed into action by the antagonist, Cluny. The time of crisis supplies the motivation for him to mature with heroic qualities. The changes in Matthias are foreshadowed early in the story when he expresses his admiration for Martin the Champion, the mouse who once drove off enemies of Redwall Abbey with his ancient sword. Matthias later sets out on a mission to locate the missing sword.

Cluny is a foil character whose personality traits contrast, those of Matthias. Cluny is depicted as completely evil, without any redeeming qualities. Events do not alter his character or lead him to reveal any finer dimensions of personality; therefore, readers feel justice is served when he dies. There are also a number of flat, one-dimensional characters who interact with the main character. Father Abbot is a wise monk who sees Matthias as a comical character. The Churchmouse family, Cornflower, and Constance the Badger are good characters who help Matthias, while Cluny's ragtag camp includes Fangborn, Ragear, Mangefur, and Cheesethief who are just as bad as their names suggest. The foxes are double agents who eventually meet a just fate.

The author uses each of these characters to work together in creating a story that is entertaining and compelling. Each character, even those that are not drawn with the same in-depth detail as Matthias, contributes to the development of the story and of the main character.

## Revealing character through narration

Readers come to know characters the way they come to know an acquaintance—from the way the character talks and acts. Character traits are revealed through a number of narration techniques. First-person narration, in which the main character is usually the narrator, allows readers to infer traits from what the main character says and how others react. Similarly, a limited narrator may tell the story from the main character's point of view. An omniscient narrator, on the other hand, may tell all about the main character and also tell about others from their points of view.

Walter Dean Myers uses a first-person narrator in *Me, Mop, and the Moondance Kid* to reveal the main character, Tommy, and his brother, Moondance: "Most of the kids at the Academy are young. Mop and me were just about the oldest. When kids get to be eleven or twelve, they're usually sent out to another home. I would have been sent out to Tiverhead except for Moondance. They like to keep brothers together" (p. 2).

Authors often use conversations to help readers know characters; manner of speaking and subject matter are revealing, especially when combined with the characters' actions, and build the readers' understanding of the characters. The following interchange occurs between Tommy and his brother Moondance after Moondance drops his teddy bear, Dinky, in the toilet and stops it up. Tommy rescues the bear and unstops the toilet.

> "The toilet's still stopped up, isn't it?"
>
> "I don't think so," I said.
>
> Mom gave me one of those is-something-strange-going on looks and went into the bathroom. She flushed the toilet and it worked fine.
>
> That night just before I went to sleep, . . . Moondance came to my bed and shook me.
>
> "What's the matter?" I asked.
>
> "Thanks a lot for saving Dinky," he said.
>
> "We had to save Dinky," I said. "He's your best friend."
>
> "No," he said. "You're my best friend. Dinky's my second-best friend." (p. 49)

Authors sometimes reveal aspects of characters' personalities through their thoughts. Tommy's thoughts reveal some of his character in this quotation: "I didn't get any hits because I was nervous on account of Rocky. He was hanging around watching

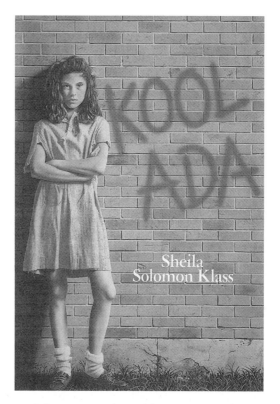

Ada never speaks and has no answer but her fists. That is the situation until she meets and comes to know Mrs. Walker, a teacher in Chicago who is as fierce and strong in her way as Ada is in hers.

the game. I was standing near the fence talking to Mop when he came up on the other side of the fence" (p. 35).

A character's traits may be revealed through the eyes of another character. Sheila Klass uses this technique in *Kool Ada:* "Since I cut school fairly regular, I didn't spend much time with Ms. Walker. But I already understood her better'n any other teacher I ever had. It wasn't hard. Ms. Walker said what she meant and she meant whatever she said. Every time. She was famous all over the school for that. If she gave her word—promise or punishment—you could count on it. No use pouting, or whining, or apologizing" (p. 8).

Character traits, descriptions, and actions are usually developed through illustrations in picture books. In these books, the words and the pictures are integrated to reveal character. In *Little Penguin's Tale*, written and illustrated by Audrey Wood, we see a penguin dancing with gooney birds; his mischievous, carefree nature is apparent in the pictures.

## Setting

**Setting** is *the time and place of a story*. Vivid settings give a story reality; they give readers a sense of being there. The importance of setting varies from story to story. In some it creates the stage for the characters' actions, while in others it is indefinite, a universal setting that is secondary to the story. The story itself dictates the importance of setting.

In creating setting, authors choose a location (an urban, rural, or small town and a country) and time (past, present, or future). Contemporary settings take place in the here and now, while historical settings occur in the past—for example, post–Civil War Virginia, as in *Shades of Gray*.

Once the general location and time are identified, authors decide on details of a specific time and place: perhaps a very specific designation such as a certain district in London, England, in the summer of 1993, or a more universal setting requiring fewer details and a more indefinite time and place. Time and location dictate many of the rest of the details of the story: the type of home and furniture, the scenery, and the flora and fauna of the surrounding countryside. The social environment, foods, newspapers, magazines, and games are all aspects of the setting. Authors depict setting through sensory imagery, using visual, auditory, tactile, and olfactory images.

In fantasy, the time and place of a story may be a make-believe setting that no one has ever seen. Writers of fantasy create imaginary worlds, people, and events. For instance, Phillipa Pearce creates a clock that strikes 13, signaling the appearance of a garden that does not exist at other times, in *Tom's Midnight Garden*. This fantasy garden is a playground for Tom and his friend, who is an old woman during the day and a young girl at night. On the other hand, setting in fantasy may be as ordinary as everyday life, as it is in E. B. White's *Charlotte's Web*.

Setting is especially significant in historical fiction; these stories depend on setting perhaps more than any other genre. Authors must carefully research such common things as food, clothing, housing, social attitudes, and language to ascertain the appropriate details for the historical period. Authentic historical settings permit readers to move into other times and places and to develop greater understandings about other people and times. For example, in *Sing Down the Moon*, Scott O'Dell re-creates a time in American history when Indians were oppressed and forced onto reservations. Navaho culture is important to this book because the wealth of a family was based on the sheep, which were owned and cared for by the women. Readers experience the brutality of the soldiers against the Indians and come to understand the anger the Indians felt.

### Developing setting

Illustrations develop setting in some books, while others portray it through words. Some stories are closely tied to the setting, while others are not. The sounds, sights, and feelings of night in the country are the story of *Night in the Country* by Cynthia Rylant; Mary Szilagyi's exquisite illustrations combine with the language to convey the mood of a night in the country. This story revolves around the setting.

Settings for fantasy are a special challenge: authors must not only imagine places and times that do not exist, they must make readers see them, as Donn Kushner does in this excerpt from *A Book Dragon*: "Nonesuch was—and still is, for that matter—the last of a family of dragons that lived over five hundred years ago in a limestone hill, honeycombed with caverns. . . . The dark mouth of the family's cavern opened towards an ugly tangled scrub forest that ended, at the lap of the hill, in an evil bog" (p. 2).

### Creating mood

The mood or tone of a story is created through the setting. The author uses words and the artist uses illustrations to create the feelings reader should experience. Consider the following excerpt from Ruth White's *Sweet Creek Holler*: "The holler was skinny between the mountains. The road was

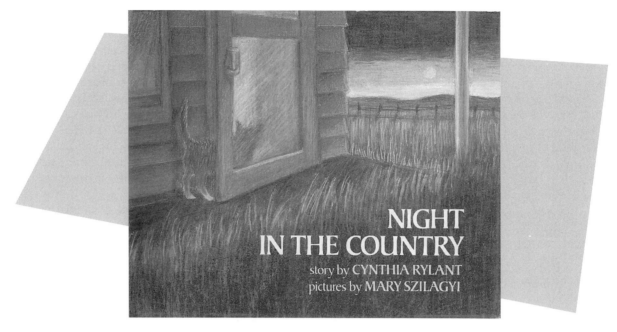

*Through the night a river flows, an owl swoops, a rabbit patters.
The author and illustrator of this book give readers a night — melodious, mysterious, alive — fringed at each end by the colors of day.*

chiseled out of the side of one mountain base. . . . houses were stuck on the sides of the hills, many with stilts underneath to prop them up level. . . . Some were made of cinder blocks, a few were whiteboard, or brick, but most of them were tar-paper shacks" (p. 6).

The words and phrases used here—such as *skinny, chiseled, stuck, sides of the hills, and tar-paper shacks*—create a feeling for the hard life in a depressed area of the United States. These words and phrases express the author's interpretation of the significance of the place and time. Moreover, the author's language reflects the tone and theme of the story (Sebesta and Iverson, 1975).

## Theme

The word *theme* identifies a statement about the story that steps back from the literal interpretation (Lehr, 1991). **Theme** is *the important idea, the meaning, the significance behind a story*. It is a central or dominating idea in a work. In nonfiction prose it may be thought of as the general topic of discussion, the subject of the discourse, or the thesis. In poetry, fiction, and drama it is the abstract concept that is made concrete through its representation in person, action, and image in the work. No proper theme is simply a subject or an activity. The theme of a story has both a subject and a predicate. For instance vice cannot be used as a theme without some proposition about vice posited by the author. For instance, the statement "vice seems more interesting than virtue but turns out to be destructive" (Holman et al., 1986) is an adequate theme, as it has both a subject (vice) and a position on the subject.

Theme is the melody, the motive, or the dominant idea developed in the story (Wyndham and Madison, 1988). Fine writers weave theme subtly into their stories. Children, like adults, prefer authors who trust their readers to infer theme from story events, characters, and setting rather than preaching or explicitly stating the theme. In *Charlotte's Web*, the theme emerges through the animals' actions and the cycle of life and death, and the continuity of life is paralleled in the cycle of the seasons. Readers experience the dominant idea that death is as necessary as birth; both are part of the life cycle. Every event and every character in the story resonates with this theme.

In Mavis Jukes's *Like Jake and Me*, every action and image of the protagonist, Alex, portray a boy who is insecure about his stepfather's affections and his mother's pregnancy (Hearne, 1990). Alex tries to prove that he is competent and helpful, but his stepfather, Jake, refuses his assistance. Finally Jake asks Alex to help find a wolf spider and they develop a new sense of closeness. This theme about the way respect gradually grows between people emerges naturally from this story.

## Multiple themes

Stories may have multiple themes that intertwine as elements of a story. In *Like Jake and Me*, the gradual growth of respect between stepfather and stepson is a major theme related to the need to belong. An additional theme is the loving relationship between mother and son related to the need to love and be loved. Alex's mother tries to build a better understanding between her son and his stepfather because she understands her son's need to belong.

The most common themes in children's books are associated with fundamental human needs, including:

1. the need to love and be loved
2. the need to belong
3. the need to achieve
4. the need for security—material, emotional, spiritual
5. the need to know (Wyndham and Madison, 1988)

These universal themes are expressed through the ideas, characters, plots, and settings developed in fiction, nonfiction, and poetry.

## Children's response to theme

Building meaning is a complex developmental process. A three-year-old understands a story dif-

ferently from an eight-year-old; younger children can, however, identify theme. In kindergarten, children are "able to identify thematically matched books 80% of the time for realistic fiction and 35% for folktales, thus indicating that thematic identification is a fairly early developmental strategy," but older children are better able to talk about the themes in stories (Lehr, 1991, p. 67). Developmentally, children move from responding at a concrete level to a more abstract response. Children who have more exposure to literature are better able to talk about meaning in books.

Themes are subject to readers' interpretation, so different individuals may identify different themes in the same book; the dominant idea or theme, however, should be apparent to readers. Individuals respond differently to the same story because their response is based on their individual experience, which they use to interpret and understand the material. Individuals remember what is important to them and see what they expect to see or are capable of seeing. Readers who have experiences with stepparents may interpret *Like Jake and Me* in different ways: those who have had positive experiences with stepparents would respond differently from those who have had negative experiences. The varying responses of students are explored in greater depth in Chapter Four.

Many stories offer readers opportunities to respond at different levels of understanding. Readers can take as much or as little from literature as their developmental level and experiential background permit. *Charlotte's Web* offers many layers of meaning to readers. Younger children are apt to understand this book as an animal fantasy. Older children are ready to apprehend the cycle of life and death, while adults recognize the irony in a situation that gives one character credit for the creativity of another. This is why we recommend using *Charlotte's Web* in the third or fourth grade, when children are ready to understand its major theme.

Some adults mistake sentimental books that reflect on the "cuteness" of childhood, such as Joan Walsh Anglund's *Morning Is a Little Child*, as books for children. These books, however, are *about* children rather than *for* them. Nostalgia rarely appeals to children, who are usually future oriented. Such books are more appropriate as gifts for adults who enjoy childhood memories.

## Style

Authors express their **style** through the *language they use to shape their stories: the words they choose, the sentences they craft, the dialogue they create, and the amount and nature of the descriptive passages.* Authors arrange words in ways that express their individuality. "Style is a combination of the two elements: the idea to be expressed and the individuality of the author" (Holman et al., 1986, p. 487). No two styles are exactly alike. Ultimately it is the author's use of language that determines the lasting quality of a book (Saxby, 1987).

### Language devices

Author style is most apparent in the language devices used to achieve special effects or meanings, stimulating their readers through use of figurative language, imagery, allusion, hyperbole, understatement, and symbolism. Readers then use these devices to infer and connote individual interpretations based upon their experiential background. *Connotation* refers to an association or emotional response a reader attaches to a particular word that goes beyond the dictionary definition or denotation; it is a meaning drawn from personal experience. For example, many people associate warm, loving feelings with the word *mother* that go far beyond the literal denotation of a female parent.

*Figurative language.* **Figurative language** is *connotative, sensory language that incorporates one or more of the various figures of speech* such as simile, metaphor, repetition, and personification (Holman and Harmon, 1986). Figurative language is used to develop character, show mood, and create setting. Katherine Paterson uses figurative language to great effect in *The Great Gilly Hopkins.* Gilly moves to Mrs. Trotter's home, the latest in a long line of foster homes. There she meets William Ernest, another foster child living in the same home: "He was rattling the tray so hard that the milk glass was threatening to jump the edge" (p. 47). Paterson's

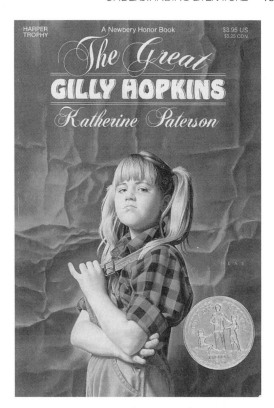

Brash and sassy Gilly Hopkins yearns desperately for a real family and a place to call home, eventually learning that life usually is not the way it is supposed to be.

figurative language implies that William Ernest is a scared, nervous, timid person far more vividly than mere telling would achieve.

Her figurative language also creates mood when she describes Gilly's new foster home: "Inside, it was dark and crammed with junk. Everything seemed to need dusting" (p. 4). The words *dark, junk,* and *dust* have connotative meanings for most people that conjure visions of a dank, uninviting place. This clearly gives the reader a sense of Gilly's negative feelings about her new foster home without explicitly stating "Gilly had negative feelings about her new home," which is a drab and uninteresting way of conveying meaning.

*Imagery.* Sensory language widens the mind's eye and helps the reader build images that go beyond the ordinary to new and exciting experiences.

These experiences can be the sensory kind in which one sees or hears new things; they can be an intellectual kind in which one thinks new things (Saxby and Winch, 1987).

Pamela Allen's book *Bertie and the Bear* (1983) illustrates the role of imagery. In this noisy book, the pages are full of shapes, colors, and movement (Saxby and Winch, 1987). Dramatic noises like *yip yipping*, *shoo shooing*, and *boom booming* stretch our imagination to think of the IN-CRED-IBLE visions these wonderful sounds create.

*Allusion.* **Allusion** is *a figure of speech that makes brief reference to a historical or literary figure, event, or object* (Holman and Harmon, 1986). In an amusing passage, Gilly alludes to godfathers and the Mafia in reference to William Ernest, but it is the direct contrast to William Ernest's actual personality that makes the idea even funnier. "An inspiration came to [Gilly]. . . . It was William Ernest. She laughed out loud at the pleasure of it. Baby-Face Teague, the frog-eyed filcher. Wild-eyed William, the goose-brained godfather. . . . The midget of the Mafia" (p. 48). Paterson also uses allusion to describe Mrs. Trotter: "Trotter smiled impatiently and closed the door quickly. When she turned back toward Gilly, her face was like Mount Rushmore stone" (p. 97). Through this allusion, readers learn that Trotter is impassive to Gilly's efforts to antagonize her.

*Hyperbole.* **Hyperbole** is *exaggeration used to make a point*, as shown in this passage: "Gilly gave her the 300-watt smile that she had designed for melting the hearts of foster parents. 'Never better!' She spoke the words with just the right musical lilt" (p. 48). In this instance, the size and impact of Gilly's smile and the sound of her voice are exaggerated to make the point that she is on the surface at least trying to be congenial with her foster parent.

*Understatement.* **Understatement** is almost the opposite of hyperbole. It *plays down a situation or person and is often used for comic effect.* Gilly deliberately wrecks her own hair with chewing gum to antagonize Trotter, who ignores it. Gilly then shakes her head dramatically to draw attention, to which Trotter calmly says, "You got a tic or something, honey?" (p. 18). Trotter's understatement creates a comical situation—she appears not to notice Gilly's dreadful hair—which is embellished when Gilly tries to remove the chewing gum, further ruining her hair.

*Symbolism.* **Symbols** are *persons, objects, situations, actions, or words that operate on two levels of meaning.* A symbol has both a literal meaning—a denotation—and an inferential meaning, one that is implied. Gilly's mother is described as a "flower child," which literally refers to someone who lived a free-spirited lifestyle in the 1960s, but Paterson uses the phrase as a symbol in two separate instances: (1) "Miss Ellis suddenly looked tired. 'God help the children of the flower children,' she said" (p. 119); and (2) "Her hair was long, but it was dull and stringy—a dark version of Agnes Stokes's, which had always needed washing. A flower child gone to seed" (p. 145). In the first instance, Paterson implies that the children of flower children need help that will not be forthcoming from these free spirits. The second suggests that Gilly's mother is stuck in an adolescent stage of development and continues to live as she did in her younger days, in spite of the fact that she is growing older.

## Point of view

**Point of view** is *the perspective or stance from which the author tells a story.* It is the eye and mind through which the action is perceived (Morner and Rausch, 1991). The point of view determines the vocabulary, sentences, and attitudes expressed. Essentially, there are two general narrative points of view, first and third person. A first-person narrator actually appears within the story and tells the tale using the pronoun *I*. The first-person point of view has some advantages; one is its conversational nature, which makes readers feel they know the narrator. First-person narrators tells the reader what they are thinking and feeling, giving readers an intimate feeling. Plot, setting, and character are likely to be unified when the main character says, "This is what happened to me, this is where it happened, this is how I felt" (Sebesta and Iverson, 1975, p. 78).

Vivien Alcock chose first-person narration for the main character in *The Monster Garden*, Frankie Stein. Frankie tells the readers about the problems she faces in feeding and caring for a monster she has grown and must keep secret from the hostile world. The author gives Frankie graphic descriptive narration to make the monster a very real being to the reader: "There was no safe place for Monnie anywhere on land. It was too large and alien and gentle to live among us. It stood up, a huge royal figure with its shining crest. Perhaps it would make its own kingdom under the sea, a kinder, friendlier place than we have made on earth" (p. 134).

A third-person narrator, unlike a first-person narrator, stands outside the story and tells the tale using pronouns such as *he*, *she*, and *they*. Third-person narration has two commonly used variations: *omniscient perspective* and *limited omniscient perspective*. Children's literature most frequently uses omniscient perspective to tell stories.

With omniscient perspective, the narrator sees all, knows all, and reveals all to the reader. This narrator has access to and reveals the thoughts and motives of all the characters, knows the present, past, and future, and also comments on or interprets the actions of all of the characters. A major advantage of this style lies in the unlimited scope and relative freedom the narrator has in unfolding the story. With omniscient perspective, authors can speak to readers directly, telling whatever they choose to tell or speaking over the heads of the characters in an aside to help readers understand the significance of an event or a character (Sebesta and Iverson, 1975). Dianne Snyder uses this point of view in her picture book *The Boy of the Three-Year Nap*: "All day long the widow sewed silk kimonos for the rich ladies in town. As she worked, her head bobbed up and down, up and down, like the heads of the birds hunting for fish. ... Her only son, Taro, was, oh, such a clever lad and as healthy as a mother could wish. But, alas! He was as lazy as a rich man's cat. All he did was eat and sleep, sleep and eat" (p. 7). Throughout the story, the narrator's attitude toward Taro is apparent through the asides to the reader. The author's style is just right for the story.

Narrators with limited omniscience, on the other hand, focus on the thoughts of a single character and present the other characters externally (Morner and Rausch, 1991). In this approach, the author typically follows one character throughout

THE BOY OF THE THREE-YEAR NAP

Dianne Snyder                    Illustrated by Allen Say

*The story is told in this book by a third-person narrator who hatches a scheme to marry his rich next-door neighbor's daughter, only to find that laziness does not pay . . . or does it?*

the story; the reader knows only what this one character knows and sees only those incidents in which that character is involved. Betsy Byars uses this style in *The Burning Questions of Bingo Brown*: "As Bingo sat down, he made a decision. If Mr. Markham called on another girl, he was going to put his fingers in his ears. He could not fall in love a fourth time. He understood now his weakness for powerful women" (p. 9). The entire story is told from the perspective of the main character, Bingo. This style permits authors to present the story through the eyes of a central character while retaining some distance.

## STORY GRAMMAR

Stories can be analyzed not only through the structural elements of literature (plot, theme, etc.) but also with **story grammar,** *a set of rules that describes the possible structures of well-formed stories* (Stein and Glenn, 1979; Rumelhart, 1975). Although researchers describe story grammars in various ways, many of the differences are merely semantic. Most researchers agree that story grammars include character, setting, a problem or conflict, and a series of one or more episodes (Black and Wilensky, 1979).

Story grammars give readers a way of describing and discussing what they read, which helps refine their comprehension and gives them a means of organizing their recollections. Readers who understand story structure expect to encounter characters, setting, problems, and efforts to solve problems in books; these anticipations enrich their comprehension.

Writers also use story grammars for generating stories (Meyer and Rice, 1984), to plan the elements and organization of the tale. The story grammar in Figure 2.3 is based on Russell Erickson's *A Toad for Tuesday*, in which Warton, a toad, sets out to take beetle brittle to his Aunt Toolia but is captured by an owl who plans to eat him on Tuesday. Warton attempts to avoid his fate through a variety of strategies, but he is unsuccessful until he helps the owl escape death and earns the owl's gratitude. The story grammar clearly shows that Warton has a problem and makes specific efforts to solve it.

## FIGURE 2.3

Story grammar.

Title: A Toad for Tuesday

Author: Russel Erickson

Setting

Who: Warton (toad), Morton (toad), George (owl), mice

Where: The woods

When: Winter

Problem: Warton is captured by George the Owl, who plans to eat him on Tuesday.

Efforts to solve the problem (also called events):

1. Warton tries to make friends.
2. Warton makes a ladder.
3. The mice try to help.
4. Warton saves George from the fox.

Resolution: Problem or conflict solution ...George decides not to eat Warton

The story winds down ...George flies Warton to visit his aunt.

## EXPERIENCING LITERATURE

Although reading seems like a solitary activity, it has social dimensions that are apparent when readers discuss their literary experiences. When a group of seven or eight students discusses a book they have all read, they stimulate one another to think about the story, enhancing the understanding and response of each person in the group. Moreover, each time a different group of children discusses a story, they bring up ideas that no one has mentioned before. The elements of fiction and story grammar are useful concepts for guiding children's discussions of literature and writing experiences.

Teachers, librarians, parents, and other concerned adults serve as children's guides to literary experiences. They cannot teach literature; they can only attempt to increase children's awareness of the inner world of ideas and feelings through literary experiences, which encourage children to build their own understanding of genre and to express their own response to the story. When planning activities, consider the following guidelines, which are adapted from Routman (1991):

- What is the purpose for using this activity or strategy?
- Does this activity relate to the true nature of the book?
- How does this activity fit with my philosophy of literature?
- How will this activity enhance the children's knowledge and response to the literature?

The best literature-based activities are those that grow naturally out of the literature and relate to the plot, theme, setting, characters, or style of the book. Activities that grow out of the literature encourage students to think critically and enable readers to demonstrate or share their response to the book. Later chapters discuss experiencing literature in much greater detail.

## CLASSROOM ACTIVITIES TO ENHANCE UNDERSTANDING OF LITERATURE

### Genre

When working on developing understanding of genre, select titles that are clear examples of the genre being studied. Picture books are useful for developing genre activities because they are appealing as well as clear and direct examples for teaching genre. They are also useful for developing understanding of plot, theme, style, characterization, setting, and style.

### Literary Experience

The suggested activities are suitable for individuals, pairs, small groups, or whole classes. Extensive

## FIGURE 2.4

Map of literary activities.

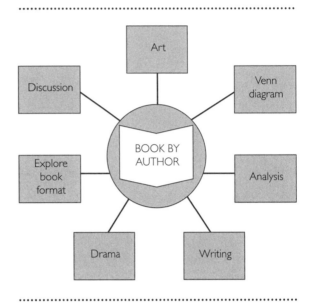

directions are not included because in most instances the best way to introduce an activity is through demonstration and example. When planning literary experiences, think of ways to enhance appreciation of the literature, for instance, ask a few appropriate discussion questions to enhance understanding. You are, after all, guiding children to respond to a book; you are not conducting an inquisition. Questions for each chapter are undesirable.

The map in Figure 2.4 shows some of the many appropriate literary activities. Do not do all of these activities with a single work of literature, however, but choose the most appropriate activity or activities in a specific instance.

*ACTIVITIES*

## 2.1   Analyzing literary elements

This activity deals with analyzing the literary elements of a piece of realistic fiction. Although all of the elements are mentioned here, in an actual classroom you would probably choose to discuss only one of the elements, such as plot or characterization or setting.

BOOK: *Return to Bitter Creek*
        by Doris Buchanan Smith

1. Introduce the book, asking questions to help students predict the elements of the story.
    a. What might the title indicate about the story?
    b. What can the dust jacket help you predict about it?
    c. Where do you think the story takes place? Who is the main character? How old is the main character?
2. Students read the story silently.
3. Discuss the story with the students, stimulating them to think about the story.
    a. Describe Lacey at the beginning of the story. How does she change in the story? What events caused her to change?
    b. What is the theme of this story? What makes you think this is the theme?
    c. What is the setting? How does the setting relate to the story?
    d. What is the tragedy in this story?
    e. Do you know anyone like Lacey's grandmother? What characteristics does that person share with her grandmother? Do you think her grandmother changed after Lacey's birth? Why or why not?
    f. Now that you have read the story, what do you think the significance of the title is?
    g. On the last page of the story, the author writes "The silence was louder than any thunder." What was the author referring to and what does that statement mean?
    h. Did you anticipate the tragedy in this story? Why or why not?
4. Use extension activities to allow students to respond to the story.
    a. Make a time line for this story that begins with Lacey's birth.
    b. Read *Where the Lilies Bloom* or *Trial Valley* by Vera and Bill Cleaver. Compare one or both of these books to *Return to Bitter Creek*.
    c. Write a sympathy letter to Lacey.
    d. Write a review for this book that will cause another person to want to read it.
    e. Read another book by Doris Buchanan Smith. Discuss similarities between the two books.

## 2.2.  Exploring a book with young children

BOOK:  *Together* by George Ella Lyon, with pictures
by Vera Rosenberry

1.  Introduce the book to the children, focusing on the words *author, illustrator,* and *title,* and on the book's theme.

    a.  Hold up the book, identify the author and illustrator, and explain that the illustrator used her daughter and her daughter's best friend as models for the pictures.

    b.  Ask the children what the title means to them. Discuss togetherness and how it makes them feel.

    c.  Ask what things they like to do together with their best friends. Have them tell about or draw a picture of their favorite things to do together.

2.  Read the book aloud.

3.  Discuss the story with the students, stimulating them to think about the story.

    a.  What did the author and illustrator say to you through this story?

    b.  What was your favorite part of the story?

    c.  What is your favorite thing to do with a friend?

    d.  Can friends dream the same dreams?

    e.  What are some dreams that you and your friends have?

4.  Use extension activities to allow students to respond to the story.

    a.  Sing or chant the story to a familiar tune. (This story is easily adaptable to music. Ask the music teacher for assistance if necessary.)

    b.  Act out a favorite scene.

    c.  Think of new scenes and act them out.

    d.  Paint a mural about things to do together or about their dreams.

    e.  Draw or write about their dreams.

...........................................

## 2.3  Suggested activities for individual literary experiences

These are activities that teachers can suggest for students to perform on their own or in groups of two or three.

1.  Prepare discussion questions for the book. (Students may need to be given models of open-ended questions until they become adept at creating such questions.)

2.  Prepare a Venn diagram that compares and contrasts this book with another.

3.  Prepare a diorama of an important scene or setting from the book.

4.  Act out a scene from the book.

5.  Prepare a poster or commercial for the book.

6.  Keep a reading journal summarizing each day's reading and responding to the reading experience.

7.  Prepare a story grammar or story map. (See the model in this chapter.)

8.  Draw a plot line for the story. (See the models in this chapter.)

## SUMMARY

Genre are classifications of literature, with each member of a classification exhibiting common characteristics. Genre classifications give teachers, librarians, and students the language to discuss and analyze books. The genre of children's literature includes picture books, traditional literature, fantasy, realistic fiction, historical fiction, poetry, and informational literature; all these categories of genre have the same characteristics as adult literature.

Initially, readers like or dislike the books they read for indefinable reasons, responding emotionally to literature. Through many experiences with stories, they gradually discover the elements that make up literature: story, plot, characters, setting, theme, and style. As their experience with literature grows, they develop schemata, cognitive structures that enable them to make sense of what they read and to anticipate what the author will say, thus enriching their understanding. Children's understanding of literature exceeds their ability to verbalize story knowledge, but concerned adults can help them expand their appreciation and understanding. As one of those concerned adults, your understanding of the elements and organizational patterns of fiction discussed in this chapter will assist you in choosing books and planning literary experiences. The box *"Elements of Fiction"* reviews the elements of fiction and suggests some questions to ask yourself when reviewing a piece of literature.

## THOUGHT QUESTIONS

1. How can teachers use the elements of literature?
2. What is author style? Identify the components of style that you would expect to find in a novel.
3. Compare a picture book character with a character in a novel. How do they differ in development and the amount of detail included?
4. What themes have you discovered in the children's books you have read thus far?
5. Why do you think teachers choose to read fiction aloud more often than nonfiction?

## ENRICHMENT ACTIVITIES

1. Choose a fiction book to read and identify each of the elements of literature in that book. Then map the story grammar of the book.
2. Choose a nonfiction book and identify the patterns of organizing information in it.
3. Compare characters in two different fiction books.
4. Read a book of fiction, nonfiction, and poetry to a group of children. Ask them to identify the aspects of each type of literature that they enjoy.
5. Survey an elementary school class. Ask the students to identify the structures in various types of literature. Which type of literature do they seem to know the most about? Why do you think this is true?
6. Compare a poem, a story, and an informational book that are about the same topic.

# Elements of Fiction

## Plot

1. Does the plot grab the reader's attention and move quickly?
2. Are the story events sequenced logically, so that cause and effect are clear?
3. Is the reader prepared for story events?
4. What is the conflict in this story? (character with another character, character and society, character and a group, within the character)
5. Is there a climax?
6. Is the denouement satisfying?

## Character

1. Does the main character seem like a real person?
2. Is the main character well rounded, with character strengths and weaknesses revealed? (In a shorter story fewer traits are exhibited.)
3. How are character traits revealed? (conversation, thoughts, author tells reader, actions) Does the author rely too much on a single strategy?
4. Does the character grow and change?
5. Is the character a delineated character?
6. Are the character's conversations and behavior consistent with age and background?

## Setting

1. Where does this story take place?
2. When does this story take place?
3. How are time and place related to the plot, characters, and theme?
4. Is this a universal setting?

## Theme

1. What is the theme?
2. Is the theme developed naturally through the actions and reactions of story characters?
3. Does the author avoid stating the theme in words (except in traditional literature)?
4. Is the abstract theme made concrete by the story?

## Style

1. What stylistic devices characterize the author's writing? (connotation, imagery, figurative language, hyperbole, understatement, allusion, symbol)
2. What is the mood of the writing? (gloomy, happy, evil, mysterious)
3. What point of view is used?
4. Is the point of view appropriate to the story?

# RECOMMENDED CHILDREN'S BOOKS

Alcock, Vivien. (1988). *The Monster Garden*. New York: Delacorte. (4–6)

Frankie uses a sample from one of her father's experiments in genetic engineering to create a baby monster that grows at an alarming rate. She must keep the monster a secret or her father will take it away from her.

Avi. (1994). *The Barn*. New York: Orchard. (5–8)

This short novel shows the relationships among three children as they cope with their father's illness and impending death.

Banks, Lynne Reid. (1980). *The Indian in the Cupboard*. New York: Doubleday. (3–6)

A nine-year-old boy receives a cupboard, an old plastic toy Indian, and a key for his birthday. The Indian comes to life in the cupboard and the boy has a series of adventures living with the Indian. There are two sequels to this book: *The Indian Returns* and *The Secret of the Indian*.

Burnett, Frances Hodgson. (1962). *The Secret Garden*. Philadelphia: Lippincott. (4–6)

A spoiled, self-centered girl and a pampered invalid find themselves in an abandoned garden. In the process of coming to terms with themselves, they learn compassion for others.

Byars, Betsy. (1988). *The Burning Questions of Bingo Brown*. New York: Viking Kestrel. (4–6)

Bingo Brown struggles with the confusing and sometimes funny problems of youth. He frequently becomes a magnet for trouble. He also acquires some disturbing insights into adult problems.

Cleary, Beverly. (1984). *Ramona Quimby Age 8*. New York: Morrow. (2–4)

This is a book in a continuing series about Ramona. In this book her mother is employed and her father is going to college. Ramona and her sister resist the changes that come with having a working mother and an unemployed father.

Cole, Brock. (1987). *The Goats*. New York: Farrar, Straus & Giroux. (5–7)

Two children attending different camps are made the "goats" of their respective camps and stranded without clothing on a nearby island. They find each other and join forces to survive physically and emotionally.

Erickson, Russell. (1974). *A Toad for Tuesday*. New York: Lothrop, Lee, and Shepard. (2–4)

Morton and Warton Toad make beetle brittle for Aunt Toolia. Warton starts off to take it to his aunt, but he is captured by an owl, who intends to eat him on Tuesday. Warton struggles with his problem and escapes in an unexpected ending.

Fox, Paula. (1988). *The Village by the Sea*. New York: Orchard. (4–7)

Ten-year-old Emma must stay with her aunt and uncle while her father has open-heart surgery. She escapes from her aunt's problems by going to a nearby beach where she makes a friend.

George, Jean Craighead. (1959). *My Side of the Mountain*. New York: Dutton. (4–6)

A city boy chooses to spend a winter alone in the Catskill region that his ancestors farmed. Through his studies he acquires the knowledge necessary to obtain food, shelter, and clothing.

Howe, Deborah, and James Howe. (1979). *Bunnicula: A Rabbit Tale of Mystery*. Illustrated by Alan Daniel. New York: Atheneum. (3–5)

This hilarious story is a tale of three pets—Harold, a dog; Chester, the cat; and Bunnicula, who may be a vampire bunny.

Jacques, Brian. (1986). *Redwall*. New York: Philomel. (3–6)

Matthias, a bumbling mouse-apprentice at Redwall Abbey, becomes an unlikely hero when Cluny, the terrible one-eyed rat, and his battle-seasoned horde vow to conquer the Abbey.

Jukes, Mavis. (1984). *Like Jake and Me.* Illustrated by Lloyd Bloom. New York: Knopf. (1–3)

At the outset the boy in this story and his stepfather seem far apart, but when they search for a wolf spider together, they come to a greater understanding. Superb illustrations.

Kesey, Ken. (1990). *Little Tricker the Squirrel Meets Big Double the Bear.* Illustrated by Barry Moser. New York: Viking Penguin. (all ages)

The author retells a story that his grandmother had told him. Big Double is a grizzly bear who is outwitted by Little Tricker the squirrel.

Klass, Sheila. (1991). *Kool Ada.* New York: Scholastic. (4–6)

Ada's only relatives die. She never speaks, so teachers assume she is slow, but Ada is determined to overcome her problems.

Kushner, Donn. (1987). *The Book Dragon.* New York: Holt Rinehart Winston. (4–6)

Nonesuch is a dragon whose life spans six centuries. This book chronicles his adventures from a treasure-strewn cave to a lofty Gothic cathedral, from plague-stricken London to a cozy 20th century bookshop.

Lindgren, Astrid. (1957). *Pippi Longstocking.* Translated by Florence Lamborn. Illustrated by Louis S. Glanzman. New York: Viking. (3–5)

This book and others in the series were translated from Swedish. Pippi is a hilarious character who lives alone with a monkey and a horse, doing whatever she pleases without adult interference. Pippi has many unusual, funny adventures.

Lowry, Lois. (1979). *Anastasia Krupnick.* Boston: Houghton Mifflin. (4–6)

The plot focuses on Anastasia's list of things she loves and hates. However, the story events change her mind about some of the items on the list, especially the new baby brother she was certain she would dislike.

Lyon, George Ella. (1989). *Together.* New York: Orchard Books. (K–2)

Two friends can do almost anything. They churn ice cream, build a house, and paint a boat. They also sometimes dream the same dream.

McCloskey, Robert. (1949). *Blueberries for Sal.* New York: Viking. (K–2)

Sal and her mother go to Blueberry Hill to pick blueberries to can for the winter. Little Bear and her mother go to the same place to store up food for the winter by eating it. The mothers and children become mixed up on Blueberry Hill.

McCord, David. (1986). *One at a Time.* Illustrated by Henry B. Kane. Boston: Little, Brown. (1–6)

This collection of McCord's poetry illustrates his use of rhythm to convey the essence of a subject.

Myers, Walter Dean. (1988). *Me, Mop, and the Moondance Kid.* Illustrated by Rodney Pate. New York: Delacorte. (3–5)

Tommy and his younger brother Moondance are adopted, but their friend Mop remains at the Dominican Academy in spite of her relentless efforts to become adopted. They share a love of baseball and work hard to overcome their opponents.

Myers, Walter Dean. (1988). *Scorpions.* New York: Harper & Row. (5–7)

Jamal is forced into taking on the leadership of a Harlem gang, the Scorpions, when his brother goes to jail. Jamal finds that he is treated with respect when he acquires a gun. Tragedy forces him to realize that he cannot keep the gun or lead the gang.

Naylor, Phyllis Reynolds. (1991). *Shiloh.* New York: Atheneum. (4–7)

A boy tries to prevent abuse to a dog that he befriends.

O'Dell, Scott. (1970). *Sing Down the Moon.* Boston: Houghton Mifflin. (4–7)

Bright Morning is the main character and the narrator in this story. Bright Morning and Tall Boy have a wonderful life planned until white men destroy their village, sheep, and crops, and then force them to move to the reservation.

Parken, Steve. (1992). *Whales and Dolphins*. San Francisco: Sierra Club. (4–8)

This informational book is illustrated with color photographs. The author provides fascinating information about whales and dolphins and their lives.

Paterson, Katherine. (1985). *Come Sing Jimmy Joe*. New York: Crowell. (4–6)

Jimmy Joe is raised by his grandmother and his uncle in the mountains. He is forced into performing country music by his parents. In spite of his fears, he comes to recognize the weakness and betrayal in his parents' actions.

————. (1978). *The Great Gilly Hopkins*. New York: Crowell. (4–6)

Gilly is a foster child who has moved from foster home to foster home. Her most recent move is to Mrs. Trotter's, where she meets William Ernest and Mr. Randolph. Her goal in life is to live with her mother, but she eventually comes to respect and love her foster mother.

————. (1977). *Bridge to Terabithia*. New York: Crowell. (4–6)

Jess is not happy with his family and has few friends. When Leslie moves into the neighborhood and his class, they become fast friends. They build a special kingdom, Terabithia. But Leslie ventures there when the creek is swollen with heavy rains and drowns. Jess must cope with her loss and his feelings of guilt.

Paulsen, Gary. (1987). *Hatchet*. New York: Puffin. (5–7)

Thirteen-year-old Brian survives a plane crash in the Canadian wilds. He spends 54 days learning to survive with the aid of a hatchet his mother gave him. He also learns how to survive his parents' divorce.

Pearce, Phillipa. (1958). *Tom's Midnight Garden*. Philadelphia: Lippincott. (4–6)

This time fantasy is about a boy who plays in a garden at midnight and becomes friends with a girl who also plays there. The garden, however, exists in the past and the little girl is now an old woman living in the same house as Tom.

Prelutsky, Jack. (1988). *Tyrannosaurus Was a Beast*. Illustrated by Arnold Lobel. New York: Greenwillow. (2–5)

This collection of humorous poems about dinosaurs conveys the essence of many common dinosaurs. For example, Brachiosaurus is described as a "perpetual eating machine." Arnold Lobel's illustrations strike just the right note.

————. (1983). *Zoo Doings*. New York: Greenwillow. (K–4)

A collection of Prelutsky's animal poems that are fine and funny.

Reeder, Carolyn. (1989). *Shades of Gray*. New York: Macmillan. (5–7)

When he is orphaned by the Civil War, the main character is forced to live with an uncle who is a pacifist. Through the incidents in this story, he gradually develops a grudging respect for his uncle's beliefs and chooses to stay with the family even when he has an opportunity to move.

Rylant, Cynthia. (1988). *Night in the Country*. Illustrated by Mary Szilagyi. New York: Bradbury. (K–2)

The rich illustrations join with the language to convey the mood of night in the country. In this book, the description of the sounds is so accurate that they truly help the reader share the experience.

Selden, George. (1960). *Cricket in Times Square*. New York: Farrar, Straus & Giroux. (4–6)

Chester Cricket travels by train into Times Square where he becomes friends with a cat and a mouse. He saves the newspaper vendors with his operatic voice.

Sendak, Maurice. (1963). *Where the Wild Things Are*. New York: Harper & Row. (K–2)

Max is sent to bed without his supper when he acts like a wild thing. He escapes in his imagination to a place where the wild things are and he can do whatever he pleases. He is king of all the wild things, but he discovers that he would like to go where someone loves him best of all.

Service, Pamela. (1988). *Stinker from Space*. New York: Scribner's. (3–5)

Tsynq Yr crashes his spaceship in Midwestern America, resulting in injury to his current body. He must seek another and moves into the only body available—that of a passing skunk. Later he makes friends with Karen and her friend Jonathan, who dub him Stinker. With the help of his friends, Stinker manages to divert a NASA project to return to his home planet, accompanied by the local skunk population.

Slote, Alfred. (1978). *My Trip to Alpha I*. Illustrated by Harold Berson. Philadelphia: Lippincott. (3–5)

This story is set in the future. Jack, the hero, travels to another planet via VOYA-CODE body travel. When he arrives, he discovers a sinister plot.

Smith, Doris Buchanan. (1988). *Return to Bitter Creek*. New York: Viking Kestrel. (4–6)

Lacey is an illegitimate child who has never met her grandparents, aunts, uncles, and cousins. Finally, her mother decides to take her to meet the family. Through a tragedy, Lacey learns about love and family life.

Snyder, Dianne. (1988). *The Boy of the Three-Year Nap*. Illustrated by Allen Say. Boston: Houghton Mifflin. (2–4)

This traditional Japanese folktale introduces a lazy character who uses his wits to acquire a fortune. The beautiful illustrations are in keeping with a traditional Japanese folktale.

Van Allsburg, Chris. (1981). *Jumanji*. Boston: Houghton Mifflin. (1–3)

Two children begin playing a jungle-adventure board game after being warned that once the game is started they cannot stop. They have a python on the mantel and a rhinoceros crashing through the living room, but they survive and return the game to the place where they found it.

Walsh, Jill Paton. (1982). *The Green Book*. New York: Farrar, Straus & Giroux. (3–6)

This science fiction adventure follows the adventures of pioneers who must leave the dying planet Earth and travel on an out-of-date spaceship. After arriving at a nearby planet they discover that they cannot grow edible food. The strange-looking objects they discover are living beings rather than food.

White, E. B. (1952). *Charlotte's Web*. New York: Harper & Row. (3–5)

The farmer plans to make bacon of Wilbur the pig, but Charlotte the spider thinks of a scheme to save her friend's life. She spins a web that identifies him as such a special pig that he should live. Unfortunately, Charlotte has completed her life span and dies at the end of the book.

White, Ruth. (1988). *Sweet Creek Holler*. New York: Farrar, Straus & Giroux. (4–8)

Ginny tells about living in an Appalachian town in 1948. She and her best friend, Lou Jean Purvis, are certain nothing can happen to them as long as they are together.

Wood, Audrey. (1988). *King Bidgood's in the Bathtub*. New York: Harcourt Brace Jovanovich. (K–2)

The king refuses to leave the bathtub in spite of the inducements offered by various members of his court. Finally, the pageboy pulls the plug to solve the problem. This cumulative story has a repeated refrain throughout.

————. (1989). *Little Penguin's Tale*. New York: Harcourt Brace Jovanovich. (K–2)

Granny Penguin tells a story to all the little ones about a penguin who danced with the gooney birds and participated in other dangerous activities. The illustrations show Little Penguin is a joyful, carefree character.

Yolen, Jane. (1990). *Dinosaur Dances.* Illustrated by Bruce Degen. New York: Putnam. (1–6)

This collection of poems about all kinds of dinosaurs dancing has wonderful rhythms and captivating illustrations. The dinosaurs do all sorts of dances, from ballet to a chorus line.

Zolotow, Charlotte. (1980). *Say It!* Illustrated by James Stevenson. New York: Harper & Row. (K–6)

A little girl and her mother go walking together on an autumn day in this book-length poem. The youngster begs her mother to "say it!" Finally, her mother tells her, "I love you, I love you, I love you."

# Three

## KEY TERMS

bibliotherapy

BIR

Caldecott Medal

catharsis

censorship

Children's Choices

great books

identification

insight

literary criticism

Newbery Award

readability

videos

Young Adult Choices

## GUIDING QUESTIONS

How do you choose books to read? You may read different types of books on vacation than for class. Do you read best-sellers? Why or why not? How do you think parents and grandparents choose books for children? Understanding your criteria for personal book selection will help you better understand how to choose books for others, especially children. As you read this chapter, keep in mind these questions:

1. What are some appropriate criteria adults can use when selecting books for children?

2. How do children's interests influence the books they choose and the ones adults choose for them?

3. How can parents, librarians, and teachers create effective environments for promoting children's interest in literature?

## OVERVIEW

Your own enthusiasm and passion for children's literature will help you cultivate a lasting love of literature in your students. Your sense of children and their needs and how they respond to books will serve you well in connecting children with books, and will help you develop their love of books. Knowing children's interests at various ages and stages of development helps you create a good fit between readers and books. Using this knowledge, you can create experiences and environments that promote children's interest in reading and literature.

In this chapter you will formulate a basis for selecting quality literature through consulting reviews, reading books, viewing films, and understanding children and their reading interests. This chapter explores the kinds of literature appropriate for children—whether classics, award winners, or books with popular appeal—and provides a framework for evaluating books, considering such issues as literary criticism, popularity, physical format, social appropriateness, and readability. There is a wide array of resources to consult when selecting literature. Keep in mind also, that literature is more than books: computers, cassette tapes, films, videos, and newspapers and magazines are different forms of literature, but they are literature.

This chapter also addresses children as readers and includes generic information about their interests. All children are individuals, however, and have differing backgrounds and experiences and unique interests. Knowing individual students and their preferences will help you find the right book for each of them. Parents, teachers and schools, and librarians and libraries also have roles in promoting reading interests. Book selection is a never-ending quest for works that will develop children's love of literature and help them grow into lifelong readers.

# Connecting Children and Literature

## EVALUATING AND SELECTING BOOKS

......................... ## INTRODUCTION

As you will see from the opening vignette, book selection is a complex process requiring considerable thought and effort. The search for quality literature is complicated by the fact that some 50,000 children's books are currently in print and more than 6,000 new ones are published each year. Adults must consider a variety of factors and consult numerous resources to find the connections that will spark children's interest in literature. These considerations include such factors as the content of the books, readers' interests, and the purposes for integrating literature in our classrooms.

Children's reading interests are a powerful influence on their overall literacy development. Children learn to read by reading, and the more they read the better they read; it follows that developing children's reading interests is beneficial to their reading habits. Children who are interested in reading are more likely both to read and to become more fluent readers. Reading interest is a complicated topic, however, because children's reading interests hinge on their stage of development as well as their individual experiences. These factors make it difficult to generalize regarding reading interests.

In most classrooms, teachers try to provide for a range of reading experiences and abilities. They seek to create experiences that entertain, provoke thought, expand knowledge, develop language, serve as models for writers, and provide many other benefits to students. Above all, teachers hope to create experiences that will motivate children to read more books. To this end, teachers and librarians select great books, classic books, and books that are good but not necessarily great. A teacher who is seeking to entertain students may elect to read Norman Bridwell's *Clifford the Big Red Dog* to first graders. This book is very popular with children, although it is not a great literary work. A teacher who seeks to motivate further reading might select Louis Sacher's *Wayside School Gets a Little Strange* for third graders. After listening to one of the Wayside School books, many children are motivated to read other books in this hilarious series. In addition, the use of videos such as Beverly Cleary's "Ramona" series motivates children to read the books on their own.

If the goal is to develop students' appreciation for the author's craft, a fifth-grade teacher might choose to read *Johnny Tremain* by Esther Forbes for its exemplary literary quality and timeless appeal. This experience with courage and war can be extended by comparing the Revolutionary War depicted in *Johnny Tremain* with the World War II experience of the Japanese American battalion depicted in *Heroes* by Ken Mochizuki.

Literature selection criteria are dynamic and change with the goals and purposes of the individual making the choices. Teachers give their students opportunities for meaningful encounters with literature when they maintain a flexible approach to book selection and expose children to a wide variety of reading materials. As children read books with differing levels of quality, they begin to develop a sense of those that have greater literary quality. In addition, providing children with many opportunities to choose books they would like to read encourages them to choose reading as a leisure-time activity when they are not in school.

····················· *Vignette*

While he was planning his lesson, Jim Smith glanced at his calendar and noted the date. It was November 1, and at least half of his class read no better than they had at the beginning of the school year. The reading skills of these students were well below their grade level and they were unmotivated to read. Mr. Smith knew their best hope for developing reading fluency lay in encouraging them to read extensively in books they enjoyed.

At the beginning of the school year, he had given the class an interest inventory, but they had joked around rather than doing the inventory. He had considered engaging them in a group discussion to learn more about their reading interests but was concerned that they might not discuss their interests any more seriously than they had completed the inventory. Instead, he decided to consult some references in order to identify books that appealed to this age group, then read some books aloud to the class to see what sparked their interest. After consulting *Best Books for Junior High Readers* (Gillespie, 1991), *The Read Aloud Handbook* (Trelease, 1989), and the databases *Bookwhiz* (Educational Testing Service, 1987) and *Children's Reference Plus* (Bowker, 1991), he identified three books to read aloud: *Slake's Limbo* by Felice Holman, *Hatchet* by Gary Paulsen, and *Incident at Hawk's Hill* by Alan Eckert.

He started the read-aloud sessions with *Slake's Limbo*. When his students pleaded "keep on reading, please" he knew he was on the right track. They were interested! He returned to his references to find other books with the same appeal. After obtaining copies from the public and school libraries, Mr. Smith prepared brief synopses of each book and created a display of the books and their synopses, so the students could choose the ones they wanted to read.

He continued reading aloud and watching the students' responses, gathering ideas for other displays to spark their interests. He purchased multiple paperback copies of the most popular books. The students read more and more as the school year progressed, and their fluency increased as they read.

## EVALUATING CHILDREN'S LITERATURE

Literary quality is a primary consideration in evaluating any literature. However, book selection based on literary quality should never preclude consideration of whether children will have an interest in the book. Bauer and Sanborn (1981) believe that literary quality and popularity are both important in choosing literature for children. Children must want to read, view, or listen to the work, and evaluating this factor should be as important as evaluating the literary quality of the work. Current **literary criticism** reflects the growing interest in children's books and book selection. In general, literary criticism *falls into three categories: work-centered criticism (focused on the quality of the work), child-centered criticism (focused on children's response to the work), and issues-centered criticism (focused on the appropriate presentation of various social issues in the work)*. All three components of criticism are important to consider when choosing literature for children: a book may present social issues accurately while failing to achieve excellence in storytelling; a book of excellent literary quality may not appeal to children's interests. A comprehensive approach emphasizes the importance of finding the perfect fit between reader and story.

## WORK-CENTERED CRITERIA

One of the first criteria applied by most adults in selecting children's literature is that of quality. "We should put in their hands only the books worthy of them: the books of honesty, integrity, and vision—the books on which they can grow.

Reading which does not stir their imagination, which does not stretch their minds, not only wastes their time but will not hold them permanently" (Smith, 1967, p. 13). Such quality books have come to be regarded as **great books,** those that *have stood the test of time and continue to attract readers generation after generation.* These books possess high literary quality as well as transmitting the significant values of the culture (Hill, 1986). Despite children's changing tastes and interests, great books continue to attract a wide audience and sell large numbers. According to *U.S. News and World Report,* "Sales of old favorites remain the backbone of the [children's book] market" (Rachlin, 1988, p. 50). Books from every genre are included among these favorites.

The Children's Literature Association has identified the 10 best American children's books of "enduring quality" published during the past 200 years. The list includes older books such as Mark Twain's *The Adventures of Tom Sawyer* and Louisa May Alcott's *Little Women* along with more recent titles such as *Island of the Blue Dolphins* by Scott O'Dell and *Julie of the Wolves* by Jean George. This illustrates the point that a book can be a great book even though it is not a venerated classic. In fact, some books attain the status of great books within a relatively short time span. Maurice Sendak's *Where the Wild Things Are,* a book that is a standard in most children's libraries today, is an example of this phenomenon.

What is the appeal of a truly great children's book? Why do so many children return to these books year after year? First of all, they are magnificent stories. Today's children find the adventures of Tom Sawyer and Robinson Crusoe as intriguing as did earlier generations. Second, the characters, memorable and well drawn, live on in our adult minds—consider Peter Pan and Captain Hook. Third, although great books generally cross genre lines, many are fantasies. *Charlotte's Web, The Secret Garden,* and *The Borrowers,* by E. B. White, Frances Hodgson Burnett, and Mary Norton, respectively, continue to capture children's imaginations, proving the lasting appeal of excellent fantasy. Fourth, many great books combine memorable text with vivid illustrations. Books such as Beatrix Potter's *The Tale of Peter Rabbit* and Maurice Sendak's *Where the Wild*

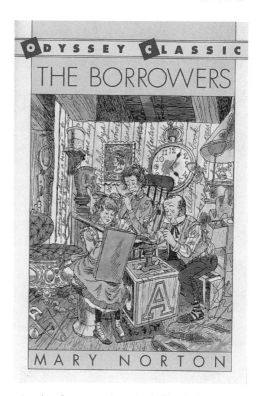

In this fantasy, the Clock family lives in a miniature world furnished with things they have "borrowed" from the "human beans": spools of thread for chairs and postage stamps for paintings.

*Things Are* illustrate this union of text and illustration. The true classics of literature are books that remain popular because children want to read them.

## Award Books and Recommended Reading Lists

Some adults believe the best way to choose books for children is to focus on award winners. The majority of children's literature awards, such as the Newbery Award, are given by adults, who tend to choose books based on authors and titles they have heard of previously and favorites from their own childhood (Stoodt, 1993), and professional adults (teachers, librarians, and professors) who tend to select books that reflect high literary standards.

*The story of a six-year-old girl whose Aunt May has died, this book is the winner of the 1993 Newbery Award.*

### Newbery Award

**Newbery Awards** are *given to books that have outstanding literary quality.* Each year this award goes to the author of a book published in the United States that represents the most outstanding contribution to the field of children's literature. This prestigious award is named after John Newbery (1713–67), the first British publisher of books intended expressly for children It is a sought-after award because it represents artistic achievement and carries significant media attention.

A 15-member committee of the Association for Library Service to Children of the American Library Association determines the winners. Although the award is given to only one book, others are identified as runners-up, called honor books. (See the Appendix for a list of winners and honor books.) Criteria for the award are shown in the box on page 64.

Newbery Award books are fine examples of literature; as previously noted, however, they are selected by adults. Research indicates that many Newbery titles are beyond the reading ability of elementary children. In fact, Shafer (1976) found the readability of almost one-third of the Newbery titles to be fifth grade or above. Newbery books are often best presented as read-alouds to younger children or less able readers.

### Caldecott Medal

The **Caldecott Medal**, named for the great British illustrator Randolph Caldecott, *is awarded annually to the illustrator of the most distinguished picture book published in the United States.* (See the Appendix for the list.) The criteria require that the award be given not only for excellence in artwork, but also for the effective interaction of text and illustrations (see the box on page 64). Books featuring a wide range of media have won the Caldecott Medal; watercolor, pen and ink, and collage have all been represented. Caldecott Medal winners are typically suitable for younger children, but some, such as Chris Van Allsburg's *The Polar Express*, appeal to all age groups. Caldecott names honor books as well.

### Other awards

While the Newbery Award and the Caldecott Medal are the best known of all children's book awards, a number of additional awards are presented each year to exemplary children's books (see the Appendix). The list below identifies a few of these.

- The Hans Christian Andersen International Medal is awarded to living authors and artists by the International Board on Books for Young People.
- The International Reading Association presents the Children's Book Award to authors with unusual promise.
- The Laura Ingalls Wilder Award is given to authors or illustrators who have made lasting contributions to children's literature.
- The Boston Globe/Horn Book Award is presented to authors of fiction and nonfiction and to illustrators.

*In this Caldecott Medal winner, the author has created an otherworldly classic of the Christmas season, which is full of strange and moving shades of full-color art.*

## Recommended reading lists

A number of educational organizations offer lists of recommended books that include great books, good books, and classics. For instance, The American Library Association compiles lists of notable books. The Teachers' Choices project, administered by the International Reading Association, identifies outstanding trade books for children and adolescents that effectively enhance the curriculum. Regional teams of teachers field test between 200 and 300 books annually and compile a list of 30 books categorized as primary (grades K–2), intermediate (grades 3–5), and advanced (grades 6–8). Books are selected on the basis of literary quality and presentation, the need for teachers to guide children to such books, and appropriateness for use across the curriculum.

The Child Study Children's Book Committee of Bank Street College compiles an annual list, as does the California State Department of Education. Each year the Children's Book Council works with the National Science Teachers Association and the National Council for the Social Studies, respectively, to compile "Outstanding Science Trade Books for Children" and "Notable Children's Trade Books in the Field of Social Studies," annotated bibliographies published in *Social Education* and *Science and Children*.

*School Library Journal* also publishes lists and book reviews: for instance, "Reference Book Roundup" appears in the May issue each year. In addition to these lists, children's books are regularly reviewed and recommended in periodicals like *The Horn Book*, *The Horn Book Guide to Children's and Young Adult Books*, *The Bulletin of the Center for Children's Books*, *Reading Teacher*, *Journal of Reading*, *Language Arts*, *Perspectives*, and *The New Advocate*.

In addition to these periodicals, a number of reference books have been published to help adults choose books for children. The following list identifies some of the best of these guides.

- Dreyer, S. S. (Ed.). *The Bookfinder: A Guide to Children's Literature About the Needs and Problems of Youth Aged 2–15.* American Guidance Service.
- Hearne, Betsy. *Choosing Books for Children.* Delacorte Press.
- Isaacson, R., F. Hillegas, and J. Yaakov. *Children's Catalog.* H. W. Wilson.
- Jensen, Julie M. and Nancy L. Roser (Eds.). *Adventuring with Books: A Booklist for Pre-K–Grade 6.* National Council of Teachers of English.
- Liggett, Twila C. and Cynthia Mayer Benfield. *Reading Rainbow Guide to Children's Books.* Citadel Press.
- Lima, C. W. and J. A. Lima. *A to Zoo: Subject Access to Children's Picture Books.* R. R. Bowker.
- Miller-Lachmann, Lyn. *Our Family Our Friends Our World.* R. R. Bowker.
- Oppenheim, Joanne. *Choosing Books for Kids. (A Bank Street Book).* Ballantine Books.
- *Subject Guide to Children's Books in Print.* R. R. Bowker.
- Thomas, James L. *Play, Learn & Grow.* R. R. Bowker. (Books for young children.)
- Winkel, L. (Ed.) *The Elementary School Library Collection: A Guide to Books and Other Media.* Brodart Foundation.

# Criteria for the Newbery Award

1. In identifying distinguished writing in a book for children committee members must:

   a. consider:

      - interpretation of the theme or concept
      - presentation of information including accuracy, clarity and organization
      - development of plot
      - delineation of characters
      - delineation of setting
      - appropriateness of style

   NOTE: Because the literary qualities to be considered will vary depending on content, the committee need not expect to find excellence in each of the named elements. The book should, however, have distinguished qualities in all the elements pertinent to it.

   b. consider excellence of presentation for a child audience

2. Each book is to be considered as a contribution to literature. The committee is to make its decision primarily on the text. Other aspects of a book are to be considered only if they distract from the text. Such other aspects might include illustrations or overall design of the book.

   NOTE: The committee should keep in mind that the award is for literary quality and quality of presentation for children. The award is not for didactic intent or for popularity.

From: Peterson, Linda K. and Marilyn L. Solt. (1982). *Newbery and Caldecott Medal and Honor Books,* p. 399. New Providence, NJ: R. R. Bowker.

# Criteria for the Caldecott Medal

1. In identifying a distinguished picture book for children committee members must:

   a. consider the excellence of:

      - execution in the artistic technique employed
      - pictorial interpretation of story, theme, or concept
      - appropriateness of style of illustration to the story, theme, or concept
      - delineation of plot, theme, characters, setting, mood, or information through the pictures

   b. consider the excellence of presentation in recognition of a child audience

2. The only limitation to graphic form is that the form must be one that may be used in a picture book (film photography is not considered, but still photography is).

3. Each book is to be considered as a picture book. The committee is to make its decision primarily on the illustrations, but other components of a book are to be considered, especially when they make a book less effective as a children's picture book. Other components might include elements such as the written text or the overall design of the book.

   NOTE: The committee should keep in mind that the award is for distinguished illustrations in a picture book and for excellence of pictorial presentation for children. The award is not for didactic intent or for popularity.

From: Peterson, Linda K. and Marilyn L. Solt. (1982). *Newbery and Caldecott Medal and Honor Books,* p. 400. New Providence, NJ: R. R. Bowker.

*Criticism of award books and reading lists*

Some children's literature authorities advocate the exclusive use of books with superior literary quality. Indeed, literary quality is an important consideration in selecting books. But there are many fine children's books that contribute to children's developing appreciation of literature, although they may not achieve the highest standards of literary excellence. For instance, a book may address the problems of a child whose parents are divorcing in spite of the fact that its literary qualities are not outstanding.

Children's book awards and recommended lists have been criticized on several counts. First, such awards are often given to books appealing to only a small segment of the population, selected not on the basis of popularity with children but only on the basis of their quality. This can create the problem of elitism: "The times have changed, but not so children's librarians. . . . We have our high standards of literature to maintain. We have our Newbery winner . . . that reflects the judgment of adults with little regard for what children are reading" (Kalkoff, 1973, p. 15).

Second, many children's favorites are outstanding works that did not receive Newbery Awards. For example, the Little House books by Laura Ingalls Wilder and *Charlotte's Web* by E. B. White were not recipients. Research also shows that Newbery books are not popular with children (Laurence, 1956) and that the Newbery honor books (the runners-up) are more popular than the winners (Lacy, 1980).

Third, the vast majority of awards and lists reflect the standards and taste of adults; they should be viewed as resources rather than prescriptions for children's reading. Ohanian (1990) points out the dangers of such lists: "Rather than including children in some sort of common cultural foundation, they exclude [children] from the rich possibilities of language and literature. . . . Lists . . . end up driving the curriculum, making us forget the needs of individuals" (p. 176). Bauer and Sanborn (1981) believe that both children's preferences and adult preferences should be considered in giving awards. One example of a children-selected award is *Children's Choices* by the International Reading Association. "Adult-selected awards set literary standards, whereas awards selected by young readers represent interests and needs. Both types of awards are important, as they celebrate achievement in children's literature, bring attention to the importance of children's books in the total body of literature available in our country, and stimulate young people's reading" (p. 56).

Betsy Hearne (1991) also stresses the importance of personal appeal and involvement in selecting children's books. She suggests that adults begin choosing books that meet their standards but that also appeal to children. She maintains that children's responses to books are as important as experts' recommendations. The power of personal attraction to a book cannot be under- estimated. During their school years, children will read many types of literature, some of which will have enormous personal value for them, in spite of the fact that adults do not understand the attraction. Many teachers and librarians recognize that reader response is central to literary experience. (Response to literature is explored further in Chapter Four.)

The goal in connecting children and literature is to include them in the "literacy club" (Smith, 1988). Great books, award-winning books, and recommended books can serve as guides toward books of excellence. When used to the exclusion of other guidelines, however, these books may expose children to an extremely limited view of the world and the people who inhabit it.

## CHILD-CENTERED CRITERIA

Many teachers who use trade books in their classrooms advocate children's free choice of literature as an important element for promoting reading in classrooms. Some suggest that children themselves should be the ultimate critics of their literature, that children's preferences for certain kinds of books should not only be honored but also should form a basis for evaluating books. Children's reading selections often differ widely from the books adults select for them, and frequently include series books such as Nancy Drew, Hardy Boys, and Babysitter's Club as well as books based on television shows and movies. Thousands of teachers and librarians compiled bibliographies of what their children read, revealing that "the respondents became momentarily addicted to both the series and comic books. . . .

---

# *Guidelines for Literature Selection*

Remember to consider not only literary quality when selecting children's books but children's reading interests and issues as well. This will help create a well-balanced literary experience for the children.

1. Is the book of high literary quality?
   a. Fiction
      - Is the plot well developed?
      - Are characters well drawn and memorable?
      - Does the setting accurately reflect the time and place?
      - Is the theme significant?
      - Is the book carefully crafted and well written?
   b. Nonfiction
      - Is the author qualified to write this book?
      - Is the information clearly organized and presented?
      - Is the information accurate?
      - Is this book appropriate to a child audience?
2. Does the book appeal to children's reading interests?
3. Does the book avoid stereotyping on the basis of race, sex, age, and other discriminatory factors?
4. Is the book's readability level appropriate to the audience that is expected to read it?
5. Is the book's physical format appealing to children?
6. Will this book enhance the child's personal growth and development?
7. Will this book contribute to the child's development as a reader?
8. Will this book help foster a love of reading in this child?
9. Am I creating an environment that will help promote love of literature?

---

These materials seem to be as much a part of one's literary maturation as are the children's classics" (Carlsen and Sherrill, 1988, p. 16).

How do we explain the popularity of such books? First, they possess predictable language, action, and characters. This predictability, coupled with following the same characters' adventures through several books, creates a familiarity that many children enjoy. Second, children identify readily with the characters in these books. While the characters are often one-dimensional, they do possess the larger-than-life characteristics of mythological heroes that are important in traditional literature. As Purves and Monson (1984) indicate, series characters in children's books are not terribly real, but they consistently outsmart adults, they are seldom depressed, and are unfail-

ingly "nice," and they seem to represent characteristics that we admire and find agreeable. Although they are clichés, they sustain us in the same ways that *Cinderella* and *Little Red Riding Hood* do (Purves and Monson, 1984).

Although these books lack literary quality, they do have value for young readers. "The experience of making patterns, putting stories together, extrapolating and confirming may be providing a crucial step towards more substantial reading" (Mackey, 1990, p. 44). Series books also help children see connections between books from a variety of genre. The effective teacher can help children discern similarities between series book characters and those found in myths, legends, and other traditional literature. Moreover, such books simply add to "the reservoir of experiences and ideas created from the sum total of all their reading"; the richer this reservoir of experience and ideas, the more effective children's transactions with literature will become over time (Purves and Monson, 1984).

## Children's Choices

The Children's Choices project, mentioned earlier, is a national survey of children's reading preferences. It identifies the interests of 10,000 children nationwide in grades K–8 and is conducted by the International Reading Association/Children's Book Council Joint Committee. The winners are published each October in *The Reading Teacher*. Books are grouped by reading levels: all ages, younger readers, middle grades, and older readers. The label **BIR** indicates *books that are especially useful for beginning independent readers*. In addition, results of the **Young Adult Choices** project, similar in design to the **Children's Choices** project, are published each October in the *Journal of Reading*.

## What Children Like

What attracts children to certain books? Lehman (1991) studied nine award-winning books that appeared on the Children's Choices list (International Reading Association). After analyzing and categorizing the theme, style, and structure of each, she generalized the following:

1. Substantial differences do exist between award-winning books children prefer and do not prefer. The following items identify some of the reasons for this phenomenon.
2. Children prefer predictable qualities, optimistic tone, and a lively pace.
3. Children prefer action-oriented structures and complete plot resolutions.
4. Children do not choose books with unresolved endings, tragic tones, or slow-paced, introspective plots.

### Physical characteristics

The physical appearance of books is important to children. Their choice of books is influenced by type size, style, illustrations, and covers. Children in grades 3–8 select books on the basis of appearance,

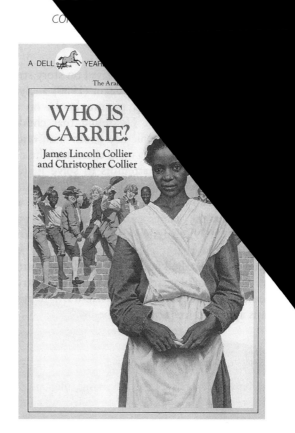

Elementary grade children prefer paperback books like *Who Is Carrie?* the story of a young girl who has been a kitchen slave in a New York City tavern for as long as she can remember.

author, recommendation, or some combination of these factors. Older children base their decisions on peer recommendations and the informational blurb on the book jacket (Burgess, 1985). Elementary children prefer paperback to hardcover when selecting books for individualized reading (Campbell, Griswold, and Smith, 1988). Fifth graders made different choices depending upon whether they saw the actual book or merely read an annotation (Brown, 1971).

Illustrations are important to children's choices at all grade levels. Cappa (1958) found that illustrations are the most important source of appeal for kindergartners. Young children generally prefer color illustrations (Stewig, 1972). Even middle-school students prefer books with illustrations to those without (Robbins, 1982).

...tation-
...the list.

## Reading Interests

Content is typically regarded as the most important criterion children use in selecting books. Studies over a period of years yield surprisingly consistent results about the topics that appeal to children (Wolfson, Manning, and Manning, 1984). The general interests of children of all ages include animals, humor, action, suspense, and surprise (Huck et al., 1987). There is also research to indicate that reading ability affects reading interests (Swanton, 1984).

Although the individual nature of reading interests makes it impossible to generalize about the interests of any particular reader, the many investigations of children's reading interests that have been conducted over the years are useful in generating general guidelines for selecting books for children. The studies of children's reading interests are somewhat dated, but the most pertinent are summarized here to help concerned adults think about the reading interests of children (Greenlaw and Wielan, 1979).

### Influences on children's reading interests

Many factors influence children's reading interests; age, sex, home environment, teacher, classroom environment, accessibility of books, and academic ability are just a few. Children's reading interests are an important aspect of their response to literature, and adults have a better chance of creating pleasurable reading experiences for children when they understand children's reading interests, as this knowledge can help them motivate children to read more. Students who enjoy books spend more time reading. Also, children comprehend interesting books better than they do books that are less interesting (Asher and Markell, 1974).

*Age.* Age is clearly related to reading interests. Children's book preferences gradually change as they mature. Younger children exhibit narrow reading interests that gradually broaden as they move from the primary to the elementary grades and then to middle school. Younger children generally have narrower reading interests because they have had fewer life experiences and thus have not developed a range of interests. Research indicates that younger children enjoy fairy tales, animals, make believe, and stories about children. They prefer fiction to nonfiction, although this finding may change in the future because of the increasing numbers of nonfiction books for younger children. First and second graders in 10 countries preferred fairy tales and fantasy to other types of stories (Feeley, 1981). Favat (1977) posits that young children enjoy fairy tales because these stories reflect their thinking patterns. Research also suggests that these children enjoy humorous books and poetry (Sebesta, 1979), particularly poetry with rhyme (Fisher and Natarella, 1982).

Children in grades four through six consistently exhibit a wider range of interest than their younger counterparts. As children mature they become more interested in realistic literature (Purves and Beach, 1972). Elementary students enjoy adventure stories, fantasies, social studies and history, mysteries, animals, and humor (Pieronek, 1980). Table 3.1 summarizes the research regarding elementary- and middle-school students' preferences. Students between the ages of 10 and 13 generally are more interested in recreational reading and develop a broader range of interests because they dip into many different genres that reflect their range of experiences. In fact, students at this age probably indulge in more recreational reading than they will at any time during their educational lives. As students progress through school,

## TABLE 3.1

Elementary- and middle-school reading preferences.

| TOPIC | EXAMPLE |
| --- | --- |
| Adventure | *The Righteous Revenge of Artemis Bonner* by Walter Dean Myers |
| Animal stories | *Shiloh* by Phyllis Reynolds Naylor |
| Fantasy | *Mariel of Redwall* by Brian Jacques |
| History | *Shades of Gray* by Carolyn Reeder |
| Humor | *The Boy Who Owned the School* by Gary Paulsen |
| Mystery | *The Man Who Was Poe* by Avi |
| Social issues | *The Coldest Winter* by Elizabeth Lutzeier |

## TABLE 3.2

Gender differences in children's reading interests.

| BOYS' INTERESTS | GIRLS' INTERESTS |
| --- | --- |
| *Male characters* | *Female characters* |
| *Nonfiction topics* | *Fiction topics* |
| ■ science | ■ families |
| ■ animals | ■ home |
| ■ history | ■ romance |
| ■ biography | ■ historical fiction |
| ■ geography | ■ mystery/adventure |
| ■ sports | ■ fantasy |
| ■ cars | ■ multiethnic |
| ■ war | *Nonfiction topics* |
| ■ machines | ■ sports |
| ■ applied science | ■ arts |
| ■ adventure | ■ multiethnic |

the academic and social demands of their lives leave less and less time for recreational reading.

*Gender.* Although the role of gender in reading interests is unclear because of the individual nature of children's reading interests, research indicates that these differences become more prominent at about age nine (Haynes, 1988), with the greatest number of differences appearing between the ages of 10 and 13. The impact of gender on reading interests has been observed in many different countries (Fisher, 1988). Sex stereotypes in reading preferences have been observed in preschool children as well as school-age students (Kropp and Halverson, 1983). Boys prefer the main characters to be male and girls prefer them to be female. The same preferences were observed in fifth-grade students (Hopkins, 1988). It is difficult to determine whether these are actual differences or a reflection of culturally transmitted behavior.

In general, elementary girls prefer fiction about home, family, and animals (Haynes, 1988). Elementary girls enjoy fantasy, while boys in these grades exhibit a growing interest in nonfiction. Boys like action and adventure stories and sports stories (Haynes, 1988). The gender differences in children's reading interests are summarized in Table 3.2.

*Environment.* The home, school, teacher, and community are all powerful influences on children's interests, motivations, and development. Morrow (1983) finds that young children who express interest in literature come from homes with environments supportive of literacy: books are available and parents read for themselves and to their children and use the public library. According to Morrow, "Before the child gets to school many background characteristics that have been linked to high and low interest in literature have been established" (p. 229).

The school, classroom, and teacher also have substantial impact on children's reading interests. More and more studies point to the positive effects of teachers' influence on children's reading interests. Blatt's (1981) longitudinal study of classroom environments in which children learned to read finds that teachers are most successful in fostering reading interests when they give children time to read, use literature to teach reading, or read aloud regularly to students. Fielding, Wilson, and Anderson (1986) find that avid readers belong to communities of readers that begin at home but expand to include peers and teachers. In fact, Zimet (1966) finds that peers have the greatest influence on children's reading.

Hiebert, Mervar, and Person (1990) find that second graders whose classrooms contain many trade books and commonly use literature give more detailed reasons for their book selections and have specific books in mind when they visit the library. Morrow (1983) finds that kindergartners from classrooms with literature programs that rate as good or excellent show higher interest in books than children who do not come from such classrooms.

Family and school have a stronger influence on children's interest in reading than some other factors. Studies of the reading interests of urban and suburban children, however, show that there are other factors at work as well. Feeley (1981) reports that suburban boys prefer sports and historical fiction more than urban boys. Suburban females prefer social empathy and animal stories, while urban females show higher preference for books related to the arts. Emans (1968) finds that inner-city children enjoy books about families, friends, and pets rather than city themes. Johns (1975), studying inner-city children's preferences for books representing inner-city environments and characters, reports that intermediate graders prefer books with middle-class settings and characters, characters with positive self-concepts, and positive group interaction.

*Race and ethnicity.* The research results regarding the racial and ethnic differences in children's reading interests are dated and inconclusive. The availability of literature with minority characters as protagonists was so limited in the past that children had little opportunity to exhibit differences in reading interests. We do know, however, that children enjoy reading about people who are like themselves, so there is a good chance that with exposure to multicultural literature, minority children will prefer it.

*Reading ability.* The influence of reading ability on reading interest is unclear. A number of studies indicate that reading interests of students at different achievement levels do not differ (Stanchfield and Fraim, 1979; Hawkins, 1984). Swanton (1984), however, finds that gifted readers prefer mysteries, fiction, science fiction, and fantasy, while average readers prefer mysteries, comedy/humor, realistic

fiction, and adventure. She also finds that children in different groups choose different favorite authors. Style may contribute to these differences; for example, some authors write in abstract language, which appeals to some children, while others prefer authors who use concrete language. Readers with higher ability select longer books than less able readers (Anderson, Higgins, and Wurster, 1985) and choose books that are enjoyed by children who are two to three years older but have less ability (Russell, 1961).

*Readability.* Books with too many unknown words daunt even the most determined readers. Some books are meant to be read aloud to children and others to be read independently. Although children with a strong interest in a topic can compensate for difficult readability, it is unwise to expect too much of readers.

**Readability** refers to *the reading level of a book*, and this level should be considered not only by teachers, parents, and librarians when selecting books for children to read but also by children themselves as they select books to read on their own. Readability formulas provide a rough measure of the range of difficulty of a book based on the number of difficult words and the average sentence length. There are several different formulas for teachers to apply to books, but a simple one can be applied by children themselves to check the difficulty of a particular book. The "five-finger test" simply involves selecting a page in a book and counting on the fingers of one hand the number of unknown words. If there are five or more unknown words, the book may be too difficult.

Some children's books include information regarding the readability level on the dust jacket or cover. "RL 4.0" means that the book is written at a fourth-grade reading level. This does not mean the book is appropriate for every fourth grader, since reading abilities in a fourth-grade classroom may range from first to seventh grade. Moreover, children must be able to pronounce 98 to 100 percent of the words and answer 90 to 100 percent of the questions asked about the book if they are to read with understanding. Therefore, if the book is to be read independently, it might well be appropriate for an average reader in fifth grade.

## Identifying reading interests

Teachers can identify individual children's reading interests through three different techniques:

1. Observe children as they engage in classroom activities, noting and recording interests exhibited during class assignments, oral discussions, group projects, and so forth.

2. Informal discussions with the children themselves, their parents, peers, and others will reveal some interests.

3. Interest inventories, which take a variety of forms, ask children directly about their reading interests. Children can list favorite book titles, respond to questions through a multiple-choice format, or complete sentence starters (illustrated in Figure 3.1).

## ISSUES-CENTERED CRITERIA

Our society has changed significantly in recent years. In the United States we are moving toward greater concern for all racial and ethnic groups. We are trying to provide a better quality of life for the people who are challenged physically, mentally, or emotionally. Although we have not yet achieved these goals, we are moving forward. Children's literature should reflect respect and concern for all people in our world.

The Council on Interracial Books for Children, for instance, states that books should promote human values "that lead to greater human liberation" (1976, p. 4), and this is the primary criterion whereby this group evaluates children's books. They evaluate children's literature for the presence of racism, sexism, ageism, classism, materialism, and elitism, based on their understanding of human liberation. This section addresses some aspects of evaluating children's books to ensure appropriate portrayal of the diversity in our culture. (These issues will be examined further in Chapters Four and Fourteen.)

### FIGURE 3.1

Interest inventory.

1. I like to read about _____ .
2. I go to the library every _____ .
3. I like to read when _____ .
4. I like to read more than I like to _____ .
5. I like to watch television every _____ .
6. I like television shows about _____ .
7. Books about sports are _____ .
8. I think horse stories are _____ .
9. I think mysteries are _____ .
10. My favorite author is _____ .
11. Books bore me when _____ .
12. I read funny stories about _____ .
13. When I have spare time, I _____ .
14. I like to read in _____ .
15. Good books make me feel _____ .
16. The best books are about _____ .
17. I own _____ books.
18. My favorite video is _____ .
19. The best taped book I have heard is _____ .
20. I read these books on computers _____ .

Scoring:

Score one point for each positive answer. Positive answers are answers that indicate the student enjoys reading and has identifiable reading, listening, and viewing interests.

13–17 = child has positive attitude toward reading

9–12 = child has average interest in reading

1–8 = child needs guidance in developing greater interest in reading

## Racial and Ethnic Issues

Children's books are powerful allies in socialization, so they should present positive and accurate portrayals of minority cultures. Huck, Hepler, and Hickman (1987) suggest that in addition to evaluating books for literary quality, adults need to consider whether they (1) provide diversity and range of representation, (2) avoid stereotyping, (3) use appropriate language, and (4) have appropriate cultural perspectives.

In order to provide diversity and range of representation, children's books should portray minorities in a wide variety of economic circumstances, lifestyles, and occupations. Consistent portrayal of Asian Americans as studious scientists or engineers stereotypes them in a way that is just as inaccurate and damaging as portraying all Hispanics as poor migrant workers. Members of particular cultural groups must be regarded as unique individuals with their own values, beliefs, and opinions, not merely as representatives of those groups. (This topic is treated in greater depth in Chapter Fourteen.)

In a recent study of multicultural picture books, Costello (1992) reports that African American adults have specific criteria in mind when they select books for children: accurate portrayal of their culture, lives, and concepts of beauty, and illustrations that look like their children. In a study of children's responses to picture books, Costello finds that minority readers identify with a main character who is a member of a minority group. However, children's discussion of the main character was important to their understanding of and identification with that character. This topic is discussed in greater detail in Chapter Fourteen.

In order to avoid stereotyping, authors should refrain from using certain items that traditionally have been associated with particular ethnic groups, such as *sombreros*. Customs and values of each group should be accurately portrayed. Illustrations should capture the distinctive characteristics of a particular group and should portray scenes containing members of many cultures. Illustrations of nonwhite characters should be readily recognizable as members of a particular racial or cultural group.

Excellent multicultural literature tells the story from the perspective of a member of the cultural

*African American adults choose this book for their children because it portrays the true story of the importance of the Negro baseball leagues.*

group told about in the story rather than from the perspective of the white majority. It depicts characters as capable of making their own decisions and meeting their own needs without the intervention of white benefactors. Nonwhite characters are represented as being equal to white characters, not subservient or inferior.

## Gender Stereotyping Issues

Evaluation of children's books includes attention to gender stereotyping. Many children's books have traditionally depicted women only in traditional roles such as housewives, reflecting the culture that existed at the time they were written. Traditional literature sometimes portrays helpless, vulnerable female characters waiting for strong, capable men to rescue them, as in *Snow White* and *Cinderella*.

While we often point to such works as examples of female stereotyping, they also stereotype men as perpetually strong, capable, and competent. Although it is unfair to criticize such works for reflecting the needs, values, and mores of people long ago, it is important, especially in selecting contemporary literature, to offer students a wide variety of all types of literature, ensuring that they have access to plenty of books that carefully avoid the use of gender stereotypes.

Appropriate portrayal of females includes presenting them in a variety of occupations, accurately portraying their contributions to society, showing them deriving satisfaction from their achievements, and describing them as intelligent, independent, and strong. *Little Miss Muffet Fights Back* (Feminists on Children's Media, 1972) provides an excellent list of nonsexist books for girls. Modern folktales are reversing the stereotyping found in the aforementioned examples from this genre. Robert Munsch provides a view of a contemporary princess who takes charge of her own life in *The Paperbag Princess*; other stories, such as Jane Yolen's *Dove Isabeau* and Charlotte Huck's *Princess Furball*, portray women as strong and capable.

Additional examples of books that avoid stereotyped portrayals of women include *The Hero and the Crown* by Robin McKinley and *Sarah, Plain and Tall* by Patricia MacLachlan. The heroine of *The Hero and the Crown* is a strong, capable female who slays dragons and overcomes an evil magician. While the setting of this epic is common to traditional literature, the heroine is not depicted in a stereotypical manner. Sarah, of *Sarah, Plain and Tall*, describes herself as "not mild mannered" in a letter to her prospective husband. While Sarah is a "mail order bride," there is no sense that she is desperate for marriage, only that she welcomes the opportunity for adventure provided by her trip west. Conversely, Steven Kellogg's modern picture book *Can I Keep Him?* promotes stereotyping through illustrations of an aproned mother who is devoted to housework.

Literature that avoids stereotyping men and boys portrays them as sensitive human beings with a wide range of emotions. In addition, males as well as females should be portrayed in a variety of occupations, including those traditionally reserved for women. Books such as Gary Paulsen's *Hatchet* show an adolescent boy learning to survive in the

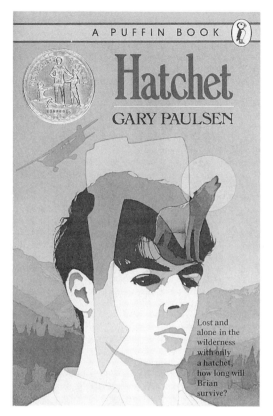

This adventure shows an adolescent's struggle to survive, lost and alone as he is in the wilderness after a plane crash, with nothing to draw upon but a hatchet.

wilderness while coping with his parents' divorce. The boy lacks the skills and knowledge he needs in this situation because he has been sheltered. In *On My Honor*, Marion Dane Bauer describes a young man's emotional struggle to come to terms with his friend's death. These characters exemplify nonstereotyped character development.

## OTHER EVALUATION CONSIDERATIONS

### Developmentally Appropriate Literature

It is important that adults selecting books for children have a sound knowledge of child development. Such knowledge can help them select

*Elementary-grade children ages 9 through 12 prefer informational books like Chimney Sweeps, which looks at the folklore and history of the colorful and fascinating occupation of the chimney sweep.*

books appropriate to children's individual needs and abilities and can help promote their progress toward greater literary appreciation. A child who is not developmentally ready for a particular book will benefit less from reading or listening to it than a child who is ready. While all children pass through all levels, they do so at their own speed. Even though different age groups are associated with particular developmental levels, these levels are approximate and all children have individual preferences.

Several child development models have been postulated by authorities in the field. For example, Piaget's (1969) levels of cognitive development provide one means of evaluating how children change and grow. Current theory suggests that children are in the process of becoming literate from birth and are capable of learning to understand written language before attending school (Adams, 1990; Harste, Burke, Woodward, 1982).

Schlager (1978) examines the relationship between child development and children's literature, analyzing the relationship between the characteristics of middle childhood (ages 7–12) and the children's book choices. She found a clear correlation between the books that were most read and the developmental characteristics of middle childhood; the children's interest was aroused by the developmental characteristics displayed by the main characters in the story rather than the literary quality of the books.

Table 3.3 summarizes children's stages of development and the developmental characteristics for each stage and it includes books appropriate to each level.

## TABLE 3.3

Appropriate literature for each developmental stage.

| AGE AND STAGE | CHARACTERISTICS | BOOK TYPES | SAMPLE BOOKS |
|---|---|---|---|
| 0–6 prereading | acquire language rapidly; | concept | *Planting a Rainbow*, Lois Ehlert |
| | understand simple concepts, environmental print, signs, brand names | | *Airport*, Donald Crews |
| | recognize letters, numbers, their own names | alphabet | *A. B. See*, Tana Hoban<br>*One Day Two Dragons*, Lynne Bertrand |
| | enjoy listening to stories | simple, predictable | *Goodnight Moon*, Margaret Wise Brown<br>*Brown Bear, Brown Bear*, Bill Martin, Jr. |
| | engage in pretend reading | wordless books | *The Snowman*, Raymond Briggs<br>*Deep in the Forest*, Brinton Turkle |
| 6–7 initial reading | learn letters and associate them with words | easy to read | *Mine's the Best*, Crosby Consall<br>*A Dark, Dark Tale*, Ruth Brown |
| | develop concepts of print bring meaning to print | animal books | *Go Dog Go*, P. D. Eastman<br>*Little Bear*, Else Minarick |
| | | predictable | *Hop on Pop*, Dr. Seuss |
| 7–8 confirmation fluency | read to increase fluency | high frequency words | *Frog and Toad*, Arnold Lobel<br>*Henry and Mudge*, Cynthia Rylant<br>*Babar's Little Circus Star*, Laurent de Brunhoff |
| | | nonfiction | *Going on a Whale Watch*, Bruce McMillan<br>*Wagon Wheels*, Barbara Brenner |
| 9–12 | read for knowledge, information, ideas, and experiences | more complex and sophisticated fiction | *Lon Po Po*, Ed Young<br>*Bunnicula*, James Howe<br>*Tuck Everlasting*, Natalie Babbitt |
| | word meanings and prior experiences are important | nonfiction | *Honest Abe*, Edith Kunhardt<br>*The Hospital Book*, James Howe |
| | longer, more complex sentences | | *Whales and Dolphins*, Steve Parker<br>*A Medieval Feast*, Aliki<br>*The Great Barrier Reef*, Carolina Arnold<br>*The Great Little Madison*, Jean Fritz |

## Using Literature to Meet Children's Needs

**Bibliotherapy** literally means *helping with books*. A book that presents a story or information about a problem that is troubling a child is often helpful to the child in working through the trouble. Historically, doctors, therapists, and other health care professionals have used bibliotherapy. According to Bernstein (1989), bibliotherapy involves the "self examination and insights gained from reading" (p. 159). Such experiences may result from planned or unplanned encounters with print. They may occur when an individual seeks out a book relating to a particular problem or when a teacher or librarian directs a student to a specific book.

Bibliotherapy can help meet children's most basic human needs. Children's needs for love, belonging, esteem, and self-actualization can be met through the three fundamental responses associated with bibliotherapy: identification, catharsis, and insight. Through **identification,** readers *associate themselves with story characters*, recognizing similarities to their own lives. Sometimes talking about the problems that book characters encounter enables children to reveal their own difficulties. **Catharsis** is the *emotional release* that occurs when readers identify with a character. Some readers express their response orally, an important part of the therapeutic process; others find it easier to write about their experience, which can lead to and facilitate discussion. **Insight** is a form of *self-discovery* whereby attitudinal and behavioral changes occur; it is therefore often regarded as the crucial factor in bibliotherapy (Stephens, 1981). When children respond to their reading, they may grow and change as a result of the experience of reading.

For the child experiencing the fear, loneliness, and confusion created by the loss of a parent, a book such as *How It Feels When a Parent Dies* by Jill Krementz may be helpful. This book is a collection of interviews with children who describe their feelings about this traumatic event. A child who has recently experienced this loss may identify with all of the children in the book or with the particular feelings of one child. Identification may help the child feel less alone with the grief and may ultimately result in catharsis and insight. Moreover, this process can enhance children's sense of self, thereby contributing to their self-esteem.

Children's response to books is central to the concept of bibliotherapy, but the response of a particular individual to a particular book cannot be predicted with accuracy. Teachers often find that a book that appealed to a previous class holds no interest for this year's class. Often a book that one individual does not enjoy is of particular interest to another person to whom the book speaks. For instance, one student commented to a teacher that she had enjoyed a certain book more than any other she had ever read. The teacher was puzzled because in her opinion the book had no redeeming qualities. The student explained, however, that she had blamed herself for her mother's suicide until she read this book, in which the same tragic event had happened. The student developed insight about her own life through reading this book. Unfortunately, such responses are not predictable, so, although teachers can make suggestions, children should choose books that appeal to them and seem to meet their needs.

Bernstein (1989) suggests guidelines for selecting books to use therapeutically in the classroom:

1. Allow children to select their own books.
2. Discuss books with the students and listen with empathy rather than sympathy.
3. Use group discussions to help children generate new solutions to problems. Group discussions should focus on expressing and clarifying feelings. Children who are uncomfortable with discussing feelings should not be forced into revelations.

## Censorship

Censorship is an issue in children's reading because it limits their access to books and thus the development of their reading interests. When literature is censored, children's reading interests are limited to books that are approved by the adults around them. Book selection and censorship are opposite concepts since book selection is concerned with choosing books to include, while censorship is concerned with exclusion of books.

**Censorship** is usually based on *removing a book from circulation because of sexual references, profanity, sexism, racism, ageism, nudity, drugs, or violence.* A number of children's books have been the subject of censorship. In 1970, law-enforcement officials objected to William Steig's portrayal of policemen as pigs in *Sylvester and the Magic Pebble.* Several groups have requested the removal of Helen Bannerman's *Little Black Sambo* on the basis of racism. Jean Fritz's use of the word "damn" in *And Then What Happened, Paul Revere?* is objectionable to some critics.

Teachers and librarians may find books of significant literary value challenged, so they should be aware of community feelings regarding literature. M. Jerry Weiss (1989), chairperson of the International Reading Association's Intellectual Freedom Committee, makes the following suggestions for dealing with this issue in a professional manner:

1. Communicate with parents regarding their concerns about certain books. This might include forming a book discussion group for parents so that they can read and discuss children's books.

2. Provide a variety of books for children so that if parents prefer their child not to read a specific book, there are plenty of others from which to choose. A well-balanced library collection will contain many books about a given subject.

3. Clearly state and write down the school's adoption and purchasing policy for classroom and library books. The school may create an advisory board to assist in decisions about purchasing books and include parents on the board. Provide forms for parents to complete when they have concerns about a book, with room to detail specific objections.

4. Objections to books should be considered by a school review committee using the questionnaire shown in Figure 3.2, or a similar one, to guide deliberations regarding objections.

## FIGURE 3.2

Questionnaire for concerned parents.

1. Have you read the entire book? _____

2. What is the teacher's purpose for this material? _____

3. Identify the specific passages that you find objectionable: _____

   _____

4. In your view, what problems would reading this material cause? _____

   _____

5. What action do you think should be taken? _____

6. Can you suggest an acceptable substitute? _____

## MEDIA-BASED LITERATURE

Audio books, computerized books, television, and movies and videos are legitimate forms of literature that are here to stay. High-quality media actively involve children with the literature they are experiencing—an advantage for many children that they may carry into other literary experiences. Programs such as the *Little House on the Prairie* television series have increased the popularity of an already popular series of books and led to the publication of additional books.

The availability of media-based literature is growing rapidly: Listening Library now offers over 200 unabridged children's recordings. Although these media do not replace books, they do offer a different dimension, and narrators and actors can make stories come alive for children. Many children will go on to read books they have been exposed to through various media; others will not because the media offer an alternative route to literature they would otherwise miss.

The growth of literature available on the computer has surged since CD-ROM drives have been added to many computers. *Living Books*, featuring children's authors such as Mercer Mayer, are very popular (Random House/Broderbund). *Busy Town*, by Richard Scarry, has received the Parents Award for quality (Paramount International). Microsoft published some of the *Magic School Bus* titles on CD-ROM and children find them fascinating. The interactive, involving nature of computerized books adds to their popularity and their value for children.

Media-based literature is not simply alternate versions of existing books, however. Some writers create original literature for the computer rather than converting existing literature to a media format. Shelley Duvall writes computer-based adventure stories centered on Digby, a little dog with a big bark (Sanctuary Woods). *Where in the World Is Carmen Sandiego?* is an interactive detective story that also provides geography lessons to participants (Broderbund). *Freddie Fish and the Case of the Missing Kelp Seeds* is another entertaining and original computer story (Humongous Entertainment).

Some exceptional audiotapes for upper elementary students are *Anapao* by Jamake Highwater (Recorded Books), Gary Paulsen's *Canyons* (Bantam Doubleday Dell Audio), and Scott O'Dell's *Island of the Blue Dolphins* (Recorded Books). Peter Coyote narrates *Canyons*, a parallel story of two boys, one contemporary and one an Apache who lived a century earlier. Audio recording is the perfect medium for *Anapao*, which was intended to be read aloud, and this recording captures the distinctive style of Native American storytelling. Listening to the recording of *Island of the Blue Dolphins* brings the story alive even for those who have read it many times before.

Some of these media stories will become classics for future generations. Certainly the movie *Fantasia* is a Disney classic and Disney's *Jungle Book* has led to a resurgence of interest in the original writing of this wonderful story, popularizing Rudyard Kipling's book for a new generation. Raffi, a singer and storyteller, is a superstar to many in the younger set, who flock to his concerts, listen to his audiotapes, and watch his videos.

## Evaluating Media-Based Literature

The standards for literature identified earlier in this chapter are applicable to media presentations of literature. Some children's bookstores and companies that distribute media to schools will allow teachers to try out or preview their materials, an advantage since catalog descriptions and advertising materials cannot predict how the children will respond. In addition to trying before buying, the following guidelines should be helpful in selecting media-based literature. The literature

1. must tell a good story or a wonderful poem or give accurate, interesting information (check the guidelines established in the genre chapters)
2. must actively involve viewers or listeners
3. should convey the essence of the literature so that plot, theme, characterization, and setting are authentic, although style may differ according to the medium
4. should meet all of the standards set for written literature: for instance, informational literature should meet nonfiction standards and the difference between theory and fact should be apparent
5. should have all illustrations in scale and accurately identified
6. should not be simplified, so that it loses literary quality; literature prepared for film, computer, video, and so forth may require changes but these can be achieved without loss of quality
7. should not trivialize the literature, for instance, by making the presentation too "cute."

## Using Media-Based Literature

Media-based literature is easy to present: it can be done by turning a switch. It should always, however, be a part of a planned literary experience. Parents, teachers, or librarians presenting the literature should share the experience with the children. First creating a context for the experience by introducing the piece and helping the children see connections to themselves will help ensure their active involvement and response; afterward, adults can discuss the experience with the children and share their responses. Discussion and opportunities to respond are just as important for media as for books. The suggestions in Chapter Four will be helpful in planning responses to media-based literature.

## SUMMARY

Connecting children with literature they will enjoy and appreciate is both an art and a science. There are no simple formulas to aid this process, but the goal can be achieved through careful book evaluation and selection. Knowledge of students and literature helps concerned adults match children and books in ways that will enhance their appreciation and response and enables understanding of students' reading needs and purposes as well as their abilities and interests. Books should be evaluated from a variety of perspectives. A book that entices one student to read may not do the same for another student in the same class.

## THOUGHT QUESTIONS

1. What factors should be considered when selecting children's books?
2. Summarize the research related to children's reading interests.
3. What books did you enjoy as a child? How old were you when you enjoyed these books? How do you think these books related to your development?
4. Why is it important to avoid books that have sexual or racial stereotyping?
5. Describe some ways that teachers, parents, and librarians can promote children's reading interests.

## ENRICHMENT ACTIVITIES

1. Select several books for a child with whom you are well acquainted. Consider the criteria listed on page 57. Which of these criteria did you apply when choosing these books? Which were least important?
2. Read six Newbery and six Caldecott books. Evaluate each one according to the award criteria, then rank the books according to your own evaluation.
3. Interview children who have read Newbery or Caldecott winners. Find out which were their favorites and why, and then ask them to use the award criteria to evaluate the books.
4. Imagine that a parent has challenged you for using a particular children's book. Role-play the meeting between the parent and you.
5. Plan a bibliotherapy lesson based on a book you particularly liked. Consider what problem you might address and how you will lead student discussion over the book.
6. Plan a presentation for parents of preschool children designed to show them the importance of introducing books to their children.

## RECOMMENDED CHILDREN'S BOOKS

Alcott, Louisa May. (1868). *Little Women*. Boston: Little, Brown. (5–8)
   This is a classic tale of a warm, loving family.

Arnosky, Jim. (1983). *Secrets of a Wildlife Watcher*. New York: Lothrop, Lee & Shepard. (2–5)
   This children's manual teaches how to observe wildlife, animals' tracks, and so forth.

Babbitt, Natalie. (1975). *Tuck Everlasting*. New York: Farrar, Straus & Giroux. (4–7)
   The Tuck family has a secret spring that gives them everlasting life. Trouble begins when an evil stranger discovers their secret.

Bannerman, Helen. (1923). *Little Black Sambo*. Philadelphia: Lippincott. (preschool–2)
   This book is a commonly cited example of racist literature.

Bauer, Marion Dane. (1986). *On My Honor*. New York: Clarion. (4–7)
   A boy must cope with guilt and self-blame when his friend drowns.

Bridwell, Norman. (1985). *Clifford the Big Red Dog*. New York: Scholastic. (K–2)
This story details the comical adventures of a large red dog.

Brown, Laurie Krasny, and Marc Brown. (1986). *Dinosaurs Divorce*. Boston: Little, Brown. (1–5)
This book helps children understand the problems they may experience when parents divorce.

Burnett, Frances Hodgson. (1909). *The Secret Garden*. Philadelphia: Lippincott. (4–7)
A young girl becomes enthralled with a secret garden that ultimately transforms her life and the lives of her friends.

Collier, James, and Christopher Collier. (1974). *My Brother Sam Is Dead*. New York: Four Winds Press. (5–7)
This historical fiction, set during the Revolutionary War, shows the tragedy that occurs when a family is divided.

Eckert, Alan. (1971). *Incident on Hawk's Hill*. Boston: Little, Brown. (3–5)
Set in Canada, this story tells about a boy who is lost and befriended by a mother badger.

Forbes, Esther. (1943). *Johnny Tremain*. Boston: Houghton Mifflin. (5–7)
This historical fiction about the American Revolution tells of the war through the eyes of a boy.

Fritz, Jean. (1989). *The Great Little Madison*. New York: Putnam. (2–4)
This book tells about the life of James Madison.

———. (1973). *And Then What Happened, Paul Revere?* New York: Coward, McCann. (2–4)
This biography tells about Paul Revere's life.

George, Jean. (1972). *Julie of the Wolves*. New York: Harper & Row. (5–7)
This is a survival story about a young girl lost in the Alaskan wilderness.

Grimm, Brothers. (1981). *Cinderella*. New York: Greenwillow. (1–3)
This is one of the older versions of this well-known folktale.

———. (1972). *Snow White and the Seven Dwarfs*. New York: Farrar, Straus & Giroux. (2–4)
This is one of the older versions of this well-known folktale.

Holman, Felice. (1986). *Slake's Limbo*. New York: Dell. (5–7)
Slake goes underground in the subway system when life overwhelms him aboveground. He learns about life in this unusual setting.

Huck, Charlotte. (1989). *Princess Furball*. New York: Scholastic. (2–4)
This is a variation on the Cinderella story.

Kellogg, Steven. (1971). *Can I Keep Him?* New York: Dial. (K–2)
A young boy repeatedly asks his mother to keep various animals, but she rejects all of his pleas.

Krementz, Jill. (1981). *How It Feels When a Parent Dies*. New York: Knopf. (3–6)
This book tells children about personal experiences with a parent's death.

Lewis, C. S. (1961). *The Lion, the Witch, and the Wardrobe*. New York: Macmillan. (4–7)
This allegorical fantasy explores the experiences of four children who enter the kingdom of Narnia.

MacLachlan, Patricia. (1985). *Sarah, Plain and Tall*. New York: Harper & Row. (3–6)
Sarah, a mail-order bride from Maine, comes to live with a man and his two children in their prairie home.

McKinley, Robin. (1984). *The Hero and the Crown*. New York: Greenwillow. (3–5)
Aerin, the daughter of the Damarian king and a witchwoman of the North, wins her birthright with the assistance of a wizard.

Mochizuki, Ken. (1995). *Heroes*. New York: Lee and Low. (4–6)

A young Japanese American has friends who make him play the enemy because he is Japanese. He knows that his father and uncle were heroes in World War II, but his playmates refuse to believe it.

Munsch, Robert. (1980). *Paperbag Princess.* Toronto: Annick Press. (1–4)

A princess with a modern attitude decides not to marry a prince.

Norton, Mary. (1953). *The Borrowers.* New York: Harcourt Brace Jovanovich. (2–4)

This fantasy describes the life of a family of tiny people who live by borrowing from the "human beans."

O'Dell, Scott. (1960). *Island of the Blue Dolphins.* Boston: Houghton Mifflin. (4–6)

This true story tells how a girl survives alone on a Pacific island.

Paulsen, Gary. (1987). *Hatchet.* New York: Bradbury (5–7)

In this compelling adventure story, the main character must survive the Canadian wilderness after an airplane crash.

Potter, Beatrix. (n.d.). *The Tale of Peter Rabbit.* New York: Frederick Warne. (preschool–2)

This classic tale of Peter Rabbit continues as a favorite of modern children.

Sacher, Louis. (1995). *Wayside School Gets a Little Strange.* New York: Morrow. (2–5)

This is another volume in the hilarious Wayside School series. Not only is the school strange, but the teachers are as well.

Sendak, Maurice. (1963). *Where the Wild Things Are.* New York: Harper & Row. (preschool–2)

In this classic favorite, a boy visits the land of wild things, tames them, and returns home.

Simon, Seymour. (1987). *Mars.* New York: William Morrow. (4–7)

This book contains beautiful photographs accompanied by excellent text containing a variety of facts about Mars.

Speare, Elizabeth George. (1983). *Sign of the Beaver.* Boston: Houghton Mifflin. (4–6)

A boy left alone in the wilderness is befriended by a Native American boy who teaches him how to survive.

Steig, William. (1969). *Sylvester and the Magic Pebble.* New York: Windmill.

This story describes how the donkey Sylvester becomes a rock and his family comes to believe that he is gone forever. (1–3)

Tolkien, J. R. R. (1938). *The Hobbit.* Boston: Houghton Mifflin. (6–adult)

A hobbit and 13 dwarves seek to overcome the evil dragon, Smaug.

Twain, Mark. (1981). *Tom Sawyer.* New York: Putnam. (7–adult)

The story of Tom Sawyer, a boy growing up on the Mississippi River, continues to be a classic tale.

Van Allsburg, Chris. (1981). *Jumanji.* Boston: Houghton Mifflin. (2–4)

Two children discover a board game that they decide to play in spite of the mysterious directions that accompany it.

White, E. B. (1952). *Charlotte's Web.* New York: Harper. (3–6)

This classic book describes the friendship between Charlotte and Wilbur, a spider and a pig.

Wilder, Laura Ingalls. (1932). *Little House in the Big Woods.* New York: Harper & Row. (3–6)

This is the first book in the Little House series based on the life of Laura Ingalls Wilder.

Yolen, Jane. (1989). *Dove Isabeau.* New York: Harcourt Brace Jovanovich. (2–4)

This original fairy tale has the traditional elements, including a stepmother and a dragon. Beautiful Dove marries her prince.

# $F$*our*

## KEY TERMS

| | |
|---|---|
| aesthetic reading | language charts |
| character map | literate environment |
| community of response | plot relationships chart |
| efferent reading | prediction charts |
| engaging with literature | response |
| envisionment | stance |
| inferencing | story map |
| intertextuality | story pyramid |
| knowledge charts | |

## GUIDING QUESTIONS

Think about your responses to the different kinds of literature you read. What aspect of that literature arouses the strongest response? As you read this chapter, think about the following questions and answer them after you complete the chapter.

1. Why is response to literature important?

2. How do literary experiences change over time?

3. How can teachers nurture children's response to literature?

## OVERVIEW

Children's response to literature is a relatively young area of study. Prior to 1979, researchers studied only the literary responses of adults and adolescents because they did not view children's books as "real" literature. Moreover, they assumed that children did not have a sufficient store of experience to respond to literature (Holland, Hungerford, and Ernst, 1993). Since then, children's literature has gained stature, and adults who work with children recognize that children who have opportunities to become acquainted with books do respond to literature.

The meaning that readers create depends on what they already know. The text does not tell them the exact meaning; they must actively create the meaning. This is the basis for the theory that a work of literature is created through the interaction (transaction) between reader and literature (Rosenblatt, 1978) and the impetus behind developing a response-centered literature program.

Readers who are actively involved with literature and constructing meaning respond to the literary text they create. Not only that, but they continue to respond as they rethink and reread the book or parts of the book, or even read another book that is somehow related. **Response** refers to the *reader's reactions and feelings about a book or books*. This chapter explores ways of creating literary experiences and nurturing children's response to literature.

Teachers, librarians, and parents can plan engaging literary experiences, make literature available, create a warm, literate environment, and guide children in choosing, interpreting, and responding to literature. In this chapter, the term *literature* includes fiction, nonfiction, and poetry. Drama and other media are included in the discussion since they all contribute to literary experience and offer avenues for expressing response.

# Encouraging Children's Response to Literature

## INTRODUCTION

The opening vignette portrays children responding to various types of books in ways that express their understanding and appreciation. Christopher demonstrated his response to the story plot in his discussion of Ralph S. Mouse's adventures. Annie identified the primary character's main problem and responded to his efforts to solve it in another animal fantasy. Jimmy and Patsy shared an informational book, explaining they wanted to read this book because flying kites at the beach is a favorite activity of theirs. Their response culminated in kite construction and the desire to read further about kites, demonstrating a variety of literary transactions and responses.

## VIGNETTE

It's language arts time in Jane Morrison's third-grade classroom. Christopher finishes his book, Beverly Cleary's *The Mouse and the Motorcycle*, and holds it up. "This book is really good! I'm going to read *Runaway Ralph* next, and then I'm going to read *Ralph S. Mouse*."

"Have you read any other books with a mouse as a main character?" Ms. Morrison asks.

"No, but I really like this one. He does so many exciting things!"

In another part of the classroom Annie is engrossed in *A Toad for Tuesday* by Russell Erickson. She looks up and a friend asks, "Is that a good book?"

"Oh, yes!" she answers. "Warton is so smart! I really like the way he keeps his head and thinks of ways to save his life. But I don't like the owl. He's mean."

Jimmy and Patsy are on the floor doing something with paper. The teacher assistant observes them for a time, then asks, "What are you making, kids?"

"We just finished reading the Gail Gibbons book, *Catch the Wind!* and it has directions for making a cool kite, so we're making it. Then we're going to read a book about Japanese kites."

"Do you enjoy flying kites?"

"Oh, yeah! We fly kites at the beach whenever we can."

## LITERARY THINKING

Meaning in literature is expressed in several unique ways (Langer, 1992a): through written language, the conventions of language, and literary structures such as characters, setting, plot, theme, and so forth. Developing literary thinking is a natural and necessary part of the well-developed intellect. Langer maintains that readers use distinct patterns of thinking to understand literature. These patterns of thinking entail relating prior knowledge, experiences, and the text to understand genre, content, structure, and language. Readers use meaning to create more meaning (Langer, 1992b).

### Literature as a Means of Knowing

Literary thinking encourages five kinds of knowing (Probst, 1992): knowing about self, knowing about others, knowing about books, knowing about contexts, and knowing based on what kind of thinker an individual is—concrete or abstract.

*Self.* First, the reader learns about self through literature. This occurs when the reader recalls experiences related to the text and integrates them with the text, thus expanding self-understanding. For instance, after reading *Family Pictures* by Carmen Lomas Garza, nine-year-old Julia recalled her family's activities and thought how much her family was like the Mexican family in the book.

*Others.* Children also begin to realize that each reader has different experiences. For instance, Julia's classmate Josh said the family portrayed in *Family Pictures* was not real because he could not relate to their activities. Both Julia and Josh discovered new ideas about one another from this experience and deepened their understanding of the book.

*Books.* Literary thinking helps readers understand books and literary devices used by authors to stimulate readers' thinking. In *Who Came Down That Road?*, George Ella Lyon uses the image of a road to stir readers to imagine all the different people and animals that came down an old, old, old road—all the way back to before the Native Americans, when mastodons roamed the earth. These images invite students to respond by

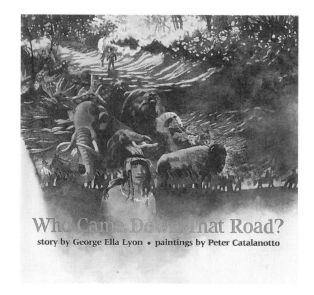

*The narrative of this story develops from a mother's attempt to answer her son's question: "Who came down that road, Mama?"*

thinking about roads they have encountered, to look at the text more carefully, and to think about related historic images.

*Contexts.* Literature helps learners know about contexts. A five-year-old reader has a different perspective than a fifteen-year-old. The younger child reading *Who Came Down That Road?* might think of Native Americans or cowboys, while the older one might think of settlers in covered wagons. Each of these readers brings a different context or background to the book depending on the extent of their personal experiences. Discussion helps readers clarify and activate their contexts.

*Ways of thinking.* Each reader thinks about text in a unique way. Some students are highly analytical, concrete thinkers, while others are subjective and abstract. Some readers race through the text, while others proceed slowly, reflecting as they read. In time, children come to understand that each individual thinks differently about text, which leads to different understandings of the same text. One child reading *Family Pictures* will reflect on happy family outings; another may think of family gatherings made sad by anger and disputes.

## Envisionment: Individual Meaning

Understanding of literature depends on the individual reader's memories, associations, thoughts, and questions; the author stimulates this within the reader by the words and sentences. All of this is part of the literary experience (Probst, 1992). A single text yields diverse meanings to different readers. Individuals use their personal backgrounds to construct and shape meaning in their minds as they read and think (Adams and Collins, 1986; Anderson et al., 1985; Rumelhart, 1981). Research shows that individuals with dissimilar background experiences construct different meanings for the same text (Steffensen, Joag-Dev, and Anderson, 1979). The text does not hold the meaning; the text guides the reader but the meaning comes from the reader (Galda and Pillar, 1983). Approaching literature with this understanding is essentially different from approaching literature through literary criticism, which is based on an authority determining the meaning of a text and passing the meaning on to teachers, who then convey the meaning to their students.

Langer uses the word **envisionment** to refer to this *reader-derived meaning*. In her theory, an envisionment is created as the child reads and understands the text (Langer, 1992a, b). The box *Envisioning "The New Kid on the Block"* describes how one reader creates an envisionment from Jack Prelutsky's poem.

Another reader might emphasize different words and fill the gaps in meaning from a dissimilar set of world experiences, creating an entirely different envisionment of the poem. This reader might not know any bullies or might not know what the word *bully* means. A reader well acquainted with Jack Prelutsky's poetry will have different expectations of the poem than one who does not and will expect a funny poem with a surprise near the end.

Involved readers actively pursue meaning from the first instant of reading, thinking about the book and predicting its meaning. As they make sense of the written language, they confirm or cancel their predictions of meaning. Active, involved readers constantly build and synthesize meaning, paying attention to the words and attending to the images and emotions within the text (Iser, 1978). The words and the particular patterns of words stir up

---

> ## Envisioning *"The New Kid on the Block"*
>
> In Jack Prelutsky's poem "The New Kid on the Block," I first read that the new kid is *real tough.* These words create an image of a muscular bully in my mind. The next few lines tell how the new kid *punches hard, pulls hair,* and *likes to fight,* which elaborates on my envisionment of a neighborhood bully. Then the poet describes the bully's behavior with the words *swiped* and *bad,* so my interaction with the text adds the fact that the bully is also unpleasant to my envisionment. But the surprise in the last line of the poem makes me reconsider my earlier envisionments: "I don't care for *her* at all."

---

their memories and activate related parts of memory. Meaning is infused into the author's words from the reader's intellectual and emotional experiences (Rosenblatt, 1983).

When readers think, rethink, reread, and discuss books, they discover what a book means to them and how they feel about it. They select aspects of the text to remember based on their understanding and response; they fill in gaps in meaning from their world knowledge (Iser, 1978). They infer, interpret, and think critically as they revise and sharpen their understanding of the text. They discover their sense of the text, their ideas about it, their understanding of what it is and means. Even the details they remember change and shift and come to them in different arrangements (Chambers, 1983). This is why communities of readers, discussed later in this chapter, are important. Although response is individual, community discussions encourage individuals to share their unique verbal, artistic, dramatic, and written interpretations of and responses to literature.

## Intertextuality: Individual Connections

Literature is woven with quotations, references, and echoes of prior literary experiences that give it

THE TALKING EGGS
*by Robert D. San Souci   pictures by Jerry Pinkney*

*The wondrous talking eggs in this story prove that beauty may hide great ugliness while, the plainest of objects may conceal treasures within.*

virtually unlimited meaning (Barthes, 1975). Meaning in each new book an individual reads is enriched in some measure by the shadows of texts read previously. This process, called **intertextuality,** is *the process of interpreting one text by means of another* (Kristeva, 1980; De Beaugrande, 1980). Two or more texts, written or oral, are involved in the intertextuality process (Bloome and Bailey, 1992), and may include films, videos, class lectures, conversations, and books (Hartman, 1992).

San Souci's *The Talking Eggs* clearly demonstrates intertextuality. Readers of this story commonly focus on plot and character in this story, realizing its similarities to *Cinderella*. In *The Talking Eggs* the characters are a widow and her two daughters, one mean and cross and the other, Blanche, sweet and kind. The widow pampers Rose, the bad-tempered daughter who puts on airs, while the sweet-spirited daughter must do all of the work. The story is set in the rural South rather than a palace, and the magic character is an old woman who blesses Blanche. In the end, the widow and her bad-tempered daughter run into the woods, chased by whip snakes, toads, frogs, yellow

jackets, and a big gray wolf. The plot and characters in *The Talking Eggs* give the reader intertextual links that facilitate comprehension.

The student reading *A Toad for Tuesday* in the opening vignette built part of her understanding through intertextuality as well as through her personal experience. She compared Warton's beetle brittle to peanut brittle and decided it was a confection more appealing to toads than to people. As Warton bundled up against the winter weather, she remembered northern winters and felt a sympathetic shiver. The plot reminded her of *Little Red Riding Hood*, and she compared these stories on several points: for instance, when the owl captured Warton and announced his plan to eat the toad on Tuesday, she was reminded of the wolf. She admired Warton's ingenious efforts to escape. Her understanding grew as she read and used her experiences to understand the text.

A two-year study in Australia worked to identify and describe the intertextuality process. "There is incredible diversity in the links that are made" (Cairney, 1990, p. 483). Based on the writing of children aged 6–12 years, Cairney concludes:

1. All children poach from stories they have read previously, and almost all children are aware that this intertextuality influences their writing.

2. There are only minor differences in awareness of intertextuality among children of different achievement levels.

3. The most common intertextual links include genre, character, plot ideas, and combining several narratives.

4. The majority of intertextuality links students use are related to ideas and plot.

Like creating meaning, readers apply intertextuality differently from one individual to the next. Intertextuality is not a linear process; even when reading exactly the same stories, readers identify different links to use in constructing meaning. There is no way to predict which links will occur to a specific reader. Each reader creates a highly personal mosaic of intersecting texts with intertextual relationships that may not be apparent to others who may have read the same texts. As Margaret Meek (1988) points out, the use of intertextual links is implicitly learned. This is among the unteachable lessons acquired from prior reading experiences. It seems highly plausible, however, that teachers, librarians, parents, and other involved adults can encourage readers to use ideas from previous literary activities to build meaning as they read new texts.

## REASONS FOR READING

All readers have *a purpose for reading,* or **stance** (Holland et al., 1993). Stance indicates what the reader is paying attention to in the reading process and influences the reader's response. Response gives form to these literary experiences and a mode for expressing them. Response shows us what has caught the reader's attention. There are two major stances, aesthetic and efferent.

The purpose of **aesthetic reading** is to have *a pleasurable, interesting experience for its own sake.* Aesthetic readers center on the sound and rhythm of the words and the personal feelings, ideas, and attitudes created during reading (Rosenblatt, 1982). They create new experiences as they live through the literature: participating in the story, identifying with the characters, sharing their conflicts and their feelings. As a byproduct of the aesthetic reading stance, readers may acquire values, information, or related benefits, but these are not the purpose of the reading.

The **efferent reading** stance *focuses on the meanings and ideas in the text* (Rosenblatt, 1982). Efferent reading has a narrow focus because the readers are seeking information, directions, or conclusions and attempting to build these into memory to use in another situation.

Rosenblatt points out, however, that any reading event may fall anywhere on a continuum between the aesthetic and the efferent poles, so a stance cannot be only aesthetic or only efferent because most reading experiences have elements of both (see Figure 4.1).

## UNDERSTANDING RESPONSE

In the opening vignette, Jimmy and Patsy chose to read a book about kites because they had enjoyed

**FIGURE 4.1**

Reading stance continuum.

| Mostly aesthetic | Half efferent, half aesthetic | Mostly efferent |

previous experiences with kites. They already knew something about kites, which motivated them to read more about kites. Their previous reading and knowledge created intertextual links that assisted them in constructing meaning from the new reading. They acquired some new understandings about kites after reading *Catch the Wind!,* and they responded to the experience by following the directions in the book to build kites and planning to read more books about kites. Both of these responses to literature further extended their understanding.

Response to literature is many things: what readers make of a text as they read; how it comes alive and becomes personal; what happens during reading; how they feel about what they have read. Response is also the pleasure and satisfaction readers feel and the way they display these feelings (Galda, 1988b). "It is this combination of personal, social, and cultural contexts which have tremendous influence on the reader's interpretation" (Largent, 1986, p. 17).

Literature affects readers in all sorts of ways. We really cannot read without responding in some way: excitement or pleasure or boredom. We may go to sleep or become so fascinated that we read all night long. Young children are responding to literature when they plead "read it again, read it again."

Literary experience does not stop when the last page is read, however (Martinez and Nash, 1991). The reader's feelings remain and continue to evolve after completing the book, sometimes long after the book is read (Rosenblatt, 1978). A young girl who likes Audrey Wood's book *Heckedy Peg,* for example, listens to the book over and over. She also pretends to be Heckedy Peg and invents new adventures and powers for the character.

Heckedy Peg, inspired by a sixteenth-century game still played by children today, is about seven children, a wicked witch's intrusion into their lives, and a spell that only their mother can break.

## Dimensions of Response

Children's response to literature is developmental, meaning that it changes with age and stage of development (Meek, Warlow, and Barton, 1977). The number and nature of literary experiences and the readers' feelings about those experiences enhance the growth of response. At the Dartmouth Conference of English teachers, the developing nature of response was described in terms of the aspects of literature to which children respond (Purves and Rippere, 1968). Preschool children, for instance, enjoy the rhythms and sounds of nursery rhymes—Mother Goose is developmentally appropriate for children in this age group. The various facets of response include sound, event, and world.

## Sound

Children who respond to *sound* are sensitive to the words and rhythms of language in a book. They hear the text in their head as they read, listening to the dialogue as they would conversation. This is why "reading aloud to children of all ages is vital . . . because this is the way we learn how to turn cold print into a dramatic enactment in the theater of our imagination" (Chambers, 1983, p. 163).

The dialogue in Edith Thacher Hurd's *I Dance in My Red Pajamas* is so realistic that many children reading the story identify with the conversations between grandchild and grandparents. Dick King-Smith uses British dialect in *Babe the Gallant Pig* and most of the conversation occurs among farm animals; nevertheless the language has an appealingly authentic sound, as shown in this excerpt:

> "What's your name?"
>
> "I don't know," said the piglet.
>
> "Well, what did your mother call you, to tell you apart from your brothers and sisters?" said Fly. . . .
>
> "Babe," said the piglet, and the puppies began to giggle when their mother silenced them with a growl.
>
> "But that's a lovely name," she said. "Would you like us to call you that? It'll make you feel more at home."
>
> At this last word the little pig's face fell even further.
>
> "I want my mum," he said very quietly. (p. 20)

### Event

Readers who respond to *event* are sensitive to the form of story, poem, or nonfiction. They can anticipate events, characters, and setting when they read. They expect stories to have characters, setting, problems or conflicts, and efforts to solve problems. Experienced readers have learned many things, such as that biographies are based on the life of a person who actually lived and that fantasies have elements that could not actually happen in the real world. Their expectations are based on genre, story elements, story grammar, poetic form, and expository grammars, which are discussed in Chapters Eight and Fifteen.

Children identify with the roles of story characters, which is why they enjoy reading about characters near their own age or a bit older. Children who have a close relationship with their grandparents will identify with Jenny, who stayed overnight with her grandparents in *I Dance in My Red Pajamas*. Her grandmother cooked her favorite foods and played her favorite games, and she helped her grandparents with their chores. Children often reshape and revise a story to fit their own reality and their personal experiences.

### World

The world response occurs when readers incorporate aspects of all dimensions of response.

When reading the poem "If I Were in Charge of the World" by Judith Viorst, children connect it with their own lives and with other literature that gives them similar feelings. They respond to sounds in the poem, such as the alliterative phrases "healthy hamsters" and "basketball baskets." As they read the poem, they relate it to their world and to real events and personal experiences. Children who have allergies identify with the author's desire to "cancel" allergy shots, and both children and adults identify with the author's similar wish to eliminate "Monday mornings." Anyone who has had several hamsters with short lifespans as pets can also relate to the author's desire for "healthier hamsters."

## GUIDING RESPONSE

This book emphasizes the individual nature of creating literary meaning, a theory that implies respect for individual, unique understandings of literature and an attitude that welcomes individual response. The ways adults guide literary experiences can encourage students actively to make meaning of the texts they read, awakening their reading interests by planning literary encounters that invite them to respond.

Literary experiences have much to offer the growing mind (Langer, 1992b). The major reason for providing children with literary experiences is to help them read with more pleasure and understanding. "Helping children to read for themselves, widely, voraciously, and indiscriminately" is something every adult can do (Chambers, 1983, p. 48). Although they cannot directly teach literature to children, they can set the stage for children to experience literature so that the children can actively construct their own knowledge and beliefs.

Well-read teachers share their enthusiasm with their students. They create literary experience through the literature they select and present in the classroom. They create a **literate environment** *that encourages children to engage with books and gives them opportunities to express their responses to literature.* (The dimensions of creating literary experience are presented in Figure 4.2.) To develop

## FIGURE 4.2

Dimensions of creating literary experience.

| Processes for enhancing literary experience | Ways of Organizing Literature Study | | | | |
|---|---|---|---|---|---|
| | Genre studies | Studies of outstanding books | Studies of the elements of literature | Illustrator studies | Author studies |
| Read aloud Reader's Theater | × | × | × | | × |
| Read silently | × | × | × | × | × |
| Drama | | × | × | | × |
| Writing | × | × | × | × | × |
| Art | | × | × | × | |
| Music | | × | × | × | × |
| Discussion | × | × | × | × | × |
| Movement | | × | | × | |

literary experiences, teachers, librarians, and parents encourage children to make meaning of the texts they read, choosing books that will facilitate this process. Focusing the way readers feel about a book and providing ways of expressing their responses is a part of guiding the literary experience. Books that support literary experiences will

- invite dialogue
- awaken memories
- raise questions
- stimulate connections with other literature and with life
- encourage problem solving

Guiding children's literary experiences involves encouraging them to think about and respond to literature: literary thinking is not linear, nor is it predictable (Langer, 1990). Children's literary experiences are guided by helping them connect with books and build the background needed for understanding. Leading discussions and encouraging readers to lead discussions clarifies their understandings and assists them in learning from one another. Students build their own understanding of literature and raise their own questions rather than focusing on content questions created by someone with different experiences and knowledge. Enhance children's experiences through selecting and introducing books for children to hear, read aloud, or read silently; and through stimulating their thinking beyond the book after reading.

## Community of Response

*Although each individual reader creates a unique understanding of text, each relies on common understandings and language for discussions and sharing responses.* These shared understandings emerge from a mutual focus that Sebesta and Iverson (1975) call a **community of response.** Readers externalize their response best when their discussion focuses on the literary work itself (Chambers, 1983). For instance, a community of readers can agree that stories include plot and character, and they can agree about the identity of the principal character, but they may disagree agree about character motivation.

As children share their individual understandings with one another, they learn that a story can have many different interpretations. One person's interpretation of an incident or a character might not occur to another individual without the opportunity for discussion (Petrosky, 1977). Sharing individual perceptions of literature with one another in discussion or conversation enhances understanding and response to literature. Giving students such occasions to share their personal understandings and responses will inspire their response.

Story structures such as plot, setting, characterization, theme, and writer's style are common understandings that readers share, just as main ideas and supporting details are common understandings they share about nonfiction. Genre characteristics are another source of agreement. Identifying a book as historical fiction, poetry, or nonfiction is a relatively concrete task. Such knowledge influences the way readers engage with a book as well as the way they respond to it.

Without shared understandings "there would never be the sort of agreement that makes a book well-loved or well-hated. Children as well as adults seem to seek this commonality" (Sebesta and Iverson, 1975, p. 412). They talk over their thoughts and reactions to a best-selling book, a television show, or a play; they may even argue the finer points of the piece. Chambers (1983) says the need to recreate the story in our own words is so strong that "when two friends discover they have both read and enjoyed the same book their talk often consists simply of sharing retellings: "I especially liked that part where . . . ." These discussions clarify understanding and response; therefore, the community of response is an important issue for those who work with children. These adults nurture students' response when they give them opportunities to form a community of readers. They can also give them time to share thoughts about their reading.

## Warm, Literate Environment

A warm, literate environment sets the stage for children's engagement with and response to literature. In this setting, students are surrounded with many appealing, interesting books that set the stage for pleasurable experiences. Both centralized school libraries and classroom library centers are essential to literacy experiences. The classroom reading center gives children immediate access to literature, increasing their interest in reading. Parents and caregivers create warm, literate environments when they have books and magazines in the home.

Pleasing arrangements of books, displays, posters, and bulletin boards in the library center invite children to explore books. Books displayed open at eye level encourage more reading than book shelves lined so that only the spines show. Reading environments are discussed in more detail in Chapter Three.

## Book Selection

Choosing well-written, interesting books for classrooms and libraries is basic to creating successful literature programs. Such a large number of children's books are published each year, and these books vary so widely in quality, that book selection is too important to be left to chance. Carefully selected literature engages readers' minds and interests and feelings (Altwerger, Edelsky, and Flores, 1987; Rosen, 1986). Considerations in selection include interests, age, grade, and developmental stage.

A broad collection of literature of excellent literary quality, drawn from all genre, is the cornerstone of literary experience. Books selected should be both readable and listenable (Galda and Pillar, 1983). In selecting books, consider the elements that make a story, a poem, or an informational book excellent literature. Children's reading interests are important considerations in choosing literature. Students' interests can be identified through discussion and interest inventories. (Chapters Three and Six examine children's reading interests and stages of development and the elements of book evaluation and selection.)

In stocking a library, remember that literature is not confined to print. Media such as films, videos, audiotapes, filmstrips, recordings, puppets, reader's theater, dramatizations, and storytelling are forms of literary experience and ways of bringing literature to children. Cox and Many (1989) find that children's response to film and literary narrative are related. Experiencing literature through various media expands background knowledge, deepens students' response, and strengthens their understanding (Kulleseid and Strickland, 1989). Students often say that a particular story reminds them of a movie or television show. Informational books often remind readers of newscasts and programs on the Discovery Channel.

## Engaging with Literature

Children must engage with literature in order to respond to it. **Engaging with literature** *makes the characters and events come alive for readers.* Engagement activities focus on what the story, poem, or nonfiction is really about so that readers can understand and respond to it. The following are some typical engagement activities:

- discussion
- story grammar
- story map
- predicting
- compare/contrast (Venn diagram)
- problem solving
- plot maps
- story summary
- story pyramid
- character maps
- student-generated questions

# NURTURING RESPONSE

Nurturing children's response to literature means creating pleasurable experiences with books in a warm, accepting setting. Chambers (1983) sums up the literary experience as one in which adults and children share what they read and discover together what is "entertaining and revealing, recreative, re-enactive, and engaging" (p. 40). The focus of a literary experience is discovering the meaning, thinking about it, and discovering the reader's feelings about the experience. Literature is an experience "to be entered into, to be shared and contemplated" (Chambers, 1983, p. 39).

Appropriate literary experiences are essential to children's development and thinking. These experiences are not an effort to teach children the content of a book, but rather are intended to develop understanding and appreciation. As Rosen (1986) states,

"receiving a story is an exploration . . . not a set of responses to someone else's questions in right/wrong format" (p. 229). We are concerned with *why* children remember a story, not simply *what* they remember. C. S. Lewis (1961) makes a distinction between "using" and "receiving" literature: "A work of (whatever) art can be either 'received' or 'used.' When we 'receive' it we exert our senses and imagination and various other powers according to a pattern invented by the artist. When we 'use' it we treat it as assistance for our own activities" (p. 44).

Response activities sustain the reader-text interaction and nurture literary development (Martinez and Nash, 1991). Morrow (1989) finds that in a literature-based after-school program including response activities such as storytelling, puppets, drama, writing, and art, primary-grade students develop deeper understandings, greater interest in reading, and read more books than their peers not in the program; they are also more interested in literature when they can interact with and share their responses with adults.

Response may be written or oral and formal or informal and may make use of a variety of media. Teachers and other concerned adults can create opportunities for varied responses to literature through activities before reading, during reading, and after reading. Strategies and activities for introducing books, experiencing books, and encouraging response to literature are explained in later sections.

Literature loses its appeal when it is misused. Chambers (1983) offers an example of such abuse when he tells of an English teacher who taught 12-year-olds to parse with a paragraph from J. M. Falkner's novel *Moonfleet.* No doubt this activity taught many students to dislike literature. Misuse of literature involves deliberately reading and questioning a piece of literature in order to teach specific information or skills. This violates its integrity. Creating comprehension exercises from literary passages, phonics drills that focus on the sounds of words in a fine book, and spelling lists from great books are the stuff of which literary abuse is made. Questions and activities such as *What color was the main character's dress, why did the dog run away,* and *pretend you are the main character and write a letter to . . .* do not contribute to literary

## A First-Grade Literature Experience

### Introduction

Ms. Osaka showed her first-grade students a picture of a mouse to introduce them to the poem "Mice" by Rose Fyleman. After reading the first line of the poem, she asked them what reasons they thought the poet would give for saying that mice were nice, and she listed their reasons on the chalkboard. She then read the entire poem aloud.

### Discussion and Understanding

After reading the poem through a second time when the children asked to hear it again, Ms. Osaka asked them what the poet said she liked about mice. She listed their responses next to the earlier list on the board. Several children said their families didn't like mice, so Ms. Osaka let the class discuss the reasons for this.

Afterward, she asked them what kind of words the poet used to help listeners see mice in their mind. Some of the children recognized "scurrying" words in the poem.

*Mice*

I think mice
Are very nice.

   Their tails are long,
   Their faces are small,
   They haven't any
   Chins at all.
   Their ears are pink,
   Their teeth are white,
   They run about
   The house at night.
   They nibble things
   They shouldn't touch
   And no one seems
   To like them much.

But *I* think mice
Are nice.

### Response Activities

Ms. Osaka asked the children to think about the things they could do to show another person how they felt about this poem. Many of the children chose to draw pictures. Some of them selected mouse puppets and acted out the poem. Some others remembered the book *Whose Mouse Are You?* by Robert Kraus and asked the teacher to read it again.

---

experience; these activities treat literature as content. The literary experience is not a quest for a predetermined right answer. The process of making meaning is not one of learning a correct interpretation prescribed by an authority in the field (Langer, 1990).

### Introducing Books

Introductions may be elaborate or very simple. They may consist of a question, discussion, or picture; a comparison to another book, a film, or a piece of music; reading the opening paragraph or paragraphs; or presentation of an object that symbolizes some aspect of the book. Introductions arouse children's interest in the text and give them background that enriches their comprehension. The teacher, parent, or librarian acquaints children with the genre, content, structure, and language of the text (Langer, 1990). Children will usually meet the main character and identify the setting during the introduction.

The first step in planning a book introduction is considering what readers need to know to understand the book. To understand a fantasy such as Madeleine L'Engle's *A Wrinkle in Time* requires preparing readers to imagine places and people outside of their experience. Their understanding will depend on their ability to follow the story when it switches from reality to make-believe; it might help to demonstrate how one *tesseracts*, or travels through a wrinkle in time, as described in the book. Skilled writers of fantasy make us believe that such things could happen.

Children form different expectations for a book introduced as a fantasy, as *The Indian in the Cupboard* by Lynne Reid Banks, than for a book introduced as realistic fiction or poetry. Familiarizing children

When his grandchildren follow Grandpa up
the stairs, a dazzling show, better than any
on TV, begins. From a dusty trunk Grandpa
extracts the makings of a vaudeville man and
Grandpa brings new life to days gone by.

with *The Indian in the Cupboard* would include background for the British setting and language, and it could include reading about Native American traditions. Introducing Karen Ackerman's *Song and Dance Man*, a realistic fiction picture book, could be as simple as reading the dust jacket, which tells about a vaudeville song and dance man who is also a grandfather. A derby hat and a cane or a film clip showing a vaudeville act could be useful. When planning introductions, consider children's experiences, background, and the other books they have read or heard, so you can provide the information that will enhance understanding.

Creating a relationship between a piece of literature and previous reading develops intertextuality and facilitates response. Use Robert Kraus's *Whose Mouse Are You?* to introduce Karen Numeroff's *If You Give a Mouse a Cookie*, or refer to a mouse poem such as Rose Fyleman's "Mice." Literary experience is not based on a single book, but the ideas, experiences, and understandings that come from reading many books.

Children learn to preview books themselves from the techniques used to introduce books to them. By the time students reach the middle grades, they are ready to explore independently a book before reading and know that the dust jacket usually provides background information.

## Experiencing Books

After the introduction, the children read or listen to the book or poem. As they read and listen, children link their prior knowledge with the new information presented, building their comprehension and creating a new understanding. Readers who immerse themselves in the literature gradually build an understanding of the piece, identifying and coming to understand the main character's personality. As the story unwinds, readers recognize the escalating tension in the plot, the cause and effect, and the problem or conflict that builds suspense. Readers who ask themselves why and who relate literature to their own experiences will increase their comprehension.

Understanding is related to **inferencing** or *interpretation of literature*, which is concerned with meanings that are not directly stated in the text. The author suggests and hints at ideas rather than stating them directly, and the reader must interpret the author's words to understand the intended meaning. Authors cannot tell readers everything: the stories would be too long and the detail would make them too boring. Authors must rely on their audience to fill in the empty spaces. In *Circle of Gold*, when Mattie says, "I can't write fifty-dollar essays. I can't write fifty-cent essays" (p. 46), Candy Dawson Boyd, the author, is telling the reader that Mattie lacks confidence in her writing ability. The reader interprets this statement to understand her point.

Critical thinkers make judgments about the quality, value, and validity of text. They evaluate the accuracy of the material, synthesize information, make comparisons and inferences, and suspend judgment until they have all the information they need. Critical readers recognize the author's purpose, point of view, and use of language. They

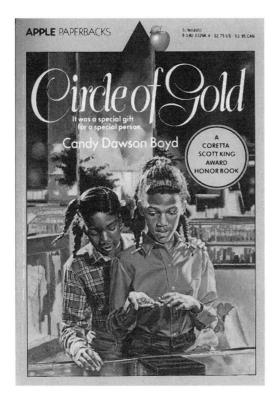

*Similar to the main character in her story, the author at age 12 entered a writing contest sponsored by the local newspaper with the great hope of winning it for a very special reason.*

distinguish fact from opinion and test the author's assertions against their own observations, information, and logic. For instance, a critical reader would probably conclude that Mattie was a much better writer than she realized, since she won the essay contest even though she didn't believe she could write a fifty-cent essay.

## CLASSROOM ACTIVITIES TO ENHANCE ENGAGEMENT AND RESPONSE

Students who are members of a community of readers who discuss, dramatize, and share books with one another engage and respond with literature more fully (Hancock and Hill, 1988).

Engagement and response activities focus on readers' responses rather than detailed analysis. "Students will not be dissecting the text, nor will they inspect it; rather they will be focused on such literary elements as the main characters, the setting, the problem to be resolved, the major events, the problem solution and what the story is really about" (Macon, Bewell, and Vogt, 1991). "The purpose of engagement activities is to get students immersed, engrossed, absorbed, and totally involved in literature" (Macon et al., 1991, p. 3). Response to literature grows from literary experience and is expanded through engagement activities.

The understanding and responses generated through the activities in this section will increase students' comprehension as well as create a springboard for discussion and writing. "Students must understand that they should complete the assigned reading *prior* to tackling the assigned activity rather than interrupting the flow of the story to record their data. Preserve the integrity of the text, then work on the activities" (Macon et al., 1991). Unless readers complete reading the entire story, article, poem, or informational piece *before* exploring it in discussion or response activities, they lack full understanding of the piece. Understanding grows as the reader follows the unfolding of character, the story problem and its resolution, or the full development of the theme. This is how they learn how the story works, or how the informative pieces fit together.

The activities described in this section may be conducted as individual activities, small group activities, or whole class activities. Pencil-and-paper activities help students organize and remember their thoughts for discussion. Activities for engagement and response should not be overused because overdoing even the most interesting ones can discourage reading. Students who are required to *do* something with everything they read will lose interest in literature—the main purpose of reading should be simply to read.

### Discussion

Discussion is an integral part of developing understanding and engagement with literature. The questions raised by fellow students, interaction with others in the discussion process, and the teacher's thoughtful questions increase comprehension (Macon et al., 1991). Child-centered discussion allows students many occasions to raise questions and make comments about the literature they read. Friendly debate regarding various reactions fosters readers' response to literature (Larrick, 1991a). The teacher's role is to facilitate discussion, keep it going, encourage full participation, and inspire children to talk about literature. Plan thoughtful questions based on *listening to the voice of the book* rather than analyzing it. The most useful questions are broad and open-ended, as these questions help students develop a sense of the entire story, poem, or informational piece. Thoughtful questions avoid the trivial and obvious (Sebesta and Iverson, 1975) and instead focus on a few significant ideas and stimulating higher levels of understanding and response. Higher levels of understanding involve inferential thinking, critical thinking, and creative thinking. Lower levels concentrate on "right" answers.

### Developing discussion

A few thoughtful questions, especially those that the students ask, will stimulate a good discussion. The inquisition approach of asking many, many questions is guaranteed to destroy children's response to literature. The teacher who comments, "I feel like I have wrung the life out of this book and neither the students nor I ever want to see it again," has assuredly overanalyzed the book and ensured that her students will never enjoy that book, even though it may be a favorite of many children who have not been subjected to overteaching or overanalysis.

Discussions that focus on the characters suggest that readers wonder what kind of person the main character will turn out to be (Hansen, 1991). The well-developed characters in Katherine Paterson's books invite this kind of response. When focusing on character, develop questions to guide students' thinking, such as:

- What kind of character is the main character?
- What words describe the character?
- What character have you read about that is like the main character in this book? How are they alike?

- Do you know anyone who is like the main character? How so?

Some books are plot driven, so students read for the story events or the adventures. Many of these stories are action-packed and have story events that build suspense. Guiding children's response to these stories could involve questions such as:

- What events create suspense?
- What is the main problem or conflict in this story?
- What is the climax of this story?
- How is the problem or conflict solved?

Prompts, such as the ones listed in the *"Discussion Prompts"* box, can elicit children's oral and written responses to literature. Using these prompts for a full year in a third-grade class shows that the students are more actively involved in learning and more enthusiastic about literature than their peers, with an observable difference in fluency and

---

## Discussion Prompts

Kelly's prompts:

1. What did you notice about the story?
2. How did the story make you feel?
3. What does the story remind you of in your own life?

Borders' and Naylor's prompts:

1. Talk about what you notice in the story. This may include any aspect of the book such as text, format, illustrations, characters and so forth. Children will notice things that teachers never noticed.
2. Talk about how the story makes you feel. When members of a group share feelings and thoughts they bond and the group is a safer place to explore issues.
3. Talk about what the story reminds you of in your own life. Our own experience helps us understand a book and the book helps us understand our experience.

increased reflection of emotional involvement as the students use the process (Kelly, 1990). Adapting the prompts to statements shows that they are effective for discussion and that the more the prompts are used, the more effective they are. Children as young as three respond to the prompts; moreover, the children involved in the latter study used the prompts on the teachers and asked what they noticed in the story (Borders and Naylor, 1993).

## Writing

Discussion and writing are valuable literary response activities (Hancock, 1991). Students who read well usually write well because literature stimulates background knowledge, thinking, and writing. Reading gives students models for organizing writing and language to express their thoughts. The response journal is one of many appropriate writing response activities.

### Response journals

Literature response journals, also called reading journals or dialogue journals, are a form of response activity that leads students to engage with literature, since the journals consist of students writing down their thoughts about their reading. Flitterman-King (1988) defines the response journal as "sourcebook, a repository of wanderings and wonderings, speculations, questionings . . . a place to explore thoughts, discover reactions, let the mind ramble—in effect, a place to make room for the unexpected." Response journals are an effective means of linking writing with the active reading process (Bauso, 1988). Researchers find that response journals extend children's writing and thinking (Barone, 1990; Kelly, 1990). Some students find it difficult to get started writing in their journal, or they may say the same things over and over, so plan ways to encourage their responses when they seem to have difficulty thinking of something to write.

Hancock (1991) reports an analysis of a sixth-grade girl's literature response journal. The journal reveals the student's personal meaning-making process as well as insights into her personal feelings,

which the teacher had rarely seen. This student was encouraged to record all of the thoughts going on in her head as she read the book and not concern herself with correct spelling or the mechanics of writing because the objective was to capture her thoughts. Her entries were classified in these ways: (1) character interaction, (2) character empathy, (3) prediction and validation, (4) personal experiences, and (5) philosophical reflections (Hancock, 1991). When writing about character interaction, the student wrote comments directly to the character she was reading about. The researcher notes her responses were of the quality of reading and writing that teachers hope to inspire. After the student wrote entries, the researcher made encouraging, nonevaluative responses to her entries. Students are motivated by teachers' comments. They try to repeat the kind of writing to which the teacher responded.

Literature response journals can have several different formats. A few are suggested here, but teachers can try anything that fits the situation. Langer (1992b) suggests a two-part journal, with a student entry on one side and the teacher's response (or the response of another student) on the other side. (See the sample entry in Figure 4.3.) Another format suggested by Langer is based on research by Stoodt and Amspaugh (1994) showing that children's responses change over time as they relate new information, feelings, and ideas to previous knowledge. Immediate response is more detailed, while longer reflection permits children to relate these data to a larger context. In this journal format, the students would make entries under three headings: immediate reaction, later reaction, reading and writing. A third approach might be for a student to make comments in the journal and then pass it to another person who has read the book to respond to the comments.

### Other forms of writing

The preferred writing response differs from student to student and teacher to teacher. Some students enjoy writing letters to the characters or to their friends about the books they enjoy. Others like to create diaries or journals from the character's point of view. Some find writing additional adventures or chapters for favorite characters

## FIGURE 4.3

Two-part literature response journal.

Book: <u>Owl Eyes</u> by Yoshi Miyake

| Notes | Comments |
|---|---|
| Mohawk legend<br>Funny story because the owl is always complaining. The story explains why the owl looks like it does and why it sleeps at night. | The art is beautiful! I guess the Master of All Spirits and Everything Maker is like God. Raweno made the owl sleep at night so that he wouldn't bother him. |

interesting. After reading nonfiction books, some students become so interested in the information that they want to learn all they can about the subject, which could lead to writing an article about it. Students may decide to develop their own original information and create a nonfiction book to share with classmates. Basically, writing response activities are unlimited. Students will think of their own when they have the opportunity.

## Oral Language

Dramatic activities are important response activities for children. These activities are explored more fully in Chapter Eleven. They give children opportunities to act out their interpretations of characters and events. They can see how the action evolved.

## Maps and Charts

Literature may be mapped or charted (sometimes called diagrams) as a means of summarizing and organizing thoughts and responses to the text. There are many different kinds of maps and charts to use.

### Story maps

The sample **story map** in Figure 4.4 is based on *Stonewords* by Pam Conrad. A story map is *a diagram of a story grammar.* Readers complete the

various parts of the map based on the story structure (grammar) of the book they have read.

### Character maps

**Character maps** *focus on the main character in a story.* They assist children in developing a more thorough understanding of characters in a story and their actions, thereby helping readers identify character traits (Toth, 1991). They also serve to summarize the story.

This exercise may be conducted as an individual activity, a cooperative group activity, or a paired activity. Students write or cut and paste the character's name on the map. Then they write in qualities, such as honesty, loyalty, bravery, of that character. Finally, they identify the actions that support the qualities identified.

This activity can be varied by having students draw pictures or locate magazine photographs that illustrate a character's behavior. Figure 4.5 shows a sample character map based on *Amazing Grace* by Mary Hoffman.

### Language charts

**Language charts**, originally developed as part of the Language to Literacy Program designed for at-risk students in kindergarten through fifth grade, are *a means of introducing discussion and writing to children in a literature response program* (Roser, Hoffman, Labbo, and Farest, 1991;

## FIGURE 4.4

A sample story map for *Stonewords*.

............................................................................................................

Setting:  A house connected by a back staircase to the past. Zoe lives in the present, and her best friend, Zoe Louise, lives in the past. Zoe lives with Grandma and PopPop.

---

Problem:  Zoe wants to solve the mystery of Zoe Louise and her haunting.

---

Event 1:  Zoe discovers Zoe Louise.

Event 2:  Zoe finds a mysterious tombstone.

Event 3:

Event 4:

---

Solution:  Zoe learns about herself through Zoe Louise.

---

Theme:  The power of love

............................................................................................................

Hoffman, 1992). The program focuses on literature units with clusters of books that have some common element (such as theme, genre, or author). Each unit includes 10 children's books read over a two-week period, and the unit guide includes background information and suggestions for sharing and discussing books as well as response activities. The organization of the units provides a framework for the children's discoveries of the connections among the literature selections. The language charts help children and teachers explore many aspects of literature and response to literature. At the close of story-time talk, children's responses to the stories are gathered and written on a language chart that the students may use to recall other stories in the unit and to find similarities and differences among stories. (See Figure 4.6 for a sample language chart.) The charts have several functions:

- show the importance of sharing and studying literature
- make a record of classroom literacy experiences
- show oral to written language connections
- stimulate children to express personal responses to literature
- connect the individual books to the unit theme or topic
- encourage students to reflect on a literary experience
- create a bridge between trade books and content area study
- serve as a springboard for other responses to literature
- encourage students to use higher-order thinking skills

## FIGURE 4.5

Character map based on *Amazing Grace*.

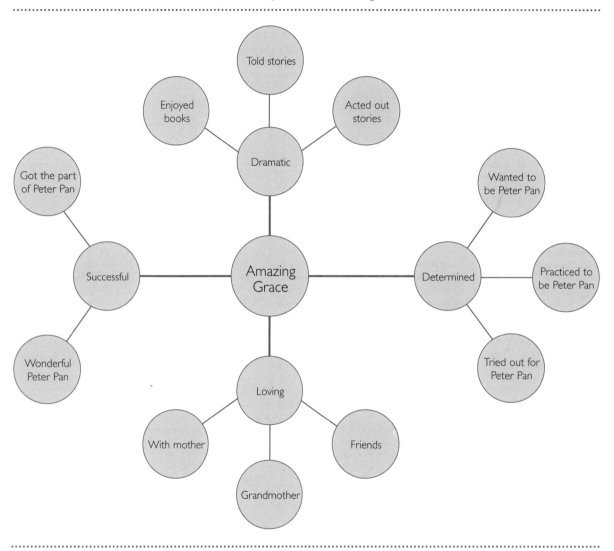

### Plot relationships charts

This **plot relationships chart**, similar to one developed by Barbara Schmit and Marilyn Buckley (1991), *categorizes story information under four headings:* somebody, wanted, but, *and* so. The chart guides children as they identify the major elements of a selection they have heard or read and helps them understand relationships between characters, problems, and solutions. A sample plot

relationships chart for the book *Journey* by Patricia MacLachlan is shown in Figure 4.7.

### Story pyramids

A **story pyramid** (Waldo, 1991) gives students a *convenient way to summarize a story. Each line of the pyramid gives specific information about the story in a specific number of words: the first line has one word,*

**FIGURE 4.6**

Native American language chart.

Meanings and origins of state names from your reading:

| | | |
|---|---|---|
| Alaska | "great land" | Aleut |
| Arizona | little spring place | Pima |
| Connecticut | long river place | Algonquin and Mohican |
| Idaho | Comanche | Kiowa Apache |
| Illinois | men or soldiers | Algonquin |
| Indiana | land of the Indians | English |
| Iowa | beautiful land | Sioux |
| Michigan | great water | Chippewa |
| Minnesota | sky-tinted water | Sioux |
| Mississippi | great river | Chippewa |
| Missouri | muddy water | Algonquin |
| Ohio | good river | Iroquois |
| Tennessee | tanasi | Cherokee Village |
| Utah | upper | Navajo |

Illustrate these Native American words:

| | |
|---|---|
| canoe | squash |
| hickory | toboggan |
| moccasin | totem |
| moose | wigwam |
| skunk | woodchuck |

**FIGURE 4.7**

A sample plot relationships chart for *Journey*.

JOURNEY

| Somebody | wanted | but | so |
|---|---|---|---|
| Journey | his mother to remember his father, | she went away and tore up the family photographs, | Journey became interested in photography. His grandfather made a darkroom and found negatives to copy the destroyed photographs. |

*the second line has two words, and so forth.* (See Figure 4.8 for a sample pyramid based on *Journey*.) This format forces the student to encapsulate the plot. The lines of the pyramid should describe the following:

1. the main character's name
2. description of the main character
3. setting
4. statement of the problem
5. one main event
6. a second main event
7. a third main event
8. solution to the problem

### FIGURE 4.8

A sample story pyramid for *Journey*.

| | |
|---|---|
| 1 | Journey |
| 2 | young boy |
| 3 | farm fields barn |
| 4 | wants to see mother |
| 5 | mother sends money no words |
| 6 | Journey adopts cat named Bloom |
| 7 | Journey discovers torn photographs of his family |
| 8 | grandfather finds negatives, Journey becomes photographer, replaces photographs |

Adapted from Waldo, 1991

### FIGURE 4.9

A sample story prediction chart for *Three Names*.

| | WHAT DO YOU REALLY THINK WILL HAPPEN? | WHAT DID HAPPEN? |
|---|---|---|
| Part I | The dog's name has three parts like Harold the Third. | The reason for the Three Names is that three people call the dog three different names. |
| Part II | Three Names will run away with another dog. | Three Names goes to school with the children in the family. |
| Part III | Three Names will really like school. | Three Names misses school when it closes for vacation. |

## Prediction charts

**Prediction charts** *guide children to predict what will happen next as they move through a story.* Prediction charts activate prior knowledge and establish purposes for reading (Hammond, 1991).

When using a prediction chart, the teacher introduces the book to students. Students predict orally or in writing what will happen next in the story. They also summarize what actually did happen and compare the results to their predictions.

This activity can be individual or group. Younger children not able to write can dictate their predictions. For longer books, predictions can be broken into smaller parts (part I, part II, part III) or into the book's chapters. Figure 4.9 shows a sample prediction chart based on *Three Names* by Patricia MacLachlan.

## Knowledge charts

**Knowledge charts** are quite useful with nonfiction, but they also apply to fictional materials. *The purpose of knowledge charts is to engage and focus students' reading, as well as to help them access the knowledge they already have regarding the topic* (Jim and Joan Macon, 1991). If students do not have previous knowledge regarding a particular topic, then as part of this study teachers need to help them acquire background knowledge.

Figure 4.10 shows a sample knowledge chart based on *The Egg* by Gallimard Jeunesse and Pascale de Bourgoing.

## Unit and Book Introductions

The following sample introductions are models for engaging children with literature. The related discussion questions and response activities show ways to guide readers through and beyond the text.

### FIGURE 4.10

A sample knowledge chart for *The Egg*.

| Prior Knowledge About Eggs | New Knowledge About Eggs |
|---|---|
| 1. Eggs come from chickens. | 1. Eggs form in chickens. |
| 2. Eggs break easily. | 2. Female chickens lay eggs. |
| 3. Eggs have yolks. | 3. Chicks form in eggs. |
| | 4. The hen sits on eggs. |
| | 5. A chick grows in 21 days. |
| | 6. The shell cracks, and the chick comes out of the egg. |
| | 7. Many fowl and birds lay eggs. |
| | 8. Turtles and alligators lay eggs. |

ACTIVITIES

## 4.1  Sample book introduction for historical fiction

BOOK: *Lyddie* by Katherine Paterson

Synopsis (for teachers): This historical fiction relates the struggles of Lyddie, the oldest child of impoverished parents. Her father has disappeared and her mother seems very confused, so Lyddie and her brother must look after their mother and two little sisters. Lyddie is sent to work in a local tavern. Later she leaves this job to become a factory girl in a mill where workers weave fabric. The focus of this literary experience is to analyze character growth and historical setting and to understand the relationship between them. The following topics will aid in the discussion and help children apply new insights gained to their own lives.

1. The life of girls and women during this historical period. (This focus is both setting- and theme-related.)

2. The central character and character growth (the causes and effects of character growth, as well as the relationship of setting to character development).

3. How have children's work and women's work changed?

4. Why do you think these changes occurred?

1. Introduce *Lyddie*.

   a. Ask students if they know any children who have jobs. Discuss the age at which children can legally work today.

   b. Explain that *Lyddie* is about a girl who had to go to work at the age of 13. She was paid only fifty cents a week and the money she earned was paid to her mother.

c.  Read the first few pages of the book that tell about the bear incident. This incident portrays Lyddie as a courageous girl who, with the help of her brother, protects her mother and little sisters from a marauding bear.

d.  Read or write on an overhead the note on page nine that Lyddie's mother wrote after taking the younger children to live with her sister and brother-in-law, leaving Lyddie and her brother to fend for themselves.

e.  Introduce the language in the book. Explain that it is characterized by expressions that are uncommon today. For example, Lyddie used the expression "ey" at the end of many sentences.

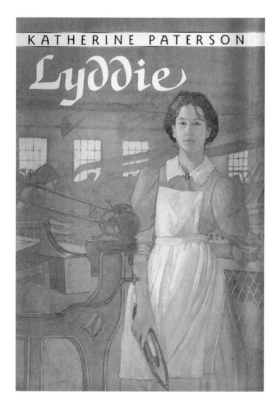

*Tension in this story develops as Lyddie becomes friends with another girl who is fighting for better living conditions, thereby risking Lyddie's own job and her family's future.*

f.  Explain that Lyddie used sentences that we would consider incorrect, such as "It were only a black bear." Discuss Lyddie's dialect and the reasons for it (age, story setting, lack of education, and historical period). Readers will notice there is some change in her language near the end of the book. In addition to Lyddie's dialect, Quaker expressions are used, and during Lyddie's factory work, she encounters Irish immigrants whose language reflects this heritage.

2.  Students read the story silently. Discussion will prepare them to read with greater understanding. Focus their silent reading by reading Lyddie's statement that she is no better than a slave and ask the students to think about it as they read the story. The meaning of this statement evolves as the story unfolds, thus focusing silent reading.

3.  Discuss the story with the students, stimulating them to think about the story. Follow-up discussion takes place after the students have read the entire story. Focus on the following:

a.  What did Lyddie mean when she said that she was no better than a slave?

b.  Describe Lyddie's personality. How does she change during the story?

c.  How did the setting influence Lyddie and the changes she displays?

4.  Use extension activities to allow students to respond to the story. Mrs. Daniels's class did the following after reading *Lyddie*:

a.  The class discussed whether this story could happen today. Students researched the child labor laws, unions, legal work days, overtime, and related topics. They interviewed some legally employed 16-year-olds and discovered that some local businesses violated the law by making the students work more hours than the law permitted. The students were afraid to complain because they believed they would lose their jobs. The sixth graders were incensed at some of the violations they discovered and several of them wrote reports and some others wrote stories about modern-day Lyddies.

b. Compare *Lyddie* to other stories. Mrs. Daniels suggested *Homecoming* by Cynthia Voigt and *The Mill Girls* by Bernice Selden. Some students who had seen the movie *Norma Rae* recognized the connection and asked if they could compare the movie to *Lyddie*. Several parents arranged to rent the videotape and the students watched it as an out-of-school activity and reported on it in class.

---

One sixth-grade classroom had the following discussion after reading *Lyddie*. (The discussion is somewhat abridged because of space constraints.)

Mrs. Daniels: How would you describe Lyddie?

Sally: She seemed very brave at the beginning and at the end, but it was hard to understand why Lyddie did what her mother told her even when she knew her mother was wrong.

Jeremy: You have to remember she was only 13 years old and didn't have any education. She couldn't do anything else.

Christopher: The people working in that factory didn't have any rights. They can't treat people like that today, can they?

Mrs. Daniels: What do you think? Can they? Do you know anyone who has a job at 13? Do you know anyone who works for fifty cents a week?

Children: We don't know.

Mrs. Daniels: Would you like to find out?

Children: Yes!

Mrs. Daniels: After our discussion, we'll go to the library and find out about child labor laws. You may want to interview some people about this subject too. Let's go back to Lyddie's character now.

Sally: You know—I thought she was getting her dream when she got the factory job. But then things got worse and I was sorry that she was afraid to sign the petition.

Christopher: But the factory owners and bosses had too much power; she couldn't do anything else. Would you have been as brave as she was?

Sally: I don't know, but I want to be.

Sarah: But she really got a lot of self-confidence and education in this story and she did finally sign the petition. That really took a lot of courage. I think she was brave and a good friend.

Mrs. Daniels: Why did she say that she was no better than a slave?

Richard: Because she was the same as a slave when she worked at the tavern and the factory job wasn't much better—she still didn't have any freedom.

---

## 4.2  Sample book introduction for an informational book

BOOK: *Sea Otter Rescue* by Roland Smith

Synopsis (for teachers): This book is based on the oil spill in Prince William Sound, Alaska. The author headed a team of people who worked at the Otter Rescue Center in Valdez, Alaska, which gave him firsthand information and opportunities to photograph the otters.

1. Introduce *Sea Otter Rescue*.

   a. The photographs, the author's note, and the dust jacket give background information that establishes the author's credentials and experiences.

   b. The irresistible photographs in this book are the best introduction. Let students browse through the pictures and discuss the problem of preventing the death of "oiled" otters.

   c. Give background information and statistics concerning the oil spill, the otters, and ways the otters were located and taken to the rescue center.

2. Students read the story silently. The students look at the photographs over and over as they read the book and see different things each time.

3. Discuss the story with the students, stimulating them to think about the story.

a. Ask them to think about and discuss the relationship between the oil spill and ecology and between the otters' death and ecology.

b. Ask them to raise questions about the book.

4. Use extension activities to allow students to respond to the story.

---

One fourth-grade classroom generated the following questions:

- How do oil spills influence our lives and our environment?
- What other animals and birds are injured by this kind of disaster?
- What can we do to prevent future oil spills?
- What is the current state of the cleanup operation in Prince William Sound?
- Why are otters important?

This class discussed their questions and in order to answer them did additional reading for a week after reading the book.

The fourth-grade students also chose and created the following extension activities in response to reading the book.

- They did additional research on oil spills and otters.
- They created an oil spill experiment in the classroom to develop their own understanding.
- They researched the oils spills that took place during the Gulf War.
- They read related conservation books of their individual choice, including *Going Green* by John Elkington, Julia Hailes, Douglas Hill, and Joel Makower; *A Box of Nothing* by Peter Dickinson; *Coastal Rescue* by Christina G. Miller and Louise A. Berry; *Wildlife Rescue* by Barbara Ford and Stephen Ross; and *Endangered Animals* by John Bonnett Wexco.

---

## SUMMARY

This chapter examines children's understanding of and response to literature. The ultimate response, of course, is pleasure in reading. Teachers, librarians, parents, and other concerned adults can guide children's literary experiences and inspire their response to literature by selecting good literature and creating a warm, literate environment. They can introduce literature, provide activities to develop understanding, and encourage follow-up activities to enhance response, including discussion, writing, drama, and further reading. Response activities are discussed further in subsequent chapters.

Literary experiences may involve children reading or listening to stories or experiencing media. Focusing on text meaning to address their reading purpose enhances their response to literature. This is influenced by the child's stance, or purpose for reading. Readers have individual understanding of and response to literature based upon their experiences and interactions with text, but they must also have the knowledge that enables them to share their understanding and discuss their response with a community.

## THOUGHT QUESTIONS

1. Explain understanding as it relates to literature.
2. What is response to literature?
3. Why is response to literature important?
4. What is the teacher's role in creating literary experiences?
5. Why is discussion essential to literary experience and response?
6. What are the characteristics of appropriate discussion of books? What should be avoided in book discussions?
7. How is community of response related to individual response?

## ENRICHMENT ACTIVITIES

1. Read a book to a group of children and observe their responses to the book. Note facial expressions, attentiveness, and comments. Write a paper that describes their responses. Tape-record your reading if possible.
2. Read a book to a small group of children. Have each child retell the story individually and tape-record them if you can. How are their understandings alike? How are they different?
3. Make plans for introducing three books to a group of children, using a different technique for each. Identify the introduction needed for each book (for example, character introduction, plot introduction, setting introduction, or story problem or conflict introduction).
4. Plan questions that could be used to guide the discussion of a book. If possible conduct the discussion with a group of children and tape it for further analysis.
5. Create a discussion plan that fosters children's questions and comments about a book rather than a teacher-directed discussion. If possible conduct this discussion with a group of children and tape it for further analysis.
6. With one student or a small group of students, conduct a teacher-directed discussion. Using the same book and a different student or group, hold a student-focused discussion. Tape both discussions and compare them.
   a. Which discussion involved the most students?
   b. Which discussion revealed the greatest depth of understanding?
   c. Which students appeared to be the most interested in the book?
   d. How were the discussions similar?
   e. How were the discussions different?
7. Use one of the maps or charts presented in this chapter as an introduction or a follow-up to a book with a group of children. Bring their products to class and discuss them.

## RECOMMENDED CHILDREN'S BOOKS

Ackerman, Karen. (1988). *Song and Dance Man.* Illustrated by Stephen Gammell. New York: Knopf. (2–4)

> Grandfather was a song and dance man in the vaudeville theater. He still enjoys entertaining his grandchildren with his routines and magic tricks, and they enjoy his show as well.

Banks, Lynne Reid. (1985). *The Indian in the Cupboard.* Illustrated by Brock Cole. New York: Doubleday. (3–6)

> Omri received a miniature plastic toy Indian for his birthday, which came to life in a cupboard. The tiny character creates interesting problems for Omri.

Boyd, Candy Dawson. (1984). *Circle of Gold.* New York: Scholastic. (3–5)

> This realistic fiction story was a Coretta Scott King Award Honor Book. Mattie Benson wants to buy her widowed mother a special gift for Mother's Day, a beautiful gold pin.

Cleary, Beverly. (1982). *Ralph S. Mouse.* Illustrated by Paul Zelinsky. New York: Morrow. (3–5)

> Ralph goes to school in this sequel to *The Mouse and the Motorcycle.*

———. (1970). *Runaway Ralph.* Illustrated by Louis Darling. New York: Morrow. (3–5)

> Ralph, a mouse who rides a toy motorcycle, is tired of his life in an old hotel. He decides to run away in this sequel to *The Mouse and the Motorcycle.*

———. (1965). *The Mouse and the Motorcycle.* Illustrated by Louis Darling. New York: Morrow. (3–5)

> Ralph the mouse lives in an old hotel and makes friends with a visiting boy who owns a toy motorcycle. They become friend, and Ralph is able to help out his friend.

Conrad, Pam. (1990). *Stonewords.* New York: HarperCollins. (4–6)

> In this suspense story, Zoe and Zoe Louise are best friends in spite of the fact that one of them is a ghost from the past. Zoe must discover the mystery of Zoe Louise and her ghostly presence.

Dickinson, Peter. (1985). *A Box of Nothing.* New York: Delacorte. (3–5)

> James buys a box of nothing, which catapults him into a bizarre world of rubbish in this hilarious and terrifying fantasy.

Elkington, John, Julia Hailes, Douglas Hill, and Joel Makower. (1990). *Going Green.* New York: Penguin. (3–6)

> This informative book guides children to reuse, recycle, and refuse. It provides simple explanations of conservation issues from the greenhouse effect to vanishing rain forests, and how we reuse and misuse energy.

Erickson, Russell. (1974). *A Toad for Tuesday.* New York: Lothrop, Lee & Shephard. (2–4)

> Warton the toad sets out to take beetle brittle to Aunt Toolia but is captured by an owl who plans to eat him on Tuesday.

Fyleman, Rose. (1931). "Mice." In *Fifty-one New Nursery Rhymes.* New York: Doubleday. (1–3)

> This is a poem about mice and their activities in homes.

Garza, Carmen Lomas. (1990). *Family Pictures.* San Francisco: Children's Book Press. (K–4)

> This picture book is illustrated with paintings of family doings in Mexico. The paintings capture the artist's family involved in picking oranges, family dinners, and so forth.

Gibbons, Gail. (1989). *Catch the Wind!* New York: Little, Brown. (K–3)

> Two children visit a kite shop to buy kites for a festival. In the process they learn all about kites and how they are made and used. This informational book provides directions for children to make their own kites.

Hoffman, Mary. (1991). *Amazing Grace*. Illustrated by Caroline Binch. New York: Dial. (1–3)

Grace loves to pretend and hopes to be Peter Pan in the school play. One person tells her she can't because she is a girl, another says she can't because she is African American.

Houghton, Eric. (1989). *Walter's Magic Wand*. New York: Orchard. (1–3)

Walter goes to the library with his mother and discovers the joys of reading. He is so engrossed in the books he samples that he has many adventures.

Hurd, Edith Thacher. (1982). *I Dance in My Red Pajamas*. New York: Harper & Row. (1–3)

Jenny visits her grandparents, who prepare her favorite foods, play games with her, and allow her to assist them. But perhaps best of all, Grandma plays the piano, and they sing and dance.

Jeunesse, Gallimard and Pascale de Bourgoing. (1989). *The Egg*. New York: Scholastic. (K–2)

This informational book is beautifully illustrated. It tells all about eggs and the creatures that produce them.

King-Smith, Dick. (1983). *Babe the Gallant Pig*. New York: Dell. (3–6)

This fantasy has elements that are both funny and serious. Babe the pig does not realize that she is to become a part of the farmer's menu, then she thinks she is a dog.

Kraus, Robert. (1970). *Whose Mouse Are You?* Illustrated by Jose Aruego. New York: Macmillan. (K–1)

This picture book features a mouse who has lost all his family. However, he is able to reclaim them.

L'Engle, Madeleine. (1963). *A Wrinkle in Time*. New York: Dutton. (5–9)

The father of the Austin family, a scientist, disappears, then the younger brother disappears. Meg sets out to find her father and brother and must journey through wrinkles in time to reach them.

Lyon, George Ella. (1992). *Who Came Down That Road?*. Illustrated by Peter Catalanotto. New York: Orchard Books. (1–4)

A mother tells her son about an old, old road and they reflect about the people who came down that road through the years.

MacLachlan, Patricia. (1991). *Journey*. New York: Delacorte. (4–6)

Journey and his sister, Cat, live with their grandparents because their mother has gone away. Journey has difficulty adjusting and his mother sends money but no words.

———. (1991). *Three Names*. Illustrated by Alexander Pertzoff. New York: HarperCollins. (2–4)

Three Names is a dog who has three names because different people in the family have individual names for him.

Miller, Christina G. and Louis A. Berry. *Coastal Rescue*. New York: Atheneum. (4–6)

This informational book addresses the crises of the coasts in the United States. The book explores the natural activities of tides and erosion as well as coastal resources.

Numeroff, Laura Joffe. (1985). *If You Give a Mouse a Cookie*. New York: Harper & Row. (K–2)

This picture book tells a circle story. When the main character gives the mouse a cookie, he requests milk and the story builds.

Paterson, Katherine. (1991). *Lyddie*. New York: Dutton. (4–7)

This story portrays the life of a New England factory girl who labors under conditions that were almost like slavery.

Prelutsky, Jack. (1984). *The New Kid on the Block*. New York: Greenwillow. (1–6)

This collection of poems introduces unusual things and unusual ways of viewing things. Readers encounter jellyfish stew, a bounding mouse, a ridiculous dog, and a boneless chick, to name a few.

San Souci, Robert. (1989). *The Talking Eggs*. Illustrated by Jerry Pinkney. New York: Dial. (1–4)

This book was a Caldecott honor book and a Coretta Scott King Award winner. This colorful folktale is a version of the Cinderella story.

Smith, Roland. (1990). *Sea Otter Rescue*. New York: Dutton. (3–6)

This photographic account of rescuing animals after an oil spill graphically illustrates the process in a step-by-step sequence.

Taylor, Mildred D. (1987). *The Friendship*. New York: Bantam. (3–6)

This story addresses race relations in the South of the 1930s. Taylor writes about the rude treatment of an elderly black man as seen through the eyes of some black children who know that the rude man owes his life to the old black man.

Viorst, Judith. (1981). *If I Were in Charge of the World and Other Worries*. New York: Alladin. (1–6)

This collection of poems addresses the everyday problems of children and their parents. It includes such topics as goodbye, wicked thoughts, thanks and no thanks, facts of life, and night.

Wood, Audrey. (1987). *Heckedy Peg*. New York: Harcourt Brace Jovanovich. (K–3)

This picture-book story is about a witch named Heckedy Peg.

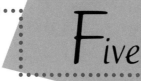

# Five

## KEY TERMS

| | |
|---|---|
| benchmark | picture book |
| compositions | visual literacy |
| illustrated book | wordless picture book |
| medium | |

## GUIDING QUESTIONS

1. What was your favorite picture book when you were a child? Why did you like this book?

2. Why are picture books called unique works of art?

3. What is a picture book?

4. How do picture books differ from other genre?

5. What challenges do authors and illustrators face when creating picture books?

## OVERVIEW

Most adults who hear the words *children's literature* think of picture books. "Today the picture book is a part of growing up, a teaching tool, an entertainment medium, a memory to treasure" (Lima and Lima, 1993). Picture books are, after all, the first literary experience for most of us. Picture books are an art form combining literature and art. In picture books, visual and verbal language come together to tell a story, share a poem, or convey information. Reader, author, and artist jointly create meaning and the reader responds to that meaning.

Books with pictures have three main forms: some have written language and illustrations that work together to tell the story; others are **wordless picture books** *in which the pictures take the place of any text;* and still others are **illustrated books,** *whose pictures illustrate parts of the text but are not integral to it, nor do they add to or elaborate on the text.* In what are generally thought of as **picture books,** *illustrations are an integral part of the story, poem, or information.* Writers use a few hundred words to tell their story, and artists work with the basic elements of line, shape, color, texture, and value, envisioning the text they are interpreting. They organize these elements into compositions that include eye movement, balance, rhythm, and pattern (Ocvirk, Bone, Stinson, Wigg, and Wigg, 1991). *Owen,* by Kevin Henkes, shows this blend of story and art: Owen, a young mouse, has difficulty giving up his security blanket until his mother thinks of a unique solution to his problem. Young children identify with this delightful character and his problem. Owen's facial expressions, his body language, and his blanket evoke readers' understanding and response.

This chapter includes examples of excellent picture books to enrich your understanding of picture books and their values in the classroom. The exemplary

# Picture Books

books discussed in this chapter represent **benchmarks** or *standards of quality to which you can compare* the books you read. Your ability to distinguish between outstanding picture books and those of lesser quality will increase with experience.

## INTRODUCTION

Picture books bring images and ideas together in a unique and exciting art form that adults and children can explore at many different levels (Kiefer, 1995). "The picture book is a book in two media—words and paint or whatever media the artist uses" (L. H. Smith, 1991, p. 106). Children construct meaning and respond to illustrations even before they learn to read words: illustrations evoke both cognitive and aesthetic understanding and response, and children as young as 14 months of age express preferences for specific types of illustrations (Stoodt, 1995). Moreover, art stimulates children to participate actively in literary experiences, cultivates their aesthetic responses, exercises their imagination, and expands their experience. Fine picture books give children a window on the wider world, enabling them to know and learn things outside their own limited domestic experience (Lanes, 1980).

## VIGNETTE

After a restroom break, Pam Peterson said to her second graders, "Everyone who has had a good day so far hold up your right hand." Almost every hand in the classroom went up. "Think of some ways that you can show other people that you are having a good day. Then think of your favorite way to tell other people how you feel."

Jerome volunteered, "I like to sing when I'm feeling good."

Mary Katherine spoke up and said, "I like to play games."

Several other children told about their "happy" time activities.

"Today I'm going to read a book about a mole who wants to dance because he's happy and he's tired of digging tunnels. The title of this book is *Moles Can Dance*. Richard Edwards wrote it and Caroline Anstey created the illustrations." She turned to the first double-page spread and asked, "Do you see any patterns in the art on these pages?"

Several of the children noticed the circles on both pages of the spread.

"Why do you think Caroline Anstey used circles in her illustrations?" asked Ms. Peterson.

Lester said, "'Cause a tunnel would be like a circle, I think."

The teacher responded, "Good idea, Lester!"

Eric volunteered, "Because the mole wants to dance instead of digging holes."

*(continued)*

Ms. Peterson said, "As I read the story to you, think about Eric's prediction. Please look carefully at the illustrations. Notice the shapes, patterns, colors, and feelings you see in the pictures."

When she had finished reading the story aloud, Ms. Peterson asked, "Well, do you agree with Eric's prediction?"

"Yes!" the children chorused.

Ms. Peterson showed them the pictures again and they found the circles and patterns in the illustrations. After discussing the circles, the teacher asked the children to think of their own questions about the story. They thought of a number of questions such as: "Why do moles dig holes?" "Why did the animals think they couldn't dance?" "Can moles really dance?" and several others.

"What was Daisy's problem in this story?"

Several of the children said, "She could not find anyone to teach her to dance."

"Also they told her that moles don't dance," Emily said.

"What happened when Daisy learned to dance?" the teacher asked.

"All the moles found out they could dance!" the children said.

"Tell me about the pictures," Ms. Peterson asked.

The children pointed out that the artist used circles throughout the book. They noted that the pictures were happy pictures and that the artist used bright colors. One child pointed out that the moles looked like they were laughing, moving, and dancing in the pictures.

Ms. Peterson held the book up and showed the pictures again, asking them to think about Daisy's feelings in the pictures and how the artist showed her feelings. She invited them to compare how they felt when they were told that they could not do a certain thing.

The following day, Ms. Peterson introduced *Mole's Hill* by Lois Ehlert.

## THE NATURE OF PICTURE BOOKS

Illustrations contribute greatly to the meaning derived from picture books (Thomas, 1983). Children realize illustrations can tell stories and they use them to construct meaning, the foundation for responding to literature. In the opening vignette, children perceived the meanings and feelings expressed in the illustrations and related them to their own responses. They appreciated the artist's ability to express Daisy's carefree feelings and movements after she learned to dance. Words alone could not express the moles' joyful feeling: the illustrations extended the text and the readers' responses.

Caldecott medalist Ed Young believes that "there are things that words do that pictures never can, and likewise, there are images that words can never describe" (1992). He cites the Chinese philosophy of painting as the inspiration for his work as an artist and writer, explaining, "A Chinese painting is often accompanied by words . . . . They are complementary" (1991). Illustrators and authors are actually co-authors, since they work together to create picture books. The illustrations in picture books are an integral part of each page, adding dimension to the text. Although the text itself is brief, the interaction of text and illustrations make picture books a complex genre.

*In the Haunted House* by Eve Bunting is an example of the blending of text and art that occurs in this genre. Only 280 words were used in telling this story; it takes only ten minutes to read the entire book. Susan Meddaugh's art amplifies the rhythmic language and creates visual and auditory images. The book opens with the text: "This is the house where the scary ones hide. Open the door and step softly inside." Readers see two pairs of sneakers, one large and one small, step through the door, building suspense and moving the plot along.

The language increases the suspense: "An organ is playing a funeral air. It's playing and playing, but nobody's there." The picture shows an organ, a spider, an arrow, and sneaker-clad feet. The author and illustrator establish a dramatic situation through implied questions: What is this house? Who is in the sneakers? Readers next see ghosts, witches, and bats. Sneakers appear in each

*In a true picture book like this one, the illustrations tell as much of the story as do the words.*

FIGURE 5.1

Relationship between text and illustrations, from *In the Haunted House.*

Halloween Houses are so much fun!

illustration; the author and illustrator communicate the wary feelings of the person wearing the large sneakers and the confidence of the person wearing the small sneakers.

The text goes on: "faces that don't look like faces at all," accompanied by running feet; the tension mounts. A mummy appears, while readers see only the characters' shadows. The shadow of a werewolf gargles in the bathroom, and the sneakers run downstairs and outside. The climax occurs when the people wearing the sneakers step "into the day that's asparkle with sun," and the text continues, "Halloween Houses are so much fun!"

Readers see a father and daughter in the illustrations—the father pauses and wipes his brow (see Figure 5.1). The little girl looks back at the house, while her father heads down the sidewalk. The falling action shows the little girl stepping through the front door of the haunted house, followed by a large sneaker. In true picture book style, readers encounter an interesting twist at the end.

## THE HISTORY OF PICTURE BOOKS

### Picture-Book Pioneers

Three great 19th-century British illustrators, Walter Crane, Randolph Caldecott, and Kate Greenaway, are the great-grandparents of modern picture books (Townsend, 1990). Walter Crane designed and illustrated many books, but it was his books of nursery rhymes that paved the way for modern picture books. Caldecott, for whom the American Picture Book Award is named, illustrated traditional nursery rhymes with pictures that communicate a feeling of action and great fun. The Caldecott Medal, awarded each year to an outstanding picture book, is engraved with one of his illustrations. Kate Greenaway's illustrations of nursery rhymes portray gentle, old-fashioned children in formal British gardens, dressed in the soft, pastel-colored clothing in vogue for fashionable children of her day. The Kate Greenaway Medal is the British equivalent to the American Caldecott Medal.

Beatrix Potter, whose *Peter Rabbit* is one of the most popular children's books of all time, was influenced by these early artists. Peter Rabbit originated in Beatrix Potter's letters to her former governess's child (Townsend, 1990). Potter, a skillful wordsmith, wrote with elegant, rhythmic language and enhanced readers' understanding of unfamiliar words with context. Her watercolors enriched the text of these small books that fit so well in little children's hands.

Like Max in Maurice Sendak's contemporary picture book *Where the Wild Things Are*, Peter is anxious to escape parental authority. Both children are curious about forbidden places, and both return home to the warmth of food: Peter to chamomile tea and Max to a warm dinner. The publication of *Where the Wild Things Are* signaled a change in picture books and children's literature in general. With the publication of this book, it became acceptable to write about and illustrate children's conflicts, internal struggles, and feelings of frustration (Scott-Mitchell, 1987). Max's struggle for autonomy is illustrated when he tames the wild things he creates. Although the theme of *Peter Rabbit* was similar, a rebellious bunny was more acceptable to the adults who chose books than was a rebellious child (Scott-Mitchell, 1987). This is a significant change because adults are still the ones who purchase books or check them out of the library for young children.

## Contemporary Picture Books

The short text of picture books (usually 2,000 words or less, with 60 words per page and only 32 pages per book) allows the author to give only the bare bones of a story (Ardizonne, 1980). These textual constraints mean that writers must be downright stingy with their words, yet they have to create enough suspense to make readers turn the pages. The excitement of an outstanding picture book is created through the constant tension between the moments isolated by the pictures and the flow of words joining those moments together (Lukens, 1986). Artists do not "make pictures" for books, they show parts of the story that writers cannot put into words. Artists embellish—and often even establish—story elements such as plot,

character, setting, mood, and style. Picture book illustrators are often artists who find that this medium offers them another form of creative expression (Schwarcz and Schwarcz, 1991).

## ILLUSTRATORS

Illustrators are artists who create visuals that tell or interpret stories. The key to "writing with pictures" is creating a flow of graphic images that are readable, coherent, and obviously related to the text (Shulevitz, 1985). The sequential flow of art is an important aspect of illustrating picture books (Egielski, 1992). Artists strive to evoke the essence of a work rather than to simply "make pictures" (Thomas, 1983). For instance, for May McNeer's picture biography, *America's Abraham Lincoln*, Lynd Ward chose to illustrate with lithography in order to convey Lincoln's strength of character.

Pictures stimulate dramatic, active responses in children that compare with responses to theater or film. Don and Audrey Wood (1986, p. 556) suggest that picture books exist in a literary twilight zone as "the spectacular child of the marriage of images and text. As such, it is probably as close to drama or a thirty-two page movie, as it is to either literature or art." For this reason the picture book makes unique demands on its creators. They must carefully choose which parts of a story to tell through art (Cummings, 1992). They explore various media to identify the best way to interpret a piece of literature (Dillon, 1992a) and make careful selection of color, technique, and style for their illustrations, considering the nature of the subject at hand.

Although artists can choose from the entire world of art when illustrating a picture book, many artists develop new techniques, media, and style to express their ideas. Leo and Diane Dillon frequently examine the history of art from the locale in which a story is set to find ideas for the style they will use (Dillon, 1992b). For instance, in Katherine Paterson's *The Tale of the Mandarin Ducks*, they used a style inspired by *ukiyo-e*, a Japanese art form based on woodcuts.

Art can be used to get a novel perspective on a familiar story. James Marshall used cartoonlike

*This wonderful picture book is the story*
*of how a loving couple risk their lives to*
*save a beautiful drake from a greedy lord.*

illustrations for his retelling of the traditional folk-tale *Goldilocks and the Three Bears*, showing the bears riding a bicycle built for two with a baby seat. He includes entertaining details such as the hair that the bears shed on their chairs. Goldilocks is portrayed as a naughty little girl who is always in trouble.

Artistic styles create a different "feel" for different books. In illustrating Gloria Houston's historical fiction *The Year of the Perfect Christmas Tree*, Barbara Cooney chose soft colors to illuminate the Appalachian setting and the traditions of an old-time Christmas celebration. Peter Parnall focuses readers' attention on Byrd Baylor's poem in *The Other Way to Listen* with clean pen-and-ink drawings and spare use of color, creating a desert feeling with his artistic style. In *Stellaluna* Janell Cannon used liquitex acrylics and Prismacolor pencils on bristol board to express the love and respect she has for bats. She shows the little fruit bat as a lovable and loving character, so that readers struggle with her as she learns to live in a bird nest. She put so much character in Stellaluna's face and body that the bat comes alive for the reader.

## Working with Authors

Because illustrators extend the authors' meaning and go beyond the language, they become essential contributors to picture books. The integration of pictures and language is the vital dimension of picture books. Illustrators and authors meld written text with images to clarify and explain the facts presented (Thomas, 1983). Dress and countenance reveal more than a name does. Both the author and the illustrator work to make the reader care about a character and what happens to that character. The setting is depicted in illustrations and language that establish the time and place as well as the mood and atmosphere of the story.

FIGURE 5.2

A rainy day in *The Napping House.*

FIGURE 5.3

The sun comes out in *The Napping House.*

*The Napping House,* written by Audrey Wood and illustrated by Don Wood, shows how an illustrator and author work together to tell a story. Figure 5.2 depicts a rainy day from the exterior of a house. The picture in Figure 5.3 has more yellow in it, showing that the sun is emerging. Figure 5.4 shows the last page of the story: an exterior view of the napping house with a rainbow in the background. The author did not describe in words the setting change from outside the house to inside the bedroom, the return to the outside, or identify the child as a boy or girl. Further, the cumulative language in the story does not mention rain, sun, or rainbow, but the mood gradually changes as the sun comes out, and an entirely different feeling is conveyed by the last page of the book.

There are other dimensions illustrators can add to an author's words. In Karla Kuskin's informational book, *The Philharmonic Gets Dressed,* Marc Simont managed to instill a bit of humor while con-

veying information through his drawings. His illustrations interact with the text to communicate information about an orchestra and to spark readers' interest in the subject. The illustrations show male musicians shaving and getting into their underwear and trousers and female musicians wiggling into their slips and skirts as they get ready for a performance.

## ILLUSTRATIONS

Fine illustrators use their talents to create original, interesting pictures that speak to children. They arrange the art and text to create meaningful **compositions,** *well-planned designs that help readers understand and visualize the text,* which encourages them to create their own interpretation of literature. The art enlarges the personal experience of its viewers, heightens their awareness of the world around them, and helps them understand their

FIGURE 5.4

A rainbow in *The Napping House.*

in the napping house,
where no one now is sleeping.

own experiences. Trina Schart Hyman's detailed drawings place the setting of Lloyd Alexander's *The Fortune-Tellers* in central Africa in a way that words alone could not.

Artists express their thoughts, feelings, and interpretations through illustrations. In much the same way that authors choose words and sentences to create a certain story, artists choose style, medium, technique, and color to create their own interpretation of a particular piece of literature. Leo and Diane Dillon, who used a Japanese style to such great effect in *The Tale of the Mandarin Ducks*, used an airbrush technique to illustrate Verna Aardema's African folktale *Why Mosquitoes Buzz in People's Ears* because it created the mood they wanted for the story.

Illustrators may choose from an array of styles—from impressionism that suggests and implies ideas, to literal representation that is very

detailed and specific—to fit the mood of the story. The artist Thomas Allen uses pastel chalk and muted colors to evoke a nostalgic feeling for *In Coal Country* by Judith Hendershot and *Climbing Kansas Mountains* by George Shannon. Photographs are representational art appropriate for books such as Tana Hoban's *Circle, Squares, and Triangles*, a concept book that uses photographs of common objects to explore these common shapes. Some children prefer photographs as illustrations (Stoodt, 1995).

## Style

"Style in its simplest sense is a manner of expressing" (Kiefer, 1988, p. 261). The illustrations in picture books are works of art that express meaning through medium, technique, color, line, and design. The Japanese style of the art in *The Tale of the Mandarin Ducks* fits this Japanese story. Even listeners who are too young to recognize artistic style can sense the unity of text and artistic style in this book. Even very young children respond to an artist's ability to express meaning (Applebee, 1978) and use it to actively construct both cognitive and affective meaning. Kiefer (1988, 1986, 1984, 1983) devoted six years to studying children's response to picture books in kindergarten through fourth grade. Her observations enabled her to document children's growing awareness of aesthetic factors and of the artist's role in choosing these factors to express meaning. She found that children increased their understanding of picture book art when they had chances to compare and respond to artistic style, media, and color in various books.

## Medium

**Medium** refers to *the material used in creating the illustrations for a story*, including pen and ink, watercolor, pastels, woodcut, fabrics, and many other materials; artists may select a single medium or a combination of media from an almost unlimited range to enable them to interpret an idea. John Steptoe uses pencil and wash drawings, which fit the theme and mood of the traditional

*The shadowed trees and trails painted by the illustrator in Jane Yolen's story* Owl Moon *are landmarks past which he and his family trudged on winter nights searching for the magnificent and elusive owl.*

Native American legend in *The Story of Jumping Mouse*. In *Tar Beach* Faith Ringgold uses acrylic on canvas paper, similar to the canvas fabric she used to create the original quilt paintings on which the story is based, and the page borders are reproduced from her original story quilt. Her bright colors and primitive style communicate the spirit of her childhood. Some of the more popular media for children's picture books are listed in Table 5.1, which also cites examples of books illustrated in each medium.

Identifying the particular medium an artist has used in illustrating a picture book is often difficult and sometimes impossible. However, consulting the dust jacket, the book's introductory material, reviews, and author–illustrator interviews may

help. Refer to Chapter Three for additional information regarding illustrations in Caldecott Award and Caldecott honor books. Chapter Ten discusses both illustrators and authors.

### Technique

Technique refers to the way a medium is used. Although David Ray chose acrylic paint to illustrate Jane Yolen's *Greyling*, his thick application created a texture similar to oil or oil pastels (Kiefer, 1995). Some artists consistently use the same technique—their trademark, so to speak. Others use many different techniques to illustrate books. For example, in *The Three Billy Goats Gruff* Marcia Brown uses crayon and gouache drawings

## TABLE 5.1

Popular media for illustrations in children's picture books.

| MEDIUM | EXAMPLE BOOK | MEDIA COMBINATIONS |
|---|---|---|
| pastels | *The Polar Express*, Chris Van Allsburg | |
| watercolors | *Owl Moon*, Jane Yolen | |
| colored pencil | *The Great Kapok Tree*, Lynne Cherry | colored pencil, watercolors |
| woodcuts | *Shadow*, Marcia Brown | woodcuts, cut paper, tissue paper |
| oil paints | *Heckedy Peg*, Audrey and Don Wood | |
| crayon | *Fish Is Fish*, Leo Lionni | |
| gouache* | *Arrow to the Sun*, Gerald McDermott | gouache, tempera |
| pen and ink | *Always Room for One More*, Nonny Hogrogian | |
| photographs | *Look Again*, Tana Hoban | |

*Gouache is an opaque watercolor created by using a white base with tempera.

to dramatize the story. In the folktale *Once a Mouse*, woodcuts and bold colors convey the animals' strength. Delicate drawings and soft colors, however, illustrate *Cinderella*.

## Color

Color is a very expressive element of illustration, conveying temperature, personality, and emotion. Red signifies danger in *Once a Mouse*, but it can also be used to convey anger. Artists generally use the warm colors—red, yellow, and orange—to create feelings of excitement, energy, friendship, and anger, while the cool colors—blue and green, the colors of sky and water—create peaceful, quiet moods and sometimes sad or depressed moods. Barbara Cooney used light, warm green and light blue with touches of white and warm brown to portray spring in the mountains and warm family feelings in *The Year of the Perfect Christmas Tree*. She portrays winter using white touched with warm brown and blue gray.

Sometimes the absence of color is significant. Maurice Sendak, illustrating *A Very Special House* for Ruth Krauss, used flat line drawings for the imaginary incidents in the story, but drew the main character with a three-dimensional shape, wearing blue trousers with a white shirt.

*Intensity.* Intensity, which refers to the brightness or dullness of color, affects the meaning and mood of illustrations. In illustrating *Dreamplace*, by George Ella Lyon, Peter Catalanotto chose low intensity, muted colors to create a dreamlike quality in the illustrations, appropriate because most of the story takes place in a child's imagination: as she tours old, abandoned pueblos, she imagines how the original inhabitants lived. In contrast, for *Night in the Country* by Cynthia Rylant, Mary Szilagyi used deep, rich shades of blue and other deep colors to create the feeling of a summer night.

*Contrast.* Contrast is an aspect of color value and is developed through the use of opposite colors. This also affects the final illustration and the reader's perception of it. Rachel Isadora used high contrast black and white art deco illustrations to give readers a 1930s feeling in the historical fiction

*Ben's Trumpet.* In Eloise Greenfield's poetry book, *Honey, I Love, and Other Love Poems,* the poetry and the low contrast of brown illustrations on a soft white background convey the beauty of the principal character's face and focus on its energy.

## Line

Line is the most common artistic element (Kiefer, 1995). Lines are very expressive: they communicate meaning, mood, and movement. Thin lines speak of fragility and thick lines convey weight and strength. Curves and circles suggest warmth and softness. In Ruth Krauss's *The Happy Day,* Marc Simont creates circles on every page to suggest the warmth of animals sleeping contentedly, drowsy awakening from sleep, and the joy of laughing and dancing. Vertical lines convey stability, while sharp, diagonal lines establish excitement and movement. Horizontal lines are calm and peaceful, which is why Barbara Cooney used them to create peaceful feelings for spring and winter pictures in *The Year of the Perfect Christmas Tree.*

## Design

In design, or composition, the layout and size of pictures are chosen to create a rhythm that expresses the meaning of the book. Design is used to create both unity and variety. Finally, a well-designed book balances and creates a satisfying pattern between pictures and text.

*Size.* Size communicates a variety of ideas in children's books. Maurice Sendak used size to show that Max was dreaming in *Where the Wild Things Are:* the illustrations grow larger as Max moves into his imagination until they fill two pages with the wild rumpus; when Max begins to return to reality, the pictures gradually grow smaller and calmer.

*Placement and perspective.* Leo Lionni uses placement and color in *Swimmy* to create a feeling of loneliness. He places the little fish in the corner of a page with a dull gray background to establish a lonely mood. Then Lionni creates vertical movement using the lines and colors of undersea

*Characteristic of many picture books, this one has a surprise ending, which is why children love it.*

plants and fishes to raise readers' spirits. In *The Napping House,* Don Wood gradually changes the perspective of the illustrations until the reader has the feeling of looking down on the bed when the story climax occurs. Chris Van Allsburg uses this same technique in *The Polar Express.* The reader has the feeling of looking down on Santa and his sleigh, generating a feeling of distance.

## TYPES OF PICTURE BOOKS

Realistic fiction, modern fantasy, traditional literature, biography, historical fiction, poetry, and informational books—all genre of children's literature are represented by picture books, and the illustrations clarify concepts and ideas in all of them. The category is often thought to be somewhat limited, however, perhaps because authors and illustrators frequently choose the picture book format to communicate the simplicity of folktales, and many traditional stories are told in a picture book format. The illustrators of these tales create individual interpretations from a wide variety of art styles and colors: lush, jungle colors illustrate Mwenye Hadithi's folk tale *Hot Hippo*, while Steven Kellogg uses soft colors and detailed drawings to interpret *Chicken Little*. Only the imagination and talent of the artist and the author, however, can define the limits of picture books, as shown by the sampling listed here.

- *What Mary Jo Shared* by Janice Udry tells a realistic, albeit fictional, story about a kindergartner who puzzles over the problem of what to share in kindergarten sharing time. Evelyn Mill's soft illustrations nicely portray Mary Jo's family and kindergarten classroom.

- Karla Kuskin's *City Noise* is a picture book poem. Renee Flower uses bright colors, busy pictures, and geometric patterns to illustrate a "noisy" poem, in which a little girl holds a tin can to her ear to hear city noise just as a child at the beach would hold a shell to her ear to hear ocean sounds. The artist and the poet created an analogy through language and image.

- *Tight Times*, a realistic fiction by Barbara Hazen with black-and-white line drawings by Trina Schart Hyman, tells the story of a young boy who experiences tight times when his father loses his job.

- Photographs illustrate Ann Morris's informational book *On the Go*, part of a series about the ways people around the world live their daily lives.

- Tomie dePaola frequently communicates information through art. *The Popcorn Book* and *The Cloud Book* provide extensive, comprehensible information about these subjects.

Although picture books may be on any subject and may fall into any genre of children's literature, there are basically only two categories of picture books: those with and those without words.

## Wordless Picture Books

**Wordless picture books** *tell stories entirely through pictures.* This format is very appealing for today's

*The author of this picture book has created an urban symphony full of life and energy that give a city its city sound.*

children, whose experiences with television and film orient them to visual communication. Teachers find wordless picture books to be invaluable for developing vocabulary, comprehension, and critical reading (Cianciolo, 1990). These books are like other picture books: they delight all age groups, address all subjects, and belong to all genre.

Illustrators of wordless picture books use their artistic talents to create character, setting, plot, theme, and style without using any words at all. Each frame or page leads readers to the next. Mercer Mayer is a master of funny wordless picture books. His hilarious book, *A Boy, a Dog and a Frog*, tells the story of a boy's relationship with his dog and his acquired frog. These characters also appear in some of his other books: in *One Frog Too Many*, for example, he develops a theme of sibling rivalry guaranteed to make even adults laugh. Figure 5.5 shows an illustration from this book—

## FIGURE 5.5

A page from *One Frog Too Many*.

try to identify the story conflict from the illustration. Other artists who create wonderful wordless picture books include Raymond Briggs, John Goodall, Pat Hutchins, Peter Spier, and Paula Winter.

Peter Spier explores many dimensions of rain in his book by the same name. It opens with raindrops on the title page and he goes on to portray rain in many ways: from splashing raindrops to the glistening drops caught in a spider's web to children's delight with playing in the rain. Spier captures a rainy-day mood that makes the reader think of cozily enjoying cookies and cocoa while warm and dry inside—and he never writes a single word.

Brinton Turkle uses a novel perspective in *Deep in the Forest*, an interpretation of the traditional folktale *Goldilocks and the Three Bears*. Children are delighted when they recognize that he has reversed the roles of Goldilocks and the little bear.

### Picture Books with Words

Picture books can combine art and language to tell a story or share information. Preschoolers who experience the joys of literature early in life often identify with characters such as Don Freeman's *Corduroy*, the toy bear with green overalls who loses a button, but finds it and a home at the same time. Many young children connect Ezra Jack Keats's *The Snowy Day* with their own lives. They respond to the principal character's joy in the first snowfall of winter and to the rich colors of the simple illustrations. Shirley Hughes has written a number of enchanting books for preschool children. In *Out and About*, she illustrates 18 simple rhymes with watercolor paintings featuring families and the seasons of the year.

A variety of picture books is available for older students too. Susan Jeffer's interpretation of Robert

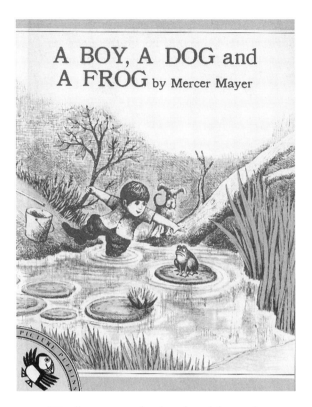

*Wordless picture books rely solely on the artists talent to tell a story.*

Frost's poem, *Stopping by Woods on a Snowy Evening*, is a stunning picture book with ageless appeal. Her illustrations create the silence of a snowstorm and a feeling of eternity. Allen Say illustrated the Japanese folktale *The Boy of the Three-Year Nap* with colorful, detailed pictures that create an Asian setting. This traditional story, written by Diane Snyder, is excellent for children in third or fourth grade. Chris Van Allsburg's *The Mysteries of Harris Burdick* has full-page pictures with interesting captions that stir the imagination. This wonderful book is just right for intermediate grade children.

## SELECTING AND EVALUATING PICTURE BOOKS

What makes a picture book an outstanding example of the genre? This question is at once simple and complex, just as are fine picture books. Young children, of course, enjoy picture books, leading many adults to think they are only for young children. It is important to remember, however, that "the best children's writers say things to a five-year-old that a fifty-year-old can also respect" (Hearne, 1990, p. 9). Both a five-year-old and a fifty-year-old can enjoy picture books, although they probably appreciate them in different ways.

Excellence in narrative is difficult to achieve in picture books because they must be short and simple and yet interesting enough to retain freshness and quality even through many readings (Lobel, 1981). Certainly, quality picture books have well-drawn characters, suspenseful plots, authentic settings, and all of the factors that contribute to literary excellence in all categories of literature. The art is integrated with the narrative and is appropriate to the mood and subject matter. Arnold Lobel (1981) established the most important standard: "A good picture book should be true. That is to say, it should rise out of the lives and passions of its creators" (p. 74).

In choosing picture books to read, consider the visual components of color, line, shape, space, texture, and perspective (Lacey, 1986), as well as the standards suggested for that particular genre, since picture books encompass all genre. The best indicators for picture books that children will enjoy, however, are these qualities:

1. The book is appropriate for the age and stage of development of the potential readers or listeners. Fine picture books are works of art appropriate for a broad range of students.

2. Children can identify with the main character. Consider whether the main character is developed as a rounded character or a stereotype. (Stereotypes are appropriate characters in traditional literature, of course.)

3. Children can understand the plot, which has an identifiable climax and an identifiable ending.

4. The theme grows out of characters and plot and is appropriate for children.

5. The story is told in interesting, expressive language with simple narrative, and the author avoids long descriptions—it is a "page turner."

6. The illustrations enrich the text, are integrated with the text, and are appropriate to the mood and subject matter.

## CLASSROOM ACTIVITIES TO ENHANCE LITERARY EXPERIENCE

Picture books are written to be read aloud while the listeners look at the pictures—an integral part of the literary picture-book experience. (Chapter Eleven gives information regarding oral presentations of literature.) Children often cluster in a group to listen so that they can better see the illustrations, frequently asking the teacher to read it again; they do benefit from multiple hearings. They like to pick up the books they have heard read and pore over the pictures at their own pace. This section presents strategies and activities to engage students with picture books, encourage response, and develop visual literacy. Many of the suggestions focus on the illustrations and careful observation of them. Although these activities are based on picture books, they are applicable to other literature.

### Visual Literacy

Children today live in a complex visual world. Visual communication and visual literacy are extremely important because our eyes are major avenues of communication. Eighty percent of our information comes to us visually, through billboards, signs, television, pictures, and photographs (Debes and Williams, 1974). Children who have many opportunities to describe, compare, interpret, and value illustrations in picture books learn to interact with visual information (Stewig, 1992). Giving them many experiences with picture books will help them *sort out, recognize, and understand visual information*, which is **visual literacy.** The guidelines given in Activity 5.1 will assist in planning picture-book experiences for students.

ACTIVITIES

## 5.1  Reading a picture book to children

1. Introduce the book to the children. The introduction can motivate listeners and anticipate the ideas in the book. Show them the cover and title and tell them the author's and illustrator's names.

2. Read the story aloud to give them the opportunity for appreciative listening. Make sure that all the children have the chance to view the pictures as you read.

3. Discuss the story with the children, stimulating them to think about the story. Discussion following appreciative listening enhances understanding. Ask them what things they noticed in the book.

Encourage them to compare themselves and their experiences to the picture book and its illustrations. Does the main character look like them? Act like them? Would they do the same things as the character did? Would they like to have the character as a friend?

4. Use extension activities to allow students to respond to the story. Students can enrich their own understanding through examining the ways that authors and artists make meaning in text and illustrations.

   a. Studying various versions of the same story can facilitate this understanding. Traditional

## FIGURE 5.6

Hyman's Little Red Riding Hood.

## FIGURE 5.7

de Regnier's Little Red Riding Hood.

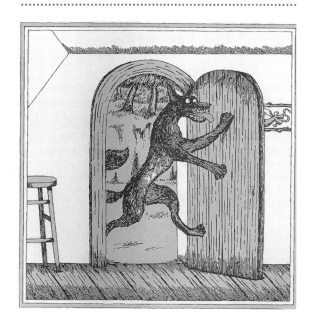

literature is especially appropriate for this experience because many children know these tales already, and because the stories have been told, retold, and illustrated so many different ways. Figures 5.6 and 5.7 show two ways that different artists have interpreted the traditional tale of Little Red Riding Hood. Compare the interpretations of the wolf by these two author/illustrators. Little Red Riding Hood could be compared in the same way. In the discussion of the art include consideration of line, shape, texture, color, value, and layout used in each version. Find other versions of this story for children to compare.

b. Older students can do the above activity as a writing activity.

c. Students can create their own versions of Red Riding Hood (or of another favorite).

d. Students can compare the written text of various versions of Red Riding Hood.

e. Additional aesthetic experiences can involve making puppets, drawing or painting pictures, painting friezes, designing bulletin boards, creating posters, and doing craft projects.

f. Retelling stories through creative drama and storytelling gives children opportunities to respond to the language of picture books. Encourage students to relate prior knowledge to picture clues to construct understanding.

g. Writing stories, poems, or informative pieces based on picture books gives children additional literary experiences. They could even develop their own illustrations to accompany their written response.

h. Choosing music that fits the mood of a book extends the aesthetic experience.

### *Artists' Differing Interpretations of Little Red Riding Hood*

Trina Schart Hyman drew on her childhood love of the Little Red Riding Hood story when creating her Caldecott honor book. Her elegantly detailed illustrations are rich in color. She framed the text and illustrations with elaborate designs of flowers, hearts, and plaids.

Beatrice Schenk de Regniers used a more primitive style: her long, sharp lines for drawing Red Riding Hood, the mother, the wolf, and the grandmother contrast with Hyman's softer, more rounded characters. The spare, simple settings create a vastly different mood than the lushness of Hyman's illustrations.

*Lon Po Po,* a Caldecott Medal winner, written by Ed Young, is a Chinese version of the Red Riding Hood story, although it does not have a Red Riding Hood character. In this version, three little children stay at home while their mother goes to visit their grandmother, Po Po. The wolf plans to eat the children while their mother is away, but they outwit him. Young renders a more realistic treatment of the wolf than either Hyman or de Regniers.

........................................

## 5.2   Developing a unit study on the topic of dogs

Select several appropriate books for a teaching unit on dogs. A partial list of good picture books about dogs appears at the end of this activity. A unit of study such as this one could extend over a week or more. Although this unit focuses on dogs, the topic could be virtually anything—trees, giants, boys, girls, teachers, mothers, fathers.

1. Introduce the book you have selected to the children, encouraging them to make predictions from the title and the cover of the book or from the opening sentences.

2. Read the story aloud to give them the opportunity for appreciative listening. Ask them to think about the pictures of the dog in the book and what the text says about the dog. Ask them to think about how this dog is like dogs they know or have seen.

3. Discuss the story with the children, stimulating them to think about the story. Ask appropriate questions to start discussion.

    a. Do the pictures look like real dogs or make-believe dogs?
    b. Is this a big dog or a little dog?
    c. What colors are the dog?
    d. What is special (unique) about this dog?
    e. What things did the dog do in the story?
    f. What is special about the things the dog did?
    g. Does this dog remind you of any dog that you know?
    h. How is it different from dogs that you know?
    i. If you could talk to the author or illustrator, what questions would you like to ask?

4. Use extension activities to allow students to respond to the story.

    a. After reading several books to the children and letting them enjoy the illustrations, have them think of ways to compare and contrast dogs. They may suggest such things as size, color, personality (some dogs are gentle, some are not), or whether they are real or make believe, and so forth.
    b. They can draw pictures of their favorite dog and tell or write why this is their favorite.
    c. They can tell or write about which dog they would like to have as a pet and why.
    d. Older students may compare the dog characters by creating grids such as the one in Figure 5.8.
    e. Ask students to write about the things that make dogs good pets or ways of caring for pet dogs.
    f. Suggest that children make up stories about dogs that they can tell aloud, dictate to the teacher, or write on their own.

## FIGURE 5.8

Grid for comparing characters, in this case dogs.

| Title | Dog's Looks | Dog's Personality | Dog's Actions | Dog's Likable Characteristics |
|-------|-------------|-------------------|---------------|-------------------------------|
|       |             |                   |               |                               |
|       |             |                   |               |                               |
|       |             |                   |               |                               |
|       |             |                   |               |                               |
|       |             |                   |               |                               |

The following are suggested picture books to use in a unit on dogs.

- Blegvad, Lenore. (1979). *Hark! Hark! The Dogs Do Bark! Rhymes About Dogs.* Illustrated by Erik Blegvad. New York: Atheneum.

- Burningham, John. (1976). *The Dog.* New York: T. H. Crowell.

- Galdone, Paul. (1960). *Old Mother Hubbard and Her Dog.* New York: McGraw-Hill.

- Hill, Eric. (1980). *Where's Spot?* New York: Putnam.

- Jones, Rebecca C. (1982). *The Biggest, Meanest, Ugliest Dog in the Whole Wide World.* Illustrated by Wendy Watson. Greenwich, CT: Macmillan.

- Mayer, Mercer. (1967). *A Boy, a Dog and a Frog.* New York: Dial.

- Ormondroyd, Edward. (1971). *Theodore's Rival.* Illustrated by John Larrecq. Boston: Houghton Mifflin.

- Rosen, Michael J. (Ed.). (1993). *SPEAK! Children's Illustrators Brag About Their Dogs.* New York: Harcourt Brace Jovanovich.

- Wagner, Jenny. (1977). *John Brown, Rose, and the Midnight Cat.* Illustrations by Ron Brooks. New York: Puffin Books.

- Wildsmith, Brian. (1979). *The Hunter and His Dog.* New York: Oxford.

- Zion, Gene. (1956). *Harry the Dirty Dog.* Illustrated by Margaret Bloy Graham. San Francisco: Harper & Row.

## 5.3  Exploring a single book in depth

Story Synopsis: Two children become separated from their mother in a Paris train station. A friendly gendarme (policeman) tries to rescue them. He asks, "What does your mama look like?" They answer that she is the most beautiful woman in the world. He searches for someone who fits this description. Each woman he locates is the wrong one—until the children figure out on their own how to go back to their mama.

1. Introduce the book *Where's Our Mama?* to the children. The book was written and illustrated by Diane Goode and tells the story of a boy and girl at the Paris train station who have a problem.

2. Read the story aloud to give them the opportunity for appreciative listening.

3. Discuss the story with the children, stimulating them to think about the story.

   a. Which picture is this book do you like the best? Why?

   b. What words would you use to describe your mama?

   c. Why did the gendarme have so much trouble finding mama?

   d. How did the children describe their mama? Why did they describe her this way?

   e. How would you describe the children's mama?

   f. How did the children feel when they finally found their mama?

4. Use extension activities to allow students to respond to the story.

   a. Compare this story with *Mama, Do You Love Me?* by Barbara M. Joosse, illustrated by Barbara Lavallee. How are these stories alike? How are they different? Compare the settings.

   b. The children may tell or draw pictures of where they would look for their mama if they became separated.

   c. Have the children draw pictures of ways they show their mothers they love them. This would be a very good experience for Mother's Day.

...........................................

## 5.4  Introducing art concepts

To introduce the art concepts of media, technique, line, color, and perspective, you may wish to first refer to *Words About Pictures: The Narrative Art of Children's Picture Books* (Nodelman, 1988), *Art Fundamentals* (Ocvirk et al., 1991), or *The Potential of Picture Books* (Kiefer, 1995).

Use examples from picture books (any mentioned throughout the chapter or those listed at the end of this activity) to illustrate these various concepts for children. Discuss the concepts with the children, using stimulating questions like the ones listed below. They may complete a grid like the one in Figure 5.9 to compare the illustrations in various books. This will give them a basis for comparing illustrations and choosing ways of illustrating their own work. Once they understand the various concepts, have them experiment in creating illustrations for their compositions.

1. How do artists create setting in pictures?

2. How do pictures of night settings differ from daytime settings?

3. How can pictures contribute to the plot?

4. How do artists create characters in pictures?

5. How are the pictures like you and things you have done?

The following are some suggestions for picture books to use in a study of particular art concepts.

### Art—General

- Briggs, Raymond. (1978). *The Snowman.* New York: Random House.

- Carle, Eric. (1992). *Draw Me a Star.* New York: Philomel.

- Cooney, Barbara. (1990). *Hattie and the Wild Waves.* New York: Viking Penguin.

- dePaola, Tomie. (1989). *The Art Lesson.* New York: Putnam.

- Fisher, Leonard Everett. (1986). *Look Around: A Book About Shapes.* New York: Viking Penguin.

- Hart, Kate. (1994). *I Can Paint.* Portsmouth, NH: Heinemann.

- Micklethwait, Lucy. (1993). *A Child's Book of Art.* New York: Dorling Kindersley.

- Micklethwait, Lucy. (1992). *I Spy: An Alphabet in Art.* New York: Greenwillow.

## FIGURE 5.9

Grid for comparing illustrations.

| Title | Line | Color | Shape | Texture |
|---|---|---|---|---|
|  |  |  |  |  |
|  |  |  |  |  |
|  |  |  |  |  |
|  |  |  |  |  |
|  |  |  |  |  |

- Roalf, Peggy. (1994). *Looking At Paintings: Dogs.* New York: Dorling Kindersley.
- Rylant, Cynthia. (1988). *All I See.* New York: Orchard Books.
- Wick, Walter, Jean Marzollo, and Carol Carson. (1994). *I Spy: A Book of Picture Riddles.* New York: Greenwillow.
- Wolkstein, Diane. (1992). *Little Mouse's Painting.* New York: Morrow.

### Element—Line

- Arnosky, Jim. (1986). *Deer at the Brook.* New York: Lothrop, Lee & Shepard.
- Brown, Marcia. (1954). *Cinderella.* New York: Scribner's.
- Carle, Eric. (1977). *The Grouchy Lady Bug.* New York: T. H. Crowell.
- Fleming, Denise. (1991). *In the Tall, Tall Grass.* New York: Henry Holt.
- Yenawme, Phillip. (1991). *Lines.* New York: Delacort.

### Element—Color

- Ehlert, Lois. (1990). *Color Farm.* New York: HarperCollins.

- Serfozo, Mary. (1988). *Who Said Red?* New York: McElderry.
- Walsh, Ellen. (1989). *Mouse Paint.* New York: Harcourt Brace Jovanovich.
- Wood, Audrey and Don Wood. (1984). *The Napping House.* San Diego: Harcourt Brace Jovanovich.

### Element—Texture

- Ehlert, Lois. (1991). *Red Leaf, Yellow Leaf.* San Diego: Harcourt Brace Jovanovich.
- Hoban, Tana. (1984). *Is It Rough? Is It Smooth? Is It Shiny?* New York: Greenwillow.
- Steptoe, John. (1987). *Mufaro's Beautiful Daughters.* New York: Lothrop, Lee & Shepard.

### Element—Shape

- Baker, Keith. (1991). *Hide and Snake.* San Diego: Harcourt Brace Jovanovich.
- Bang, Molly. (1980). *The Grey Lady and the Strawberry Snatcher.* New York: Four Winds.
- Baylor, Byrd and Peter Parnall. (1979). *Your Own Best Secret Place.* New York: Scribner's.
- Hoban, Tana. (1986). *Shapes, Shapes, Shapes.* New York: Greenwillow.

## 5.5 Illustrating a text

Read a picture book to the class without showing them the pictures, then ask them to create appropriate illustrations to accompany the story. Compare their illustrations with those in the book.

## 5.6 Identifying illustration techniques

Show the children wordless picture books and ask them to identify which details change from picture to picture to show progression in the story and to illustrate character, setting, and plot. Have students create their own wordless picture books, making certain to include details that will help to tell the story.

## 5.7 Creating a story map

Create a story map using a format similar to the one shown in Figure 5.10 for a picture book or a wordless picture book. Both the illustrations and the narrative will contribute to the story map. (See Chapter Fifteen for more information on story maps.)

### FIGURE 5.10

Blank story map.

Setting: (time, place, character)

_____

Problem:

_____

Efforts to Solve the Problem:

1.

2.

3.

_____

Resolution:

## 5.8 Reciting in unison

After students have listened to a picture book of a traditional story, have them read the refrain in unison from a chart you have prepared. Paul Galdone's picture book versions of traditional stories such as *The Little Red Hen, Henny Penny,* and *The Three Little Pigs* are good choices for this activity because he includes refrains in the story narrative. Many of the children will then join in to read the entire story.

## 5.9 Creating a finished picture book

Older students may choose a Grimm folktale, another traditional story, or a poem and create their own illustrations for it. They should be prepared to explain their choices of media, technique, colors, and lines. They should include the text of the story or poem with their illustrations, so this would be a good opportunity for them to work on penmanship or even calligraphy. This is also a good opportunity to teach book binding, so they can produce a finished-looking book. They may read their picture books to younger children.

## 5.10 Teddy bear and doll week

Plan a week for bears or dolls. Have students bring their favorite teddy bear or doll to school. Students can help prepare bulletin boards announcing the activity to the rest of the school and write invitations to other classes to visit the classroom during the week. Children may read about toys and read to their own toys. They may write stories about their toy's adventures. Younger children may draw their stories or dictate them to a teacher or teacher assistant. Older children may study the histories of teddy bears and dolls.

The following are some suggestions for picture books to use in a teddy bear and doll theme week.

- Alexander, Martha. (1973). *I'll Protect You From the Jungle Beasts.* New York: Dial.

- Bond, Michael. (1958–1994). *Paddington* (series). Boston: Houghton Mifflin.
- Carlstrom, Nancy White. (1980). *Jessie Bear What Will You Wear?* Illustrated by Bruce Degen. New York: Macmillan.
- Freeman, Don. (1968). *Corduroy.* New York: Viking.
- Milne, A. A. (1954). *Winnie the Pooh.* Illustrated by Ernest H. Shepard. New York: Dutton.
- Wells, Rosemary. (1983). *Peabody.* New York: Dutton.
- Williams, Margery. (1983). *The Velveteen Rabbit.* Illustrated by Michael Hague. New York: Henry Holt.
- Zolotow, Charlotte. (1972). *William's Doll.* Illustrated by William Péne du Bois. New York: Harper & Row.

---

## 5.11 Stimulating interest in the arts

Picture books are works of art and therefore are particularly useful vehicles for generating interest in the arts. Picture books give visual images to music. Young children love to sing, hum, and chant so books based on music are highly motivating for them. Many picture books build aesthetic appreciation.

The following are some suggestions for picture books you can use to stimulate interest in the arts.

- Aliki. (1974). *Go Tell Aunt Rhody.* New York: Macmillan. Illustrates a traditional ballad. The patchwork quilt end papers contribute to the mood of this book.
- Horwitz, Elinor. (1975). *When the Sky Is Like Lace.* Illustrated by Barbara Cooney. Philadelphia: J. B. Lippincott. Describes night.
- Isadora, Rachel. (1976). *Max.* New York. Macmillan. Introduces the world of ballet.
- Isadora, Rachel. (1980). *My Ballet Class.* New York: Greenwillow. Introduces the world of ballet.
- Prokofiev, Sergei. (1987). *Peter and the Wolf.* Illustrated by Jorg Muller. Orlando, FL: Holt. This Russian tale tells about a boy named Peter who goes into the forest and the wolf who hopes to catch him. The birds and forest animals try to warn Peter.
- Spender, Stephen. [1966]. *The Magic Flute.* New York: G. P. Putnam's Sons. Illustrates Mozart's life.
- Udry, Janice May. (1959). *The Moon Jumpers.* Illustrated by Maurice Sendak. New York: Harper & Row. Gives readers the feeling of movement and dance.
- Williams, Vera. (1984). *Music, Music for Everyone.* New York: Greenwillow. Addresses the importance of music in our lives.
- Williams, Vera. (1983). *Something Special for Me.* New York: Greenwillow. Addresses the importance of music in our lives.
- Zemach, Harve. (1966). *Mommy Buy Me a China Doll.* Illustrated by Margot Zemach Fullett. New York: Farrar, Straus & Giroux. Illustrates a traditional ballad.

## 5.12 Using illustrations to learn more about stories

Students can examine the illustrations in a book to glean information that is not presented in the story. Answering questions like the following will guide their studies (Stewig, 1992). These questions and their answers are based on the illustration in Figure 5.11 from *Chicken Little* by Steven Kellogg.

1. What can we tell from the characters' clothing? (The animals are wearing clothing, which suggests that the story is make-believe. They are not wearing cold-weather clothing, so it is probably not winter.)

2. Where do you think Chicken Little is going? Why? (She is carrying a lunch box and pencil, which suggest that she is going to school.)

3. How did the fox happen to see Chicken Little? (He is using binoculars.)

4. Why does the fox have a book in the car? (It is a poultry recipe book: he is planning to cook Chicken Little.)

5. What can we infer about the time of year? (It is probably fall, since school is in session, but it is not cold yet because the leaves are green and acorns are on the tree.)

6. How does the fox plan to kill Chicken Little? How do you know? (With a hatchet, because the picture of his imagination shows one.)

7. What do we learn about the fox? (He likes to eat chickens.)

FIGURE 5.11

The first page from *Chicken Little.*

## 5.13 Exploring the use of color in picture books

Explore the ways that artists use color throughout an entire book (Marantz, 1978). Look, for example, at the shades of tan and brown found throughout the pictures in Molly Bang's *The Paper Crane. King Bidgood's in the Bathtub* by Audrey Wood uses tones of purple to give the book visual unity (Stewig, 1992). Children can analyze how colors are used to create unity, to establish mood and changes of mood, and to extend the story. Teachers can refer to Marantz for additional information about exploring color. They can also choose a group of colorful picture books and have children work in cooperative groups to identify colors that are important in the pictures and the ways the artists have used art to give the stories meaning. Also the children can create their own writing with pictures to illustrate the ways color gives meaning to their stories and reports.

## 5.14 Experimenting with media

Students can experiment with the various media that artists use and make their own picture books. You may choose to involve the art teacher in this experience and explore such media as paint, collage, chalk, photographs, pencil, lithograph, water color, fabric, or quilt paintings. Students could create a picture book or photographic essay using photographs they have taken. They can create a composition based on the photographs, write the text, make a cover, and bind the book.

## SUMMARY

The picture book genre includes books in which the illustrations and the text interact to tell a story or in which there are no words, only pictures. Picture books usually have less than 2,000 words and no more than 32 pages. These constraints force authors to choose their words carefully and make the illustrations very important in developing the story, information, or poetry in the book. Picture books are complex art forms. Many artists experiment with a variety of style, media, and color to achieve the interpretation they feel is appropriate for the text. Their interpretations of literature are very important because picture books are usually children's first experience with literature.

## THOUGHT QUESTIONS

1. Which picture-book illustrations are your favorites? Why?
2. How did the work of Beatrix Potter influence today's picture books?
3. Identify three reasons for using picture books with older children.
4. How can you use picture books to extend children's aesthetic experience?
5. Compare the aesthetic aspects of language in picture books.

## ENRICHMENT ACTIVITIES

1. Make a bibliography of picture books that children could use to compare and refine their understanding of art. You may wish to categorize the books by color, line, style, and so forth.
2. Read three picture books to a group of children. Ask them to choose their favorites and explain why it (or they) is their favorite.
3. Read *Talking with Artists*, compiled and edited by Pat Cummings, and identify ways you could use it in the classroom.
4. Interview the parents of preschoolers to determine how many of them regularly read to their children.
5. Visit a children's bookstore and study the picture books. Which genre had the most selections? Can you identify any trends in the art work?
6. Create a picture book of your favorite traditional story.
7. Write a book and have a friend illustrate it, then discuss why your friend chose a particular style for this story.
8. Develop a picture book teaching unit based on suggestions from the "Activities" section beginning on page 126.
9. Make up a list of picture books that parents could read to their children.

## RECOMMENDED CHILDREN'S BOOKS

Aardema, Verna. (1975). *Why Mosquitoes Buzz in People's Ears: A West African Tale.* Illustrated by Leo and Diane Dillon. New York: Dial. (1–3)

This West African folktale is a *pourquoi*. It explains the "why" of the buzzing of mosquitoes.

Ahlberg, Allan and Janet Ahlberg. (1983). *The Baby's Catalogue.* Boston: Little, Brown. (preschool)

These illustrations show all kinds of parents, all kinds of breakfasts, and all kinds of activities for children.

Alexander, Lloyd. (1992). *The Fortune-Tellers.* Illustrated by Trina Schart Hyman. New York: Dutton. (1–5)

This African tale is about a young man who accidentally becomes a fortune-teller.

Anno, Mitsumasa. (1977). *Anno's Counting Book.* New York: Harper Trophy. (1–3)

This wordless counting book is beautifully illustrated.

Asch, Frank. (1978). *Turtle Tale.* New York: Dial. (P–2)

Block shapes and bright colors tell the story of a turtle making his way to a pond and learning when to stay in his shell and when to come out of it.

Bang, Molly. (1987). *The Paper Crane.* New York: Mulberry Books. (3–5)

This Japanese tale is about kindness and its rewards. The author shows the importance of cranes in Japanese culture.

Baylor, Byrd. (1978). *The Other Way to Listen.* Illustrated by Peter Parnall. New York: Scribner's. (3–6)

This book-length poem tells about a boy who learned how to listen from an old man. The illustrations and mood of the book are Native American.

Bowen, Gary. (1994). *Stranded at Plimouth Plantation 1626.* New York: HarperCollins. (4–6)

This informational book shows the hard life of the Pilgrims through a boy's journal.

Brown, Marcia. (1982). *Shadow.* New York: Scribner's. (1–3)

This is a picture book of shadows.

————. (1961). *Once a Mouse.* New York: Scribner's. (1–3)

This traditional folktale of Hawaii is illustrated with woodcuts.

————. (1957). *The Three Billy Goats Gruff.* New York: Harcourt Brace Jovanovich. (1–3)

The traditional story is interpreted with strong line drawings and tempera paints.

————. (1955). *Cinderella.* New York: Scribner's. (1–3)

This traditional story is done in delicate colors and line drawings. Caldecott medal winner.

Burton, Virginia Lee. (1945). *The Little House.* Boston: Houghton Mifflin. (1–3)

The main character is a shiny new house, but the city gradually encroaches on it. The great-great-granddaughter of the original owner happily moves it to the country.

————. (1939). *Mike Mulligan and His Steam Shovel.* Boston: Houghton Mifflin. (preschool–2)

Mike Mulligan and his steam shovel Mary Ann dig the foundation for a new city hall. They don't plan carefully and Mary Ann is stuck in the basement.

Cannon, Janell. (1994). *Stellaluna.* New York: Harcourt Brace Jovanovich. (1–3)

Stellaluna is a young fruit bat who gets lost and has to adjust to living in a bird nest.

Cherry, Lynne. (1990). *The Great Kapok Tree.* San Diego: Harcourt Brace Jovanovich. (1–3)

A boy dreams that jungle animals tell him to save their habitat.

Cooney, Barbara. (1982). *Miss Rumphius.* New York: Viking. (1–3)

Miss Rumphius travels all over the world to see its many wonders. As she grows older, she stays at home and beautifies the New England coast with flowers.

dePaola, Tomie. (1978). *The Popcorn Book*. New York: Holiday House. (K–3)

This picture book provides a large amount of interesting facts about popcorn.

————— . (1975). *The Cloud Book*. New York: Holiday House. (K–3)

This informational book provides scientific information about clouds in a picture book format.

de Regniers, Beatrice Schenk. (1972). *Red Riding Hood*. Illustrated by Edward Gorey. New York: Macmillan. (1–3)

This version of the traditional tale is told in verse. The illustrations are stark in color and line.

Edwards, Richard. (1994). *Moles Can Dance*. Illustrated by Caroline Anstey. Cambridge, MA: Candlewick Press. (K–3)

Daisy, a young mole, is determined to learn to dance and she does.

Freeman, Don. (1968). *Corduroy*. New York: Viking. (preschool–1)

Corduroy is a teddy bear who wears green corduroy overalls. One day a little girl points out that he needs a new button for his overalls. Corduroy has many adventures while hunting for a button.

Friedrich, Priscilla, and Otto Friedrich. (1957 text; 1983 illustrations). *The Easter Bunny That Overslept*. Illustrated by Adrienne Adams. New York: William Morrow. (K–2)

The Easter bunny oversleeps and tries to deliver Easter eggs on the fourth of July, Christmas, and so forth. He learns that the only time to deliver Easter eggs is Easter.

Gag, Wanda. (1928). *Millions of Cats*. New York: Coward McCann. (K–2)

This traditional story tells about an old man and an old woman who want a cat, but so many cats want to live with them that they don't know what to do. Eventually, the cats get in a fight over who will live with the couple.

Goode, Diane. (1991). *Where's Our Mama?* New York: Dutton. (K–2)

Two children became separated from their mother in a busy Paris train station. A gendarme tries to help them find her but is unsuccessful. The children think of a way to find her.

Greenfield, Eloise. (1978). *Honey, I Love, and Other Love Poems*. Illustrated by Diane and Leo Dillon. New York: Harper & Row. (all ages)

This book of poetry demonstrates an African American child's enthusiasm for life and love.

Hadithi, Mwenye. (1993). *Hot Hippo*. Boston: Little, Brown. (preschool–2)

The story of a hippo living in Africa who gets cooled off in the river.

Hendershot, Judith. (1987). *In Coal Country*. Illustrated by Thomas Allen. New York: Knopf. (3–5)

This picture book tells of the author's experiences growing up in a coal mining region.

Hendrick, Mary Jean. (1993). *If Anything Ever Goes Wrong at the Zoo*. Illustrated by Jane Dyer. New York: Harcourt Brace Jovanovich. (K–2)

Leslie loves the zoo so much that she invites the zookeepers to bring the animals to her house if anything ever goes wrong at the zoo. And they do.

Hoban, Tana. (1987). *Dots, Spots, Speckles, and Stripes*. New York: Greenwillow. (preschool–2)

This concept book is illustrated with photographs that shows shapes, colors, lines, and textures.

————— . (1974). *Circles, Triangles, and Squares*. New York: Macmillan. (preschool–2)

This concept book illustrates circles, triangles, and squares.

————— . (1971). *Look Again*. New York: Macmillan. (preschool–2)

Hogrogian, Nonny. (1971). *Always Room for One More*. New York: Macmillan. (K–2)

This Scottish folk song is enhanced by the use of color in the purple heather and green fields. The pen and ink crosshatching makes the illustrations unusual and adds to the feeling of shadows emerging from the mists of Scotland.

Houston, Gloria. (1988). *The Year of the Perfect Christmas Tree.* Illustrated by Barbara Cooney. New York: Dial. (all ages)

This historical fiction piece is set in the mountains of North Carolina. In this warm family story we learn about mountain customs of the early 1900s.

Howe, James. (1994). *The Hospital Book.* Photographs by Mal Warshaw. New York: Morrow. (3–7)

The energetic text and photographs introduce children to all aspects of the hospital experience.

Howe, James, and Deborah Howe. (1979). *Bunnicula.* New York: Atheneum. (3–4)

Harold the dog wrote this story about a small rabbit found in a movie theater. Chester the cat is convinced the rabbit Bunnicula is a vampire. This hilarious story tells about Chester's efforts to eliminate Bunnicula. There are several sequels to this book that include the same characters.

Hughes, Shirley. (1988). *Out and About.* New York: Lothrop, Lee & Shepard. (preschool)

The rhymes in this book are illustrated with families shown in all four seasons of the year.

Hyman, Trina Schart. (1983). *Little Red Riding Hood.* New York: Holiday House. (1–3)

This version of Little Red Riding Hood is traditional in tone. Hyman's rich colors and decorative page frames give it a European feeling appropriate to a traditional Grimm's fairy tale. This book was a Caldecott honor book.

Isadora, Rachel. (1979). *Ben's Trumpet.* New York: Greenwillow. (K–3)

This historical fiction book, set in the 1930s, is enhanced by black and white art deco illustrations. An African American child wants to become a trumpet player and learns that he can aspire to this goal.

Jeffers, Susan. (1978). *Stopping by Woods On a Snowy Evening.* New York: Dutton. (all ages)

This is Jeffers' interpretation of Robert Frost's well-known poem.

Joosse, Barbara. (1991). *Mama, Do You Love Me?* Illustrated by Barbara Lavallee. San Francisco: Chronicle Books. (K–2)

A young Inuit girl asks her mama whether she will love her if she does things she should not. Her mother reassures her.

Jukes, Mavis. (1984). *Like Jake and Me.* New York: Knopf. (1–3)

A boy and his stepfather come to understand one another as they search for a wolf spider.

Keats, Ezra Jack. (1962). *The Snowy Day.* New York: Viking. (preschool–1)

A boy experiences the very first snowfall of the winter doing the things that children have always enjoyed in the snow. The rich colors and collage-style illustrations help tell the story.

Kellogg, Steven. (1985). *Chicken Little.* New York: Morrow. (preschool–1)

This is Steven Kellogg's version of the cumulative folktale, wherein the sky is falling because a helicopter goes awry.

Kiser, SuAnn. (1993). *The Catspring Somersault Flying One-Handed Flip-Flop.* Illustrated by Peter Catalanotto. New York: Orchard Books. (1–3)

Willy does a remarkable catspring somersault flying one-handed flip-flop. She is so excited that she wants to demonstrate it for her parents and her 11 brothers and sisters.

Krauss, Ruth. (1953). *A Very Special House.* Illustrated by Maurice Sendak. New York: Harper & Row. (K–2)

In this story, the main character escapes to a special house in his imagination where he can do anything he wants.

———. (1949). *The Happy Day.* Illustrated by Marc Simont. New York: Harper & Row. (preschool–2)

This Caldecott honor book tells of sleeping animals, running animals, and happy animals who find a flower blooming in the snow.

Kunhardt, Edith. (1993). *Honest Abe*. Paintings by Malcah Zeldis. New York: Greenwillow. (1–4)

This biography of Lincoln portrays the key events in his life with primitive paintings.

Kuskin, Karla. (1994). *City Noise*. Illustrated by Renee Flower. New York: HarperCollins. (K–3)

A young girl holds a tin can to her ear to hear the city noises in this poetic picture book.

————. (1982). *The Philharmonic Gets Dressed*. Illustrated by Marc Simont. New York: Harper & Row. (1–4)

This informational book tells about the clothes orchestra musicians wear and how they get into them.

Lionni, Leo. (1970). *Fish Is Fish*. New York: Pantheon. (K–2)

A fish dreams about exploring the land but he discovers being a fish is best.

————. (1963). *Swimmy*. New York: Pantheon. (K–2)

Swimmy is a little fish whose family is eaten by a shark. He is frightened and hides, but soon regains his perspective and swims off to enjoy the undersea world.

Lyon, George Ella. (1993). *Dreamplace*. Illustrated by Peter Catalanotto. New York: Orchard Books. (2–4)

This book shows what a visitor to a pueblo believes life must have been like for the original inhabitants.

Mahy, Margaret. (1986). *The Boy Who Was Followed Home*. Illustrated by S. Kelly. New York: Dial. (K–2)

Robert, the hero of this tale, is followed home from school by a growing number of hippopotami. He sends them out of the house, where they take up residence on the lawn.

Marshall, James. (1988). *Goldilocks and the Three Bears*. New York: Dial. (preschool–2)

This is a traditional version of the story. The illustrations are less traditional than the text because Marshall used a detailed cartoon approach to the illustrations.

Mayer, Mercer. (1967). *A Boy, a Dog and a Frog*. New York: Dial. (P–2)

This wordless picture book tells about the friendship of three characters.

Mayer, Mercer, and Marianna Mayer. (1975). *One Frog Too Many*. New York: Dial. (preschool–2)

This wordless picture book tells a classic story of jealousy.

McDermott, Gerald. (1974). *Arrow to the Sun*. New York: Viking Penguin. (3–5)

This is a popular Native American folktale.

McNeer, May. (1957). *America's Abraham Lincoln*. Illustrated by Lynd Ward. Boston: Houghton Mifflin. (3–6)

This picture biography of Lincoln begins with Abe entering school at the age of seven and ends with his assassination.

Melmed, Laura Krauss. (1993). *The First Song Ever Sung*. New York: Lothrop, Lee & Shepard. (1–3)

Set in ancient Japan, this book explores the idea of what the first song was.

Morris, Ann. (1990). *On the Go*. New York: Lothrop, Lee & Shepard. (K–2)

This picture book shows the various conveyances people use to travel in countries around the world.

Paterson, Katherine. (1990). *The Tale of the Mandarin Ducks*. Illustrated by Leo and Diane Dillon. New York: Dutton. (1–3)

A pair of mandarin ducks is separated by a cruel lord. But a compassionate husband and wife risk their lives to aid the ducks.

Pryor, Bonnie. (1988). *Porcupine Mouse.* Illustrated by Maryjane Begin. New York: Morrow. (K–2)

Two mice set out to find a new home because their home is so crowded with brothers and sisters. They encounter a dangerous cat, but escape him through good thinking.

Ringgold, Faith. (1991). *Tar Beach.* New York: Crown. (1–4)

The tar beach is the rooftop of Cassie Louise Lightfoot's apartment building. She imagines that the stars lift her up and she flies over the city, solving family problems. This book weaves together fiction, autobiography, and African American history and literature.

Rylant, Cynthia. (1986). *Night in the Country.* Illustrated by Mary Szilagyi. New York: Bradbury. (K–2)

This book explores night feelings, sounds, and views in pictures.

Scieszka, Jon. (1989). *The True Story of the Three Little Pigs.* Illustrated by Lane Smith. New York: Viking. (all ages)

Mr. A. Wolf gives his version of what happened to the three little pigs. Of course, he was grossly misjudged in the original story.

Sendak, Maurice. (1963). *Where the Wild Things Are.* New York: Harper & Row. (K–2)

Max is sent to bed without his dinner because he was a "wild thing." He escapes in imagination to a place where he can be a wild thing and he is the wildest thing of all.

Shannon, George. (1993). *Climbing Kansas Mountains.* Illustrated by Thomas Allen. New York: Bradbury. (4–6)

The author's reflections bring the past to life as seen through a child's eyes.

Slote, A. (1978). *My Trip to Alpha I.* Illustrated by Harold Berson. Philadelphia: Lippincott. (4–6)

In this futuristic story Jack visits his aunt on another planet via body travel. While there he uncovers a sinister plot to defraud his aunt.

Snyder, Diane. (1988). *The Boy of the Three-Year Nap.* Illustrated by Allan Say. Boston: Houghton Mifflin. (2–4)

This traditional story tells how a lazy but cunning son becomes successful by marrying well and providing for his mother.

Spier, Peter. (1982). *Rain.* New York: Doubleday. (preschool–3)

This book explores the concept of rain from many perspectives. The artist portrays rainy day fun, rainy day moods, and the many visual effects of rain.

Steptoe, John. (1984). *The Story of Jumping Mouse.* New York: Lothrop, Lee & Shepard. (2–4)

This traditional Native American legend tells how Jumping Mouse became an eagle.

Turnbull, Ann. (1993). *Too Tired.* Illustrated by Emma Chichester Clark. San Diego: Gulliver/Harcourt Brace Jovanovich. (K–2)

In this delightful version of the Noah's ark story, everyone is on board except the sloths, who are too tired.

Turkle, Brinton. (1976). *Deep in the Forest.* New York: Dutton. (K–2)

This is a reversal of the traditional Goldilocks and the Three Bears; this time, Little Bear goes into Goldilocks' house.

Udry, Janice. (1966). *What Mary Jo Shared.* Illustrated by Evelyn Mill. Morton Grove, IL: Whitman. (K–2)

Mary Jo cannot think of anything for sharing time, but she eventually has a great idea. Everyone agrees that bringing her father was a good idea.

Van Allsburg, Chris. (1985). *The Polar Express.* Boston: Houghton Mifflin. (K–adult)

This Christmas story is about a train full of children who go to the North Pole where they meet Santa Claus. One boy receives a special present of a bell.

_____ . (1984). *The Mysteries of Harris Burdick*. Boston: Houghton Mifflin. (4–6)

This book consists of a series of pictures with captions which were left with an editor by Harris Burdick.

_____ . (1981). *Jumanji*. Boston: Houghton Mifflin. (2–4)

Two children find a game in the park. The instructions caution them that once begun the game must be completed, but they ignore this and play the game. Fortunately, their parents are out for the evening because they have all sorts of wildlife in the living room.

Wells, Rosemary. (1985). *Max's Breakfast*. New York: Dial. (P–3)

Max and his sister Ruby are rabbits. Their activities are so amusing because they are just like little children.

Williams, Vera. (1982). *A Chair for My Mother*. New York: Greenwillow. (preschool–1)

After losing their furniture in an apartment fire, a little girl, her grandmother, and her mother save money to buy a new chair.

Wood, Audrey and Don Wood. (1987). *Heckedy Peg*. New York: Harcourt Brace Jovanovich. (1–3)

This story of good versus evil is about a conflict between a loving mother and a bad witch.

Wood, Audrey. (1985). *King Bidgood's in the Bathtub*. New York: Harcourt Brace Jovanovich. (K–3)

The king will not leave his bathtub for any reason, but a young page solves the problem by pulling the plug.

_____ . (1984). *The Napping House*. Illustrated by Don Wood. New York: Harcourt Brace Jovanovich. (K–2)

This is a cumulative story about a nap on a rainy day in which a flea bites a mouse, who wakes all of the nappers.

Yolen, Jane. (1991). *Greyling*. Illustrated by David Ray. New York: Philomel. (3–5)

This is a story about the selkie (seal) of Scotland that is transformed into human form.

_____ . (1990). *Dinosaur Dances*. Illustrated by Bruce Degen. New York: Putnam. (all ages)

The poetry in this book is based on dance rhythms and Degen's illustrations capture the feeling of these rhythms.

_____ . (1987). *Owl Moon*. New York: Philomel. (1–3)

A little girl and her father search for an owl in the snowy woods.

Yorinks, Arthur. (1986). *Hey Al*. Illustrated by Richard Egielski. New York: Farrar, Straus & Giroux. (1–3)

Al and his dog escape their mundane life when they fly to a fantasy island. They soon discover that home is best.

Young, Ed. (1992). *Seven Blind Mice*. New York: Philomel. (preschool–3)

This is a new interpretation of the ancient story from India about the blind men and the elephant.

_____ . (1989). *Lon Po Po*. New York: Philomel. (1–3)

This is a Red Riding Hood Story from China. In this version mother goes off to visit the granny. The wolf knocks on the door of the children's home and they do him in.

Zelinsky, Paul. (1986). *Rumpelstiltskin*. New York: Dutton. (1–3)

This is the traditional Grimm Brothers' version of this well-known tale.

# $S_{ix}$

alliteration

assonance

concrete poetry

connotative meaning

epics

figurative language

free verse

haiku

imagery

metaphor

meter

narrative poem

nonsense poetry

onomatopoeia

personification

rhyme

rhythm

simile

## GUIDING QUESTIONS

Think about your early experiences with poetry—did you enjoy poetry as a child and if you did, what types of poems did you enjoy and why? Do you think your early experiences affected whether you like or dislike poetry now? What was the last poem you read? Keep your own experiences in mind as you read through this chapter. Remembering how you felt about poetry as a child will help you understand how your students feel about poetry. Keep these questions in mind as you read:

1. What are at least three ways of describing poetry?

2. What are some common misconceptions about poetry?

3. Who are some of the popular contemporary children's poets?

## OVERVIEW

The imaginative, artistic forms of poetry are rooted in ancient ballads and chants. Many people consider poetry to be the highest form of literature. It is literature in its most intense, imaginative, and rhythmic form (Morner and Rausch, 1991), expressing and interpreting the essence of experience through language (Perrine, 1969). The rich imagery of poetry permits a far greater concentration of meaning than is found in prose (Morner and Rausch, 1991).

Young children have a natural affinity for poetic language. They are intrigued with the sounds of language and enjoy the unusual combinations of words found in poetry, responding to its musical, rhythmic qualities. Poets use language in ways that not only re-create the rhythms of oral language children hear daily in conversation and play, but extend language to include novel and unusual applications. Childhood songs and nursery rhymes are natural springboards into poetry (Peck, 1979). These initial poetry experiences are followed a little later with jump rope rhymes and nonsense verse. As children mature, they especially enjoy chanting simple, rhythmic conversational poems as they go about daily activities. This kind of language play is a natural activity for young children, who relish inventing words and rolling them over their tongues.

Children's poetry has experienced a renaissance in recent years. Contemporary children's poets such as Jack Prelutsky, Paul Fleischman, Paul Janeczko, and Eloise Greenfield are very popular (Crisp, 1991). Books of poetry are the largest-growing market in children's literature (Gregory, 1988). "More than ever before, poetry for children has climbed to its proper station" (Hopkins, 1987, p. 4). Teachers, librarians, and parents have the opportunity to choose from a wide variety of poems and poetry books to nurture children's interests. Poetry can be categorized according to various

# Poetry

criteria: poetic form, content, theme, and audience appeal. Developing a broad acquaintance with poetry that appeals to children will help nurture children's appreciation for poetry, and experimenting with various ways of sharing poetry will help build children's responses to poetry.

## INTRODUCTION

Children's poetry holds an important place in literature for children. Contemporary poetry introduces children to the various poetic forms and addresses an infinite number of subjects—from insects to garbage. The opening vignette demonstrates the infusion of poetry into a classroom. The children's appeals to Ms. Andrews to read it again show their pleasure in poetry. They respond to the content and the illustrations, comparing the poem with the story they had read earlier. Their comments and discussion reveal their response to the poetry.

At no time does the teacher ask them to analyze the form or meter. Instead, she chooses poetry related to their lives and classroom experiences to engage their interest and stimulate their response.

## VIGNETTE

Gayle Andrews's first graders enjoyed listening to *Whose Mouse Are You?* by Robert Kraus, so she decided to surprise them with *Mice Are Nice*, a book of poems about mice compiled by Nancy Larrick.

When the children returned to their classroom after lunch, Ms. Andrews directed them to the story rug. "I'm going to read you a poem called 'Mice,' which Rose Fyleman wrote."

As she read, the room was so quiet the only sound was the rustling of wiggling children and an occasional cough. When she had finished, Mark asked, "Did you read that poem because we read *Whose Mouse Are You?* this morning?"

"What do you think?" she asked in return.

"Yes, yes," the children chimed in.

"Are the mice in the poem the same as the mouse in the story?" the teacher asked.

"No," Richard said.

"Why do you say that?" Ms. Andrews asked.

"The mice in the poem are like real mice; they ran around the house and got into all kinds of stuff," he answered.

"But the mice in the story did all kinds of things that mice can't really do," Shirley mentioned. "In the story, the mice were talking."

Sarah added, "In the poem, it was like someone was talking about the mice."

*(continued)*

"The pictures of the mice in the poem are different from those in the story," Andrea said.

"How are they different?" Ms. Andrews asked.

"The ones in the story were like newspaper drawings and they were gray, but the pictures in the poetry book were like mouse fur," Serena said.

"Please read some more poems about mice," Michael pleaded.

Later in the day, Ms. Andrews realized that almost every child in the class had drawn pictures of mice, so she decided to make a bulletin board of the drawings.

## THE NATURE OF POETRY

Poetry allows readers to perceive objects, experiences, or emotions in new and unique ways. Poets use rhythm, rhyme, sound, imagery, and figurative language to capture the very essence of life experience in words. Poets share their inner life through poetry. It is a more complex form of literature than can be easily defined or described. Poetry, however, must be distinguished from mere verse: "The best poetry is a union of beauty and truth. . . . The best poets speak to us with beauty that we can appreciate and in truths we can understand" (Russell, 1991, p. 77). Putting words to feelings makes them visible to the rest of the world so that many readers can recognize and identify with the feelings and images expressed. Recognizing these shared emotions helps us appreciate and express our own feelings.

Poetry is the simplest form of literature, according to Peck (1979). Its simplicity is deceptive, however: the language may be unpretentious and the number of words limited, but each word is carefully chosen to imply a range of ideas, images, and feelings. "You can't say anything much more briefly than a poem or folktale says it, nor catch a fact or feeling much more expressively" (Hearne, 1991, p. 107). Imagery enables poets to create dense meaning with a few words. They use words economically, choosing and polishing each one like a gem to create associations in readers' minds.

They do not have to *say* "I love you" because they arrange words and rhythms and pictures to express the *feeling* of love (Livingston, 1991). Poetry's economy of expression is comparable to the terseness of a conversation between longtime friends—it relies for meaning on the ring of familiarity, the voice inflections, and images.

In *Stories I Ain't Told Nobody Yet*, Jo Carson's poems are conversations like those most of us hear daily. Paul Janeczko relies on these same qualities in *The Music of What Happens*. Karla Kuskin demonstrates the poetry of conversation in "Where Have You Been Dear?" from her book *Dogs & Dragons Trees & Dreams* (see box).

### Emotional Intensity

Poetry, rooted in the world of emotions as well as in the mind, is emotionally intense. Poets capture universal feelings, writing about experiences that have affected them in such a way that the experiences

### Where Have You Been Dear?

Where
Have you been dear?
What
Have you seen dear?
What
Did you do there?
Who
Went with you there?
Tell me
What's new dear?
What's
New with you dear?
Where
Will you go next?
What
Will you do?
"I do this and I do that.
I go here and I go there.
At times I like to be alone.
There are some thoughts that are my own
I do not wish to share."

Kuskin, 1980

will affect readers as well. The experiences are often everyday happenings seen and commemorated with an emotional intensity that meets the emotional needs and interests of listeners and readers, evoking their response. For instance, Charlotte Zolotow expresses an emotional need for many children in *Say It!* In this book poem, a little girl and her mother celebrate the joy of walking on a beautiful autumn day.

> "Say it," shrieked the little girl. "Say it say it say it!"
>
> "I love you," said her mother. "I love you I love you I love you!" And she twirled around and around with the little girl in her arms until they were both dizzy.

## Expressing Feelings

The emotional intensity of poetry makes it a natural form for expressing feelings. *Honey, I Love, and Other Love Poems* by Eloise Greenfield shares an African American child's love for members of her family and her enthusiasm for life. Leo and Diane Dillon's illustrations enhance these poems by helping us visualize these emotions in her face. Judith Viorst also explores feelings in *If I Were in Charge of the World and Other Worries: Poems for Children and Their Parents*, which focuses on situations and people that worry and frustrate children in their everyday lives. Lee Bennett Hopkins collected poems about growing up from a variety of sources for *Through Our Eyes: Poems and Pictures About Growing Up*. Shel Silverstein addresses the fears and joys of childhood in his enormously popular book *Where the Sidewalk Ends: The Poems and Drawings of Shel Silverstein*. His humor and the zany illustrations help us examine our feelings with a light heart. "Sick," a popular poem in this collection, tells about a character who is gravely ill—until she realizes that it is Saturday. Sleep and nighttime are popular topics in a number of books, explored by Lee Bennett Hopkins in *Still as a Star* and by Michael Hague in *Sleep, Baby, Sleep: Lullabies and Night Poems* which include both lullabies and night poems.

Jean Little gives voice to the sensibilities of children in her exuberant book, *Hey World, Here I Am!* The title poem is the voice of Kate, introduced in Little's earlier works, telling readers her feelings

A Book of Nighttime Poems

STILL ★ AS ★ A ★ STAR

*selected by Lee Bennett Hopkins*
*illustrated by Karen Milone*

*This collection of poems and lullabies perfectly captures the dreamy nighttime mood when a child leans out of her window to gaze at the moon, and a boy dreams of giants up in the mountains.*

about growing up in her world—she is an individual who is thrilled with life. Cynthia Rylant also explores growing up in her book *Waiting to Waltz*. She tells of the crises of a girl growing up in a small mountain town, who loses a spelling bee and is punished for swearing. Rylant shares her personal experiences, her joys, and her sorrows in this book, which is related to her autobiography *But I'll Be Back Again!* Readers who share her experiences in these books will respond to them in a variety of ways.

## ELEMENTS OF POETRY

Poets use words in melodious combinations to create its singing, lyric qualities. The sound patterns, figurative language, and emotional intensity contribute to poetry's uniqueness among the literary genre. Poets use sound patterns and **figurative**

## Poem to Mud

Poem to mud—
Poem to ooze
Patted in pies, or coating your shoes.

Poem to slooze...
Poem to crud—
Fed by a leak, or spread by a flood.

Wherever, whenever, wherever it goes,
Stirred by your finger, or strained by your toes,

There's nothing sloppier, slipperier, floppier,
There's nothing slickier, stickier, thickier,

There's nothing quickier to make grown-ups sickier,
Trulier coolier
Than wonderful mud.

Snyder, 1969

**language** *to connote sensory images appealing to sight, sound, touch, and smell.* These types of images build on children's experiences and relate to their lives, as shown in "Poem to Mud" by Zilpha Keatley Snyder (see box), which addresses a subject with which children are well acquainted in language that is natural to them. All of this enables them to appreciate poetry.

### Poetic Language

Poetic language is compact—each word infers and suggests more than it says. Poetic language builds rich metaphors that stimulate readers by summoning hundreds of associations. Readers' individual connotative understandings are based on their emotional responses to words or concepts. In writing, poets concentrate greater meaning in individual words, relying heavily on imagery to convey meaning and on readers to associate sensations with those images. For instance, readers who grew up in the Blue Ridge Mountains will have many and more varied responses to poetry about mountains than those who have never seen mountains.

One way of stimulating these associations in readers involves the use of sensory language, language that will arouse the senses of the readers and remind them of concrete experiences. Poets are always searching for fresh imagery to arouse the senses, a sample of which are shown below.

| Sense | Imagery |
|---|---|
| vision | fire-engine red, gigantic, elongated |
| touch | soft, hard, rough |
| sound | crunch, rumble, squeak |
| smell | rotting leaves, wet dog, bread baking |
| movement | hop, skip, trudge |
| taste | sweet, salty, bitter |

### Sound Patterns

Children learn the sound patterns of language before they learn words; in fact, it appears that sound patterns are instrumental in children's acquisition of language. The sounds of poetry attract young children, who realize early on that words have sounds as well as meanings. "They love to rhyme words, to read alliterative tongue twisters, to laugh at funny-sounding names" (Fleischman, 1986, p. 553). Sound patterns are a delight to the ear of everyone, young and old. Rhyme, alliteration, onomatopoeia, and assonance are several devices commonly used by poets to achieve these sound patterns, and are often combined to give sound effects to a poem.

The delightful sound patterns of nursery rhymes, combined with their brevity and simplicity, invite children to roll them over their tongues. "Hickory Dickory Dock" is a good example. Repeat it aloud to yourself or read it to a young child. Think about your own or the child's response to its patterns of sound. How many devices can you identify in this verse?

> Hickory, dickory, dock,
> The mouse ran up the clock.
> The clock struck one,
> and down he run.
> Hickory, dickory, dock.

*Rhyme.* Rhyme is one of the most recognizable elements in poetry, although poetry does not have to rhyme. **Rhyme** is based on *the similarity of sound between two words* such as *sold/mold* or *chrome/foam.* "When the sounds of their accented syllables and all succeeding sounds are identical, words rhyme" (Morner and Rausch, 1991). A good rhyme, a repetition of sounds, pleases readers. It gives order to thoughts and pleasure to the ears (Livingston, 1991). Rhyme gives poetry an appealing musical quality.

The most common form of rhyme in poetry is *end rhyme*, so named because it comes at the end of the line of poetry (Morner and Rausch, 1991). End rhyme is illustrated in Rhoda Bacmeister's poem "Galoshes" (see box), which appears in May Hill Arbuthnot's collection *Time for Poetry*. *Internal rhyme* occurs within a line of poetry and is illustrated in the poem "Hughbert and the Glue" in Karla Kuskin's *Time for Poetry*. Rhyming patterns in poetry are grouped in stanzas. A common end rhyming pattern is to rhyme the last word in every other line. The stanzas thus formed have special names depending on the number of lines in the rhyming pattern:

- two lines: couplet
- three lines: tercet
- four lines: quatrain
- five lines: quintet
- six lines: sextet
- seven lines: septet
- eight lines: octave

---

### Galoshes

Susie's galoshes
Make splishes and sploshes
And slooshes and sloshes,

As Susie steps slowly
Along in the slush.

They stamp and they tramp
On the ice and concrete,
They get stuck in the muck and the mud;

But Susie likes much best to hear
The slippery slush

As it slooshes and sloshes
And splishes and sploshes,
All round her galoshes!

Bacmeister, 1940

---

*Alliteration.* **Alliteration** is achieved through *repetition of consonant sounds at the beginning of words or within words*. It is one of the most ancient devices used in English poetry to give unity, emphasis, and musical effect. This technique is also shown in the poem "Galoshes."

*Onomatopoeia.* Onomatopoeia gives poetry a sensuous feeling. **Onomatopoeia** refers to *words that sound like what they mean*. For example, the word *bang* sounds very much like the loud noise to which it refers. The words *splishes, sploshes, slooshes*, and *sloshes* in the poem "Galoshes" create the sounds of walking in slush.

*Assonance.* **Assonance** is *the close repetition of middle vowel sounds between different consonant sounds* such as the long /a/ sound in *fade* and *pale*. Assonance creates near rhymes rather than true rhymes commonly found in improvised folk ballads (Morner and Rausch, 1991). Assonance gives unity and rhythmic effect to a line of poetry.

## Rhythm

**Rhythm** is *the patterned flow of sound in poetry* created through combinations of words that convey a beat. Rhythm can set the sense of a story to a beat, but it can also emphasize what a writer is saying or even convey sense on its own, as in a speaker's gestures (Fleischman, 1986). In traditional English poetry, rhythm is based on **meter,** *the combination of accent and numbers of syllables* (Morner and Rausch, 1991). Patterns of accented and unaccented syllables and of long and short vowels work together to create meter and rhythm (Lukens, 1986). Karla Kuskin demonstrates this meter in her poem "Thistles," which appears in *Dogs & Dragons Trees & Dreams*.

Rhythm is natural to children. In the first months of life they wave their arms and legs to the rhythm of nursery rhymes. By 18 months, they enjoy marching in circles to "ring around the rosie, all fall down." In school, primary-grade children use rulers and pencils to tap out the rhythm of David McCord's "Song of the Train" which appears in *Far and Few*. McCord shows his mastery of the rhythms of children's playground activities in "Bananas and Cream" (see box on page 148). As you read this poem, think about the recurring stress and the repeated words that create a rhythmic pattern.

## Word Play

*Word play* is an inviting characteristic of children's poetry. The patterns of sound in poetry create the playful language patterns that are a source of pleasure for children. They enjoy rolling interesting words over their tongues and repeating them to savor their flavor. Laura Richards' poem "Eletelephony," which appears in Jack Prelutsky's *Random House Book of Poetry for Children*, exemplifies poetic word play (see the box on page 149).

## Figures of Speech

Writers use *figures of speech*, also called *figurative language*, to express feelings and create mental pictures (images). Figures of speech offer writers many possibilities for expressing themselves. One of the major challenges in creating poetry is to choose figures of speech that offer fresh images and that uniquely express the writer. In fact, a poet's facility in using figures of speech is what makes the major difference between pleasant verse and fine poetry (Livingston, 1991). The best known figures of speech are *simile*, *metaphor*, and *personification*.

*Simile.* A **simile** is a *figure of speech using* like *or* as *to compare one thing to another.* Most of you will recognize that "white as snow" is a simile, but this one is so timeworn that it has become a cliché. Poets must be acute observers, seeing and hearing in new ways in order to offer fresh figures of speech. Look for similes used by Valerie Worth in "Frog," a poem from her book *Small Poems* (see the box on page 149). Think about the observations that enabled the poet to create these comparisons.

*Metaphor.* **Metaphor,** like simile, is a *figure of speech comparing two items*, but instead of saying something is *like* something else, metaphor says that something is something else. Langston Hughes uses

### Bananas and Cream

Bananas and cream,
Bananas and cream:
All we could say was
Bananas and cream.

We couldn't say fruit,
We wouldn't say cow,
We didn't say sugar—
We don't say it now.

Bananas and cream,
Bananas and cream,
All we could shout was
*Bananas and cream.*

We didn't say why,
We didn't say how;
We forgot it was fruit,
We forgot the old cow;
We *never* said sugar,
We only said WOW!

Bananas and cream,
Bananas and cream,
All that we want is
*Bananas and cream!*

We didn't say dish,
We didn't say spoon;
We said not tomorrow,
*But NOW and HOW SOON*

Bananas and cream,
Bananas and cream,
We yelled for bananas,
*Bananas and cream!*

McCord, 1952

metaphor to arouse the reader's feelings and imagination in his poem "Dreams," calling life a "broken-winged bird" and a "barren field/Frozen with snow" (see box). These metaphors construct images that clarify the concept of dreams. The reader recognizes, of course, that life is not actually a bird or field (Livingston, 1991), but these comparisons communicate images and feelings that are vivid and unique.

### Eletelephony

Once there was an elephant,
Who tried to use the telephant—
No! no! I mean an elephone
Who tried to use the telephone—
(Dear me! I am not certain quite
That even now I've got it right.)

Howe'er it was, he got his trunk
Entangled in the telephunk;
The more he tried to get it free,
The louder buzzed the telephee—
(I fear I'd better drop the song
of elephop and telephong!)

Richards, 1983

### Dreams

Hold fast to dreams
For if dreams die
Life is a broken-winged bird
That cannot fly.

Hold fast to dreams
For if dreams go
Life is a barren field
Frozen with snow.

Hughes, 1932

*Personification.* **Personification** *attributes human characteristics to something that does not actually have these qualities.* Poets have a talent for endowing inanimate objects with life, as Myra Cohn Livingston does in the poems in her book *A Circle of Seasons.*

> Spring brings out her baseball bat, swings it through the air,
> Pitches bulbs and apple blossoms, throws them where it's bare,
> Catches dogtooth violets, slides to meadowsweet,
> Bunts a breeze and tags the trees with green buds everywhere.

In this instance, the poet endows spring with the attributes of a baseball player, using the words *swings, pitches, throws, catches, slides, bunts,* and *tags* to give human characteristics to a season of the year.

## TYPES OF POETRY

Free verse has become the popular form for contemporary children's poetry, while older poetry follows traditional forms. Authorities divide poetry into the categories of narrative, lyric, and

dramatic, although these elements are often combined in a single poem (Bagert, 1992). Poets choose and combine poetic forms to create a form that best tells their ideas and feelings. This means that attempts to categorize poems by type are usually impossible. In this section we examine poetic form and introduce examples to clarify understanding.

### Narrative Poems

*Narrative poems* tell stories. The story elements—plot, character, setting, and theme—make narrative poems especially appealing, because everyone enjoys a good story. Narrative poems that tell about the adventures of characters who are children or childlike are compelling reading for children. A. A. Milne, who created Winnie the Pooh, also created the narrative poems found in *Now We Are Six* and *When We Were Very Young.* These poems tell stories about children and their experiences.

Narrative poems may be short or long. *Book-length narrative poems are called* **epics.** Byrd Baylor and her illustrator Peter Parnall share their love of nature with readers in their illustrated epics *The Other Way to Listen; Hawk, I'm Your Brother;* and *The Way to Start a Day,* all of which have a desert setting and a Native American ambiance.

Aileen Fisher, the nature poet, immerses herself in the natural world and shares her feelings in narrative poems that tell stories about her observations of animals, insects, and birds. Through her writing, children who may not have thought about the happenings in their natural world prior to reading her poetry become sensitized to the natural world. Her epics *Listen Rabbit, Going Barefoot, Anybody Home,* and *Sing, Little Mouse* encourage all of us to experience nature in extraordinary ways.

Sorche Nic Leodhas's fanciful narrative poem *Always Room for One More* is quite different from Fisher and Baylor's nature poetry. In rhyming language, the poet tells a story about Lachie MacLachlan and his wife and ten children, who live in a tiny house happily until Lachie invites so many guests that the family is crowded out of their own home. Humorous narrative poems like this one are great favorites with children.

## Dramatic Poetry

Dramatic poetry often appears in the form of a monologue in which a single character tells about a dramatic situation (Morner and Rausch, 1991). The poet sometimes pretends to be something or someone else in a dramatic poem (Livingston, 1991). Poets have pretended to be the wind, bugs, and seashells among other things. Many examples of dramatic form are found in traditional ballads, as well as in the work of Carl Sandburg, T. S. Eliot, and Robert Frost. Dramatic poetry often appears in anthologies of children's poetry.

Some dramatic poems are heard as a dialogue between two characters. An example of dialogue is seen in the dramatic poem in *Stories I Ain't Told Nobody Yet,* by Jo Carson. Others, like "A Bug Sat in a Silver Flower" by Kuskin are narrative as well as dramatic (see box above).

## Lyric Poetry

Lyric poems are short, personal poems expressing the poet's emotions and feelings. They speak of personal experience and comment on how the writer sees the world. Originally such poems were written to be sung to the music of a lyre, so it is not surprising that lyric poetry has a feeling of melody and song (Livingston, 1991). Lyric poetry is the most common form for children's poetry. It can be identified through the use of the personal pronouns *I, me, my, we, our,* and *us* or related words (Livingston, 1991). The distinguishing characteristics of these poems are emotion, subjectivity, melodiousness, imagination, and description (Morner and Rausch, 1991).

## Haiku

Authentic **haiku,** *a poetic form that originated in Japan, describes nature and the seasons.* Haiku are patterned poems based on syllables, words, and lines. The first line contains five syllables, the second contains seven, and the third contains five, for a total of 17 syllables in three lines. The following haiku, "Fly with the Wind, Flow with the Water," was written by Ann Atwood, who illustrates her poetry with photography in her book by the same title as the haiku.

> Looking straight ahead
> going some definite Where—
> the geese goose-stepping.

Several exemplary books of haiku appear in the Children's Literature section at the end of this chapter, including three by Ann Atwood, *Haiku: The Mood of the Earth, Haiku—Vision in Poetry and*

---

### A Bug Sat in a Silver Flower

A bug sat in a silver flower
Thinking silver thoughts.
A bigger bug out for a walk
Climbed up that silver flower stalk
And snapped the small bug down his jaws
Without a pause
Without a care
For all the bug's small silver thoughts.
It isn't right
It isn't fair
That big bug ate that little bug
Because that little bug was there.
He also ate his underwear.

Kuskin, 1980

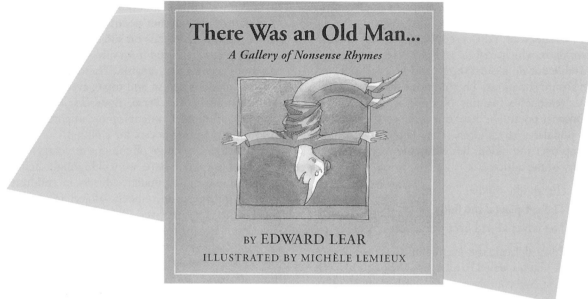

# There Was an Old Man...
## A Gallery of Nonsense Rhymes

BY EDWARD LEAR

ILLUSTRATED BY MICHÈLE LEMIEUX

Edward Lear's wit has amused readers for
more than 150 years.

*Photography*, and *My Own Rhythm: An Approach to Haiku;* Harry Behn's *More Cricket Songs;* and Richard Lewis's *In a Spring Garden*, which contains authentic haiku.

## Free Verse

**Free verse** differs from traditional forms of poetry in that it is *"free" of a regular beat or meter* (Morner and Rausch, 1991). Free verse usually does not rhyme, usually does not follow a predetermined pattern, and often contains fragmentary syntax. Free verse incorporates many of the same poetic devices that writers of structured poetry employ, but writers of free verse are more concerned with natural speech rhythms, imagery, and meaning than with rhyme and meter. "Treehouse," by Ted Kooser, appears in *Pocket Poems* by Paul Janeczko.

> Whose kite was this?
> It must have caught here
> summers ago. Winters
> have tugged it apart.
> Here is its tail,
> this piece of knotted rope
> is still blowing.

## Concrete Poetry

The form of concrete poetry is inseparable from the content. **Concrete poetry** *merges visual, verbal, and auditory elements, arranging the words and letters to suggest something about the subject of the poem.* For example, a poem about a rock might be written in the shape of a rock, or a poem about a cloud is written in a cloud shape. Or several carefully selected words may be suspended on a mobile so that as the air moves the mobile, the words move and a poem evolves, but each individual sees a different poem. As with all poetry, each reader brings his or her own ideas, feelings, and experiences to the poem.

## Nonsense Poetry

**Nonsense poetry** *ordinarily is composed in lyric or narrative form, but it does not conform to the expected order of things. It defies reason. It is playful poetry in which meaning is subordinate to sound* (Morner and Rausch, 1991). "Nonsense is a literary genre whose purpose is to rebel against not only reason but the physical laws of nature. It rejects established tenets and institutions, pokes fun at rational behavior, and touts destruction. It champions aberrations" (Livingston, 1981, p. 123).

Writers of nonsense poetry create unusual worlds in which objects and characters are recognizable but do absurd things and become involved in absurd situations. They do not behave in a sensible, reasonable manner. Nothing is impossible in nonsense poetry; perhaps this is the very reason it is so popular with children. They know cows cannot jump over the moon, but enjoy the very implausibility of the antics:

> Hey diddle diddle,
> The cat played the fiddle,
> The cow jumped over the moon.

Edward Lear, the master of nonsense, wrote poems that appealed to all ages. Although his *The Complete Nonsense Book* was published in 1958, it remains popular today. Lewis Carroll, another skilled writer of nonsense, wrote the delightful poems, "The Walrus and the Carpenter" and "Jabberwocky," which appear in *Through the Looking Glass*. The popular contemporary poets Shel Silverstein and Jack Prelutsky also have created outstanding nonsense verse.

Nonsense writers use a variety of strategies in their craft. They invent words, as Laura Richards does in "Eletelephony." Lear frequently uses alliteration, a common technique, in his "Pelican Chorus." Personification lends itself well to nonsense verse, as animals, objects, even furniture take on human characteristics. Exaggeration is a useful device to writers of nonsense, as Shel Silverstein shows in "Sarah Cynthia Sylvia Stout Would Not Take the Garbage Out," one of many nonsense poems in his book *Where the Sidewalk Ends*.

## CONTENT OF POETRY

Poems are written on every subject in the world—subject matter is unlimited. Poetry embodies life and reveals its complexity; it is a part of the fabric of life. Poets look at ordinary things and events more closely than the rest of us and see things that we overlook. Mary Ann Coleman demonstrates this ability to see and present ordinary things in a new light in *The Dreams of Hummingbirds: Poems From Nature*, which communicates the sheer beauty of nature through her poems and illustrations.

A plethora of poems on subjects ranging from garbage to fairy tales and from side-splittingly funny to serious are readily available. There are poems to fit every mood, interest, and topic, available in any form: narrative, free verse, limericks, ballads, or whatever is desired. Content is more important than form when selecting poetry for children.

Although the range of content in poetry is far too broad to catalog here, we will highlight humor as one of the most popular subjects in children's poetry. Garbage is an unlikely subject for poetry, but Dennis Lee received the Canadian Library Association Award for the best book of the year in 1978 for *Garbage Delight*. The delightful poetry in this book derives its appeal from humor, exaggeration, nonsense, and strong rhythm, all aspects of poetry that children particularly enjoy. Jack Prelutsky is a poet well known for his zany poems. He uses splendid words such as *disputatious* and *alacrity*, and his poems have unexpected twists that delight his readers. Perhaps most importantly, all children (including boys, who are sometimes hard to interest in poetry) love his poems. His book *Something Big Has Been Here* has many ridiculous images to delight readers. In "The Turkey Shot Out of the Oven," a turkey is shot out of an oven because it is stuffed with unpopped popcorn. Then there is the character in "Denson Dumm" who planted lightbulbs in his hair so that he would be forever bright. Like all of Prelutsky's books, however, this one offers a diverse range of topics, including serious poems such as "Don't Yell at Me."

Again, space constrains us from cataloging the variety of ways of treating subjects in poetry, but we will briefly discuss three poems on a topic elementary children love: dinosaurs (see box). Each poet chose different stylistic devices to portray dinosaurs: the first two poems could be identified as realistic fiction or even informational compositions, because they communicate the essence of actual dinosaurs, while the third poem is delightful fantasy.

The first poem, "When Dinosaurs Ruled the Earth" by Patricia Hubbell, uses repeated words to create rhythm and to tie the verses together. The phrases "rolled his evil eye, bared his long

## Brachiosaurus

Brachiosaurus had little to do
but stand with its head in the treetops and chew,
it nibbled the leaves that were tender and green,
it was a perpetual eating machine.

Brachiosaurus was truly immense,
its vacuous mind was uncluttered by sense,
it hadn't the need to be clever and wise,
no beast dared to bother a being its size.

Brachiosaurus was clumsy and slow,
but then, there was nowhere it needed to go,
if Brachiosaurus were living today,
no doubt it would frequently be in the way.

Prelutsky, 1988

## Dinosaur Dances

When the lights went low
Over prehistoric plains,
And the music beat
In rhythm with the rains,
All the mud and ooze
Showed the scientist remains
Of a prehistoric party.

Here's Tyrannosaurus
Dancing on his toes.
Here is Stegosaurus
In a ballet pose.
And with airy Pterodactyls
Anything goes
At a prehistoric party.

Brontosaurus sits
And waits this number out.
But here's Allosaurus
Doing "Twist and Shout"
And seven little coelurosaurs
Hopping all about
At the prehistoric party

"Goodness gracious,
It's Cretaceous
Party time again!"

Yolen, 1990

and yellow teeth, teeth were made for tearing flesh, his teeth were made to gnash" and "dabblers in the slime" create visual and auditory images. The poet dramatizes the dinosaurs' sizes by comparing the beasts with buildings and trees. In contrast, the phrases, "he roamed and slew his friends, eaters of their friends and foe" and "their pygmy brains were slow to grasp" create images of dinosaurs that go beyond the visual and auditory.

In "Brachiosaurus," Jack Prelutsky describes the dinosaur as a "perpetual eating machine, truly immense" and " clumsy and slow." These phrases give us visual images. However, Prelutsky also says "its vacuous mind uncluttered by sense, it hadn't the need to be clever and wise," and he points out that today it would "frequently be in the way." These phrases reiterate the idea of "pygmy brain" found in the first poem. But Prelutsky uses fewer words and rhymes every other line in his poem, distinguishing it from Hubbell's "When Dinosaurs Ruled the Earth." The third poem, "Dinosaur Dances," is bound to be a hit with children. In this poem, Jane Yolen writes about make-believe dinosaurs in costumes, dancing everything from ballet to a hula. She creates a rhythmic beat with words and rhymes in the title poem, telling readers that "anything goes" at a prehistoric party with "lights low, couples doing Twist and Shout" and

"hopping all about." Bruce Degen's illustrations create unusual images—clumsy dinosaurs dancing a refined minuet. Each of the poems in this book has a different dance beat that makes it unique and delightful. The beat of these poems makes toes tap and leads to movement.

## CHILDREN'S RESPONSE TO POETRY

Poetry speaks to the emotions and the intellect. It is pleasurable and comfortable, amusing and relaxing. Poetry can be an important part of children's literary life, clarifying and illuminating experience and enriching daily life. The rhythms of poetic language

*The poet and artist create images of dinosaurs dancing to the beat of a hard rock band.*

stick in memory and children repeat the words over and over, savoring the feel of them on their tongues. Poetry lifts their spirits and stimulates their imaginations, stirring them to communicate in interesting ways (Peck, 1979). Poetry can be enjoyed at any grade, any age. It addresses the interests and abilities of anyone, anywhere, whether gifted or reluctant readers. Poetry appreciation is personalized—even more so than response to other literary forms. A single poem may arouse different responses in each reader, based on the highly individual images called up by the carefully selected imagery packed into the poem.

Children should be given many opportunities to respond to poetry that covers a wide variety of content and language patterns. Positive attitudes toward poetry are built when interesting poetry is presented in meaningful ways. Poetry appreciation begins with the premise that it merits a prominent

place in children's lives. Unfortunately, many teachers and other adults believe poetry to be dreary and uninteresting because formal structured experiences they had with it involved memorizing, dissecting, and analyzing such works as *Romeo and Juliet* (Bugeja, 1992). When adults have such expectations, many children learn the same expectations— poetry is obscure, meaningless, and irrelevant. And then, unfortunately, their expectations become a self-fulfilling prophecy. Giving children many and varied experiences with poetry that relates to their own lives helps overcome this attitude. "Poetry must flow freely in our children's lives; it should come to them as naturally as breathing, for nothing—nothing—can ring and rage through hearts and minds as does poetry" (Hopkins, 1987, p. 4).

Extensive technical knowledge about poetry is not necessary to engage children's interest. Although

*This collection of hilarious poems
about food invites children's responses.*

sometimes helpful, expertise in poetic form is not as important as many experiences with interesting poetry, since response to poetry is largely a matter of experience. Presenting a variety of poems gives children opportunities to identify individual favorites and, over a period of time, teachers, librarians, and parents can acquire a discriminating sense for the poetry children enjoy. Eve Merriam tells us how to enjoy poetry in "How to Eat a Poem," which appears in *It Doesn't Always Have to Rhyme.*

## SELECTING AND EVALUATING POETRY

Children should be immersed in poetry, but many teachers are insecure about their own poetry know-how and are therefore reluctant to use it, much less make their own selections of poems to use in their classrooms. Fortunately, poets and poetry authorities have come to their rescue, writing books that expand teachers' knowledge of poetry and ways of integrat-

ing it into their classrooms. Many of these volumes offer exemplary poetry and suggestions for classroom activities: *Let's Do a Poem!* (1991) by Nancy Larrick and *Pass the Poetry, Please* (1988) by Lee Bennett Hopkins are only two. Other writers focus on writing poetry: how they got started, sources of ideas, and the processes they use to create fresh ideas. *The Place My Words Are Looking For* (1990) by Paul Janeczko and *Near the Window Tree* (1975) by Karla Kuskin are two good examples. Myra Cohn Livingston gives poetry a more formal treatment in *Poem Making: Ways To Begin Writing Poetry* (1991). Books such as these will help you develop more confidence in selecting poetry for children.

One of the very best ways to cultivate confidence is through reading many poems and deciding which poems and poets *you* like the best. Once you have discovered a poem or a poet who speaks to you, look for more by the same poet. Through this process your own taste will evolve, and it is always easier to interest children in something that you really enjoy. Develop your own wide collection of

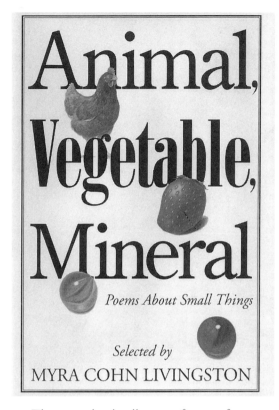

*This specialized collection of poems focuses on small, hardly noticed things.*

poems, including anthologies, specialized collections, and book-length poems, both for your own use and to stimulate the interest of the children. Ready access to a wide selection will give the children opportunities to develop their own taste. Children who have access to poetry books explore and discover their personal preferences gradually, over a period of time (Sebesta, 1983). Identify appealing kinds of poetry and offer a variety of poems in read-aloud sessions. A particular poem or book, however, may not be for everyone. It is for that person who relates to the feelings and ideas expressed. In the introduction to *A Tune Beyond Us* (1968), Myra Cohn Livingston cautions readers: "Every poem in this collection will not speak for you./But perhaps one, or two, will./And that will be enough (p. iv)."

The brevity of poems is a stimulus to reading. Readers find them less demanding than other forms of literature. Despite their brevity, however, poetry should be read at a leisurely pace to allow readers to savor the words and ideas (Hearne, 1990). Children relish poetry in classrooms and other settings where it is cultivated as a natural happening, a part of daily life. Spontaneous experiences with poetry cultivate opportunities to read and listen. Since poets carefully choose each word for its sound and meaning, poems should be read as complete entities rather than fragmenting and analyzing them word by separate word (Dias, 1987).

## Locating Poetry

Poetry appears in several different types of books: anthologies, specialized collections, and book-length poems. *Poetry anthologies* are collections of poetry that include many types of poems on many different subjects. One of the most comprehensive is *The Random House Book of Poetry for Children*, edited by Jack Prelutsky and illustrated by Arnold Lobel, which includes 572 poems arranged in broad categories. *Specialized collections* are books of poems that focus on a specific theme or topic. All of the poems in Jane Yolen's *Dinosaur Dances*, illustrated by Bruce Degen, relate to dinosaurs—more specifically, dancing dinosaurs. A lengthy single poem may be published as an entire book, usually a picture book, as is Byrd Baylor's *The Other Way To Listen*, illustrated by Peter Parnall.

Evaluating poetry anthologies can be especially difficult because the poems represent such a broad range of subject matter and style, but the range of topics can be identified by reviewing the table of contents and examining the literary quality of a few poems in different sections. An anthology that is able to provide appropriate poetry at a moment's notice for everyday reading needs—holidays, weather, daily incidents—can be considered a good anthology. Of course, one or two good anthologies cannot be solely relied on to fulfill all the poetry needs of children, and the use of poetry should be planned as well as incidental. Table 6.1 presents several examples each of good anthologies, specialized collections, and book-length poems.

## TABLE 6.1

Examples of books of poetry.

| AUTHOR | TITLE | GRADE LEVEL |
|---|---|---|
| **Anthologies** | | |
| Beatrice de Regniers | *Sing a Song of Popcorn* | K–8 |
| Tomie dePaola | *Tomie dePaola's Book of Poems* | 1–6 |
| Jack Prelutsky | *The Random House Book of Poetry for Children* | 1–8 |
| Ann McGovern | *Arrow Book of Poetry* | 3–7 |
| Nancy Larrick | *Piping Down the Valleys Wild* | 3–7 |
| **Specialized Collections** | | |
| Zena Sutherland | *The Orchard Book of Nursery Rhymes* | Preschool–1 |
| Valerie Worth | *All the Small Poems* | K–2 |
| Mary Ann Hoberman | *Yellow Butter Purple Jelly Red Jam Black Bread* | K–3 |
| Nancy Larrick | *Mice Are Nice* | K–3 |
| Edward Lear | *Of Pelicans and Pussycats: Poems and Limericks* | K–4 |
| Jack Prelutsky | *Something Big Has Been Here* | K–4 |
| Aileen Fisher | *When It Comes to Bugs* | K–6 |
| Karama Fufula | *My Daddy Is a Cool Dude* | 1–5 |
| Robert Froman | *Seeing Things: A Book of Poems* | 1–6 |
| Nancy Larrick | *On City Streets* | 1–6 |
| David McCord | *One at a Time* | 1–6 |
| Jack Prelutsky | *Rolling Harvey Down the Hill* | 1–6 |
| Paul Fleischman | *Joyful Noise: Poems for Two Voices* | 2–6 |
| Arnold Adoff | *Sports Pages* | 4–7 |
| Cynthia Rylant | *Waiting to Waltz: A Childhood* | 4–8 |
| **Single-Book Poems** | | |
| Nadine Bernard Westcott | *Peanut Butter and Jelly: A Play Rhyme* | K–2 |
| Myra Cohn Livingston | *Up in the Air* | K–4 |
| Robert Frost | *Stopping by Woods on a Snowy Evening* | 1–6 |
| Arnold Adoff | *All the Colors of the Race* | 3–8 |
| Byrd Baylor | *The Desert Is Theirs* | 3–8 |
| Byrd Baylor | *The Other Way to Listen* | 3–8 |
| George Ella Lyon | *Together* | K–6 |

## Considering Preferences

Children's appreciation of poetry is motivated by careful choice of poems on the part of the teacher, librarian, or parent. This entails considering children's poetry preferences, which in turn emerge from their experiences and interests. Of course, asking children what they like has obvious value. Research also offers information about children's poetry preferences. Children seem to appreciate poems that are generously spaced and tastefully illustrated, suggesting that visual appeal is a factor to consider (Sebesta, 1983). Fisher and Natarella (1982) report that primary-grade children's poetry preferences include narrative poems and limericks, poems about strange and fantastic events, traditional poems, and those that use alliteration, onomatopoeia, or rhyming. Intermediate grade students like poems related to their experiences and interests, humorous poems, and those with rhythm and rhyme (Bridge, 1966). They respond better to contemporary poems than to traditional ones and also prefer poems that address familiar and enjoyable experiences, funny poems, and those telling a story (Terry, 1974). Narrative poems and limericks are the most popular form with fourth, fifth, and sixth graders, while haiku and free verse are among the least popular (Terry, 1974).

Later studies of children's poetry preferences are consistent with the earlier studies (Ingham, 1980; Simmons, 1980), although their conclusions are limited to the geographic area used in the study. Both report that children prefer humorous poetry and poetry that addresses familiar experiences. Poems by Shel Silverstein and Dennis Lee are preferred to traditional poetry (Ingham, 1980). The weight of research therefore indicates that humorous poetry—that of Shel Silverstein, Jack Prelutsky, and Dennis Lee, for instance—should be included in a poetry collection because it attracts children to poetry, and that collections should be up-to-date because children find contemporary poetry more appealing than traditional poetry. This is not to suggest that only research-validated poetry be used, but the research does provide an obvious beginning point for building children's appreciation of and pleasure in poetry. In the final analysis, good poetry speaks to children. It communicates, inspires, informs, and tells of things that are, were, may be, and will never be (Peck, 1979).

## Finding Winners

The top ten books of poetry of the 1980s, as identified by Crisp (1991) from teachers' reports, were:

1. *Joyful Noise: Poems for Two Voices* by Paul Fleischman
2. *Under the Sunday Tree* by Eloise Greenfield
3. *Brickyard Summer: Poems* by Paul Janeczko
4. *Did Adam Name the Vinegarroon?* by X. J. Kennedy
5. *Knock at a Star: A Child's Introduction to Poetry* by X. J. and Dorothy M. Kennedy, editors
6. *American Sports Poems* by R. R. Knudson and May Swenson, compilers
7. *Poems for Jewish Holidays* by Myra Cohn Livingston, editor
8. *Fresh Paint: New Poems* by Eve Merriam
9. *Tyrannosaurus Was a Beast: Dinosaur Poems* by Jack Prelutsky
10. *A Visit to William Blake's Inn: Poems for Innocent and Experienced Travelers* by Nancy Willard

*Dinosaurs are long gone, but fourteen of them live again in this book of lilting verses and captivating pictures.*

Honorable mentions on her list included:

- *Tomie dePaola's Book of Poems* by Tomie dePaola, compiler and illustrator
- *The Music of What Happens: Poems That Tell Stories* by Paul Janeczko, compiler
- *Dogs and Dragons Trees and Dreams: A Collection of Poems* by Karla Kuskin
- *Overheard in a Bubble Chamber and Other Science Poems* by Lillian Morrison
- *Waiting to Waltz: A Childhood* by Cynthia Rylant
- *Small Poems Again* by Valerie Worth

Books of poetry such as these can serve as a beginning for exploring poetry, but remember that students should be given many experiences with all kinds of poetry, because appreciation for poetry develops slowly. Use the following questions to help you in selecting poetry:

1. Will the subject matter appeal to children?
2. Are the images, rhythms, rhymes, and emotions expressed understandable for children in this stage of development? (See Chapter Three for additional information.)
3. Does the poem represent an imaginative use of language (reflected in language flow, word choice, figurative language, imagery, and rhyme if used)?
4. Is the style appropriate to the subject?
5. Does the poet make the subject live? (Literary critics agree that fine poets bring an experience or emotion to life, making it live for the reader or listener.)
6. Will this poem motivate children to read other poetry?
7. Does the poetry evoke a response in the listener/reader?

Using such guidelines, however, is no substitute for old-fashioned observation: children's eyes light up over a splendid poem that speaks directly to them, they grimace over ones they do not like. The clearest signal that you have read a winner is, of course, a request to read it again.

## CLASSROOM ACTIVITIES TO ENHANCE POETIC EXPERIENCE

Children respond to poetry in various ways. Their responses are closely linked to the ways in which they customarily explore the world: observing and manipulating. As they explore the nature and parameters of language, poetry can give them access to specific characteristics or elements not found in their everyday experience (Parsons, 1992).

Experiencing poetry begins with reading it aloud. This permits students to "hear" the musical qualities of the poetic language. Young children enjoy repeating and intensifying the magic of poetry; they like to hear it over and over again and will often object to changes in delivery or any attempt to leave out verses (Parsons, 1992). They love to chime in with the reader, clap with the rhythm, mime facial expressions, act out events, or just repeat the words. Such oral experiences intensify their appreciation of the rhythm, rhyme, figurative language, and imagery of poetry.

Reading poetry aloud, however, can be complicated by the poet's use of unfamiliar words and combinations of words, definite rhythms, vocal stress on words and syllables, and even the ideas. Stumbling over words or rhythm can interfere with children's experiences of the poem, so prepare for reading poems aloud by being thoroughly familiar with the language of the poem so that you can read fluently and well all at a comfortable rate. A tape recorder can be helpful in practicing reading aloud.

Children need to hear poetry read aloud *daily*. Particularly appealing poems should be read over and over to enable children to develop an ear for the rhythm and sound of poetry. Daily readings of poetry should be both incidental and planned. *Incidental poetry reading* occurs when an event is taking place: someone is celebrating a birthday or the birth of a new baby. Holidays and events like the first day of spring and the first day of winter are good reasons to read a poem. Rain, sunshine, snow, and the first robin of the spring are all events to be marked with poetry. *Planned poetry reading* occurs when the teacher chooses poetry that fits the curriculum or develops thematic units with poetry; the diversity of subject matter and form in poetry makes such planning easy. A few unit suggestions are included at the end of this chapter.

## Rhythm

*Sound effects.* Students can express the rhythms of poetry through sound effects. Organize a team to create background sound effects as a poem is read aloud (Larrick, 1991b); for instance, for "The Merry-Go-Round Song" a sound effects team could recreate the up-and-down rhythm of a carousel by repeating the sounds OOM-pa-pa, OOM-pa-pa in the rhythm of the song. Encourage the children to vary the sound effects and work at identifying the most effective ones for poems they enjoy. Groaning, snapping fingers, stomping feet, and hands rubbed together may be appropriate sound effects for some poems. For other poems, students might make crying sounds, or laugh, moo, or cluck; or they may even invent sounds.

*Repetition.* Young children enjoy repeating sounds, words, and phrases they hear. Joining in on the repeated lines in nursery rhymes, ballads, camp songs, spirituals, and traditional play rhymes is a fine way to involve them with poetry. Invite them to join in on the repeated parts during reading or singing such songs and rhymes as "The Muffin Man," "John Brown's Baby Had a Cold Upon His Chest," "The Wheels of the Bus Go Round and Round," or "He's Got the Whole World in His Hands."

*Echo.* Echoing lines and words are another way of inviting children into poetry. Repeated words or phrases can be treated like an echo or a series of echoes (Larrick, 1991b), as shown in the traditional folk song "Miss Mary Mack" (see box). The echo can be developed in a number of ways: one individual can read or recite the poem, with another individual echoing the repeated words; or groups can do the parts instead of individuals. Another variation is to emphasize the beat on the repeated words by clapping with the chant on those words.

*Choral reading.* Activities such as repetition and echoing prepare children for choral reading of

### Miss Mary Mack

Miss Mary Mack, Mack, Mack
All dressed in black, black, black
With silver buttons, buttons, buttons
All down her back, back, back.

She asked her mother, mother, mother
For fifteen cents, cents, cents,
To see the elephant, elephant, elephant
Jump the fence, fence, fence.

He jumped so high, high, high
That he touched the sky, sky, sky
And never came back, back, back
Till the Fourth of July, July, July.

Hubbell, 1991

poetry. Many poems lend themselves to choral reading. "Bananas and Cream," shown on page 148 can be a choral reading involving two or three groups of students. Assign the various stanzas to different groups and have the repeated words chanted in unison by the entire group. "The Poor Old Lady Who Swallowed a Fly" is another good poem for choral reading. There are literally hundreds of poems for this and similar activities; the examples here are provided to give you an idea of what to look for. If you try a poem and it does not work out, try others until you find some that you and the students enjoy. Material for choral reading should be meaningful, have strong rhythm, have an easily discernible structure, and perhaps rhyme (McCracken and McCracken, 1983). Some good ones are:

- "The Pickety Fence" by David McCord, in *Far and Few, Rhymes of Never Was and Always Is*
- "The Umbrella Brigade" by Laura Richards, in May Hill Arbuthnot's *Time for Poetry*
- "Godfrey, Gordon, Gustavus Gore" by William B. Rand, in May Hill Arbuthnot's *Time for Poetry*
- "Yak" by William Jay Smith, in Jane Yolen's *Oh, That's Ridiculous*

For additional suggestions for choral reading, see Jeannette Miccinati's article "Using Prosodic Cues to Teach Oral Reading Fluency" (1985).

## Movement

The rhythm of poetry gives it a feeling of movement, making it difficult for children to be still when listening to it. "Poetry is not irregular lines in a book, but something very close to dance and song, something to walk down the street keeping in time to" (Frye, 1964). "Or jog down the trail keeping time to. Or do the dishes by. Or jump rope on the playground with" (Hearne, 1990). Being involved with poetry makes it more appealing. "Doing" creates opportunities for children to respond to, to participate in, to be involved with the poetry. "Doing" can involve chanting, singing, dancing, tapping, and swinging to the rhythms of poetry (Larrick, 1991b). Children appreciate the rhythmic aspect of poetry and rhymes. Tapping, clapping, and swinging arms with poetry sensitizes participants to the rhythms and involves them with poetry. They need opportunities to hop, skip, jump, and march to poetry. They enjoy trying out various assignments such as: "Walk with confidence. Tiptoe stealthily. Walk flatfoot like a clown. Walk like a sad old man. Imagine you are picking up a heavy sack of apples and carry it on your shoulder. . . . Swim like a fish. Fly like a bird" (Larrick, 1991b).

Movement is a natural introduction to poetry. Some traditional singing games such as "If You're Happy and You Know It, Clap Your Hands" and "The Wheels on the Bus Go Round and Round" are excellent vehicles for making students more aware of rhythm. Movement is an important element in Lillian Morrison's *Rhythm Road: Poems To Move To*. This fresh, inventive collection of nearly 100 poems is an excellent introduction to the genre and to motion for all ages. Morrison has arranged the poems in sections that include dancing, riding, watching water, and hearing music; other sections include the topics of living things, active entertainments, sports, work, TV, technology, and the mind. When using this book in the classroom, read the poems aloud and encourage listeners to move with the sounds.

Lillian Morrison has accommodated the need for movement in much of the poetry she has written. *The Breakdance Kids* is just one of her books that stimulates poetic movement. *A Rocket in My Pocket*, compiled by Carl Withers, is a collection of

### Bedtime

Hop away
Skip away
Jump away
Leap!
Day is all crumpled
And lies in a heap.
Jump away
Skip away
Hop away
Creep!
Night comes and coaxes
The world to sleep

Hubbell, 1991

rhythmic chants, songs, and verses that are part of the folklore of the United States; all works in it are effective for developing movement activities in classrooms. Nancy Larrick (1991b) recommends the poem "Bedtime," by Patricia Hubbell (see box), for encouraging children to experiment with different movements.

## Themes and Topics

One way of organizing poetry experiences and activities is through themes and topics (Parsons, 1992). By identifying a topic and using that focus to integrate classroom experiences, teachers encourage, support, and reinforce children's learning. Theme or topic exploration may include activities such as field trips, art, dramatic play, music, and further reading. Themes and topics for poetry explorations can focus on any number of topics, including colors, animals (wild animals, imaginary animals, zoos), myself, out-of-doors, or any other content area that is of interest. Even houses can be a theme for poetry, as Mary Ann Hoberman demonstrates in her picture book *A House Is a House for Me*. She explores the concept of houses with such interesting ideas as a glove (a house for a hand) and a hand (a house for money).

Quiet is Peter Parnall's theme in his book *Quiet*. In this book-length poem a boy sprinkles apple cores and seeds on his chest while lying in the grass so that he can observe the life around him. A chip-

*This volume of poetry is for two voices.*

munk, a mouse, a bumblebee, and a chickadee see the treats from different perspectives, shown in the charcoal-and-colored-pencil illustrations. After reading this poem, children may want to lie in the grass themselves, observing what happens and writing their own poems or stories about the experience. They could also examine the meaning of some other word in the same way that Parnall did in *Quiet*.

Another book-length poem, *Train Song* by Diane Siebert, contrasts with Parnall's *Quiet*. The rhythm and rhyme of the rolling wheels of a train create the movement, sights, and sounds of a train. Richly colored paintings illustrate this picture book. *Train Song* could be the beginning of a transportation unit along with *Truck Song*, also by Diane Siebert, or of a train unit with George Ella Lyon's picture book *A Regular Rolling Noah* and Robert Welber's *The Train*.

Two thematic units that are highly popular with children and that offer plenty of material for study are animals, birds, and bees, and holidays. (For other specific unit suggestions, see the section "Discussion" on page 164.)

*Animals, birds, and bees.* Animals, birds, and insects are frequent subjects for poets and often favorite subjects of children, and there is no shortage of books from which to build a thematic unit on this topic. William Jay Smith's *Birds and Beasts* is both a poetry collection and an art book. Smith's poems and the graphic images created by Jacques Hnizdovsky's woodcuts combine to create a funny, lighthearted tone. Myra Cohn Livingston's *If the Owl Calls Again: A Collection of Owl Poems* views owls from many different perspectives. Many readers will be surprised at the number of great poets from various cultures who have chosen to write about owls.

Insects are the theme of Paul Fleischman's Newbery Award book, *Joyful Noise: Poems for Two Voices*. These poems are wonderful fun in the classroom because they must be read by two or more individuals, and they can be the basis for creating choral readings. In these poems, sounds create the images, movements, and appearance of many different insects.

Aileen Fisher writes about many kinds of wildlife in her nature poems: bees, spiders, rabbits, and weather are just a few of her topics. The sensory images in her poems help children see their natural world in a new light and encourage them to observe carefully. *Feathered Ones and Furry* includes many of her nature poems.

*Holidays.* Poetry is a natural part of holiday celebrations, and holidays are a good time for integrating poetry in classrooms. Almost every holiday or season has more than enough poetry written about it to serve as the basis for a unit study at the appropriate time of year. A number of poets and compilers have created holiday poems and collections, a few of which are listed below.

- *New Year's Poems* by Myra Cohn Livingston
- *Valentine Poems* by Myra Cohn Livingston
- *Easter Poems* by Myra Cohn Livingston
- *Merrily Comes Our Harvest In* by Lee Bennett Hopkins
- *Best Witches: Poems for Halloween* by Jane Yolen
- *Halloween A B C* by Eve Merriam
- *Halloween Poems* by Myra Cohn Livingston
- *Hey-How for Halloween* by Lee Bennett Hopkins
- *Thanksgiving Poems* by Myra Cohn Livingston
- *Christmas Poems* by Myra Cohn Livingston
- *Diane Goode's American Christmas* by Diane Goode
- *Sing Hey for Christmas Day* by Lee Bennett Hopkins
- *Celebrations* by Myra Cohn Livingston

## Writing

Children are natural poets because poetic language comes naturally to them. Those who are immersed in poetry often express their own ideas in the same patterns as their favorite poems. Writing models encourage children to run with their imaginations—to take off with a concept and see where it goes. They may write or dictate concept poems to be bound into a class book to share with visitors to the classroom.

Myra Cohn Livingston (1976) suggests another method for encouraging children to write and respond to poetry, an approach that expedites children's discovery of their own poetic voice. First, share with them many poems that will stimulate their imagination, then give them observation sheets on which they can record their own responses, guided by the questions *what I saw* and *what I thought about what I saw*. These sheets create a bridge between the facts observed and the feelings related to the observations. Writing requires keen observation, and Livingston's method builds students' ability to scrutinize their environment. For instance, she recommends prompting them to consider sounds, smells, and tastes in their surroundings by bringing in potato chips and other noisy foods. In Livingston's plan, children keep a daily observation journal in which they record feelings and observations. The teacher works on inspiring students to turn their observations and feelings into poems, working with the children in conferences to help them make their writings look like poetry and pointing out the parts that work and those that need additional polishing.

Students can learn about the mechanical differences between poetry and prose by comparing the treatment of a subject in a poetry selection, a prose selection, and an informational selection. Ideas and information are imparted in different ways in each form of literature. Students can write sentences that tell about the similarities and differences in various literary forms on the same subject or create a chart like that in Figure 6.1 to demonstrate the comparisons. This figure compares three picture books on the topic of flying:

- *First Flight* by David McPhail. This picture book fantasy features a naughty teddy bear who is taking a first flight with his very well-behaved owner. The teddy bear breaks all the rules for flying.
- *Up in the Air* by Myra Cohn Livingston. This picture book is a poem illustrated by Leonard Everett Fisher. The illustrations are from the perspective of a person looking down toward the earth from an airplane.
- *Flying* by Donald Crews. This informational picture book follows an airplane flight from the passengers boarding the plane to their arrival at a destination.

## FIGURE 6.1

Chart comparing three kinds of literary forms in three picture books.

| Titles | Genre | Theme | Language |
|---|---|---|---|
| First Flight | Fantasy | How to behave on an airplane | Imaginative; child's emotions expressed through his teddy bear |
| Up In the Air | Poetry | The emotions and feelings about looking down on the earth | Poetic language that succinctly expresses feelings |
| Flying | Nonfiction | Information about airplanes and airports | Straightforward, descriptive. |

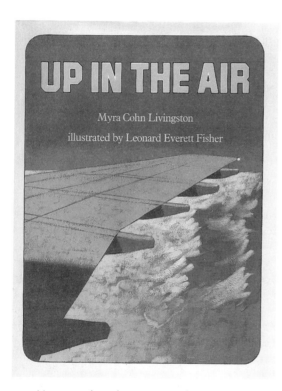

*Using triplets that capture the excitement of rising "up in the air," the poet evokes with words what the illustrator captures in dramatic pictures of air and space.*

## Discussion

Many people are unsure about discussing or asking questions about poetry. Poetry is art and many of us agree that it should not be overanalyzed, but does that mean it cannot be discussed or examined at all? Sebesta and Iverson call poem discussion a risky venture (1975). Discussions of poetry should avoid overanalysis as well as overgeneralization. The best guide for poetry discussion comes from Perrine (1963):

1. Consider the speaker and the occasion. Discuss who wrote the poem, whether the speaker or character is the same person as the poet, and the point of view the poet uses.
2. Consider the central purpose of the poem. Discuss why the poet wrote it and what type of poem it is: a circus poem, a wildlife poem that celebrates nature, and so on.
3. Consider the means by which that purpose is achieved: rhythm, rhyme, imagery, or repeated words, phrases, or lines, and so on.

*UNIT SUGGESTIONS*

As children become fluent readers, they can prepare poems to read aloud either as individuals or as groups, implementing some of the suggestions in this activity section. One way of generating student participation in poetry is to write a poem on a chart, then cut it apart and give each student the part they are to read. The parts can be numbered to assist the students. Playing music as a background when reading poetry dramatizes it. Puppets, pantomime, and creative drama are appropriate activities for many poems because they tell stories. Nursery rhymes such as Jack and Jill or Humpty Dumpty are appropriate to these activities as are many other poems. "The Poor Old Lady Who Swallowed a Fly" works well for puppets or drama. Children may experiment and explore with the sounds of poetry through their voices, create their own poetry, examine various themes, relate poetry to the arts.

## 6.1 Humor

Suggested Book List:

- *Faint Frogs Feeling Feverish* by Lillian Obligado
- *If I Were in Charge of the World* by Judith Viorst
- *New Kid on the Block* by Jack Prelutsky
- *Rolling Harvey Down the Hill* by Jack Prelutsky
- *The Complete Nonsense of Edward Lear* by Edward Lear
- *Where the Sidewalk Ends* by Shel Silverstein
- *You Read to Me, I'll Read to You* by John Ciardi

Guiding Questions:

1. What makes you laugh? Think about television shows, books, poems, and real-life events. Some people laugh at exaggeration, word play, jokes on other people, or unexpected events.
2. Can you think of other things that make people laugh? Make a list with your classmates.
3. Listen to the poems that your teacher reads. Which ones did you think were the funniest? Which ones were not funny?
4. How did the poet make you laugh? (techniques, elements, forms, etc.)
5. Why did the poet write this poem?
6. What poems made your classmates laugh? Why did they laugh?
7. Vote for the funniest poem or poems of those your teacher reads. Find out why these were the funniest.
8. Make a bulletin board display to tell the school about funny poems and the ways authors make them funny.
9. Find more funny poems and make a class book.
10. Read funny poems to your family and friends to find out what poems make them laugh.

## 6.2 Weather

Suggested Book List:

- *A Circle Of Seasons* by Myra Cohn Livingston
- *Go with the Poem* by Lilian Moore
- *I Like Weather* by Aileen Fisher
- *Rain Talk* by Mary Serfozo
- *Rainbows Are Made: Poems* by Carl Sandburg, Lee Bennett Hopkins, and Fritz Eichenberg
- *Season Songs* by Ted Hughes
- *Sky Songs* by Myra Cohn Livingston

Guiding Questions:

1. What is your favorite kind of weather? Why?
2. What is your least favorite kind of weather? Why?
3. In the poem you have selected for study, what is the poet's favorite weather? How do you know?
4. How does weather in the poem make us feel?
5. Why did the poet write this poem?
6. How did the poet help us experience a particular kind of weather?
7. Compose a poem of your own that is parallel to one of those studied in this unit.

## 6.3 Animals

Suggested Book List:

- *Animals, Animals* by Eric Carle
- *A Gopher in the Garden and Other Animal Poems* by Jack Prelutsky
- *Birds and Beasts* by William Jay Smith
- *Cat Poems* by Myra Cohn Livingston
- *Circus! Circus!* by Lee Bennett Hopkins
- *Dinosaurs* by Lee Bennett Hopkins
- *My Mane Catches the Wind: Poems About Horses* by Lee Bennett Hopkins
- *Turtle in July* by Marilyn Singer
- *Tyrannosaurus Was a Beast* by Jack Prelutsky

Guiding Questions:

1. What kinds of animals are good pets? Why?
2. Do you have a pet? What is it?
3. How does the poet feel about animals? How do you know?
4. What did the poet tell us about animals?
5. How did the poet tell us about animals?
6. Why did the poet write this poem?
7. What did you learn about animals from the poems your teacher read?
8. Which animal poem did you like best? Why?
9. Do you have different ideas about animals after hearing poems about them? How did your ideas change?
10. How are animals in poems similar to those in stories? How are they different?
11. Write a poem about your favorite animal.

## SUMMARY

Poetry is compressed language and thought that implies more than it says. Poetry is literature in verse form. The good news about children's poetry is its plentiful supply. Current poetry addresses contemporary themes and experiences that children can appreciate. Children see poetic language as natural unless they have had negative experiences that turn off their interest in this form. Unfortunately, many adults view poetry with a mixture of awe and insecurity because they believe they must have academic knowledge in order to do justice to it in the home or classrooms. However, teachers, librarians, and parents can read poetry with and to children as an organic part of their daily experiences and celebrations. Oral read-aloud experiences are the best way to introduce poetry to children.

Adults must carefully choose poetry for students. They need a wide acquaintance with all forms and types of poetry so they can discover that which will entice children to read. Children enjoy the rhyme, humor, rhythm, and movement of poetry; however, response to poetry is more personal than to other literary genre, so a wide-ranging collection of poetry enhances children's opportunities to respond to it. Emphasizing meaning, response, and enjoyment is important in incorporating poetry into children's lives.

## THOUGHT QUESTIONS

1. How is poetry different from prose?
2. What are the major characteristics of poetry?
3. Why does poetry appeal to children?
4. How can you as a teacher prevent children from disliking poetry?
5. Do you think poetry is natural to children? Why or why not?
6. How should poetry be presented in classrooms? Why?
7. Identify three strategies for presenting poetry that you plan to use as a classroom teacher. Why do you like these strategies?

## ENRICHMENT ACTIVITIES

1. Start a poetry file or collection for use in your classroom. This collection should relate to everyday events, holidays, and the curriculum.
2. Start a thematic collection of poetry. The themes you identify will depend upon the ages of the children you will be working with.
3. Compare the treatment of a single subject in poetry, prose, and informational writing.
4. Survey the teachers in an elementary school. Ask them how often they use poetry in their classrooms and what the children's favorite poems are. What conclusions can you reach based on your results?
5. Survey students at one grade level. Ask them to identify their favorite poems. Create a graph that shows the titles, poets, and types of poems they enjoy most.
6. Practice reading three poems aloud. Tape yourself, so that you can realize your progress in the oral interpretation of poetry.
7. Examine three or more anthologies of poetry. Which one would you find most useful in the classroom? Why?

......................... RECOMMENDED CHILDREN'S BOOKS

Adoff, Arnold. (1982). *All the Colors of the Race*. Illustrated by John Steptoe. New York: Lothrop, Lee & Shepard. (3–7)

> This collection of poetry celebrates individuals who have mixed racial heritage.

————. (1986). *Sports Pages*. Illustrated by Steve Kuzma. Philadelphia: Lippincott. (3–7)

> This is an interesting volume of sports poetry.

Arbuthnot, May Hill, compiler. (1959). *Time for Poetry*. Glenview, Ill: Scott Foresman. (K–6)

> This anthology of poems addresses many topics and experiences, which makes it very useful.

Atwood, Ann. (1971). *Fly with the Wind, Flow with the Water*. New York: Scribner's. (3–5)

> A collection of this author's nature haiku.

————. (1971). *Haiku: The Mood of the Earth*. New York: Scribner's. (3–5)

> The poet's haiku expresses her feelings about the earth.

————. (1977). *Haiku—Vision in Poetry and Photography*. New York: Scribner's. (3–5)

> Photographs are used to express the haiku moods.

————. (1973). *My Own Rhythm: An Approach to Haiku*. New York: Scribner's. (1–3)

> The book of haiku illustrates the rhythms of the art form.

Bacmeister, Rhoda W. (1940). *Stories to Begin On*. New York: E. P. Dutton. (1–3)

> This is a collection of poems for young children.

Baylor, Byrd. (1976). *Hawk, I'm Your Brother*. Illustrated by Peter Parnall. New York: Scribner's. (2–5)

> A boy talks with a hawk in poetic language.

————. (1976). *The Way to Start a Day*. Illustrated by Peter Parnall. New York: Scribner's. (1–3)

> This book tells readers how to greet the sun.

————. (1978). *The Other Way to Listen*. Illustrated by Peter Parnall. New York: Scribner's. (2–adult)

> This is a book-length poem that explores ways of listening and knowing. The theme is respect for all things.

————. (1975). *The Desert Is Theirs*. New York: Scribner's. (3–9)

> This book-length poem portrays the lives of desert animals.

Behn, Harry. (1971). *More Cricket Songs*. New York: Harcourt Brace Jovanovich. (1–4)

> This collection of Japanese haiku was narrated by Harry Behn.

Carroll, Lewis. (1946). *Through the Looking Glass and What Alice Found There*. New York: Random House. (7–12)

> This delightful book contains many wonderful nonsense poems.

Carson, Jo. (1989). *Stories I Ain't Told Nobody Yet*. New York: Orchard Books. (5–8)

> This book of poetry includes 49 poems that are really conversations that the poet eavesdropped on in grocery store lines, beauty parlors, and emergency rooms in east Tennessee and the Appalachian region. (5–9)

Ciardi, John. (1985). *Doodle Soup*. Illustrated by Merle Nacht. Boston: Houghton Mifflin. (2–5)

> A collection of nonsense and humorous poetry.

————. (1962). *You Read to Me, I'll Read to You*. Illustrated by Edward Gorey. Philadelphia: Lippincott. (2–4)

> Poems for paired reading.

de Regniers, Beatrice Schenk, Eva Moore, Mary Michaels White, and Jean Carr. (1988). *Sing a Song of Popcorn*. New York: Scholastic. (K–6)

Many of these poems are well known. Each one is illustrated by a different well-known illustrator.

Fisher, Aileen. (1960). *Going Barefoot*. New York: T. H. Crowell. (1–6)

This book-length poem celebrates the joys of going barefoot in the out-of-doors.

_____. (1964). *Listen Rabbit*. Illustrated by Simeon Shimin. New York: T. H. Crowell. (1–6)

This book-length poem is about a child talking to a wild rabbit.

_____. (1961). *Sing, Little Mouse*. New York: T. H. Crowell. (1–6)

These poems are songs a mouse might sing.

_____. (1986). *When It Comes to Bugs*. Illustrated by Chris and Bruce Degen. New York: Harper & Row. (1–6)

This collection of poems shows how much the poet likes bugs.

_____. (1963). *I Like Weather*. New York: T. H. Crowell. (1–6)

These poems reflect the pleasures of all kinds of weather.

_____. (1971). *Feathered Ones and Furry*. Illustrated by Eric Carle. New York: T. H. Crowell. (1–6)

This is a collection of animal and insect poetry created by Fisher. The poems have images that appeal to children.

Fleischman, Paul. (1988). *Joyful Noise: Poems for Two Voices*. Illustrated by Eric Beddows. New York: Harper. (3–6)

This Newbery Award book is composed of poems to be read by at least two people creating playful sound effects. The poems focus on insects and their movements, voices, appearance, and metaphoric significance.

Froman, Robert. (1974). *Seeing Things: A Book of Poems*. New York: T. H. Crowell. (1–3)

Poetry about observation.

Frost, Robert. (1978). *Stopping by Woods on a Snowy Evening*. Illustrated by Susan Jeffers. New York: Dutton. (4–adult)

A picture book of this popular poem.

Glazer, R. (1973). *Eye Winker, Tom Tinker, Chin Chopper: Fifty Musical Fingerplays with Piano Arrangements and Guitar Chords*. (preschool–K)

This is an excellent collection of movement songs to help children understand rhythm in poetry.

Goode, Diane. (1990). *Diane Goode's American Christmas*. New York: Dutton. (all ages)

Poems, songs, and traditional stories. The entries reflect the different cultural groups in our country.

Greenfield, Eloise. (1988). *Under the Sunday Tree*. Illustrated by Amos Ferguson. New York: Harper & Row. (1–5)

This collection of poems focuses on family and the Caribbean islands.

_____. (1978). *Honey, I Love, and Other Love Poems*. Illustrated by Diane and Leo Dillon. New York: Harper. (1–4)

This book of poems shares an African American child's enthusiasm for love and family life. The Dillons' illustrations show the love and enthusiasm in the child's face.

Hague, Michael, compiler and illustrator. (1994). *Sleep, Baby, Sleep: Lullabies and Night Poems*. New York: Morrow Junior Books. (preschool–2)

This is a poetic lullaby.

Hoberman, Mary Ann. (1982). *A House Is a House for Me.* Illustrated by Betty Fraser. New York: Penguin. (preschool–2)

This picture book explores the concept of house. For example, a hive is a house for bees, and a glove is a house for a hand. An imaginative treatment of a concept.

Hopkins, Lee Bennett. (1982). *Circus! Circus!* New York: Knopf. (1–3)

These poems tell about the circus.

_____ . (1979). *My Mane Catches the Wind: Poems About Horses.* New York: Harcourt Brace Jovanovich. (3–6)

Twenty two poems about horses.

_____ . (1978). *Merrily Comes Our Harvest In.* New York: Harcourt Brace Jovanovich. (1–6)

These poems celebrate Thanksgiving and the fall season.

_____ . (1977). *Beat the Drum: Independence Day Has Come.* Illustrated by Tomie dePaola. New York: Harcourt Brace Jovanovich. (all ages)

This is a collection of poetry for the Fourth of July holiday.

_____ . (1974). *Hey-How for Halloween.* New York: Harcourt Brace Jovanovich. (1–4)

Children will enjoy this collection of Halloween poetry.

Hopkins, Lee Bennett, editor. (1992). *Through Our Eyes: Poems and Pictures About Growing Up.* Boston: Little, Brown. (1–6)

This collection of poetry is about the feelings associated with growing up.

_____ . (1988). *Still as a Star: A Book of Nighttime Poems.* Illustrated by Karen Milone. Boston: Little, Brown. (K–3)

This is a collection of poems for bedtime.

_____ . (1987). *Dinosaurs.* Illustrated by Murray Tinkleman. New York: Harcourt Brace Jovanovich. (3–6)

This anthology includes 14 poems about dinosaurs. The poems are widely varied in their reflections about these beasts and are enhanced by pen-and-ink drawings.

Hopkins, Lee Bennett, selector. (1990). *Good Books, Good Times.* Illustrated by Harvey Stevenson. New York: Harper. (K–5)

The theme of this collection of poems is books and reading. Many of these poems are from magazines or single-author collections. They range from serious to humorous, but all testify to the joys of reading. The poems are enhanced by double-page pastel watercolor illustrations.

Hubbell, Patricia. (1991). "Bedtime." In *Let's Do a Poem!* Edited by Nancy Larrick. New York: Delacorte. (K–3)

_____ . (1987). "When Dinosaurs Ruled the Earth." In *Dinosaurs.* Edited by Lee Bennet Hopkins. Illustrated by Murray Tinkleman. New York: Harcourt Brace Jovanovich. (3–6)

_____ . (1991). "Miss Mary Mack." In *Let's Do a Poem!* Edited by Nancy Larrick. New York: Delacorte.

Hughes, Langston. (1932). "Dreams." In *The Dream Keeper and Other Poems.* New York: Knopf. (3 and up)

This wonderful poem is almost ageless.

Hughes, Ted. (1975). *Season Songs.* New York: Viking. (2–5)

These are poems about the seasons.

Janeczko, Paul B. (1988). *The Music of What Happens: Poems that Tell Stories.* New York: Orchard. (4–adult)

The poems in this book are "storytelling" poems. They address all ages, times, and places. Included are poems about a 17-year-old killed by the Comanche Indians, an organizer of the student resistance movement in Nazi Germany, and a woman who lived 80 years without human contact. Their lives and others create the music in this poetry collection.

_____ . (1985). *Pocket Poems*. New York: Bradbury. (1–5)

These short poems would fit in a pocket.

Kennedy, X. J. (1982). *Did Adam Name the Vinegarroon?*. Illustrated by Heidi Johanna Selig. Boston: David Godine. (1–3)

These poems tell about unusual animals.

Kennedy, X. J. and Dorothy M. Kennedy, editors. (1982). *Knock at a Star: A Child's Introduction to Poetry*. Illustrated by Karen Ann Weinhaus. Boston: Little, Brown. (K–2)

This is a collection of sleepytime poetry.

Knudson, R. R. and May Swenson, editors. (1986). *American Sports Poems*. New York: Watts. (4–6)

Athletes and sports fans will enjoy these poems.

Kraus, Robert. (1970). *Whose Mouse Are You?* Illustrated by Jose Aruego. New York: Macmillan. (preschool–2)

The hero of the story is a mouse whose family is gone. His father is inside the cat, his sister is in a trap, is brother is far from home. But he rescues them and gets a new baby brother in the bargain.

Kuskin, Karla. (1992). *Soap Soup*. New York: HarperCollins. (K–2)

This new collection of poetry for young readers expresses a child's enjoyment of exploring the world and making discoveries of such things as clouds, sand, and knees.

_____ . (1980). *Dogs & Dragons Trees & Dreams: A Collection of Poems*. New York: HarperCollins. (1–3)

This collection of poems by Karla Kuskin includes her introductions to each poem.

_____ . (1975). *Near the Window Tree*. New York: Harper. (4–6)

Kuskin is a popular, well-known poet who writes about the concerns of childhood for all ages. This collection is special because each poem is accompanied with an explanation of why she wrote it.

Larrick, Nancy, editor. (1990). *Mice Are Nice*. Illustrated by Ed Young. New York: Philomel. (K–3)

This collection of poetry includes 25 verses that describe mice, their habits, and their houses. The illustrations are in rich charcoal and pastels, which give the mice the earthy color of mouse fur and a look of velvet softness.

Lear, Edward. (1990). *Of Pelicans and Pussycats: Poems and Limericks*. New York: Dial. (all ages)

This is a book of nonsense poetry.

_____ . (1958). *The Complete Nonsense Book*. New York: Dodd, Mead & Company. (all ages)

This classic book of nonsense verse continues to delight readers of all ages.

Lee, Dennis. (1977). *Garbage Delight*. Illustrated by Frank Newfeld. Boston: Houghton Mifflin. (K–6)

This winner of the Canadian Book of the Year Award is a collection of poetry with an unlikely theme. The poet uses exaggeration to create humor.

Leodhas, Sorche Nic. (1965). *Always Room for One More*. Illustrated by Nonny Hogrogian. San Diego: Holt. (2–5)

A delightful book-length poem.

Lewis, Richard. (1965). *In a Spring Garden*. Illustrated by Ezra Jack Keats. New York: Dial.
This book contains authentic haiku poetry. (2–6)

Little, Jean. (1989). *Hey World, Here I Am!* Illustrated by Sue Truesdell. New York: Harper. (4–7)
Kate, the main character (who was introduced in *Through My Window* and *Kate*), is revealed through the poems and anecdotes in this book, which speak to children who are having the same experiences.

Livingston, Myra Cohn. (1991). *Poem-Making: Ways to Begin Writing Poetry*. New York: Harper. (5–8)
Livingston has created a guide to the sounds, shapes, and structures of poetry. She discusses the practices and principles of voice, rhyme, metrics, imagery, and form, including quatrains, ballads, haiku, cinquain, limerick, and free verse. She uses examples of excellent poetry, as well as examples of what not to do.

————. (1989). *Up in the Air*. Illustrated by Leonard Everett Fisher. New York: Holiday House. (K–3)
In this book-length story told in poetic language, the poet relates how the earth looks from an airplane.

————. (1987). *Valentine Poems*. New York: Holiday House. (K–adult)
This is a collection of poems for celebrating Valentine's Day.

————. (1985). *Celebrations*. Illustrated by Leonard Everett Fisher. New York: Holiday House. (K–6)
These poems are appropriate for all types of celebrations.

————. (1983). *Sky Songs*. Illustrated by Leonard Everett Fisher. New York: Holiday House. (2–5)
These poems tell about what we see in the sky.

————. (1982). *A Circle of Seasons*. Illustrated by Leonard Everett Fisher. New York: Holiday House. (2–5)
A collection of seasonal poetry.

Livingston, Myra Cohn, compiler. (1990). *If the Owl Calls Again: A Collection of Owl Poems*. Illustrated by Antonio Frasconi. New York: McElderry. (6–10)
As the title indicates, this is a collection of poetry about owls compiled by Livingston. The wide-ranging collection includes Native American chants, and humorous verse.

Livingston, Myra Cohn, editor. (1987). *Cat Poems*. Illustrated by Trina Schart Hyman. New York: Holiday House. (1–4)
This collection contains poems about different kinds of cats.

Livingston, Myra Cohn, editor. (1985). *Thanksgiving Poems*. Illustrated by Stephen Gammell. New York: Holiday House. (K–adult)
This is a book of holiday poems.

————. (1984). *Christmas Poems*. Illustrated by Trina Schart Hyman. New York: Holiday House. (K–adult)
These poems are for Christmas celebrations.

Lyon, George Ella. (1986). *A Regular Rolling Noah*. Illustrated by Stephen Gammell. (1–3)
A boy travels with farm animals on a train from Kentucky to Canada. His trip with the animals in a box car is compared with Noah and his ark in this picture book.

————. (1992). *Together*. New York: Orchard Books. (all ages)
This picture book celebrates the joys of friendship.

McCord, David. (1952). *Far and Few, Rhymes of Never Was and Always Is.* Illustrated by Henry B. Kane. New York: Little, Brown. (all ages)

This collection includes many of McCord's best rhythmic poems.

McCord, David, and Marc Simont. (1967). "Bananas and Cream." In *Every Time I Climb a Tree.* Boston: Little, Brown. (K–3)

———. (1977). *One at a Time.* New York: Little, Brown. (2–5)

These are poems to enjoy "one at a time."

McGovern, Ann. (1985). *Arrow Book of Poetry.* New York: Scholastic. (1–5)

This collection is a useful resource for the classroom.

Merriam, Eve. (1987). *Halloween A B C.* Illustrated by Lane Smith. New York: Macmillan. (3–8)

This is a Halloween alphabet book.

———. (1986). *Fresh Paint: New Poems.* New York: Macmillan. (1–4)

This collection has 45 poems that range from squat mushrooms to the new moon.

———. (1964). "How to Eat a Poem." In *It Doesn't Always Have to Rhyme.* New York: Atheneum (1–4)

This collection of poems has a lilt and rhythm for primary grades.

Moore, Lilian. (1979). *Go with the Poem.* New York: McGraw Hill. (2–5)

A collection of 90 poems by outstanding 20th-century poets, this rhythmic poetry is designed for children's pleasure.

Morrison, Lillian. (1985). *The Breakdance Kids.* New York: Lothrop. (all ages)

The poems in this collection were written by Morrison. The title indicates their strong rhythms and motivation to move.

Morrison, Lillian, editor. (1988). *Rhythm Road: Poems to Move To.* New York: Lothrop. (all ages)

This is a collection of poetry to encourage motion. The poems are arranged into sections that include dancing, riding, watching water, hearing music, living things, active entertainments, sports, work, TV and technology, and the mind.

Parnall, Peter. (1990). *Quiet.* New York: Morrow Junior Books. (3–6)

Peter Parnall explores the meaning of "quiet" in this book-length poem.

Prelutsky, Jack. (1990). *Something Big Has Been Here.* Illustrated by James Stevenson. New York: Greenwillow. (K–4)

This collection of poetry ranges from the hilarious boy who planted lightbulbs in his hair so that he would always be bright to the more serious subjects of "Don't Yell at Me!"

———. (1988). *Tyrannosaurus Was a Beast: Dinosaur Poems.* Illustrated by Arnold Lobel. New York: Greenwillow. (K–4)

Humorous poems about dinosaurs.

———. (1984). *The New Kid On The Block.* Illustrated by James Stevenson. New York: Greenwillow. (all ages).

The title poem in this delightful collection of Prelutsky's poetry is especially good.

———. (1980). *Rolling Harvey Down the Hill.* Illustrated by Victoria Chess. New York: Greenwillow. (2–7)

A favorite collection for young children.

———. (1966, 1967). *A Gopher in the Garden and Other Animal Poems.* Illustrated by Robert Leyden Frost. New York: Macmillan.

Poems about all sorts of animals.

Richards, Laura. (1983). "Eletelephony." In *The Random House Book of Poetry for Children*, edited by Jack Prelutsky. Illustrated by Arnold Lobel. New York: Random House. (all ages)

   This is a large thematic collection of poems.

Rylant, Cynthia. (1989). *But I'll Be Back Again: An Album*. New York: Orchard Books. (4–9)

   This autobiography of Rylant's childhood deals directly with her painful experiences. Many youngsters will identify with her experiences.

_____ . (1984). *Waiting To Waltz: A Childhood*. Illustrated by Stephen Gammell. New York: Bradbury. (4–8)

   These are autobiographical poems composed from Rylant's childhood in a small Appalachian town. She writes of small and large crises in the life of a child.

Sandburg, Carl, Lee Bennett Hopkins, and Fritz Eichenberg. (1982). *Rainbows Are Made: Poems*. New York: Harcourt Brace Jovanovich. (4–8)

   This is a collection of poetry by Carl Sandburg.

Serfozo, Mary. (1990). *Rain Talk*. Illustrated by Keiko Narahashi. New York: Macmillan. (K–3)

   This book-length poem expresses the sensory images of rain.

Siebert, Diane. (1990). *Train Song*. Illustrated by Mike Weimmer. New York: T. H. Crowell. (2–5)

   This book-length poem has the rhythm of the train wheels. The poet conveys the movement, sights, and sounds of trains through rhyme and rhythm.

_____ . (1989). *Truck Song*. Illustrated by Mike Weimmer. New York: T. H. Crowell. (2–5)

   This book-length poem expresses the rhythm of wheels on the road.

Silverstein, Shel. (1974). *Where the Sidewalk Ends: The Poems and Drawings of Shel Silverstein*. New York: Harper. (5–12)

   Through humorous poems, the poet explores the joys and fears of childhood. This poetry is probably ageless.

Singer, Marilyn. (1989). *Turtle in July*. New York: Macmillan. (all ages)

   Sixteen poems about the twelve months of the year and the four seasons.

Smith, William Jay. (1990). *Birds And Beasts*. Illustrated by Jacques Hnizdovsky. Boston: Godine. (3–6)

   This collection of 29 poems is illustrated with 32 woodcuts. The verses and illustrations in this creative book are funny.

Snyder, Zilpha Keatley. (1969). "Poem to Mud." In *Today Is Saturday*. Illustrated by John Arms. New York: Atheneum. (1–4)

   This is a collection of poems about activities kids do out of school.

Sutherland, Zena. (1990). *The Orchard Book of Nursery Rhymes*. New York: Orchard Books. (all ages)

   This collection includes 77 classic nursery rhymes.

Viorst, Judith. (1981). *If I Were in Charge of the World and Other Worries: Poems for Children and Their Parents*. Illustrated by Lynne Cherry. New York: Atheneum. (1–6)

   The pains and pleasures and people who frustrate in everyday life is the subject of this collection. Both parents and children are likely to see themselves and their feelings in these poems.

Welber, Robert. (1972). *The Train*. New York: Pantheon. (K–2)

   This picture book explores everyday things such as trains and noises that frighten children.

Westcott, Nadine Bernard. (1987). *Peanut Butter and Jelly: A Play Rhyme*. New York: Dutton. (preschool–1)

   A picture book of the rhyme with accompanying hand motions.

Willard, Nancy. (1981). *A Visit to William Blake's Inn: Poems for Innocent and Experienced Travelers.* Illustrated by Alice and Martin Provensen. San Diego: Harcourt Brace Jovanovich. (2–6)

Withers, Carl, compiler. (1988). *A Rocket in My Pocket.* Illustrated by Susanne Suba. New York: Henry Holt. (K–4)

This collection of rhythmic chants, songs, and verses are a part of the folklore of the United States. They are effective for developing movement activities in classrooms.

Worth, Valerie. (1987). *All the Small Poems.* Illustrated by Natalie Babbitt. New York: Farrar, Straus & Giroux. (preschool–K)

This collection includes all small poems.

———. (1978). *Small Poems Again.* New York: Farrar, Straus & Giroux. (preschool–3)

This is another volume of small poems.

———. (1976). *Small Poems.* New York: Farrar, Straus & Giroux. (preschool–3).

Young children like small poems.

Yolen, Jane. (1990). *Dinosaur Dances.* Illustrated by Bruce Degen. New York: Putnam. (1–6)

This collection contains poems about all kinds of dinosaurs dancing. They dance everything from ballet to a chorus line. The poems have wonderful rhythms and the illustrations are captivating.

———. (1989). *Best Witches: Poems for Halloween.* New York: Putnam. (K–3)

These are modern witches who do aerobics and fly on vacuum cleaners.

———. (1972). *Oh, That's Ridiculous.* New York: Viking Press. (1–4)

This is a collection of nonsense poems.

# Seven

## KEY TERMS

| | |
|---|---|
| ballad | legend |
| fable | modern fantasy |
| fantastic elements | myth |
| folktale | pourquoi tales |
| high fantasy | science fiction stories |

## GUIDING QUESTIONS

Consider the reading material of your own childhood. Do you have favorite folktales from your childhood? What are they? Do you still like these stories? Do children still enjoy these stories? Remembering what you enjoyed reading as a child will help you to understand what children today enjoy. As you read, keep the following questions in mind:

1. What types of traditional literature can be used in elementary classrooms?

2. How are traditional literature and modern fantasy alike?

3. Why is fantasy an important type of literature for children?

4. Why is traditional literature so popular?

## OVERVIEW

Traditional tales are the foundation of modern literature. Frye (1964) claims that all literature is rooted in these original stories. Traditional literature and modern fantasy are treated together in this chapter because these genre are closely related: traditional literature is ancient make-believe, while modern fantasy is contemporary make-believe.

Traditional literature includes **folktales** from all the cultures in the world. It differs from other *literature* in that it was *transmitted orally from generation to generation*. Although folk literature now exists in both written and oral forms, it survived for centuries only in the memory of storytellers who shared their personal versions of the same stories with different audiences, perpetuating them in much the same way a pebble sends out ripples in a pool. The Cinderella story alone has nearly a thousand variants (Thompson, 1951).

We owe a debt of gratitude to people like the Brothers Grimm and Charles Perrault, who collected folktales and put them in print, preserving them for the pleasure of later generations. Authors of fine fantasy must convince readers to suspend their disbelief in order to believe in magic, at least for a little while. "The more fantastic a piece of fiction is, the harder the writer must work to make it believable" (Hearne, 1991, p. 84). In creating fantasy, authors must adhere to strict rules; they cannot wave a wand to solve all of the dilemmas confronting the protagonist. Fantasy does not automatically appeal to all children or adults, but many are devoted fans. Fantasy stimulates the imagination and should be an important part of children's lives so that they can develop an appreciation for it.

# Make-Believe

## TRADITIONAL LITERATURE AND MODERN FANTASY

................ INTRODUCTION

Traditional literature and modern fantasy originate in humanity itself, in stories of the "folk" that mirror the culture of origin, as well as the mores and values of that culture. The make-believe in traditional literature and fantasy both entertain and serve as instruments for disseminating cultural beliefs and mores to other generations and cultures. The Molly Whuppie story in the opening vignette is ancient. Many folk literature authorities believe it is based on the character of the first wife of Henry VIII. This story teaches children to keep trying and to take care of siblings.

................ VIGNETTE

Robin Haynes put her storytelling shawl around her shoulders and settled into her rocking chair to tell the story of Molly Whuppie. Her fourth graders were comparing different versions of folktales from various cultures and this was one they hadn't heard before. "Girls and boys, today I am going to tell you the story of Molly Whuppie. This tale is about a girl who performs brave deeds."

Once upon a time in a faraway country, there lived a man and woman who had so many children they couldn't feed them all. So they told the three youngest children to put on their warmest clothing and took them deep into the forest. When they reached a huge castle in a clearing, the parents told their children to sit on the grass and wait until they had gone, and then to knock on the door and ask for food. The obedient little girls did just as their parents told them. When they knocked on the door a woman answered it.

The children said, "Please give us something to eat. We're so hungry."

The woman said, "My husband is the two-faced giant! He can see everything and he will kill you as soon as he comes home."

"Please, please give us food! We're starving!" they cried.

So the giant's wife gave them milk and bread. They had just begun to eat when they heard a thunderous knock and a terrible

*(continued)*

voice said: "Fee, fie, fo, fum, I smell the blood of an Englishman!"

"Who is in my house?" the giant demanded.

"It's three starving little girls, and they'll go away. You're not to touch 'em," his wife replied.

The giant said nothing until he had eaten an enormous supper; then he said they could stay the night.

Molly Whuppie, the youngest child, was suspicious when the giant told them to share the bed with his three children, so she stayed awake. After Molly was sure everyone was sleeping, she got out of bed and took the straw ropes off her and her sisters' necks and exchanged them for the gold chains around the necks of the giant's daughters.

In the middle of the night, the giant got up and felt for the straw ropes. When he found them, he put the girls in a bag and left them in the forest.

Molly woke her sisters and told them to be quiet. They tiptoed out of the house and ran away. They ran and ran and never stopped all night long. In the morning they saw a grander castle than the giant's. They went in and found out that it was the king's castle, so they told him their story. He said, "Molly, you're a smart girl, and you did well to get away from the giant, but if you go back and steal the giant's sword that hangs on the back of his bed, I'll marry your oldest sister to my oldest son."

Molly said, "I'll try." So she went back to the giant's house and slipped quietly inside and crawled under his bed. She waited until he had eaten his supper and went to bed. As soon as she heard his snores, she crawled out and reached over the giant to get the sword, but the golden chain on the sword rattled and woke him. He leaped out of bed and chased Molly. She ran and ran and the giant ran and ran, till they came to the Bridge of One Hair. Molly crossed over, but the giant couldn't. He shouted at her, "Woe on you Molly Whuppie! Never come back again.

But she said, "Twice again I will come to Spain." Then Molly took the sword to the king and her sister married the king's son.

The king said, "You were very brave, Molly, but if you are truly brave, you'll go back and steal the purse that is under the giant's pillow. Then your second sister can marry my second son." Molly agreed to try again. She went back to the giant's house, crept in, and hid under the bed again. Again she waited while he ate and waited for him to snore. When he commenced to snoring, she slid out of her hiding place and slipped her hand under the pillow and grabbed the purse. But as she went out the door the giant awakened and ran after her. She ran and ran and he ran and ran until they came to the Bridge of One Hair; again she crossed over, but he couldn't. The giant said, "Woe on you Molly Whuppie, never come back here again."

Molly said, "Once again I'll come to Spain." Then Molly took the purse to the king and her second sister married the king's second son.

After the wedding, the king said to Molly, "Molly, you are such a smart girl, but if you are truly smart you could steal the giant's finger ring. Then I will give you my youngest son to marry." Molly agreed to try. So back she went to the giant's house and hid under the bed. The giant came home, ate a big, big supper and went to bed. Pretty soon he was snoring away. Molly slid out and took the giant's hand, and pulled on the ring and pulled on the ring, but when it came off the giant awakened.

The giant said, "Now I've got you, Molly Whuppie! How would you punish me if you caught me doing all that you have done to me?"

Molly said, "I would put you in a sack and . . . with you, . . . and a needle and thread and scissors, and I'd hang you up on the wall and I'd go to the forest and get the thickest branch I could find and I would bring it home and hit you until you were dead."

The giant laughed, "That's just what I'm going to do to you, Molly!"

So he put Molly and the needle and thread and scissors in a bag and hung it on the wall while he hunted for a branch.

Molly called out to the giant's wife, "You should see what I can see."

*(continued)*

"Oh, what do you see, Molly?"

Molly didn't answer, so the giant's wife begged her to tell what she saw. So Molly took the scissors and cut a hole in the bag and took out the needle and thread and helped the giant's wife into the sack and sewed up the hole.

The giant's wife saw nothing and asked to get down, but Molly didn't answer her. The giant came home with a tree branch and started hitting the bag.

His wife cried, "It's me!" but the giant didn't hear her.

Molly went out the back door, but the giant saw her. He chased her until she came to the Bridge of One Hair, and she crossed over, but he couldn't. Once again he said, "Woe on you Molly Whuppie! Never come here again."

"Never again will I come to Spain," she answered. Molly took the ring to the king and she married his youngest son and never saw the giant again.

After they listened to the story, Ms. Haynes asked the children to think of stories similar to *Molly Whuppie*. They immediately recognized that it was like *Jack and the Beanstalk*, and *Hansel and Gretel*. They discussed the specific similarities and differences and prepared a chart, shown in Figure 7.1, comparing the three tales.

## UNDERSTANDING REAL AND MAKE-BELIEVE

Children's understanding of the difference between real and make-believe is vital to their appreciation of both folk literature and fantasy and also to their ability to discriminate fact from fiction (Applebee, 1978). Children eventually learn there are underlying patterns in both fiction and fact. Pitcher and Prelinger (1963) studied children's stories to identify formal openings or titles, formal closings, and consistent use of past tense. They discovered that even two-year-olds understood some story structures and used introductions such as

"once upon a time" and closings like "they lived happily ever after," showing the early influence of folktales. Fantasy is important in children's lives: even very young children who are protected from fairy tales and exposed only to informative literature invent their own fantasies, which include many of the same characteristics as traditional folktales (Chukovsky, 1963).

Ability to understand make-believe is linked to development, and children exhibit a wide range of individual differences in acquiring this ability. Five-year-olds generally are still developing concepts of fantasy and realism, while seven- and nine-year-olds usually have acquired these concepts (Harms, 1972). Some children are still confused about fantasy and reality as late as age six: many six year-olds recognize that Cinderella is not real, although they tend to think that she once lived, and some 73 percent in one study were uncertain whether story characters and events were real (Applebee, 1978). The same study, however, reports that children recognize nonsense at quite an early age.

## TRADITIONAL LITERATURE

Traditional literature has been popular for thousands of years. It is a chain of communication through the centuries—a long folk memory stretching from ancient times to the present (Hunter, 1975). "Before writing there was story. Before story there was language" (Saxby, 1987). Folk literature is as old as humanity. It represents the accumulated wisdom and art of humankind springing from the many cultures in the world. Primitive humans shared, celebrated, and remembered experiences through story, art, and dance. Stories in these early days were transmitted by word of mouth—in fact, the word *tale* means "oral" in the original Anglo-Saxon language. Storytellers entertained and instructed with timeless tales of greed, jealousy, love, and need for security as they relaxed around nightly campfires. Storytellers, bards, minstrels, poets, and rhymers of old were venerated; they were welcomed into palaces and huts alike and accorded places of honor.

The identities of the actual originators of these folktales are lost in the passage of time; therefore the written versions that we have today of these

## FIGURE 7.1

Chart comparing *Molly Whuppie* to other traditional tales.

| Title | Characters | Setting | Villan | Hero/Heroine | Conclusion |
|---|---|---|---|---|---|
| *Molly Whuppie* | Three girls | Woods/giant's castle/king's castle | Giant | Molly | Molly saves herself and her sisters |
| *Jack and the Beanstalk* | Jack, his mother, the giant's wife, the giant | Giant's house | Giant | Jack | Jack saves himself and gets the means to support his mother |
| *Hansel and Gretel* | Hansel and Gretel, stepmother, father, and witch | Woods, witch's hut | Wicked stepmother and witch | Hansel and Gretel | Hansel and Gretel escape and get to eat all the food they want |

tales are credited to *retellers, collectors,* and *illustrators* rather than authors. The tales we enjoy today have survived for hundreds of years, polished and edited by storytellers throughout history who shared their own idioms, perspectives, and particular ways of knowing, clothing their folk memories with imagination. Every time a storyteller tells a story, the story changes, giving rise to thousands of variations of a single tale, which grows or shrinks over time as portions are added or deleted by different tellers. The significance of a story, its symbolism, may change over time because its original inspiration—often a particular event or a social or political issue—disappears. A folktale is a living thing that frequently lives longer than the issue leading to its birth.

Since all humankind shares in these folk memories, people throughout the world appreciate the stories (Hunter, 1976). The form and content of folktales, even from vastly different cultures, appear to be remarkably similar: people of all times and places share common concerns, fears, desires, and wishes. The universal themes mirror the hopes, dreams, fears, and values of humans in all cultures. For example, there are hundreds of versions of the Cinderella story from such diverse cultures as the German, French, and Chinese.

The details and modifications that appear in variants of folktales reflect the society or culture that produced them; therefore these variations provide anthropologists with a window to each culture. Folklore says a good deal about the times in which its creators lived and about their needs (Schwartz,

1977). It is concrete. Folktales have to do with accomplishing impossible feats, escaping from powerful enemies, outwitting the wicked people in the world, earning a living, securing food, and protecting the weak. They illustrate the traits and ethics valued by a culture: *The Fisherman and His Wife* teaches that wishing is foolish and that we should be satisfied with what we have. They help perpetuate the cultural values: *Little Plum*, a modern picture-book version of the Tom Thumb story by Ed Young, teaches children that size has very little to do with success and ability. Taboos and concepts of right and wrong are passed from one generation to the next through stories. Cinderella stories teach unselfishness, and "The Golden Goose" tale teaches the evils of greed.

## The Contemporary Value of Traditional Literature

Traditional literature has many contemporary values. It continues to entertain modern children, just as it once entertained both children and adults around the campfires of long ago. Folktales celebrate imaginary feats that would be impossible in real life. They explore good and evil, taboos, and the supernatural. Stories give us heroes, wise men, wizards, and magicians, as well as monsters, giants, and dragons. They may comfort children or frighten them depending upon the teller's purpose. In traditional stories, characters can do things not permitted in real life (Dundes, 1965). They can

According to this Navajo tale, all who
traveled up the steep mountain hoped to
dream of power. But what of the boy
who dreamed of an acorn?

express anger and frustration without fear of reprisal. "Nothing in the entire range of 'children's literature'—with rare exceptions—can be as enriching and satisfying to child and adult alike as the folk fairy tale. . . . A child can learn more about the inner problems of man and about solutions to his own (and our) predicaments in any society, than he can from any other type of story within his comprehension" (Bettelheim, 1975, p. 76).

Traditional literature is a rich source of content for multicultural studies and global education that can be used to develop children's cultural awareness and understanding. Leigh Casler's Native American tale *The Boy Who Dreamed of an Acorn* teaches that all children are searching for their place in the world and that all children have dreams. *Oh, Kojo! How Could You!*, an African folktale by Verna Aardema, can play an important role in developing understanding of some of the many cultures in our country and our world. Marc Brown's illustrations for this story were greatly influenced by his studies of West African cave paintings. Mirra Ginsburg's translations and adaptations bring Russian folktales to children; *The Old Man and His Birds* is borrowed from a nineteenth-century Russian collection of folklore.

## Controversy over Traditional Literature

Folktales have been and continue to be controversial. Early in the nineteenth century they were controversial because they did not provide direct, specific moral instruction (Saxby, 1987), but the efforts to eliminate or rewrite them failed. More recently, parents and teachers have expressed concern about the violence in folktales; some versions of traditional stories have been rewritten to "launder" or "sanitize" them (Rothman, 1990). In some instances, the vocabulary of traditional tales is changed; in others the plot is altered. A recent puppet show of "Little Red Riding Hood" punished the wolf by sending him to the zoo. Fortunately, traditional tales seem to be resilient and indestructible; they have withstood all assaults. Perhaps this is true because children seem to need fantasy in their lives, as discussed earlier.

## Elements of Traditional Literature

Traditional stories include the same elements as fiction: plot, setting, characters, theme, and style. Folktales based on oral tradition, however, differ in their use of these elements: characters are usually stereotypes and always few in number, plots and settings lack subtle nuances and development, and description is kept to a bare minimum. Storytellers include just enough events to make the story interesting. Plot and setting can be sketched quickly and the stereotyped characters dropped into place quickly. If there were too many attempts to solve a problem or conflict, the story could become boring; therefore, storytellers move quickly into the conflict that incorporates a minimum number of characters.

One way that the story is kept brief is through the use of a "magic" number. In folk literature from the European tradition, three is the magic number. There are three attempts to climb the glass mountain, three riddles to answer, three brothers to seek their fortune, or three wishes. In the opening vignette, Molly Whuppie used the Bridge of One Hair three times. In Asian folktales, the magic number is usually four. Three or four attempts or incidents seem to be just the right number to make most stories interesting without dragging them out too long.

### Plot

A well-structured plot has conflict, suspense, and action. The conflict or problem and the suspense appear early in the story. The suspense builds as the hero or heroine makes a series of attempts to resolve the conflict or problem. Plot development is logical within the framework of the story: each incident builds on the preceding action. The mounting suspense surrounding the problem solution or conflict resolution holds attention. After the climax, story action winds up with the falling action of the denouement.

Plots in traditional literature, although they follow the usual structure, are always extremely brief and highly predictable. The characters are usually symbolic of good and evil. After a quick start, the plot moves forward rapidly and the principal character moves the plot along to a quick climax. Although magic may be used to move the plot forward, it must be logical within the framework of the story. The listener expects good to reign supreme, and it always does, so there are few surprises regarding story outcomes.

Typical story structures in traditional tales are sequential (beginning, middle, end), circular (ends up about where it began), and cumulative (additions and repetitions build the story). In Figure 7.2 *Goldilocks and the Three Bears* illustrates the sequential building of events to a quick resolution. The circular structure of *The Little Red Hen* is shown in Figure 7.3.

### Setting

Brevity is a hallmark of story introductions in traditional literature. Descriptions of times and places are unnecessary to the fast-moving plot. Time is developed with stock phrases such as *once upon a time, long ago and far away*, and *once there was and was not*. In *Molly Whuppie* the introduction was "Once upon a time in a faraway country." This brevity sets a stage for the story that would be difficult to improve upon. The setting may be a castle, a peasant's hut, or a forest, but again brevity is the key word. In *Molly Whuppie*, the setting jumps from a peasant's hut to the forest then to the giant's castle and finally the king's castle, with no more description than that the king's castle was grander than the giant's castle, which was simply described as being huge. The most important aspect of place in traditional literature is as a backdrop for characters' actions.

### Characters

Only a few characters are needed to tell most folktales. These flat, stereotyped characters are clearly recognizable as symbols of good or evil who spring

## FIGURE 7.2

A sequential plot structure map of *Goldilocks and the Three Bears.*

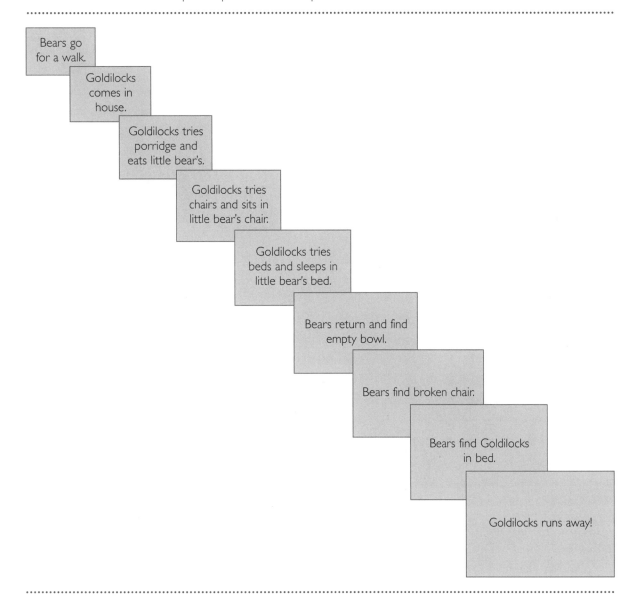

into action at the outset of the story to solve a problem or end a conflict without much in the way of character development. The good characters are totally good and the bad ones are altogether bad. Listeners learn almost nothing, for instance, about Molly Whuppie herself other than that she is brave and determined and wants to provide for her sis-ters. She braves the giant's wrath once to save her sisters' lives and her own and then three more times to earn security for the three of them. Nevertheless, these stereotypically "good" traits are all that the storyteller reveals. Molly is a flat rather than a round character, and we do not know anything about her personality.

## FIGURE 7.3

A circular plot structure map of *The Little Red Hen*.

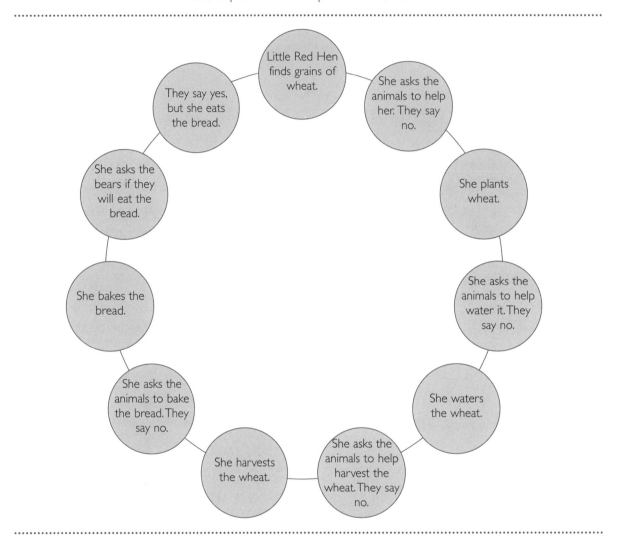

The flat characters are one reason children enjoy folktales. Good characters are rewarded and bad characters are punished, as when the wolf villain in *Little Red Riding Hood* is killed to rescue the Grandma he ate. These moralistic stories appeal to children, who tend to see people as completely good or completely bad. They love to cheer when the "bad guys" gets what they deserve and when dreams come true for good characters. Small, weak characters win and often receive rewards, while evil characters are losers, which appeals to children's sense of justice.

### Theme

Traditional stories have significant themes, such as cultural values and mores. Characters who exhibit traits of humility, courage, honesty, patience, and hard work are honored with riches, magical powers, palaces, and delicious banquets. Traditional literature teaches lessons such as the importance of the inner qualities of love and kindness as more important than outward appearance. Seemingly small, weak characters have virtues that enable them to achieve success in the face of violence and cruelty.

## Style

One of the hallmarks of folktale styles are the formulaic beginnings used to establish setting and characters and invite listeners: *long ago and far away* or *once there was and was not*. Folktales also have formulaic endings, such as *they lived happily ever after*, or the ending of *Three Billy Goats Gruff*: "snip, snap, snout; this tale's told out."

The language style is succinct and direct. These stories are compact; they sound as if they are being told aloud even when they are actually being read. Some folktales include stylistic devices such as rhymes, verses, or repetition. *The Three Little Pigs* is built around these devices, with a repeated rhyming verse appearing several times:

Wolf: "Little pig, little pig, let me come in!"

Pig: "Not by the hair of my chinny chin chin."

Wolf: "Then I'll huff, and I'll puff, and I'll blow your house in."

## Types of Traditional Literature

The term *folk* can refer to any group of people whatsoever who share at least one common factor (Dundes, 1965). Folklore exists where people share an identity, when they recognize themselves as members of a group united by race, nationality, occupation, class, geography, or age (Opie and Opie, 1974). Consequently, the category of folklore embraces the lore of such groups as lumberjacks, railroad workers, African Americans, Jews, Armenians, and schoolteachers, because each of these groups shares common factors and has its own stories.

According to Dundes (1965), folklore includes myths, legends, folktales, jokes, proverbs, riddles, chants, charms, blessings, curses, oaths, insults, retorts, taunts, teases, toasts, tongue-twisters, greeting and leave-taking formulas, folk costume, folk dance, folk drama, folk art, folk superstition, folk medicine, folk instrumental music, folk songs, folk speech (slang), folk similes (blind as a bat), folk metaphors (paint the town red), and names (nicknames).

Folk poetry ranges from oral epics to autograph-book verse, epitaphs, latrinalia (writings on the walls of public bathrooms), limericks, ball-bouncing rhymes, jump-rope jingles, finger and toe rhymes, dandling rhymes (to bounce children on the knee), counting-out rhymes (to determine who will be "it" in games), and nursery rhymes.

Folk literature is published in two forms, picture books of single tales and collections of folktales, also usually illustrated. Both collections and single tales generally identify retellers rather than authors, since these are retellings or reinterpretations of existing stories rather than original tales. In some instances, an illustrator is creating new pictures for a well-known folktale, which may also constitute a new interpretation of a story.

Traditional literature is classified in various ways and authorities differ in the terminology they use. However, folktales (also called wonder tales and household tales) consist of all kinds of narrative originating in the oral tradition (Thompson, 1951). In this sense, the category of folktales encompasses all traditional literature. Fairy tales, animal tales, myths, legends, tall tales, and ballads are all folktales. These forms of folktales, discussed in this section and summarized in Table 7.1, represent the majority of traditional literature in print for children today.

Folktales in general express and reinforce the way people think, feel, believe, and behave; they teach children what is proper and moral. They put the stamp of approval upon certain values held by the group (Arbuthnot, 1964). In these stories, lowly heroes win fame and fortune in an unreal world of improbable characters. Such tales often include magical transformations, ogres, and superhuman feats of valor. *Jack and the Beanstalk* is just one example of the many folktales for children.

## Fairy tales

*Fairy tales* are unbelievable stories featuring magic and the supernatural. Fairies, giants, witches,

TABLE 7.1

Common types of traditional literature.

| TYPE | CHARACTERISTIC | EXAMPLE |
|---|---|---|
| Folktales | giants, witches, magic, tasks, ogres | *Jack and the Beanstalk* <br> *Goldilocks and the Three Bears* |
| Cumulative folktales | repeat actions, refrains in sequence | *Henny Penny, Johnny Cake* |
| Fairy tales | magic and wonder | *Cinderella, Beauty and the Beast* |
| Animal tales | animals who outwit enemies | *Little Red Hen, Three Billy Goats Gruff* |
| Fables | animal stories that teach a lesson | *The Hare and the Tortoise* |
| Trickster tales | tales in which characters are able to dupe other characters (especially rabbits and coyotes) | *Brer Rabbit* |
| Noodlehead tales (humorous folktales) | silly humans, stupid characters | *The Princess and the Pea, Simple Simon* |
| Myths | explain the origin of the world and natural phenomena | Greek myths |
| Pourquoi tales | explain why certain things are the way they are | *How the Snake Got Its Rattles* <br> *How the Rabbit Got a Short Tail* |
| Legends | often based on historical figures with embellished deeds | *Robin Hood*, King Arthur |
| Tall tales | larger-than-life characters | Daniel Boone, Paul Bunyan |
| Ballads | rhyme and rhythm set to music | |

dwarves, good people, and bad people in fairy tales live in supernatural worlds with enchanted toadstools and crystal lakes. Heroes and heroines in these stories have supernatural assistance in solving problems. *Snow White and the Seven Dwarfs* is a typical fairy tale.

### Animal tales

Folktales are often told with animals that have human characteristics as the main characters. *The Little Red Hen* falls into this category of folktale. One of the most ancient types of story, **fables,** *are animal tales. In these stories, the animals symbolize humans, often to make a specific point or teach a moral lesson, which is explicitly stated at the end of the fable.* *Aesop's Fables* are among the best-known fables in the Western culture, while *Jataka Tales* are well known in the Eastern culture.

Trickster tales are also animal tales. The principal character in these stories is amoral, neither good nor bad. Tricksters laugh when they should not and are always "up to" something, but tricksters are charming and likeable and often escape punishment. The trickster's function in folk literature is to keep us from taking ourselves too seriously (Lester, 1988). Trickster tales appear in every culture, although the trickster animal varies from culture to culture. Brer Rabbit is a popular trickster character with American children. Native Americans identified the coyote as a trickster, while tales from the African tradition have a spider as trickster.

### Noodlehead tales, drolls, and simpleton tales

The principal character in these stories is an engaging fool. They are popular because they represent the underdog who wins, the good-hearted fool who triumphs. A common theme in noodlehead stories is the simpleton or fool who trades something of value for a worthless object. "Lazy Jack," one of the most famous of these characters, trades a cow for

*"The Tortoise and the Hare" is a famous Aesop fable, one of more than one hundred fables collected in this book.*

some worthless beans in one popular story. Of course, in the end the worthless objects turn out to be valuable—they grow a giant beanstalk.

## Myths

**Myths** *are stories about gods and supernatural beings. Myths explain human origins and events in nature, and the relationships between humans and the supernatural.* Myths occur in all cultures. Perhaps the best-known myths are **pourquoi tales,** *also called "why" stories.* These myths explain why the rabbit has a short tail, why the elephant has a long trunk, and so forth.

## Legends

**Legends** *are closely related to myths, but the main characters are frequently based on actual historical figures, such as religious saints, rather than supernatural beings.* Although usually based in truth about a person, place, or event, legends tend to embellish and embroider the truth in order to showcase a partic-

ular virtue, so that the character's wonderful feats grow more amazing with each telling. For instance, King Arthur and his knights of the Round Table exemplify chivalrous behavior; Joan of Arc exemplifies courage and conviction; Robin Hood and his Merry Men exemplify taking care of the poor. A famous American legend involves George Washington, who refused to lie about chopping down a cherry tree despite the fact that he would be punished for admitting the crime. Other types of legend explain rocks, mountains, and other natural features, as do the Australian writer Oodgeroo's stories about Mother Earth's features as well as her legends about trees (Oodgeroo, 1994).

Published and unpublished legends exist throughout the United States, and local and regional legends are often especially interesting to students. Charles Harry Whedbee collected stories about the North Carolina coast in *Outer Banks Mysteries and Seaside Stories.* One story, "The Gray Man of Hatteras," tells about the Gray Man who appears between Cape Point and the Hatteras Lighthouse every time a hurricane threatens. He appears to be trying to warn the residents to take shelter from the approaching storm and always walks on a particular part of the beach. He never fails to give his warning and is never wrong about the storm. Local people who encounter him believe the Gray Man cares about people and seeks to protect them from the storms.

## Tall tales

Tall tales are based on lies and exaggerations about larger-than-life characters such as Fin M'Coul, John Henry, Mike Fink, Davy Crockett, Johnny Appleseed, and Daniel Boone. Like legends, some of the characters in tall tales actually lived, while others may be a composite of several people; many are entirely fiction. These stories are probably the precursors of the larger-than-life characters in modern novels (Saxby and Winch, 1987) such as *Crocodile Dundee, Pocahontas,* and *Swamp Angel* (Isaacs, 1994).

## Ballads

**Ballads** are essentially *dramatic poems that tell stories handed down from one generation to the next through song.* These narrative poems have marked rhythm and rhyme. They often include passages of dialogue, a chorus or a refrain, and formalized phrases that recur from ballad to ballad. Ballads usually tell stories about heroes, murders, love, tragedies, and feuds. "The Streets of Laredo" is a ballad that tells of a cowboy's exploits (Sutherland and Livingston, 1984). "Stagolee" is an African American hero who is the subject of both ballads and folktales (Lester, 1969). The Australian ballad "Waltzing Matilda," which is popular with American children, tells about life in the Australian bush. Traditional ballads can serve as a good introduction to literature in general and to poetry in specific: ballads introduce children to the themes of great literature and tune their ears to the rhythms of poetry.

## Selecting and Evaluating Traditional Literature

The factors to consider when selecting and evaluating traditional literature are basically the same as for all literature. Some specific guidelines to keep in mind as you add to your collection are:

1. Does the book tell a good story?
2. Does the dust jacket or the foreword identify the book as traditional literature and tell the original, cultural source of the selection? Does the reteller identify the source of the tale?
3. What characteristics of traditional literature does it have? (formulaic beginning or ending, universal setting stated briefly, little or no description, etc.)
4. Does the story have rapid plot development?
5. Are the characters symbolic? Can children relate to them?
6. Is the style simple and direct?
7. Does the story express universal values?

## MODERN FANTASY

The word *fantasy* brings to mind dreamy make-believe—imagination, inventiveness, playfulness, humor, surprise, and the unexpected. All of these describe fantasy, but these words do not fully convey the essence of this genre. Authors of **modern fantasy** are like poets: they *use exquisite language and sensory imagery to create literature that communicates basic human values and feelings.* Charlotte Huck et al. (1987) believe that "fantasy, like poetry, means more than it says.... Underlying most of the great books of fantasy is a metaphorical comment on society today" (p. 344). The form of modern fantasy is extremely varied. It ranges from simple stories of magic to profound and complex stories (Townsend, 1990). Writers use imaginary elements to tell their stories so skillfully that readers willingly suspend disbelief to enter stories and believe for a time that it can happen, characters can create magic, and other worlds do exist. Readers must believe that pigs fly, animals talk, entire villages appear and disappear, and clocks do strike 13.

Many modern fantasies are metaphors of life. For instance, toys and animals like those in *Little Bear* by Else Holmeluna Minarik and *Bedtime for Frances* by Russell Hoban represent children. Stories like these make children feel secure and loved. Dick King-Smith also uses animals to parallel human nature in his books. The pig, dog, and sheep in *Babe, the Gallant Pig* have many human qualities, as do his cats and mice in *Martin's Mice*. His affectionate understanding of the creatures he writes about shows him the qualities to point up and those that are telling parallels with human nature (Townsend, 1990).

Modern fantasy takes for granted not only the physical world and the real world that we see and feel, but also the supernatural world with all sorts of possibilities. Fantasy has special qualities distinguishing it from other genre. It concerns things that cannot happen, places that cannot exist, and people and creatures who do not exist, yet each story has its own self-contained logic that is its own reality. In fantasy, an entirely imaginary land like C. S. Lewis' Narnia can exist; visitors can come from other worlds as in Alexander Key's *Forgotten Door*; and you can wake up in Mary Rodgers's *Freaky Friday* as your own mother. Almost anything can happen in fantasy.

## The Historical Roots of Fantasy

**Modern fantasy** *is rooted in traditional literature. From traditional literature fantasy receives its common*

DICK KING-SMITH
MARTIN'S MICE
Illustrated by Jez Alborough

*A cat with a mouse for a pet? Dick King-Smith has a different view of life.*

themes: *the struggle between good and evil; the importance of kindness and love, basic human values, and perseverance in the face of adversity.* Like the characters in folktales, many fantasies feature characters who are symbols of good, beauty, and wisdom or of ugliness, bad, and evil. The quality of make-believe is shared as well, as are many of their stylistic features. Some authors of modern fantasy make extensive use of the folktale style. For example, Jane Yolen chose this style in *The Girl Who Cried Flowers*, a collection of five tales of magic with a formulaic beginning ("Far to the North where the world is lighted only by softly flickering snow") and a "happily ever after" ending.

Traditional literature communicates universal truth, values, and mores in the ancient oral tradition, while **modern fantasy** *is an art form that communicates the truth of contemporary life.* Both folktales and modern fantasy have elements of magic that are contrary to life as we know it. Traditional literature and modern fantasy are so closely related that children who have experiences with folktales are more likely to appreciate modern fantasy (Yolen, 1981a).

The first author of modern fantasy was Hans Christian Andersen. His stories, written in the early 1800s, were first translated into English in 1846 and were a mixture of folktale adaptations and fantasies that grew out of his own troubled childhood. The Grimm Brothers' tale *The Six Swans* was probably the stimulus for his popular story *The Wild Swans*. *The Ugly Duckling* and *The Steadfast Tin Soldier* are make-believe stories, but they are based on Andersen's experiences. *The Emperor's New Clothes* comments on the falseness he observed in society.

George MacDonald is another early writer of fantasy. *At the Back of the North Wind*, published in 1871, was one of the foundations of modern fantasy. *The Golden Key* and *The Light Princess* have been interpreted by various illustrators including the contemporary Maurice Sendak. Modern writers of fantasy build on folktales and on the work of authors such as these. Among the most popular stories of all time are fantasies such as *Charlotte's Web* by E. B. White, *Winnie the Pooh* by A. A. Milne, *A Wrinkle in Time* by Madeleine L'Engle, *A Bear Called Paddington* by Michael Bond, *Charlie and the Chocolate Factory* by Roald Dahl, and *The Wizard of Oz* by Frank Baum.

## Children and Fantasy

Fantasy stretches the imagination and encourages dreams, helping children know they can do anything. It stimulates creative thinking and problem-solving abilities. Fantasy is important in children's lives and in their classrooms because it furnishes new ways of looking at life and the problems of life (Britton, 1977). In fantasy, children learn about good and evil, peace and conflict. They develop more open-minded attitudes that enable them to understand other peoples' perspectives. The student in the boxed vignette is no different from many others who think fantasy is not for them. Perhaps they realize that it is a demanding genre or they lack experience with it. Fantasy, of all the genres of writing for children, offers the greatest challenge and the greatest rewards to both readers and writers (Smith, 1987). Through fantasy children verify

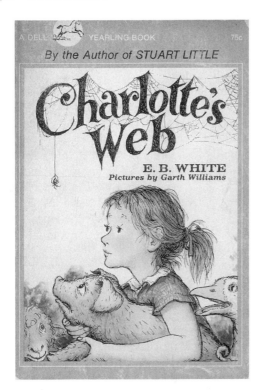

*Charlotte's Web is a classic fantasy and provides some children their first acquaintance with the loss of something loved.*

The only sounds in James Livingston's sixth-grade classroom were the rustles of pages turning. Sustained silent reading (SSR) had this effect on his students: they really enjoyed reading, he thought. When he called time, all of the students put their books away and pulled out their notebooks—except Jared, who continued to read. Finally Mr. Livingston tapped him on the shoulder.

"Time to stop."

"But I don't want to stop! This is the best book I ever read in my whole life!" Jared said.

"What're you reading?"

*"A Wrinkle in Time."*

"What do you like about it?" Mr. Livingston asked.

"It's so real, I feel like I'm there! They feel the same way I would if I were in the story," Jared answered. "I can't really explain—it's so real, but I know it's make-believe. I never liked make-believe before. I just read this book because Chris said it was really good. I didn't know it wasn't real."

"I'm glad you discovered how good fantasy is," Mr. Livingston said.

"It seems like it's about good and evil. Has she written any other books like this one?"

"You're in luck! *A Wrinkle in Time* is the first book in a trilogy. The second book is *A Wind in the Door* and the third one is *A Swiftly Tilting Planet.* She has some other books that I think you'll like too."

their understanding of the external world they share with others: imagination is an important dimension of fantasy and it helps children construct a coherent picture of their immediate world (Smith, 1987). Fantasy also gives children a way of examining their inner world and comparing it with the inner worlds of others (Britton, 1977). Children vary in imaginative ability, however. Some take pleasure in the ingenuity of fine fantasy, while others read fantasy simply because it tells a good story. Some children reject fantasy because it is not real. Gifted children choose to read fantasy more frequently than children who are not gifted (Swanton, 1984). A taste for fantasy must be cultivated in most children.

Activities such as reading aloud from fine fantasy develops children's appreciation for this genre; choose fantasies that are likely to have the broadest appeal and are a good "read." William Steig's *Sylvester and the Magic Pebble* is a wonderful fantasy for the younger set. In this book, Sylvester, a don-

key, finds a magic pebble that enables him to make wishes that come true. When he wishes to become a boulder to escape a fierce lion, he cannot hold the magic pebble to wish himself back. His family thinks he is lost until the day they have a picnic and find the magic pebble he dropped. His parents, who are mourning for Sylvester, wish for him to return as they are holding the magic pebble—and he does.

Young children enjoy listening to *The Fortune-Tellers* by Lloyd Alexander and looking at vivid, detailed illustrations. In this picture book, the author and illustrator have created an imaginary

*The artist has filled her brilliant illustrations of the country of Cameroon with the bountiful humor and wisdom of the West African people.*

world peopled by witty characters. One of these, the fortune-teller, gives interesting prophesies. His wisdom is illustrated in his forecast of wealth for a man if he earns large sums of money and of marriage to a true love for another if the man finds his true love and she agrees to marry him. In Deborah and James Howe's *Bunnicula*, a read-aloud fantasy for third or fourth grade, a bunny is found in a movie theater with a message written in a Transylvanian language attached to his neck. After Bunnicula arrives, the vegetables in the house begin to appear drained of their juices. The plot thickens when Chester the cat (who is well read) concludes that Bunnicula is a vampire and sets out to protect the family from vampire attack. The entire story is written from the point of view of the dog, Harold.

Readers in fifth and sixth grade enjoy the originality of plot and character in the several short stories included in William J. Brooke's *Untold Tales*. "A Prince in the Throat" is a clever play on traditions in which a queen yearns for the days when her husband was a modest frog. Science fiction readers find "Into the Computer" an entertaining and challenging story. Middle-grade readers who enjoy ghost stories especially enjoy Patricia McKissack's *The Dark-Thirty: Southern Tales of the Supernatural*. These stories stir the imagination but are not so gruesome as to make children fearful.

## The Nature of Fantasy

The main function of fantasy, like that of fairy tales, is to express imaginative experiences and insights into the human condition. Two things set excellent fantasy apart from other genre. First, the author must have a strongly realized personal vision, a perspective or belief about the meaning, significance, symbolism, allegory, a moral, message, or lesson in the fantasy, which is the second aspect (Langton, 1977). For instance, L'Engle addresses the theological meaning of the role of love in the conflict between good and evil in *A Wrinkle in Time*. Despite this moral or lesson, the author must avoid moral pronouncements—children do not tolerate this any better than do adults. Instead, these truths must emerge naturally from the story, providing insights about the human condition without preaching (Smith, 1987).

"The best stories are like extended lyrical images of unchanging human predicaments": life and death, love and hate, good and evil, courage and despair (Cook, 1969, p. 2). These basics of human existence are dramatized in fantasy. Fantasy must communicate a sense of truth, as well as telling us something about ourselves and our world. For example, in *The Forgotten Door* by Alexander Key, readers confront their fear of the unknown and different. A truth clothed in the fantastic is often easier to understand and accept than a baldly stated fact.

The images, ideas, and possibilities in fantasy must, however, remain essentially true to life and good and evil; the fantasy must maintain a consistent logic throughout to allow readers to believe that magic and impossible happenings are plausible. Obviously, fantasy always includes at least one element of the impossible, one element that goes against the laws of the physical universe, as we currently understand them (Alexander, 1992); it concerns things that cannot really happen, people or creatures that do not really exist. Nevertheless, each story must have its own self-contained logic that creates its own reality. Cameron (1983) believes that authors of fantasy must establish a premise and an inner logic in their stories. They need to draw boundary lines outside which the fantasy may not wander. For example, in *Charlotte's Web* the animals talk among themselves, but not to the human beings. White created this logic at the outset of the story, and it is never violated. Although the author is free to create any specific boundaries or logic, writers of fantasy must be hard-headed realists. "What appears gossamer is, underneath, solid as prestressed concrete. Once committed to his imaginary kingdom, the writer is not a monarch but a subject" (Alexander, 1965, p. 143).

## Elements of Fantasy

Like traditional literature, authors of fantasy use all of the normal stylistic devices to make readers believe in fantasy. They skillfully craft language that will cause readers to suspend their disbelief and enjoy fantasy, inviting readers to enter their fanciful worlds.

### Characters

Well-rounded, believable characters are essential in fantasy. To be believable they must be multidimensional characters who grow and develop through their experiences in the story. Meg, the protagonist in *A Wrinkle in Time*, is such a character. She is fearless at times and falters at other times; nevertheless, she is courageous and determined to find her father at any cost. Meg learns lessons, changes, and develops her character throughout the book.

Readers come to know characters' personalities through their dialect, vocabulary, and speech rhythms. For instance, in *Eva*, Peter Dickinson creates much of the principal character's personality by revealing her thoughts. Eva awakens from a coma induced by an accident thinking, "Waking . . . Strange . . . Dream about trees? Oh, come back! Come . . . Lost . . . . But so strange . . . . Relief and joy in the voice not but something else still, underneath . . . . Oh, darling, said Mom's voice, farther away now. There was something in it—had been all along, in spite of the happiness in the words. A difficulty, a sense of effort" (p. 35). Dickinson creates a mood through what is *not* said. Eva senses that something is not normal long before she or the readers realize exactly what has happened: Eva survived the accident because her brain was placed in the body of a chimpanzee. After Eva realizes that she is living in a chimpanzee's body, she thinks,

*Eva wakes up from a coma and finds that she is forced to live a wholly new kind of life.*

"Okay, it *was* better than dying, but that wasn't enough. You had to awaken and open your eyes and see your new face and like what you saw. You had to make the human greeting and the chimp greeting and mean them" (p. 31).

The principal character in a fantasy establishes the logic of the fantasy and helps readers enter into the make-believe by expressing a confidence and belief in the unbelievable events and characters. Eva recognizes her dilemma and suffers as she becomes more aware and must adjust to her situation. The fact that she is living in a chimpanzee's body is logical because her father is a researcher who studies them. In fact, Eva grew up with Kelly, the chimpanzee in whose body her brain was placed. Both the masterful characterization and Eva's reactions to the situation make readers believe.

Another technique (in direct contrast to the previous one) authors use to entice readers into accepting make-believe is through characters who

*Tom discovers more excitement than he
could have imagined in this British fantasy.*

refuse to believe in fantasy, despite the fact that they may be fantasies themselves or at least taking part in a fantasy. In *Tom's Midnight Garden* by Philippa Pearce, strange events that defy the laws of time take place: when a clock strikes 13, a garden appears with a young girl in it. Tom and the girl play together and become friends, but Tom himself is puzzled by the appearance of the garden and the girl. This aspect of the fantasy convinces readers to suspend their disbelief, as Tom does, until the mystery unfolds.

## Setting

Detailed settings make readers believe in fantasy. The author's use of sensory imagery helps readers hear, smell, and taste the sounds, odors, and tastes of the imaginary place. In *Babe, the Gallant Pig*, King-Smith's detailed descriptions of the farm animals and their habits make readers believe that indeed a pig could herd sheep and

actually participate in dog trials. E. B. White uses sensory imagery in his descriptions of the barn in which Charlotte and Wilbur lived. Readers who are well acquainted with farms can smell the barn when reading about it in *Charlotte's Web*. Peter Dickinson invites readers to believe in his stories by describing unusual characters, places, and events in detail. His skill is illustrated in *A Box of Nothing*:

> It took a whole day for the Burra's green arm to come to life again. In the meanwhile it made do with a monkey arm, which wasn't as useful. The table set firm at the same time, and the fridge out on the slope had "gone fossil" a little earlier. By then James was almost used to eating food that cooked itself and watching a TV that switched itself off and on when it felt like it and sleeping on a living bed. The bed was especially good. It snuggled around you when you got into it, and the blankets tucked themselves around

your spine to keep the drafts out, and in the morning they folded themselves tidy while you were having breakfast.

## Plot

Characters and setting must be brought together in an original plot to create excellent fantasy, as Natalie Babbitt does in *Tuck Everlasting*. The central characters drink at a secret spring, which allows anyone who drinks from it to live forever; they befriend Winnie, a girl of 11. The carefully drawn characters are as convincing as the descriptions of an unreal world in this tightly wound novel.

One of the most common strategies that authors use for making a fantastic plot believable is starting the story in reality and gradually moving into fantasy. Readers may not even realize the book is fantasy until the second or third chapter. Both *Charlotte's Web* and *A Wrinkle in Time* use this technique to draw the reader into the plot.

Authors sometimes choose to convince us to believe in their fantasy by having characters move back and forth between their real environment and the make-believe environment. In *Fog Magic*, Julia Sauer creates a character who lives in a normal home but visits a make-believe village, Blue Cove, when it is foggy. Philippa Pearce also uses this strategy effectively in *Tom's Midnight Garden*. Tom lives in a present-day house, but he visits in a long-ago garden and plays with an imaginary character when the old hall clock strikes 13. On the clock's face is the motto "Time No More" and indeed the natural laws of time are defied in this splendid fantasy. It is only as he is leaving to return home that Tom realizes his friend, Hatty, grew up to be the strange old lady upstairs.

This technique is useful in books for younger children as well. Chris Van Allsburg begins the picture book *Jumanji* in a realistic setting. The fantasy starts when the children begin playing a game that cannot be stopped before the entire game is completed. In this potentially dangerous game many unbelievable events seem real as a hippopotamus crashes through the living room and a python slithers onto the mantel.

Authors must make their plots credible and consistent, retaining their inner logic, if readers are to believe in their fantasy. George Selden achieves this in the imaginative plot of *The Cricket in Times Square*, in which insects and animals work together to solve problems. When Chester the cricket arrives in Times Square, Tucker the mouse and Harry the cat join forces to help him settle into the urban environment. Chester and the animals talk among themselves, but they do not converse with the humans. The characters stay within the logical boundaries created at the outset and they solve problems with their own powers: Chester rubs his back legs together to generate the music for his concert. The setting is described in great detail to create a realistic context for the story.

## Theme

Theme is a significant aspect of fantasy. Universal themes such as wishes, dreams, the struggle between good and evil, and the importance of love are most common in modern fantasy. Symbolism is often used to help further the theme of a fantasy. In *Tuck Everlasting*, Babbitt uses Ferris wheels and other wheels in the story as symbols of the cycle of the seasons and of life and death. The point of the symbolism is that the hub of a wheel is a fixed point that is best left undisturbed, and helps establish Babbitt's major theme: *everlasting life can be a burden.*

## Style

The language authors use, one of the major components of style, is especially important in fantasy because authors must find a way to tell about places, things, and people that do not exist in such a way that readers will see it in their imagination much as authors see it in their own. William Steig's elegant language easily encompasses this goal. His animal fantasy *The Amazing Bone* tells about Pearl, a "succulent" pig, who "dawdled" on the way home from school and seemed "destined" to become dinner for a fox. Steig's wonderful use of language, however, always stays within the logic of his story. Pearl may talk to amazing bones, but she always remains a pig. Steig is not the only author noted for superb language styling. C. S. Lewis, Lloyd Alexander, Susan Cooper, John Christopher, and many others exhibit exceptional ability in expressing fantastic ideas.

The point of view, determined by the person telling the story, is in fantasy as in other literature,

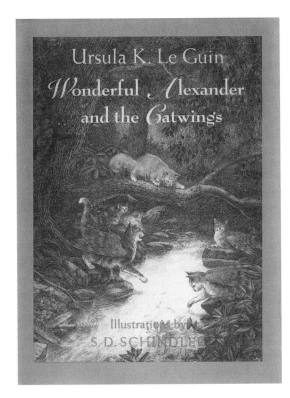

*With well-observed feline detail, the author introduces readers to the Catwings family, who both purr and fly.*

another aspect of the style. In *The Space Ship Under the Apple Tree*, Louis Slobodkin writes from the point of view of Eddie, struggling to understand a Martian and desperately attempting to communicate with his deaf grandmother. Mary Norton tells *The Borrowers* from the point of view of tiny people called Borrowers. Norton must look at the world from the perspective of tiny persons and consider the dangers they would face in a human-sized world. A 12-year-old girl who travels back 100 years in time narrates *The Root Cellar*, necessitating that the author, Janet Lunn, research how people lived at that time, what they ate, their clothing, the language used, and the issues of the day, which in this instance included the Civil War. In some stories, the point of view switches from one character to another or from a character to an omniscient storyteller. In *Wonderful Alexander and the Catwings*, Ursula K. LeGuin uses an omniscient point of view to tell about kittens who are born with wings that permit them to escape the slums of a city. The point of view changes when they go to the country and find children who will cherish them.

## Types of Fantasy

All forms of fantasy are important in children's lives. Classroom experiences with fantasy are essential because they educate children to the importance of imagination in their lives. Two forms of modern fantasy are: high fantasy and science fiction.

### High fantasy

**High fantasy** *is a complex, philosophical form of literature that focuses on themes such as the conflict between good and evil.* The complexity and abstractness of high fantasy make it most popular with a middle-school audience. Creators of fantasy write of myth and legend, of science and technology, and of human life as it is lived, might be lived, and ought to be lived (LeGuin, 1979). The characters in high fantasy are often symbolic of good people who battle evil, as Meg does in *A Wrinkle in Time*, or as C. S. Lewis's characters do in "The Chronicles of Narnia" series. The four principal characters enter Narnia, a strange new world, through an old wardrobe in the first book, *The Lion, the Witch, and the Wardrobe*. In the land of Narnia, the four children become kings and queens who are entangled in an endless battle between good and evil. After living in Narnia for many years, they return to their own world and discover they have not been missed because time is calculated differently in Narnia.

The theme of Jackie Koller's *The Dragonling* is peace. At the beginning of the story, Darek hopes to slay a dragon, but instead he finds a baby dragon in the pouch of a dragon his brother killed. This discovery leads him to see the dragons in a new light and changes his attitude. In this high fantasy, the protagonist's goal changes and he strives to make peace between his people and the surviving dragons.

### Science fiction

**Science fiction stories** *are based on scientific advancements and imagined technology.* The detailed descriptions of the technology created by the author help readers suspend their disbelief. In science fiction, the story builds around events and problems that would not have happened at all without the scientific content (Gunn, 1975). Sylvia Engdahl also wrote about rebuilding a life in *Beyond the Tomorrow Mountains*, in which the protagonist escapes an earth doomed to destruction to create a new life in a different world. Alfred Slote's *My Robot Buddy* is set in a future where robots are an everyday part of life, but so are robotnappers. The protagonist receives a robot friend for his birthday who is quickly robotnapped. The police pursue the criminals in solar-powered vehicles.

There is some crossover between high fantasy and science fiction: much, although not all, science fiction is also high fantasy. Vivian Alcock's *The Monster Garden* is a science fiction story that is also high fantasy. In this story, matter produced in a lab grows into a monster that is kind-hearted and wise. But, Monny the monster has to go away because she is different, therefore unacceptable to people in the community.

## Selecting Fantasy

When selecting fantasy for your classroom consider the following factors in addition to the guidelines for all literature.

1. Does it tell a good story?
2. What are the elements of fantasy in this story? (setting, magic powers, time, etc.)
3. How is this story different from the real world?
4. How has the author made the story believable?
5. What is the theme of this fantasy?

# CLASSROOM ACTIVITIES TO ENHANCE MAKE-BELIEVE

## Activities for Traditional Literature

Traditional stories are quite compatible with classroom activities and teaching. Their brevity, simplicity, and directness make them particularly well suited to teaching children the elements and structures of literature. Furthermore, their oral quality and universal appeal make superior materials for learning activities (see Activities 7.1–7.18 on pages 196 through 204).

ACTIVITIES

## 7.1 Chanting

Folktales are ideal vehicles for teaching students to chant refrains. *The Little Red Hen* works well for this activity because it has repetitive events and repeated, rhythmic phrases. Write the repeated phrases on the chalkboard or on charts and encourage the children to join in on repeated parts as you read aloud. Show them the charts that will guide their part of the activity. Read the story with the children's assistance several times. Vary this activity by having them prepare to read the story and the other children join in on the refrain.

## 7.2 Mapping

Mapping is a good activity for developing understanding, even if the students will not be telling a story. This activity summarizes and organizes students' understanding of stories. You may have the students create their own maps using the model given in Figure 7.4.

## 7.3  Storytelling

Storytelling, a natural activity to use with traditional literature, develops children's oral language and communication.

1. Let the children choose stories. Tell them to choose ones that they especially enjoy.

2. Have them learn their stories, but not memorize them. Tell them to be concerned with the outline of the story initially. After identifying the bare bones, they can list them, map them, or outline them with drawings. A story map is a graphic display showing the organization of events and ideas in the story (see Figure 7.4).

3. After the students have a map or plan for their stories, group them in pairs so that the pairs can tell their stories to each other from the map or plan.

4. Once they can remember their story outlines, ask them to elaborate on their storytelling using these techniques:

   a. Visualize the setting, the people, and the action. Think about what you would see, hear, and feel if you were there. Choose words that will make the story more vivid so that your listeners can visualize it as you do. Retell the story with the more vivid language.

   b. Think of ways that you can make the story more exciting for the audience and get them more involved.

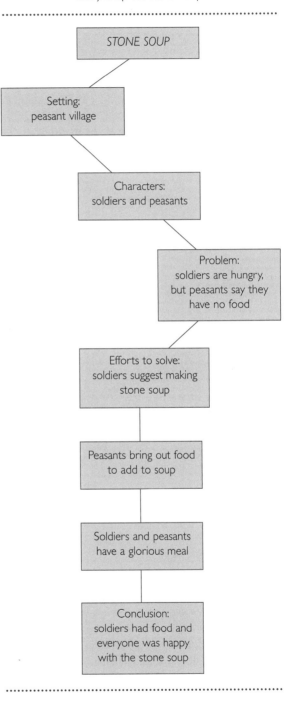

**FIGURE 7.4**

Story map for *Stone Soup*.

STONE SOUP

Setting: peasant village

Characters: soldiers and peasants

Problem: soldiers are hungry, but peasants say they have no food

Efforts to solve: soldiers suggest making stone soup

Peasants bring out food to add to soup

Soldiers and peasants have a glorious meal

Conclusion: soldiers had food and everyone was happy with the stone soup

## 7.4 Composing folktales

Students can compose their own folktales. This activity is a variation of one suggested by Livo and Rietz (1987). Write setting, character, and problem or conflict ideas on slips of paper, and put each in a separate pile (all the settings together, all the characters together, etc.). Group students into pairs or trios and let each group draw one idea from each pile of slips, then develop a spontaneous story using the setting, characters, and problem or conflict provided. Once they are used to working this way, the activity can be varied by giving the students one slip of paper only so that they have just part of the story and must build the rest of it. On the slips of paper you might write such ideas as:

- Characters: mean witch, spider, trickster rabbit, good fairy
- Setting: enchanted forest, a peasant hut, a giant toadstool, a castle
- Problem: can't break evil witch's spell, lost in a forest, can't find family, hungry

## 7.5 Prediction

Folktales are quite predictable, so anticipation and prediction are good ways to involve children with the stories. Select a story such as *Henny Penny* or *The Three Billy Goats Gruff* by Paul Galdone, *Who's in Rabbit's House* by Verna Aardema, or *Fin M'Coul* by Tomie dePaola. Introduce the story to the children. Ask them to predict what the story will be about from the title and the book cover. Then read the story aloud, stopping at various points in the story to ask them to predict what will happen next. After they predict, tell them to listen to determine whether their predictions were correct. In *The Little Red Hen* you might stop for predictions after each of these points in the story:

a. The hen asks for help planting the wheat.
b. The hen asks for help watering the wheat and pulling the weeds.
c. The hen asks for help cutting the ripe wheat.
d. The hen asks someone to take the wheat to be ground into flour.
e. The hen asks for help making the wheat into bread.
f. The hen asks for help eating the bread.

A variation of this activity might be to have the children write down their predictions and then discuss them after the story is completed.

## 7.6 Illustrating folktales

Children enjoy creating their own illustrations for their favorite folktales. Many folktales have variants that have been illustrated in many different ways, often resulting in a reinterpretation of the tale. Prepare them for this activity by presenting several picture-book versions of the same folktale (see Figure 7.5 for a sample list). After the students examine the tales, ask them to identify the media, style, colors, and lines used to illustrate the various tales and to think about the various illustrators' reasons for choosing these various styles. (See Chapter Five for more discussion of the elements of pictures.) Give them copies of the text for a traditional story and have them think about the colors, style, media, and lines they will use in illustrating this tale and why they choose them before proceeding to create the illustrations. They may like to add the text to their illustrations and bind the stories to make their own books.

## FIGURE 7.5

Illustrated folktales to compare.

| | |
|---|---|
| Brer Rabbit | *The Tales of Uncle Remus: The Adventures of Brer Rabbit* by Julius Lester, illustrated by Jerry Pickney |
| | *The People Could Fly: American Black Folktales* by Virginia Hamilton, illustrated by Leo and Diane Dillon |
| The Three Billy Goats Gruff | *The Three Billy Goats Gruff* by Peter Asbjornsen, illustrated by Marcia Brown |
| | *The Three Billy Goats Gruff* by Paul Galdone |
| Jack and the Beanstalk | *Jim and the Beanstalk* by Raymond Briggs |
| | *Jack and the Beanstalk* by Tony Ross |
| | *Jack and the Bean Tree* by Gail E. Haley |
| Cinderella | *Yeh-Shen* by Louie Ai-Ling |
| | *Cinderella* by Charles Perrault, illustrated by Errol Le Cain |
| | *Cinderella* by Charles Perrault, illustrated by Marcia Brown |
| | *Cinderella* by the Brothers Grimm, illustrated by Nonny Hogrogian |
| | *Cinderella* by Paul Galdone |

## 7.7 Writing folktales

Folktales are exceptional models for writing. Study of folktales can teach story parts (beginning, middle, end), story form, and story structure as well as the elements of story grammar: setting, problem, actions, and resolution. Folktales also provide models of story content. Through studying legends, myths, animals tales, fairy tales, and other folktales, students can learn to understand and to write them.

Introduce each type of folktale to the students (fables, pourquoi, trickster tales, legend, myths, etc.) and give examples of each. Then have the students identify additional examples of each type, specifying the characteristics that helped them identify the various types of folktales. Ways of applying this activity to specific types of folktales are listed below.

1. Have the students identify cumulative stories, structured around repetition: *Bringing the Rain to Kapiti Plain* by Verna Aardema, *The Gingerbread Boy* by Paul Galdone, and *The House That Jack Built* by Janet Stevens are several examples. Read or have the students read the tales aloud then discuss the cumulative aspects of the stories. Write the repeated portions on the chalkboard or charts. They may want to act out the repeated lines. Have them identify these elements of cumulative stories:

- The stories are short.
- The stories have a strong rhythmic pattern.
- The story events are in a logical order and related to the preceding events.
- All of the story events are repeated and accumulated until a surprise ending is reached.

Once the structure of cumulative stories has been learned, the children may write their own cumulative tales, conforming to the story elements identified above. This activity is a variation of one suggested by Kennedy and Spangler (1987).

2. A journey story is one in which characters set out to travel to a specific place and have adventures along the way. *The Bremen Town Musicians* by Donna Diamond and *The Fat Cat* by Jack Kent are examples of this story type. Use the pattern developed in the preceding activity as a basis for having children write journey stories. Have them identify these elements of cumulative stories: In journey stories a character or characters go on a journey far from home, and they mature as a result of their experiences. They may also draw a line that illustrates the route taken on the journey (Kennedy and Spangler, 1987).

3. Fables are especially easy to write because they are short and moralistic. After reading fables such as *Aesop's Fables* by Heidi Holder, *Fables* by Arnold Lobel, or *Three Fox Fables* by Paul Galdone, children may write their own fables. Have them identify these elements of fables:

- Fables contain a moral or lesson.
- Fables have animals as the main characters.
- The animals act like a humans.
- Fables are short with fast action.

- The last line of the story contains the moral.

4. Wishing stories are common in traditional literature. One of the most popular is *The Fisherman and His Wife*. Other wish stories teachers might choose to use in the classroom are *The Rainbow-Colored Horse* by Pura Belpre and *Three Wishes* by Paul Galdone. Have the students identify these elements of wishing stories: wishing stories involve characters who have wishes they misuse.

## 7.8 Comparing variant folktales

A large number of variants exist for many popular tales, often as many as 900 different interpretations of a single tale. (For example, see the list of Noah and the Flood variations at end of the Recommended Children's Books section at the end of this chapter.) Variants can be compared by noting the points of similarity and difference in the various aspects of the story structure (setting, character, problem, resolution, conclusion) and the way they are written or illustrated.

Read variants of a folktale aloud, and let students individually prepare charts to compare them, like the one shown in Table 7.2. Other elements that can be compared are the differences in language in folktales from different countries, the differences in formulaic beginnings and endings, and the themes. Another possibility is comparing the text, illustrations, and cultural characteristics in the variants.

### TABLE 7.2

Comparison chart for folktale variants.

| Author/ illustrator | Main character | Setting | Other characters | Beginning | Problem | Ending |
|---|---|---|---|---|---|---|
| Jakob and Wilhelm Grimm Nonny Hogrogian Greenwillow, 1981 | Cinderella | Germany | Stepmother Doves Hazel tree | Invitation to ball | Cinderella mistreated | Marries prince |
| Marcia Brown Scribner's, 1954 | Little glass slipper | France | Stepmother Stepsisters | Invitation to ball | Cinderella mistreated | Marries prince |
| | | | | | | |
| | | | | | | |

## 7.9 Collecting regional folktales

Children enjoy collecting legends and stories related to the region in which they live. They can do this through library study, talking with and listening to storytellers, or asking older people in the community if they know about any local stories. As they collect the stories, they may create a class or school book recording the region's stories. They may want to dramatize these stories to entertain and publicize their books. Activities such as this can build students' interest in social studies and science as well as in literature and language.

## 7.10 Comparing written and film versions of folktales

A number of traditional stories have been made into films. Children will enjoy watching the film as a class after having heard or read the book version. Class discussion after viewing the film can focus on questions such as:

- What scenes were in the book that were not in the film?
- Why did the filmmaker omit these scenes?
- Were the characters the same in the book and the film?
- How did the colors and art style vary between the two media?
- Describe the overall differences between the two versions.
- Why did these differences occur?
- How would they have filmed the story?

If a camcorder is available, they can film their own version of the story.

## 7.11 Dramatizing folktales

Traditional stories are easy to dramatize. The class can be divided into groups and each group can dramatize a different tale using improvisation, puppets, pantomime, reader's theater, or another forum to present the stories.

## 7.12 Responding with art

Art activities are an excellent medium for responding to traditional literature. Students can make papier-mâché masks, objects representing magic objects in the stories, dioramas, posters, and pictures related to their stories.

## 7.13 Studying cultures

Students in the upper elementary grades can discuss the aspects of culture that appear in traditional stories (values, manners, beliefs, traditions, holidays, character roles). This activity can easily be integrated with social studies lessons.

### Activities for Fantasy

More than other genre, fantasy needs to be introduced and read aloud. Introductions explain the context of the story, encourage listeners to predict story events, and prompt listeners to engage with and respond to the story. Key characters, themes, and elements may be included in an introduction. Fantasy often includes many unknown or unusual words that students need help understanding. Context clues are especially helpful when reading fantasy as the meaning of invented or unusual words is usually revealed in the text. For instance, *tesseract,* a made-up word, is defined within the story in *A Wrinkle in Time.*

## 7.14 Reading journals

Reading journals are important vehicles to facilitate children's response to fantasy and other genre as well. At the close of each reading session, the students summarize and respond to the reading completed that day by writing in their journals. In addition to writing about what they read and responding to the reading, they should include any questions they have for subsequent discussions and identify words and phrases that are new to them or that need further exploration. Reading journals can be used during discussions to refresh their memory.

## 7.15 Exploring fantasy through the arts

Sensory imagery is a prominent aspect of fantasy and many children respond well to sensory imagery, making the arts an important element in exploring fantasy. Children may draw or paint their own interpretation of the settings and characters they read about. They may reinterpret stories or create illustrations where none exist in the original story. Children may choose mood music that reflects their interpretation of the story mood; musical students may even want to write their own score for a story.

## 7.16 Thematic units

Thematic units also develop children's response to fantasy. A thematic unit may explore the **fantastic elements** *such as time travel, miniature worlds, futuristic settings, and other strange happenings.* The Recommended Children's Books section at the end of this chapter supplies some titles that could be used in this kind of thematic unit. Through comparing the plot, theme, characterization, setting, and style students achieve a greater understanding and appreciation for fantasy. Other units may be developed around books with themes of peace, good versus evil, or other common ideas in fantasy. Group or class charts can compare thematic development in different works.

## 7.17 Writing fantasy

Authors create detailed descriptions in fantasy because they are picturing nonexistent things. This detailed writing can serve as a model for students who want to create their own fantasies. When writing fantasy, help children understand that they must establish a framework or a set of rules that cannot be broken by the magic in their story. Refer to the Lloyd Alexander (1965) article "The Flat-Heeled Muse."

## 7.18 Discussion

Class discussion of fantasy is important to building children's understanding and response. Eight or nine students is an excellent size group to encourage active participation when they have read the same book. Instead of leading the discussion, the teacher may be a group member and let the students take turns starting the discussion, using significant questions such as *What do you think?* and *Why do you think this?* The students may have enough questions in their journals to stimulate the discussion or may need help in coming up with good open-ended discussion questions such as:

- What do you predict will happen next in the story?

- What did you learn about the characters, setting, and other parts of the story in today's reading?
- What experiences of your own did you remember in relation to today's reading?
- What other books could you compare this one to?

Another approach is for students to complete individually discussion webs such as the one shown in Figure 7.6.

### FIGURE 7.6

Example of a discussion web.

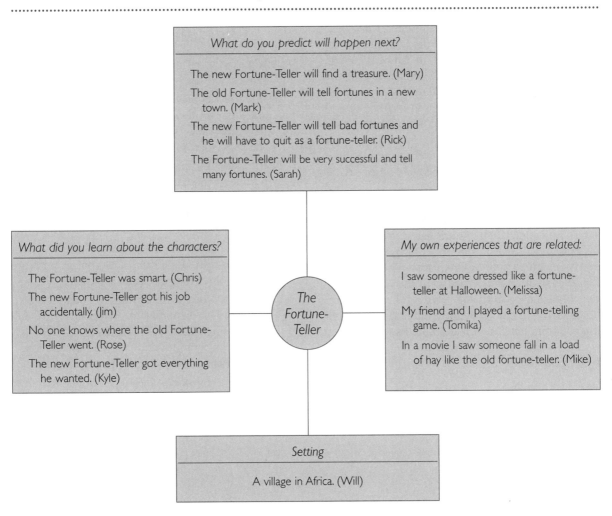

**What do you predict will happen next?**

The new Fortune-Teller will find a treasure. (Mary)

The old Fortune-Teller will tell fortunes in a new town. (Mark)

The new Fortune-Teller will tell bad fortunes and he will have to quit as a fortune-teller. (Rick)

The Fortune-Teller will be very successful and tell many fortunes. (Sarah)

**What did you learn about the characters?**

The Fortune-Teller was smart. (Chris)

The new Fortune-Teller got his job accidentally. (Jim)

No one knows where the old Fortune-Teller went. (Rose)

The new Fortune-Teller got everything he wanted. (Kyle)

*The Fortune-Teller*

**My own experiences that are related:**

I saw someone dressed like a fortune-teller at Halloween. (Melissa)

My friend and I played a fortune-telling game. (Tomika)

In a movie I saw someone fall in a load of hay like the old fortune-teller. (Mike)

**Setting**

A village in Africa. (Will)

## SUMMARY

Both traditional literature and modern fantasy are make-believe. Both are important in children's lives as well as adult lives. For young and old they serve the function of play, dreaming, and imagining better worlds and solutions to problems. Lloyd Alexander shares his view of this genre: "Fantasy touches our deepest feelings, and in so doing, it speaks to the best and most hopeful parts of ourselves. It can help us learn the most fundamental skill of all—how to be human" (1965, p. 43).

Traditional literature is based on the oral tradition. The stories, ballads, and tales in this genre are descendants of the original oral stories, created by storytellers around campfires long ago. These stories have traveled all over the world from storyteller to storyteller, teaching listeners about life and about people. The favorites of the past continue to be popular today. The characters, settings, and events in folktales are symbolic and they differ from other forms of fiction in that they teach more direct lessons. Other forms of literature develop themes more subtly, but even the more direct teachings of folktales must avoid preachy-teachy stories.

Modern fantasy is make-believe set in more recent times. It usually has more developed characters and plots than traditional stories, but the make-believe is still developed through magic events, characters, time, and places. The themes of fantasy are often concerned with the age-old battle between good and evil. The abstract, imaginative nature of fantasy educates children's imagination, but children are more likely to appreciate it when teachers introduce the stories and read them aloud.

## THOUGHT QUESTIONS

1. How are fantasy and traditional literature alike?
2. How do fantasy and traditional literature differ?
3. What are the major characteristics of high fantasy?
4. Why is traditional literature so popular?
5. Why is it important for teachers to motivate children to read fantasy?
6. How does traditional literature relate to culture?

## ENRICHMENT ACTIVITIES

1. Identify ways to motivate children to read fantasy.
2. Interview children at various grade levels and ask them to identify the books of fantasy they have enjoyed. Ask them what they like about the particular books they enjoy?
3. Interview teachers—ask them to identify the number of fantasies they read in one year to their class and the number of traditional literature stories they read.
4. Read a fantasy to a group of children or a class and conduct a discussion following the read-aloud session. Tape the discussion, so you can analyze the strengths and weaknesses.
5. Students who are interning in a school classroom may experiment with having the students or a group of students keep a reading journal for a month and analyze how the journal influences their reading response.
6. Create a bibliography of fantasies for one grade level.
7. Identify various versions of a single folktale that students could compare in a classroom.

# RECOMMENDED CHILDREN'S BOOKS

This literature section is the same as that in other chapters, except that at the end of the main list there is a "Specialized Children's Literature Lists" section.

Aardema, Verna. (1981). *Bringing the Rain to Kapiti Plain.* Illustrated by Beatriz Vidal. New York: Dial. (1–3)

An African cumulative tale, this book describes a delightful day of rain.

————. (1977). *Who's in Rabbit's House?* Illustrated by Leo and Diane Dillon. New York: Dial. (2–4)

This traditional story tells how rabbit and his friends save rabbit's house.

Alcock, Vivian. (1988). *The Monster Garden.* New York: Delacorte. (4–6)

Using a sample from one of her father's experiments in genetic engineering, Frankie creates a baby monster that grows at an alarming rate. She must care for the monster while keeping it secret so her father won't take the monster away from her.

Alexander, Lloyd. (1992). *The Fortune-Tellers.* Illustrated by Trina Schart Hyman. New York: Dutton. (K–5)

This picture book has rich, detailed illustrations. Readers have the opportunity to experience a new world peopled with witty children, women, and men. The fortune-teller prophesies that one man will be rich if he earns large sums of money. His other advice is equally edifying.

————. (1964). *The Book of Three.* New York: Dutton. (5–7)

This is the first of the five-book Prydain cycle. Taran the Assistant Pig-Keeper, the hero of the cycle, is introduced in this book. The major theme of this book and the others in the series is the battle against evil. The other books in order are *The Black Cauldron, The Castle of Llyr, Taran Wanderer,* and *The High King.*

Andersen, Hans Christian. (1992). *The Steadfast Tin Soldier.* Illustrated by Fred Marcellini. New York: HarperCollins. (K–3)

This is a story of a tin soldier's love for a paper doll and his courage in reaching her.

————. (1991). *Thumbelina.* New York: Putnam. (K–3)

Tiny Thumbelina has many adventures.

————. (1990). *The Ugly Duckling.* Illustrated by Troy Howell. New York: Putnam (all ages)

In this story an ugly duckling becomes a swan.

————. (1986). *The Emperor's New Clothes.* Illustrated by Dorothee Dunlze. New York: North South Books. (2–5)

A little boy points out that the king does not have wonderful new clothing, he has no clothing.

Asbjornsen, Peter Christian. (1957). *The Three Billy Goats Gruff.* Illustrated by Marcia Brown. San Diego, CA: Harcourt Brace Jovanovich. (preschool–2)

Three goats want to eat grass, but a troll tries to keep them from crossing the bridge.

Babbitt, Natalie. (1975). *Tuck Everlasting.* New York: Farrar, Straus and Giroux. (4–7)

In this fantasy, Winnie Foster runs away from her parents and meets the Tucks. All of the Tucks drank from the spring that gives them the magic of everlasting life.

Baum, L. Frank. (1972). *The Wizard of Oz.* New York: World Publishing Co. (4–8).

Originally published in 1900, this book has been called the "first American fantasy." Children enjoy the Tin Man, the Scarecrow, the Cowardly Lion, and Dorothy, in the Land of Oz.

Begay, Shonto. (1992). *Ma'ii and Cousin Horned Toad.* New York: Scholastic. (2–4)

This traditional Navajo story is a trickster tale.

Belpre, Pura. (1978). *The Rainbow-Colored Horse*. Illustrated by Antonio Martorell. New York: Frederick Warne. (1–6)

This is a collection of Spanish folktales.

Bond, Michael. (1960). *A Bear Called Paddington*. Illustrated by Peggy Fortnum. Boston: Houghton Mifflin. (K–4)

These well-loved stories tell of a bear from darkest Peru who visits London and has many adventures.

Boston, Lucy M. (1955). *The Children of Green Knowe*. Illustrated by Peter Boston. New York: Harcourt Brace Jovanovich. (4–6)

These fantasies are set in the past and in the present. Tolly, a lonely child, is sent to live with his great-grandmother in an ancient manor house, Green Knowe.

Briggs, Raymond. (1989). *Jim and the Beanstalk*. New York: Putnam. (all ages)

This story is an updated version of *Jack and the Beanstalk*.

Brooke, William. (1992). *Untold Tales*. New York: HarperCollins. (5–9)

This collection of short stories includes interesting wordplay as well as clever play on traditions.

Brown, Marcia. (1972). *The Three Billy Goats Gruff*. New York: Harper & Row. (K–2)

This book tells the traditional story of three billy goats going to pasture who meet a troll. The biggest billy goat puts the troll in his place.

————. (1961). *Once a Mouse*. New York: Scribner's. (2–4)

This Caldecott Medal winner tells a traditional fable in woodcut illustrations. The mouse tries to escape a crow in this fable.

Brown, Marcia, reteller. (1954). *Cinderella*. New York: Scribner's. (K–2)

Brown's illustrated version of the traditional Cinderella story gives the story a delicate, feminine feeling.

Casler, Leigh. (1994). *The Boy Who Dreamed of an Acorn*. Illustrated by Shonto Begay. New York: Philomel. (3–6)

In this Native American folktale, a boy who dreamed about an acorn discovers that small, weak things can have great power.

Christopher, John. (1967). *The White Mountains*. New York: Macmillan. (6–9)

This story is set in the future when the world is ruled by machine creatures called Tripods who maintain their mastery over humans by placing steel caps on the humans' skulls.

Cooper, Susan. (1973). *The Dark Is Rising*. New York: Atheneum. (6–9)

The principal character in this story is Will Stanton, the seventh son of a seventh son. He is the youngest of an ageless people who are destined to fight evil so long as they live.

Dahl, Roald. (1964). *Charlie and the Chocolate Factory*. New York: Knopf. (2–6)

This fantasy has an unusual collection of characters whose vices lead to their downfall.

dePaola, Tomie. (1981). *Fin M'Coul: The Giant of Knockmany Hill*. New York: Holiday House. (1–3)

This is an Irish folktale.

Dickinson, Peter. (1988). *Eva*. New York: Delacorte. (6–9)

This science fiction story has a principal character who survives an accident by having her brain implanted into the body of a chimp.

————. (1985). *A Box of Nothing*. New York: Delacorte. (3–5)

James purchases a box of nothing for $0.00 in the Nothing Shop. This box leads him to the Dump, where he discovers mysterious objects and characters.

Engdahl, Sylvia. (1973). *Beyond the Tomorrow Mountains*. Illustrated by Richard Cuffari. New York: Atheneum. (5–7)

This is a story of a young man who matures in the world that is being built after the earth is doomed to destruction.

Galdone, Paul. (1979). *Henny Penny*. New York: Clarion. (preschool–1)

Henny Penny thinks the sky is falling when she is hit by an acorn.

_____ . (1979). *The Gingerbread Boy*. New York: Clarion. (preschool–1)

The gingerbread boy escapes only to be eaten by a fox.

_____ . (1979). *The Three Billy Goats Gruff*. New York: Clarion. (preschool–1)

Three billy goats are attacked by a troll.

_____ . (1978). *Cinderella*. New York: McGraw-Hill. (1–4)

The classic French version of Cinderella.

Ginsburg, Mirra. (1994). *The Old Man and His Birds*. New York: Greenwillow. (1–3)

An old man has a robe that changes colors and strange birds fly out of his sleeves.

Grimm, Jakob. (1980). *The Fisherman and His Wife*. Translated by Randall Jarrell. Illustrated by Margot Zemuch. New York: Farrar, Straus & Giroux. (2–4)

The magic fish gives a selfish woman wishes that she misuses.

Grimm, Jakob, and Wilhelm Grimm. (1988). *The Six Swans*. Retold by Robert San Souci. New York: Simon & Schuster. (K–3)

Six brothers are turned into swans by a sorceress. Their sister is the only one who can rescue them.

Haley, Gail E. (1986). *Jack and the Bean Tree*. New York: Crown. (preschool–4)

An Appalachian version of the traditional tale.

Hamilton, Virginia (reteller). (1985). *The People Could Fly: American Black Folktales*. Illustrated by Leo and Diane Dillon. New York: Knopf. (4–adult)

A collection of African American tales that address flying, a common theme in these tales.

Hoban, Russell. (1960). *Bedtime for Frances*. New York: Harper. (K–2)

Frances, like many children, does not like to go to bed.

Holder, Heidi. (1981). *Aesop's Fables*. New York: Viking. (3–6)

A collection of the best known of these fables.

Howe, Deborah, and James Howe. (1979). *Bunnicula*. New York: Atheneum. (3–5)

This fantasy features a dog narrator. The well-read cat believes that the rabbit Bunnicula is a vampire who sucks the juice from vegetables.

Isaacs, Anne. (1994). *Swamp Angel*. Illustrated by Paul Zelinsky. New York: Dutton. (1–3)

The Swamp Angel is a prodigious heroine who can disarm men and bears.

Kellogg, Steven (reteller). (1991). *Jack and the Beanstalk*. New York: William Morrow. (all ages)

This is a hilarious version of the original Jack and the Beanstalk story.

Kent, Jack. (1971). *The Fat Cat*. Chicago: Parents. (1–3)

This cumulative tale was translated from the Danish.

Key, Alexander. (1965). *The Forgotten Door*. Philadelphia: Westminster. (4–6)

A strange boy appears in a farming community, and no one knows where he came from. A family takes him in, but they quickly realize that he has unusual powers.

King-Smith, Dick. (1989). *Martin's Mice*. Illustrated by Jez Alborough. New York: Crown. (3–6)

Martin is a cat who decides to raise mice to save the effort of catching them. He imprisons Drusilla, a mouse, in a bathtub and his problems begin.

_____ . (1988). *Foxbusters*. New York: Delacorte. (3–5)

Some very special chickens who have evolved though survival of the fittest develop the skills necessary to bomb the foxes with their eggs. This humorous book is an excellent read-aloud.

_____ . (1983). *Babe, the Gallant Pig*. New York: Dell. (3–5)

A pig comes to Farmer Hogget's farm destined to become bacon, but Babe is no ordinary pig. Babe becomes friends with a sheep dog who teaches him about sheepherding.

Koller, Jackie. (1990). *The Dragonling*. Illustrated by Judith Mitchell. New York: Little, Brown. (3–5)

Darek dreams of going on a dragonquest and slaying a dragon. He discovers a baby dragon in the pouch of a dead dragon and takes care of it, and gradually his opinion of dragons changes.

LeGuin, Ursula K. (1988). *Wonderful Alexander and the Catwings*. Illustrated by S. D. Schindler. New York: Watts. (1–3)

This modern fantasy features kittens who fly. The four flying kittens escape a city slum and find a loving home with a boy and girl in the country.

L'Engle, Madeleine. (1962). *A Wrinkle in Time*. New York: Farrar, Straus & Giroux. (5–8)

Meg and her brother set out to find their father, who has disappeared. They learn that they must journey through time in order to find him.

Lester, Julius (retold by). (1988). *More Tales of Uncle Remus: Further Adventures of Brer Rabbit, His Friends, Enemies and Others*. Illustrated by Jerry Pinkney. New York: Dial. (10–adult)

This a retelling of the adventures of Brer Rabbit and Brer Fox, stories in the African American folk tradition.

_____ . (1987). *The Tales of Uncle Remus: The Adventures of Brer Rabbit*. Illustrated by Jerry Pinkney. New York: Dial. (10–adult)

These tales are retellings of these popular stories.

_____ . (1969). *Black Folktales*. Illustrated by Tom Feelings and Richard W. Baron. New York: Pantheon. (3–12)

This collection of folktales includes pourquoi such as "How the Snake Got Rattles," and hero tales such as "Stagolee."

Lewis, C. S. (1951). *The Lion, the Witch, and the Wardrobe*. New York: Macmillan. (all ages)

The classic fantasy of four children who discover the enchanted land of Narnia.

Lobel, Arnold. (1980). *Fables*. New York: Harper & Row. (all ages)

This collection contains different versions of popular fables.

Louie, Ai-Ling. (1982). *Yeh-Shen*. New York: Philomel. (1–3)

A magic fish is Cinderella's confidant in this 1,000-year-old tale.

Lunn, Janet. (1983). *The Root Cellar*. New York: Scribner's. (4–8)

Twelve-year-old Rose is sent to live with her aunt in a country home on the shores of Lake Ontario. Rose is not very happy in her new situation until she discovers an overgrown root cellar.

MacDonald, George. (1966 [1871]). *At the Back of the North Wind*. Illustrated by Arthur Hughes. New York: Dutton. (4–6)

The story of a boy who seeks help from the cold north wind.

Marshall, James. (1988). *Goldilocks and the Three Bears*. Illustrated by James Marshall. New York: Dial. (1–3)

This interpretation of the traditional story has cartoonlike illustrations.

McKissack, Patricia C. (1992). *The Dark-Thirty: Southern Tales of the Supernatural*. Illustrated by Jerry Brian Pinkney. New York: Knopf. (2–6)

This very popular collection focuses on scary stories.

Merrill, Jean. (1964). *The Pushcart War*. Illustrated by Ronni Solbert. New York: Harper. (4–6)

This fantasy tells of a war between truck drivers and pushcart vendors on the streets of New York.

Milne, A. A. (1954). *Winnie the Pooh*. Illustrated by Ernest H. Shepard. New York: Dutton. (preschool–4)

These are classic stories of a bear who gets into difficulties, but his friends help him out.

Milnes, Gerald. (1990). *Granny, Will Your Dog Bite, and Other Mountain Rhymes*. New York: Knopf. (2–6)

This book contains an interesting, funny collection of Appalachian mountain rhymes.

Minarik, Else Holmelund. (1957). *Little Bear*. Illustrated by Maurice Sendak. New York: Harper & Row. (preschool–2)

Little Bear has adventures with his family and friends.

Norton, Mary. (1953). *The Borrowers*. Illustrated by Beth and Joe Krush. New York: Harcourt Brace Jovanovich. (3–5)

The Borrowers are small creatures who live in old houses. Their surnames are derived from the places they live within the house.

Oodgeroo. (1994). *Dreamtime Aboriginal Stories*. Illustrated by Bronwyn Bancroft. New York: Lothrop, Lee & Shepard. (3–8)

This is a collection of aboriginal folklore that Oodgeroo heard as a child.

Pearce, Philippa. (1958). *Tom's Midnight Garden*. Philadelphia: Lippincott. (4–7)

This time fantasy won the British Carnegie Medal. Tom stays in an apartment in an old house with his aunt and uncle when his brother is ill. He discovers a clock that strikes 13 and a mysterious garden that appears at midnight with a young girl in it.

Perrault, Charles. (1989). *Cinderella and Other Tales from Perrault*. Illustrated by Michael Hague. New York: Henry Holt. (all ages)

The familiar French version of Cinderella.

Rodgers, Mary. (1973). *Freaky Friday*. New York: Harper. (4–7)

Annabel, who is 13 years old, awakens one morning to discover that she has switched bodies with her mother.

Rohmer, Harriet, adapter. (1989). *Uncle Nacho's Hat*. Illustrated by Veg Reisberg. Children's Book Press. (1–3)

Uncle Nacho cannot get rid of his old hat in this traditional tale.

Sauer, Julia. (1943). *Fog Magic*. Illustrated by Lynd Ward. New York: Viking. (4–6)

Ten-year-old Greta discovers the village of Blue Cove, only to realize that it just exists in the fog.

Selden, George. (1960). *The Cricket in Times Square*. Illustrated by Garth Williams. New York: Farrar, Straus & Giroux. (2–4)

Chester Cricket catches a train into New York from his home in the country. Once in Times Square he makes friends with a cat and a mouse.

Service, Pamela. (1985). *Winter of Magic's Return*. New York: Atheneum. (4–7)

This book is set 500 years after a nuclear holocaust that brought on a nuclear winter. Humanity has survived and people live in a cluster of petty kingdoms.

Slobodkin, Louis. (1955). *The Space Ship Under the Apple Tree*. New York: Macmillan. (3–4)

Eddie is the protagonist in this humorous science fiction story. When a Martian space ship crashes in his grandmother's orchard, Eddie meets a Martian who is about the same age.

Slote, Alfred. (1975). *My Robot Buddy*. Philadelphia: Lippincott. (4–6)

This science fiction story is set in the future, when people can purchase robots. Danny, the main character, receives a robot for his birthday that is stolen by robotnappers.

Steig, William. (1976). *The Amazing Bone*. New York: Farrar, Straus & Giroux. (2–4)

A succulent pig and a talking bone outwit a wily fox in this animal fantasy.

Steig, William. (1969). *Sylvester and the Magic Pebble*. New York: Windmill. (1–3)

This animal fantasy won the Caldecott Award. Sylvester the donkey finds a magic pebble that grants his every wish. Unfortunately, he wishes himself to be a boulder to escape a lion and then cannot hold the pebble to wish himself back.

Stevens, Janet. (1992). *The Bremen Town Musicians*. New York: Holiday House. (K–2)

A scraggly group of animals take a trip and have an adventure with a gang of robbers.

————. (1985). *The House That Jack Built*. New York: Holiday House. (preschool–2)

The cumulative tale about Jack building a house.

Turkle, Brinton. (1976). *Deep in the Forest*. New York: Dutton. (K–2)

This wordless picture book reverses the traditional Goldilocks and the Three Bears story.

Whedbee, Charles Harry. (1978). *Outer Banks Mysteries and Seaside Stories*. Winston-Salem, NC: John F. Blair, Publisher. (4–8)

This collection of folktales revolves around the geographical area of the North Carolina coast.

White, E. B. (1952). *Charlotte's Web*. New York: Harper & Row. (3–8)

This story of the friendship between Charlotte and Wilbur, a spider and a pig, is a classic in American children's literature.

Yolen, Jane. (1974). *The Girl Who Cried Flowers*. Illustrated by David Palladini. New York: Crowell. (4–6)

This is a collection of five tales of magic that are modern fantasy written in the style of traditional literature.

Young, Ed. (1994). *Little Plum*. New York: Philomel. (1–3)

This modern version of Tom Thumb in picture book format teaches children that size has very little to do with ability or accomplishments.

## Specialized Children's Literature Lists

### Folktales

Bierhorst, John. (1988). *The Naked Bear: Folktales of the Iroquois*. Illustrated by Dirk Zimmer. New York: William Morrow. (5–8)

Grimm, Jakob, and Wilhelm Grimm. (1973). *Clever Kate*. Illustrated by Anita Lobel. New York: Macmillan. (3–6)

————. (1973). *The Juniper Tree*. Illustrated by Anita Lobel. New York: Macmillan. (3–6)

Haley, Gale. (1986). *Jack and the Bean Tree*. New York: Crown. (5–9)

Lester, Julius. (1989). *How Many Spots Does a Leopard Have? And Other Tales*. Illustrated by David Shannon. New York: Scholastic. (9–adult)

————. (1988). *More Tales of Uncle Remus*. Illustrated by Jerry Pinkney. New York: Dial. (10–adult)

_____ . (1987). *The Tales of Uncle Remus: The Adventures of Brer Rabbit.* Illustrated by Jerry Pinkney. New York: Dial. (10–adult)

Lurie, Allison. (1980). *Clever Gretchen and Other Forgotten Folktales.* New York: T. H. Crowell. (9–11)

McDermott, Gerald. (1972). *Anansi the Spider: A Tale from the Ashanti.* San Diego: Holt, Rinehart and Winston. (5–8)

Milnes, Gerald. (1990). *Granny, Will Your Dog Bite, and Other Mountain Rhymes.* New York: Knopf. (7–11)

Scieszka, Jon. (1989). *The True Story of the Three Little Pigs!* Illustrated by Lane Smith. New York: Viking. (ageless)

Snyder, Dianne. (1988). *The Boy of the Three-Year Nap.* Illustrated by Allen Say. Boston: Houghton Mifflin. (5–9)

Steptoe, John. (1987). *Mufaro's Beautiful Daughters: An African Tale.* New York: Lothrop, Lee & Shepard. (5–8)

Yep, Laurence. (1989). *The Rainbow People.* Illustrated by David Wiesner. New York: Harper & Row. (9–adult)

Yolen, Jane, editor. (1986). *Favorite Folktales from Around the World.* New York: Pantheon. (3–adult)

Young, Ed, translator. (1989). *Lon Po Po: A Red Riding Hood Story from China.* New York: Philomel. (ageless)

## Fairy Tales

Huck, Charlotte. (1989). *Princess Furball.* Illustrated by Anita Lobel. New York: Greenwillow. (ageless)

Watts, Bernadette. (1989). *Tattercoats.* New York: North-South. (7–9)

## Fables

Bierhorst, John. (1987). *Doctor Coyote: A Native American Aesop's Fables.* Illustrated by Wendy Watson. New York: Macmillan. (8–adult)

Brown, Marcia. (1961). *Once a Mouse.* New York: Scribner's. (5–8)

Cauley, Lorinda Bryan (reteller). (1984). *The Town Mouse and the Country Mouse.* New York: Putnam. (1–8)

Galdone, Paul. (1973). *The Little Red Hen.* Boston: Houghton Mifflin. (K–2)

Holder, Heidi. (1992). *Carmine the Crow.* New York: Farrar, Straus & Giroux. (8–adult)

Zwerger, Lisbeth. (1991). *Aesop's Fables.* New York: Picturebook Studio. (8–11)

## Legends

Alexander, Ellen. (1989). *Llama and the Great Flood: A Folktale from Peru.* New York: HarperCollins. (6–8)

Bryan, Ashley. (1989). *Turtle Knows Your Name.* New York: Atheneum. (5–7)

Goble, Paul. (1988). *Her Seven Brothers.* New York: Bradbury. (5–8)

Hamilton, Virginia, reteller. (1985). *The People Could Fly: American Black Folktales.* Illustrated by Leo and Diane Dillon. New York: Knopf. (9–adult)

Sanfield, Steve. (1989). *The Adventures of High John the Conqueror.* Illustrated by John Ward. New York: Watts. (9–12)

Steptoe, John. (1984). *Story of Jumping Mouse: A Native American Legend.* New York: Lothrop, Lee & Shepard. (5–7)

## Myths

Hamilton, Virginia. (1988). *In the Beginning: Creation Stories from Around the World.* Illustrated by Barry Moser. San Diego: Harcourt Brace Jovanovich. (12–adult)

Haviland, Virginia. (1979). *North American Legends.* Illustrated by Ann Stugnell. New York: Philomel. (9–12)

Lattimore, Deborah Nourse. (1989). *Why There Is No Arguing in Heaven: A Mayan Myth.* New York: HarperCollins. (6–10)

Lester, Julius. (1969). *Black Folktales.* New York: Pantheon. (9–adult)

Van Laan, Nancy. (1989). *Rainbow Crow.* Illustrated by Beatriz Vidal. New York: Knopf. (6–9)

## Tall Tales

Chase, Richard (reteller). (1945). *The Jack Tales.* Illustrated by Berkeley Williams, Jr. Boston: Houghton Mifflin. (7–12)

Dewey, Ariane. (1983). *Pecos Bill.* New York: Greenwillow. (5–8)

Keats, Ezra Jack. (1965). *John Henry: An American Legend.* New York: Pantheon. (5–8)

## Ballads

Goode, Diane. (1990). *The Diane Goode Book of American Folktales and Songs.* New York: Dutton. (7–11).

Hart, Jane. (1982). *Singing Bee! A Collection of Favorite Children's Songs.* Illustrated by Anita Lobel. New York: Lothrop. (5–8)

Langstaff, John. (1957). *Frog Went a-Courtin'.* Illustrated by Feodor Rojankovsky. New York: Harcourt. (all ages)

————. (1957). *Over in the Meadow.* Illustrated by Feodor Rojankovsky. New York: Harcourt Brace Jovanovich. (5–7)

Rounds, Glen. (1968). *Casey Jones: The Story of a Brave Engineer.* San Francisco: Golden Gate. (5–7)

————. (1973). Sweet Betsy from Pike. Chicago: Children's Press. (9–12)

Spier, Peter. (1961). *The Fox Went Out on a Chilly Night.* New York: Doubleday. (5–7)

## Noah and the Flood Variations

Bollinger, Max. (1972). *Noah and the Rainbow.* Illustrated by Helga Aichinger. New York: Crowell. (K–3)

Baynes, Pauline. (1988). *Noah and the Ark.* New York: Henry Holt. (K–3)

dePaola, Tomie. (1983). *Noah and the Ark.* New York: Harper. (K–3)

Diamond, Jasper. (1983). *Noah's Ark.* Englewood Cliffs, NJ: Prentice-Hall. (K–3)

Eborn, Andrew. (1984). *Noah and the Ark and the Animals.* Illustrated by Ivan Gantschev. Natick, MA: Picture Book Studio. (K–3)

Fussennegger, Gertrud. (1982). *Noah's Ark.* Illustrated by Annegert Fuchshuber. Philadelphia: Lippincott. (K–3)

Fischetto, Laura. (1989). *Inside Noah's Ark.* Illustrated by Laura Fischetto. New York: Viking Kestrel. (K–3)

Geisert, Arthur. (1988). *The Ark.* Boston: Houghton Mifflin. (K–3)

Haley, Gail E. (1971). *Noah's Ark.* New York: Atheneum. (K–3)

Hogrogian, Nonny. (1971). *Noah's Ark*. New York: Atheneum. (K–3)

Hutton, Warwick. (1977). *Noah and the Great Flood*. New York: Atheneum. (K–3)

Lenski, Lois. (1948). *Mr. and Mrs. Noah*. New York: Crowell. (K–3)

Mee, Charles L., Jr. (1978). *Noah*. Illustrated by Ken Munowitz. New York: Harper. (K–3)

Ray, Jane. (1990). *Noah's Ark*. New York: Dutton Children's Books. (K–3)

Rounds, Glen. (1985). *Washday on Noah's Ark*. Holiday House. (K–3)

Singer, Isaac Bashevis. (1974). *Why Noah Chose the Dove*. Illustrated by Eric Carle. New York: Farrar, Straus & Giroux. (2–5)

Spier, Peter. (1977). *Noah's Ark*. New York: Doubleday. (K–3)

Wildsmith, Brian. (1980). *Professor Noah's Spaceship*. New York: Oxford. (K–3)

# Eight

## KEY TERMS

contemporary fiction      historical fiction

didacticism      realistic fiction

## GUIDING QUESTIONS

As you read, think about whether you strongly identify with the story characters and their problems. Keep the following questions in mind as you read through this chapter.

1. Can you see relationships between the problems presented in these realistic books, which are set in the present, and the historical fiction books, which are set in the past?

2. How are these problems related to those that are currently facing the society at large?

3. Can you think of any reasons for giving contemporary problems a historical setting?

4. Why is realistic fiction so popular with children?

## OVERVIEW

Realistic fiction and historical fiction both describe events, people, and relationships as they might have happened—in the present or in the past. In these stories, problems are solved through hard work, persistence, and determined efforts rather than magic, as in fantasy. There are no fantastic elements, no magical spells, and no supernatural powers. However, there are occasional serendipities—because truth is often stranger than fiction.

The protagonists succeed or fail as a result of their own strengths or weaknesses. As children read contemporary and historical fiction, they have opportunities to gain insights about people in current times or in times past; to learn about events, past and present, and how they influence young people; to become aware of the similarities of the human spirit in all contexts; and to experience the way that real people have survived and learned from their challenges. They learn about the problems and the tragedies—and sometimes the comedies—of growing and living in the real world. Readers can walk in another person's shoes to learn what that person thought and felt about experiences.

Both contemporary and historical realistic fiction address the problems that are often faced in the real world. Although contemporary realistic fiction is set in the present and historical fiction in the past, the characters tend to face the same issues. Readers discover that Esther Forbes's Revolutionary War title character in *Johnny Tremain* grapples with rights and issues quite similar to those facing Avi's contemporary character Philip Malloy in *Nothing but the Truth*. Each of them has to learn that rights carry responsibilities.

# People Then and Now

## HISTORICAL FICTION AND CONTEMPORARY REALISTIC FICTION

················· INTRODUCTION

"The more things change, the more they stay the same." This familiar quotation is a good description of the genre discussed in this chapter. When reading about events described in historical fiction, you will be struck by the similarities to events in contemporary realistic fiction. Often, only the details and the contexts have changed and the events seem parallel.

Katherine Paterson (1992), author of many award-winning books for children, notes, "I've been writing a chapter this year for a book entitled *The World in 1492*. My assignment is 'Asia in 1492.' What I discovered about the world in 1492 and Asia in 1492 was that it looked depressingly like the world in 1992" (p. 165). In both historical and contemporary realistic fiction, events reflect what has happened or could have happened. The similarities exist because throughout time, the same kinds of events occur over and over.

The interactions among people are also similar. Some people in the past were governed by greed and self-interest just as some people are today. Mean-spiritedness and the desire to take advantage of those who may be weaker are not limited to any historical era—and these characteristics certainly are evident in historical fiction as well as in contemporary realistic fiction. On the other hand, one reads about characters in past and present settings who exemplify many positive characteristics. They are compassionate, unselfish, and benevolent. Characters are most realistic when they have a reasonable mix of good and not-so-good characteristics—because then they are most like real people.

················· VIGNETTE

Jeff McKenzie held up Minfong Ho's *The Clay Marble* so his fifth graders could see the cover.

Jennifer exclaimed, "Oh no! Another war book? I'm tired of war!"

"Cool," chorused several of the male class members.

"Jennifer, why do you think this is a war book?"

"Because the kids look like Vietnamese."

Mr. McKenzie replied, "Well, you're right in a way, but this story is really about refugees."

"What's a refugee?" asked Sheila.

"A homeless person," said Randolph.

"No it isn't! I never heard anyone call the people at the homeless shelter refugees," Gina said.

Cameron said, "Well, refugees wander around because they don't have a place to go. Isn't that being homeless?"

After several minutes of this discussion among the students, Mr. McKenzie mentally changed his plans and asked the class, "Have you decided what a refugee is?"

"No, no," the class answered.

"Let's figure out what you want to know about refugees and then decide whether you want to read this story."

The class brainstormed the following questions about refugees:

1. Are refugees homeless?
2. Are homeless people refugees?

*(continued)*

3. Why are refugees homeless?

4. What happens to refugees? Are they homeless forever?

5. What's a refugee camp?

6. Does every country have refugees?

7. Do we have refugees in the United States?

The literature-based unit that the students and Mr. McKenzie created based on these questions is presented in the last section of this chapter.

## CONTEMPORARY AND HISTORICAL REALISTIC FICTION

The characters in **contemporary and historical realistic fiction** could actually exist. *Some of the stories are unpleasant, but they reflect real life.* Many books in this genre are not for the faint of heart. Death and dying, cruelty and abuse, racism and sexism are integral elements of many plots. All books of this genre, however, are not so intense; many present life experiences have to do with the conflict inherent in growing up in families and the problems of peer relationships. Although not life threatening, these family and peer problems are often perceived by the protagonists (and the readers as well) as ones that will alter their lives forever. Betsy Byars, who draws on her experiences with her own children to write about real life, sensitively deals with these problems and characters' feelings while capturing the absurdities of situations with her special talent for looking at sad situations from a good-humored perspective. *The Burning Questions of Bingo Brown* addresses first love between two classmates and also takes a serious look at a teacher's integrity.

Much of the genre, however, and especially much of the historical genre, deals with the uglier side of life. Hester Burton (1973), author of several books of historical fiction, reflects, "History is not pretty. The Nazi concentration camps aside, I think people were far more cruel to each other in times past than they are today. The law was certainly more cruel. So was poverty. So was the treatment of children. . . . The brutality of times

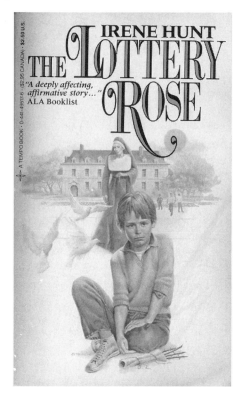

Georgie, an abused child who dreams of flowers, slowly learns to give—and to receive love.

past may shock the oversensitive" (p. 303). The level of physical abuse described in books with modern settings may be less than in historical settings but often the mental and emotional abuse is still present, as it is in Irene Hunt's *The Lottery Rose*. As you read historical fiction, you will discover that it is often more acceptable to address sensitive subjects in a historical setting, thus removing the immediacy of the abuse.

### Controversy over Realistic Fiction

Authors of children's **realistic fiction** are committed to telling the truth in whatever genre they write. Fine literature *portrays honest interpretations of actual events, characters, and conflicts.* After all, "The world has not spared children hunger, cold, sorrow, pain, fear, loneliness, disease, death, war, famine, or madness. Why should we hesitate to make use of this knowledge when writing for them?" (Steele, 1973, p. 290). A growing number of people, however, believe that books for children and young adults need to be censored—or at least rewritten—to protect the children from the harsh realities portrayed or because the ideas conflict with their view of the world. Robert Burch's (1973) reply to this idea is, "If we could guarantee children that the world out there would be completely safe, then fine, we could afford to give them only stories that leave the impression. But until we can, in whatever we present as being realistic, is it not cheating for it to be otherwise?" (p. 284). Well-written realistic fiction gives an honest description of life, as perceived by the author.

Children, no less than adults, experience the effects of slavery, war, segregation, and similar kinds of stresses. How these are dealt with can give children insight for recognizing and dealing with conflicts that they will face in current societal situations. Books can give them a vision of a better world as well as a vision of how they can be a part of changing their world. One of the distinguishing characteristics of children's realistic fiction is the message of hope and possibility that is always present. Even though life may be hard, survival and the possibility of better things is never out of the question. People, especially children, need hope to be able to sustain the will to live, and children's realistic fiction encourages positive expectations of fulfillment. "Writings for young people are about maturing in the real world. The important thing is that things do change; whatever is can be made better" (Hamilton, 1992, p. 678). Chapter Thirteen addresses some of the problems that impinge on all of our lives.

## Similarities and Differences in Contemporary and Historical Realistic Fiction

Historical fiction and contemporary realistic fiction have many common features, although they are classified as different genre by the majority of children's literature textbooks, which make explicit distinctions between them. Their shared characteristics include:

1. The plot contains events and incidents that could actually occur in the particular setting of the book. These events and incidents are *possible*, but need not be *probable* (Russell, 1994).

2. The characters demonstrate both strengths and weaknesses in their actions. They are not perfect.

3. The language used is typical of the language used in the setting, either in the past or the present.

4. The theme is one that readers can relate to. They can make connections between the ideas in the book and their own lives.

The major difference between the two genre lies in the story setting.

The setting is very important to the story. It influences the language used, the interactions among people, the social traditions displayed, the cultural behaviors, and the conflicts that occur. Rosemary Sutcliff (1973) suggests that "the way people act is conditioned by the social custom of their day and age—even the way they think and feel" (p. 308). It becomes quite obvious then that, when writing about a setting that is historically quite different from the present, authors must include more details about the context. The integration of these details into the story is a distinguishing characteristic between well-written and mediocre historical fiction.

Choice of characters, both the main characters and those who support them, is particularly important. It is not realistic fiction if an author uses actual people from a period of the past and creates conversations and actions in which they did not participate. It is acceptable to place fictional characters in actual events and create actions and conversations for them; it is not acceptable to do the same with actual historical people. An author must have documentation of actions and conversations in order to use actual historical figures in realistic fiction.

Historical fiction then has additional characteristics that distinguish it from realistic fiction:

1. The details describing the historical setting are portrayed so that readers are drawn into the times.

2. The actions, thoughts, conversations, and feelings accurately reflect the historical period.

3. Although actual historical events may be used, no conversations or actions of actual people are included unless the conversations or actions can be documented.

## When Does the Present Become the Past?

Students in children's literature classes are often confused when attempting to classify books as realistic fiction or historical fiction: Just when does the present become the past? Books that were contemporary when they were published may over time become historical. Children who are currently in the third grade think of the historical past as any time before they were born. Adults have very different perspectives regarding the historical past!

Many books are easy to classify. Scott O'Dell places *My Name Is Not Angelica* in 1733; in *Waiting for Anya*, Michael Morpurgo uses a World War II setting. Both of these books are obviously historical fiction. On the other hand, Paula Danziger obviously puts *Not for a Billion Gazillion Dollars* in the present day, as Jean Van Leeuwen does in *Dear Mom, You're Ruining My Life*. There is no question that these books are contemporary fiction.

Various children's literature authorities employ different schemes for categorizing books as historical or contemporary fiction. Some authors classify anything set after World War II as contemporary fiction (Russell, 1994; Norton, 1995), while other authors classify everything up until the Gulf War as historical fiction (Cullinan and Galda, 1994; Reed, 1994; Huck, Hepler, and Hickman, 1993). Perhaps the most sensible solution is for readers to decide whether the book is contemporary or historical, which permits them to use their experience and judgment as they respond to a book. As long as readers can support a classification, it should be honored.

## ISSUES IN REALISTIC FICTION

As mentioned earlier, many adults do not appreciate the sometimes graphic reality portrayed in both historical and contemporary realistic fiction. This is an important issue to be considered by adults who choose literature for children. You will find yourself disagreeing with friends, families, and colleagues because there are no right and wrong answers and no easy answers.

## Didacticism

**Didacticism,** *giving readers obvious, heavy-handed moral messages or instructions*, turns readers off. Some authors find realistic fiction an irresistible platform for sharing their beliefs and values. Some believe young people lack values and should be taught through didactic literature. The issue here is not a concern for the specific values espoused, but the way in which they are presented. One of the differences between well-written and poorly written fiction is the way beliefs and values are expressed. In well-written fiction, the beliefs and values are implicit. They emerge from the characters' actions, conversations, and decisions. In poorly written fiction, the theme or message gets in the way of the story itself.

Susan Sharp (1992) suggests, "It is the values and ideas we think children might miss if we don't assert them that lead us into didactic stories"; however, "in the works of the greatest writers, unresolved issues can make the best stories" (p. 696). Didacticism usually puts readers off; therefore, it is best to avoid it when selecting literature.

## The Value of Realism

Values portrayed in many books of realistic fiction can be a major issue in children's literature. In Chapter One we introduced this issue, which cannot be resolved in a simple fashion. Certainly authors express values one way or another every time they write. Knowing this places greater responsibility on the adults who guide children's reading. An open marketplace of ideas encourages children to think critically and express their own values. Clearly, this is a multifaceted issue that is an ongoing concern, and values are an especially important issue in realistic fiction. The depiction of families has moved from the "Ozzie and Harriet" and "Leave It to Beaver" types to single-parent families, unwed mothers, and alcoholic parents. Should we pretend that these families do not exist or should authors tell it like it is? Should authors allow the characters in children's books to use profanity? Would Gilly, the foster child in *The Great Gilly Hopkins*, be the same character if she didn't use some profanity? The author, Katherine Paterson, is a minister's wife and the daughter of missionaries. No matter what the arguments are in favor of such realism or who writes it, some adults may be very upset if their children are allowed to read such things.

## Violence

Violence is an issue throughout our society and the depiction of violence in realistic and historical fiction is a concern in selecting literature. This issue is addressed in Chapter Thirteen also. Although violence appears in all genre of children's literature, it seems to appear most frequently in realistic fiction and traditional literature (see Chapter Seven for a discussion of violence in traditional literature).

Can children's books exclude violence while portraying realistic contemporary life? Walter Dean Myers includes guns, gangs, and violence in *The Scorpions*, as well as depicting teachers and principals in a negative light. Nevertheless, this is a too-good-to-miss book that raises important issues for children in grades four through eight. The author writes out of his own experience and a reality that many youngsters experience in contemporary society.

## TYPES OF REALISTIC FICTION

The categories of realistic fiction in this section emerged from the literature itself as we read thousands of books for children and young adults and asked this question: Is the struggle one in which the focus is on the main character's growth and development and in which the setting is almost incidental, or is the reason for the problem the result of societal events? Four broad categories emerged from the literature: (1) families past and present, (2) challenges from outside the family, (3) societal issues, and (4) books to meet special interests. Subcategories are developed based on the kinds of conflicts within the books and by modifying some

of the historical periods described by Crabtree, Nash, Gagnon, and Waugh (1992).

## Families Past and Present

Stories grow out of authors' experiences and are greatly influenced by the times and values of the society in which the author writes. Taxel (1994) states, "Like other cultural artifacts, children's literature is a product of convention that is rooted in, if not determined by, the dominant belief systems and ideologies of the times in which they are created" (p. 99). Family structure in books, both past and present, gives evidence of these belief systems and values.

### Nuclear families

Although many families no longer consist of two parents with their children, this is still society's norm. It is not surprising, then, to see this structure mirrored in numerous books. For some children and adults, these books confirm the belief that families provide needed support and guidance as children mature.

Books in which the family interactions are the focus of the story have many variations. They range from "happily ever after" books to those with a less optimistic ending. Beverly Cleary's books have a long-standing popularity with children and adults, and children can easily identify with many of the situations in her books. In *Beezus and Ramona*, Beezus learns that having bad thoughts about a pesky little sister who always seems to get her own way is quite normal. The entire Quimby family learns to adjust to Mr. Quimby's unemployment in *Ramona and Her Father*, and the feelings of unease, irritation, and worry are eventually resolved and replaced with joy, understanding, and insight. Some readers may think the solutions are too easy; others gain a sense of relief and comfort as problems are solved.

In 1991, Judith Caseley introduced readers to the Kane family: two parents, two daughters, and one son. The series begins with *Hurricane Harry*, told from the perspective of the son. The middle Kane child tells the story in *Starring Dorothy Kane*, and the oldest Kane child tells the story in *Chloe in the Know*. Baby Arney's birth was the motivation for *Harry and Arney*. The events, conflicts, and challenges in this series occur among family members and friends of the children, as when Harry decides that since Chloe's fish like bubbles they would be especially happy if he added bubble bath to their fish tank. Worries and fears arise because of Mrs. Kane's pregnancy, but the family adjusts and thrives in the process.

*Extended family*. Grandparents play an integral part in the family in some books, as in Barbara Dugan's *Good-Bye, Hello*, in which Bobbie faces a series of problems after her grandmother moves in. First she faces a difficult adjustment to sixth grade, then Gramma is ill and Bobbie has to accept the fact that she may not get well. Bobbie's teacher helps her cope with the reality of her grandmother's illness.

*Holidays*. Holidays are an integral part of all types of families. Virginia Hamilton writes about a traditional family Christmas in *The Bells of Christmas*, set in southwest Ohio in 1890 with aunts, uncles, and cousins joining in the celebration: caroling, eating, exchanging gifts, and attending church. Hamilton gives the readers a picture of a warm family celebration of this special holiday.

*Family misfits*. Finding one's place in a nuclear family can be a problem. Louise Fitzhugh portrays this problem in *Nobody's Family Is Going to Change*. Emma Sheridan wants to be a lawyer like her father, and her brother Willie wants to be a dancer like his Uncle Dipsey. But their parents want them to choose more traditional careers. The father is particularly upset because as an African American he has fought prejudice to become an attorney. He views his son's desire to dance as an affront because the youngster will be accepting a stereotyped role for African Americans.

Frankie, in Avi's *Who Was That Masked Man, Anyway?*, has a hard time getting along with his family. He identifies closely with the radio heroes he listens to—Captain Midnight, The Lone Ranger, Sky King, and others popular in the 1940s—and often assumes their personas. This causes problems at home and at school. When Frankie devises an outrageous plan to introduce his teacher to his older brother, who was wounded in World War II, a catastrophe nearly occurs. Frankie learns that being a hero isn't always heroic and that reality is as important as fantasy.

Betsy Byars tells the story of another misfit in *The Glory Girl*. Anna Glory is the misfit in her family, the Glory Gospel Singers, because she cannot carry a tune. "There are lots of people who didn't fit into their families. Anna reminded herself of this all the time—the dumb one in a family of brains, the ugly one in a family of beauties. But no one—Anna was sure of this—felt as left out as she did when her family sang together (p. 29)." Since she can't sing, she is responsible for selling the family's tapes and records. Anna Glory's family is portrayed as quite artificial. It is only after Anna and another family misfit, Uncle Newt, save the rest of the family that the reader sees a growing realization that each person is important.

*Family problems*. Members of intact families do not escape serious problems either. In *A Summer to Die* by Lois Lowry, Meg and her family move to the country so that her father can finish his book. There are many adjustments to make with school, friends, and the country setting. The family is just beginning to feel comfortable when Molly, Meg's older sister, falls ill. After each bout of illness, she seems to recover, but then has relapses. Finally, she is diagnosed with leukemia and dies at the end of the summer.

In *Francesca, Baby*, Joan Oppenheimer vividly describes the family illness of alcoholism. The mother of Francesca and Mary Kate begins drinking heavily after their brother Robbie dies. Their father travels more and more because he doesn't know how to deal with his own grief or his wife's drinking. Francesca has to assume most of the family responsibilities. A teacher intervenes and helps Francesca seek help through Alateen. As she learns about alcoholism, she is able to confront the serious problems involved. Readers who are unfamiliar with programs like Alateen and Alcoholics Anonymous may find the solutions contrived and simplistic, but those who are familiar with these programs will recognize that the events are not unusual or exceptional.

Susan has two sets of parents in Eve Bunting's *Sharing Susan*. Susan and another baby girl were mixed up in the hospital nursery at birth. When the other girl dies, her parents discover the mix-up.

After an investigation, the parents find Susan and both families go through a tumultuous time trying to adjust to reality.

Unfortunately, real-life families have children who disappear. This problem is the Jeffer family's focus in *The Year Without Michael* by Susan Pfeffer. Michael goes to visit a friend and disappears. The family, disturbed before the disappearance, is left in almost complete chaos. Finally they seek help to cope with the loss and their family problems. Even though Michael has not returned, the reader is left with hope at the conclusion.

## Alternative family structures

In many books published prior to the 1960s, the typical family structure included two parents, children, and perhaps a few close family members. Alternative structures were the result of the death of a parent, often the mother. Contemporary and historical fiction published today portrays alternative family structures much more frequently, and death is not the sole reason for these changes. Divorce, desertion, or sexual preference of parents all create families that are not "typical." Homelessness, single-parent families, children raised by family members rather than parents, foster children, and families with stepparents are all portrayed with increasing frequency as family structures in realistic fiction. All of the children and young people in these books struggle as they learn to survive. For some of the children, the struggle is physical; for others, it is emotional. In addition to the normal challenges of growing up, these children have extra responsibilities, different expectations, and circumstances over which they have no control. The ways they cope with these life conditions gives readers insights about life. Some of these topics are explored in Chapter Thirteen.

Most of the characters in these books have some sort of family structure or adult support. Through their experiences the characters begin to develop an understanding of themselves and those around them. They come to realize that they are not the only people in the world facing these problems, a realization that helps them feel connected to the world. Connectedness to others is a main theme in many of these books.

*Single parents.* Single-parent families are an important part of today's society, as they were in the past. In *Sarah, Plain and Tall* by Patricia MacLachlan, a single father advertises for a wife. Sarah answers the advertisement. After she visits, the children are afraid she will return to Maine rather than staying with them in their small house on the prairie. But the family bonds and Sarah marries the father. The interactions among the characters are the primary emphasis in this book. Sarah is depicted as a strong, independent woman, a significant theme for today's readers.

In *Bride for Anna's Papa*, Isabel Marvin emphasizes the interactions of the characters within the context of the setting, which is 1907 in the iron range of Minnesota. After Anna's mother dies, Anna must take responsibility for the house and for her younger brother, which prevents her from attending school until the new teacher convinces her to come for a few hours each week. Anna and her brother decide their father needs a wife, but when the teacher and their father marry, Anna is resentful. When a great fire destroys the surrounding area, Anna begins to change her attitude: "She would always mourn her mother, but Mae was now an important part of their family, someone she had come to accept and even to love. Their house might not be standing after this fire, but they were together, a family" (p. 136).

In William Armstrong's *Sourland*, Anson Stone is raising his three children alone. Moses Waters, a black man, who believes that a person of integrity does what is right regardless of the consequences, becomes an important influence on the lives of the whole family. The children learn to respect differences among themselves and others; they also learn the ugliness of racism and narrowmindedness. The family grows stronger because of their values.

*Divorce and stepfamilies.* In a more modern setting, Beverly Cleary tells the story of a child of divorce. *Dear Mr. Henshaw* features sixth-grader Leigh Bott's letters and diary entries. Readers recognize Leigh's struggles to respect his father even though the father largely ignores Leigh. In the sequel, *Strider*, Leigh continues to write in his diary. Although his family relationships are important, he is changing. Leigh is now more concerned with his dog, his peers, and school.

Divorce and remarriage place many children into stepfamilies. Children must struggle to make sense first of the divorce and then of becoming a member of a different family. In *What Hearts*, Bruce Brooks introduces Asa, an excited seven-year-old coming home to share the prizes he has won in first grade. When he arrives home, his mother is sitting on a suitcase on the porch, the house is empty, and his parents have separated. Almost immediately he is introduced to his mother's friend, David, who soon becomes Asa's stepfather. Asa and David are not two of a kind and at times life is almost unbearable. By the time Asa and his stepfather have made the first steps toward what might be a good relationship, his mother has decided to divorce David and once again Asa is set adrift.

In the book *Like Jake and Me*, Mavis Jukes writes about a six-year-old dealing with divorce. His stepfather Jake does not approve of his desire to take ballet lessons. To add to the complexity of the situation, his mother is expecting twins. But when he is able to rescue Jake from a wolf spider, a relationship begins to grow.

Maggie visits her father, stepmother, and baby half-sister in Avi's *Blue Heron*. She anticipates tensions when she arrives, but does not anticipate the problems that she actually must deal with once she is there. Her father has lost his job, he is ill and refuses to take his medicine, and then he has a serious car accident. Maggie's only peace during the summer comes from observing a blue heron. As she works with her stepmother to save her father, they begin to develop a positive relationship. In the end, all of the main characters develop greater self-awareness.

*Long-distance fathers.* *Jim Ugly* by Paul Fleischman deals with the unfortunate topic of absentee fathers. Jake Bannock's father supposedly dies and Jake is to live with his cousin, Aurora. The only reminder Jake has of his father is his dog, Jim Ugly. Jake overhears Aurora planning to kill Jim Ugly and runs away. After he gets away and begins to think about the situation he comes to the conclusion that his father isn't really dead. Then he discovers that a bounty hunter is searching for his father by following Jake and Jim Ugly. Eventually Jake and Jim Ugly are reunited with his father.

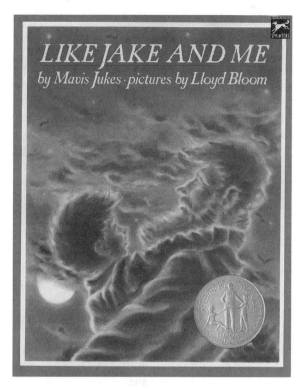

*This is the story of a young child coming to terms with a stepparent named Jake.*

Unlike Jake, Jimmy Little in *Somewhere in the Darkness* by Walter Dean Myers has never really known his father, who is in jail. After his mother's death, he lives with Mama Jean. Then Crab, his father, escapes from a hospital where he was placed for treatment and insists that Jimmy accompany him so they can escape from the authorities. During the escape, he hears his father's side of the incident that resulted in his prison sentence. When Crab is caught, he returns to the hospital and dies. Jimmy returns to live with Mama Jean, but he has learned the importance of parent and child relationships.

Although Marion Dane Bauer's focus in *Face to Face* is the relationship between father and son, the conflict also is between stepfather and stepson. Michael's mother remarries and her new husband adopts Michael. But when his biological father calls for a visit, Michael is more than ready to go. He is angry because his stepfather took the new rifle Michael received for his birthday. During the visit, Michael's father, Dave, constantly tests him for bravery. Even when he "wins" a test, he doesn't have a good feeling. At one point, Michael is swept overboard during white water rafting and his father rescues him. But later that evening, Michael discovers that his father dumped him on purpose. The situation deteriorates and Michael returns home early. At home, he finds his gun and tries to commit suicide. The gun fires, but doesn't kill him. His stepfather finds him and helps him finally understand that his father truly does care for him.

### Living with family members other than a parent

Many times children must live with relatives and not their parents. Sometimes parents die, some parents are dysfunctional, or both war and military careers may separate children from either or both parents. In *The Cookcamp*, Gary Paulsen writes about a boy living with his grandmother because his father is a soldier in World War II, and his mother is unable to cope. The boy learns to help his grandmother, who cooks for nine roadbuilders. He learns to love his grandmother and gets used to the men, who become a part of his life. When his mother is able to take him, he returns with a mixture of happiness and sadness.

In *Child of the Owl* by Laurence Yep, Casey's father is always planning "big deals" that will make him rich. After he is hospitalized as a result of a beating, he sends Casey to live with her uncle, but streetwise Casey and her big-shot lawyer uncle don't hit it off. He sends Casey to live with her eccentric Chinese grandmother, Paw-Paw. From her grandmother, Casey learns about the discrimination her father has faced. She also learns about her culture and comes to love her grandmother.

Although *Journey*, the title of a Patricia MacLachlan book and the name of the main character, is from a different cultural background from Casey, he has some of the same problems. Journey and his sister live with their grandparents. They wait for promised letters from their mother that never come. Grandfather takes many photographs that chronicle the family, and through studying these photos, Journey comes to realize that his grandparents love him deeply. He also realizes that his mother is not likely to return. In the end, Journey develops an interest in photography.

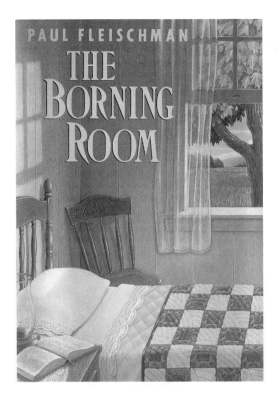

*The eternal cycle of birth, courtship, giving birth, and death is portrayed in this story of an Ohio farm girl's life.*

Summer, the main character in *Missing May* by Cynthia Rylant, has lived with a series of relatives. Finally, elderly Aunt May and Uncle Ob find her and take her home to their trailer in the mountains of West Virginia. When Aunt May dies six years later, Summer faces another crisis because she loses the security she finally had developed. Eventually, both Summer and Uncle Ob gain the strength to accept May's death.

### Generations of families

Some excellent literature follows generations of the same family, giving readers insight into a family over many years. They are given the rare opportunity to see the positive changes that occur over decades. Other times, however, readers see the changes and are dismayed by them. Paul Fleischman's *The Borning Room* is a book in which changes are positive. The focus of this story is a

*Jericho is the story of four generations of women told through the sketchy memories of a great-grandmother.*

room that represents coming into and leaving life. Georgina Caroline Lott was born there in 1851, and she dies in the same bed in 1918. During the intervening years, her mother delivers a baby with the help of a runaway slave; their beloved grandfather dies; her mother dies in childbirth; her brother recovers from diphtheria; and Georgina delivers her own baby there. Not only do readers identify with the family, but they also are caught up in the events of the times—slavery, wars, women's rights—as well as weddings, social gatherings, and daily chores.

In *Jericho*, Janet Hickman presents the lives of four generations of women, focusing primarily on GrandMin, the great-grandmother, and Angela, the great-granddaughter. GrandMin's mind is back in Jericho, the town where she grew up. She has only fleeting periods of living in the present and requires the help of her daughter, granddaughter,

and Angela. Through a series of flashbacks, we see GrandMin's life from childhood through adulthood and we develop an understanding of the family.

Walter Dean Myers portrays the generations of survivors that make up the Lewis family in *The Glory Field*. He traces the family from 1753 on the coast of Sierra Leone, West Africa, to the present in Harlem, New York. They were slaves in 1864 during the Civil War. By 1900, they live on eight acres of land called the Glory Field. By 1964, the Civil Rights Movement has started and the family joins in this battle. Tommy finds the shackles that were on the legs of the first family member brought to this country and chains himself to the sheriff. In the final section, the Lewis family gathers for a last reunion at Glory Field; a resort is going to be built there. Malcolm, a family member, attends the reunion and becomes custodian of the shackles that symbolize the bond among all generations.

## Challenges Outside the Family

As children grow up, the family—whether nuclear or alternative—assumes less importance in children's lives and the peer group takes on greater importance. These changes represent children's growing need for independence. Parents, siblings, other family members, and other adults who have been the focus of a child's interactions may now become part of the background. A common theme in books dealing with this area of life are problems within the family: family members who "don't understand" or who try to interfere with peer relations. In general, however, despite conflicts the characters still see their families, especially parents, as integral partners in resolving problems. Other books address problems outside the family with peers, school, and nonfamily adults; the family is less involved as the characters seek to define who they are becoming. In these books the characters need support, that they may receive from peers or other adults or, in some circumstances, an understanding family. A third kind of problem occurs as the characters face emotional or physical challenges which they must meet by themselves, without family or peers. Their ultimate survival depends on how they overcome the hardships. They may not have the support of adults or others; they may be alone by choice or because of circumstances beyond their control. The books for children and young adults reviewed here reflect these three kinds of problems or conflicts. Of course, it is possible to place a book in a different category than is done here. As in true in life, many books cannot be neatly pigeonholed.

### Families and peers

All of the families portrayed in this section are supportive of their children, although this support is not always appreciated. As youngsters begin to identify more closely with their peers and develop some independence, conflicts begin to arise with their parents and their siblings, which is the case with Samantha Slayton, a sixth grader often embarrassed by her parents' actions. She doesn't want her friends to see them or to have them chaperon any of her school activities. For years, Samantha and her parents have used letters as a way of communicating to address conflicts before they are blown out of proportion. *Dear Mom, You're Ruining My Life* is both the title of Jean Van Leeuwen's book and the opening of the letter Samantha writes to let her mother know her feelings. Samantha and her parents both end up with a better understanding of each other's perspectives.

Ben Tucker has a different set of problems in *Different Dragons* by Jean Little. First, he must stay with Aunt Rose, whom he hardly knows; second, he's afraid of dogs and Aunt Rose keeps Gully, one of the biggest dogs he's ever seen. To make matters worse, Hana, the neighbor girl, loves Gully and makes fun of Ben. During a storm that frightens Ben, he discovers that Gully is equally frightened and surprises himself as he tries to comfort the dog. Ben recognizes that Hana has fears, too, when they climb to the attic and the ladder falls down. Through a series of events, Ben grows out of some of his fears and develops a better understanding of himself and others. When his family returns, he has gained the confidence to accept Gully as his birthday present.

Paula Danziger wrote a series of books that follow Matthew as he moves from fourth grade through junior high: *Everyone Else's Parents Said Yes, Make Like a Tree and Leave, Earth to Matthew,* and *Not for a Billion Gazillion Dollars.* These books show the changing patterns of peer relationships as Matthew develops. In the early years, Matthew has almost exclusive interactions with boys; over time girls gradually are included in the activities. The major emphasis in this group of books is peer relationships, but issues such as conservation, ecology, and responsibility are addressed also.

Walter Dean Myers uses an urban setting for *Won't Know Till I Get There*, portraying different situations through 14-year-old Steve's diary entries. Steve's parents believe that it is their responsibility to share their home and love with a child who is less fortunate. They choose Earl, a 13-year-old who has a criminal record. When Steve and his friends spray paint a train to show off for Earl, they are caught and sentenced to spend the summer working in a senior citizens' home. Over the course of the summer, all of the children learn to respect each of the seniors as individuals. They also learn about the harm that stereotypes can cause and that personal values can make life worthwhile. Steve's parents support both boys. Earl's birth mother refuses to sign the adoption papers, but the family assumes legal custody of him.

Betsy Byars addresses abusive behavior through an 11-year-old boy in *Cracker Jackson.* Cracker seeks to help his former babysitter, Alma, convinced that she is in trouble because she has bruises. Finally she agrees to go to a battered women's shelter, but changes her mind halfway there and insists that Cracker take her home. Later, when Cracker's mother goes to Alma's house she finds both Alma and Alma's baby have been badly beaten and takes them to the hospital. When the two recover, Cracker and his parents take them to a shelter so Alma can begin a new life.

### Peers

Bette Bao Lord gives us insight into how one little girl overcomes prejudice and stereotyping in the book *In The Year of the Boar and Jackie Robinson.* Shirley Temple Wong and her mother move to the United States to join her father in 1947. Shirley's adjustment to school is difficult. She gets two black eyes from Mabel, one of the biggest girls in fifth grade, but refuses to tell who hit her. After that, Mabel becomes Shirley's guide and guard. With her help, Shirley learns to play baseball and becomes a fan of Jackie Robinson. In sixth grade, she makes another friend, Emily, and helps her get elected to class president. When Jackie Robinson comes to the school, Shirley gets to present him with the key to the school. It is a proud moment for Shirley when she meets her hero and recognizes the opportunities that are available to her.

The theme of Katherine Paterson's *Flip-Flop Girl* is friendship between two misfits. Vinnie moves to a new school after her father's death. During the difficult first days in school she meets Lupe, a fellow misfit, and the two form a tenuous relationship. After Lupe helps Vinnie in a crisis, she learns to accept responsibility for her own actions and she begins to mature.

Like Vinnie, Alice has many school-related problems in *Reluctantly Alice*, by Phyllis Reynolds Naylor: boys, teachers, homework, and taking showers in gym. Alice gains the respect of an older girl by choosing her as a partner for classroom activities. As she gains confidence, she is able to resolve some of her problems and family relationships by facing them. She discovers the support and friendship she needs from her widowed father, older brother, and two close friends.

Ten-year-old Blaze faces major life changes after his mother's death in Kevin Henkes's *Words of Stone*. Blaze is a fearful child who is easily upset. He is very disturbed to see his mother's name written in stones on the hillside. Then he learns that Joselle, who is visiting her own grandmother, did it. He also learns that she embellishes the truth, but she does help him get over some of his fears. He realizes that she too feels lonely and abandoned.

Jerry Spinelli writes about very different experiences in *There's a Girl in My Hammerlock*. Eighth grader Maisie was not chosen for the cheerleading squad, so she decides to sign up for the wrestling team. Maisie is taunted in the school and community and most of her friends abandon her, but she is feisty, determined, and a good wrestler. She earns her teammates' respect as well as that of her coach, the school, and the community. The experience is not easy, but Maisie earns self-respect and insights about the important things in life.

Friendships make a positive contribution to growing up, but they can have negative consequences as well. In *Out of Control*, Norma Fox Mazer describes a friendship among three boys that began in elementary school and continues into high school. These three popular boys are accustomed to impressing girls, but Valerie is not impressed with their behavior and confronts them. They decide to get even and attack her in the hall. They are surprised when she reports the attack and they are suspended from school. Valerie explains why she goes public about the attack: "Because you guys did what you wanted to me and you're home free" (p. 216). Rollo begins to question himself, his actions, and his friends. Finally he breaks with his friends at the end of the story.

Although many of the books discussed in this section fit in the category of contemporary realistic fiction, similar themes appear in historical fiction. Theodore Taylor describes Ben's life in the late 1890s on the coast near Cape Hatteras in *Teetoncey*, *Teetoncey and Ben O'Neal*, and *The Odyssey of Ben O'Neal*. In the first book, Ben rescues Teetoncey from nearly drowning after a shipwreck. He takes her home to his mother where she remains in a coma. In the second book, Teetoncey comes out of the coma and the British consul tries to take her back to England. She is well hidden and stays with the O'Neals. Teetoncey, Ben, and his friends try to find the chest of gold bullion that went down with the ship. When the local men discover their plan, they get the chests, but Ben's mother cuts a rope and sinks the chests in the ocean. Ben's mother dies of pneumonia. In the third book, Ben signs on a ship as a galley boy and Teetoncey follows him. Thirteen years later, they return to North Carolina and marry. This series portrays relationships and growing up and it also gives a picture of life in the 1890s and early 1900s.

In a very different setting, Jan Hudson tells about the challenges of growing up in the Native American culture. *Sweetgrass* is the story of a 15-year-old Blackfoot girl. She and her friends are beginning to have their marriages arranged. They face constant problems in finding food and another Nation attacks them. The greatest challenge occurs when the family is exposed to smallpox during the coldest part of the winter. Sweetgrass is spared the smallpox, but the entire responsibility for her family's care falls on her shoulders. She must find food and bury the dead. She copes so well with these challenges that her father recognizes her as an adult.

*Clay was homeless at eleven but couldn't leave the streets for fear that he would never find Ma or Daddy again.*

## Survival

The young people in these books must rely on their own wits, intelligence, and strength to survive. Except for brief intervals they do not have family, peer, or other adult support. Clay Garrity, abandoned by his parents, is befriended by homeless men in Paula Fox's *Monkey Island.* After some hoodlums trash the park, Clay becomes ill and goes to the hospital. While there, a social worker comes to interview him and places Clay in a foster home. His foster parents are kind, but Clay depends on his street friends. Then social services locates his mother and reunites Clay with her.

Harley Nunn's mother has regularly abandoned him since he was a young child. His saga is revealed in *Out of Nowhere* by Ouida Sebestyen. At the beginning of the story, Harley's mother is living with a man who will not take Harley with them. When Harley is abandoned in a roadside park, an old woman offers him food. Then he finds a dog and the three form an unlikely trio. They travel to the old woman's home and add two more people to the group. Over time they build a kind of dependence and trust among themselves and Harley experiences the responsibilities and stability of love.

Slake, age 13, lives with an abusive aunt in Felice Holman's *Slake's Limbo.* He escapes a gang and stays in a subway, where he remains for 121 days. He earns money by selling papers the subway passengers leave and by scavenging items people leave on the subway. He gradually develops a routine and lives relatively well until he becomes ill. After he recovers in the hospital, he runs away to escape social services. However, he has matured to the point that he wants to stay aboveground.

In a book by Jerry Spinelli, Jeffrey becomes *Maniac Magee* when he runs away from his aunt and uncle's dysfunctional family, at the age of 11, to the town where he lived before his parents' death. He receives his the nickname because of the things he does: he borrows a book from Amanda Beale, which he carries around with him; intercepts a pass at the varsity football game; saves a child from the Finsterwalds; runs on the railroad rails; hits every one of John McNab's pitches; and hits the Little League team bully. He lives with the animals at the zoo; with the Beales, a black family in a segregated town; with a groundskeeper at the bandshell; and with the racist McNabs. In a completely unconventional manner, Maniac becomes a bridge between the white and black sides of town. The book ends as Maniac follows Amanda, knowing "that finally, truly at long last, someone was calling him home" (p. 184).

Jean George has written many wonderful books for children. *My Side of the Mountain*, a revered favorite of many children and adults, is an account of how Sam creates a house in the roots of a tree to survive the winter and tames a falcon to help him gather food. Although Sam has occasional guests, he is self-sufficient. In the sequel, *On the Far Side of the Mountain*, Sam's sister Alice joins him on the mountain. Alice has her own treehouse, but she and Sam work together on projects. Sam's falcon has disappeared, but Alice is able to free it and Sam contacts the sheriff who arrests the men who stole the bird to sell it illegally. Through their experiences, Sam and Alice learn to appreciate each other and other people as well.

Gary Paulsen has written a number of survival books with young men as protagonists. In *Tracker*, John Borne's grandfather is dying of cancer and John must go deerhunting alone. He knows his grandparents need the food to survive the winter, but he has a hard time killing an animal. He tracks a doe, thinking about life, death, and dying, but he is unable to kill the deer. He returns and tells his grandparents that he couldn't kill. Sam is surprised at his grandfather's pride in him. At this point, he is able to accept the inevitability of death.

In another of Paulsen's books, *Hatchet*, Brian Robeson is stranded in a wilderness when the plane he is a passenger on crashes in a lake. He is injured but survives. He learns to make a fire, gather food, and build a shelter. He survives animal and insect attacks, a hurricane, and illness. Brian is forever changed by his experience and comes out of it

more mature. In the sequel to *Hatchet*, *The River*, Brian returns to the wilderness with a psychologist, Derek, because Derek wants to study the mental processes that enabled Brian to survive. Lightning strikes both Derek and Brian and puts Derek in a coma, so Brian is again in a desperate situation. He builds a raft, lashes Derek to it, and is able to save himself and Derek.

In *The Iceberg Hermit*, a historical fiction book by Arthur Roth, 17-year-old Allan Gordon signs on a whaling ship working north of Greenland. The captain is a stubborn man and does not start the return trip until bad weather sets in. The ship hits an iceberg and sinks; Allan is the sole survivor. The ship surfaces and provides him with food, but he lives in a cave well away from the ship. A young polar bear adopts him and helps him find food. Later he is discovered by Eskimos and lives with them for several seasons. After seven years he returns to Scotland via a whaling ship.

Roth uses a very different setting for a survival theme in *The Castaway*. Daniel has a misunderstanding with his brother and runs away to sea. His ship crashes, and Daniel washes up on a small rock reef in the southern Pacific Ocean. He learns how to get food and shelter and makes friends with some of the animals. Five years later, he is rescued when a ship is blown off course.

## Societal Issues

The story characters in this section face many of the same challenges as those in the previous section—growing up with or without families, establishing relationships with peers and adults, and surviving on their own. However, these young people have no control over the events they are caught up in. Slavery, war, economic hardships, and political upheavals change their entire way of life and create new challenges.

The books in this section are organized in a chronological order of sorts, but there is considerable overlap in the years included in the various categories. History resists neat categorization when considered from an issues perspective and impact of those issues on people's lives. The books on slavery, war, exploration, and similar issues could easily have fit into a category of societal impact.

PAM CONRAD

*PEDRO'S JOURNAL*

*A Voyage with Christopher Columbus*
*August 3, 1492 - February 14, 1493*

*Illustrated by* PETER KOEPPEN

*Pedro de Salcedo was a cabin boy aboard the Santa Maria when Columbus sailed to the new world.*

### Pre-Colonial Era

*Pedro's Journal* by Pam Conrad and *I Sailed with Columbus* by Miriam Schlein both tell about Columbus's voyages from a cabin boy's point of view. In both books, the cabin boy is aware that Columbus is keeping two sets of records and each is ashamed of the mistreatment of the natives. Overall, each writer gives a relatively positive view of Columbus and his goals. There are similarities in authors' descriptions of events, although they differ in the emphasis placed on some events, so both books suggest interesting possibilities for critical reading.

Jane Yolen offers a very different perspective of Columbus in *Encounter*. A native boy dreams of strangers who are coming to the village and the problems they will bring with them, but since he is only a child the elders ignore him. When the strangers arrive he and several others are taken captive. He is able to escape, but disease and colonization doom his people.

Michael Dorris also writes about Columbus's arrival from Taino's perspective in *Morning Girl*. Readers have an opportunity to live through the problems Morning Girl and her brother face when the strangers arrive. They welcome these new people, but they have no way of knowing that their lives are changed forever.

### Colonial Era

Elvajean Hall chronicles the struggles and successes of the Pilgrims from 1606 to 1621 in *Margaret Pumphrey's Stories*. They did not have religious freedom in Holland, where they had gone to escape religious persecution in England and feared that the children were becoming Hollanders. Readers learn about their problems in obtaining the money they needed to move to the New World. Gary Bowen uses diary entries to describe the same period in *Stranded at Plimoth Plantation 1626*. The storyteller is 13-year-old Christopher Seals, an indentured orphan who stays with the Brewster family. This time period is also explored by Cheryl Harness in *Three Young Pilgrims*, a story about a fictional family, carefully researched to be representative of the *Mayflower* Pilgrims and their struggles.

*The Witch of Blackbird Pond* by Elizabeth George Speare is set in the time of the New England witch hunts. Kit is one of those named as a witch, but she is finally acquitted and accepted in the community. In Kathryn Lasky's book *Beyond the Burning Time*, Mary Chase's widowed mother is named a witch and sentenced to hanging. Although they are terrified, Mary and her brother are determined to save their mother, who is imprisoned under terrible conditions, awaiting execution. In the end, their mother must have a foot amputated, but she escapes and the family starts a new life in Bermuda. This is a very carefully researched book and includes interesting documentation.

Avi explores the way children were treated in the late 1700s in two books, *Night Journeys* and *Encounter at Easton*. In the first, 12-year-old Peter lives with his guardian Everett Shinn, who is a justice of the peace. When two bondsmen escape, Peter joins his guardian in the hunt to try to gain the reward. When he learns the runaways are children, he changes his mind and tries to help them escape. Elizabeth, the girl, was branded with an *M* on her thumb because she stole to get food. Robert was sentenced because he helped her. In *Encounter at Easton*, the story is told through the recorded testimony in this case. Eventually, Elizabeth is killed, but Robert survives.

Sally Keehn carefully documented *I Am Regina*, a fascinating true story. Regina is captured by Indians during the French and Indian War. During the eight years of her captivity she grows to love the woman with whom she lives. However, eventually she is returned to her real mother, who identifies her through a song she sang to Regina when she was a child.

## Revolutionary War

Children's authors have written about many of the dimensions of the Revolutionary War, including the colonists, the loyalists, the Native Americans, adults, children, and many more. Literature helps children understand complex periods of history such as this by helping them identify with the characters and their emotions as they hear or read the stories of this period.

Avi documents a 24-hour period of the American Revolution in *The Fighting Ground*. In this story, 13-year-old Jonathan runs away to join the fighting, but three Hessians capture him and imprison him in a house with the bodies of a small boy and his parents. After burying them, Jonathan escapes, only to be recaptured. He is finally able to return home, wiser than when he left.

Tempe Wick is a feisty girl who hides her horse in her bedroom so the British soldiers will not take it in *This Time Tempe Wick?* by Patricia Gauch. On the other side of the war is an equally feisty Tory, Katie, whose story is related by Ann Turner in *Katie's Trunk*. This story is based on a true incident in the life of one of the author's ancestors. Katie's family flees when a group of colonists threatens their home, but young Katie returns to protect their property. Finally realizing her efforts are futile, she hides in a trunk.

James Lincoln Collier also gives a Tory point of view of the Revolution in *My Brother Sam Is Dead*. Tim witnesses his Tory father's imprisonment and

*Set in seventeenth-century Salem, this is an unforgettable story about good and evil and an individual's power to make moral choices.*

the massacre of his neighbors by British troops; then his brother, a Continental soldier, is convicted of a crime he didn't commit. This story shows the human cost of war and that everyone loses in war.

The Native American perspective on the Revolution is portrayed in *The Valley of the Shadow* by Janet Hickman. This story is based on the Delaware Nation in Ohio which converted to Christianity and tried to remain neutral in the war. Tobias and the group experience a daily struggle to live; eventually they are captured and methodically murdered. Tobias and his friend Thomas escape and make their way to the missionaries, who help them.

The difficulties of African Americans during the Revolutionary period is the theme of *Jump Ship to Freedom* by James Lincoln Collier and Christopher Collier. The main character of this story is Dan, who is trying to buy his family's freedom. His maturation and growing confidence are an important aspect of the theme. He does finally achieve freedom.

## Building and expansion

Following the Revolutionary War, a period of building and expanding our country emerged. Some families remained to put down roots where their families had settled originally; others moved to settle the frontier. Life in New England is portrayed by Barbara Cooney in *Island Boy*. Matthais' father built the first house on Tibbets Island and Matthais returns to the island again and again during his long life. Children and adults have loved the Laura Ingalls Wilder Little House series, based on her family life, for many years. These books based on her family tell about a family moving and living in frontier America. The family is introduced in *Little House in the Big Woods* and follows the moves of her family to frontier America, ending with Laura's adulthood in *The First Four Years*.

The exploits of Laura and her family have become a real part of Americana. A popular television series, *Little House on the Prairie*, was based on one of her books by the same name. More recently, T. L. Tedrow wrote another series of books, "The Days of Laura Ingalls Wilder." He states in the foreword of *Good Neighbors*, "While this book is a fictional account of Laura's exploits, it retains the historical integrity of her columns, diary, . . . and the general history of the times in which she lived" (p. 10). Roger Lea MacBride has written another series about the Wilders from the perspective of Laura's daughter, Rose. MacBride was Rose's only heir and has her books, diaries, and letters, which served as the basis for his books, *Little House on Rocky Ridge* and *The Little Farm in the Ozarks*.

As the pioneers moved west, they often encountered Native Americans. This is the theme of *Thunder Rolling in the Mountains* by Scott O'Dell and Elizabeth Hall, which tells about the westward movement from the Native American perspective. When Sound of Running Feet and her friends see a white family's cabin they know there is danger from the whites and their soldiers. The community is forced to move and they battle the soldiers as they are moved from camp to camp and eventually to a reservation in Idaho.

A number of popular books tell about the daily life in pioneer families. In *Aurora Means Dawn*, Scott Sanders introduces young children to a family moving from Connecticut to Ohio to build a new home, and in *Warm as Wool* he recreates the story of the Ward family, the first pioneers to own sheep in their township. *Going West* helps young readers understand the hardship of traveling in wagons. Jean Van Leeuwen depicts brutal weather, deprivation, and isolation in this story, but the pioneers never lose hope.

## A nation at war with itself

The themes of slavery and the Civil War are inextricably tied together and influence the entire history of our nation. Slavery was the pivotal force in the Civil War and in the following period of Reconstruction, and without these turning points, much else in our history would have never occurred.

*Slavery.* Understanding slavery is essential to understanding all of the history of our country. Scott O'Dell develops the reader's sensitivity to slavery in *My Name Is Not Angelica*, the story of Raisha and Konje, prominent members of their African tribe who were to marry in three years time. After they are taken captive and sold on St. John Island in 1733, they suffer cruel treatment as slaves. Konje is treated so badly that he joins the other runaway slaves, who jump off a cliff rather than go back to the plantations when they are discovered. Raisha later was taken to Martinique, where, under the law there, she is no longer a slave.

Jennifer Armstrong gives another view of slavery in *Steal Away*. Susannah lives in Vermont, but her parents' deaths make it necessary to live with her uncle's family in Virginia. In his household she meets a young slave, Bethlehem Reid, with whom she becomes friends. The two girls decide to dress as boys and escape to Vermont. This exciting story is told through journals and letters and follows the two girls from 1855 through 1896.

Mary Lyons also uses letters to tell about the life of an African American child born into slavery in *Letters from a Slave Girl: The Story of Harriet Jacobs*. She portrays a life of great injustice, hope, and courage. As an adult, Harriet runs away and hides in an attic crawlspace for seven years.

Although this book shows slavery's brutality, the main character's spirit is uplifting.

*The Civil War.* So many fine books have been written about the Civil War and its battles that it is difficult to choose a brief sampling. As with other historical events, literature helps children experience the drama and sorrow of this war. In *Cecil's Story*, author George Ella Lyon shares a child's concerns and fears about his father going off to the Civil War. The sensitive illustrations help young readers visualize the child's fears. Battles seem exciting until we think about the human toll.

*Bull Run*, a famous battle, is interpreted by Paul Fleischman in the book of the same name. He tells about this battle from the perspectives of eight Southern characters and eight Northern characters. Each of these individuals shares his or her expectations and hopes of what will happen when the two armies meet. This book is an excellent one for reader's theater.

Carolyn Reeder's *Shades of Gray* shows how family disagreements about the Civil War tore families apart. In this book, a boy who is orphaned when his father dies in the war must live with his uncle who refuses to fight. The reader sees him come to understand himself and his uncle as the story unfolds.

## Industrialization

When peace finally returned to our nation, it was time to rebuild. The war forwarded the movement toward industrialization and the peace made raw materials available. The industrial movement, however, was built on the labor of men, women, and even children who were in many ways enslaved to the factory owners and managers. In *Lyddie*, Katherine Paterson shows readers the life of a girl working in the weaving room of a factory. When Lyddie defends a friend from the advances of the overseer, she is fired. Her strong character prevails through hard work and perseverance, and she eventually goes to Oberlin College, the only college admitting women at that time.

Joan Aiken shows readers a horrifying view of mill workers' lives in *Midnight Is a Place*. In this instance, the owner of a mill teaches Lucas, his ward, how to run the mill so that Lucas can take over when he is older. Lucas, however, is appalled by the lack of regard for human life that he sees. Lucas and another character go to work in the mill and discover that "accidents" regularly occur when managers are not paid bribes. Lucas and his friend are able to gather enough evidence to displace the people in control.

## Immigration

Many of the immigrants who came to the United States fled lives of injustice and poverty to come to work in the factories and farms of this country, as did Rebekah Levinsky and her Jewish family, who fled Russia with only the clothes they could carry. Joan Lowery Nixon tells their story in *Land of Hope*. Through Rebekah's eyes we see the pain of families whose members were denied admittance to this country. As the story unfolds, it appears that Rebekah also will be denied an education so that her older brother can go to school. When he refuses an education, she is finally able to realize her dream.

## 20th-Century Wars

The 20th-century wars are the subjects of many books, but many more of these books focus on World War II than World War I, the Korean War, Vietnam, or the more recent Gulf War. Perhaps this is because during World War II everyone living at that time was involved at some level and it so drastically changed people's lives. Also, authors tend to write about their childhood experiences and memories, so this far-reaching event became the subject of many books. This section includes a sampling from several of these wars, but consult a card catalog or a computer database to locate books that fit your educational needs.

*World War I.* Gloria Skurzynski portrays life in the United States of World War I through the lives of two boys in *Good-Bye, Billy Radish*. In a steel town of 1917, the men who are not soldiers work 12 hours a day, seven days a week. Boys as young as 14 work these long shifts as well. The heavy work schedule led to factory accidents and deaths. But accidents were not the only threat to life: the dreaded flu epidemic swept through the United States and takes Billy's life.

Pieter Van Raven's *Harpoon Island* explores the American hysteria about Germans during World War I. The main character is Frank, whose grandfather was German. When a submarine is sighted, the islanders assume Frank is a German sympathizer. After the island dwellers learn the truth, they vote for Frank to stay on the island.

*World War II.* Selecting the books for this section was most difficult because of the many fine pieces of literature focusing on this period. We have tried to select books that show the war's impact on different people. The themes in this section are concerned with the prejudice that fear creates, the importance of freedom, and the courage to prevail in the face of great difficulty.

The prejudice against Germans during World War I was prevalent throughout the United States during World War II as well, and the prejudice extended to the Japanese living on the West Coast. Because of fear and prejudice, Japanese Americans were interned in camps located in remote areas of the United States. Yoshika Uchida brings these events to life in *Journey to Topaz* and *Journey Home*, fictional accounts based on her own family's experiences. In the first, we see life in the camp through Yuki's eyes. She vividly describes their fears, the privations of living in the camp, and their desire to prove their loyalty to the United States. *Journey Home* tells about the mistreatment the Japanese Americans faced once they were released and returned home. This great injustice in our history is commemorated in a mural that depicts the internment of 120,000 Japanese Americans, which in turn inspired Sheila Hamanaka to write the picture book *The Journey: Japanese Americans, Racism, and Renewal.* The text accompanying the dramatic illustrations in this book describes the indignities and degradation suffered by these innocent people.

The United States was not the only country affected by World War II, of course. Vilna, Poland, and Siberia are the sites of *The Endless Steppe*, a true story by Esther Hautzig based on her family's trials during this war. This powerful book about human survival and adaptability tells the story of a close-knit Jewish family transported to Siberia when their country is occupied by the Russian army. They survive transportation in a cattle car,

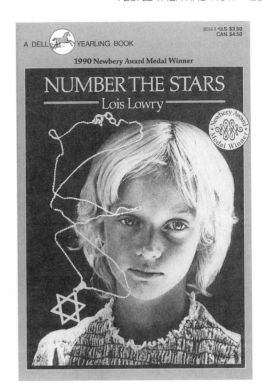

In this World War II story, Annemarie helps to save her best friend from Nazi soldiers.

degrading work, and a starvation-level existence. Esther Hautzig now lives in the United States.

Lois Lowry set *Number the Stars* in Copenhagen during the war. In this story the Johansen family "adopts" Ellen, a ten-year-old Jewish child. They are able to do this because an older daughter was killed working for the Resistance Movement, and the Jewish girl takes her place in the family. Eventually, Ellen is able to sail to Sweden and freedom.

Michael Morpugo set *Waiting for Anya* in France. The theme is a village's response to the killing of Jews. When the Germans become suspicious that villagers are helping Jewish children escape to Spain, the entire town becomes involved. Only two of the children are unable to escape, but they survive.

During World War II some men who were drafted as soldiers refused to fight because of conscientious objections; these men were assigned to noncombat positions. Other soldiers went AWOL—absent without leave from the army—for various reasons. Men in both of these categories were often the victims of prejudice during this extremely patriotic period. Mary Downing Hahn writes about these conflicts in *Stepping on the Cracks.* Margaret and Elizabeth are angry with Gordy, the meanest boy in their class. They decide to get even and in the process they discover that his brother is AWOL and use that against him. Then Margaret's family receives word that her brother is dead. After they learn that Gordy's alcoholic father abuses the entire family, they realize that many human elements affect judgments about people.

*Vietnam.*  The Vietnam War is a little-understood chapter in our history; nevertheless it influenced all of our lives. One perspective on this war is given by Katherine Paterson in *Park's Quest.* Park can't understand why his mother will not discuss his father, who died in Vietnam. Finally, during a brief visit with his father's family, he discovers that his father had another family in Vietnam and Park has a half-sister, Thanh. The other family lives near his grandparents and Park gets acquainted with Thanh; gradually they come to accept each other.

In *The Wall*, Eve Bunting portrays a boy and his father searching for a name at the Vietnam Veterans Memorial. This picture book helps young children understand the significance of the wall as a disabled veteran, a mourning couple, and children on an outing visit it.

Another context for Vietnam is presented by Minfong Ho in *The Clay Marble.* The story is set in a refugee camp on the border of Thailand and Cambodia. Countless refugees have fled to the camp in search of free food and farming supplies. The children quickly become acquainted and try to create a peaceful world although a peaceful life is so dim and distant that they can scarcely remember it. All too soon, the fighting and destruction move near the camp. Families are separated and family members struggle to reunite with the people they love.

## Special Interests

Many children develop interests during the elementary years that they retain throughout their lives; others explore a different interest each month. Whichever is true of the children you are dealing with, literature is means of exploring and expanding children's interests.

### Sports

This section identifies books that help readers look at sports in a larger context. The games and game practice create events and contexts that show readers the importance of telling the truth, of racial appreciation, of accepting one's weaknesses as well as strengths. Readers will enjoy these stories even if they are not involved in sports.

Baseball is important in two of Walter Dean Myers's books, *Me, Mop, and the Moondance Kid* and *Mop, Moondance, and the Nagasaki Knights.* The first book focuses on the lives of two adopted children and their experiences before adoption. Through baseball they learn to share both good and bad times. They also learn to deal with people they do not respect. In the second book, the same children are playing teams from other countries. The team members find it difficult to communicate with the other teams, but they meet these challenges with the strategies of 12-year-olds. When the problems grow too big, their parents help.

Some children learn to cope with failure through sports. Jason Ross is despondent when he is cut from the baseball team. He seeks coaching assistance from a school custodian in *Finding Buck McHenry* by Alfred Slote. This story includes some interesting history of players in the old Negro leagues.

Basketball is the sport of choice in Matt Christopher's *Johnny Long Legs.* Johnny has many adjustments to make in this story because his mother has just remarried and they have moved to a small town. His new classmates make his life miserable. Fortunately, his new family supports him. *Takedown*, by the same author, is a wrestling story. Sean is a successful wrestler, but he has a new stepfather, a new stepbrother, and a bully who picks on him. Through his wrestling experiences he develops a better understanding of himself and his family.

Basketball from a coach's perspective is the theme of *The Rebounder* by Thomas I. Dygard. The coach, Doug Fulton, encounters a natural basketball player, Chris Patton. The player refuses to play because he is afraid of injuring other players. Eventually, the student manager is able to help Chris work through his fears and he joins the team.

## Mysteries

Mysteries are popular with children. However, teachers, librarians, and parents have often regarded them with suspicious eyes, concerned about literary quality. Fortunately, children's mysteries include those by several notable authors such as Betsy Byars, Joan Lowery Nixon, Gary Paulsen, Phyllis Reynolds Naylor, and Virginia Hamilton—adults can rest easy when giving children books by authors of such quality.

Betsy Byars writes about Herculeah Jones, whose father is a police detective and mother is a private investigator in *The Dark Stairs*. Herculeah becomes suspicious of one of her mother's clients and launches her own investigation. After falling into a hidden stairway, she is able to answer a series of puzzling questions.

Joan Lowery Nixon is a well-known mystery writer and the only three-time winner of the Edgar Allan Poe Award. In *The Other Side of Dark*, 17-year-old Stacy awakens after a four-year coma. Her mother was killed by the same person who wounded Stacy and she is the only person who has the information to identify the killer. Stacy is able to give the necessary evidence and survives the killer's attempt to murder her.

In addition to all the other books he writes in different genre, Gary Paulsen writes mystery series. In the "Culpepper Adventures" series, Duncan Culpepper and his best friend Amos embroil themselves in mysterious situations. In *The Case of the Dirty Bird*, they search for hidden treasure but find a building filled with gunpowder instead.

## CLASSROOM ACTIVITIES TO ENHANCE LITERARY EXPERIENCES

Fiction, both in contemporary and historical settings, is particularly useful in developing children's understanding of themselves, their families, their cultural setting, their values, and issues addressed in the social studies. Trade books provide children with multiple human perspectives that textbooks do not. Moreover, literature permits readers to experience historical and current events in a very personal way. This is why more and more teachers are incorporating trade books, reader's theater, literature study groups, read-alouds, storytelling, and informal drama in their classes.

Realistic fiction and historical fiction are frequently used to develop social studies concepts, cultural studies, and geography. Historical fiction turns facts and statistics into living human experience (Tunnell and Ammon, 1993). Moreover, historical fiction and realistic fiction draw readers into reality, so that students can feel the joys, triumphs, and hopes, as well as the pain, suffering, and despair of others. Trade books from all genre are resources for integrating curriculum studies.

## Social Studies Standards

The National Council of the Social Studies and the National Center for History in the Schools (1994) have developed standards for children in kindergarten through grade 12. These standards include teaching suggestions and trade book examples like using "historical fiction such as *Trouble at the Mines* by Doreen Rappaport (1993) to investigate the strikes in the coal mines and the organizing efforts of Mother Mary Jones" (p. 154).

## Resource Guides for Using Trade Books in Classrooms

The increasing use of trade books in classrooms has encouraged publishers to provide excellent resources for teachers. This section lists guides that provide multiple approaches to integrating literature in classrooms.

- The "Exploring the United States Through Literature" series, published by Oryx Press, includes books, periodicals, and videos. Two of the titles included in this series are *Exploring the Great Lakes Through Literature* (Latrobe, 1994) and *Exploring the Southeast States Through Literature*.
- *The Story of Ourselves: Teaching History Through Children's Literature* (Tunnell and Ammon, 1993) is a practical resource that provides a

rationale for understanding history and integrating literature and history in the classroom.

- *War and Peace Literature for Children and Young Adults* (Walter, 1993) describes techniques for sharing books, suggestions for classroom activities, and comprehensive bibliographies.
- *Using Literature to Teach Middle Grades About War* (Kennemer, 1993) includes six units about the major American wars.
- *Social Studies Through Children's Literature* (Fredericks, 1991) is a helpful resource. The author includes a rationale for connecting social studies and children's literature along with units for the classroom.
- *Understanding American History Through Children's Literature* (Perez-Stable and Cordier, 1994) focuses on American history. The authors include lesson plans and activities.
- *Literature-Based Reading* (Laughlin and Swisher, 1990) presents objectives, book titles, and follow-up activities.

## Literature-Based Teaching

Teachers who use literature as a basis for their teaching use the same principles as those used when literature is the basis for learning to read. Instead of textbooks, trade books are the primary sources of information. Textbooks become reference material, just the way encyclopedias are. Although the teacher will have objectives that are to be met, much of the direction for learning comes from the interests and motivation of the children. They share the responsibility for planning with the teacher, and they help decide on activities and projects.

UNIT
SUGGESTIONS

## 8.1 Refugees

The fifth-grade students described in the opening vignette generated questions about refugees, and the teacher, Jeff McKenzie, decided to create a literature-based unit around their curiosity. One student realized that three refugees attended their school and asked to invite them into the classroom. After talking with these children, the class decided they wanted to know more and they chose to read Minfong Ho's *The Clay Marble* and Margy Burns Knight's *Who Belongs Here?* They studied formal definitions that identified refugees as people who flee from one place to another for safety. Through discussion, the students heard one another's questions, which stimulated more thinking and questioning. At this point, they had a better concept of what a refugee was, but they wanted to know more. They generated additional questions to study, such as "Could we ever become refugees?"

The teacher believes that learning is social inquiry and that students who investigate real questions are truly learning (Copenhaver, 1993). He works to structure, guide, and coach his students as they investigate. In this instance, he created a set of readings (listed below) that would provide a diverse view of refugees. The students formed cooperative groups and each group selected questions to study and books to read.

Reading List

- Cormier, Robert. *Other Bells for Us to Ring.*
- Dillon, Eilis. *Children of Bach.*
- Gregory, Kristina. *Earthquake at Dawn.*
- Hesse, Karen. *Letters From Rifka.*

- Karr, Kathleen. *It Ain't Always Easy.*
- Kerr, Judith. *When Hitler Stole Pink Rabbit.*
- Leighton, Maxine. *An Ellis Island Christmas.*
- Levitin, Sonia. *Silver Days.*
- Lutzeier, Elizabeth. *The Coldest Winter.*
- Turner, Ann. *Katie's Trunk.*

Reading, discussion, writing, and meeting with actual refugees were the major activities the cooperative groups used for learning. Each group wrote papers that summarized the things they had learned about refugees. They added the concepts of *displaced person* and *immigrant* to their discussions. After they answered the original questions (listed in the chapter vignette), each student wrote an explanation of refugees.

Each group summarized everything they had learned and created a way of sharing their conclusions with the class. One group created a frieze that showed the countries many refugees came from and a large papier-mâché globe with flags identifying the countries of origin. Another group made and illustrated a chart that showed the problems that refugees face and a list of organizations that help refugees. Another group focused on the parts of the United States that were home to refugees, exploring why refugees chose those particular places to live. Another presented a skit to the class that gave reasons for people becoming refugees, such as war or natural disasters. The students concluded that they too could become refugees through no fault of their own. Some members of the class learned that their ancestors came to this country as refugees.

## 8.2 Wagon Wheels

Third graders reading Barbara Brenner's historical fiction *Wagon Wheels* can explore a variety of social issues including interdependence, friendship, disasters, life after the Civil War, life on the frontier, and racism, as well as exploring the literary element of setting. In this story, the Muldie family is traveling to Nicodemus, Kansas, because black families can homestead land there. The family must survive many difficulties to reach their goal.

1. Introduce the book to the children. The story can be introduced with a map, so they can trace the route the Muldie family traveled. Create a bulletin board with pictures of prairies, dugouts, and other scenes from the areas they traveled through.

2. Have students read the story silently.

3. Discuss the story with the children, stimulating them to think about the story. Discuss the reasons the family traveled to Nicodemus, Kansas. Possible focus questions for discussion include:

   a. Why didn't the boys travel with their father? How would you feel if you were the boys?

   b. Why do you think Johnny told the ladies that the boys could take care of themselves?

   c. Why did the Osage Indians help the settlers?

   d. Would your parents allow you to travel 150 miles by yourself?

   e. What difficulties did the boys face in making the trip? Which was the most difficult problem?

   f. How is racism related to this story?

Questions related to setting may include:

   a. What was the time of this story?

   b. What was the place of the story?

   c. How was life different from today in the time and place of this story?

   d. What were the difficulties of living in a dugout house? What were the good things about this kind of house?

   e. What kind of research would a writer have to do to create this setting?

4. Use extension activities to allow students to respond to the story.

   a. Students can make models of a dugout.

   b. Students can make a model of Nicodemus, Kansas.

   c. Cook cornmeal mush for the students to try.

   d. Study the Osage Indians and their way of life. Create a frieze that shows the information gathered.

   e. Have each student identify one difficulty the brothers faced and write about the way they would overcome it.

   f. Compare this story with another book.

Other stories that can be included in this unit are:

- Freedman, Russell. *Children of the Wild West.*
- Rowan, James P. *Prairies and Grasslands.*
- Wilder, Laura Ingalls. *Little House on the Prairie.*
- Wilson, Terry. *The Osage.*

## SUMMARY

**Realistic** and **historical fiction** are *"tell it like it is" genre that deal with a broad range of topics that are enjoyable to read, provide insights about oneself and others, and increase understanding of events and issues.* These genre play an important role in the curriculum because this literature puts the reader in the shoes of the characters who are having different experiences and living in different times. Such experiences help children understand themselves and others. Trade books motivate students to read more than textbooks do and give readers a feeling of the emotions, the time, and the place so they have a deeper understanding than they would from merely reading facts.

Because of the range of topics and the controversial issues these books address, questions are regularly raised about their suitability for children. However, the issues addressed are the very reasons that realistic fiction and historical fiction can be the backbone of personal, school, and public libraries. Children can read them simply for enjoyment or for supplementing and enriching curricular material. They encourage readers to reflect on themselves and on contemporary issues in ways that few other genre do.

## THOUGHT QUESTIONS

1. What preparations will you make as you select books to be used in your classroom? Are there written guidelines for book selection in your school district? Is there an approved book list? Is there a policy that addresses what to do if a book is challenged by a parent or other adult?

2. What policy, if any, exists in your school district about using specific text books or basal readers? If you are required to use a basal reader, how will you adapt it so the children can read authentic literature?

3. How can you integrate literature with a social studies textbook?

4. What are your favorite contemporary realistic fiction books? Historical fiction?

5. Why do you think that some historical periods have many more books written about them than other periods? What are the implications for children and teaching?

6. What subject do you think is most neglected in historical fiction? In realistic fiction?

## ENRICHMENT ACTIVITIES

1. Find movies that have been adapted from realistic fiction. After reading the books, make Venn diagrams that illustrate the likenesses and differences in the book and film version of the story.

2. Identify an issue or topic. Using one of the resource books cited or other sources, identify books that are available on that topic. Compile an annotated bibliography for your present or future use.

3. Read several of the contemporary and historical fiction works that have received the Newbery Award. Explain why you think these books received the award.

4. Collect several books that are written in the form of journals or letters such as *A Gathering of Days*, *Pedro's Journal*, *I Sailed with Columbus*, *Dear Mr. Henshaw*, and *Strider*. Plan ways that you could use these as models for your students' journals.

5. Many realistic fiction books refer to school and school experiences as an integral part of the plot. Identify several of these books, such as *A Bride for Anna's Papa*, *Earth to Matthew*, *Scorpions*, and *Flip-Flop Girl*, and analyze the portrayal of the school. Is it positive or negative? What are the implications of the portrayal?

# RECOMMENDED CHILDREN'S BOOKS

Aiken, Joan. (1974). *Midnight Is a Place.* New York: Viking. (4–8)

The owner of a mill teaches his ward about running a mill. The ward is horrified by the lack of regard for human life that he observes.

Armstrong, Jennifer. (1992). *Steal Away.* New York: Orchard Books. (4–6)

Susannah and her slave escape to the North and become lifelong friends.

Armstrong, William H. (1971). *Sourland.* New York: HarperCollins. (4–8)

This sequel to *Sounder* shows a single parent raising a family.

Avi. (1994). *Night Journeys.* New York: Morrow. (4–7)

This story is set in the late 1700s and focuses on the search for and treatment of escaped bondsmen.

———. (1994). *Encounter at Easton.* New York: Morrow. (4–7)

The sequel to *Night Journeys* tells what happened to the bondsmen.

———. (1992). *Who Was That Masked Man, Anyway?* New York: Macmillan. (4–7)

The setting is 1945. Frankie listens to so many radio programs that he has an imaginary persona.

———. (1992). *Blue Heron.* New York: Macmillan. (4–7)

Maggie visits her father, stepmother, and baby half-sister and discovers problems she did not expect.

———. (1991). *Nothing but the Truth: A Documentary Novel.* New York: Orchard Books. (4–8)

Philip Mallory hums along with "The Star-Spangled Banner" in school and is suspended. The author tells the story through the letters and memos written about it.

———. (1984). *The Fighting Ground.* New York: HarperCollins. (4–8)

Bauer, Marion Dane. (1991). *Face to Face.* Boston: Houghton Mifflin. (4–6)

This story explores the relationship between Michael and his father and his stepfather.

Blos, Joan. (1979). *A Gathering of Days: A New England Girl's Journal.* New York: Scribner's. (3–8)

Life in early New England is depicted through journal entries.

Bowen, Gary. (1994). *Stranded at Plimoth Plantation 1626.* New York: HarperCollins. (2–4)

This historical fiction portrays the daily life of a boy at Plimoth Plantation.

Brenner, Barbara. (1978). *Wagon Wheels.* Illustrated by Don Bolognese. New York: Harper & Row. (1–3)

An African American family moves from Kentucky to Kansas after the Civil War.

Brooks, Bruce. (1992). *What Hearts.* New York: HarperCollins. (4–8)

This Newbery honor book addresses four major problems that Asa the protagonist faces: divorce, moving, stepfather, and learning about love.

Bunting, Eve. (1991). *Sharing Susan.* New York: HarperCollins. (4–7)

Susan is mixed up with another infant in the hospital nursery. The mix-up is discovered when the other child dies and the parents of the dead girl seek her out.

———. (1990). *The Wall.* Illustrated by Ronald Himmer. New York: Clarion. (4–8)

A boy and his father visit the Vietnam Veteran's Memorial to search for a name on the memorial. During the visit they encounter many different veterans.

Byars, Betsy. (1994). *The Dark Stairs: A Herculeah Jones Mystery.* New York: Viking. (4–6)

Herculeah Jones has a father who is a police detective and a mother who is a private detective. In this story she gets involved in one of her mother's cases.

_____ . (1991). *Wanted . . . Mud Blossom*. Illustrated by Jacqueline Rogers. New York: Delacorte. (4–8)

Mud, the Blossom family dog, is accused of eating the class hamster.

_____ . (1988). *The Burning Questions of Bingo Brown*. New York: Viking. (3–6)

This very funny story tells about first love between classmates, and a teacher who has some serious problems.

_____ . (1985). *Cracker Jackson*. New York: Viking. (3–7)

Eleven-year-old Cracker helps his former babysitter, who is the victim of beatings.

_____ . (1983). *The Glory Girl*. New York: Viking. (4–7)

Glory is the misfit in her family until she joins forces with another family misfit.

Carter, A. (1989). *The Shoshoni*. New York: Franklin Watts. (4–7)

The author has created a portrait of tribal life including history, hunting, gathering, religion, culture, customs, games, and art.

Caseley, Judith. (1994). *Harry and Arney*. New York: Greenwillow. (2–5)

Harry is the big brother in this book.

_____ . (1993). *Chloe in the Know*. New York: Beech Tree. (2–5)

Chloe is the middle child in the Kane family and this book is told from her point of view.

_____ . (1992). *Starring Dorothy Kane*. New York: Beech Tree. (2–5)

Another story in the Kane family series. This story is from the oldest child's perspective.

_____ . (1991). *Hurricane Harry*. New York: Beech Tree. (2–5)

Harry is an only son in the Kane family when he tells this story.

Christopher, Matt. (1990). *Takedown*. New York: Little, Brown. (4–7)

Sean is a successful wrestler whose experiences help him develop a better understanding of himself and his family.

_____ . (1970). *Johnny Long Legs*. New York: Little, Brown. (5–8)

Johnny is a basketball player, but when he moves to a new town he encounters many adjustments. His new classmates make his life miserable, but his family supports him.

Cleary, Beverly. (1991). *Strider*. New York: Morrow. (3–5)

Leigh Botts and a friend find a dog and agree on joint custody.

_____ . (1983). *Dear Mr. Henshaw*. New York: Morrow. (3–5)

Leigh Botts writes a series of letters to his favorite author in an attempt to deal with his parents' divorce.

_____ . (1977). *Ramona and Her Father*. New York: Morrow. (2–5)

The focus of this story is Ramona's relationship with her father. They deal with unease, irritation, and worry, and solve their problems.

_____ . (1968). *Beezus and Ramona*. New York: Morrow. (2–4)

Beezus and her little sister Ramona are the main characters in this episodic story.

Collier, James Lincoln. (1974). *My Brother Sam Is Dead*. New York: Macmillan. (5–8)

This is one of several books about the American Revolution that Collier has written. In this story, the reader learns about the Revolution from the Tory perspective.

Collier, James Lincoln, and Christopher Collier. (1981). *Jump Ship for Freedom*. New York: Delacorte. (4–8)

Dan, a young African American, is the central figure in this story that shows the American Revolution from a different perspective.

Conrad, Pam. (1991). *Pedro's Journal.* Honesdale, PA: Boyds Mill. (4–6)

This story is about Columbus's voyage and is written from the point of view of a cabin boy.

Cooney, Barbara. (1988). *Island Boy.* New York: Viking. (K–3)

This story follows a New England child's growth into a father and a grandfather.

Cormier, Robert. (1990). *Other Bells for Us to Ring.* New York: Delacorte. (3–6)

Danziger, Paula. (1992). *Not for a Billion Gazillion Dollars.* New York: Delacorte. (4–6)

In this story Matthew's peer relationships are the focus as well as issues of responsibility.

_____ . (1991). *Earth to Matthew.* New York: Delacorte. (3–6)

Matthew is beginning to experience the pangs of love in this story.

_____ . (1990). *Make Like a Tree and Leave.* New York: Delacorte. (3–6)

Matthew Martin is serving as the chair of the Mummy Committee on the Egypt Unit Project.

_____ . (1989). *Everyone Else's Parents Said Yes.* New York: Delacorte. (4–6)

Matthew Martin is planning big things for his 11th birthday, but his plans go awry.

Dillon, Eilis. (1992). *Children of Bach.* New York: Scribner's. (2–4)

Reading this book about Bach will increase children's music appreciation.

Dorris, Michael. (1992). *Morning Girl.* New York: Hyperion. (3–6)

This story is set in 1492 and is told by 12-year-old Morning Girl and her brother, who live on a Caribbean island.

Dugan, Barbara. (1994). *Good-bye, Hello.* New York: Greenwillow. (4–6)

Bobbie Callahan faces many adjustments after her grandmother moves in and also has to cope with the fact that her grandmother is ill.

Dygard, Thomas J. (1994). *The Rebounder.* New York: Morrow. (5–9)

A basketball coach is perplexed about why a "natural" basketball player refuses to be on the team.

Fitzhugh, Louise. (1974). *Nobody's Family Is Going to Change.* New York: Farrar, Straus & Giroux. (4–7)

Emma faces the fact that her family will not change, and she will have to live with their problems.

Fleischman, Paul. (1993). *Bull Run.* New York: HarperCollins. (4–7)

Seven different perspectives on the Civil War battle.

_____ . (1992). *Jim Ugly.* New York: Greenwillow. (4–7)

The main character has his father's dog, Jim Ugly, but his aunt plans to get rid of the dog.

_____ . (1991). *The Borning Room.* New York: HarperCollins. (4–7)

This story follows the people who died and various infants who were born in one room over the years.

Forbes, Esther. (1943). *Johnny Tremain.* Illustrated by Lynd Ward. Boston: Houghton Mifflin. (5–8)

This historical fiction book set in the Revolutionary War tells about a handicapped apprentice silversmith. He learns how to make his way in the world with his handicap.

Fox, Paula. (1991). *Monkey Island.* New York: Orchard Books. (4–7)

Clay's parents abandon him and he is befriended by street people. He later reunites with his mother.

Freedman, Russell. (1983). *Children of the Wild West.* Burlington, MA: Clarion. (3–6)

This nonfiction book shows what it was like for settlers and Native American children living and going to school in the West.

Gauch, Patricia. (1974). *This Time Tempe Wick?* New York: Putnam. (2–4)

    Tempe Wick bravely saves her horse from the British soldiers.

———. (1975). *Thunder at Gettysburg.* New York: Putnam. (2–6)

    Historical fiction set during the Civil War.

George, Jean. (1959). *My Side of the Mountain.* New York: Dutton. (4–7)

    In this old favorite, Sam becomes self-sufficient in the house he creates in the roots of a tree.

———. (1990). *On the Far Side of the Mountain.* New York: Viking. (4–7)

    This sequel to *My Side of the Mountain* tells what happens when Sam's sister joins him on the mountain.

Gregory, Kristina. (1992). *Earthquake at Dawn.* New York: Harcourt Brace Jovanovich. (4–8)

    A fictionalized account of two young women witnessing the San Francisco earthquake of 1906.

Hahn, Mary Downing. (1991). *Stepping on the Cracks.* New York: Clarion. (5–8)

    Men who avoided military service during World War II are the focus of this story.

Hall, Elvajean. (1991). *Margaret Pumphrey's Pilgrim Stories.* New York: Rand McNally. (4–7)

    The author chronicles the Pilgrims' experiences from 1606 to 1621.

Hamanaka, Sheila. (1990). *The Journey: Japanese Americans, Racism, and Renewal.* New York: Orchard. (5–8)

    The mural commemorating the internment of Japanese Americans during the Second World War is depicted in this picture book.

Hamilton, Virginia. (1989). *The Bells of Christmas.* New York: Harcourt Brace Jovanovich. (4–7)

    This historical fiction story tells about a family Christmas celebration in 1890.

Harness, Cheryl. (1992). *Three Young Pilgrims.* New York: Bradbury. (1–4)

    The Allerton family, *Mayflower* Pilgrims, are followed in this historical fiction book.

Hautzig, Esther. (1968). *The Endless Steppe.* New York: Crowell. (4–7)

    This story of a young Jewish girl and her family who were exiled to Siberia actually happened.

Henkes, Kevin. (1992). *Words of Stone.* New York: Puffin. (3–6)

    A lonely boy discovers another child with the same problems.

Hesse, Karen. (1992). *Letters from Rifka.* New York: Henry Holt. (5–adult)

    Rifka and her family flee the oppression against Jews in Russia. The details of her journey are written in letters to her cousin.

Hickman, Janet. (1974). *The Valley of the Shadow.* New York: Macmillan. (4–7)

    This story is based on the daily life of a Delaware Nation in Ohio who converted to Christianity. They were murdered in the end.

———. (1994). *Jericho.* New York: Greenwillow. (4–7)

    This book focuses on four generations of women in one family.

Ho, Minfong. (1991). *The Clay Marble.* New York: Farrar, Straus & Giroux. (4–8)

    A refugee camp on the Thailand and Cambodian border is authentically portrayed in this novel.

Holman, Felice. (1974). *Slake's Limbo.* New York: Aladdin. (4–7)

    Slake lives underground in the subway and matures.

Hudson, Jan. (1984). *Sweetgrass.* New York: Philomel. (3–6)

    A 15-year old Blackfoot Indian girl living in Alberta, Canada, is the heroine of this tale.

Hunt, Irene. (1976). *The Lottery Rose*. New York: Scribner's. (4–8)

Georgie, an abused child, is sent to a private school where he begins to heal and build some permanent relationships.

Jukes, Mavis. (1984). *Like Jake and Me*. Illustrated by Lloyd Bloom. New York: Knopf. (2–4)

Jake and his stepson have an uneasy relationship until the wolf spider gets on Jake and his stepson saves him.

Karr, Kathleen. (1990). *It Ain't Always Easy*. New York: Farrar, Straus & Giroux. (4–up)

In this story, two orphans travel from New York City to Pennsylvania, searching for love and for a family.

Keehn, Sally M. (1984). *I Am Regina*. New York: Philomel. (4–7)

This story about a girl who was captured by Native Americans during the French and Indian War is based on fact, but some of the details elaborated are fictitious.

Kerr, Judith. (1972). *When Hitler Stole Pink Rabbit*. New York: Coward McCann. (3–5)

This is the story of a Jewish family that escaped Hitler's Germany. They lived as refugees in Switzerland.

Knight, Margy Burns. (1994). *Who Belongs Here?* Tilbury House. (2–5)

This picture book portrays the confusion of a Vietnamese child who struggles to come to the United States, only to be rejected by his classmates.

Lasky, Kathryn. (1994). *Beyond the Burning Time*. New York: Scholastic. (5–8)

The widow Virginia Chase is named a witch and sentenced to be hanged. Her children determine to save her and they succeed.

Leeuwen, Jean Van. (1989). *Dear Mom, You're Ruining My Life*. New York: Viking. (4–7)

Samantha, a sixth grader, is often embarrassed by her parents. However, she and her parents have a unique way of communicating that helps her solve the problem.

————. (1992). *Going West*. New York: Dial. (2–4)

This book depicts the hardships of pioneer life in terms that young children can understand.

Leighton, Maxine. (1992). *An Ellis Island Christmas*. New York: Viking. (2–up)

This is a story of a family of immigrants who have to spend Christmas on Ellis Island.

Levitin, Sonia. (1970). *Journey to America*. New York: Aladdin. (4–7)

A German Jewish family become refugees when Hitler comes to power and suffer many difficulties but are reunited in America.

————. (1989). *Silver Days*. New York: Atheneum.

This book tells about the further adventures of a Jewish family that escapes Nazi Germany.

Little, Jean. (1986). *Different Dragons*. New York: Penguin. (4–7)

Ben Tucker is afraid of dogs, but he finally makes peace with his aunt's big dog and accepts the dog as a present after he learns the dog is afraid too.

Lord, Bette Bao. (1984). *In the Year of the Boar and Jackie Robinson*. New York: HarperCollins. (4–7)

Shirley Temple Wong and her family move to the United States in 1947. Shirley must make many adjustments to her new country.

Lowry, Lois. (1977). *A Summer to Die*. Boston: Houghton Mifflin. (6–9)

Meg and her family move to the country and are just beginning to adjust when they learn that her older sister has leukemia.

————. (1989). *Number the Stars*. Boston: Houghton Mifflin. (4–6)

This Newbery Award winner is about a Danish family helping a Jewish girl escape the Nazis.

Lutzeier, Elizabeth. (1991). *The Coldest Winter*. New York: Holiday House. (4–up)

The story is set in the Irish Potato Famine of the 1840s. An Irish family is evicted from their farm in the dead of winter because the landlord wants more grazing land.

Lyon, George Ella. (1991). *Cecil's Story*. Illustrated by Peter Catalanotto. New York: Orchard Books. (1–3)

This is a story about a child's fears about his father going to fight in the Civil War.

Lyons, Mary. (1992). *Letters from a Slave Girl: The Story of Harriet Jacobs*. New York: Scribner's. (4–8)

A fictionalized account, this story is told through letters written by an African American child born into slavery.

MacBride, Roger Lea. (1993). *Little House on Rocky Ridge*. New York: HarperCollins. (3–5)

This is one of the series MacBride did about the Wilder family. It is based on the diaries and letters of Rose Wilder, Laura's daughter.

_____ . (1994). *Little Farm in the Ozarks*. New York: HarperCollins. (3–5)

More about the Wilder family told from the perspective of Laura's daughter Rose. These books are based on Rose's diaries and letters.

MacLachlan, Patricia. (1985). *Sarah, Plain and Tall*. New York: Harper & Row. (3–7)

Sarah, a mail-order bride, becomes very important to her stepchildren.

_____ . (1991). *Journey*. New York: Delacorte. (2–4)

This is the story of a boy whose mother leaves him with his grandparents and about his loneliness for her.

Marvin, Isabel. (1994). *A Bride for Anna's Papa*. Minneapolis: Milkweed Editions. (3–6)

Anna's widowed father marries her teacher and Anna has mixed feelings, but she comes to accept her stepmother.

Mazer, Norma Fox. (1993). *Out of Control*. New York: Morrow. (5–8)

Three high school friends who are disappointed that Valerie was unimpressed with them decide to attack her. One of the boys realizes the error of his ways.

Morpurgo, Michael. (1990). *Waiting for Anya*. New York: Puffin. (5–8)

French villagers help Jews during the Second World War in this story.

Myers, Walter Dean. (1982). *Won't Know Till I Get There*. New York: Puffin. (5–8)

Fourteen-year-old Steve's family take in a street-tough foster child named Earl and both boys get in trouble. The author uses a humorous style.

_____ . (1988). *Scorpions*. New York: Harper & Row. (5–7)

Jamal is forced into taking on the leadership of a Harlem gang, the Scorpions, when his brother goes to jail. Jamal finds that he is treated with respect when he acquires a gun. Tragedy forces him to realize that he cannot keep the gun or lead the gang.

_____ . (1991). *Me, Mop, and the Moondance Kid*. New York: Delacorte. (3–7)

Two adopted children must make adjustments to their new family.

_____ . (1992). *Mop, Moondance, and the Nagasaki Knights*. New York: Delacorte. (3–7)

In this sequel to *Me, Mop, and the Moondance Kid*, the two adopted children play ball against a team from another country.

_____ . (1993). *Somewhere in the Darkness*. New York: Scholastic. (5–9)

Jimmy Little never knew his father, who is in jail. Then his father escapes and comes for Jimmy. Although his father is recaptured, Jimmy has an opportunity to meet him.

_____ . (1994). *The Glory Field*. New York: Scholastic. (5–9)

This book traces the Lewis family from 1753 in Sierra Leone, West Africa, to the present in Harlem, New York.

Naylor, Phyllis Reynolds. (1991). *Reluctantly Alice*. New York: Atheneum. (4–7)

Alice has many problems, but she discovers help in her family and from her friends.

Nixon, Joan Lowery. (1986). *The Other Side of Dark*. New York: Delacorte. (5–8)

Seventeen-year-old Stacy awakens after a four-year coma. She is the only person who can identify her mother's murderer, which puts her in danger.

————. (1992). *Land of Hope*. New York: Bantam. (5–8)

This book addresses the trials of immigrants who fled poverty and injustice to enter the United States.

O'Dell, Scott. (1989). *My Name Is Not Angelica*. Boston: Houghton Mifflin. (5–8)

Raisha and Konje were captured and sold into slavery. Eventually Raisha is able to escape.

O'Dell, Scott, and Elizabeth Hall. (1992). *Thunder Rolling in the Mountains*. Boston: Houghton Mifflin. (4–7)

This story tells about the westward movement from the Native American point of view. It tells of the Native Americans' struggles and their eventual settlement on a reservation in Idaho.

O'Neal, Zibby. (1980). *The Language of Goldfish*. New York: Viking. (5–8)

Thirteen-year-old Carrie suffers a mental breakdown and retreats from life.

Oppenheimer, Joan L. (1976). *Francesca, Baby*. New York: Scholastic. (4–7)

Francesca has to assume family responsibilities as a result of her mother's alcoholism. She joins Alateen.

Paterson, Katherine. (1978). *The Great Gilly Hopkins*. New York: Harper & Row. (4–7)

Gilly is a hardened child of the foster care system until she meets Trotter, a foster parent. She finally meets her biological mother and matures through the experience.

————. (1988). *Park's Quest*. New York: Dutton. (5–7)

Park learns about his father, who died in Vietnam, and meets his half sister, who is half-Vietnamese.

————. (1991). *Lyddie*. New York: Viking. (4–8)

Lyddie's mother forces her to work in a mill. She discovers that she has no freedom and eventually is able to leave the mill.

————. (1994). *Flip-Flop Girl*. New York: Lodestar. (4–7)

This is the story of two misfits and their relationship, which contributes to their maturing.

Paulsen, Gary. (1984). *Tracker*. New York: Puffin. (5–7)

This story is of a young man living in the woods, close to nature.

————. (1987). *Hatchet*. New York: Viking. (5–7)

Brian was traveling to visit his father when he survived an airplane crash. Alone he has to make his way in the wilderness. In the process he solves some other problems.

————. (1991). *The River*. New York: Delacorte. (5–7)

The sequel to *Hatchet* has Brian returning to the scene of his survival experience so that a psychologist can study his mental processes.

————. (1991). *The Cookcamp*. New York: Orchard Books. (5–7)

A young boy lives with his grandmother because his father is a soldier in World War II and his mother is unable to cope.

————. (1992). *The Case of the Dirty Bird*. New York: Dell. (4–7)

Duncan Culpepper and his friend Amos are involved in a search for hidden treasure in this mystery.

Pfeffer, Susan. (1987). *The Year Without Michael*. New York: Bantam. (5–9)

Michael is kidnapped on the way to visit a friend. This book portrays the family's difficulties in coping.

Roth, Arthur. (1974). *The Iceberg Hermit*. New York: Four Winds. (5–8)

Allan Gordon is the protagonist in this survival story. He is on a whaling ship working off Greenland when the ship hits an iceberg and sinks.

_____ . (1983). *The Castaway*. New York: Scholastic. (5–8)

Daniel runs away to sea and his ship crashes. This story tells about his survival.

Rylant, Cynthia. (1992). *Missing May*. New York: Orchard Books. (4–6)

A child mourns after her aunt's death, but she has wonderful memories of Aunt May.

Sanders, Scott. (1989). *Aurora Means Dawn*. Illustrated by Jill Kastner. New York: Bradbury. (1–3)

This picture book account of early pioneer life follows a family moving from Connecticut to Ohio.

_____ . (1992). *Warm as Wool*. New York: Bradbury. (2–4)

Using facts drawn from a nineteenth-century record book, the author recreates the story of a pioneer family.

Schlein, Miriam. (1991). *I Sailed with Columbus*. New York: HarperCollins. (4–7)

A cabin boy tells his story about sailing with Columbus.

Sebestyen, Ouida. (1984). *Out of Nowhere*. New York: Orchard Books. (4–7)

Harley Nunn has been abandoned by his mother, but he develops a relationship with an old woman and a dog.

Skurzynski, Gloria. (1992). *Good-bye, Billy Radish*. New York: Bradbury. (4–7)

This story is set in the United States during World War I. It is the story of two men who work long hours in steel factories.

Slote, Alfred. (1991). *Finding Buck McHenry*. New York: HarperCollins. (5–8)

After Jason Ross is cut from the baseball team, he gets help from the school custodian.

Speare, Elizabeth George. (1958). *The Witch of Blackbird Pond*. Boston: Houghton Mifflin. (6–9)

Kit is accused of being a witch during the time of the New England witch hunts.

Spinelli, Jerry. (1990). *Maniac Magee*. New York: Little, Brown. (4–7)

Jeffrey runs away from his dysfunctional family, gets the nickname Maniac Magee, and finds a home.

_____ . (1991). *There's a Girl in My Hammerlock*. New York: Simon & Schuster. (5–8)

After she fails to make the cheerleading squad, Maisie decides to become a wrestler.

Taylor, Theodore. (1974). *Teetoncey*. New York: Doubleday. (4–7)

Ben saves a nearly drowned Teetoncey from a shipwreck.

_____ . (1975). *Teetoncey and Ben O'Neal*. New York: Doubleday. (4–7)

Teetoncey comes out of a coma and the British consul tries to take her back to England.

_____ . (1977). *The Odyssey of Ben O'Neal*. New York: Doubleday. (4–7)

Ben joins a crew as a cabin boy and later marries Teetoncey.

Tedrow, T. L. (1992). *Good Neighbors*. Nashville, TN: Thomas Nelson. (4–8)

This fictionalized account of Laura Ingalls Wilder's exploits retains historical integrity.

Turner, Ann. (1992). *Katie's Trunk*. New York: Macmillan. (2–4)

Set during the Revolutionary War, this book tells the story of a young Tory girl whose home is threatened by the colonists.

———. (1989). *Grasshopper Summer*. New York: Macmillan. (4–7)

This book portrays the Dakota territory of 1874 through a family's experiences. They build a sod house and plant crops only to have them destroyed by grasshoppers.

Uchida, Yoshiko. (1971). *Journey to Topaz*. New York: Scribner's Sons. (4–7)

This is the story of a Japanese American family held in an internment camp in Utah during World War II.

———. (1978). *Journey Home*. New York: Atheneum. (4–7)

This sequel to *Journey to Topaz* tells about the lives of Japanese Americans after they were released from the internment camps.

Van Raven, Pieter. (1989). *Harpoon Island*. New York: Scribner's. (5–8)

The American hysteria about Germans is the focus of this World War I story.

Wilder, Laura Ingalls. (1971). *The First Four Years*. New York: Harper & Row. (4–7)

This tells the story of the first four years of Laura's marriage.

———. (1935). *Little House on the Prairie*. Illustrated by Garth Williams. New York: Harper & Row. (4–7)

The story tells of the Ingalls family during their years on the prairie.

Yep, Laurence. (1977). *Child of the Owl*. New York: HarperCollins. (4–7)

Casey's father sends her to live with her uncle, who sends Casey to live with her Chinese grandmother.

Yolen, Jane. (1992). *Encounter*. New York: Harcourt Brace Jovanovich. (5–8)

In this story that gives a different perspective on Columbus's voyages, a Native American boy realizes that his tribe will become victims and escapes their fate.

# Nine

........................................................

## KEY TERMS

biography                    experiment and activity books
biographical fiction         informational book
concept books                life cycle books

## GUIDING QUESTIONS

1. What kinds of information interested you as an elementary student? Did you find books in the library on this subject?

2. What biographies of famous people did you read?

3. What are the major characteristics of nonfiction? How do informational books and biographies differ from the other genre?

4. Why do children need to experience both nonfiction and fiction?

## OVERVIEW

We live in an information age. Not only is information multiplying at a rapid rate, but information retrieval is essential to people in all walks of life. Up-to-date information makes the world go around. Of course, children have always found information about their world fascinating: they are curious, they ask questions, they gather facts. Nonfiction can fulfill their need to know.

Excellent nonfiction books animate the subject matter and infuse it with life. They are just as compelling as a good story (Freedman, 1988). However, nonfiction for children has been slow to gain momentum. In 1921, the first Newbery Award was awarded to a nonfiction book, *The Story of Mankind*. After this recognition, children's nonfiction was largely ignored by award committees and by those who purchased books. Skilled authors such as Russell Freedman, however, who was given the 1988 Newbery Award for *Lincoln: A Photobiography* and the 1993 Award for *Eleanor Roosevelt*, are bringing much-deserved attention to nonfiction. Authors like Kathryn Lasky, James Cross Giblin, Seymour Simon, Aliki, Jean Fritz, Gail Gibbons, Patricia Lauber, and others have also focused their considerable talents on this genre. Moreover, instructional changes such as literature-based teaching and integrated curricula have contributed to the growing popularity of nonfiction.

This chapter teaches about the qualities of fine nonfiction and how to choose nonfiction for classrooms and media centers, as well as about the types of nonfiction and the authors who have written outstanding books in this genre.

# Nonfiction

## BIOGRAPHY AND INFORMATIONAL BOOKS

## INTRODUCTION

We live in an information age fueled by a flood of knowledge. Information drives our society. We gulp and gobble it and wait for the next wave to come. Moreover, information quickly grows obsolete. This means that nonfiction is more important in all our lives than ever before. Today's children will have to read and understand massive amounts of information throughout their lives.

Nonfiction books are a tool for satisfying children's curiosity about their environment (Hearne, 1990). Moreover, nonfiction provides the answers to children's questions. It whets their appetites for more study, as will be demonstrated in the opening vignette where the children demonstrate how factual content fascinates and motivates children's interests. Well-written nonfiction holds a genuine fascination for children. To capitalize on this compelling interest, teachers, librarians, and parents must put the right books into children's hands at the right moment, something that requires a solid knowledge of children's nonfiction.

## VIGNETTE

We began our visit in a kindergarten classroom. An eager kindergarten boy greeted us: "Hi, my name's Daniel. I'm your host. See our shoes!"

He guided us around the classroom, identifying shoes of every size, color, and description, including jogging shoes, football shoes, ballet shoes, tap shoes, tennis shoes, baby shoes, clogs, moccasins, safety toe work shoes, and golf shoes.

Daniel explained, "We're reading books about shoes, too."

"Which books are your favorites?" I asked.

He showed us *Shoes from Grandpa* by Mem Fox, *Shoes* by Elizabeth Winthrop, and *My Two Feet* by Alice Shertle. Daniel said that Ms. Greene read all of the books aloud and then put them on the reading table for the children to read.

As we walked around the kindergarten, we saw Ms. Greene and her students engaged in a wide range of activities. They studied shoes from many cultures. The children engaged in free reading, wrote in journals, created posters and paper sculptures, and dramatized events they thought the shoes would have experienced. They counted the shoes displayed in the classroom, discussed the shoes required for different occupations, and drew pictures of shoes they designed for special purposes. The children's interest in shoes was evident as they explained their activities.

*(continued)*

In another corridor of the school, we found a fourth/fifth grade combination classroom, in which cooperative groups were working at tables around the classroom. Each group of students had a stack of informational books and a list of questions the group had generated about reptiles. I joined a group of students who were deeply involved in a discussion of snakes. They referred to 10 different books as they completed their questions. As the group put the finishing touches on their work, I asked one of the students, "What was the most interesting thing that you learned about snakes?"

He pointed to an illustration in the book he was reading and said, "Did you know snakes used to have feet?"

"No, I didn't!"

He enthusiastically explained that, during one period of the evolutionary history of snakes, they had feet, which gradually disappeared because they didn't need them. Then snakes developed into the form we recognize today.

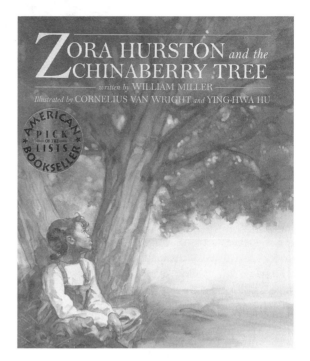

*This biographical account of an incident in Zora Hurston's life is an American Bookseller "Pick of the Lists" book.*

## THE CHANGING PERSPECTIVE ON NONFICTION

Nonfiction has often been treated as a poor relative in children's literature in spite of the fact that creating a nonfiction book requires the same quality of imagination as is essential to the writing of fiction. Imagination, invention, selection, language, and form are just as important in making a good volume of biography, history, or science as it is to the making of a piece of fiction (Meltzer, 1994). Russell Freedman addressed this issue in his acceptance speech for the Newbery Award:

"Nonfiction has never been completely ignored; for a long time it was brushed off and pushed aside, as though factual books were socially inferior to the upper crust stuff we call literature. . . . If a nonfiction book were talented and ambitious enough, it could rise above its station. But for the most part, children's nonfiction was kept in its place" (p. 422).

Several developments have contributed to the changing place of nonfiction in children's literature. First, the quality of children's nonfiction is impressive. Today's nonfiction is characterized by effective writing and attractive layouts, and it addresses a wide range of subject matter. In addition, librarians and educators have realized that children truly enjoy nonfiction and even prefer nonfiction to fiction. As a result, nonfiction is assuming a place of greater prominence in the world of children's literature, evidenced by such developments as the Horn Book Graphic Gallery competition to honor outstanding nonfiction books for excellence in design. The National Council of Teachers of English bestows the Orbis Pictus Award to an outstanding children's nonfiction book each year. The lists of honor books for such prestigious awards as the Newbery Award the Caldecott Medal, and the Boston Globe/Horn Book Awards are including nonfiction books more frequently than before.

When nonfiction is used in many elementary classrooms, it is used exclusively in content areas to help children acquire information about specific topics (Duthie, 1994) but there is no good reason for not using it throughout elementary schools. It is an important read-aloud for all grade levels. Good expository text is born of deep investment and passion (Meltzer, 1994). Well-written, well-researched nonfiction is exciting and creative. Excellent nonfiction makes readers want to know more, inviting them to reexamine the topic at hand, be it history, geography, the arts, or whatever area it deals with.

Extensive use of nonfiction establishes children's familiarity with this genre early, permitting them to read nonfiction with confidence (Duthie, 1994). Research shows that students who did not have these experiences exhibit more difficulty comprehending expository text than narrative text and are less sensitive to important information in expository text (Ballantyne, 1993). Children who are exposed to various genre of literature recognize the differences among the various genre as young as age four, and children who have experiences with nonfiction enjoyed it and chose to read more nonfiction than their peers (Stoodt and Amspaugh, 1994). Young children who read nonfiction can grow to be excited, competent, creative readers and writers of nonfiction across all curriculum areas (Duthie, 1994). Nonfiction not only provides rich experiences but also has implications for lifelong learning (Walmsley, 1993).

## Trends in Current Nonfiction

James Cross Giblin (1987), author and publisher of numerous nonfiction children's books, identifies four factors that characterize recent nonfiction: (1) a clear focus on a single aspect of the subject, (2) tightly written text designed to hold children's interest, (3) emphasis on illustration, and (4) careful attention to book design.

These elements are present and apparent in Aliki's *A Medieval Feast*. From the very first page, Aliki maintains a clear focus on the topic—a medieval feast—while creating clearly written, absorbing prose that holds children's attention. Her detailed descriptions of the preparation, pre-sentation, and devouring of each course of the feast make up the middle of the book. She includes interesting facts about what was eaten and how it was eaten, with detailed illustrations. For instance, she described a cockatrice: "It was really a capon and a suckling pig that were cut in half, stuffed and sewn together again each to the other's half." The book concludes with: "They ate and ate until dark. It was a feast fit for a king, and there would be more tomorrow." The magnificent illustrations are based on art from the medieval era. Her illumination style is characteristic of art in the Middle Ages, and the flora and fauna used in the illustration borders are from that time period. The design and layout of the book are also noteworthy. Many of the illustrations resemble paintings enhanced with borders and friezes. The text is laid out line by line on each page, giving it the appearance of poetry. The captions beneath the illustrations expand the informational nature of the text. Informational books such as this are valuable resources for helping students understand people's lifestyles in various times and places.

## THE VALUE OF NONFICTION

*Provides information.* **Informational books** *provide up-to-date facts.* Students can explore such timely topics as global warming in books such as Laurence Pringle's *Global Warming*. The color illustrations, maps, graphs, and text present this topic in ways that children can comprehend, as well as increasing their awareness of these issues as they impinge on the global community.

*Expands background knowledge.* Through wide reading on content area topics, children learn the concepts and terms associated with these topics. Nonfiction books present topics in greater depth and detail than textbooks can. Social studies textbooks mention Eleanor Roosevelt only in passing, but the library has entire books devoted to her life. Moreover, trade books are usually written in a more interesting style. Nonfiction books provide children with a rich context for understanding many aspects of some real time, place, animal, person, or event, thus enhancing their schema.

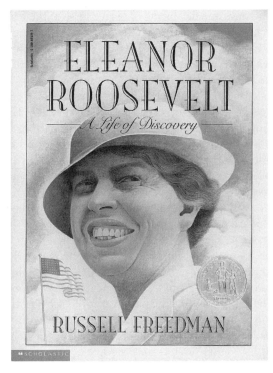

*Titles or subtitles of biographies often reveal the author's theme.*

*Promotes exploration.* Millicent Selsam (1967), who writes many science books for children, believes that a good book simulates direct experience—it makes the child want to go out and experience the observation or discovery firsthand. Many of today's nonfiction books for young readers promote that kind of firsthand discovery by explaining how to participate in particular activities through clear, easy-to-follow directions. For example, in *Simple Simon Says: Take One Magnifying Glass*, Melvin Berger provides easy directions for a variety of fascinating experiments whereby children examine fingerprints, dollar bills, and crystals with a magnifying glass.

*Enhances emotional development.* Nonfiction promotes the emotional development of its readers (Hearne, 1990). Books such as *Dinosaurs Divorce*, by Marc and Laurene Krasny Brown, can help children understand some of the emotions they experience when parents separate. Nonfiction, as well as fiction, helps children realize they are not the only ones in the world facing problems and gives them characters with whom they can identify.

## BIOGRAPHY

**Biography** *is the story of a life, the "history of the life of an individual"* (Lukens, 1995). When biography is working, it sparks the reader's interest—even for a reader who initially had no interest in the subject. Reading a well-written biography becomes an absorbing human encounter with a person whose achievement is out of the ordinary. Children's fascination with this phenomenon is no different from that of adults (Wilms, 1978). In addition, biographies allow children to identify with people of the past and the present. Readers "learn about life by tapping the experiences of others. If it is possible for the people described in biographies to overcome obstacles such as ignorance, poverty, misery, fear and hate, then it must be possible for the rest of us. This is the very optimistic message that children find in biographies" (Zarnowski, 1990, p. 9). Children can see others' lives as models of achievement and career goals; they may learn about courage and tenacity in the face of adversity and difficulty.

Biographers do not simply tell the stories of individual lives, as their subjects do not live isolated lives. Their lives are shaped through their interactions with other people and through events that form the backdrop of their story. Certainly, it would be impossible to describe the subjects of children's biographies without considering the personal and historical contexts of their lives. "When you write biography, you present history through the prism of a single life, a life, that is, of course, connected to other lives" (Meltzer, 1987, p. 15). Thus, when children read biographies, they learn about not just one but many lives, as well as about different times and places, as author Pam Conrad illustrates. When Conrad researched her historical fiction book *Prairie Songs*, she discovered that a man named Solomon Butcher had taken photographs of Nebraska pioneers. This discovery inspired the biography *Prairie Visions: The Life and Times of Solomon Butcher*, which explores the life of ordinary settlers, outlaws, and cowboys. The reader learns about a patent medicine man and a frontier photographer as well as the people and events that shaped life on the Nebraska prairie. In addition, children learn about locust swarms and life in soddies.

## Writing Biography

The first requirements of a good biography are that it be accurate, up-to-date, and authentic. Objective biographers research their subjects carefully. They also, however, assume an attitude or theme in writing toward the subject, which guides them in selecting the events and details to include. Once the research has been done and the attitude decided, the writer shapes the biography to make the subject come alive.

Biography may appear to be a simple writing task, essentially a reporting of actual people, events, and life stories. Biographers, however, must decide on a style of writing appropriate to the subject, a theme, a point of view, how much detail to include about the subject's life, whether to use illustrations, which friends or enemies of the subject to write about, and many other details. Biographers use many of the same techniques as other storytellers: They "set their scenes descriptively, develop their characters completely, and give us the impression of life unfolding" (p. 6). Because children have experienced these literary techniques, "biographies are a comfortable, somewhat familiar type of material for children" (Zarnowski, 1990, p. 6).

When writing a biography of any type, the author must determine which facts are appropriately omitted or included in telling the subject's story. Sometimes they elect to omit or to only mention particular facts about a person that may be controversial or deemed inappropriate for children. For example, in his biography of *Franklin Delano Roosevelt*, Russell Freedman chose to mention, but not elaborate upon, Roosevelt's well-known extramarital affair with Lucy Mercer.

## Types of Biography

One of the most important decisions a biographer must make is the type of biography to write. This decision entails other decisions, such as how much of the subject's life to include, how much to include about other people in the subject's life, and even how much to interpret the subject's life.

### Complete versus partial biography

Complete, or cradle-to-grave, biographies describe a subject's life from birth to death. In *Lost Star*, Patricia Lauber traces Amelia Earhart's life from her birth in Atchison, Kansas, in 1897, to her disappearance in 1937. Partial biographies, on the other hand, focus on a particular time or specific event in a subject's life. In *Leonardo da Vinci: The Artist, Inventor, Scientist in Three Dimensional Movable Pictures*, Alice and Marten Provensen describe the events of the year 1492 in da Vinci's life. During this year he developed a flying machine, created a statue, studied the heavens, and painted the Mona Lisa. William Miller's picture book *Zora Hurston and the Chinaberry Tree* tells of a little-known episode in the childhood of the renowned writer Zora Neale Hurston. Another picture book, Edith Kunhardt's *Honest Abe*, depicts only major events in the life of Abraham Lincoln through unforgettable primitive paintings and simple language. The text and illustrations are uniquely suited to the subject's life.

### Single versus collective biography

Single biographies such as Russell Freedman's award-winning *Eleanor Roosevelt: A Life of Discovery* and James Cross Giblin's exceptional picture biography of *Thomas Jefferson* focus on the life of one individual. On the other hand, a collective biography describes in a single book several subjects with some connection among them that addresses the theme of the book. Brent Ashabranner's *People Who Make a Difference* profiles ordinary people who made a difference in the lives of the needy, in the environment, through community service, and through personal example. In *Biography Today*, Laurie Lanzen Harris has collected profiles of current figures who are of interest to young readers, such as Macaulay Culkin, the movie star, and Avi, the children's author. These profiles include photographs and are written in a factual style.

# Honest Abe

Paintings by **Malcah Zeldis**
Words by **Edith Kunhardt**

*Lincoln's story is told in this extraordinary biography through unforgettable paintings and simple words.*

## Autobiography

Many autobiographies are written for children as well. For example, Eloise Greenfield and her mother, Lessie Jones Little, tell the story of their own lives and of Eloise's grandmother in *Childtimes: A Three-Generation Memoir.* The story of these three women, which spans the years 1800–1940, provides a fascinating glimpse of how childhood changes and yet remains the same over time.

## Authentic versus fictionalized biography

How to interpret an individual's life is a very important decision on the biographer's part. The author may adhere to the facts in authentic biography or dramatize the subject's life through fictionalized biography. In authentic biography, the only facts included are those verifiable through research. Any dialogue is substantiated by historical documents (Russell, 1991). Biographer Jean

Fritz (1990) explains her stance: "I would make up nothing, not even the dialogue, and I wouldn't even use dialogue unless I had a source. I would be honest. If there was a fact I wasn't sure of, or if it was unknown, I would say so" (p. 25).

Most children's biography, however, is fictionalized. This style, often called **biographical fiction,** *represents a middle position between strict adherence to known facts and completely invented narrative:* The "facts are the bricks with which a biographer builds" (Coolidge, 1974, p. 141). In fictionalized biography, dialogue and events can be invented based upon historical documents (Zena Sutherland and May Hill Arbuthnot, 1991). Margery Fisher points out that "to draw a line too sharply between known fact and reasonable deduction would be to deny [children] a great deal of persuasive detail" (p. 304). Barbara Brenner's *On the Frontier with Mr. Audubon,* for example, records the story of Audubon's journey down the Mississippi in 1821. She uses the character of his real-life assistant, Joseph Mason, to create imaginary journal entries, as though he were recording their trip. In the "Note from the Author," Brenner explains that "almost every incident in the book actually happened. Although the conversations are fictional, they are based upon facts about Audubon and Joseph" (p. 95).

## Selecting and Evaluating Biography

Biography has not enjoyed the popularity with children that other literary genre, such as realistic fiction, has in the past (Meltzer, 1987). Part of this lack of enthusiasm may be a relic of the poor quality of many children's biographies of the past (Carr, 1982; Fisher, 1972), which were often characterized by inaccuracies, poor writing, and overglorification of historical figures. For instance, Russell Freedman (1988) cites an older Lincoln biography that includes this exchange between 11-year-old Abe and his father: "Books!" said his father. "Always books! What is all this studying going to do for you? What do you think you are going to be?" "Why," said Abe, " I'm going to be President" (p. 424).

This contrived dialogue illustrates the writing commonly found in older biographies. Moreover, this author made it appear that Lincoln was different from other 11-year-old children—that he was somehow predestined to be president. This is not an uncommon approach in these older works, but today there are some children's biographies of excellent quality that teachers can seek out to introduce in their classes. In selecting biography of good quality, consider the subject of the biography, the accuracy of the information, the characterization, the theme, and the author's style.

## Subject

For many years, the subjects of children's biographies were confined largely to historical figures considered worthy of emulation. This is changing, however, and the subjects of biography today are often people who have done or been something special or discovered or demonstrated something that made their lives significant, whether that significance was commendable or not (Lukens, 1995). Thus, biographies focus on admirable characters like Paul Revere in Jean Fritz's *And Then What Happened, Paul Revere* and also on less than admirable subjects, as in her *Traitor: The Strange Case of Benedict Arnold.*

In writing about both of these characters, the author included "specific, unexpected facts, the kind that give the past a pulse" (Fritz, 1990, p. 25), such as the fact that Revere forgot his spurs on the way to his historic ride and his dog saved the day. "Paul wrote a note to his wife, tied it around the dog to go home. . . . The dog [came] back with Paul's spurs around his neck." (Fritz, 1973, p. 30). Children enjoy these fascinating footnotes to history as much as adults. These interesting details also give readers a different understanding of the subject than a simple recounting of the major events in the individual's life.

Historical figures continue to have a strong presence in many biographies. Jean Fritz writes about great explorers in *Around the World in a Hundred Years.* In *America Alive*, a remarkable history of the United States, Jean Karl celebrates the greatness of people like Thomas Edison, Henry Ford, Martin Luther King, Jr., and Elizabeth Cady Stanton. She points out that America is people: people who plodded by foot across this country to settle on its frontiers, people who invented and discovered the things we needed to build our nation.

*Jean Fritz brings to life the explorers who changed the map of the world.*

Other books describe ordinary people in extraordinary circumstances. Eleanor Coerr's *Sadako and the Thousand Paper Cranes* extols the bravery of a 12-year-old girl dying from leukemia as a result of radiation from the atomic bomb dropped on Hiroshima in World War II. Sadako's statue still stands in the Hiroshima Peace Park, and each year Japanese children celebrate her courage.

Members of minority cultures have often been omitted from biography and history. "Not that long ago . . . American children learned American history minus Black people. The same is certainly true of women, Hispanics, and Native Americans" (Hearne, 1990, p. 136). However, excellent biographies that include these groups are increasing. In *Teammates*, Peter Golenbeck describes the friendship between Jackie Robinson, the first African American to play professional baseball in this country, and Pee Wee Reese, his white teammate. Jeannette Winter's children's biography of Diego Rivera, one of the greatest muralists in the world, dramatizes his life story with vibrant miniature paintings.

There are also more and more excellent biographies about women, who have also been little represented in biography. Lillian Gish's *An Actor's Life for Me* is a fascinating account of this silent-film star's childhood as an actress. *Ragtime Tumpie* by Alan Schroeder is a fictionalized biography of jazz entertainer Josephine Baker's childhood in St. Louis. Faith Ringgold's painted quilts illustrate her autobiographical picture book, *Tar Beach*.

## Accuracy

Accuracy is the linchpin of excellent biography. The best biographers conduct exhaustive research to document their books. Russell Freedman began his research for the Newbery Award–winning *Lincoln: A Photobiography* at the Abraham Lincoln Bookshop in Chicago. He read widely from the many books on Lincoln's life, examined original documents, and conducted eyewitness research at sites in Kentucky, Indiana, Illinois, and Washington, D. C. (Freedman, 1988). He documents his research in three sections of the book, "In Lincoln's Footsteps," "Books About Lincoln," and in the acknowledgments and credits, so that others can find the same facts he did while doing his research.

In the past, children's biographers created idealized versions of the lives of famous Americans. Today's biographers, however, create more realistic portraits of their subjects, as Freedman did in *Lincoln: A Photobiography:* "His untidiness followed him home from the office. He cared little for the social niceties that were so important to his wife. He was absent-minded, perpetually late for meals. He was away from home for weeks at a time. . . . And he was moody, lapsing into long, brooding silences" (p. 41). Freedman explained that he was never tempted to write an idealized, hero-worshipping account. Recognizing Lincoln's weaknesses throws his strengths and his greatness into sharper relief (Freedman, 1988).

Fictionalization in biography, discussed earlier, is also an issue of accuracy. The dialogue constructed for characters is the most common use of fiction. England and Fasick (1987) suggest that writers use caution when creating dialogue, expressions of emotion, and imagined minor events to advance the narrative. Biographers differ regarding the amount of fictionalization that is appropriate. You will develop a better understanding of this point after reading a number of benchmark biographies.

## Characterization

Biographers often choose to use the main characteristic of a subject as a focal point and a theme for their writing. Freedman has done this in his biographies of Lincoln and Eleanor Roosevelt. Jean Fritz focused on Revere's compulsive activities in *And Then What Happened, Paul Revere?* Her theme and style in this biography meld together seamlessly: her short sentences and informal tone mimic Revere's compulsive, breathless speech.

The goal of biographers is to create characters who come alive for children. To achieve this, a biographer selects facts that effectively tell the subject's story and help children feel they know the character described. Authors use various devices to help us understand their subjects. In *The Librarian Who Measured the Earth*, Kathryn Lasky depicts Eratosthenes' extremely curious nature, a trait with which many children can identify, as they too are filled with wonder and questions.

Another stylistic technique for helping readers "see" a subject is telling the story from a child's point of view. In *Me and Willie and Pa*, Ferdinand Monjo tells Lincoln's life through the voice of his son Tad. Children understand this characterization through comparing different biographies of the same individual. Allen Say compares his life and his grandfather's life in the Caldecott Award–winning book *Grandfather's Journey*, telling about his grandfather's journey to the United States and his return to Japan. His grandfather loved both countries, and when he was in one country he yearned for the other. Say explains that he feels the same way. Although Say is not a child, his point of view makes his grandfather's biography warm and personal.

Older students can learn about different points of view about a single character by reading *A Proud Taste for Scarlet and Miniver* by E. L. Konigsburg, a biography of Eleanor of Aquitaine told from the different perspectives of three people who knew

*This book celebrates Eratosthenes, the man with a questioning mind who measured the earth standing still.*

her in life. In the book, they and Eleanor are in heaven comparing their different points of view about her life.

### Theme

Biographers identify a unifying thread or theme to bind the characterization of their subject together. Various authors go about this in various ways. In some instances, research into the subject's accomplishments reveals an obvious theme, but in most cases there is so much research that the biographer must select the most prominent or appropriate theme from several possibilities. This then determines the facts to include and exclude and shapes the authors' interpretation of their subjects. Freedman's biography of Eleanor Roosevelt focuses on her discoveries about herself and her own strengths. He chose to exclude extensive discussion of her husband's infidelity.

### Style

A lively, interesting style makes the subject of a biography come alive for readers. Children generally enjoy facts woven into narrative style (Russell, 1990). They find it easier to understand biography that reads like a story, albeit a real-life story. Adopting narrative style, however, does not excuse the biographer from the research needed to create authenticity in daily life, food, games, clothing, and conversation. For example, the language created in conversation should be appropriate to the era, and discussions must reflect the issues of the time. Some of the vocabulary used may be foreign to young readers and impede their understanding. Jean Fritz (1990) explains that in her biographies she limits vocabulary to make the books readable, but she does not omit important words just because they may be strange to young readers. Some authors include glossaries to help children.

## INFORMATIONAL BOOKS

One of the most exciting trends in children's literature today is the burgeoning informational book market. Outstanding writers are creating exemplary nonfiction. At their best, these books show the authors' deep-seated interest in their chosen subjects. The authors' personal interest in their subjects is contagious for young readers, who want to know more and more. Their hours of research, thoughtful writing, well-chosen graphics, and balance between fact and narrative result in books that are truly literature (Elleman, 1991).

England and Fasick (1987) suggest these books are written for at least three different purposes. One purpose is to introduce young children to specific ideas and concepts. Such books are designed to engage "browsers" and as a result have large print, colorful illustrations, and simple, clearly explicated text. Lynn Reiser's *Any Kind of Dog* is an example of a such a book. In this book children learn about the many kinds of dogs they might choose as a pet. Another purpose of nonfiction is to supply information; this type of book is intended for children already interested in a particular topic or area of study. Gail Gibbons' book *Nature's Green Umbrella* is an excellent example. In it, she explains one of the world's most complicated

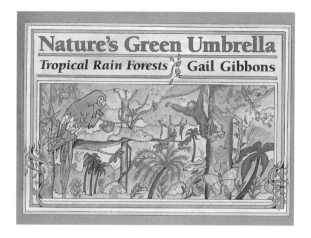

*To protect our endangered rain forests, we need to understand how important they are to the whole world.*

ecosystems with lucid language and lush illustrations. She shares information about tropical rain forests, such as the fact that 240 inches of rain may fall there in a single year. The third purpose of a nonfiction book is to summarize and organize information. Laurence Pringle's book, *Living Treasure: Saving Earth's Threatened Biodiversity,* summarizes and organizes information about our planet's unique organisms.

## Types of Informational Books

**Informational books** appear in a variety of formats: concept books, nature identification books, life cycle books, experiment and activity books, books derived from original documents and journals, photographic essays, and reference books and periodicals. They *focus on many subjects including the arts, animals, mathematics, man-made objects, language, sex, the life cycle, and every other topic imaginable* (Stewig, 1988). Many nonfiction books cannot easily be categorized as they deal with specialized information that does not obviously belong to a specific type.

### Concept books

**Concept books** *explore abstract ideas and categories of ideas.* For example, in *Twenty-Six Letters and Ninety-*

*Nine Cents,* Tana Hoban explores the concept of alphabet through letter associations. The first half of this book uses photographs juxtaposed with photographs of objects to explore upper and lowercase letters. In *The Shape of Things* by Dayle Dodds and *Circles and Spheres* by Allen Morgan, the concepts of shapes are explored through photographs and drawings that show the shapes in everyday activities and objects.

### Nature identification books

The nature identification books, as the name implies, show children things from nature and the outdoor world. The primary-grade *The Big Bug Book* by Margery Facklam illustrates big bugs in their actual size, showing common objects along with the bugs to give children a better sense of their size. Older children will appreciate Elizabeth Lacey's *The Complete Frog: A Guide for the Very Young Naturalist*, which goes beyond mere frog identification, detailing the frog's anatomy and life cycle, providing guidelines for catching frogs, and describing "the frog in fact and fiction" as well as frog "folklore." Colorful illustrations enhance this book.

### Life cycle books

The **life cycle books** *trace the growth of animals and plants.* Susan Bonners traces the panda's life cycle and its amazing growth and development in *Panda.* Books such as *Oak and Company* by Richard Mabey trace the life cycle of an oak tree and its impact on the surrounding forest.

### Experiment and activity books

**Experiment and activity books,** *another category of nonfiction, provide children with hands-on exploration of a variety of concepts.* Such books include a safety precaution statement, a list of sequential steps to follow, a list of required materials or equipment, and an illustration of the finished project. In *Exploring Space: Using Seymour Simon's Astronomy Books in the Classroom*, Barbara Bourne and Wendy Saul guide children through space-related projects that will extend their knowledge of astronomy. These projects are addressed to children and offer them activities that are integrated across the curriculum.

## Books from original documents and journals

Books derived from research involving original documents and journals interest children because of their authenticity. Julius Lester's *To Be a Slave* is a touchstone for this type of book. To learn about the slavery experience, Lester consulted many sources, including especially valuable interviews with slaves recorded by members of the Federal Writers Project in the late 1930s and early 1940s. This was a part of Roosevelt's WPA. The actual words of the former slaves were used to describe their experiences.

## Photographic essays

Photographic essays are an increasingly important form of informational book. Sally Ride's *To Space & Back*, Patricia Lauber's *Volcano: The Eruption and Healing of Mt. St. Helens*, and Russ Kendall's *Eskimo Boy* are outstanding examples of books in which color photography lends an air of authenticity to the information. Caroline Arnold, a notable author of informational books, also effectively uses color photographs to illustrate her ideas, conveying a real sense of desert life in *Watching Desert Wildlife*. Richard Wormser uses black-and-white photographs to illustrate *Hoboes*, which are just right for the tone of the book and the subject. In *Comets, Meteors, and Asteroids*, Seymour Simon combines drawings, photographs, and simple language to create an informational book that elementary school children can understand.

## Reference books and periodicals

Reference works, available for virtually all areas of information, include encyclopedias, bibliographies, dictionaries, atlases, and almanacs for all age groups. These resources are important for their content and for teaching students how to search for information (England and Fasick, 1987). *The Children's Animal Atlas* by James Lambert explains how animals have evolved, where they live today, and why so many are in danger. *The Children's Atlas of Exploration* enables readers to follow in the

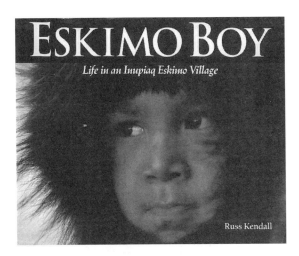

*This photographic essay is the fascinating account of life with Norman Kokeok and his family in a small Alaskan village.*

footsteps of the great explorers. *The Kingfisher First Picture Atlas* represents the trend to publish reference books for younger students. *All About Our World*, intended for kindergarten and first-grade students, examines where and how people live all over the world; its pictorial table of contents makes it especially useful. Encyclopedias on CD-ROM are an exciting addition to traditional reference works. When using these reference materials, students may actually listen to a speech or piece of music, they can see people and machines moving, and many other exciting innovations.

Some reference works are recommended for all age groups. *Exploring Your World: The Adventure of Geography* has 334 encyclopedia entries on a variety of geographical topics, with more than 1,000 photographs, diagrams, and charts. Specialized bibliographies such as *Science Experiments Index for Young People* includes science activities and experiments drawn from 700 books. *The Facts on File Junior Visual Dictionary* contains visual information on a variety of subjects.

Kingfisher publishes a variety of reference works. *The Kingfisher First Picture Atlas* includes information about map scale as well as reading and making maps. This book was written as a first atlas for young readers. *The Kingfisher Young People's Encyclopedia of the United States* has 1,200 entries that reflect the school curriculum. *The Kingfisher*

*Exploring Space* is one of many books in
the interacive arts and sciences series
called "Voyages of Discovery."

*Young People's Encyclopedia of Animals* has 450
entries about animals. Kingfisher also publishes an
*Illustrated Thesaurus*.

Dorling Kindersley publishes a variety of
reference works as well, including *The Dorling
Kindersley Children's Illustrated Dictionary*.

## Innovative Informational Books

"The Magic School Bus" series is well known
among schoolchildren and teachers for a humorous approach to science for children. Joanna Cole,
the author, is the winner of the 1991 Washington
Post/Children's Book Guild Nonfiction award for
the body of her work. In *The Magic School Bus in the
Time of the Dinosaurs* and *The Magic School Bus on
the Ocean Floor* as well as other Magic School Bus
titles, readers meet Ms. Frizzle, an unusual teacher
who wears outrageous clothes and drives a magic
school bus on incredible journeys. Although the
bus trips are fanciful, the science reported is accurate and carefully documented. These books are
also available on CD-ROM.

J. Young's *The Most Amazing Science Pop-Up
Book* is an interactive book with a working record
player, compass, microscope, camera, sundial,
kaleidoscope, and periscope. This book is rich with
accurate information as well.

In its Voyages of Discovery series, Scholastic
Books also offers an interactive approach to information. For example, in *Exploring Space*, published
by HarperCollins, there are movable maps of the
constellations, plastic overlays, fold-out maps, 3-
D glasses, and a sky clock students can rotate to
tell time as 16th-century astronomers did. A time
line and extensive references for further reading
are included, and the information is up-to-date
and accurate. Other titles in this series are fascinating as well; they include *Taming Fire, Paint and
Painting*, and *Musical Instruments*.

## Selecting and Evaluating
## Informational Books

What standards distinguish excellent informational
books from mediocre ones? Most of all, the best

informational books make us think. Facts abound in our information-dense world, but books that make readers think are not as prevalent. Several criteria guide the evaluation of informational books: the literary style and technique; the authority of the author; and the accuracy, appropriateness, and attractiveness of the book.

## Style

Literary style refers to an author's use of language, sometimes called "voice." A distinctive, interesting voice is crucial to informational books. Clarity, accuracy, organization, scope, currency, objectivity, honesty, authority, illustration, documentation, holistic treatment, and readability are all important factors in informational books, but without voice, nonfiction too often goes unheard (Hearne, 1993).

Karen Wallace's *Think of an Eel* is a book that does have a voice, one "that is a distinctive blend of verbal and artistic styles that shapes the subject, from the selection of facts to the progression with which they're presented. The end papers depict developmental stages of eel growth in eye-catching watercolors and suggest a mysterious dynamic about to unfold" (Hearne, 1993, p. 273). Readers are involved with the subject from the first line, but the author never romanticizes the subject. She includes information about the gulls who eat eels and about the worn-out and wasted bodies of the eels after they lay their eggs. *Think of an Eel* is a part of the Read and Wonder Series published by Candlewick. Each book in the series has a distinctive voice and is a fine example of a top-quality informational book. Other books in the series include *The Wheeling and Whirling-Around Book* by Judy Hindley, *A Piece of String Is a Wonderful Thing* by Judy Hindley, and *Bears in the Forest* by Karen Wallace.

A concise style that presents facts in simple, direct language is appropriate for most informational books. Quality nonfiction authors use correct terminology, present information simply, and do not talk down to their readers. Books of this quality inspire readers in the same ways that great teachers do (Stodart, 1987). They present the subject in an understandable form while remaining true to the content. A good voice, however, consists of more than conveying information as a "basket of facts," no matter how accurate and direct the information is. The best nonfiction is literature; it combines factual information with literary devices that make the ideas come alive. The writing in these books has an aesthetic dimension similar to good fiction (Purves and Monson, 1984). Jane Yolen (1973), who writes fiction, poetry, and nonfiction says, "It is the . . . writer's problem to turn . . . data into information. Data is useful only to the trained ear and eye. As information it speaks to anyone who takes the time to listen. Changing data into information is a creative process. It is the first of a series of processes that make the writing of nonfiction as creative as the writing of fiction" (p. 69).

The best writers of informational books convey an enthusiasm and passion about their subject that is passed on to their readers. It is this transformation from data to information through literary style that distinguishes the writing typical of textbooks from that of quality informational trade books. Compare the quality of writing on the same topic from a textbook and a trade book:

*Textbook.* "So the Pilgrims decided to look for a place where they could have their own church and also live as English men and women.

After thinking about a number of places, the Pilgrims decided to go to North America. . . .

In 1620, about a hundred people crowded onto a small ship called the *Mayflower*" (McAuley and Wilson, 1987, p. 69).

*Trade book.* "The *Sparrowhawk's* crew set sail from London in hopes of reaching Jamestown, Virginia. Amongst the 26 passengers, mostly Irish servants, were Masters Fells and Sibsey. I was indentured to Captain Sibsey by my unscrupulous uncle. On November 6 our ship crashed in fog on what the captain told us was a New England shore" (Bowen, 1994, p. 1).

The textbook description is factually accurate, but it does not make the past come alive in ways that children can understand. The trade book, however, gives a vivid and lively portrayal of this period in American history. Moreover, the trade book stimulates children to read more of the book. Bowen's writing creates the sense of adventure that those early settlers must have felt in coming to a new land.

## Technique

Closely related to style is the literary technique authors employ to make their subjects interesting. All of the techniques used by authors of fiction books are employed by authors of nonfiction: narrative, metaphor and simile, relating known information to new information, imagery, and "hooks" to engage readers' interest.

Karla Kuskin combines narrative and exposition in *Jerusalem, Shining Still* to tell the 4,000-year history of Jerusalem through text, prose, and poetry. She explains, "The Moslems, like the Christians and the Jews, thought that Jerusalem was a special place in the world, a holy city" (p. 16).

In *Think of an Eel*, Karen Wallace compares eels to familiar things to help children who probably have never seen an eel to understand what they are like:

> Think of an eel.
> He swims like a fish.
> He slides like a snake. . . .
> He looks like a willow leaf,
> clear as a crystal. . . .
> He eats like a horse.

David Schwartz achieves the same in *How Much Is a Million?* He uses details to relate the abstract concept of a million to familiar concepts. He explains that if a million kids climb onto one another's shoulders, they would be "taller than the tallest buildings, higher than the highest mountains and farther up than airplanes can fly." He offers several other examples to lend reality to this concept. Children can expand their understanding by collecting a million flip tabs from soda cans or a million tea-bag tags.

Visual imagery helps readers see the sod houses that settlers built in Freedman's book *Children of the Wild West*. He describes the inside of a sod house: "During heavy rains, water seeped through the roof and dripped down on the settlers and their furnishings" (p. 33).

Authors often use the journalistic device of a "hook" to capture children's interest. For example, "Launch morning. 6... 5... 4... The alarm clock counts down. 3... 2... 1... Ring! 3:15 A.M. Launch minus four hours" (Ride and Okie, 1986). The countdown, juxtaposed with the alarm-clock ring, draws children's interest. It also relates the unfamiliar countdown with the familiar ring of an alarm clock.

## Authority

The author's qualifications for writing an informational book are usually given on the back flap of the book jacket or the book itself. When this information is not available, readers can consult reviews in journals such as the *Horn Book*, the *New Advocate*, *Language Arts*, and the *Bulletin of the Center for Children's Books* to learn more about an author's expertise.

Some children's authors are themselves authorities on the subjects about which they write, as are Jean Craighead George, a naturalist, and Millicent E. Selsam, a botanist. Many authors of informational books, however, are not experts in the fields they have chosen to write about. Instead, these authors thoroughly research the topic and consult with experts to ensure accuracy and credibility in their text. They usually credit the authorities who assisted them in their research on the opening or closing pages of the book. For example, on the copyright page of the book *Volcano: The Eruption and Healing of Mt. St. Helens*, Patricia Lauber acknowledges the help of 13 different individuals, including geologists, naturalists, and foresters.

## Accuracy

Accuracy is essential in nonfiction. Clear, correct, and up-to-date facts and concepts are the hallmarks of fine children's nonfiction, and illustrations, diagrams, charts, maps, and other material in the book should meet these requirements as well. Accuracy includes more than correct factual information, however. Effective authors of informational books distinguish between theories and facts and make it clear that there are various points of view regarding controversial subjects. Recency of information, illustrations, and examples in the book are also important considerations, as information in older books may have been revised by current research; check the copyright date to ensure obtaining the most up-to-date information possible.

David Macaulay's *The Way Things Work*, winner of the Boston Globe/Horn Book Award for

Nonfiction, received praise for its attention to detail and accuracy. Macaulay deftly illustrates the functioning of more than 400 different machines. The author includes more than 300 pages of detailed diagrams of almost every possible instrument. In addition, the book includes a glossary of technical terms. The text is lucid and clear while using a limited number of words.

Accuracy of information can be checked with a recent encyclopedia or a current textbook, but concern for accuracy is often a confusing issue. In *America Alive: A History*, Jean Karl has created an excellent informational book that gives children a sense of historical continuity in a narrative chain that reads like a story. However, there a few small "bloopers," such as saying Sutter's Mill is west of San Francisco instead of east as it should be. As Roger Sutton points out, however, "that's a quibble in a book filled with telling detail" (Sutton, 1994). Certainly, accuracy is essential in evaluating nonfiction, but in this book the inaccuracies are small and do not invalidate its quality.

Another consideration in selecting and evaluating nonfiction is the author's use of anthropomorphism, or attribution of human characteristics to animals or objects. Some authors use anthropomorphism because they think this will make their animal subjects more human and interesting to readers (Lukens, 1995). However, as Millicent Selsam (1967) points out, animal behavior is fascinating in and of itself and does not have to be obscured by ascribing human characteristics to animals. The best authors avoid this pitfall in their writing. Anthropomorphism can confuse children and lead them to believe that animals think and behave in the same ways as human beings. For instance, in *I Am a Wild Animal*, by Jose Sanchez and Miguel Pacheco, a baby elephant asks its mother, "Hey mama, how come we don't work?" The mother answers, "Some of us don't work because we're not tamed animals." The elephant later says, "Although my mother told me many stories about famous elephants, I could never forget the jungle stories."

## Appropriateness

The concept of appropriateness in informational books encompasses several issues. Excellent

*A whole window into the past is opened when a sunken treasure ship is discovered and explored.*

informational books suit their audience. They are organized well and include bibliographies and suggestions for further reading. The literary style corresponds to the subject and the audience for which the book is intended.

Clearly organized text enables children to understand the author's presentation of information. An author may organize the text by moving from the familiar to the unfamiliar, moving from the general to the specific, or through a question-and-answer format. A common organizational pattern is presenting facts in chronological order. Gail Gibbons uses this pattern in her informational book, *Sunken Treasure* which details the discovery of the *Atocha*, a Spanish treasure ship. Seven sections organize the information: the sinking, the search, the find, the recording, the salvage, the restoration and preservation, and the cataloging and distribution.

Bibliographic data, which includes tables of contents, indices, glossaries, appendices, and lists of related readings, help children understand the information presented. These aids can help readers locate specific information within a book without having to read the entire book. Effective bibliographic aids provide the starting point for gathering additional information on a particular topic. It does little good to whet children's appetite for further study if they cannot proceed to locate more information on the topic. Realizing this, Gail Gibbons provides appendices at the end of *Sunken Treasure*, describing four other famous treasure hunts through minimal text and illustrations. She also includes a brief history of diving, extending children's understanding of the concepts introduced in the book.

## Attractiveness

Attractiveness or appeal is important to children. They are more likely to pick up a book that is attractive than one that is not. Modern children have been conditioned to visual images by television and computers and expect a fast pace and dramatic impact. Informational books can include attractive, colorful illustrations that range from photographs to paintings to line drawings. Attractiveness cannot remain the sole criterion, however. Illustrations, charts, and diagrams must be accurate and should mesh with the text, faultlessly depicting the ideas, concepts, and facts presented in the book. Moreover, although illustrations can be used to enhance the text and attract readers, illustrations cannot replace strong organization and well-written text to present information.

Leonard Everett Fisher (1988), who has illustrated many nonfiction books, explains his purpose in illustrating nonfiction: "Today what interests me . . . is giving youngsters a visual memory of a fact rather than just the fact. I am trying to present a factual mood. The Tower of London, for instance, is a creepy place, and if I can establish the creepiness of the place so that the youngster gets an unsettled feeling about the tower. . . . I'm trying to create the emotion of the history, the dynamics of history, together with the facts of history. I'm trying to communicate what events in history felt like" (p. 319).

Photography is increasingly common in children's nonfiction. Stodart (1987) points out that

This book uses photographs and drawings to tell the true story of a little boy who, with his toy bear, survived the sinking of the Titanic.

photographs add a sense of direct reporting and are very important in documenting history and biography. Effective use of photographs in scientific informational books is one hallmark of Seymour Simon's work. The photographs he obtained from the *Viking I* and *Mariner I* space probes give his readers a sense of "being there" in *Mars*. Photographs and drawings also create a feeling of authenticity in Daisy Spedden's *Polar, the Titanic Bear*, an interesting book written 80 years ago about a toy bear and a boy who survived the sinking of the *Titanic*.

Both illustrations and layout are instrumental in guiding children's response to nonfiction. Appropriate placement of the illustrations and text on the page influences the facts, ideas, and concepts readers will focus on and the importance they attribute to the information presented. Illustrations should prepare readers to understand the text. Innovative layouts like the use of three-dimension in *The Human Body* by Jonathon Miller and David Pelham and the interactive format in *Exploring Space* are significant to readers' response to a nonfiction book.

## CLASSROOM ACTIVITIES FOR ENHANCING NONFICTION EXPERIENCE

All literature is taking an increasingly important role in classrooms because of current views of teaching. More and more educators are integrating literature in all areas of the curriculum, using it to extend content area knowledge and to develop basic concepts. More and more integrated units of study are being introduced in elementary classrooms. Exploring a theme or topic through trade books permits students to discover the connections among the types of knowledge belonging to particular domains. These units help children understand how knowledge is organized, used, and related (Pappas, Kiefer, and Levstik, 1990). They contribute to children's fundamental understanding of science, social studies, mathematics, art, and music. Informational books help promote children's critical thinking, suggest methods of study, and provide a writing model for children to use when reporting information.

Nonfiction literature has distinct benefits in developing students' knowledge, skills, and interests. Trade books permit teachers to use books of different reading levels that address the same subject so that all children can study materials at a level appropriate for their ability (Shanahan, 1989; Hillerich, 1987). Trade books are usually more up-to-date than textbooks, which is appealing to students who are usually more interested in the present than the past. Trade books are likely to depict the latest scientific and social science discoveries. Moreover, the writing styles used in trade books are more appealing to readers than textbook style. Nonfiction books have both content and visual appeal for students. Their interesting cover designs, graphics, and choice of topics appeal to children. Trade books provide greater depth of information whether they are exploring places, cultures, people, or science. They can address controversial issues and sensitive subjects. For example, trade books explore prejudice, the Holocaust, and Vietnam in depth, while textbook authors often give such topics superficial attention. Finally, trade books tend to arrange information in a more logical and coherent fashion than textbooks (Fielding, Wilson, and Anderson, 1986).

### Trade Books and Science

Many of today's students spend most of their science class time engaged in hands-on experiences. They ask questions, make observations, infer, measure, and think. They record their work, their thinking, their observations, and their conclusions in science journals. For homework, they may read from a textbook or trade book and answer teacher- or student-generated questions that tap reasoning skills. Nontextbook science experiences predominate today. Both the National Science Teachers Association (1986) and the American Association for the Advancement of Science (1989) endorse a scientific-inquiry-based approach to instruction. Both organizations recognize the importance of scientific literacy.

Trade books, both nonfiction and fiction, play an important role in current concepts of teaching science. Children can learn basic science concepts, scientific thinking, the relationship of science to their lives, the excitement of the new and unknown, and the beauty of nature from trade books. The quality and readability of science trade books is increasing. Each year *The Science Teacher* publishes "Outstanding Science Tradebooks for Children," a list selected by a committee from the National Science Teachers Association. A number of excellent authors write science trade books: Aliki, Caroline Arnold, Jim Aronsky, Barbara Bash, Melvin Berger, Lynne Cherry, Joanna Cole, Helen Cowcher, Margery Facklam, Jean Craighead George, Patricia Lauber, Laurence Pringle, and Seymour Simon are just a few.

To get a sense of what makes a science trade book outstanding, read some that are identified as exemplary, such as those listed below. The quality of an individual book depends upon the author of that book, so if the book is part of a series, evaluate the quality of each book in the series.

- The Sierra Club publishes children's nonfiction books related to the study and protection of the earth's scenic and ecological resources—mountains, wetlands, woodlands, wild shores, rivers, deserts, and plains. These books are consistently high-quality trade books for children in grade four and above. Some examples are Mary Batten's *Nature's Tricksters: Animals*

*A shell is just the right sort of home for snails and turtles and crabs and clams.*

*and Plants That Aren't What They Seem* and *Urban Roosts: Where Birds Nest in the City* by Barbara Bash.

- The "Let's-Read-and-Find-Out" Science series, published by HarperCollins, has been researched and validated by authorities in the field. This series is divided into Stage 1 books, which explain simple and easily observable science concepts for preschool and kindergarten children, and Stage 2 books, which explore more challenging concepts for children in the primary grades and include hands-on activities that children can do themselves. *My Five Senses* by Aliki and *What Lives in a Shell* by Kathleen Weidner Zoehfeld are Stage 1 books. Stage 2 books include *Elephant Families* by Arthur Dorros and *The Planets in Our Solar System* by Franklyn M. Branley.

- Thomson Learning publishes a variety of interesting hands-on books. The "Make It Work!" series includes titles such as *Insects, Body, and Machines*. The "Science Activities" series includes such titles as *Electricity, Heat, and Light*. This company has a number of series and titles within the series that are very useful in teaching science.

- Joanne Cole's "The Magic School Bus" series, illustrated by Bruce Degen and published by Scholastic, is popular with children and teachers. The majority of her titles are concerned with science, as is *The Magic School Bus at the Waterworks.*

- Each of the books in the "Read and Wonder" series, published by Candlewick, has been carefully developed. The writing style and illustrations are superb. You will enjoy titles such as *A Piece of String Is a Wonderful Thing* and *The Wheeling and Whirling-Around Book*, both by Judy Hindley.

- The "Real Kids/Real Science" series of children's science trade books includes such titles as *Ornithology, Vertebrate Zoology*, and *Woods, Ponds, and Fields*. These books are produced in association with the Children's School of Science in Woods Hole, Massachusetts, and Thames and Hudson publishing house.

- There are also many excellent individual science trade books not associated with a series; these too will develop children's scientific literacy and their understanding of the interdependence of science, mathematics, and technology.
  - *A River Ran Wild* by Lynne Cherry
  - *How Green Are You?* by David Bellamy
  - *Germs Make Me Sick!* by Melvin Berger
  - *Nature All Year Long* by Clare Walker Leslie
  - *Tree Trunk Traffic* by Bianca Lavies
  - *Whales and Dolphins* by Steve Parker
  - *Wildlife Rescue: The Work of Dr. Kathleen Ramsay* by Jennifer Owings Dewey

## Trade Books and Social Studies

Milton Meltzer (1994), a master of nonfiction, believes that young readers need to be informed about how houses are built, how trucks run, how flowers grow, how birds fly, how weather is formed, and how physical handicaps are overcome, but he also believes they need to know how character is shaped and how the world works. Moreover, he believes that disasters of nature (hurricanes, floods, droughts) and of human society (Vietnam, the Holocaust, poverty) are worthy of attention as causes of suffering to human victims. He believes that all children will encounter fundamental problems of race and class and tyranny in their lifetime and that they should prepare for this by reading about such things.

Literature contains all the great stories of humanity and can be used in social studies to help students develop a sense of history, a sense that the past influences the present, and a sense that various cultures each contribute in an important way to the global society (Cullinan, 1992). Social studies curricula are moving toward this idea of global education, of helping students understand the relationships in their immediate environment and in the world. Nonfiction writers can create an awareness of society and culture that reaches beyond mere facts, helping children understand this country and others in the light of their historical development. Nonfiction writers can create a vision of what might be which excites the imagination and stretches the mind. This is why trade books are a rich resource for teaching social studies; they enable children to develop social studies concepts in a memorable way.

The books mentioned in the "Notable Children's Tradebooks in the Field of Social Studies" offer interesting alternatives to textbooks. This compilation of books is selected each year by the National Council for the Social Studies in conjunction with the Children's Book Council and appears in *Social Education*. Margy Burns Knight has written several good examples of the exciting trade books available for social studies. *Talking Walls* tells the story of 14 walls that exist in our world. Each of the walls gives teachers opportunities to integrate social studies with all areas of the curriculum in a fascinating study. The walls included in this book are:

- The Great Wall of China
- Aborigine Wall Art
- The Western Wall
- Great Zimbabwe
- Canadian Museum of Civilization
- Taos Pueblo
- Nelson Mandela's Prison Walls
- Mahabalipuram's Animal Walls
- The Lascaux Cave
- Muslim Walls
- Cuzco
- The Vietnam Veterans Memorial
- Mexican Murals
- The Berlin Wall

Knight's *Who Belongs Here?* is based on the true story of Nary, a Cambodian child who dreamed of coming to the United States but was rejected when

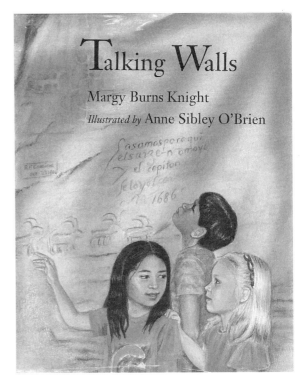

*This book shows children the impact of walls on the people who build them and are either divided or unified by them.*

he arrived. This book, like *Talking Walls*, invites young readers to explore the implications of intolerance. The author asks, "What if every American whose ancestors came from another country was forced to leave the United States? Who would be left?" She includes a compendium of detailed information at the end of the book. Both *Talking Walls* and *Who Belongs Here?* are picture books that young children can enjoy as a story, while middle-grade children can do detailed studies of the ideas, concepts, and information.

There are many books that can serve to enhance the social studies. Farris and Fuhler (1994) suggest a variety of picture books for the social studies in an article in *The Reading Teacher*. The guidelines shown in Figure 9.1 for selecting picture books for teaching social studies concepts are adapted from those suggested by Farris and Fuhler. A list appears on page 283 of the Recommended Children's Books section at the end of this chapter.

FIGURE 9.1

Picture books for social studies.

| Guideline | Example |
| --- | --- |
| The text and illustrations should appeal to readers. | Osband, G. (1991). *Castles*. Illustrated by R. Andrew. New York: Clarion. (History) |
| The facts and information are accurate, authentic, and current. | Towle, W. (1993). *The Life of an African-American Inventor*. Illustrated by W. Clay. New York: Scholastic. (Biography and History) |
| The content extends the social studies topic under study. | Burleigh R. (1991). *Flight: The Journey of Charles Lindbergh*. Illustrated by M. Wimmer. New York: Philomel. (History, detail, concepts of fear and danger) |
| The illustrations are accurate. | Cherry, L. (1992). *A River Ran Wild: An Environmental History*. San Diego: Harcourt Brace Jovanovich. |
| The book is free of stereotypes. | Wheatly, N. and D. Rawlins. (1987). *My Place*. Long Beach, CA: Australia in Print. (History and Geography) |
| The language is rich and clear. | Bruchac, J. and J. London. (1992). *Thirteen Moons on Turtle's Back*. Illustrated by T. Locker. New York: Philomel. (Culture) |
| The book motivates further reading, thinking, and studying. | Musgrove, M. (1976). *Ashanti to Zulu*. Illustrated by L. and D. Dillon. New York: Dial. (Culture) |

## Trade Books and the Arts

The arts are enjoying increasing attention in many elementary schools. Fortunately, a wide range of trade books is available to promote children's interest in the arts. The arts help children create their own visions of things through carving, painting, dancing, singing, and writing (Greene, 1992). The world of fine arts includes paint, clay, and pastels—but language, poems, stories, and riddles are arts as well. Music is an art, too: musical sounds, melody, harmony, and dissonance. Movement is art: it is the body in motion, making shapes, exerting effort, articulating visions, moving in space and time (Greene, 1992). A special list of books to help to integrate the arts into the curriculum is given in the Recommended Children's Books section at the end of this chapter.

## Teaching Strategies for Nonfiction

Trade books cover topics from multiple perspectives with imagination and interesting detail. They communicate the feelings, personal associations, imagination, and attitudes related to a topic; therefore they are excellent materials for developing higher order thinking. Higher order thinking can be developed with specific strategies (Holmes and Ammon, 1985) such as the one in Activity 9.2 on page 273 which is developed over several days and includes three stages: readiness, reading, and responses. The example in the Activity is based on a study of the Middle Ages because this topic is commonly studied in the elementary grades.

### Illustrations

Nonfiction books are usually illustrated with photographs, paintings, drawings, and prints, just as fiction is, although more photographs are used in nonfiction than other genre. The illustrations in nonfiction are especially important because they help readers understand the subject. Activity 9.3 on page 273 presents a guide for studying photographs and other forms of illustration as well (Felton and Allen, 1990).

### Drama and role playing

Creative drama is an excellent follow-up for students who are reading biographies. Children can learn a great deal from role playing or dramatizing

## FIGURE 9.2

Data chart for summarizing data from different sources.

| BOOK TITLE | What kinds of elephants are there? | What do elephants eat? | How large do elephants grow? | How dangerous are elephants? |
|---|---|---|---|---|
| *Elephant Crossing* by Toshi Yoshida | | | | |
| *Kingfisher Animal Atlas* | | | | |
| *Zoo* magazine | | | | |
| | | | | |
| | | | | |

biographies and even some informational literature as well. They may act out events in the biography; playing the part of a historical figure helps them develop a better understanding of that character and his or her role in history. Another activity is conducting television interviews. One student prepares questions while another prepares to be the character, considering the style of dress, issues of the day, and so forth. A camcorder or a tape recorder will add to the feeling of conducting a television interview.

### Summarizing important events

Provensen creates a model for summarizing and interpreting events in *The Buck Stops Here! The Presidents of the United States*, in which she gives her visual interpretation of the events and accomplishments of each president's administration. Children can study this format as a basis for creating their own visual representation of the events of a lifetime. This model could be extended to the

major events in a city or a state as well. The events should be clearly identified and labeled.

### Data charts

One of the problems children encounter when using multiple sources to gather information and write reports is how to integrate the information they collect. The concept of a data chart to help summarize information is presented by several authors (Hennings, 1994; Stoodt, 1989). The steps in preparing a data chart are:

1. Identify the topic or problem.

2. Brainstorm questions, which become the labels for each column.

3. Identify the sources of information in the left-hand column.

4. Have the students complete the chart.

   Figure 9.2 shows a sample data chart.

## UNIT SUGGESTIONS

### 9.1   What about bats? (4th grade)

This unit was the outcome of a student's question about the bat houses he saw while on vacation. He asked, "Why do people want to have bats in their yards? They're dirty, they eat blood, and they get in your hair and give you rabies." Several of the students in the class agreed with him, so this is the unit the teacher and the students planned.

1. Objective: Students will develop these basic concepts:

   a. Bats are the only mammals that fly.

   b. There are nearly a thousand different kinds of bats in the world.

   c. Some bats navigate by sight and some use sound waves.

   d. Bats eat vast quantities of insects every night.

   e. Some bats are essential for the pollination and reseeding of important plants—bananas, cashews, avocados, and figs, to name a few.

   f. Bats are some of the most helpful and fascinating creatures in the world.

   g. Bats need to be protected because through ignorance and fear many of them are being destroyed.

   h. Bats, whose wings are very much like human hands, belong to the scientific order Chiroptera, which means "hand-wing" in Latin.

2. Objective: Students will research the questions posed by their classmates.

   a. Do bats drink blood?

   b. Do bats get in humans' hair?

   c. Why are bats considered dirty?

   d. Do bats carry rabies?

   e. How well can bats see? Is it accurate to say someone is as blind as a bat?

*Books like* Stellaluna, *which is about bats, help correct children's incorrect notions about certain topics.*

The students learned so much from researching these questions that they wanted to learn more about bats and protecting them. They generated additional research questions and projects.

1. Build a model of a bat's wing to show the fingers and thumb.

2. Build models of various kinds of bats.

3. Research the bat as a symbol of good fortune and wisdom in China. Paint illustrations and be prepared to explain why the bat is a symbol of good fortune.

4. Find out about the construction of bat houses and build one.

5. Choose your favorite bat and find out all you can about this particular bat. Write a report, a story, or a poem about your bat.

6. Write a newspaper article about bat protection. Why do bats need protection? What can we do to protect bats? How can we spread the word about protecting bats?

Suggested Books

- *Shadows of Night: The Hidden World of the Little Brown Bat* by Barbara Bash
- *Bats: Night Fliers* by Betsy Maestro, illustrated by Giulio Maestro
- *Mysterious Flyers of the Night* by Dee Stuart
- *Stellaluna* by Janell Cannon

## 9.2 Developing higher-order thinking through reading, readiness, and response

1. *Reading.* In the readiness stage, children brainstorm words related to the topic. For example, children in one sixth grade came up with *armor, moat, castle, lords, ladies, jester, king, duke, prince,* and *knight.* They posed questions—Where did the people live? Were they slaves? What did they eat? How did they travel?—and categorized them.

2. *Readiness.* Next, they selected trade books for sustained silent reading in order to collect and summarize data to answer their questions. Once they chose their resource books, they wrote their bibliography of the topic using data charts (see discussion on page 271.) Some children made their own notes. Some of the books the students chose were *A Medieval Feast* by Aliki, *Quest for a King: Searching for the Real King Arthur* by Catherine Andronik, *The Truth About Castles* by Gillian Clements, and *Castle* by David Macaulay. As the children proceed with their research, discrepant information may emerge. They can reread, review, and check additional resources to resolve the discrepancies. In the process, they may generate new questions they wish to answer.

3. *Response.* In the response stage, children express their feelings and thoughts through writing, oral presentations, art, music, dance, and drama.

.........................................

## 9.3 Studying illustrations

This sample activity provides a guide to developing visual literacy with illustrations. This experience is based on ideas in "Visual Interpretation of Children's Books" (Goldstone, 1989), as well as *Stop, Look, and Write* (Leavitt and Sohn, 1964) and *Images in Language, Media, and Mind* (Fox, 1994). The visual literacy guide is applied to *Prairie Visions* by Pam Conrad.

1. Introduce the selected photograph or illustration to the students. Explain its significance and its source. After the students acquire some experience with this strategy, they can choose their own photographs or illustrations.

2. State questions to guide students' thinking. For example: Where do you think this picture was taken or what does it illustrate? What does the picture tell about the lives of the people in the book? Why were the horses on the roof of the house? What else would you like to know about the people and the way they lived?

   Students may work in pairs, small groups, or individually; they may write their answers or make notes for class discussion.

3. Describe the overall impression of the illustration. Is it dark and dreary, light and colorful, sad or happy, lively or quiet?

4. Ask students to label the people, animals, and objects in the photograph or illustration. For example, students could label different individuals, the shelter, and the horses in *Prairie Visions*.

5. Then ask students to describe the items, people, activities, structures, and so forth in the photograph or illustration. A detailed list for a photograph in *Prairie Visions* would include many items because the photographs are crowded with many objects.

6. Ask students to think about the things they have catalogued in steps 3 through 5 and use their lists and labeled items to draw inferences about the lives of the people in the book. How did they live? Where did they go to school? What did they eat? What were their homes like? What did they do for recreation?

7. When the students complete their inferences, read the text aloud.

8. The students can synthesize their thoughts with the text and the illustrations. They may decide to study the topic further. In fact, fine illustrations motivate students to further study. The students may write a paragraph about their conclusions and support them with references to the illustrations and text or their further study.

## SUMMARY

Nonfiction includes biography and informational literature. In the past, this genre has often been overlooked, but its quality is improving and its quantity is increasing. Children show a greater interest in nonfiction when they have opportunities to experience excellent nonfiction.

Nonfiction trade books are often more up-to-date and detailed than textbooks. Children find these books interesting because they answer the natural questions that children have about the world around them. Children can learn about people who have been leaders and people who have made contributions to all aspects of life from biography. They can learn about math, science, social studies, and the fine arts from informational books. These books also give them the background necessary to understand the facts presented and to relate these facts to their experiences.

## THOUGHT QUESTIONS

1. Why is nonfiction particularly appealing to many children?
2. What standards would you apply in choosing nonfiction for your library or classroom?
3. Why do you think some authors specialize in the nonfiction genre?
4. How can a nonfiction author ensure accuracy and authenticity in a work?

## ENRICHMENT ACTIVITIES

1. Compare three informational books on the same topic. What are the differences in the facts presented? What are the similarities?
2. Compare three biographies of the same person's life. What are the similarities? What are the differences?
3. Identify a topic you would like to know more about. Then identify the types of information you would collect about the topic. Create a data chart for the topic.
4. Read a nonfiction book and write a synopsis of it. Then evaluate it and list the standards you used. What were the book's strong points and its weak points?

## RECOMMENDED CHILDREN'S BOOKS

Aliki. (1983). *A Medieval Feast.* New York: Crowell. (4–8)

   Modern children get a glimpse of authentic medieval living in this book.

———. (1962). *My Five Senses.* New York: Crowell. (preschool–1)

   This is a Stage 1 book in the "Let's-Read-and-Find-Out" Science series.

Anderson, Joan. (1988). *A Williamsburg Household.* New York: Clarion. (4–8)

   Life in Williamsburg is presented from a slave's point of view.

Andronik, Catherine. (1989). *Quest for a King: Searching for the Real King Arthur.* New York: Atheneum. (4–up)

Arnold, Caroline. (1994). *Watching Desert Wildlife.* Minneapolis: Carolrhoda. (2–5)

   The author takes readers on a guided tour of desert life through clear text and stunning color photographs.

Ashabranner, Brent. (1990). *People Who Make a Difference.* Photography by Paul Conklin. New York: Dutton. (3–8)

   Everyday people who made a difference for others are profiled in this book.

Ballard, Robert. (1988). *Exploring the* Titanic. New York: Scholastic. (4–8)

   This book explores both the sinking of the *Titanic* and the discovery of its wreckage.

Bash, Barbara. (1993). *Shadows of Night: The Hidden World of the Little, Brown Bat.* San Francisco: Sierra Club Books for Children. (1–3)

This informational book with color photographs provides interesting facts.

Berger, Melvin. (1985). *Germs Make Me Sick!* Illustrated by Marylin Hafner. New York: Crowell. (K–3)

The author explains bacteria and viruses in simple terms that young children can understand.

————. (1989). *Simple Simon Says: Take One Magnifying Glass.* New York: Scholastic. (K–3)

This activity book helps children use magnification to get a different view of the world.

Blegvad, Erik. (1979). *Self-Portrait: Erik Blegvad.* Reading, MA: Addison-Wesley. (4–8)

The author created a self-portrait that provides insight into his work.

Blos, Joan W. (1994). *The Days Before Now.* Illustrated by Thomas B. Allen. New York: Simon & Schuster. (1–3)

This exquisite picture book autobiography of Margaret Wise Brown is told in her own words, adapted by the author.

Blumberg, Rhoda. (1989). *The Great American Gold Rush.* New York: Bradbury. (4–8)

The siren song of gold for Easterners and immigrants is explained in this book.

Bonners, Susan. (1978). *Panda.* New York: Delacorte. (2–6)

The life cycle of a giant panda is detailed in this book.

Bourne, B., and W. Saul. (1994). *Exploring Space: Using Seymour Simon's Astronomy Books in the Classroom.* New York: Morrow. (3–9)

Space-related projects integrated across the curriculum will extend students' knowledge of astronomy.

Bowen, Gary. (1994). *Stranded at Plimoth Plantation 1626.* New York: HarperCollins. (2–5)

This story is told through the journal entries of a 13-year-old boy who is stranded at Plimoth Plantation until passage can be found to Jamestown.

Branley, Franklyn M. (1993). *The Planets in Our Solar System.* New York: HarperCollins. (1–3)

This is a Stage 2 book in the "Let's-Read-and-Find-Out" Science series.

Brenner, Barbara. (1977). *On the Frontier with Mr. Audubon.* New York: Coward, McCann, and Geoghegan. (4–8)

Audubon's experiences are described from the point of view of his apprentice.

Brown, Marc and Laurene Krasny Brown. (1984). *Dinosaurs Divorce.* Boston: Little, Brown. (1–5)

This is an informational book about divorce for young children.

Cannon, Janell. (1993). *Stellaluna.* New York: Harcourt Brace Jovanovich. (1–3)

This is the story of a little fruit bat who is separated from her mother. She lands in a bird's nest and grows up with birds.

Cherry, Lynne. (1992). *A River Ran Wild: An Environmental History.* San Diego: Harcourt Brace Jovanovich. (1–4)

This picture book begins with the Native Americans and traces the environmental history of a river.

Cleary, Beverly. (1988). *A Girl from Yamhill: A Memoir.* New York: William Morrow. (3–6)

The author describes her early life. Interesting photographs.

Clements, Gillian. (1990). *The Truth About Castles.* Minneapolis: Carolrhoda. (3–7)

This informational book tells about life in real castles.

Coerr, Eleanor. (1977). *Sadako and the Thousand Paper Cranes.* Illustrated by Ronald Himler. New York: Putnam. (all ages)

Sadako was a victim of the atomic bomb dropped on Hiroshima. She attempted to fulfill an ancient legend to obtain good health.

Cole, Joanna. (1989). *The Magic School Bus: Inside the Human Body.* Illustrated by Bruce Degen. New York: Scholastic. (all ages)

Ms. Frizzle's class takes an unusual field trip on their magic school bus, which permits them to enter the body and observe the organs.

_____ . (1992). *The Magic School Bus: On the Ocean Floor.* Illustrated by Bruce Degen. New York: Scholastic. (all ages)

The indomitable Ms. Frizzle takes her class to the ocean floor.

_____ . (1994). *The Magic School Bus in the Time of the Dinosaurs.* Illustrated by Bruce Degen. New York: Scholastic. (all ages)

Ms. Frizzle takes her class to a dinosaur dig to look for Maiasaura nests.

_____ . (1986). *The Magic School Bus at the Waterworks.* New York: Scholastic. (3–7)

Ms. Frizzle takes her class to the waterworks via their magic school bus.

Cone, Molly. (1991). *Come Back, Salmon.* Photographs by Sidnee Wheelwright. San Francisco: Sierra Club Books. (3–6)

This book documents an actual event. The children in the book adopted a creek and brought it back to life.

Conrad, Pam. (1989). *The Life and Times of Solomon Butcher.* New York: HarperCollins. (4–8)

This book is based on the life of a frontier photographer in Nebraska during the 1800s.

Dewey, Jennifer Owings. (1994). *Wildlife Rescue: The Work of Dr. Kathleen Ramsay.* Honesdale, PA: Boyds Mills. (4–8)

This book documents Dr. Ramsey's work saving wild animals.

Dodds, Doyle Ann. (1994). *The Shape of Things.* New York: HarperCollins. (preschool–1)

This informational book explores the shapes of things through photographs and drawings of everyday activities and objects.

_____ . (1994). *The Dorling Kindersley Children's Illustrated Dictionary.* New York: Dorling Kindersley.

A colorful, useful reference.

Dorros, Arthur. (1994). *Elephant Families.* New York: HarperCollins. (1–3)

This is a Stage 2 book in the "Let's-Read-and-Find-Out" Science series.

Epstein, Sam, and Beryl Epstein. (1978). *Dr. Beaumont and the Man with a Hole in His Stomach.* Illustrated by Joseph Scrofani. New York: Coward, McCann, and Geoghegan. (4–8)

This biography tells the story of a doctor who performed unusual experiments.

*Exploring Space.* (1994). New York: Scholastic. (3–6)

Movable maps of the constellations, plastic overlays, fold-out maps, 3-D glasses, and a sky clock to rotate to tell time as 16th-century astronomers did are part of this excellent informational book. A time line and extensive references for further reading are included. This is part of the "Voyages of Discovery" series by Scholastic Books.

*Exploring Your World: The Adventure of Geography.* (1989). New York: Kingfisher. (all ages)

334 encyclopedia entries on a variety of geographical topics with more than 1,000 photographs, diagrams, and charts.

Faber, Doris. (1983). *Love and Rivalry: Three Exceptional Pairs of Sisters.* New York: Viking Press. (4–8)

This collective biography profiles three sets of sisters.

Facklam, Margery. (1994). *The Big Bug Book.* Boston: Little, Brown. (1–3)

This primary-grade book illustrates big bugs in their actual size, showing common objects along with the bugs to give children a better sense of their size.

*The Facts on File Junior Visual Dictionary.* (1989). New York: Kingfisher.

Visual information on a variety of subjects is included in this reference book.

Fox, Mem. (1992). *Shoes from Grandpa.* Illustrated by Patricia Mullens. New York: Orchard Books. (preschool–2)

This cumulative story tells how Jessie is clothed by all the members of her family.

Freedman, Russell. (1983). *Children of the Wild West.* New York: Clarion. (4–8)

This book documents life in the American West from 1840 to the early 1900s.

_____ . (1987). *Lincoln: A Photobiography.* New York: Clarion. (4–8)

Freedman superbly portrays the life of Abraham Lincoln in this picture book.

_____ . (1990). *Franklin Delano Roosevelt.* New York: Clarion. (4–8)

Freedman depicts Roosevelt's dynamic personality with text and pictures that speak to children.

_____ . (1993). *Eleanor Roosevelt: A Life of Discovery.* New York: Clarion. (4–8)

Eleanor Roosevelt is depicted as a young woman who did not discover that she was intelligent and capable until adulthood. Once she discovered her powers, she continued to discover the skills she needed in her life.

Fritz, Jean. (1973). *And Then What Happened, Paul Revere?* Illustrated by Margot Tomes. New York: Coward, McCann, and Geoghegan. (2–5)

A humorous tribute to Paul Revere's character that focuses on his skills of reporting what happened to him.

_____ . (1981). *Traitor: The Strange Case of Benedict Arnold.* New York: Putnam. (2–5)

This book explores the events in Benedict Arnold's life.

_____ . (1982). *Homesick: My Own Story.* Illustrated by Margot Tomes. New York: Putnam. (2–5)

An autobiography of Fritz's childhood in China.

_____ . (1989). *The Great Little Madison.* New York: Putnam. (4–7)

This is a biography of the fourth president of the United States.

_____ . (1994). *Around the World in a Hundred Years.* Illustrated by Anthony Bacon Venti. New York: Putnam. (3–6)

The author focuses on the great explorers, from Henry the Navigator to Magellan.

Gibbons, Gail. (1988). *Sunken Treasure.* New York: Alladin. (1–4)

This book chronologically details the discovery of the *Atocha,* a Spanish treasure ship.

_____ . (1990). *Beacons of Light: Lighthouses.* New York: Morrow. (1–4)

The author tells all about beautiful lighthouses and explains how technology has changed them.

_____ . (1994). *Nature's Green Umbrella.* New York: Morrow. (2–5)

Gibbons explains one of the world's most complicated ecosystems with lucid language and lush illustrations. She shares information about tropical rain forests.

Giblin, James. (1994). *Thomas Jefferson.* Illustrated by M. Dooling. New York: Scholastic. (3–6)

A superb portrayal of Jefferson that is enhanced by the paintings that illustrate the book.

Gish, Lillian (as told to Selma Lanes). (1987). *An Actor's Life for Me.* Illustrated by Patricia Henderson Lincoln. New York: Viking Kestrel. (4–7)

This is the autobiography of Lillian Gish, the silent-film star. The book traces her life from childhood through her years as a star of stage and screen.

Golenbeck, Peter. (1990). *Teammates.* Illustrated by Paul Bacon. New York: Harcourt Brace Jovanovich. (4–7)

The theme of this book is the friendship of Jackie Robinson and teammate Pee Wee Reese.

Greenfield, Eloise, and Lessie Jones Little. (1979). *Childtimes: A Three-Generation Memoir*. New York: T. H. Crowell. (4–7)

This is the story of three generations of African American women.

Harris, Laurie Lanzen, editor. (1993). *Biography Today*. Detroit: Omnigraphics Inc. (3–8)

This volume includes short biographies of notable people who are of special interest to students.

Haslam, Andrew. (1994). *Body*. New York: Thomson Learning. (4–7)

Part of the "Make It Work!" series, these activities help students understand the body and how it works.

———. (1994). *Insects*. New York: Thomson Learning. (4–7)

Part of the "Make It Work!" series.

———. (1994). *Machines*. New York: Thomson Learning. (4–7)

Part of the "Make It Work!" series.

Heller, Ruth. (1987). *A Cache of Jewels and Other Collective Nouns*. New York: Grossett and Dunlap. (2–5)

This book explores collective nouns.

Hendershot, Judith. (1987). *In Coal Country*. Illustrated by Thomas Allen. New York: Knopf. (2–4)

This book describes the life of a child growing up in a coal mining town.

Hindley, Judy. (1993). *A Piece of String Is a Wonderful Thing*. Cambridge, MA: Candlewick. (1–3)

This informational book is part of the "Read and Wonder" series.

———. (1994). *The Wheeling and Whirling-Around Book*. Cambridge, MA: Candlewick. (1–3)

This informational book is part of the "Read and Wonder" series.

Hoban, Tana. (1987). *Twenty-Six Letters and Ninety-Nine Cents*. New York: William Morrow. (preschool–2)

This unusual picture book teaches about counting and the alphabet.

Hoffman, Mary. (1991). *Amazing Grace*. Illustrated by Caroline Binch. New York: Dial. (1–3)

Grace loves to pretend and hopes to be Peter Pan in the school play. One person tells her she can't because she is a girl, another says she can't because she is black.

Hyman, Trina Schart. (1981). *Self-Portrait: Trina Schart Hyman*. Reading, MA: Addison-Wesley. (2–5)

The author tells about her life as an artist and illustrator.

*Illustrated Thesaurus*. (1994). New York: Kingfisher. (3–6)

Jakes, John. (1986). *Susannah of the Alamo*. Illustrated by Paul Bacon. New York: Harcourt Brace Jovanovich. (2–5)

This story is told from the point of view of a girl who survived the Alamo.

Karl, Jean. (1994). *America Alive*. New York: Philomel. (3–8)

This book is a balanced, inclusive overview of American history beginning with the first inhabitants of North America up to the present day.

Kendall, Russ. (1992). *Eskimo Boy: Life in an Inupiaq Eskimo Village*. New York: Scholastic. (1–4)

This book is about a seven-year-old Inupiaq Eskimo boy and his family.

*The Kingfisher First Picture Atlas*. (1994). New York: Kingfisher. (1–4)

An atlas in picture-book format for younger students that includes map scales, as well as how to read and make maps.

*The Kingfisher Young People's Encyclopedia of Animals*. (1994). New York: Kingfisher. (2–5)

This work includes 450 entries about animals.

*The Kingfisher Young People's Encyclopedia of the United States.* (1994). New York: Kingfisher. (3–6)
1,200 entries reflect the school curriculum.

Knight, Margy Burns. (1992). *Talking Walls.* Gardiner, ME: Tilbury House. (1–8)
Fourteen different walls around the world are the subject of this picture book.

———. (1993). *Who Belongs Here? An American Story.* Gardiner, ME: Tilbury House. (2–8)
This is a story of Nary, who escaped from Cambodia only to encounter intolerance in the United States.

Konigsburg, E. L. (1975). *A Proud Taste of Scarlet and Miniver.* New York: Atheneum. (4–8)
This is an unusual biography of Eleanor of Aquitaine.

Kunhardt, Edith. (1993). *Honest Abe.* Illustrated by Malcah Zeldis. New York: Greenwillow. (1–4)
Primitive paintings beautifully illustrate this picture-book biography of Abraham Lincoln.

Kuskin, Karla. (1987). *Jerusalem, Shining Still.* Illustrated by David Frampton. New York: Harper & Row. (2–6)
This informational book tells the 3,000-year history of Jerusalem through text, prose, and poetry.

Lacey, Elizabeth. (1989). *The Complete Frog: A Guide for the Very Young Naturalist.* Illustrated by Christopher Santaro. New York: Lothrop, Lee & Shepard. (2–5)
This guide provides detailed information and photographs of all types of frogs.

Lasky, Kathryn. (1994). *The Librarian Who Measured the Earth.* Illustrated by Kevin Hawkes. Boston: Little, Brown. (2–4)
This is a picture-book biography of Eratosthenes, who lived more than 2,000 years ago.

Lauber, Patricia. (1986). *Volcano: The Eruption and Healing of Mt. St. Helens.* New York: Bradbury. (all ages)
Through the use of photographs and text, the events before, during, and after the eruption of Mt. St. Helens are described.

———. (1988). *Lost Star.* New York: Scholastic. (3–6)
This book recounts Amelia Earhart's life.

Lavies, Bianca. (1989). *Tree Trunk Traffic.* New York: Dutton. (all ages)
Vividly describes the living things traveling up and down a tree.

Lawson, Robert. (1939). *Ben and Me.* Boston: Little, Brown. (2–4)
This humorous biography of Ben Franklin is told by a mouse who lives in Franklin's hat.

Lester, Julius. (1968). *To Be a Slave.* New York: Dial. (4–adult)
A compilation of interviews with former slaves telling about their lives as slaves.

Levinson, Riki. (1985). *I Go with My Family to Grandma's.* Illustrated by Diane Goode. New York: Dutton. (2–5)
The author describes the lives of people living in New York in the late 1800s.

———. (1985). *Watch the Stars Come Out.* Illustrated by Diane Goode. New York: Dutton. (2–4)
An immigrant family coming to the United States by boat is the focus of this story.

Little, Jean. (1988). *Little by Little: A Writer's Education.* New York: Viking Penguin. (3–5)
An autobiography of the Canadian author Jean Little, who is a writer in spite of the fact that she is nearly blind.

Mabey, Richard. (1983). *Oak and Company.* Illustrated by Clare Roberts. New York: Greenwillow. (3–6)
The life cycle of an oak tree and its impact on the surrounding forest are traced in this informational book.

Macaulay, David. (1988). *The Way Things Work*. Boston: Houghton Mifflin. (all ages)
The author describes and illustrates more than 500 different machines.

————. (1978). *Castle*. Boston: Houghton Mifflin. (all ages)
This book details the construction of a castle.

Maestro, Betsy. (1994). *Bats: Night Fliers*. Illustrated by Giulio Maestro. New York: Scholastic. (1–3)
This picture book provides interesting information about bats for younger children.

Marrin, Albert. (1987). *Hitler*. New York: Viking Penguin. (4–7)
This biography tells about the life of Hitler.

Mason, Anthony, and Keith Lye. (1993). *The Children's Atlas of Exploration*. Brookfield, CT: Millbrook Press. (2–6)

Miller, Jonathon, and David Pelham. (1983). *The Human Body*. New York: Viking. (2–4)
This three-dimensional pop-up book describes the human body.

Miller, William. (1994). *Zora Hurston and the Chinaberry Tree*. Illustrated by Cornelius Van Wright and Ying-Hwa Hu. New York: Lee and Low Books. (1–3)
This biographical picture book focuses on one incident in the life of Zora Hurston, the African American writer.

Monjo, Ferdinand M. (1973). *Me and Willie and Pa*. Illustrated by Douglas Garsline. New York: Simon & Schuster. (1–3)
Abraham Lincoln's son Tad narrates this partial biography.

Morgan, Allen. (1994). *Circles and Spheres*. Illustrated by Sally Morgan. New York: Thomson Learning. (1–3)
This informational book explores the shapes of things through photographs and drawings of everyday activities and objects.

*Musical Instruments*. (1993). New York: Scholastic. (3–8)
This is part of the "Voyages of Discovery" series by Scholastic Books.

Myers, Walter Dean. (1991). *Now Is Your Time! The African American Struggle for Freedom*. New York: Harper. (4–adult)
This book traces the history of African Americans and their struggle for freedom in this country. The book is told through the stories of people whose experiences shaped our country.

*Paint and Painting*. (1993). New York: Scholastic. (3–8)
This is part of the "Voyages of Discovery" series by Scholastic Books.

Parker, Steve. (1994). *Whales and Dolphins*. New York: Sierra Club and Little, Brown. (3–6)
Informative data and photographs of these fascinating creatures.

Peacock, G., and J. Jesson. (1994). *Electricity*. New York: Thomson Learning. (2–4)
Part of the "Science Activities" series, these science activities familiarize students with the properties of electricity.

————. (1994). *Heat*. New York: Thomson Learning. (2–4)
Part of the Science Activities series.

————. (1994). *Light*. New York: Thomson Learning. (2–4)
Part of the Science Activities series.

Peet, Bill. (1989). *Bill Peet: An Autobiography*. Boston: Houghton Mifflin. (all ages)
An entertaining autobiography of this author and Disney cartoonist.

Pringle, Laurence. (1990). *Global Warming*. Boston: Little, Brown. (4–8)
The author gives a detailed explanation of global warming.

_____. (1991). *Living Treasure: Saving Earth's Threatened Biodiversity*. New York: Morrow. (4–8)

This informational book summarizes and organizes information about our planet's unique organisms.

Provensen, Alice. (1990). *The Buck Stops Here: The Presidents of the United States*. New York: Harper & Row. (3–adult)

The term of office of each president of the United States is described.

Provensen, Alice, and Marten Provensen. (1984). *Leonardo da Vinci: The Artist, Scientist, Inventor in Three Dimensional Movable Pictures*. New York: Viking. (3–7)

This book describes one year in the life of Leonardo da Vinci.

Reiser, Lynn. (1992). *Any Kind of Dog*. New York: Greenwillow. (1–3)

In this informational book children learn about some of the many kinds of dogs they might choose as a pet.

Ride, Sally, and Susan Okie. (1986). *To Space & Back*. New York: Lothrop, Lee & Shepard. (2–5)

This book documents the life of an astronaut.

Sanchez, Jose and Miguel Pacheco. (1974). *I Am a Wild Animal*. New York: Santillana Publishing. (1–3)

This book illustrates an anthropomorphic approach to nonfiction.

Say, Allen. (1993). *Grandfather's Journey*. Boston: Houghton Mifflin. (all ages)

Say compares his life and his grandfather's life in the Caldecott Award–winning book telling about his grandfather's journey to the United States and his return to Japan.

Schroeder, Alan. (1989). *Ragtime Tumpie*. Illustrated by Bernie Fuchs. Boston: Little, Brown.

This biography describes the early years of Josephine Baker, the jazz singer.

Schwartz, David. (1985). *How Much Is a Million?* Illustrated by Steven Kellogg. New York: Lothrop, Lee & Shepard. (K–3)

This book helps children understand a million, a trillion, and a billion.

*Science Experiments Index for Young People*. (1988). New York: Kingfisher. (3–8)

This specialized bibliography includes science activities and experiments drawn from 700 books.

Shertle, Alice. (1985). *My Two Feet*. Illustrated by Meredith Dunham. New York: Lothrop, Lee & Shepard. (K–2)

This is a book about shoes.

Simon, Seymour. (1987). *Mars*. New York: William Morrow. (3–8)

The author uses NASA photographs to illustrate the information included in this book.

_____. (1994). *Comets, Meteors, and Asteroids*. New York: Morrow. (3–8)

This book provides basic information, photographs, and drawings that will help students understand these subjects.

Spedden, Daisy Corning Stone. (1994). *Polar, the Titanic Bear*. Boston: Little, Brown. (2–5)

This factual book, illustrated with photographs of the *Titanic* and written 80 years ago, follows the life of a boy named Douglas who actually sailed on the *Titanic* and survived. The information is presented from the point of view of his Teddy bear, who is included in the pictures.

Stanley, Jerry. (1992). *Children of the Dust Bowl*. New York: Crown. (4–12)

This is a compelling story about the "Okie" migration to California in the 1930s and the construction of a remarkable school.

Stuart, Dee. (1994). *Mysterious Flyers of the Night*. Minneapolis: Carolrhoda. (1–4)

This is an informative book about bats.

*Taming Fire.* (1993). New York: Scholastic. (3–8)
>   This is part of the "Voyages of Discovery" series by Scholastic Books.

Van Loon, Hendrik W. (1921). *The Story of Mankind.* New York: Liveright. (5–10)
>   The author traces the human race from prehistoric times to the 20th century.

Wallace, Karen. (1993). *Think of an Eel.* Cambridge, MA: Candlewick Press. (1–4)
>   This well-written and well-illustrated book describes the characteristics and the life cycle of eels.

————— . (1994). *Bears in the Forest.* Cambridge, MA: Candlewick. (1–3)
>   This informational book is part of the "Read and Wonder" series.

Winter, Jeanette. (1991). *Diego.* New York: Knopf. (1–4)
>   This book tells about the childhood of Diego Rivera, the Hispanic painter, and the ways that his early life influenced his art.

Winthrop, Elizabeth. (1986). *Shoes.* Illustrated by William Joyce. New York: HarperCollins. (K–2)
>   The author tells about the pleasures of new shoes for young children.

Wormser, Richard. (1994). *Hoboes: Wandering in America, 1870–1940.* New York: Walker. (5–9)
>   The author uses black-and-white photographs and well-written narrative to explore the hobo culture of the early 1900s.

Yoshida, Toshi. (1989). *Elephant Crossing.* New York: Philomel. (5–9)
>   The book follows a herd of elephants across plains to forests where they can eat. Included are the dangers found on plains.

Young, J. (1994). *The Most Amazing Science Pop-Up Book.* New York: Scholastic. (4–8)
>   This interactive informational book includes a working record player, compass, microscope, camera, sundial, kaleidoscope, and periscope. This book is rich with accurate information.

Zoehfeld, Kathleen Weidner. (1994). *What Lives in a Shell?* New York: HarperCollins. (1–3)
>   This is a Stage 1 book in the "Let's-Read-and-Find-Out" Science series.

## Social Studies Books

Ackerman, Karen. (1988). *Song and Dance Man.* Illustrated by Stephen Gammell. New York: Knopf. (1)

Allen, Thomas. (1980). *Where Children Live.* New York: Putnam. (1)

Anno. (1986). *All in a Day.* New York: Philomel. (3)

Arnold, Caroline. (1982). *What Is a Community?* Illustrated by Carole Bertole. Chicago: Watts. (3)

Berger, Melvin. (1985). *Germs Make Me Sick!* Illustrated by Marylin Hafner. New York: Crowell. (2)

Blumberg, Rhoda. (1989). *The Great American Gold Rush.* New York: Bradbury. (5)

Branley, Franklyn. (1994). *Tornado Alert.* New York: HarperCollins. (2)

Bulla, C. (1993). *Charlie's House.* New York: Knopf. (1)

Crews, Donald. (1984). *School Bus.* New York: Greenwillow. (K)

Facklam, Margery. (1993). *The Big Bug Book.* Boston: Little, Brown. (2)

Farza, Carmen (as told to Harriet Bohmer). (1990). *Family Pictures.* San Francisco: Children's Book Press. (3)

Gans, Roma. (1984). *Rock Collecting.* Illustrated by Holly Heller. New York: T. H. Crowell. (2)

Graham, Ada, and Frank Graham. (1986). *The Changing Desert.* San Francisco and New York: Sierra Club Books. (4)

Guiberson, Brenda. (1991). *Cactus Hotel.* Illustrated by Megan Lloyd. New York: Holt. (3)

Henkes, Kevin. (1987). *Once Around the Block.* Illustrated by Victoria Chess. New York: Greenwillow. (2)

Hoberman, Mary Ann. (1978). *A House Is a House for Me.* New York: Viking. (K)

Hopkins, Lee. (1992). *To the Zoo.* Illustrated by John Wallir. Boston: Little, Brown. (2)

Howe, James. (1986). *When You Go to School.* New York: Knopf. (K)

Margolies, Barbara. (1990). *Rehema's Journey: A Visit in Tanzania.* New York: Scholastic. (6)

Meltzer, Milton. (1985). *Mary McLeod Bethune: Voice of Black Hope.* New York: Morrow Junior Books. (5)

Mizumura, Kazue. (1971). *If I Built a Village.* New York: Crowell. (3)

Munro, Roxie. (1989). *The Inside-Outside Book of London.* New York: Dutton. (6)

———. (1992). *The Inside-Outside Book of Paris.* New York: Dutton. (6)

Myers, Christopher, and Lynne Myers. (1993). *McCrephy's Field.* New York: HarperCollins. (4)

Parker, Nancy W. (1987). *Bugs.* New York: Greenwillow. (3)

Siebert, Diane. (1988). *Mojave.* New York: Harper. (4)

Simon, Seymour. (1990). *Deserts.* New York: Morrow. (4)

Slawson, Michele. (1994). *Apple Picking Time.* Boston: Little, Brown. (1)

Smith, C. (Ed.) (1991). *The Explorers and Settlers: A Source Book on Colonial America.* Brookfield, CT: Millbrook. (1)

Sneve, Virginia Driving Hawk, selector (1989). *Dancing Teepees: Poems of American Indian Youth.* Illustrated by Stephen Gammell. New York: Holiday House. (5)

Stevenson, James. (1987). *Higher on the Door.* New York: Greenwillow. (K)

## Books About the Arts

Anholt, Laurence. (1994). *Camille and the Sunflowers: A Story About Vincent Van Gogh.* New York: Barrons. (1–3)

Carratello, John, and Patty Carratello. (1993). *Focus on Composers.* Chicago: Teacher Created Materials. (4–8)

Chertok, Bobbi, Goody Hirshfeld, and Marilyn Rosh. (1994). *Learning About Ancient Civilizations Through Art.* New York: Scholastic. (3–6)

DesJarlait, Patrick. (1995). As recorded by Neva Williams. *Conversations with a Native American Artist.* Minneapolis: Runestone Press.

Hart, Avery, and Paul Mantell. (1994). *Kids Make Music!* Charlotte, VT: Williamson. (K–4)

Hart, Kate. (1994). *I Can Paint!* Portsmouth, NH: Heineman. (2–5)

Hastings, Selina. (1993). *The Firebird.* Illustrated by Reg Cartwright. Cambridge, MA: Candlewick. (3–6)

Howard, Nancy. (1992). *William Sidney Mount: Painter of Rural America.* Worcester, MA: Davis. (3–6)

Hughes, A. (1994). *Van Gogh.* New York: Barron's. (3–8).

Jenkins, Jessica. (1992). *Thinking About Colors.* New York: Dutton. (1–3)

Martin, Bill. (1994). *The Maestro Plays.* New York: Henry Holt. (1–3)

Micklethwait, Lucy. *A Child's Book of Art.* New York: Dorling Kindersley. (1–5)

*Musical Instruments.* (1993). Scholastic Voyages of Discovery Series. New York: Scholastic. (all ages)

*Paint and Painting.* (1993). Scholastic Voyages of Discovery Series. New York: Scholastic. (all ages)

Prokofiev, Sergei. (1987). *Peter and the Wolf.* Illustrated by Reg Cartwright. New York: Holt. (1–5)

Rachlin, Ann. (1994). *Beethoven.* New York: Barrons. (1–5)

Thompson, Kimberly, and Diana Loftus. (1995). *Art Connections.* New York: Goodyear. (4–8)

Turner, Robyn. (1992). *Dorothea Lange.* Boston: Little, Brown. (4–8)

Turner, Robyn Montana. (1992). *Portraits of Women Artists for Children: Mary Cassatt.* Boston: Little, Brown. (3–8)

Werner, Vivian (reteller). *Petrouchka: The Story of Ballet.* New York: Viking Penguin. (3–up)

# *T*en

## KEY TERMS

author                          writing

illustrator

## GUIDING QUESTIONS

Think about your favorite childhood authors and illustrators and what you especially liked about them. Remembering what you enjoyed as a child may help you understand what the children you work with will enjoy. As you read this chapter, keep the following questions in mind.

1. What do author studies contribute to our understanding and appreciation of literature?

2. How do students get to know authors?

3. What factors should we consider in studying illustrators?

## OVERVIEW

Readers of all ages are excited to meet a favorite **author** or **illustrator**. When one visits a local bookstore, readers queue up to catch a glimpse and get an autograph. They want to know *the people who create their books.* This natural excitement works to the advantage of those who wish to involve children in literature: Learning more about creative people can motivate children to read more to become even better acquainted. "Approaching literature through writers brings a certain intimacy to the learning and enjoyment process" (Wildberger, 1993, p. 3). Learning about authors and illustrators helps children realize that these people are *members of a reading and writing "community" that readers can join.* The primary ways of getting to know authors and illustrators are through reading their works and reading interviews, articles, dust jacket information, and reference materials about them. Occasionally, an author or illustrator may appear on television.

Focusing on authors and illustrators as a means of structuring literature experiences develops thinking abilities, as readers' intellect and emotions are activated when they analyze and evaluate an author's writing or compare the work of two different authors.

This chapter examines the writing perspectives of children's authors, the works of some children's authors, and strategies for learning about authors and illustrators. Authors' and illustrators' motivations, processes of getting ideas, and artistic processes are explored. A few notable authors and illustrators are profiled in this chapter. These individuals represent a small number of a large group of wonderfully talented, interesting, dedicated, humorous, and thoughtful people. Space, of course, unfortunately prohibits including all of the fine authors and illustrators who create children's books. However, the profiles and teaching ideas presented can be used as models for studying other authors and illustrators.

# Readers, Writers, and Illustrators

## A LITERARY COMMUNITY

## INTRODUCTION

When readers open a book, they accept an invitation to collaborate with the author, to explore existing meanings, and to forge new meanings. No matter how good the writing may be, a book is never complete until someone reads it (Paterson, 1981a). All of the experiences authors have influence their writing. Paula Fox explains: "It is my view that all the moments and years of one's life are part of any story that one writes" (Elleman, 1991, p. 35). Since an author's experiences influence writing so heavily, knowing something about the author greatly enhances the reading process.

The opening vignette shows the excitement that an author's visit generates in an elementary school—but this is just a small glimpse of the enthusiasm generated. The students in this class pored over everything Jack Prelutsky published, learning all about him and his work. After the visit, they eagerly awaited his new books. And children are not the only ones to get excited: teachers are not immune, as the sketch in the box on page 286 illustrates.

Author visits are of inestimable value to children, a treat that every classroom should experience. As Byrd Baylor says, "Many schools are bringing people to talk about writing. I think it's more than just seeing a person who writes books: it's turning kids on to ideas. I see my work with children as encouragement to help them realize that they, too, have ideas and that's all they need to write" (Bosma, 1987). Unfortunately, authors cannot visit every school, but children everywhere can experience the pleasure of getting to know their favorite authors through reading their works, finding interviews or articles to read about the author, or viewing videotapes. In the process, they develop a greater appreciation for reading and writing.

## VIGNETTE

"Miss Allison, Miss Allison," five-year-old Michael said excitedly.

"What is it, Michael?" the teacher responded.

"Jack Prelutsky is coming to our school and he's my favorite poet. Look, I got *Rolling Harvey Down the Hill* from the media center."

Andrea came into the classroom next. She was carrying *The Baby Uggs Are Hatching*. "Do you think we can learn to read some of his poems, so we can do them when he visits?"

"I'm certain you can," Miss Allison answered.

"Oh boy!" Mark said. "Can we do *The Baby Uggs Are Hatching?*"

"I want to do *Rolling Harvey Down the Hill,*" Michael said.

"Do you think we could do more than one poem?" Jennifer asked.

"A real author at our school. This is so exciting!" Levonne said.

285

## FROM READING TO WRITING

Authors are inveterate readers. They marvel at the great books created by other artists (Paterson, 1981a). "Every book is a voyage of discovery. I exist in a state of continual astonishment," says Susan Cooper (1981). Weiss (1979) interviewed 17 authors for *From Writers to Students*. Each of the 17 claimed to be an avid reader. When asked to identify the authors who most influenced her work, Judy Blume cited Louise Fitzhugh, Elaine Konigsburg, Beverly Cleary, and Marilyn Sachs. Avi (1990) attributes his love of literature to the fact that he was read to constantly as a child. Katherine Paterson (1981b) explains: "I had been reading since I was five, and I am sure that I began to write not because of any ability real or imagined but because I loved to read, and that when I finally began to write books, it was not so much that I wanted to be a writer but that I loved books and wanted to be inside the process, to have a part in their making" (p. 2). Writers speak often of their love of reading; it seems that reading propels them as much as a need for creative expression. Paula Fox (1991a) says, "Writing is my work. I am impelled toward it by love of stories, by the demands of my own imagination" (p. 2).

To write well we must grow up hearing how other people have written—to get a sense of the grandeur, the playfulness, and the plain narrative strength of the English language (Zinsser, 1990). Judy Blume tells of checking out cartons of books from the public library in preparation for writing (Weiss, 1979). Vera and Bill Cleaver call the public library the "poor man's college" (Weiss, 1979) because they relied on it for their education. Gary Paulsen says, "I would have been an intellectual idiot without the library" and recommends that students "read like a wolf eats" (Handy, 1991, p. 112).

Reading influences writing in various ways. It stimulates ideas and feelings, as well as providing models for composing. For many writers, reading is essential to their art. Through enjoying many books, readers come to appreciate and understand various writers' styles. They realize that the voice, rhythms, and personality of writers come through their work.

## FROM WRITING TO MEANING

Authors use reading and writing as means of *knowing*, searching for meaning through them. "**Writing** itself *is a learning device*—a means to knowledge, self-knowledge, knowledge of life," says Ursula LeGuin (1991, p. 12). Writing as a means of self-understanding is Cynthia Rylant's (1989) theme as well: "Children who have suffered a loss too great for words grow up into writers who are always trying to find words—meaning for the way they have lived" (p. 6).

Illustrators search for meaning in their craft, as well. David Macaulay (1991), recipient of the 1991 Caldecott Award, encourages people to "ask themselves why things look the way they do" (p. 410).

The excitement of the children in the opening vignette reminded me of my own first meeting with an author, Elizabeth Yates, at a reading workshop at Ohio State University in the summer of 1963. She told about discovering the tombstone in a small church cemetery, which led her to write *Amos Fortune: Free Man*. While she told of researching this man's life, I listened spellbound, as did everyone in the large audience.

Later, someone asked where she got the ideas for her other books, and she shifted to telling about a forthcoming book, *Carolina's Courage*, and a buffalo-hide doll belonging to a little girl she knew. The doll, a family heirloom, was handed down from generation to generation in the girl's family along with the story of its origins. This doll and the family story became the impetus for *Carolina's Courage*. Later, she told the story of another book that was based on a short newspaper clipping.

Of course, I eagerly read every book that Elizabeth Yates wrote. I thought about the ways she found ideas for her stories and the research she did to validate these stories. But most of all, the beauty of her language and voice telling the stories made me want to help children experience the same excitement I felt that day . . .

The award-winning author-illustrator Maurice Sendak (1990) explains that he tries to make sense of his childhood and the disturbing figures who populated it, in many of his books. Steven Kellogg, another illustrator-author, hopes to create "a feast for the eyes, a feast for the ears, and a feast for the heart" in his books (Steffel and Zetel, 1991).

## WRITING FOR CHILDREN

Children are a more complicated audience than many people realize. In *Homesick: My Own Story*, Jean Fritz shares the thoughts, feelings, and experiences of her early years. The depth of her thoughts as a child surprise many adult readers. College students reading Betsy Byars's books for the first time often comment that they are surprised at the thoughts of nine-, ten-, and eleven-year-old characters. Although children have not lived as long as adults, they have had enough experiences to relate to the characters in their books; they also have enough experience to know when a writer does not respect their experience or intelligence. They immediately recognize shallow books or didactic, preachy books. Writers who moralize usually lose readers rather quickly.

### Respecting the Reader

Good children's writers take their craft very seriously, taking care to write honestly and truthfully. Truth is a critical quality in children's books even when the story is not literally true. In his acceptance speech for the Laura Ingalls Wilder Award, E. B. White (1970) stated, "I have two or three strong beliefs about the business of writing for children. I feel I must never kid them about anything. I feel I must be on solid ground myself. I also feel that a writer has an obligation to transmit, as best as he can, his love of life, his appreciation for the world. I am not averse to departing from reality, but I am against departing from the truth" (p. 544). Jill Krementz, a writer and photographer, says, "I would rather see children saddened by honesty than angered by omissions or lies" (Zinsser, 1990, p. 6). In discussing her own work,

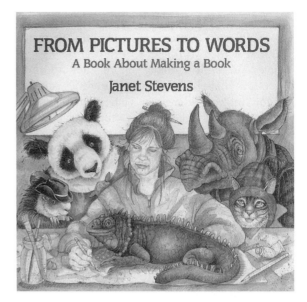

*The author and illustrator explains in this book the way she goes about writing and illustrating books.*

Lilian Moore says, "I try to tell the truth" (Glazer, 1985, p. 647). Moore's truth is based on accurate observations and is offered without sentimentality, which accounts for the popularity of her poetry.

Fine writers express truth as they understand it, through fiction, poetry, or nonfiction. Truth in literature is also expressed in the integrity of the transaction between the writer and the reader (Zinsser, 1990). It is the foundation of the picture book *Amazing Grace*, by Mary Hoffman, in which one classmate tells Grace that she cannot be Peter Pan in the school play because she is a girl, and a second classmate says that she cannot be Peter Pan because she is black. Truth in literature can help children deal with such pain, including the most painful losses of death, divorce, and illness. Fine literature helps them know they are not alone at those times. The truth of a book must be an integral feature; to omit the truth or to tiptoe around it is dishonest. Honest characters speak to children.

"To enter and hold the mind of a child or a young person is one of the hardest of all writers' tasks" (Zinsser, 1990, p. 1). The ability of outstanding children's writers to communicate with children at their own level—to respect their experience and understanding—is the key to their success, to their ability to make the stories come to life for children. They seem to be able to remember what it feels like to be a child and how the world looks when the main character is three feet tall. These writers are able to create images, language, characters, plots, themes, and settings that ring true to children, that relate to and respect their experiences. Jack Prelutsky (1991) says "the main differences between children and adults are that children have had fewer experiences—because they haven't been around long enough to have as many as we have had—and they are short. Children love to learn. They learn quickly, so I never condescend when I write for children" (p. 103).

## Tuning in to the Audience

"Good writers write out of the sum of who they are, and writers of children's books, perhaps more than other writers, write out of the emotional needs they felt when they themselves were young" (Zinsser, 1990, p. 9). Their respect for young readers is expressed in the quality of their writing. The first and most important characteristic of outstanding children's writers is their ability to tell a good story in which their audience will be interested.

Successful children's authors use a variety of strategies to tune in to their audience. Some of them write for the child they once were (Zinsser, 1990). Jean Fritz spent her early years in China, all the while yearning for her homeland. She says of *Homesick: My Own Story*, "I needed to accumulate a long American past, ... for my displaced childhood. (Fritz, 1990, p. 21). This need is also expressed in her biographies of American historical figures, such as *Why Don't You Get a Horse Sam Adams?*

Another way of entering childhood is to live around children, talking with them and observing them. Rosemary Wells, who wrote *Max's Dragon Shirt* and other Max books, finds that her own children are the impetus for the stories. A children's author need not be a parent, however. In his Newbery Medal acceptance speech, Jerry Spinelli (1991) said that his book ideas come from the children he has met and from their letters. Beatrix Potter and Margaret Wise Brown did not have children of their own, but they were talented children's authors.

## Getting Ideas

What writers write comes from their experiences, from hearsay, or from books or other arts. They use incidents, people, places, and truths from their own knowledge and experience to write. Betsy Byars says, "I always put something of myself into my books, some that happened to me. Once . . . a wanderer came by the house and showed me how to brush my teeth with a cherry twig. That went in *The House of Wings* (1972). *The Midnight Fox*, (1968) my favorite book, was written when I, like Tom, saw a fox in the woods" (Byars, 1989, p. 73). Cynthia Voigt states, "I don't know where I get my ideas," although she explains that the idea for *Homecoming* began at the grocery-store. After noticing kids in cars in grocery store parking lots, she went home and wrote it down. A year later she wrote the story (Rochman, 1985).

Many writers describe themselves as storytellers. Paula Fox (1991b) says, "I am a storyteller and I have been one for more than 30 years. When I finish one story, I watch the drift in my head, and very soon am thinking about another story. All one's experience shapes one's stories." Many writers were storytellers before they wrote. Watching children's responses and identifying what they appreciated helped these storytellers refine and expand their stories to the point that they decided to write them and eventually to publish them.

Elaine Konigsburg keeps files of ideas that are interesting and unusual, although she has no idea of exactly when or how she will use them (Jones, 1986). Don and Audrey Wood also keep extensive newspaper files. The idea for *The Napping House* came from a newspaper item in their files (Wood, 1990). When Byrd Baylor begins writing a book, she does not think about anyone reading it. She says, "If I want to write about a rock, a coyote, or a lizard—that's wonderful. I write about all the things that I truly love myself. The only thing I plan for sure in a book is the feeling that I want the book to have" (Bosma, 1987, p. 316).

Virginia Hamilton's books are quite different from those of Byrd Baylor; nevertheless, she talks about the feeling of things she writes about (Hamilton, 1991). For instance, in *The House of Dies Drear*, she writes so that readers can feel and understand the Underground Railroad, the people who helped escaping slaves, and the family histories of those involved. She wrote this book to pay tribute to her grandfather, Levi Perry, who traveled the Underground Railroad from the state of Virginia to Ripley, Ohio, and later settled in Yellow Springs, Ohio, which was the family's home.

## Making the Story Happen

The sources from which authors derive ideas are as varied as their writing styles. But even when they base their stories on actual incidents, they must make it "happen" for readers. Readers expect authors to take them "there" to help them recreate the writer's reality; what matters is what they make of it—what they do with it (LeGuin, 1991). Simply reporting incidents and characters as they took place is not enough to draw in the readers; the author must create illusions with the facts. Illusion—what writers make of their experiences—must convince readers that it is reality by resonating with their emotions and moving them to new feelings and insights (Alexander, 1981). Illusions, in fact, may be the truest things we know. Ursula LeGuin (1991) tells of writing a story with one real incident in it—which an editor identified as being untrue.

Even when a story is not based on an actual incident, however, writers still use actual experiences, objects, and people in their stories. "That is the trick hidden in 'write what you know.' Just knowing isn't enough. You 'know it for a fact'—but your job as a writer is to 'make it true.' The writer makes it *seem* true (so that the reader won't question it), and also finds out the *truth* of it (so that telling it matters)" (LeGuin, 1991, p. 12). For instance, during a vacation on Long Island, Paula Fox and a friend collected interesting beach debris, bottle glass worn smooth, bits of wood, shells, and seaweed to build a village. On the last day, they found a small balsa-wood sign in the sand, which they used to name their village. Fox's real-life

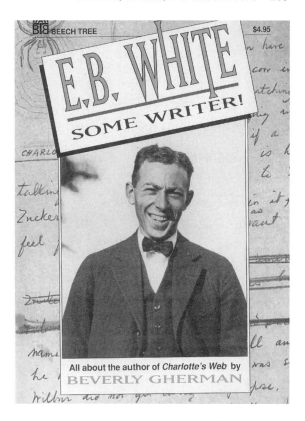

E. B. White was a dedicated father and husband, and he created children's classics such as *Charlotte's Web* and *Stuart Little*.

experience in building this village was the basis for some of the incidents in her book *The Village by the Sea*, although the main theme of the story was not based on this actual incident.

Careful observation and research provide the ideas and details that authors use to make their books come alive. Once they get an idea, most authors will research it carefully. Research provides writers the accurate information and details that give their writing integrity. After conceiving the idea for *Charlotte's Web*, E. B. White says, "I studied spiders and boned up on them" (1976, p. 644). He studied their habits, their capabilities, and their temperaments. Careful observations of a large gray spider that he knew fairly well provided a model for Charlotte. "I used to watch her weaving and her trapping, and I even managed to be present when

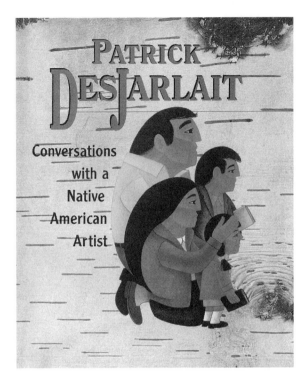

*DesJarlait's paintings demonstrate some of the traditional customs central to the Red Lake Chippewa way of life.*

she constructed her egg sac and deposited her eggs" (p. 633). His observations and research enabled him to describe Charlotte's actions in detail so that the reader can see what she does as clearly as White did himself, right down to the scene in which she is near death after making her egg sac.

## Writing the Book

Teachers and students alike are interested in knowing how long it takes an author or illustrator to create a book. The average period of time involved in the actual creation is approximately two years, but the period between conceiving the germ of an idea and producing the finished book may actually be much longer, and the final version of a book or poem may be dramatically different from the original notion. White (1976) says he took two years to write *Charlotte's Web*, but he spent 12 years creating the story *Stuart Little* (Hopkins, 1986). Betsy Byars says, "It takes me about a year to write a book, but

I spend another year thinking about it, polishing it, and making improvements" (1989, p. 43). Elaine Konigsburg explains that writing a book normally takes a year to a year and a half for her. She adds that her historical novels, *A Proud Taste of Scarlet and Miniver* and *The Second Mrs. Giaconda*, required a lot of reading and research, so they actually took longer (Jones, 1986).

## GETTING TO KNOW AUTHORS AND ILLUSTRATORS

Children can learn about authors and illustrators through many channels. They can check reference books, find magazine articles, read published interviews, write letters, view videos, and request information from publishers (allow at least six weeks for them to respond). More and more biographies and autobiographies of authors are published today. The Recommended Children's Books section at the end of this chapter includes a special listing of these resources. Check the library's card file or computer databases for additional titles.

## Author and Illustrator Profiles

This section profiles just a few outstanding authors and illustrators of children's books (space prohibits discussing more of them). The choice of those profiled here was somewhat random and was influenced by the material available by and about them, which also influenced the content of the profiles. In some instances, the profiles include information about an individual's life and work, while in others the focus is on the individual's body of work, since readers can learn about them indirectly from their works. The profiles are arranged in alphabetical order by last name. Check the Recommended Children's Books section at the end of this chapter for a sampling of books by each author.

### Mitsumasa Anno

Mitsumasa Anno is an artist who first earned his living as a mathematics teacher (Swinger, 1987). He was born in a historic Japanese village. During his childhood he had great curiosity and a vivid imagi-

*Through the months of the year, a town
grows in this wordless picture book.*

nation. He was curious about such things as what lay beyond the mountains that surrounded his hometown, and the people who lived in the cities and countries beyond the mountains. He and a friend watched other students on the school field and imagined what they might be saying to one another (Swinger, 1987). He continued to wonder about the world and everything in it and as he satisfied his curiosity, he shared his discoveries in books.

A number of Anno's books, namely *Anno's Britain*, *Anno's Italy*, and *Anno's Journey*, are based on the journey theme, which grew out of his travels and experiences with his friend Mura. These journey books include familiar images that travelers see, but Anno also included the unexpected in these books, such as viewing ordinary things from a new perspective.

Anno's vivid imagination coupled with the vast experiences brought about by satisfying his curiosity permit him to leap over human boundaries to see the world as a whole. He understands that human emotions and basic human values are the same throughout the world and that people in different countries experience different seasons, different daily experiences, and perceive life differently, although they live on the same planet. This realization led him to create *All in a Day*, in which he invited artists from different countries to illustrate the same time of day at different points around the world. Each double-page spread in this book shows the time in a different place and depicts activities of people characteristic for that time of day or night. Clothing, toys, foods, activities, and appearances all reflect the specific cultures of eight different countries. Anno's concern for international understanding is apparent in this book, as it is in most of his books.

### Byrd Baylor

Readers of Byrd Baylor's books are not surprised to learn that she lives in southwest Arizona, as many of her books are set in the desert. She lives in an adobe house that she built with the assistance of friends. Living in the desert permits her to observe desert animals and to keep in touch with nature. People often think that Byrd is a Native American because many of her books have an Native American feeling, but she is not. However, she admires their respect for the environment and their ability to adapt to their surroundings.

Byrd Baylor began writing in third grade. She says that she writes about all the things that she truly loves. When she plans a book, the most important part to her is the feeling that she creates in the book. After collecting all her notes and observations, she is ready to write. Believing that finding the right words is the hardest part of writing, she carefully chooses the words for each line of her poetic form. The visual effect forms a unity with the illustrations and portrays the mood she has developed in the story.

Many of Byrd Baylor's books are illustrated by Peter Parnall: she marvels at his ability to capture her words in his illustrations. His bold lines and brilliant colors capture the moods and desert impressions in her books. Three of their books have been named Caldecott honor books and four of their books have received American Library Association notable book awards (Bosma, 1987).

## Betsy Byars

Betsy Byars first wrote articles for the *Saturday Evening Post* and *Look* magazine. She discovered that making up stories and characters was so interesting that she never became bored (Byars, 1989). After she had children, she discovered the joy of writing for younger readers. Her own children helped her realize that her humor, compassion, and insight rang true for children.

Betsy Byars says she gets her ideas from newspapers, magazines, and people she knows (1993). Incorporating current trends into her stories is a hallmark of her writing. She is also known for creating memorable, highly individualized characters. Her realistic characters are built up layer by layer through dialogues and monologues that highlight critical moments in the characters' lives (Wilms, 1985).

Most of her books are realistic fiction aimed at middle-grade readers. Six of her novels have been dramatized for national television, and her books have been translated into nine languages. Five of her books have been named American Library Association Notable Books. In 1971, she won the Newbery Award for *The Summer of the Swans*.

## Barbara Cooney

Barbara Cooney grew up on Long Island and studied art and art history at Smith College. She is married to a retired country doctor and has grown children and grandchildren. She is an accomplished cook and gardener. In a tribute to her, Constance McClellan wrote, "She has self-discipline, drive and a motivation for independence. She is a very exciting woman, an inspiration to young illustrators and to women everywhere" (Wildberger, 1993).

Illustrating children's books was a natural step for Barbara Cooney because of her lifelong interest in art. She finds that illustrating children's books offers her great creative latitude. She has illustrated over 100 books for children. Two of her books, *Chanticleer and the Fox* and *Ox-Cart Man* were awarded Caldecott Medals.

Use of color, an eye to detail, and the meticulous research necessary to expressing feelings in art are the hallmarks of Barbara Cooney's art. She works to create illustrations that strike exactly the right tone in her books. The works closest to her heart are *Miss Rumphius* and *Island Boy*.

## Lois Ehlert

Lois Ehlert creates wonderful picture books for primary-grade children. She says that she always knew that she wanted to be an artist. As a child she enjoyed drawing and constructing things. She worked on her projects at a card table so that she did not have to stop and put them away. She still uses the same card table when working on illustrations.

Lois Ehlert knew that she wanted to illustrate children's books when she went to art school. She did illustrate a few after art school but was disappointed with the results until she studied graphic design and combined it with writing to create books like *Growing Vegetable Soup* and *Color Zoo* (Ehlert, 1991).

She likes to maintain a feeling of spontaneity in her work (Ehlert, 1991). She sketches out the concept of what she wants to do, then collects the objects to be models for her painting. She gets her ideas from watching animals and nature and interpreting them, as she did in *Feathers for Lunch*. Sometimes she expresses the joy of something she observes, as she did in *Planting a Rainbow*.

## Gail Gibbons

Gail Gibbons grew up in Oak Park, Illinois, and was educated at the University of Illinois. Her career has involved a number of positions, each of

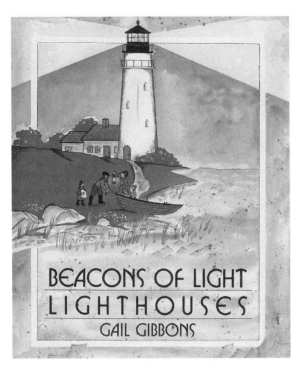

*The author carefully explains and illustrates how lighthouse technology has developed and changed over the years.*

which related to her interest in art. She has received a number of awards for her work, including The American Institute of Graphic Arts Award for *Clocks and How They Go* and The National Science Teachers Association/Children's Book Council Award for *Locks and Keys* (Metzer, 1987).

Gail Gibbons focuses on informational books in her writing. She invites readers' interest in the information she presents through colorful pictures and appropriate detail. The pictures, captions, and descriptions motivate children and help them understand otherwise complex topics. She has a talent for making information fun for students, which encourages them to seek more knowledge.

### Virginia Hamilton

Virginia Hamilton grew up in Yellow Springs, Ohio. She was named Virginia because her Grandpa Perry escaped from the state of Virginia on the Underground Railroad to Ripley, Ohio, where he

was apparently helped by the abolitionist John Rankin to start his new life (Hamilton, 1991). She is married to children's writer Arnold Adoff.

Virginia Hamilton has provided us with insights regarding her own work, explaining that her "fictions for young people derive from the progress of Black adults and their children across the American hope-scape. All of it grows from my own experience in some way" (1981, p. 638). Family history and stories her grandfather told his 10 children are rich sources of material for her writing. She describes her work as sometimes light-hearted but often "speculative, symbolic and dark, and brooding" (Hamilton, 1981, p. 638).

A great deal of research goes into Virginia Hamilton's books. *The House of Dies Drear* was created from the history of her family and community, which was settled by Quaker abolitionists and slave fugitives. She researched runaway slaves' history, Underground Railway routes, and a great deal of Ohio Underground Railroad history in addition to researching the architecture of houses used for concealing runaways. This research enabled her to create accurate, factual historical dimensions for this story, although the plot is fabricated.

### James Howe

James Howe was a literary agent when he and his late wife wrote their first book, *Bunnicula: A Rabbit-Tale of Mystery*. Neither of them had ever written a children's book—they had not even read a children's book in years (Andronik, 1991). They were simply having fun with Count Bunnicula, a character he invented, when they decided to write a children's book about him. He believes this book, which was written purely for fun, appeals to children because it has humor, mystery, and animal characters. The characters who first appeared in *Bunnicula* have appeared in several subsequent books and he expects to write additional books about them, but he is not sure about the plot of the next Bunnicula story (Andronik, 1991).

James Howe became involved in more serious writing after his wife died of cancer, an experience that precipitated his interest in writing a book to inform children about hospitals. He prepared to write this book by researching and interviewing children who had been in a hospital about their

*The illustrations in this tall tale about
Paul Bunyan, "the largest baby ever born
in the state of Maine" are hilarious.*

experiences there. The material he collected resulted in *The Hospital Book*. His second hospital book, *A Night Without Stars*, was inspired by one of the boys he interviewed for the first book, who was seriously burned.

James Howe reports that he is usually working on more than one book at a time, each at a different stage of completion. Some books seem to write themselves in a brief period of time with no major revisions, while others involve over a year of work and many drafts. He likes to stay close to his readers because their ingenuity inspires him. At schools, he demonstrates a professional writer's process for creating stories: He invites children to throw out ideas for stories, and he generates questions from their ideas, such as where the character lives, what the character's problem is, and the simple question, why.

## Steven Kellogg

Steven Kellogg reports that he has loved picture books and animals since he was a child. He was an enthusiastic artist even as a young child and dreamed of drawing as the center of his career. He tells of dreaming up stories and illustrating them for his younger sisters. He was educated at the Rhode Island School of Design and in Florence, Italy, and later did graduate work at American University. Over the last 20 years, he has written and/or illustrated 80 books (Kellogg, 1990).

Steven Kellogg believes that picture books are an art form designed specifically for children, but they can be appreciated and enjoyed by all ages. Combining diverse elements from various art forms is an exciting aspect of his work.

Currently, he lives in an old farmhouse in the hills of Connecticut, where he and his wife have raised six children, to whom many of his books are dedicated. Their family includes numerous dogs and cats. One of the dogs, a Great Dane named Pinkerton, appears in some of his books. He reports that the ideas for his books come from many different sources. His goal in creating books is to blend the illustrations and the words so that each book is a feast for the eye and ear. He says, "I want the time that the reader shares with me and my work to be an enjoyable experience—one that will encourage a lifetime association with pictures, words, and books" (Kellogg, 1990).

## Lilian Moore

Lilian Moore is a poet who received the 1985 National Council of Teachers of English Award for Excellence in Poetry for Children. She authors picture books, compiles poetry collections, and composes poetry. The truth about her feelings, accurate observations, and lack of sentimentality characterize her work. The clarity and accuracy of her observations attract many readers (Glazer, 1985).

Lilian Moore believes that "poems should be like fireworks, packed carefully and artfully, ready to explode with unpredictable effects" (Glazer, 1985). She concentrates on imagery and the play of words when writing poems. She hears the lines in her head, which permits considerable testing and revising before committing words to paper. She may rewrite a line 25 times to get it right. To her, editing is a kind of sculpture, smoothing poems to give them shape and form. Reading the work of other poets is most helpful in her work. She also enjoys talking "poet to poet" and exchanging letters with them.

## Katherine Paterson

Katherine Paterson was born in China, the daughter of missionary parents. She was educated in China and the United States. She and her husband are the parents of four children. She is a Christian who sees her work as a calling from God (Paterson, 1989).

Katherine Paterson reflects on her life and her children's books in two books about writing for children: *Gates of Excellence: On Reading and Writing Books for Children* (1981) and *The Spying Heart* (1989). In these books, she recounts stories about herself, such as the friendships, unmitigated terror, and humiliation she experienced in fourth grade. For instance, Gilly, in *The Great Gilly Hopkins*, embodies some of her life then. These experiences and her early life in China are reflected in her books.

Many of her books draw on biblical sources. For instance, she originally thought a secular publishing house would reject *Gilly* because it was a blatant rewriting of the parable of the prodigal son, but it was accepted. Similarly, although *Jacob Have I Loved* refers to the Bible, only one person has ever mentioned this fact. She draws on other sources for book ideas as well: *Bridge to Terabithia*, which received the 1978 Newbery Award, was based on the death of her son's friend. *Lyddie* is based upon research commissioned after she and her family moved to Vermont.

Katherine Paterson says about writing for children, "The hero must leave home, confront fabulous dangers, and return the victor to grant boons to his fellows. Or a wandering nobody must go out from bondage through the wilderness and by the grace of God become truly someone who can give back something of what she has been given. That—incredible as it may seem—is the story of my life" (Paterson, 1989, p. 16).

## Gary Paulsen

Gary Paulsen is a native of Minneapolis who brings a varied background to writing: a migrant farm worker, a soldier, a field engineer, a truck driver, an actor, and a magazine editor (Handy, 1982). He says that he was a miserable student whose parents were drinkers. When a librarian noticed him and gave him westerns, science fiction, and Melville to read, he discovered he could escape into books. He still reads himself to sleep every night.

Many of Gary Paulsen's books were written for middle-grade students; in fact, he dedicated *Hatchet* to the students at Hershey Middle School in Hershey, Pennsylvania. His love of the outdoors, dogs, and wildlife is apparent in all of his books. Most of his books have male protagonists, but both boys and girls enjoy his adventure stories.

## Jack Prelutsky

Jack Prelutsky is a poet. He believes he was always a poet, although he did not discover it until about the age of 24. Even then, his discovery was accidental because he was interested in illustrations and discovered his talent through writing poems to accompany his artwork (Prelutsky, 1991). He believes poems exist because a person who happens to be a poet has an experience to write about. "It exists because something occurred or was felt or dreamed or remembered and the poet chose to communicate it to other people. . . . It's the stuff that at its finest is saying things that prose cannot say" (p. 100).

Children and animals are two of his favorite things; consequently, he spends time visiting children in schools and animals in zoos. As a child he read the book *Wild Animals I Have Known* 36 times during one year of school.

He gets ideas from everywhere, everything that has ever happened, and everything he has inside. They come from everything he has dreamed, experienced, and seen on television and in movies. He points out that observing and taking notes are important secrets to writing. He also says it is important for writers to allow their imagination to work. He has various collections and toys in his studio to stimulate his own imagination. Very early in his writing career, Prelutsky learned the value of a surprise ending, and readers frequently find a little gift in the last line of his poems (Prelutsky, 1991).

## Pamela Service

Pamela Service likes to write science fiction. Her interesting educational background includes a bachelor's degree in political science and a master's degree in African prehistory. She studied Egyptology at the University of California and the University of London and has participated in several archaeological expeditions. While studying in England she became interested in the Welsh legends of Merlin and King Arthur, which led her to write the picture book *Wizard of Wind and Rock*. Her current interests are ancient history, modern political science, and futuristic science fiction (Service, 1985).

Her educational experiences and her interest in preserving the earth for future generations are apparent in her books. For instance, *Winter of Magic's Return* combines her interest in Merlin and preserving the earth. In this fantasy story, nuclear warfare has devastated the earth and mutant animals and people live in a limited area covered with snow. Welly and Heather set out to find the mythical land of Avalon, where King Arthur was taken. The story is hopeful because the earth is "beginning to revive after the long winter and beginning to move from an age of science into an age of magic."

## Doris Buchanan Smith

Doris Buchanan Smith divides her time between coastal Georgia and the mountains of North Carolina. She describes herself as rich because she lives life mostly the way she wishes to live it and earns her living doing what she wants to do (Smith, 1990).

She began to think about becoming a writer in sixth grade, when a teacher who recognized her talent asked if she had ever thought about becoming a writer. Until that time, she had thought of herself as a reader because she read all of the time, but had not thought about where books came from. Nevertheless, she responded to the suggestion and knew that was what she wanted to become. She considers writing her career but not her life's work. Her life's work is her life, she explains, and it takes a lot of practice to learn how to live, to get along, and still to be your essential self (Smith, 1990).

Her first published book was *A Taste of Blackberries*, which broke a taboo in children's literature by dealing with the death of a child. The story is set in a Maryland neighborhood and focuses on the ways that a young child deals with the death of a friend as a result of the friend's allergic reaction to a bee sting. Smith notes that people often ask why she puts sad things, mean teachers, and other unpleasantness in her books. She explains, "Life is sad and life is funny. There is meanness." Her books examine topics such as abused children, divorce, unwed mothers, handicaps, drugs, sex, and runaways. In each of the stories she writes, readers see evidence of her interests in reading, walking, pottery, music, canoeing, bicycling, and the outdoors.

*Judith Viorst*

Judith Viorst has been writing most of her life. She is married to a writer, with whom she collaborates in writing science books, poems, and magazine articles. Children's books "are a very special joy to me. I love and respect good books for kids and writing for them has always given me pleasure" (1990). Many of her books and poems have been inspired by her family life and the lives of the people, both children and adults, around her. She has won a number of awards for her writing. She recommends that people who want to be published should read widely to acquaint themselves with the kinds of books that are being written and published.

*Arthur Yorinks*

Arthur Yorinks was born on Long Island, New York, and studied social research and theater arts. His career includes writing, teaching, and performing in the American Mime Theater (Commire, 1983). He attributes his great interest in the arts to his piano teacher and his mother. He enjoys spending many hours in the art museums and galleries of New York City.

The greatest influences on his writing career came from Maurice Sendak, William Steig, Tomi Ungerer, Randolph Caldecott, Wilhelm Busch, and William Nicholson. He feels that his stories follow a basic format, asking the questions *Who am I? What does it mean to be human?* and *Why am I who I am?* (Commire, 1983). He is dedicated to the marriage of words and pictures and works directly with his illustrator, Richard Egielski, to achieve unity between text and illustration.

## THE VALUE OF STUDYING AUTHORS AND ILLUSTRATORS

Studying authors and illustrators yields many benefits to young readers. Readers who know something about the person who wrote or illustrated a literary work have a better understanding of it. Finding connections between books and their creators challenges children to think in new ways. Many authors and illustrators use their own life experiences in creating their works, so making these connections widens children's life experiences. Creators of children's literature also often project their own problems, interests, values, and beliefs into their writing, and reading and understanding that these are real concerns of real people helps readers understand how to deal with their own problems when they arise. The biographical study of Walter Dean Myers (see box on page 298) illustrates the intimate relationship between an author, his life experiences, his emotions, and his work.

Many authors project themselves into their work in this way, permitting readers to learn about them through their writing. Katherine Paterson reveals a good deal about herself in her books. She consistently develops sensitive, multidimensional characters who grow and develop through their life experiences and about whom readers care. Although the endings of her books are not "happy ever after," readers are left with hope for the future of a maturing character. Paterson says of her own writing, "I'm trying . . . to write for my readers the best story, the truest story of which I am capable" (1981b, p. 547). She will not write a book that closes in despair. Although she cannot or will not withhold from young readers "the harsh realities of human hunger and suffering and loss" neither will she neglect to plant that stubborn seed of hope that has enabled our race to outlast wars and famines and the destruction of death (p. 548).

Studying authors and illustrators yields benefits aside from learning about the author, about life, and about self. For instance, it can improve writing skills. Many writers agree they learned how to write by reading—no doubt one reason the majority of writers are inveterate readers. Authors often identify the authors who have been most influential in their work, so studying authors can help children recognize the influence of other writers in the thinking and work of their favorite writers and perhaps on themselves as prospective writers. Walter Dean Myers identifies Langston Hughes and James Baldwin as major influences in his life (Bishop, 1990). Katherine Paterson tells of the influence of the Bible and of the poet Gerad Manley Hopkins on her writing (Zinsser, 1990).

# Walter Dean Myers  *A biographical profile*

He is a well-known and highly respected writer. He is a versatile writer of fiction, fantasy, and nonfiction. Several of his books have been named Notable Books by the American Library Association, he has won three Coretta Scott King Awards, and his book *Scorpions* was named a Newbery honor book. His name is Walter Dean Myers.

Walter Dean Myers was born in Martinsburg, West Virginia. After his mother died, he was adopted and taken to Harlem, where he grew up. His literary diet included *True Romance, Classic Comics,* and the oral stories told by his father and grandfather. In high school, he discovered Honoré de Balzac, James Joyce, Thomas Mann, and Rupert Brooke. He tried to write like these white European men until he discovered the work of Langston Hughes, who lived only half a mile away in Harlem. James Baldwin's short stories were another powerful influence in his life. After reading the works of these two men, he realized he could write about his own neighborhood and the people he knew. "With few exceptions, his best-known work has tapped into the roots of his own life, his own time and place and culture" (Bishop, 1990, p. 863).

Walter Dean Myers's major strengths as a writer are his ear for dialogue and the informal language of urban African Americans, his ability to create humor, his flair for drama, and his likeable and believable characters (Bishop, 1990). His love of language is evident in his writing. The influence of Harlem is apparent in many of his books, which tend to focus on characters who are profoundly affected by the environment in which they live. In *Me, Mop, and the Moondance Kid,* he wrote about adopted children who sought to solve different kinds of problems than other characters who lived in urban neighborhoods. They were striving to create a family rather than solving the problems of urban living. This book also relates to his own experiences as an adopted child. He feels a responsibility to the children he is writing for—to be their voice and to give them images (Wildberger, 1993).

In his first nonfiction book, *Now Is Your Time!,* Walter Dean Myers traces the history of the Civil Rights Movement in America. His purpose was to present the "African-American experience as the complex, sometimes jubilant, sometimes sad, often creative effort of a people who have made important contributions to the development of the United States" (Myers, 1992, p. 22). He returned to West Virginia to research this book at "The Bower," the historical setting for an actual "great sale of slaves."

Writing enabled him to address two major concerns: (1) for the emotional burden carried by many young African Americans that the condition of their people was somehow their own fault, and (2) for what he views as the growing romanticism in much recent writing. He points out that all African Americans were not kings and queens in Africa, although they did come from a rich culture that has been maintained and has enriched the lives of all Americans. Myers says that, in coming to grips with the history involved in the period of slavery in America, he learned so much about his own people and about himself that he was able to blame and then to move beyond blame to understanding (Myers, 1992).

# CLASSROOM ACTIVITIES TO ENHANCE LITERARY EXPERIENCE

Author studies give middle-grade students opportunities to learn to read as writers read and to choose the writers who may influence their own writing. They can also read the works of writers who were major influences in the lives of other authors. For a variety of learning experiences that involve authors and their works, see Activities 10.1, 10.4, 10.5, 10.7, and 10.8 beginning on page 299.

ACTIVITIES

## 10.1 Reading a body of work

The body of an author's work differs from a single work. It is valuable to discuss how a reader's view of an author changes after examining all of the author's books. For instance, James Howe's work was humorous fantasy until his first wife's death, when his writing took a serious turn.

Reading all of an author's books in the order of publication will help readers understand the ways in which the author's work has changed over time. They can compare one or all of these factors in examining the body and significance of a single author's work: plot, character, setting, theme, and style. They may also consider whether the body of work is diverse or seems to follow a single thread. Figure 10.1 compares some of the writings of Katherine Paterson.

FIGURE 10.1

Examining an author's body of work.

Author: *Katherine Paterson*

Book:     *The Master Puppeteer* (a historical novel with a few black line drawings)

Plot      Jiro joins puppet theater during time of famine. He discovers a mysterious bandit is robbing the rich to help the poor.
Character A 13-year-old boy is the main character.
Setting   Osaka, Japan. Time is nonspecific but not contemporary.
Theme     Friendship between two boys; caring for others.
Style     Japanese words, concepts, and symbols. The language and character interactions reflect the setting and characters. Characters demonstrate their growing sensitivity and concern for others in a different social system.

Book:     *Lyddie* (historical fiction)

Plot      Lyddie and her brother are left alone on the farm to fend for themselves. Finally, she goes to Lowell, Massachusetts, to become a factory girl.
Character The main character is a 13-year-old girl.
Setting   Vermont and later Lowell, Massachusetts, in 1843.
Theme     Lyddie grows in understanding and spirit through this story of social change.
Style     The setting, conversation, and descriptions are carefully researched and authentic. Lyddie's problems in the story are based on research of factory girls' lives. Well-drawn characters, and conversation supports their development.

Book:     *The Tale of the Mandarin Ducks* (a picture book)

Plot      A beautiful duck is imprisoned by a greedy lord. The duck pines for his mate and a servant releases him and is sentenced to death. The drake and his mate save him.
Character The main character is the drake.
Setting   18th-century Japan.
Theme     Sharing happiness and trouble.
Style     This story is told in a folktale style.

## 10.2 Studying influences on illustrators

Illustrators are influenced by other artists. For example, Maurice Sendak identifies Randolph Caldecott, George Cruikshank, and Boutet de Monvel, among others (1988). Students can study an illustrator by (1) studying the illustrator's different books, (2) identifying some of the major influences on the illustrator's work, and (3) comparing the work of the illustrator to the work of the influence. Consider such concepts as color choice and use, style, media, size, and shape.

## 10.3 Studying how book illustration has changed

Study the illustrations in the book *75 Years of Children's Book Week Posters* by the Children's Book Council (1994). Compare the posters with book illustrations by the same artist, considering how the posters and slogans have changed over the years. Students can design book week posters and slogans.

## 10.4 Becoming an author expert

A student can become expert on favorite authors or illustrators by reading their works and finding articles, interviews, book reviews, and other sources of information about them. After becoming expert on a particular author, the student may write magazine or newspaper articles about the author or write and design a new dust jacket for a favorite book. In the persona of the author or illustrator, the student may participate in interviews, round-table discussions, or television talk shows staged by the class. Let students take turns conducting the interviews or directing the discussion and film the interviews or talk shows, if possible.

## 10.5 Learning about authors

Divide the class into three groups. Group One will read books written by the author; Group Two will read articles or reference materials about the author; and Group Three will read reviews of books written by the author. After the reading is completed, the students will share their information in discussion as a means of developing their understanding and appreciation of the author's work.

## 10.6 Studying author-illustrator collaboration

Study the art of your students' favorite illustrators in this activity. Have them choose a picture book to study and answer the following questions.

1. Why did the artist chose the particular color, size, style, and other design elements for this book?
2. How do these design elements affect the reading of the text? Do they enhance or detract from understanding the author's meaning?

3. How do the illustrations relate to the text?
4. Do the illustrations add anything that is not stated in the text?
5. What is the mood of the illustrations? Would you feel this mood if you had only read the text without seeing the illustrations?
6. Can you think of another way to interpret the text in art?

## 10.7 Studying author technique

Gaining a deeper understanding of an author's technique not only helps students understand the author, but it is beneficial in developing their own writing skills as well. There are several ways to go about this, including:

1. Use a single book to study a specific technique. For instance, explore the techniques Betsy Byars used to create the well-developed character of Bingo Brown.
2. Compare a specific technique in several different books by the same author. For instance, study setting in Pamela Service's books and the techniques she uses to develop it.
3. Compare how different authors achieve the same goal. For instance, study dialogue in books by two different authors to see how each author develops character through conversation.

## 10.8 Profiling an author

Learning about authors and their interests helps readers understand how they get story ideas. After studying an author or illustrator through one of the methods described in previous activities, students can write biographical profiles to summarize their research. The profile of James Cross Giblin (see box) demonstrates some of his strategies for selecting and developing writing ideas.

---

### *James Cross Giblin*  *A biographical profile*

James Cross Giblin served as editor and publisher at Clarion Books for over 20 years and has published books with several different publishers. Many of his books are nonfiction, and he points out that organizing and shaping facts into readable, interesting prose requires all the skills of a storyteller (Giblin, 1990). Many of his books deal with unusual aspects of history or information, but he always blends his research with wit and drama.

He explains how he gets his writing ideas in *Writing Books for Young People* (1990). He came up with the idea for *Chimney Sweeps* after meeting a chimney sweep on an airplane. In fact, he asked his new acquaintance to read the book manuscript for accuracy. Another book, *The Truth About Santa Claus* resulted from seeing a picture of a contemporary Santa Claus in juxtaposition with his tall, thin ancestor, St. Nicholas. *From Hand to Mouth,* which traces the story of common eating utensils, originated when Giblin was eating dinner in a restaurant and began to wonder when people first used spoons, knives, and forks.

He also points out that an idea not only should be interesting to the writer but it must also be an idea to which the writer is willing to devote a year or more. Six months of research and six months or more of writing and rewriting represent a major commitment of time and energy.

When researching a topic, Giblin looks for dramatic or amusing anecdotes that will bring the subject to life for young readers. His readers will attest to his successful use of this technique. For example, in *From Hand to Mouth* he tells how Cardinal Richelieu had his knives ground down so the points could not be used for picking teeth. When researching *The Riddle of the Rosetta Stone,* he found previously unpublished photographs to use in the book. These unusual angles on topics are a hallmark of his writing.

---

## 10.9 Using drama and creative play

The students may write and perform plays featuring their favorite authors or illustrators or featuring characters from their favorite books.

## 10.10  Celebrating authors and illustrators

There are several ways to enhance an entire classroom's interest in an author or illustrator. A few ideas are:

1. Find out when an author or illustrator's birthday is, and study that person for the entire month. Hold a birthday celebration for the author.

2. Prepare a bulletin board, author's corner, or learning station where students can display information they learn about favorite authors and illustrators.

3. Hold popularity contests to choose an author and illustrator of the year. Let the students campaign for their favorite with songs, posters, and speeches.

## SUMMARY

Studying authors and illustrators develops children's understanding of literature and their thinking skills. Getting acquainted with authors and illustrators helps students better understand and appreciate their work and develops students' respect for the body of work an author or illustrator has created. Extensive reading enables students to make connections between an author and his or her writing and illustrators and their art. Jean Fritz writes about important figures in American history because she developed a great love for her country during the years she lived in China. Steven Kellogg wrote and created art about his own dog Pinkerton. Katherine Paterson has written about events in her own life and her family's life in many of her books. Readers develop a sense of achievement as they begin to recognize the connections between the works of various authors and universal themes and topics. Learning about literature in this way enriches the curriculum.

## THOUGHT QUESTIONS

1. What are some of the values of acquainting children with authors and illustrators?

2. What can you learn about an author by reading all of his/her writings?

3. How is an author's writing connected to his/her life experiences?

4. How is an illustrator's art related to his/her life experiences?

5. What would you most like to know about your favorite author?

## ENRICHMENT ACTIVITIES

1. Create a file of articles and reviews on children's authors.

2. Make a list of authors and illustrators about whom you would like to know more and write to their publishers, requesting information about them.

3. Make an author profile of one of your favorite authors.

4. Make an illustrator profile of one of your favorite artists.

5. Read all of the books written by one author. What conclusions can you make as a result of reading the books? What can you say about the range of the author's work? How has the author's work changed over time? What are the writer's greatest strengths?

6. Write an article about an author you have researched.

7. Read three separate articles about one author from three of the reference books or journals listed at the end of the Recommended Children's Books section.

# RECOMMENDED CHILDREN'S BOOKS

Anno, Mitsumasa. (1986). *All in a Day*. London: Hamish Hamilton. (2–5)
In this book Anno illustrates the events of New Year's Day in countries around the world.

———. (1984). *Anno's Hat Tricks*. London: The Bodley Head. (1–3)
The magic of hat tricks and counting are the subjects of this book.

———. (1982). *Anno's Britain*. New York: Philomel. (all ages)
Anno illustrates a journey through Britain in this wordless picture book.

———. (1980). *Anno's Italy*. New York: Collins. (all ages)
Anno illustrates a journey through Italy in this wordless picture book.

———. (1979). *Anno's Medieval World*. New York: Philomel. (all ages)
Anno illustrates medieval life in this book.

———. (1978). *Anno's Journey*. New York: Philomel. (all ages)
Anno illustrates small towns and cities in this wordless picture book.

———. (1975). *Anno's Alphabet: An Adventure in Imagination*. New York: Crowell. (preschool–2)
Each page has either a single letter or a single object that begins with the letter.

Baylor, Byrd. (1975). *The Desert Is Theirs*. Illustrated by Peter Parnall. New York: Scribner's. (Caldecott honor, ALA notable). (all ages)
The Papago Indians are illustrated and described.

———. (1976). *Hawk, I'm Your Brother*. Illustrated by Peter Parnall. New York: Scribner's. (Caldecott honor, ALA notable). (all ages)
Rudy Soto makes the decision to release a captured hawk.

———. (1978). *The Other Way to Listen*. Illustrated by Peter Parnall. New York: Scribner's. (all ages)
Nature can be heard in these traditional and mythological beliefs of Native Americans.

———. (1978). *The Way to Start a Day*. Illustrated by Peter Parnall. New York: Scribner's. (Caldecott honor, ALA notable). (1–4)
This book discusses appropriate ways to salute the day.

———. (1985). *Everybody Needs a Rock*. Illustrated by Peter Parnall. New York: Scribner's. (ALA notable). (1–4)
The writer describes the characteristics of rocks and the pleasures they can bring to owners.

Byars, Betsy (1973). *The House of Wings*. Illustrated by Ted Schwartz. New York: Viking. (4–6)
The protagonist is left to live with the grandfather he doesn't know. The boy and the old man learn about each other through caring for the birds.

———. (1971). *The Summer of the Swans*. Illustrated by Ted CoConis. New York: Viking Penguin. (4–6)
Fourteen-year-old Sarah has a retarded brother and suffers growing pains in this Newbery Award–winning book.

———. (1973). *The 18th Emergency*. Illustrated by Robert Grossman. New York: Viking Penguin. (2–6)
When Mouse, a weakling, awaits a beating from the school bully in this story, he thinks of escapes for 17 emergencies but not for the 18th.

———. (1974). *After the Goat Man*. Illustrated by Ronald Himler. New York: Viking Penguin. (6–10)

Harold has a miserable summer dieting and playing Monopoly when the Goat Man's grandson, Figgy, joins the game. When Figgy breaks his leg Harold has to go to the Goat Man's house.

————. (1975). *The Midnight Fox*. Illustrated by Anne Grifalconi. New York: Viking Penguin. (3–6)

Tom spends the summer on a farm with relatives, while his athletic parents bicycle across Europe.

————. (1985). *Cracker Jackson*. New York: Viking Penguin. (4–8)

Cracker tries to protect his former babysitter from her husband's abuse.

————. (1989). *The Burning Questions of Bingo Brown*. New York: Viking Penguin. (3–6)

Bingo Brown got the teacher he had hoped for all summer, but the school year was disappointing.

————. (1980). *Trouble River*. Illustrated by Rocco Negri. New York: Viking Penguin. (3–6)

This historical fiction story addresses the difficulties a grandmother and grandson have understanding each other.

Cooney, Barbara. (1958). Adapted from Geoffrey Chaucer. *Chanticleer and the Fox*. New York: Crowell. (Caldecott Medal). (all ages)

Barbara Cooney's illustrations give this traditional story appeal.

————. (1982). *Miss Rumphius*. New York: Viking Penguin. (1–3)

Miss Rumphius travels all over the world. When she returns from her travels she beautifies the place where she lives.

————. (1988). *Island Boy*. New York: Viking Penguin. (Boston Globe-Horn Book Honor Book). (2–4)

A young boy explores his New England island in the early 1800s.

Ehlert, Lois. (1989). *Feathers for Lunch*. Harcourt Brace Jovanovich. (preschool–2)

A cat tries to catch birds for lunch but ends up with feathers.

————. (1991). *Color Zoo*. New York: Harper. (preschool–1)

Ehlert illustrated the zoo in geometric shapes and bright colors.

————. (1991). *Red Leaf, Yellow Leaf*. New York: Harcourt Brace Jovanovich. (preschool–2)

Collage is used to show the stages in the life of a maple tree.

————. (1993). *Nuts to You*. New York: Harcourt Brace Jovanovich. (preschool–2)

The story of Ehlert's encounter with a squirrel.

————. (1987). *Growing Vegetable Soup*. New York: Harcourt Brace Jovanovich. (preschool–2)

This book describes planting vegetable seeds and the growth of vegetables to maturity for soup.

————. (1988). *Planting a Rainbow*. New York: Harcourt Brace Jovanovich. (preschool–2)

This book describes planting flowers that make a colorful rainbow.

Fox, Paula (1988). *The Village by the Sea*. New York: Orchard/Richard Jackson. (4–6)

Emma is sent to spend two weeks with her peculiar Aunt Bea and her kindly husband. Emma and a newfound friend build a village by the sea that is destroyed by Aunt Bea.

Fritz, Jean. (1974). *Why Don't You Get a Horse Sam Adams?* Illustrated by Trina Schart Hyman. New York: Coward McCann. (2–4)

This is a humorous biography of the patriot Sam Adams.

Fritz, Jean. (1979). *Stonewall*. Illustrated by Stephen Gammell. New York: Putnam. (4–7)

This is a fine biography of Thomas (Stonewall) Jackson.

_____ . (1980). *Where Do You Think You Are Going Christopher Columbus?* Illustrated by Margot Tomes. New York: Putnam. (2–4)

This authentic illustrated biography examines the voyages of Columbus with humor and interest.

_____ . (1982). *Homesick: My Own Story.* Illustrated by Margot Tomes. New York: Putnam. (4–7)

This is an autobiography of Jean Fritz's first 11 years, which were spent in China with her missionary parents.

_____ . (1983). *Pocahontas.* Illustrated by Ed Young. New York: Putnam. (3–5)

The author helps younger children understand the tragedy of Pocahontas's life in this picture book.

Gibbons, Gail. (1982). *Tool Book.* New York: Holiday House. (2–4)

Detailed information and illustrations are provided in this book about tools.

_____ . (1983). *New Road!* New York: T. H. Crowell. (3–5)

This nonfiction book tells about building roads.

_____ . (1985). *The Milk Makers.* New York: Macmillan. (2–4)

This informational book details milk production.

_____ . (1987). *Dinosaurs.* New York: Holiday House. (preschool–3)

Young children will enjoy this well-illustrated book about dinosaurs.

_____ . (1990). *Beacons of Light: Lighthouses.* New York: Morrow. (2–5)

The history of lighthouses is described and illustrated.

_____ . (1990). *How a House Is Built.* New York: Holiday House. (1–4)

Drawings and text explain the stages of building a house.

_____ . (1990). *Weather Words and What They Mean.* New York: Holiday. (2–4)

The author identifies and illustrates words related to the weather.

Giblin, James Cross. (1982). *Chimney Sweeps.* Illustrations by Margot Tomes. New York: Harper & Row. (3–6)

The work and traditions of chimney sweeps are examined in this interesting book.

_____ . (1985). *The Truth About Santa Claus.* New York: T. H. Crowell. (3–6)

Santa Claus and the traditions surrounding him are the subject of this factual book.

_____ . (1987). *From Hand to Mouth.* New York: T. H. Crowell. (3–6)

In this historical study of eating implements, the author explains how implements and manners developed.

_____ . (1990). *The Riddle of the Rosetta Stone.* New York: T. H. Crowell. (3–6)

This informational book examines the Rosetta Stone and its history and is illustrated with photographs.

Hall, Donald. (1980). *Ox-Cart Man.* Illustrated by Barbara Cooney. New York: Viking Penguin. (Caldecott Medal). (K–3)

A family in the 1800s prepares items for sale and the farmer carries them to the market.

Hamilton, Virginia. (1967). *Zeely.* Illustrated by Symeon Shimin. New York: Collier. (3–6)

An imaginative girl thinks her uncle's neighbor is a Watusi queen.

_____ . (1968). *The House of Dies Drear.* Illustrated by Eros Keith. New York: Macmillan. (5–8)

This story of a black professor and his family who live in a house that was a former Underground Railroad station is written as a tribute to the author's grandfather, who escaped slavery on the Railroad.

———. (1974). *M. C. Higgins, the Great.* New York: Macmillan. (Newbery Medal, National Book Award). (4–10)

Strip mining threatens the family's home.

———. (1983). *Willie Bea and the Time the Martians Landed.* New York: Greenwillow. (4–10)

This story is based on the famous radio show of 1939 that led many Americans to believe the Martians had landed.

———. (1988). *Anthony Burns: The Defeat and Triumph of a Fugitive Slave.* New York: Knopf. (5–9)

Anthony Burns draws strength from his memories of his childhood as he becomes a fugitive slave and goes to trial.

———. (1990). *Cousins.* New York: Philomel. (4–7)

This story relates the intricacies of relationships among cousins.

———. (1992). *Drylongso.* Illustrated by Jerry Pinkney. New York: Harcourt Brace Jovanovich. (3–6)

During a drought in 1975, a mysterious boy appears to a farm family and helps them locate a spring.

Howe, James. (1979). *Bunnicula: A Rabbit Tale of Mystery.* New York: Atheneum. (3–6)

In this fantasy, the family cat is convinced that a bunny found in a theater is a vampire who sucks the juice out of vegetables.

———. (1981). *The Hospital Book.* New York: Crown. (4–6)

This book is based upon the author's interviews of children in hospitals.

———. (1982). *A Night Without Stars.* New York: Crown. (4–6)

This story is based on a boy that Howe interviewed when writing *The Hospital Book.* The main character is in the hospital for treatment of disfiguring burns.

———. (1982). *Howliday Inn.* New York: Atheneum. (2–4)

This book continues the adventures of Harold the dog, Chester the cat, and the vampire rabbit.

———. (1983). *The Celery Stalks at Midnight.* New York: Atheneum. (3–6)

This is a sequel to *Bunnicula* and *Howliday Inn.*

———. (1986). *There's a Monster Under My Bed.* New York: Atheneum. (preschool–1)

The story of a child who fears there is a monster waiting under the bed.

———. (1994). *When You Go to Kindergarten.* New York: Morrow. (preschool–5)

Photographs and text tell children about a day in a kindergarten.

Kellogg, Steven. (1981). *A Rose for Pinkerton.* New York: Dial. (1–3)

Pinkerton, a Great Dane, gets a kitten as a friend.

———. (1982). *Tallyho, Pinkerton!* New York: Dial. (1–3)

Pinkerton takes a trip to the woods.

———. (1984). *Paul Bunyan.* New York: Morrow. (1–4)

This is Kellogg's interpretation of the Paul Bunyan tall tale.

———. (1988). *Johnny Appleseed.* New York: Morrow. (1–4)

This is an interpretation of the traditional story about the man who planted many midwestern apple orchards.

———. (1991). *Jack and the Beanstalk.* New York: Morrow. (preschool–3)

Kellogg uses Joseph Jacobs' version of this story as the basis for his book.

_____ . (1992). *Mike Fink: A Tall Tale.* New York: Morrow. (1–3)

This is Kellogg's interpretation of tall tales about the canal boat man.

Konigsburg, E. L. (1973). *A Proud Taste of Scarlet and Miniver.* New York: Atheneum. (4–7)

This unusual biography tells about the life of Eleanor of Aquitaine.

_____ . (1968). *The Second Mrs. Giaconda.* New York: Atheneum. (5–10)

This story is a mystery about the stepdaughter of Mrs. Giancola. She returns after a long absence, but is she really the daughter?

Moore, Lilian. (1975). *See My Lovely Poison Ivy.* New York: Atheneum. (2–4)

A child shows off her poison ivy.

_____ . (1980). *Think of Shadows.* New York: Atheneum. (2–4)

Shadows fascinate children, so Lilian Moore put together this collection of shadow poetry.

_____ . (1982). *Something New Begins.* New York: Atheneum. (1–6)

Collection of new and previously published poems.

_____ . (1992). *Adam Mouse's Book of Poems.* Illustrated by Kathleen Garry McCord. New York: Atheneum.

These poems describe the adventures of a mouse.

_____ . (1992). *Sunflakes: Poems for Children.* Illustrated by Jan Armerod. New York: Clarion. (preschool–2)

This is a collection of sunshine poems.

Myers, Walter Dean. (1988). *Me, Mop, and the Moondance Kid.* Illustrated by Rodney Pate. New York: Delacorte. (3–5)

T. J. and his younger brother Moondance are adopted, but their friend Mop remains at the Dominican Academy in spite of her relentless efforts to become adopted. They share a love of baseball and work hard to overcome their opponents.

_____ . (1988). *Scorpions.* New York: Harper. (5–7)

Jamal lives in the inner city and his brother is in jail. His mother is determined that he will have a better life than his brother, but he faces many difficult decisions.

_____ . (1991). *Now Is Your Time!* New York: HarperCollins. (5–12)

This informational book begins with the history of the first slaves in America and continues with their descendants.

Noble, Trinka Hakes. (1980). *The Day Jimmy's Boa Ate the Wash.* New York: Dial. (1–3)

This picture book tells the story of an unusual class trip to a farm.

Paterson, Katherine. (1975). *The Master Puppeteer.* New York: Harper & Row. (4–7)

This story is set in Japan. The main character is the child of a poor family, but he uses his talent to succeed.

_____ . (1978). *The Great Gilly Hopkins.* New York: T. H. Crowell. (4–6)

Gilly is a foster child who is moved to a new situation with an unusual foster mother.

_____ . (1980). *Jacob Have I Loved.* New York: T. H. Crowell. (5–7)

Louise, the narrator, is a twin who lives in her sister's shadow.

_____ . (1990). *The Tale of the Mandarin Ducks.* Illustrated by Leo and Diane Dillon. New York: Dutton. (1–3)

A pair of mandarin ducks is separated by a cruel lord, but a compassionate husband and wife risk their lives to aid the ducks.

_____ . (1991). *Lyddie.* New York: Dutton. (5–9)

Lyddie and her brother are left to fend for themselves on a farm in the winter of 1843. Lyddie becomes a factory girl to support them.

_____ . (1992). *The King's Equal*. New York: HarperCollins. (3–adult)

A rich prince learns that his money cannot buy him the wife he chooses.

_____ . (1994). *Flip-Flop Girl*. New York: Lodestar Books. (5–8)

This story is based on the experiences of a Pennsylvania Dutch girl.

Paulsen, Gary. (1984). *Tracker*. New York: Bradbury. (American Library Association Best Book). (4–7)

A boy is supposed to kill a deer to supplement the family's meat supply for the winter.

_____ . (1988). *Hatchet*. New York: Bradbury. (4–7)

When a plane crashes, Brian survives in the Canadian wilderness with no tools but his hatchet. The book was given a Newbery honor award and 30 other book awards.

_____ . (1990). *The Night the White Deer Died*. New York: Delacorte. (4–7)

A hunting story about a boy who has difficulty killing animals.

_____ . (1991). *Cookcamp*. New York: Orchard Books. (3–6)

A young boy must stay with his grandmother while his father serves in World War II.

Prelutsky, Jack. (1980). *Rolling Harvey Down the Hill*. Illustrated by Victoria Chess. New York: Greenwillow. (1–6)

This humorous collection of poems focuses on five young boys.

_____ . (1982). *The Baby Uggs Are Hatching*. Illustrated by James Stevenson. New York: Greenwillow. (1–3)

These humorous poems tell about baby Uggs, Grebles, Sneepies, and Slitches.

_____ . editor. (1983). *The Random House Book of Poetry for Children*. Illustrated by Arnold Lobel. New York: Random House. (1–8)

This anthology includes over 500 poems organized by themes.

_____ . (1984). *The New Kid on the Block*. Illustrated by James Stevenson. New York: Greenwillow. (1–6)

This book of over 100 poems includes jokes, word play, monsters, and meanies.

_____ . (1989). *Poems of A. Nonny Mouse*. New York: Knopf. (1–6)

This is a book of more humorous poems.

_____ . (1990). *Beneath a Blue Umbrella*. Illustrated by Garth Williams. New York: Greenwillow. (1–6)

This is a collection of animal poetry.

_____ . (1991). *Something Big Has Been Here*. New York: Greenwillow. (1–6)

The large tracks on the cover of this book relate to the title poem, which speculates on what the something big was.

Rylant, Cynthia. (1989). *But I'll Be Back Again*. New York: Watts/Orchard/Richard Jackson. (5–8)

This memoir is based on Rylant's youth. She tells about the good times and the not-so-good times of her young life.

Service, Pamela. (1985). *Winter of Magic's Return*. New York: Macmillan. (4–6)

This story tells about a world drastically changed by nuclear war. Bands of mutant people and mutant animals wander the wilderness.

_____ . (1988). *Stinker from Space*. New York: Ballantine. (3–5)

A visitor from outer space crashes his craft on Earth. His body is dying so he moves into the only available body, that of a skunk.

_____ . (1988). *Stinker's Return*. New York: Scribner's. (3–5)

Tsyngyr returns to Earth to get help from Karen and Jonathon. The Feds pursue them in wonderful chase scenes.

_____ . (1990). *Wizard of Wind and Rock*. New York: Macmillan. (3–5)

This is a collection of folk and fairy tales of England.

Smith, Doris Buchanan. (1973). *A Taste of Blackberries*. Illustrated by Charles Robinson. New York: T. H. Crowell. (4–6)

This story tells about the ways a young child deals with the death of his friend caused by an allergic reaction to a bee sting.

_____ . (1984). *Laura Upside-Down*. New York: Viking. (4–7)

Laura does not fit in anyplace until she makes a friend who helps her.

_____ . (1984). *The First Hard Times*. New York: Viking. (4–7)

A family experiences the difficulties of living during hard times.

_____ . (1988). *Return to Bitter Creek*. New York: Viking. (4–7)

An illegitimate girl, her mother, and the mother's boyfriend visit the mother's family in the Appalachian Mountains.

Spinelli, Jerry. (1990). *Maniac McGee*. New York: Little, Brown. (4–6)

Maniac McGee earns this name because of his outrageous behavior. He searches for and finally finds a home. (Newbery Award winner).

Viorst, Judith. (1971). *Alexander and the Terrible, Horrible, No Good, Very Bad Day*. New York: Atheneum. (preschool–2)

Alexander wakes up and everything goes wrong all day.

_____ . (1971). *The Tenth Good Thing About Barney*. New York: Atheneum. (1–4)

A beloved cat dies and the family must deal with their sadness.

_____ . (1973). *My Mama Says There Aren't Any Zombies, Ghosts, Vampires, Creatures, Demons, Monsters, Fiends, Goblins, or Things*. New York: Atheneum. (1–4)

This is a collection of poems about things that frighten children.

_____ . (1974). *Rosie and Michael*. New York: Atheneum. (1–4)

Two friends learn to accept each other's good and bad characteristics.

_____ . (1978). *Alexander Who Used To Be Rich Last Sunday*. New York: Atheneum. (K–2)

Alexander's grandparents visit and give their grandson a dollar bill. The story details how he spends the dollar.

_____ . (1981). *If I Were in Charge of the World, and Other Worries: Poems for Children and Their Parents*. Illustrated by Lynne Cherry. New York: Atheneum. (all ages)

There are many everyday events that are irritating.

Voigt, Cynthia. (1981). *Homecoming*. New York: Atheneum. (4–8)

Dicey and her siblings find their grandmother after the mother abandons them in a parking lot.

Wells, Rosemary. (1991). *Max's Dragon Shirt*. New York: Dial. (preschool)

Max the little white rabbit goes shopping with his big sister Ruby.

White, E. B. (1945). *Stuart Little*. Illustrated by Garth Williams. New York: Harper & Row. (3–5)

This is the story of a baby who looked like a mouse. Stuart traveled around in a toy car and made friends with a bird named Marglo.

_____ . (1952). *Charlotte's Web*. Illustrated by Garth Williams. New York: Harper & Row. (3–5)

This American classic is the story of Charlotte, the talented spider who saves Wilbur the pig from an untimely death.

Wood, Audrey. (1984). *The Napping House*. Illustrated by Don Wood. New York: Harcourt Brace Jovanovich. (K–2)

Granny and grandson nap on a rainy day. They are joined by a cat, dog, and others in this cumulative tale.

Yates, Elizabeth. (1950). *Amos Fortune: Free Man*. Illustrated by Nora S. Unwin. New York: Dutton. (4–6)

Amos Fortune was brought from Africa in a cruel slave ship and sold to a Quaker. This book, which chronicles his amazing life, was awarded the Newbery Medal.

_____ . (1964). *Carolina's Courage*. Illustrated by Nora S. Unwin. New York: Dutton. (4–6)

Carolina and her family leave their home to join a wagon train moving west. After stopping for the night she takes her doll to a tea party with an Indian girl with surprising results.

Yorinks, Arthur. (1980). *Louis the Fish*. New York: Farrar, Straus & Giroux. (K–2)

A butcher dislikes his trade so much that he turns into a fish.

_____ . (1983). *It Happened in Pinsk*. New York: Farrar, Straus & Giroux. (4–6)

A man is having an identity crisis; no matter how successful he is he thinks someone else is more important. He finally finds himself.

_____ . (1986). *Hey, Al*. New York. Farrar, Straus & Giroux. (3–6)

A man and his dog accept an invitation to move to a pleasant island but find that home is a better place to live. This book was awarded the Caldecott Medal.


## OTHER RECOMMENDED BOOKS

### Reference Books for Researching Authors and Illustrators

Bader, Barbara. (1976). *American Picturebooks from Noah's Ark to the Beast Within*. New York: Macmillan.

Brown, Marcia. (1986). *Lotus Seeds: Children's Pictures and Books*. New York: Scribner's.

Cianciolo, P. J. (1990). *Picture Books for Children*. American Library Association.

Commire, A. (editor). *Book of Junior Authors and Illustrators*. (Volumes are numbered and dated). New York: H. W. Wilson.

*Contemporary Authors, New Revision Series*. (Volumes are numbered and dated). New York: H. W. Wilson.

Day, Frances Ann. (1994). *Multicultural Voices in Contemporary Literature*. Portsmouth, NH: Heinemann.

*Fiction*. (1990). (Volumes are numbered and dated). Detroit: Gale Research Company.

*Getting To Know You: Profiles of Children's Authors Featured in Language Arts 1985–1990*. (1991). Urbana, IL: National Council of Teachers of English.

*Illustrators of Children's Books*. (1968). Boston: Hornbook.

Kingman, L. (editor). (1975). *Newbery and Caldecott Medal and Honor Books*. Boston: Hornbook.

*More About the Author*. (Volumes, numbers, dates, and editors vary). Detroit: Gale Research Company.

*The Newbery and Caldecott Awards: A Guide to the Medal and Honor Books.* (1991 edition). Chicago: Association of Library Services to Children.

Olendorf, Donna (editor). (1991). *Something About the Author.* Detroit: Gale Research Company.

*Twentieth-Century Children's Writers.* (edition numbers, dates, and editors vary). New York: St. Martin's Press.

Wildberger, Mary Elizabeth. (1990). *Approaches to Literature Through Authors.* Phoenix, AZ: Oryx Press. (Very helpful in classroom.)

## Journals That Publish Interviews, Speeches, and Author Profiles

*Book Links.* Published by Booklist Publications, 50 E. Huron St., Chicago, IL 60611.

*Booklist.* Published by the American Library Association, 50 E. Huron St., Chicago, IL 60611.

*The Bulletin of the Center for Children's Books.* University of Illinois, University of Illinois Press, 1325 South Oak St., Champaign, IL 61820.

*Children's Literature in Education.* Agathon Press, 15 E. 26th St., New York: NY 10010.

*The Hornbook Magazine.* Hornbook Inc., Park Square Building, 31 St. James Ave., Boston, MA 02116.

*Language Arts.* Published by the National Council of Teachers of English. 1111 W. Kenyon Road, Urbana, IL 61801-1096.

*The New Advocate.* Christopher Gordon Publishers, 480 Washington St., Norwood, MA.

*School Library Magazine.* American Library Association.

## Biographies and Autobiographies

Burch, Joann Johansen. (1994). *A Fairy-Tale Life: A Story About Hans Christian Andersen.* Illustrated by Liz Monson. Minneapolis: Carolrhoda.

Cummings, Pat, compiler and editor. (1992). *Talking With Artists.* New York: Bradbury.

Fox, Mem. (1990). *Dear Mem Fox I've Read All of Your Books Even the Pathetic Ones.* New York: Orchard Books.

Gherman, Beverly. (1992). *E. B. White: Some Writer!* New York: Beech Tree.

Hunter, Mollie. (1990). *Talent Is Not Enough.* New York: Harper & Row.

Kovacs, Deborah, and James Preller. (1991). *Meet The Authors and Illustrators: 60 Creators of Favorite Children's Books Talk About Their Work.* New York: Scholastic.

Little, Jean. (1987). *Little by Little: A Writer's Education.* New York: Puffin.

Stinson, Kathy. (1991). *Writing Picture Books: What Works and What Doesn't.* Markham, Ontario: Pembrooke Publishing Limited.

Weidt, Maryann. (1994). *Oh, the Places He Went: A Story About Dr. Seuss.* Illustrated by Kerry Maguire. Minneapolis: Carolrhoda.

Williams, Neva. (1994). *Patrick DesJarlait: Conversations with a Native American Artist.* Minneapolis: Runestone.

Yolen, Jane. (1992). *Touch Magic: Fantasy, Fairy and Folklore of Childhood.* New York: Philomel.

———. (1992). *A Letter from Phoenix Farms.* (Meet the Author Series). Katonah, NY: Richard C. Owen.

# Eleven

## GUIDING QUESTIONS

1. Why is reading aloud to children important in developing literary experiences?

2. How do oral and silent reading differ?

3. What should you consider when selecting a book to read aloud to your class?

## OVERVIEW

All of the language processes—listening, speaking, reading, and writing—are means by which learners construct meaning. Being read aloud to, storytelling, drama, booktalking, silent reading—each of these art forms reveals a different facet of literature. Oral language allows the rhythm of the story and the cadence of the words to pull listeners in. Oral projects enrich children's responses to literature, contributing images that escape the devices of written language, as well as making texts accessible to both readers and nonreaders (Barton, 1986). Silent reading permits readers to understand text more rapidly and to think at higher cognitive levels.

Silent reading and oral expressions of literature are complementary processes because most readers rely on a foundation of silent reading to prepare for oral interpretation. Oral approaches to literature accommodate children's experiences with listening, telling, and acting and build their background for composing stories. Oral literature activities also enrich children's understanding of the special conventions, devices, and effects of spoken language. Listening to stories develops and expands children's comprehension, their response to literature, and their understanding of both oral and written language. This chapter covers oral and silent reading strategies that include reading stories aloud, reader's theater, choral reading, creative drama, booktalking, storytelling, and uninterrupted sustained silent reading (USSR).

# Oral and Silent Approaches to Literature

## INTRODUCTION

Discussing and sharing responses, as the children in the opening vignette do, represents the heart of the literary experience. This sharing gives children and adults a chance to intertwine their own life "stories" with the story created by the author. Oral response encourages readers to relate books to their own experiences and their other readings. It also allows them to reflect on and revise the meaning they derived from the text by hearing and considering others' views of the story's meaning. Moreover, such activities stimulate children to respond emotionally to text. Sometimes readers need to vent their feelings about what they have read; in the vignette, students needed to explore their sense of loss at the way the book ended.

For children of all ages, oral literary activities such as hearing stories, reading aloud, dramatizing, storytelling, choral reading, and reader's theater serve important purposes. These activities help them understand literature, story action, and story characters. They develop an ear for written language and a sense of the differences between the sound of book language and everyday speech and create a sensitivity to language that will serve children well when they begin to read and write on their own.

The term *literature* generally brings the thought of books, but literature is much more than just books. Storytelling is the oldest form of literature. Reading aloud is also rooted in the past, when it was a major source of entertainment and news. Young children begin their journey to literacy with listening to nursery rhymes their parents or caregivers recite aloud. Dramatic acting out of favorite characters extends children's literary experiences. Informal drama gives them opportunities to see the world from another person's perspective. Like storytelling, drama is an oral form of literature with ancient roots.

## VIGNETTE

Sally Richmond's fourth graders had just finished reading *Stone Fox* and the class was discussing the death of Willie's dog Searchlight. The teacher had gotten the class excited about producing a reader's theater, and they all wanted to do *Stone Fox*.

Denise said, "I cried my eyes out when Searchlight died!…It made me think about the time my dog died. We had to take her to the vet to be put to sleep. The story is so real for me…I think Willie hurt just like I did when my dog died."

"You could feel the tension. You were wanting Willie to win. Then when his dog died, it was so sad. The ending just left me sitting there believing that his dog just couldn't die," added Tina.

James agreed. "The ending was a real shocker. I don't think I've ever read a book with such a powerful ending before. When I look back on the book I feel different about it than when I was reading it. Now I see that Willie's grandpa had no will to live, while Willie had enough will for two people. Willie was so strong for a 10-year-old."

The children agree that the strong emotional response they all had in reading the book would be beneficial in the reader's theater they planned. They all wanted to portray the striking aspects of the story.

## READING ALOUD TO CHILDREN

Perhaps most important, hearing stories read aloud allows children to experience the enjoyment of reading and love of literature and to share that enjoyment and love with someone else. When young children curl up in a parent's lap for a good book, they share an atmosphere of trust and the reading is a pleasurable experience. Even babies in utero experience more relaxed heartbeats when they hear a familiar story (Trelease, 1989). Such enjoyable activities present natural opportunities for learning without formal instruction. When reading aloud a book such as Michael Rosen's *We're Going on a Bear Hunt*, parents and children discuss stories, ask and answer questions, and chant the refrain together: "We're going on a bear hunt. We're going to catch a big one. What a beautiful day! We're not scared." In this warm, supportive environment, children associate reading with pleasure; they begin to see reading as an activity to be enjoyed and valued. They also acquire a foundation for learning to read (Naylor and Borders, 1993).

Children as young as one year pretend to read to themselves, to their toys, and to their pets. For young children, listening to stories provides information about the reading process and motivation for learning to read. Beginning reading instruction starts by involving children in the imitating process (Peterson and Eeds, 1990). For example, after hearing Nancy White Carlstrom's story *Jesse Bear What Will You Wear?* over and over, five-year-old Jason begs to "read" the book himself. He turns the pages, points to the illustrations and the words, and pretends to read the story to his younger sister, his mother, and anyone else who will listen. "Pretend reading" helps Jason understand the reading process.

Listening to stories helps children understand structures of literature, which not only enhances their understanding of story but also provides structure for later writing of stories. Hearing stories read aloud builds literary understandings—children can listen to memorable characters and plots that they might not be able to read for themselves. It also builds a foundation for learners' response to literature. Listening to stories frees

*Jesse Bear's rhymes introduce children to literature.*

children from thinking about word identification and word meaning, permitting them to think and feel about the stories, poems, or information they hear. They find it easier to think critically about literature when it is read aloud, and daily listening to stories improves children's ability to talk about and retell stories (Morrow, 1988).

Reading aloud gives listeners of all ages opportunities for shared responses to literature—whether social, emotional, or intellectual (Trelease, 1989). Wood (1994) points out the sense of community that develops when a group shares the experience of listening to a book read aloud. Two texts exist in a read-aloud situation, the text of the book and the text the oral reader creates (Wood, 1994). Listeners experience both texts and make meaning from both texts. The reader is sharing a love of the story by giving the book to listeners.

As children grow in their ability to read and understand for themselves, hearing a story read aloud may motivate them to seek out stories by the same author or on the same topic. In this way, the

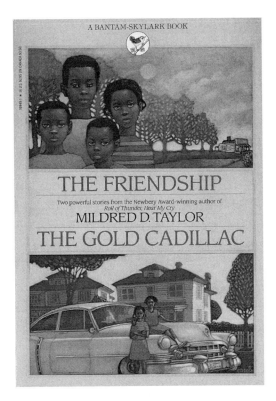

*Both of the suspenseful stories in this book are good read-alouds.*

experience of hearing a well-crafted story is not unlike throwing pebbles into a pond; the initial impact of the story provides the impetus for reading more and more books from an ever-expanding variety of genre. After hearing *Roll of Thunder, Hear My Cry* by Mildred Taylor, which describes an African American family's plight in Mississippi during the Depression, middle graders may elect to read this book on their own. Read-alouds may attract children to other books by Mildred Taylor such as *The Friendship* or *The Gold Cadillac*. They may wish to explore a topic such as racial prejudice by reading Paula Fox's *Slave Dancer* or Julius Lester's *To Be a Slave*.

## Reading Aloud in the Classroom

Providing time to read aloud to children in the school setting is just as vital as having parents read to their children at home. Children at all grade levels, including high school, should hear good literature read aloud on a daily basis. Unfortunately, time for both oral and silent reading activities is usually classified as something extra in the school curriculum—for fun after the "real" work of reading, such as doing oral and written reports, is complete. These highly motivating activities are often an afterthought in the curriculum "if there is time." This is particularly disturbing when considered in light of a number of studies (Cohen, 1968; Cullinan, Jaggar, and Strickland, 1974; Purcell-Gates, 1988; Teale and Martinez, 1987) indicating that children whose teachers read to them have higher reading and writing achievement than children who lack these experiences.

Reading aloud in the school setting presents many opportunities for positive student–teacher interactions. "The way you hold the book, the warmth you extract from it, the laughter, the interest, and the emotion—all will tell your class something about how you feel about books and the special place books and reading are going to hold in your classroom this year" (Trelease, 1989, p. 32). A reader *gives* listeners the text that is being read aloud. Trelease points out that read-aloud time in school "is often the only time when everyone is equal": all children, regardless of reading ability, are equally able to appreciate the wonder of a good story or information book (p. 61).

## Selecting Material for Reading Aloud

Some stories are for reading aloud and some are for telling. Storytelling is discussed in a later section of this chapter. Stories are for reading when the "style of the writing is so intrinsically a part of the story that it would be difficult to get the words together right by telling" (Ross, 1972, p. 217). For example, changing the words in A. A. Milne's *Winnie the Pooh* would cause the charm of the story to vanish.

Read-alouds give teachers and parents a chance to read quality literature that children might not choose for themselves or that they might be unable to read for themselves. Read-aloud materials are not confined to books. They can include magazine articles, short stories, poems, newspaper articles, or anything of interest to reader and listener. Read-aloud materials should be chosen carefully, however, so as to introduce children to motivating literature that gives them the benefits identified earlier in this chapter. Criteria for good read-aloud materials include:

1. high literary quality from a variety of genre
2. appropriate to the age and developmental level of children
3. interesting enough to hold children's attention
4. strong plot lines and characters with whom children can identify in fiction
5. accurate information in nonfiction
6. concrete subject related to children's experiences in poetry
7. reading levels of up to two or more grade levels above the grade level of the children, so long as the material interests them

Read-aloud literature is often confined to fiction or poetry, but all genre may be used as read-alouds for all ages. Many picture books are even appropriate for older children or adults. Biographies and informational books make excellent read-alouds for every grade level. Traditional literature is, of course, always a favorite read-aloud because these stories, based on the oral tradition of various cultures around the world, explore human foibles and are usually action-packed.

It is important to use all genre for read-alouds at every grade level. Even picture books are appropriate for older children and some are for children of all ages. Many adults enjoy a picture book like Chris Van Allsburg's story of a jungle board game come to life in *Jumanji* (1981, Houghton Mifflin, Boston). The book *Rose Blanche* by Christopher Galloz and Roberto Innocenti (1985, Creative Education, New York) which is about a child living during the Nazi Holocaust, is most appropriate for older children. This is also true of single-book illustrated poems such as *Hiawatha* by Henry Wadsworth Longfellow (1983, Dial, New York), which are ideal for middle graders. Similarly, books such as *The BFG* by Roald Dahl (1982, Knopf, New York) or *Fog Magic* by Julia Sauer (1943, Viking, New York) may be used successfully with younger children.

Research suggests that read-aloud choices are most often confined to fiction or poetry (Silvey, 1988; Iarusso, 1989). Popular primary-grade read-alouds included *Charlotte's Web* by E. B. White (1952, Harper & Row, New York), *Little House on the Prairie* by Laura Ingalls Wilder (1953, Harper

*In this story about a game that comes to life, the author explores the ever-shifting line between fantasy and reality.*

& Row, New York), and the *Amelia Bedelia* books by Peggy Parish (1963, Harper & Row, New York). Works by Leo Lionni, Tomie dePaola, Arnold Lobel, and poems by Shel Silverstein and Jack Prelutsky were popular. Common intermediate grade read-alouds included *Island of the Blue Dolphins* by Scott O'Dell (1960, Houghton Mifflin, Boston), *James and the Giant Peach* by Roald Dahl (1961, Knopf, New York), and *Mrs. Frisby and The Rats of NIMH* by Robert C. O'Brien (1971, Atheneum, New York).

However, biographies and information books also make excellent read-alouds for every grade level. Biographies like *Laura Ingalls Wilder: Growing Up in the Little House* by Patricia Giff (1987, Harper & Row, New York) can provide an excellent complement to oral readings of the Little House books; other biographies such as *Teammates* by Peter Golenbeck (1990, Harcourt Brace Jovanovich, New York) or *An Actor's Life for Me* by Lillian Gish as told to Selma Lanes (1987, Viking Kestrel, New York) are well suited for primary graders. *Little by Little* by Jean Little (1987, Puffin, New York), which details the life of Canadian author Jean Little, or *Franklin Delano Roosevelt* by Russell Freedman (1990, Clarion, New York) represent superb read-alouds for older children.

*Hindus all over the world celebrate an annual festival of lights called Divalia. It is a magical family time that honors the goddess who brings prosperity throughout the year.*

Informational read-alouds for primary children might include books such as *Growing Vegetable Soup* by Lois Ehlert (1987, Harcourt Brace Jovanovich, New York) or *Sarah Morton's Day* by Kate Waters (1989, Scholastic, New York). Upper-grade children might enjoy titles such as *Chimney Sweeps: Yesterday and Today* by James Giblin (1982, Harper & Row, New York). *This Land Is My Land* (1994, Children's Book Press, San Francisco) is a nonfiction book written by a member of the Plains Cree Nation named George Littlechild. The author is a renowned artist who tells about his art in this wonderful book. Children will enjoy looking at the art as well as hearing about it.

*Lights for Gita* by Rachma Gilmore (1994, Tilbury House, Gardiner, MA) combines a story with information in a picture book about the Divali, Festival of Lights which falls in October or November and is observed by Hindus all over the world. The text and the illustrations share the interesting traditions and foods of this festival.

Traditional literature interests a wide age-range of listeners. The *Uncle Smoke Stories* by Roger Welch (1994, Knopf, New York) are Native American stories about Coyote the trickster that appeal to children from third grade to junior high school. *The Corn Woman* by Angel Vigil (1994, Libraries Unlimited, Englewood, CO) is a collection of stories and legends of the Hispanic Southwest. These traditional stories share the beauty of family life before television when families passed the time by talking to each other for hours.

## Planning a Read-Aloud Session

Reading aloud to children, whether done by parents, teachers, other adults, or older children, is not difficult. Effective read-aloud sessions do not just happen, however; they are carefully planned. Aside from selecting the material, the other important factors to consider are arranging the physical setting, preparing the materials, and planning activities before, during, and after the reading. The physical setting should permit seeing and hearing readers. Very often teachers need to make sure they have enough copies of material and to plan an introduction to the story or poem. For a smooth experience, write out questions and activities.

## READER'S THEATER

**Reader's theater** *is oral presentation of literature. It is oral delivery of stories, poetry, biography, or information by two or more readers who characterize and narrate clearly and expressively.* The performers must understand the literature they are presenting so that they can structure the development of character and plot. "Reader's theater is neither lecture nor play; rather it is a staged program that allows the audience to create its own images through the skilled performance of the readers" (McCaslin, 1990, p. 263). The simplicity of reader's theater makes it appealing and effective because it does not require rehearsal or elaborate staging, yet it is so motivating that students enjoy practicing their oral reading.

The cast may be large or small. In situations with a small cast, one individual may read several different parts. During the presentation, the entire cast remains on stage, reading the various assigned portions (McCaslin, 1990). Movement is minimal, and actions are suggested through simple gestures and facial expressions. Readers usually take formal positions behind lecterns and sit on stools, often turning their backs to the audience to show that they are absent from a scene. Readers may turn around or lower their heads when not participating in a scene (Sloyer, 1982).

### Selecting Material

Many types of literature are well suited to reader's theater presentations. Both modern literature and traditional tales, including all kinds of fiction, poetry, history, biography, and unpublished materials, are effective in these readings. In some instances, related materials may be mixed in a presentation. For example, a poem and a story with related themes can be performed together. Manna (1984) suggests that reader's theater stories should have these characteristics:

1. an interesting, fast-paced story with a strong plot
2. a lot of dialogue
3. recognizable and believable characters
4. plausible language
5. distinct style

There are, of course, many appropriate pieces of literature, but a few suggestions follow.

- Andersen, Hans Christian. (1978). *The Princess and the Pea*. Illustrated by Paul Galdone. New York: Seabury. (1–3)
- Galdone, Paul. (1991). *Henny Penny*. New York: Tambourine. (preschool–1)
- Galdone, Paul. (1973). *The Three Billy Goats Gruff*. New York: Seabury. (1–3)
- Hooks, William. (1990). *The Ballad of Belle Dorcas*. New York: Knopf. (2–4)
- Lobel, Arnold. (1971). *On the Day Peter Stuyvesant Sailed into Town*. New York: Harper and Row. (K–3)
- Prelutsky, Jack. (1980). *Rolling Harvey Down the Hill*. Illustrated by Victoria Chess. New York: Greenwillow. (2–6)
- Prelutsky, Jack. (1984). *New Kid on the Block*. Illustrated by James Stevenson. New York: Greenwillow. (2–6)
- Rylant, Cynthia. (1985). *The Relatives Came*. New York: Bradbury. (2–4)
- Seuss, Dr. (1940). *Horton Hatches the Egg*. New York: Random House. (1–4)
- Suess, Dr. (1949). *Bartholomew and the Oobleck*. New York: Random House. (1–4)
- Stevens, Janet. (1992). *Bremen Town Musicians*. New York: Holiday House. (K–3)
- Thurber, James. (1990). *Many Moons*. Illustrated by Marc Simont. New York: Harcourt Brace Jovanovich. (4–8)

### Planning a Reader's Theater Performance

After selecting a piece for the performance, the next step is identifying who will read which part. If the piece is too long, the readers will choose the scenes that convey the concept or theme of the piece rather than the entire selection. After these decisions are made, details of staging must be planned and decided. A common staging device is sitting on stools in a circle and turning around on the stools when not participating in a scene. In somewhat more elaborate staging, a spotlight may be focused on the individual who is reading at the moment. Students may also sit or stand side by side, with the narrators at one side and closer to the audience.

A colored marking pen or magic marker can be used to identify the various parts to be read by individuals. Readers should practice reading in a comfortable, relaxed manner at a pace that moves the scene along, but not so rapidly that the audience is lost. Careful reading and discussion of the text during preparation is essential, as a piece of literature cannot be interpreted without understanding. The box shows an example of a fifth-grade class preparing for a reader's theater performance.

---

### *A Report on a Reader's Theater Performance*

The students chose to read *Where the Lilies Bloom* by Vera and Bill Cleaver. Eight readers took the parts of Mary Call, the protagonist; Devola, her older sister; Roy Luther, the father; Kiser Pease, the landlord and neighbor; Mary Call's younger brother and sister; the storekeeper who bought herbs from Mary Call; and a neighbor. They used stools in a circle so they could turn their backs when not participating.

They identified the following scenes as key to understanding the story.

1. Mary Call and Roy Luther discuss his impending death and his burial in the grave he has prepared.
2. Mary Call and the children pretend their father is ill when a neighbor comes to call.
3. Mary Call and Devola care for Kiser Pease when he is ill.
4. Mary Call and the storekeeper interact when Mary Call sells herbs.
5. Kiser Pease brings his car to the Luthers so that Devola can sit in it.
6. Kiser Pease asks Devola to marry him.
7. Mary Call pretends she wants to marry Kiser.
8. Devola takes charge and decides to marry Kiser.

The readers decided to serve herb tea after their performance, because Mary Call earned a living for her family by gathering herbs. They also planned to read the sequel to this story, *Trial Valley*.

---

## STORYTELLING

Oral literature includes stories, poems, and information told aloud to another person or persons. "Most modern dictionaries define a storyteller first as one who tells or writes stories, and second as one who tells fibs or falsehoods" (Pellowski, 1977, p. 3). **Storytellers** are *transmitters of stories who select, prepare, and deliver them.* The first written description of storytelling appears in the Egyptian papyrus known as the Westcar Papyrus, recorded sometime between the 12th and 18th dynasties (2000–1300 B.C.), describing a storytelling encounter between Khufu (Cheops) and his sons.

Ruth Sawyer (1962), who travels around the world to discover stories and storytellers, calls storytelling a folk art. She says enduring stories are a sharing of mind, heart, and spirit. Northrup Frye (1964) believes that traditional literature, stories in the oral tradition, are the basis of all modern stories. Cooper and Collins (1992) believe stories are the part of us that makes us human and that stories are at the heart of the teaching and learning process. Storytellers in widely different cultures tell stories with common threads running through them. Traditional stories even appear to be the basis for many television shows. Many daytime dramas owe their appeal to the ancient tales of Cinderella and Snow White.

Storytellers have a live, listening audience with whom to interact, whereas writers do not have a chance to interact directly with their readers. Listeners hear voice effects and see their storyteller move, bend, and breathe. The oral story is soft and malleable, yielding to the pleasures of the audience. Its language is not the precise and unchanging form of the written story created by a single author, but the evolving, flowing language of the community (Barton, 1986).

Storytelling is natural to human beings. Stories help us remember and understand things that have happened to us. They teach us how to behave and how not to behave. They stimulate our imagination: as the storyteller spins a tale, the listeners create pictures in their minds of the characters, the setting, and the story events. Storytelling develops an awareness of and sensitivity to the thoughts and feelings of the listeners. We can laugh and cry. Our feelings are valid and storytelling allows us to express them (Cooper and Collins, 1992). "As the teller looks right at the listeners, eyes meet and an interactive communication exists between them" (Livo and Rietz, 1987, p. xi). Storytelling appeals to everyone and can bring people of all ages together for a shared experience that actively involves both storyteller and listeners. The storyteller gets immediate feedback on how the story is received, and the storytellers' actions enrich listeners' understanding.

## The Roots of Storytelling

Traditional literature, a common source of material for storytellers, is the product of a community. One storyteller tells a story; another hears it and retells it, reshaping it in the retelling. A detail may be deleted and a new one added because of the new storyteller's personal style or perhaps to tailor-make the story for a particular audience (Lester, 1988). This is how different versions of the same story develop throughout the world.

There are literally hundreds of versions of popular stories such as Cinderella. The most common version may be the one written by Charles Perrault and illustrated by Marcia Brown. In this version, Brown creates a fairy-tale quality with ruffles and flourishes. Diane Goode's *Tattercoats* is a British version in which the prince falls in love with a dirty girl wearing a torn petticoat. The prince invites Tattercoats, her gooseherd friend, and his geese to come to the king's ball. After the prince greets

*This picture about the metamorphosis of a caterpillar into a butterfly delights and informs the very youngest reader or listener.*

them, the gooseherd plays a magic pipe, which changes Tattercoats's rags to beautiful robes and the geese to pages. *Yeh-Shen*, by Ai-Ling Louie, the oldest written version of Cinderella, is a Chinese folktale. Yeh-Shen, who must serve her stepmother and stepsister, has one friend, a fish. She feeds and talks with the fish each day. After her stepmother kills and eats the fish, Yeh-Shen discovers that its spirit is in the bones. Through the magic powers in the fish bones, she is dressed in fine clothes and feathers to go to a festival. She leaves hurriedly and loses a slipper that the king uses to claim her hand in marriage. The stepmother and stepsister are crushed by a shower of flying stones.

**Cumulative stories,** such as Eric Carle's *The Very Hungry Caterpillar,* are also frequently told as stories. A cumulative story is one that accumulates, so to speak. *Events build on events and phrases build on phrases, building to a climax at which the accumulation falls apart.* In *The Very Hungry Caterpillar* the accumulation is the food that the caterpillar eats. This builds until he grows into a huge caterpillar, when he spins a cocoon and turns into a beautiful butterfly at the climax of the story. The Woods's *The Napping House,* introduced in Chapter One, is a cumulative tale also. The nap begins with one character who takes a nap, then additional characters join the nap. Cumulative stories are highly predictable, with events and phrases repeated as new ones are added. This type of story probably descended from the first primitive efforts at conscious storytelling consisting of a simple chant set to the rhythm of some daily occupation such as grinding corn, paddling a canoe or kayak, sharpening weapons for hunting or war, or ceremonial dancing (Sawyer, 1962).

## Storytelling in the Classroom

Oral language precedes written in children's development. Children learn to talk and to explain, a form of storytelling, before they learn to read and write stories. Therefore, it is sensible to begin children's literary experiences with oral activities and to use these activities as a basis for subsequent experiences with written language. The vignette in the box shows how oral and written experiences can be intermingled.

Storytelling is valuable in elementary classrooms (Roney, 1989). It develops positive attitudes toward literature, reading, and writing. It motivates children to read and write themselves, as shown in the boxed vignette, and provides a model for children's own writing. Children enjoy participating in storytelling through telling their own stories and joining in on repeated phrases when others are telling stories. Hearing and telling different types of stories develops their awareness and comprehension of the various forms of narrative (Golden, 1984). Storytelling develops thinking abilities (Roney, 1989). Teachers can tell stories to introduce literature, to help children learn about stories, to develop children's listening and speaking skills, and to model storytelling behavior. Teachers who are storytellers can help their students learn to tell stories.

## Selecting Material

The first step in storytelling is selecting a story to learn. Traditional literature is a good starting point. *The Storyteller's Sourcebook: A Subject, Title, and Motif Index to Folklore Collections for Children* by Margaret Read MacDonald is a helpful reference in finding good traditional stories. Begin with an appealing version of a traditional story that you already know, such as *Cinderella, Three Billy Goats Gruff, Stone Soup, Jack and the Beanstalk, The Three Little Pigs,* or *Goldilocks and the Three Bears.* The

## A STORYTELLING EXPERIENCE

Jim Phillips told his first graders to make a story circle on the rug in his classroom, then he sat down on a low chair and opened the book *Brown Bear, Brown Bear* by Bill Martin. He held the book so the children could see it, told them the title and the author's name, and started reading.

"Brown Bear, Brown Bear, What do you see?" "I see a red bird looking at me."

Mr. Phillips read through the entire cumulative tale, in which each animal or bird sees another. When he finished, the children pleaded for him to read it again and he did. After the second reading, Mr. Phillips told the children they were going to make a story. They immediately asked how.

He answered, "You are going to think of new animals for the *Brown Bear, Brown Bear* story. I'll begin with 'Blue Jay, Blue Jay, What do you see?' Now, Lauren, tell us what the Polar Bear sees."

After thinking for a few moments, Lauren said, "I see a pink butterfly looking at me."

Mr. Phillips said, "Pink butterfly, pink butterfly, What do you see? Tony, tell us what the pink butterfly sees."

Tony said, "I see a striped zebra looking at me!"

Mr. Phillips and the children continued until they had completed a story, then they retold it. Afterward, Mr. Phillips said, "I am going to write your story on this chart, so you can remember it. While I am writing your story on a chart, you can draw pictures of the animals and birds that you thought of for the story and we will paste them to the chart pages."

Later in the day, he noticed that a number of the children were writing and illustrating their own *Brown Bear* stories. When the children completed their individual stories, they read them to their classmates.

most important factor in choosing a story for telling is that you enjoy the story so that you will also enjoy the telling. As a beginning storyteller, a simple story will give you security as you begin. You will find authors such as the following helpful because they retell traditional stories and write stories in a traditional literature style.

- Aardema, Verna. (1975). *Why Mosquitoes Buzz in People's Ears.* New York: Dial. (preschool–3)
- Aranda, Charles. (1993). *Dichos: Proverbs and Sayings from the Spanish.* Santa Fe, NM: Sunstone. (4–8)
- Asbjornsen, Peter Christian, and Jorgen Moe. (1967). *Norwegian Folk Tales.* New York: Viking. (all ages)
- Banks, Lynne Reid. (1988). *I, Houdini: The Autobiography of a Self-Educated Hamster.* Illustrated by Terry Riley. New York: Doubleday. (4–8)
- Barlow, Genevieve. (1992). *Latin American Tales: From the Pampas to the Pyramids of Mexico.* Chicago: Rand McNally. (all ages)
- Chase, Richard (retold by). (1943). *Jack Tales.* Boston: Houghton Mifflin. (3–adult)
- Claverie, Jean. (1989). *The Three Little Pigs.* New York: North South. (K–3)
- Cooper, Pamela, and Rives Collins. (1992). *Look What Happened to Frog: Storytelling in Education.* Scottsdale, AZ: Gorsuch Scarisbrick. (all ages)
- Fakih, Kimberly Olson. (1993). *The Literature of Delight.* New Providence, NJ: R. R. Bowker. (teacher reference)
- Holt, David. (1994). *Hairyman.* Fairview, NC: High Windy Audio. (all ages)
- Holt, David. (1994). *Tailybone.* Fairview, NC: High Windy Audio. (all ages)
- Korling, Barbara. (1989). *Cinderella.* Illustrated by James Marshall. New York: Little, Brown. (1–3)
- Kellogg, Steven. (1991). *Jack and the Beanstalk.* New York: Morrow. (all ages)
- Lester, Julius. (1968). *Black Folktales.* New York: Dial. (all ages)
- Lester, Julius. (1987). *The Tales of Uncle Remus: The Adventures of Brer Rabbit.* New York: Dial. (all ages)
- MacDonald, Margaret Read. (1982). *The Storyteller's Sourcebook: A Subject, Title, and Motif Index to Folklore Collections for Children.* Detroit: Neal-Schuman.
- O'Callahan, Jay. (1994). *The Boy Who Loved Frogs.* West Tisbury, MA: Vineyard Video. (1–3)
- O'Callahan, Jay. *Little Heroes.* Fairview, NC: High Windy Audio.
- Seeger, Pete. (1994). *Stories and Songs for Little Children.* Fairview, NC: High Windy Audio. (pre-K–2)
- Soto, Gary. (1990). *Baseball in April and Other Stories.* New York: Harcourt Brace Jovanovich. (4–8)
- Stevens, Janet. (1987). *Three Billy Goats Gruff.* New York: Harcourt Brace Jovanovich. (K–2)

Storytellers need not feel confined to traditional stories, however. Modern tales such as *Alexander and the Terrible, Horrible, No Good, Very Bad Day* by Judith Viorst is a delightful story that has broad appeal, as is Eric Carle's *The Very Hungry Caterpillar*; and there are many others. The most important factor in choosing a story for telling is that you really like it, so that you enjoy the telling.

## Planning Storytelling

The main ingredient in planning storytelling is learning the story. Storytelling confidence comes with story familiarity. Storytellers should know their story well, but it is not necessary to learn it word for word. It is important to learn the framework of a story to provide a skeleton to follow in telling it, and also to learn any phrases that are repeated or important to the story. Once these elements are learned, it is time to practice telling the story several times to polish the presentation.

Learning the framework of a story is easy, but there are some tools to help storytellers recall the story. Stories have structure, as Chapter Two mentions. They are orderly and conform to structure rules recognized as story structure or story grammar (Livo and Rietz, 1986). Stories that conform to the expected structure are easier to recall and to understand (Downing and Leong, 1982). Story patterns help readers comprehend literature; they also give form to writing. Story patterns can be mapped or diagrammed to assist storytellers in recalling and interrelating the ideas and events of a story. Story patterns and maps are especially helpful in teaching children to prepare stories for

## FIGURE 11.1

Story grammar for "The Wide-Mouthed Frog."

........................................................................................................................................

*Setting:*

The wide-mouthed frog and his wife live beside a pond with their newborn babies.

---

*The Problem:*

The wide-mouthed frog babies are hungry. Mrs. Wide-Mouthed Frog sends her husband out to get food for the babies.

---

*The Events:*

1. Mr. Wide-Mouthed frog meets a goat and asks him what his babies eat. The goat recommends tin cans, which the wide-mouthed frog rejects.
2. He meets a cat who recommends mice.
3. He meets a cow who recommends milk.
4. He meets a horse who recommends grass.
5. He meets an owl who recommends wide-mouthed frogs.

---

*Resolution:*

The wide-mouthed frog narrows his mouth and says, "Ooooooohhhhhh."

........................................................................................................................................

storytelling. Figure 11.1 illustrates a structural map of a story, "The Wide-Mouthed Frog," The box on page 325 shows the storyteller's version of this tale.

Some storytellers choose to use story maps to help them learn their stories. The following techniques will help teachers and children with storytelling.

1. When preparing to learn a story for storytelling, read several stories a week or so in advance. The story that comes back to you most frequently is the one to learn.

2. Divide the story into beginning, middle, and end. Learn it in segments, such as separate scenes or units of action. Learn the story structure in order, but do not memorize it. The ways of dividing a story differ from storyteller to storyteller. One way of dividing "The Three Little Pigs" is:
   - *Part I:* The three little pigs set out to find their fortune. One builds a house of straw, the next builds a house of sticks, and the third builds a brick house.
   - *Part II:* The wolf eats pigs one and two and goes after the third one.
   - *Part III:* The pig sends the wolf to an apple orchard and a fair and then outwits him. The wolf ends up in the kettle.

3. Learn any special catch phrases and use them in telling the story. Special phrases are phrases that may appear several times within the story or that the story hinges on, such as "I'll huff and I'll puff and I'll blow your house down" in *The Three Little Pigs.*

4. Don't worry about using the same words every time you tell the story.

5. Be expressive in storytelling, but do not be so dramatic that you overshadow the story itself (Morrow, 1979).

6. Practice telling the story several times before actually telling it to an audience to get comfortable with saying the story aloud and with the sound of your own voice.

7. Practice by tape recording yourself. Wait a day or two to listen to the tape, so you can be

objective. When you evaluate the tape think about the parts of the story and identify those that need changing or expanding. Does your voice sound pleasing and do you speak at a speed that is appropriate to the story?

8. Look directly at your audience when you are telling the story.

The National Association for the Preservation and Perpetuation of Storytelling publishes *Yarnspinner*, sponsors storytelling workshops, and provides storytelling information. Their materials are very helpful in the classroom. Their address is:

NAPPS
P. O. Box 309
Jonesborough, Tennessee 37659

## Storytelling Variations

Sitting in front of an audience and speaking with nothing but voice and expressions is not the only way to tell a story. Storytelling can be varied in many ways to give novelty to tried-and-true stories. Variations also can be used cooperatively with children to give them greater involvement with the literature presented.

### Flannel board stories

When telling stories with flannel boards, the teller sits or stands by a board covered with flannel. Cutouts of characters backed with flannel are placed on the board as they appear in the story. Some storytellers may lay the flannel board on a table to prevent the figures from falling. Children can also use flannel boards, and will enjoy taking turns telling stories with a flannel board.

Stories told with a flannel board should not have large numbers of characters or complex actions. After selecting a story, the teller decides which parts to show and which to tell. For example, in preparing *Goldilocks and the Three Bears* the teller or students could make figures for Goldilocks, the three bears, three sizes of bowls, three sizes of chairs, and three sizes of beds; some tellers may like to have a broken bowl and a broken chair to illustrate the story further. These figures can be used to present the entire story; details and actions do not have to be portrayed.

The characters can be drawn or painted on cardboard, construction paper, or any other convenient material. After cutting them out, back them with flannel or sandpaper so they will stick to the flannel board. Use yarn, buttons, or fabric to decorate and develop the characters. The board can be covered with flannel, although indoor-outdoor carpeting makes a very satisfactory backing. Figures cling to it and it wipes clean (Ross, 1972).

### Prop stories

Props such as hats, canes, stuffed animals, boxes, rocks, toys, and fruit can enhance storytelling. *The Very Hungry Caterpillar* is an excellent story to tell with props: fruit or other food mentioned in the story can later be eaten by the audience. Beans, a small harp, and a china or plastic hen are excellent props for "Jack and the Beanstalk." The props give the storyteller and the audience a focal point and help the storyteller remember the story.

### Music stories

Some stories are excellent when told with a background of music. For example, "Jack in the Beanstalk" sounds wonderful when told with the music "In the Hall of the Mountain King" playing in the background. This piece is from *Legends in Music* by Bowmar Orchestral Library. RCA Victor has an *Adventures in Music* record library for elementary schools that includes excellent selections for story background music. Musical storytellers can play their own accompaniment.

### Cut stories

Cut stories are stories told while the storyteller cuts out a piece of paper to form a character or object in the story. The figures may be drawn ahead of time on construction paper to make the cutting easier (Morrow, 1979). Some teachers are sufficiently skilled to fold the paper and cut multiple figures while storytelling. Many picture books and folktales are good choices for cut stories because the teller can cut objects to accompany the story. For example, a gingerbread boy cutout could accompany the story "The Gingerbread Boy," or a pancake could accompany "The Pancake."

---

### A Storyteller's Version of "The Wide-Mouthed Frog"

Mr. and Mrs. Willie T. Wide-Mouthed Frog lived beside a pretty pond with blue water and white lily pads. They were thrilled to have three beautiful green babies. But the babies were always hungry and crying. Mrs. Wide-Mouthed Frog was tired of hunting for food, so she told her husband to go out and hunt food for their hungry babies. Mr. Willie T. Wide-Mouthed Frog set out to find food. He hopped around the beautiful blue pond.

He met a goat and stopped. "Hello Goat, I'm a wide-mouthed frog and I'm hunting food for my babies. What do your babies eat?"

"My babies eat tin cans. They chew them right up."

"Oh! Wide-mouthed frog babies can't eat tin cans. Thank you."

The frog hops on. He meets a cat.

"Hello Cat, I'm a wide-mouthed frog and I'm hunting food for my babies. What do your babies eat?"

"My babies eat mice. They chew them up bones and all."

"Wide-mouthed frog babies can't eat mice. Thank you."

The frog hops on. He meets a horse and stops.

"Hello Horse, I'm a wide-mouthed frog and I'm hunting food for my babies. What do your babies eat?"

"My babies eat grain. They grind it up with their teeth."

"Wide-mouthed frog babies can't eat grain. Thank you."

The frog hops on. He meets a duck and stops.

"Hello Duck, I'm a wide-mouthed frog and I'm hunting food for my babies. What do your babies eat?"

"My babies eat worms. They wash them down with water."

"Wide-mouthed frog babies can't eat worms. Thank you."

The frog hops on. He sees an owl in a tree and stops.

"Hello Owl, I'm a wide-mouthed frog and I'm hunting food for my babies. What do your babies eat?"

"My babies eat wide-mouthed frogs."

The frog sucks his mouth into a narrow little circle and says, "Oooohhhh!" and then hurries home.

---

## CHORAL READING

**Choral reading** is an *oral literary activity in which a selection is read by several readers in unison with the direction of a leader.* This ancient technique has been in use for centuries. Choral reading was an important element of Greek drama. Evidence of choral speaking has been found in ancient religious ceremonies and festivals, and it is still used for ritualistic purposes in church services and on patriotic occasions (McCaslin, 1990). Ross (1972) points out that choral reading was used in early schools because there were not enough books.

Choral reading involves listening and responding to language. Through participating in choral reading, students become aware of the sounds of language, predictable language patterns, and the rhythm and melody of language, helping them understand the meaning of text (Miccinati, 1985). After choral reading experiences, children are better able to predict the words and phrases that follow one another. The purpose of choral reading is to convey meaning through sound, stress, duration, and pitch. Choral reading also develops diction and enunciation of speech sounds.

Choral reading is a group activity that gives students opportunities for social cooperation because individuals focus on a common goal. In a group activity such as this, students can participate without feelings of self-consciousness. There are no age limits for choral reading—kindergarten children enjoy it, as do high school students and adults.

### Selecting Material

Choral reading in the elementary classrooms can begin with short nursery rhymes in kindergarten. Rhythm and rhyme are the important factors in nursery rhymes, which will help children remember them. Material for choral reading should be meaningful and have strong rhythm and an easily discernible structure. The following list includes only a few of the materials that make interesting choral readings.

- *Baby-O* by Nancy Carlstrom. Illustrated by Sucie Stevenson. (1992). New York: Little, Brown.
- "So Long as There's Weather" by Tamara Kitt. (1988). In *Sing a Song of Popcorn*, edited by Beatrice Schenk de Regniers, Eva Moore, Mary Michaels White, and Jean Carr. New York: Scholastic. (K–6)
- "The Umbrella Brigade" by Laura Richards. (1952). In *Time for Poetry*, compiled by May Hill Arbuthnot. Glenview, IL: Scott Foresman. (all ages)
- "Godfrey, Gordon, Gustavus Gore" by William B. Rand. (1952). In *Time for Poetry*, compiled by May Hill Arbuthnot. Glenview IL: Scott Foresman. (all ages)
- *Laughing Time: Collected Nonsense* by William Jay Smith. (1990). Illustrated by Fernando Krahm. New York: Farrar, Straus & Giroux. (1–5)
- *Train Song* by Diane Siebert. (1990). New York: T. H. Crowell. (1–4)
- *Truck Song* by Diane Siebert. (1984). New York: T. H. Crowell (1–4)
- *I Know an Old Lady Who Swallowed a Fly* by Nadine Westcott. (1990). New York: Dutton. (1–6)
- *Peanut Butter and Jelly* by Nadine Westcott. (1987). New York: Dutton. (preschool–2)

## Planning a Choral Reading

When initiating a choral reading activity, prepare the students by giving them time to read the material silently and then aloud to themselves or their peers. After reading, lead a discussion to develop students' understanding of the selection. Once the students understand the selection, they can practice reading orally. Teachers can help young children respond to language rhythms through clapping or tapping the rhythm. Initially, the teacher may chant most of the rhyme and have the children chime in only on the last line or a repeated refrain. Use a single selection with various choral reading methods so students learn about the various ways of expressing meaning. After students have experiences with the various choral reading types, they can choose selections and plan their own choral readings.

There are four common types of choral reading: refrain, line-a-child, antiphonal, and unison. The easiest to learn is **refrain,** in which *the teacher reads most of the lines and the students read the refrain.* In **line-a-child** reading, *individual students read specific lines, while the entire group reads the beginning and ending* of the selection. **Antiphonal** or dialogue choral reading is most appropriate for middle- or intermediate-level students. It enables readers to explore pitch and duration of sound. *Boys, girls, and groups vary their pitches and sound duration for different parts of the selection.* **Unison** is the most difficult choral reading approach because *the entire group speaks all of the lines.* Without seeking perfection, the participants must practice timing so that they are producing words and sounds simultaneously. Combinations of all of the above types may be used for a single selection.

Tamara Kitt's poem "So Long as There's Weather" (see box) is a fine children's choice for choral reading. The spare use of words, frequent pauses, sound effects, emphasized words, and short lines ranging from one to five syllables create a feeling of changing weather and a child's joy in all kinds of weather. The appeal of this poem for children makes it an excellent choice for choral reading. Alert the students to the fact that dashes in the text represent pauses and that the emphasized words and pauses make the choral reading more interesting. A choral reading experience involving "So Long as There's Weather" for primary-grade children might proceed as indicated in the box.

1. Begin with crashing cymbals to simulate thunder or with water poured from container to container to simulate rain.
2. The teacher reads the first verse.
3. The children read the second verse in unison from a chart.
4. The teacher or a child who has practiced reads the third verse.
5. The children read the fourth verse in unison from a chart.
6. On the emphasized words in the fourth verse, designated children crash cymbals together.

### So Long as There's Weather

Whether it's cold
or
whether it's hot,
I'd rather
have weather
whether or not
    it's just what I'd choose.
Summer
or
Spring
or
Winter
or Fall—
any weather
is better
than
no weather
at all.
    I really like weather.
I never feel
whiney
when weather is
rainy.
And when it's
sunshiny
I don't feel
complainy.
    Weather sends me.
    So—
    Rain?
    Let it SPLASH!
    Thunder?
    CRRRASH!
    Hail?
    Clitter-clatter
    What does it
    matter—
      so long as there's weather!

Kitt, 1988

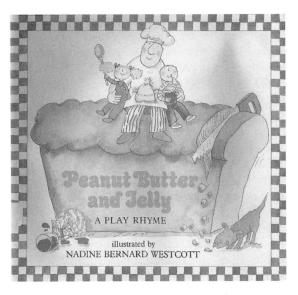

In this book, the rhythm of the popular play rhyme invites listeners to join in on the fun.

As children develop their understanding of chanting in unison, they can move to longer selections. *Peanut Butter and Jelly* by Nadine Westcott is an excellent longer piece for choral reading. After children learn to chant this play-rhyme, the teacher can introduce the hand-clap and knee-slap motions that accompany it. Still later, the teacher may choose to divide the poem into parts to be read by different groups.

## CREATIVE DRAMA

**Creative drama** is informal *drama created by the participants* (McCaslin, 1990). *This kind of drama is improvisational and process-centered rather than exhibitional.* It may be based on a story with a beginning, a middle, and an end. It may, on the other hand, be an original plot that explores, develops, and expresses ideas and feelings through dramatic enactment. The players create the dialogue whether the content is a well-known story or an original plot. "With each playing, the story becomes more detailed and better organized, but it remains extemporaneous and is at no time designed for an audience" (McCaslin, 1990, p. 5). (This avoids rehearsal and memorization.)

Reenactments allow each member of the group an opportunity to play various parts and to be part of the audience for others. Scenery and costumes have no place in creative drama, although an occasional prop or piece of costume may be permitted to stimulate the imagination (McCaslin, 1990). Similarly, there is no written script to follow. Creative drama emphasizes spontaneity and improvisation, although involvement in creative drama may lead students to write a script for a play later. When dialogue is written, the nature of the drama changes. Written drama can be very rewarding and children enjoy the creative writing involved in such enterprises.

Creative drama is done for fun, understanding, and learning, and yields many benefits. It is a way of learning and knowing; the actors become participants instead of merely observers (Heathcote, 1983). As children improvise in acting out a story they have read, an episode from a story, or an experience of their own, they participate in the literature or the incident. They comprehend and express the important details of plot, character, word meanings, story sequence, and relationships of cause and effect (Miccinati, 1985). This makes story characters and story action more concrete and comprehensible for children. In acting out stories, they use their bodies, voices, and movements to enact literature; translating words into action encourages children to interpret and respond to literature. Dramatization also increases vocabulary, syntactic flexibility, and the ability to predict aspects of story.

Creative drama also makes strong contributions to the growth of children's communication effectiveness (Busching, 1981). It requires logical and intuitive thinking; it personalizes knowledge and yields aesthetic pleasure (Siks, 1983). Drama gives children opportunities to experiment with words, emotions, and social roles. Heathcote (1983) believes that drama expands children's understanding of life experiences and that it leads them to reflect on particular circumstances and to make sense out of their world in a deeper way.

Creative drama is one of the best ways of discovering and learning to appreciate literature. Other creative drama activities include pantomime, puppets, and story creation (discussed later in this section).

*The Pushcart War is the true story of the dispute between pushcart peddlers and truck drivers in New York City.*

## Selecting Material

The story dramatized can make a lasting impression. Therefore, the opportunity to become well acquainted with good literature through dramatizing it is a major value of creative drama. Both folktales and modern stories provide fine opportunities for acting. Believable characters, a well-constructed plot, and a worthwhile theme make for engrossing drama. Any story, episode, or event that children have enjoyed is a likely candidate for dramatization. Students of all ages enjoy acting out different versions of the same story and comparing the versions. For example, they might act out three versions of Cinderella and compare the characterization, plot, and setting. Perhaps a few suggestions of specific stories for dramatization will stimulate you to think of others.

Young children enjoy dramatizing many traditional stories they have heard over and over such as

Gail Haley's *Jack and the Bean Tree*, (1986), published by Crown of New York for grades 1–4 and *Little Red Riding Hood* and *The Little Red Hen*, both by Gail Haley, published in 1976 by McGraw Hill, New York, for grades K–2. Many of John Burningham's cumulative tales such as *Mr. Gumpy's Outing* for preschoolers and first graders (1977, Macmillan, New York) lend themselves to dramatization. Middle grade students enjoy stories such as *Bunnicula* (1979, Atheneum, New York) by James and Rebecca Howe, *The Pushcart War* (1964, W. R. Scott, New York) by Jean Merrill, and *The Book of Three* (1964, Holt, Rinehart and Winston, New York) by Lloyd Alexander.

## Planning Creative Drama

Teachers should create many opportunities for children to participate in short, unstructured drama. The following guidelines will be helpful in creating these opportunities:

1. Although props are not necessary, many teachers gather a collection of props for dramatic plays. Jewelry, fabric, hats, canes, clothing, and Halloween costumes are useful props.
2. Select a story or have the children select a favorite story. A book that includes a large number of characters gives more children opportunities to participate.
3. Discuss the main events with the students. Identify and sequence the events to be included. You may wish to outline the events using a story map.
4. Identify the characters in the story. Discuss their actions, attitudes, and feelings. Explain that the children should act the way they think the character walked, talked, and so on.
5. Discuss the action in each scene and give the children opportunities to practice it. They may need to pretend to walk in heavy boots or need to practice expressive gestures such as walking happily, sadly, or so forth. Pantomime (discussed below) is a way of preparing children to move in expressive ways.
6. Assign character roles to class members. Ask the participants to think about and visualize the characters. Children who do not want to participate can be directors or stage managers.
7. Give the audience a purpose for watching the play. For example, ask them to observe characterization and character development or plot development.
8. Dramatize the story.
9. Discuss the dramatization.
10. Recast the characters and play the story again.

## Pantomime

"Pantomime is the art of conveying ideas without words"; it sharpens children's perceptions and stimulates the imagination as the players try to remember actions and characters (McCaslin, 1990, p. 71). Children can pantomime stories as they are read by another child or the teacher. They may create a character from literature or one of their own invention. Pantomime is an excellent way to begin creative drama because it is a natural means of expression for primary-grade children. In kindergarten, basic movements such as walking, running, skipping, and galloping prepare for the creative use of rhythms. Music can set the mood for people marching in a parade, horses galloping, toads hopping, race cars on a track, or children skipping on a sunny spring day (McCaslin, 1990). Older children also enjoy pantomime and children who have limited knowledge of English or who have speech and hearing problems can participate in it.

## Puppets

Puppet shows are dramas in which the actors are puppets that come to life with the assistance of a puppeteer. Children enjoy making puppets and becoming puppeteers. Puppets are excellent for children who are shy because they can express themselves through the puppet. They also work well with children who are reluctant to participate in creative drama.

A puppet show allows children to dramatize their favorite books or scripts they have written. Puppetry stimulates the imagination of the children who are creating puppets and planning to dramatize a story. Children practice cooperation as they work with others to make puppets and puppet productions.

The stage can be quite simple—a youngster kneeling behind a table and moving an object along the edge of it—or as elaborate as imagination

## FIGURE 11.2

Student-made puppets.

Stick puppet

Paper-plate puppet

Sock puppet

Styrofoam-cup puppet

Cloth or hand puppet

Paper-bag puppet

and skill can make or buy it. Similarly, you can provide commercially produced puppets, or children can make their own. They can create a puppet with nothing more than a bandanna wrapped around the first three fingers so that the thumb and little finger are the arms (McCaslin, 1990). Some of the puppets students can construct (Stoodt, 1988, p. 119) are listed below (see Figure 11.2).

- *Stick puppets:* Draw the character on tagboard, cardboard, or construction paper and decorate it with yarn, sequins, and tissue paper. Cut out the figure and attach it to a stick, tongue depressor, or dowel for manipulation.

- *Paper-plate puppets:* Draw faces on paper plates and decorate them with yarn for hair. Glue the plates on sticks, dowels, or rulers for manipulation.

- *Sock puppets:* Add yarn hair, button eyes, and felt bits for a nose, ear, or other features to the toe end of a sock. Put your hand inside the sock for manipulation.

- *Styrofoam cup puppets:* Decorate a cup as a character and attach the completed puppet to a stick or dowel for manipulation.

- *Cloth puppets:* Sew fabric to fit over a child's hand. Decorate it to create a character.

- *Paper-bag puppets:* Draw the character on the bag and put the bag over your hand to manipulate it, using the folded bottom of the bag for the mouth area; or decorate the bag as the character, stuff it with newspaper or cotton, and put a stick, dowel, or ruler into the neck of the bag and tie it shut, turning it upside down and using the stick for manipulation.

Some helpful puppeteering references include *Storytelling with Puppets* by Connie Champlin and Nancy Renfro (American Library Association, 1985); *Making Puppets Come Alive* by Larry Engler and Carol Fijan (Taplinger Publishing Company, 1973); and *The Consultant's Notebook* by Puppeteers of America (Puppeteers of America, Inc., 1989).

## BOOKTALKS

Booktalks are akin to storytelling but have a somewhat different purpose: motivating children to read. Both children and teachers should regularly share their favorite books through booktalks.

Booktalks should be based on books the teller really enjoys, otherwise, attracting readers for the book will be difficult. To prepare for the booktalk, read the book, think about the things that make it work, and listen to the voice of the book. Put the book aside and do other things. The parts that come back to you over the next few days will be the ones to include in your talk.

Booktalks may include one or more books. A common subject or theme—animals, war, survival, terror, love, secrets, outsiders—can link multiple books. A variety of reading levels, genre, and cultures will appeal to a wide range of reading interests and push readers a little beyond where they might go on their own (Rochman, 1989).

**Booktalks** *usually follow one of three styles: (1) tell highlights of the book, (2) read highlights from the book, (3) combine telling and reading.* For instance, a booktalk on *Eva* by Peter Dickinson might begin by *telling* about the hospital scene with the sobbing mother and Eva's confusion as she comes out of a coma, followed by *reading* a quotation in which Eva talks about living in a chimp body: "You had to awaken and open your eyes and see your new face and like what you saw. You had to make the human greeting and the chimp greeting and mean them."

## EVALUATING ORAL STORY EXPERIENCES

"Experience without reflection is hollow" (Cooper and Collins, 1992, p. 3). Guided discussion gives children an opportunity to reflect on oral experiences, respond to them, offer support to their classmates, and think about future experiences. They can also be used to elicit constructive criticism. For instance, questions such as these, partially suggested by Cooper and Collins, could be used to evaluate a creative drama:

1. What did you like best about this playing?
2. When were the imaginations really at work?
3. When were the characters most believable?
4. What did you learn from the playing that we didn't know from the telling?
5. What did you learn about the important ideas in this story?
6. Did we leave out anything in this playing?
7. What would you like to try in our next playing of the scene?
8. What else could our characters do or say?
9. How can we make our playing even more believable?

## SILENT READING

Understanding is the goal of all reading, whether being read aloud to, reading silently, or reading aloud for an audience. All reading is an interactive process. Being read aloud to gives children a model for reading and language development, which they use during silent reading to increase their reading and language skills. With practice, silent reading becomes more fluent and readers can readily perceive ideas in the text. Children who read more show large differences in their reading abilities as a result of their practice (Fractor, Woodruff, Martinez, and Teale, 1993). Silent reading, which precedes reading aloud to others, permits readers to focus on meaning without being overly involved with pronouncing words. Oral reading requires readers to think ahead of their voices and prepare to pronounce the next word or phrase, a skill that develops over time with extensive practice in silent reading.

### Uninterrupted Sustained Silent Reading (USSR-DEAR-SSR)

Uninterrupted sustained silent reading **(USSR),** also known as **DEAR** (drop everything and read) or **SSR** (sustained silent reading), is usually regarded as a logical counterpart to daily oral reading. USSR is *predicated on the idea that teachers regularly involve children in learning the skills of reading, but they often overlook giving children time to practice reading, thereby developing reading fluency.* USSR also makes children aware that reading and books are important; it allows them to experience whole books rather than fragments; and it gives them practice in sustaining attention, thinking, and reading.

Effective USSR programs require a foundation of reading materials that is broad enough to include materials appropriate to the age, development, and reading levels of all the children involved. These materials may include books, periodicals, magazines, newspapers, reference books, and any other type of reading material that might interest the children. They should be in the classroom library where children can readily obtain them. Select books from the school library and obtain extended loans from the local public library to stock classroom shelves.

When developing a USSR program, explain the purpose and procedures in advance. The students should understand that they may bring reading material to class or select from the classroom library, but they are not to move around the room, draw, talk, or do anything other than read. Everyone reads, there are no interruptions, and no reports will be required on their reading.

At the outset, allocate 5 to 10 minutes for first and second graders and 10 to 15 minutes for third through sixth graders. The time can gradually be increased as children grow more comfortable with the process. The time of day varies from school to school and teacher to teacher. Some schools have schoolwide programs that involve everyone in the entire school reading at the same time. In other schools individual teachers schedule USSR when it fits best in their schedules. Some teachers have students maintain records of their reading through a log of titles or number of pages read or through a reading journal. Some teachers give the students time to share poems or excerpts from their reading.

## Fostering Silent Reading

The very best way to foster silent reading is to provide many opportunities for silent reading, such as USSR. Silent reading, however, is not a directly observable skill. It is important to teach children how to read silently through guided silent reading and provide opportunities for readers to respond to silent reading through discussion and other activities.

### Guided silent reading

Begin by guiding children to read silently or "read with their eyes." Then encourage them to think about what they read as they read it. Demonstrate the thinking that occurs during silent reading by means of a "think-aloud," in which the teacher or a fluent reader verbalizes what occurs in their minds while they read silently. For example, reading "A treasure hunt—today's the day. Come on in and you can play!" (Cauley, 1994) might lead a reader to think of questions such as: *What kind of a treasure hunt? What is the treasure? Is it a Saturday or summer vacation, because these kids should be in school? Who are they inviting to the treasure hunt?* These demonstrations guide students toward understanding how to think as they read silently—which

simply admonishing them to think does not do—and enhance their response to literature.

Perhaps most important to developing silent reading skill is helping readers develop authentic reasons, or purposes, for silent reading. Silent reading that is active and purposeful enhances understanding and response. Again, purpose in reading is not directly observable, so teachers must guide readers' understanding and development of purpose. All students learn best when they create purposes for themselves. In the same way that thinking in reading can be modeled through think-alouds, a teacher or good reader can model or talk about authentic purposes. In this way, others can understand what purposes in silent reading are and can learn to develop their own purposes. Another way of modeling purpose in silent reading is to work with a group as a whole to develop purposes in listening to a story that is read aloud, as shown here with *Splash* by Ann Jonas:

1. Introduce the book to the children by reading the title, *Splash*, and asking what they think the story will be about. Such anticipation activities will give the students something to think about as they read—a purpose.
2. Write their responses on the chalkboard and ask them to think, as they hear the story, whether the splash in the story is what they expected. This will develop their sense of listening purpose and help them to actively and purposefully listen as you read.
3. Which character in the story did you like best? Answering this question develops purpose because readers see the story through the eyes of characters they like, which focuses their attention.
4. Ask them why they think Ann Jonas wrote this book. Thinking about why the author wrote the book will allow them to compare the author's purpose in writing with their purpose in listening and will develop their understanding of purpose.

Prereading discussions and purposeful listening activities such as these connect readers and books. They will be most useful and understandable for the children when they are based on the children's own questions. (Figure 11.3 shows a web of student questions generated from the title of *All*

## FIGURE 11.3

Web of student-generated questions for the title *All Pigs Are Beautiful.*

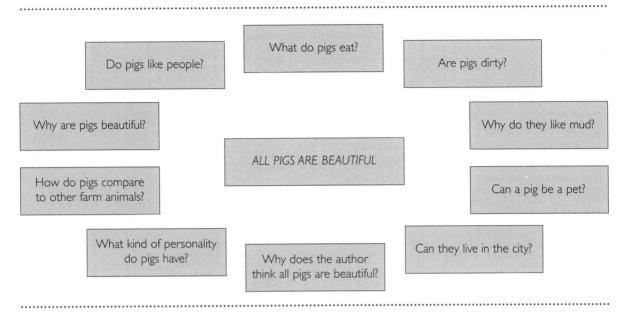

*Pigs Are Beautiful*, by Dick King-Smith.) As they begin to develop their own purposes and read silently, encourage them to read the entire story, poem, or informational piece, because they can respond more fully to a complete work than to a fragment of one. Questions and activities for silent reading should encourage this by focusing on the entire piece.

### Responding to silent reading

There are many ways for students to respond to and organize their silent reading. Class discussion is a tried-and-true method of allowing some children to respond to their reading. Prompts (discussed in Chapter Three) are useful in eliciting oral and written responses. Reflecting about a story and participating in written dialogues, and discussions develop comprehension. Participating in a community of readers, dramatizing a story, or preparing for literature circles also give opportunities for response and peer feedback. Individual response could include completing a story grammar of the book or choosing a character and explaining why this individual is their favorite.

## SUMMARY

Oral and silent reading strategies give students opportunities to experience literature and to respond to it in highly motivating situations. Both oral and silent reading strategies focus on the meaning of literature. Both are appropriate approaches to all genre. In many instances, oral and silent reading are integrated because children who are preparing for oral performances read silently in anticipation of oral reading. One of the major differences between oral and silent reading is that oral readers must think of word pronunciation and produce the appropriate sounds for a word. This makes oral reading a slower process than silent reading.

Oral reading is concerned with interpreting written literature for the appreciation of listeners, thus it is related to its artistic dimension. Oral reading serves other needs as well. For example, in the early years of schooling, children have limited reading abilities, which restrict their experiences with books, but oral reading, storytelling, choral reading, flannel board stories, dramatization, puppets, and booktalking give them a wide variety of literary experiences. Children who have experiences such as these come to books with greater understanding and appreciation. These enable children to develop an ear for the sound of written language and to understand a great deal about literature before they can read for themselves. In choosing literature for oral presentations, therefore, teachers need to consider the "sound" of the language.

Silent reading activities occur more often after children have acquired some reading abilities. An important silent reading activity is uninterrupted sustained silent reading (USSR). During USSR, students read materials of their own choosing for their own purposes. The central focus is a period of time during which everyone reads, including any adults present.

## THOUGHT QUESTIONS

1. Why are the oral strategies so motivating for children?
2. How do these activities develop literacy?
3. Which of these activities will you use most often? Why?
4. Why do some teachers rarely if ever use activities such as those presented in this chapter?
5. Write a letter to convince a teacher to use the activities described in this chapter.
6. Is reading aloud to children important? Why or why not?

## ENRICHMENT ACTIVITIES

1. Choose a poem and plan a choral reading for it that involves individual and unison reading.
2. Find *Alexander and the Terrible, Horrible, No Good, Very Bad Day* by Judith Viorst. Prepare it for oral reading. Then make a tape of your reading for your own analysis.
3. Make a story map for *The House That Jack Built* by Nadine Westcott. This map can serve as your guide for telling this story.
4. Invent five descriptive phrases for the characters in *Goldilocks*. These phrases should add color and dramatic appeal to the story when it is told aloud.
5. Choose a story for a flannel board presentation, prepare a script, and make the flannel board and the characters. Then present it to a group of children.
6. Choose a story for a puppet dramatization. Plan the script, make the puppets, practice the presentation. Present it to a group of children.
7. Listen to a recording of a professional storyteller and identify the strengths of the storyteller. Make a list of the ways that you could use this recording in the classroom.

# RECOMMENDED CHILDREN'S BOOKS

Carle, Eric. (1969). *The Very Hungry Caterpillar.* Philadelphia: Collins. (preschool–1)

   The very hungry caterpillar eats many kinds of food and gets a stomachache. Then he spins a cocoon and later becomes a beautiful butterfly.

Carlstrom, Nancy White. (1986). *Jesse Bear What Will You Wear?* Illustrated by Bruce Degan. New York: Macmillan. (preschool–2)

   A young bear's activities are described in rhymes.

Cauley, Lorinda. (1994). *Treasure Hunt.* New York: Putnam. (1–3)

   In this clever mystery for younger children, the reader must go from clue to clue to solve the mystery.

Cleaver, Vera and Bill Cleaver. (1969). *Where the Lilies Bloom.* New York: Harper & Row. (5–8)

   Mary Call is a very strong 14-year-old who takes care of her family after her father's death. The landlord wants to marry her older sister, Devola, who is "cloudy headed," and Mary Call tries to prevent the marriage.

————. (1977). *Trial Valley.* Philadelphia: Lippincott. (5–8)

   In this sequel to *Where the Lilies Bloom,* Devola and Kiser are married. They discover a child in a cage in the woods and decide to adopt him, but he prefers to stay with Mary Call.

Dickinson, Peter. (1989). *Eva.* New York: Delacorte. (6–9)

   Eva's body is destroyed in an accident, so her brain is implanted in the body of a chimpanzee. This science fiction story has a fascinating plot and characterization.

Fox, Paula. (1973). *Slave Dancer.* Illustrated by Eros Keith. New York: Bradbury. (6–10)

   Jessie is forced to play his flute on a slave ship and experiences the heartbreak of slavery.

Jacobs, Joseph. (1989). *Tattercoats.* Illustrated by Margot Tomes. New York: Putnam. (K–3)

   This is a British version of *Cinderella.* In this version Cinderella is dressed in a dirty, torn petticoat. The prince invites her, a gooseherd, and geese to a ball.

Jonas, Ann. (1995). *Splash.* New York: Greenwillow. (K–2)

   Animals and children splash in a pool while adding and subtracting.

King-Smith, Dick. (1993). *All Pigs Are Beautiful.* Illustrated by Anita Jeram. Cambridge, MA: Candlewick Press. (1–4)

   The author shares his love of pigs in this book by telling the details of their lives.

Kitt, Tamara. "So Long as There's Weather." In *Sing a Song of Popcorn,* edited by Beatrice Schenk de Regniers, Eva Moore, Mary Michaels White, and Jean Carr. New York: Scholastic. (K–6)

Lester, Julius. (1968). *To Be a Slave.* New York: Lester. (5–12)

   Descriptions of slave life based on interviews with former slaves.

Louie, Ai-Ling. (1982). *Yeh-Shen: A Cinderella Story from China.* Illustrated by Ed Young. New York: Philomel. (2–4)

   Yeh-Shen is Cinderella in this Chinese folktale. She must serve her stepmother and stepsister. Her only friend is a fish that her stepmother kills and eats, but the fish's magic is in its bones.

Martin, Bill. (1967). *Brown Bear, Brown Bear, What Do You See?* New York: Henry Holt. (preschool–1)

   This repetitive tale includes a blue horse, a yellow duck, and other animals, each of whom sees another animal or creature.

Milne, A. A. (1926). *Winnie the Pooh.* Illustrated by Ernest H. Shepard. New York: Dutton. (1–5)

   Christopher Robin is part of the adventures of Pooh and his friends.

Perrault, Charles. (1954). *Cinderella*. Illustrated by Marcia Brown. New York: Scribner's. (1–3)

The traditional European Cinderella story with the wicked stepmother and two stepsisters. Her fairy godmother gives her fine clothes for the ball and you know the rest.

Rosen, Michael. (1989). *We're Going on a Bear Hunt*. Illustrated by Helen Oxenbury. New York: Macmillan. (preschool–7)

Interesting, repetitious language encourages participation by listeners as this old chant is told.

Rounds, Glen. (1990). *I Know an Old Lady Who Swallowed a Fly*. New York: Holiday. (1–6)

In this ancient, repetitive rhyme, an old lady swallows all sorts of impossible things until she swallows a horse and "dies of course."

Shelby, Anne. (1995). *Homeplace*. Illustrated by Wendy Halperin. New York: Orchard. (1–3)

This story is about a family that from generation to generation lived in the same house for 200 years. We see the family activities and the changes in the house over the years.

Taylor, Mildred. (1976). *Roll of Thunder, Hear My Cry*. New York: Dial. (5–9)

During the 1930s it was difficult for African American families to retain their integrity and their pride when faced with overt racism and hostility.

———. (1987). *The Friendship*. New York: Scholastic. (3–adult)

The friendship between a black child and white child causes problems when they are adults.

———. (1987). *The Gold Cadillac*. Illustrated by Michael Hays. New York: Dial. (3–adult)

Driving in the segregated South was a hazardous undertaking, especially if it was a family of blacks driving an expensive car.

Viorst, Judith. (1972). *Alexander and the Terrible, Horrible, No Good, Very Bad Day*. Illustrated by Ray Cruz. New York: Atheneum. (K–6)

Alexander encounters most of the things that he dislikes in a single day. He wants to go to Australia to escape, but his mother says these things happen there too.

Westcott, Nadine. (1991). *The House That Jack Built*. New York: Little, Brown. (K–2)

This story is an example of a cumulative tale.

———. (1987). *Peanut Butter and Jelly*. New York: Dutton. (preschool–2)

This traditional play-rhyme is based on a magic chef who makes peanut butter with the assistance of elephants who mash the peanuts and stomp the grapes for jelly.

# Twelve

## KEY TERMS

board books                                    emergent literacy
developmentally appropriate

## GUIDING QUESTIONS

As you read this chapter, think about the following questions and answer them after you complete the chapter.

1. Why is literature important in the lives of young children?

2. What kinds of books should young children experience during their preschool years?

3. What is the primary caregiver's responsibility in young children's emergent literary experiences?

## OVERVIEW

The sensory data from sight, sound, and sensation spark young children's learning processes and determine in large measure the sort of people they will become. From the moment of birth, perhaps even before birth, infants begin to develop the abilities that will evolve into literacy. Children can learn to read and write as naturally as they learn to talk if the same conditions prevail (Cambourne, 1987; Jaggar, 1985; Sulzby, 1985; Clay, 1967). Thus early literacy experiences influence the entire life of individuals.

Young children's early literacy experiences shape their attitudes toward print. They are dependent on others, however, to create their literary environment and offer experiences that introduce them to the pleasures of literature. Parents are children's first and most significant teachers. Parents, primary caregivers, librarians, and grandparents play critical roles in children's literary lives (Kulleseid and Strickland, 1989; Teale and Sulzby, 1989; Baghban, 1984; Heath, 1983, 1982). Through the literary experiences parents and primary caregivers initiate, children develop **emergent literacy,** *"the reading and writing behaviors of young children that precede and develop into conventional literacy"* (Sulzby, 1991, p. 273).

The current interest in young children and emergent literacy is a natural outgrowth of recent recognition that the early years are the most important in children's lifelong development. At the same time, more and more children have primary caregivers other than their parents because approximately 50 percent of preschoolers' mothers are employed outside the home. Primary caregivers are therefore more than simply babysitters. In the best of possible worlds, they would understand child development, the values of reading and sharing books, and how to choose age-appropriate literature for young minds. They would realize that a good story nourishes minds and hearts.

# Emergent Literacy

## EARLY LITERARY EXPERIENCES

..................... ## INTRODUCTION

Books can be bridges between children and the world. Listening to stories is a delightful experience for children because this is a time when they can be close to a parent or primary caregiver and have their full attention, as well as the pleasure of a story. Dorothy Butler (1989) states, "We must find ways to reach the babies and toddlers of our world if we hope seriously to increase the ranks of the real readers" (p. 157).

The preschool years are a remarkably active period for learning about written language (Hiebert, 1988). Although learning about written language should not be confused with learning to read, educators believe that knowledge of why and how people use literacy, knowledge of story structure, attempts to make meaning of written messages, and attempts to produce meaning through writing are central to emergent literacy. These understandings emerge from learning about written language, which comes from extensive experiences with literature at an early age.

Recent research in cognitive and developmental psychology has produced different and broader conceptualizations of early literacy development than in the past. According to current theory, human beings acquire literacy in much the same way they acquire language; that is, they learn in context through interaction with a caring adult (Hiebert, 1988). The acquisition of literacy is now viewed as a social process; consequently the role of parents and primary caregivers has assumed greater importance (Greene, 1991).

The opening vignette profiled a child who had many opportunities to interact with caring adults. Her parents were readers who modeled reading behavior, read to her, and complimented her efforts to read. Printed materials abounded in her environment. Each of these elements is significant. The presence of printed materials is as important as being read to; research

demonstrates that the language and illustrations in books contribute to the development of children's cognitive and language abilities (Purcell-Gates, 1991, 1988; Sulzby, 1985). The Harvard Preschool Project clearly demonstrated the importance of children's first three years in their intellectual, emotional, and social development (White, 1988). Young children are born with the innate drive to actively seek solutions to the puzzles the world presents. "From birth the human brain is programmed to seek for meaning and to organize sensations into coherent mental structures" (Kulleseid and Strickland, 1989).

Humans search for ways to shape language that will communicate with the people in their environment. Thinking and language skills develop in an interrelated manner during the early years of life. Consider the child's language and cognitive development in this instance: A grandfather tells his three-year-old grandson to put on his shoes. After the child does so, his grandfather says, "Brian, your shoes are on the wrong feet." Brian replies, "No they aren't Grandpa; these are my feet."

............................. ## VIGNETTE

At her first birthday party, Sarah received two books, *Where's Spot?* by Eric Hill and *The Hungry Caterpillar* by Eric Carle. She unwrapped the books, turned the pages, looked at the pictures, and handed them to her mother to read aloud. As the day progressed she enjoyed "reading" her birthday

*(continued)*

cards over and over. She asked her mother to read them several times. Then she pretended to read them to her guests. These activities culminated a single year of growth and development.

From birth to three months, Sarah enjoyed nursery rhymes. Her parents, grandparents, and babysitter recited them from memory. She listened to books such as *Pat the Bunny* by Dorothy Kunhardt, *My Toys* by Dick Bruna, and *Playing* by Helen Oxenbury. Her mother and father also read traditional rhymes such as *The Wheels on the Bus* by Paul Zelinsky and did the accompanying hand motions with her. She appeared to recognize the rhythm of language in her favorites and laughed when anyone started chanting familiar rhymes. She owned many books and accompanied her mother and father, who are avid readers, to the library regularly.

Between four and nine months, Sarah began to handle books herself; her parents gave her board books printed on cardboard. She enjoyed other books as well. Her favorite was *Fish Eyes* by Lois Ehlert, which went where she went and was read over and over at her request. Her other favorites included *Brown Bear, Brown Bear What do You See?* and *Polar Bear, Polar Bear What do You Hear?* by Bill Martin and *Max's Breakfast* by Rosemary Wells. When family members read to her, they pointed to the pictures and identified them. Her parents and primary caregiver often gave Sarah books to read when she was riding in her car seat.

At 11 months, Sarah began "reading" her books to other people. Her idea of reading was to turn the pages and babble. Sarah often saw her parents, her grandparents, and her caregiver reading. Her playmate, Adam, who was nine months older, enjoyed books too. She saw books, newspapers, and magazines in her home, the caregiver's home, and the homes that she visited. She observed her parents reading books, magazines, newspapers, cookbooks, home repair manuals, and gardening books. The adults around her have also called attention to her name written on birthday cards and Christmas cards. She has seen her mother and father write notes and letters and has gone to the mailbox and the post office with family members. Sarah started scribbling with crayons, magic markers, and pencils as soon as she learned not to eat them. At the age of one year, Sarah had a joyful concept of literacy.

## THE VALUE OF EARLY LITERARY EXPERIENCE

During the early months of life, for the child who is read to, literature provides a rich source of language from which the brain takes in a lasting repertoire of sounds and nuances of the native language (Healy, 1990). The growth and development of children's thinking and language skills are enhanced through appropriate, informal experiences (Elkind, 1987; Graves, 1987; Hymes, 1987). Early experiences with literature develop children's ability to apprehend meaning. For example, Voss (1988) observed her young son's experiences with literature and noticed that his consistent experiences with literature led him to understand that letters and words hold messages and the messages should make sense. He learned that words should fit in context, which indicates that he used language knowledge derived from literature to anticipate words. By the age of three his experiences with books caused him to expect the printed label on a jar of applesauce to hold a message. Sulzby (1985) found that meaning was a factor in young children's retelling of their favorite stories. In retelling these stories, they did not merely memorize words, but used their own words, which deviated from the original text, showing that they were not merely mimicking what they had heard but were deriving meaning from the story and internalizing it.

Language experiences enable children to sort out the words, sounds, and patterns of language. They learn valuable language skills—the patterns and rhythms of language—from listening to and chanting nursery rhymes (Healy, 1990). Listening to many books teaches story patterns, which are very important in all aspects of learning and thinking (Healy, 1990). In the book *Brown Bear, Brown*

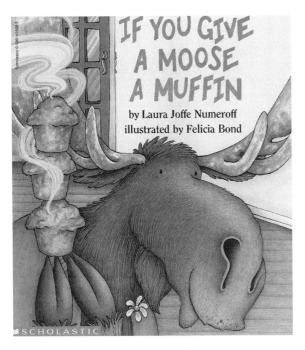

*If you give a moose a muffin, one thing
just naturally leads to another.*

*Bear, What Do You See?* the language pattern is cumulative. The first page reads *Brown Bear, Brown Bear, what do you see?* The response on the next page reads *I see a red bird looking at me.* The book develops and repeats this pattern throughout. In Laura Numeroff's *If You Give a Moose a Muffin*, readers encounter a circle story, one that ends at the same place that it began, and also a cause-and-effect pattern. Mirra Ginsburg patterns the circle story *The Chick and the Duckling* around a chick's efforts to do the same things as his friend the duckling, whose efforts are successful until the duckling swims. Children internalize common story patterns that are heard over and over again.

Literature helps young children solve language and cognitive puzzles. Young children seek to communicate meaning and have the innate capacity to make meaning. They do not merely imitate their elders when they talk, but instead create patterns of speech and thought and experiment with them until their language expresses their thoughts (Kulleseid and Strickland, 1989). Immersing children in a steady stream of language augments their language proficiency. Telling and reading stories to them and expanding on characters, events, and ideas they encounter immerses children in language, thus enriching their language and cognitive repertoire.

Listening to stories, telling stories, and conversing all help children learn that language should make sense, as well as helping them learn the words and sentences that express their thoughts. Between the ages of three and six, children recognize the difference between formal and informal language: when asked to "read" a familiar storybook, they produce formal speech rather than conversational speech (Pappas and Brown, 1987; Sulzby, 1985).

Children who learn to read early consistently exhibit certain characteristics (Kulleseid and Strickland, 1989; Clarke, 1976; Durkin, 1966):

- They hear stories from an early age.
- They live in homes that provide exposure to all kinds of reading materials and pictures.
- They see parents or caretakers reading regularly, giving them examples of reading and pleasure in reading.
- They have opportunities to talk about books, reading, and pictures with adults.
- They can choose books they want to hear and look at.

## Success in School

Literary activities afford children the interactions with speaking, listening, reading, and writing that are catalysts to language and cognitive development. Sustained experiences with books develop children's vocabulary and sense of story structure, both of which are significant factors in emergent literacy (Teale, 1981). Specific experiences with literature closely related to reading appear to have the greatest impact on emergent literacy (Mason, 1984). Parents who read to children develop their comprehension processes through discussing books and encouraging children to ask questions about books. Preschoolers ask their parents a wide variety of questions after hearing stories, ranging from story meaning and word meaning (the most frequent questions) to characters, events, story line, motives, printed word forms, letters, authors, book titles, and the act of reading (Yaden, Smolkin, and Conlon, 1989). Thus early experiences with language have profound, long-term effects on school achievement.

The impact of early literary experiences continues into the early years of school. The most significant factor in school success is hearing stories read aloud at home, before school entry age (Wells, 1986). In addition, teachers who increase the amount of storybook reading in low-socioeconomic kindergartens develop students who have greater story comprehension, attend to picture clues more frequently, infer causal relationships better, and tell more connected stories (Feitelson, Kita, and Goldstein, 1986).

Wells (1986) reports that the experiences children have with books by the age of five are directly related to reading comprehension at age seven and again at age 11. Children who hear stories regularly from an early age and whose homes are filled with reading material are ready for the literacy tasks of the school (Cullinan, Greene, and Jaggar, 1990; Smith, 1989). Morrow (1988) finds that four-year-old children who are read to for 10 weeks become better and more frequent question askers, give more interpretive responses to the stories they read, and respond more often to print and the story structure. Children who have occasions to listen and look while someone reads stories learn there is a relationship between printed and spoken words. Furthermore, children from book-oriented homes have greater interest in print, because their experiences with stories have taught them the enjoyment they can derive from books (Holdaway, 1979; Meek, 1982).

## Cognitive Development

Immersing children in literature can begin the day they are born. Although their ability to listen attentively is limited, children who are read to during the early months of life develop attentiveness to stories, rhymes, and songs sooner than those who have not been read to (Strickland and Morrow, 1990). These early experiences with print and language are the beginning of a lifelong process of developing literacy (Teale and Sulzby, 1989).

Print awareness develops as young children see their parents reading labels, cereal boxes, telephone books, magazines, and so forth. Through these experiences, they realize reading and writing are important activities that are used and valued in their homes. Exploring books enables them to discover the relationship between the print in books and the visual symbols they see around them (Smith, 1994). Exposure to and personal explorations of books are more important to young children than maturation in their ability to make sense out of print (Lundsteen, 1986). Young children learn to expect written language to make sense and to have predictable structure from their experiences (Newman, 1985). When an adult shares a book with a child and asks, "What do you think will happen?", the adult is demonstrating the cognitive process—encouraging prediction, responding, wondering, and looking for more information (Greene, 1991).

During the first months of life, children are concerned with adapting to their new environment and bonding with the primary caregiver. They spend much of their time sleeping, crying, and babbling. At this stage, infants should have soft books, soft alphabet blocks, and caregivers who read or chant rhymes and stories to them. Librarians can help parents and caregivers by making available both books on parenting and children's literature to share with infants—Mother Goose rhymes, books that show patterns, lullabies, and books that feature pictures of objects.

According to the Swiss psychologist Jean Piaget, children grow in developmental stages, progressing from the concrete to the schematic to the symbolic. He cites extensive evidence that infants learn by handling concrete objects. Providing them with books to handle at these early ages, therefore, is important to their development (Piaget and Inhelder, 1969).

Infants are also interested in the sounds of words, which expands into an interest in the meaning of words between 7 and 14 months. At this age, their vocabulary is limited, but they understand more words than they can produce. Parents of young children who read to them daily, who tell stories, who are receptive to their children's questions, who respond to children's pretend "reading," and who are readers themselves create a warm, literate environment that enhances their understanding.

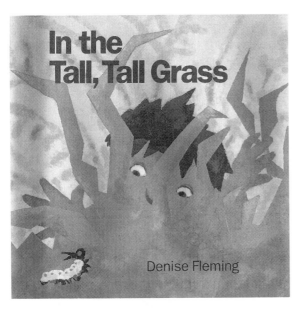

*This backyard tour in* In the Tall, Tall Grass, *is one no child will want to miss*

Children who are 15 to 24 months in age are interested in taking things apart, in action toys, and in reading pictures in books. They often engage in reading-like behavior by pretending to read stories from their books and enjoy listening to music and moving to rhythm (Greene, 1991). Popular books for this age are *The Very Hungry Caterpillar* by Eric Carle, *Have You Seen My Duckling?* by Nancy Tafuri, and *Max's Bath* by Rosemary Wells.

At about the age of two, children progress to Piaget's preoperational stage of development and enjoy books with rhythmic chants and action that invite their participation, such as Helen Oxenbury's *All Fall Down*. The preoperational stage extends to age seven, subdivided into two stages, the preconceptual stage and the intuitive stage. In the preconceptual stage (two to four years), children possess a subjective logic, classifying things on the basis of a single attribute. For instance, they associate movement with life, so they believe that moving things are alive. Children in the preconceptual stage of cognitive development can follow simple plot lines such as those in simple picture books and folktales. In Molly Bang's *Yellow Ball*, a yellow ball rolls into the water and begins a journey that can lead preconceptual

children to see objects from different perspectives. Denise Fleming's *In the Tall, Tall Grass* invites children to view the world from the perspective of a caterpillar crawling in tall grass. A spider is the main character in Eric Carle's simple story *The Very Busy Spider*, which tells about a spider, her web, and a fly.

According to Piaget, children enter the second half of the preconceptual stage of development, the intuitive stage, around the age of four and continue in this stage until about seven. During the intuitive stage, they acquire a full language system, although it will be further refined during the elementary school years. In this stage, youngsters are aware of the world around them and are less egocentric than in earlier stages. It is during this stage that children begin to explore and discover their lifelong interests. This is the ideal time to expose them to a wide range of literature types and subjects. *Corduroy* by Don Freeman is a longstanding favorite with this age group. Ezra Jack Keats' *The Snowy Day* shares a boy's delight in the winter's first snowfall. *Up in the Air* by Myra Cohn Livingston celebrates the excitement of a child's first airplane trip. A brother and sister explore New York City in Lore Segal's *Tell Me a Mitzi*. All of these books are appropriate for this developmental stage.

The general characteristics of children's development from birth through age five and developmentally appropriate literature for these ages are summarized in Table 12.1.

## EFFECT OF ENVIRONMENT ON EMERGENT LITERACY

Three major environments affect children's development: the home; the daycare, preschool, or school the child attends; and the external environment, which includes the parent's work, the neighborhood, and the church (Bronfenbrenner, 1986). Each of these environments may enhance or detract from emergent literacy. For instance, children who live in a neighborhood with a public library may have greater access to books and library programs. Children whose environments offer many opportunities to learn about written language enter school with much knowledge

## The Benefits of Literature for Young Children

Choosing appropriate literature and sharing it effectively with children gives them the benefits of literature. They learn that reading and writing are prominent parts of their world and that these abilities will help them accomplish many things. Meaningful experiences with literature help children learn:

1. To enjoy, appreciate, and respond to fine literature (Kiefer, 1988).

    *The Owl and the Pussycat* by Edward Lear and *Old Mother Hubbard and Her Wonderful Dog* by James Marshall are excellent stories for first literary experiences.

2. To understand story structure and story parts such as beginnings, middles, endings, plot, character, and setting (Morrow, 1985; Pellegrini and Galda, 1982; Brown, 1975).

    Books such as *Max's Dragon Shirt* by Rosemary Wells and *Piggies* by Audrey Wood clearly illustrate story structures and story parts.

3. To interpret literature and to understand what the author is saying to readers (Roser and Martinez, 1985).

    In *Abuela* by Arthur Dorros, children can relate to the warm relationship between grandchild and grandmother. In *In the Tall, Tall Grass* by Denise Fleming, children learn to view the world from a caterpillar's perspective.

4. To communicate more effectively using sounds, vocabulary, and language from literature (Solsken, 1985).

    Kevin Henkes shows the importance of a name in *Chrysanthemum*.

5. To broaden their understanding of different cultures and individual differences (Sims, 1982).

    Books such as *Amazing Grace* by Mary Hoffman and *At the Crossroads* by Rachel Isadora extend children's understanding of cultures and individuals.

6. To build interests and encourage selection of related books (Hepler and Hickman, 1982).

    Children who have heard *Max's Dragon Shirt* will probably want to read more stories about the white boy bunny, Max. Those who enjoy *Piggies* will want to read more books by the same author.

7. To recognize sequence.

    In *Mouse Count*, Ellen Walsh demonstrates counting; in *Cookie's Week*, Cindy Ward demonstrates sequence of days.

8. To understand and appreciate different forms of literature (fiction, nonfiction, and poetry).

    Incorporating all kinds of stories, poems, and informational materials in read-aloud sessions develops this understanding and appreciation.

9. To enhance their development in all areas: social, emotional, linguistic, cognitive, and physical (Schlager, 1978; Hepler and Hickman, 1982; Glazer, 1986).

    *Bath Time for John* by Graham explores the laughter and fun of splashing in a toddler's bath. In *A Balloon for Grandad* by Nigel Gray, Sam feels upset when his balloon disappears, but comforts himself with the idea that it is headed in the direction of North Africa, where his grandad lives.

10. To introduce a wide variety of experiences and specific facts about the world from information in stories, rhymes, and songs.

    Books like *The Very Hungry Caterpillar* by Eric Carle and *Trucks* by Byron Barton take children beyond their daily experiences. They can learn about scarecrows in *The Tale of Peter Rabbit* by Beatrix Potter.

*(continued)*

11. To develop children's cultural literacy.

Nursery rhymes such as *Michael Forman's Mother Goose* introduce children to such well-known literary figures as Mother Goose, Little Boy Blue, and Mary, Mary Quite Contrary.

12. To create a bond with parents and caregivers.

Although any book read with a child helps develop a bond, books such as *Max's Bath* by Rosemary Wells and *Goodnight Moon* by Margaret Wise Brown create especially warm feelings.

*The mice outwit the snake in this story as they "uncount" themselves one at a time and escape from the jar where the snake has trapped them.*

about literacy incidentally derived from their environment (Sulzby, 1991).

## The Family Environment

When parents hold a little one in their lap to share a nursery rhyme, a story, or a poem they create a pleasurable social event. These special moments of closeness will remain with them both for a lifetime. For children in a literate society, the foundations for learning to read and write are established in the home. A literate home environment is created by parents who talk and read to their infants and look at books with them. Parents are indispensable in this process because they are the ones who go to the library, purchase books, and read them aloud.

Parents of early readers tend to be habitual readers themselves (Strickland and Morrow, 1990). Their children respond to books, chant familiar words and phrases, and retell familiar stories without assistance.

Researchers investigating home storybook reading have identified a number of interactive behaviors between adults and young children that lead to positive effects from family reading. Adults who question, praise, offer information, discuss, share responses, and relate concepts to life experiences are encouraging cognitive and language development in children (Strickland and Morrow, 1990). Most of all, reading to and with young children gives parents and children opportunities to have fun together—to interact, thus building their interest in reading.

## TABLE 12.1

Child development characteristics and appropriate literature.

| Age | Characteristics | Appropriate Literature |
|---|---|---|
| Birth to 6 months | • cries, coos, and gurgles<br>• human voice comforts<br>• attends to musical toys and mobiles | • rhythmic language<br>• rhymes, songs, and chants<br>• Mother Goose |
| 6 months to 9 months | • laughs<br>• repeats syllables (da da, ma ma)<br>• grasps books | • rhythmic language<br>• rhymes, songs, and chants<br>• simple board books<br>• repetitive books with one object per page<br>• Mother Goose, traditional songs |
| 9 months to 18 months | • responds to words<br>• uses holophrases (one word that represents larger unit) such as "juice" for "I want some juice."<br>• plays peek-a-boo<br>• points to objects<br>• waves bye-bye | • simple stories that include family and pets<br>• stories that relate to daily life<br>• cumulative tales<br>• books with objects child can point to |
| 18 months to 24 months | • vocabulary of 50–400 words<br>• uses 2- and 3-word phrases | • all of the stories previously mentioned<br>• predictable stories |
| 24 months to 36 months | • more language is comprehended than is used<br>• uses some pronouns<br>• uses 3- and 4-word phrases | • all of the stories previously mentioned<br>• counting and alphabet books<br>• somewhat longer stories<br>• same story repeated<br>• several stories at once |
| 36 months to 48 months | • understands about 1,000 words<br>• forms sentences and questions<br>• language system complete | • all of the stories previously mentioned<br>• dramatizing<br>• puppets<br>• retelling stories to others |
| 48 months to 60 months | • understands about 1,500 to 1,800 words<br>• names objects, colors, number, and letters<br>• aware of sounds and letters | • all of the stories previously mentioned<br>• "reading" to self<br>• dramatizing<br>• recognizes hero and villain<br>• compares self to characters |

Children who grow up in literate homes or attend preschool programs that value literacy have definite advantages over children who lack these experiences. The fortunate ones have heard many stories, looked at books, listened to audiotapes, watched videos, socialized with other children, explored their environment, conversed with adults and children; in short, they have developed the language, thinking, and physical abilities, the knowledge and experience, and the interests and motivation that prepare them for entering kindergarten.

### Writing

Writing is an aspect of family literacy. Families who read to their children also provide the materials and motivation for children to experiment with writing (Teale and Sulzby, 1989). Children who see their parents writing letters and notes become aware of the importance of writing in their lives and are prepared to view writing as an understandable tool once they enter school. Moreover, children who have been read to extensively before entering school use language that has features of written language when composing stories to accompany wordless picture books (Purcell-Gates, 1988). "In these and other ways, young children are ushered into the world of literacy, viewing reading and writing as aspects of a much larger system for accomplishing goals" (Teale and Sulzby, 1989, p. 3). Both reading and writing are processes that develop through continued use. Children learn about writing through experimenting with various writing implements. They enjoy scribbling and creating pictures with crayons. Writing (scribbling) messages and reading them to others extends their interest in literacy.

### Love of literature

Children who are around people who love books learn to appreciate books themselves. Young children need to see books displayed, as well as seeing adults and other children enjoying books (Taylor, 1983). Children acquire literacy concepts and skills when given the opportunity to see adults using literacy for work and pleasure (Hiebert, 1980). Books, magazines, newspapers, and writing materials should therefore be a prominent part of children's surroundings, and the setting should foster enjoyment of these materials.

Many parents who themselves love literature do not realize its importance to infants and toddlers. They realize that books will become influential in their children's lives when they are older without understanding that literacy begins at birth. "It's amazing that children's learning to read is considered important, but children's *books* often are not. Plastic toys sell better than books. Yet if children's minds are important, so are their books" (Hearne, 1990, p. 7). Parents and grandparents emphasize the expense of books for children, although they do not hesitate to spend three times as much for a toy that may be cast aside in a few

days. But children return time and time again to fine literature when they have the chance.

## The Preschool, Daycare, and School Environment

Young children who are taken out of their home in the early months of life and entrusted to outside caretakers depend on these significant people for experiences their parents would otherwise provide. In the best situations, parents and caretakers work together to create a secure environment for these little ones. Books they enjoy can bridge the home environment to daycare. Ideally, daycare centers and preschool classrooms become communities in which home experiences are valued and used as building blocks for language and literacy development (Teale and Sulzby, 1989). Early childhood teachers and primary caregivers who provide many opportunities for children to enjoy books are planting the seeds that can develop into a lifelong fondness and appreciation for literature.

As arrangements for care outside the home for young children have become more prevalent due to parental employment, the programs of these various facilities have been scrutinized more carefully, raising awareness of the consequence of young children's environment and activities both at home and outside the home. The adults who care for children during the early years of life are responsible for their most important years—the years when they acquire language competence, cognitive abilities, social skills, emotional development, and physical skills. This growing recognition of the importance of the early years in children's lifelong learning means that all agencies and people concerned must become knowledgeable about young children, their literature, and appropriate literary experiences. There is considerable agreement among authorities that the quality of life and emergent literacy are enhanced when parents, caregivers, and preschool teachers provide young children with books and a wide variety of activities with books (Cullinan, Greene, and Jaggar, 1990). When literature and literary activities are available, children have incentives for language experimentation, dramatic play, singing, and chanting.

"The ideal environment for children to become engaged with books includes an inviting library or book center with soft cushions to sit on, stuffed animals to hold or lean on, a book shelf with a variety of choices changed frequently, a rocking chair or teacher's lap for cuddling in, and finally, a well-prepared, enthusiastic teacher who thoroughly enjoys books and reading" (Ford, 1991). The setting should also encourage children to explore books individually and with friends in a quiet uninterrupted place in the classroom. Choosing the books to place in these settings is an important task, discussed later in this chapter in the section Selecting and Evaluating Literature for Young Children and in Chapter 3.

Due to the growing recognition of emergent literacy and child development as crucial stages in a child's life, 28 states currently fund or have committed funds to prekindergarten programs (O'Neil, 1988). Teachers and caretakers of young children are teaching children and guiding them in ways that once were the province of the parents. The increasingly important role of these adults in the lives of little children is accompanied by greater responsibilities as well, since parents are relying more and more on them to both select literature for their children to read in the classroom and to suggest literature that parents should have at home.

### Early childhood programs

Early childhood education differs widely from program to program because there is a lack of uniformity in programs and personnel preparation. The National Academy of Early Childhood Programs, sponsored by the National Association for the Education of Young Children (NAEYC), is attempting to alleviate this by accrediting programs. In order to obtain accreditation, the program must promote children's learning by encouraging the use of age-appropriate literature and language arts experiences in the classroom on a daily basis (Ford, 1991). The accreditation standards require that caregivers provide a broad cross-section of children's books that includes multicultural, nonstereotypical picture books to assist children in learning about the cultural diversity of society as well as the traditional books found in childcare centers.

### The External Environment

Children's experiences are also related to the neighborhood environment, their parents' work situation, and their church. Neighborhoods with public libraries offer children opportunities to borrow books and many of them offer story hours and other programs for young children. Bookstores sometimes sponsor visits by children's authors and story reading programs. Natural science museums, art museums, and similar institutions offer stimulating activities and exhibits for children of all ages. Parents and caregivers can use current events as incentives for reading. When the circus comes to town, children are motivated to listen to and read circus stories. Local newspapers and magazines such as *Parents* magazine often include book lists and book reviews to guide parents and teachers in selecting good books. Some employers bring speakers into the workplace to help parents realize the importance of literature and of reading to children. Ministers in some churches and Sunday school teachers often include storytelling and children's literature in their presentations.

Frequent visits to neighborhood libraries for books and story hours stimulate children's interest in books. Moreover, many children's bookstores sponsor story hours, authors' visits, and related programs.

### Libraries and media centers

Librarians have a major role in helping to create a literate environment for young children. They serve as resources for children, their parents, and their caregivers by sharing enjoyable books with them. They offer programs for parents and children that introduce them to fine literature and ways of appreciating that literature. Moreover, they educate adults about childrearing and literature on that topic.

The importance of educating the adults who care for young children is being recognized in many quarters of society today. One of the libraries addressing this need is the New York Public Library, whose Children's Services created the Early Childhood Resource and Information Center (ECRIC) for children from birth to seven years and their caregivers. To develop this program, which is considered a model for other libraries, Children's Services obtained the support of a Carnegie Foundation grant and the assistance of New York University and planned a conference focusing on developing a knowledge base from which to plan and implement services to young children (Cullinan, Greene, and Jaggar, 1990). Conference participants heard authorities discuss young children and their books and became familiar with emergent literacy and research related to this topic. As a result of this experience they developed criteria for selecting print and nonprint materials and explored effective ways of working with children and caregivers from diverse populations.

## SELECTING AND EVALUATING LITERATURE FOR YOUNG CHILDREN

When confronted with rows of shelves containing books, how can parents, teachers, and librarians choose the right book, the one that will make a hit with a three-year-old? Many people select books they enjoyed as children and are dismayed when children of today don't enjoy them. While certain books like *Where the Wild Things Are* and *Goodnight Moon* are favorites of every generation, there are many newer books that children of today can also enjoy. "Evaluating children's books is a matter of practice as well as taste. The best way to start is with a few touchstone titles, surefire suggestions that rarely miss" (Hearne, 1990, p. 26). The following guidelines are helpful in selecting and evaluating literature for young children:

1. Choose **developmentally appropriate** *literature that matches the developmental level of the children.*
   a. For infants: Cloth or **board books** that *focus on single objects or simple rhymes and chants are appropriate for beginning literary experiences.*
   b. For toddlers: "Point and say" books and books with clear pictures of familiar objects as books will be enjoyed.
   c. For preschoolers: Books with characters, plots, and situations with which children can identify are appropriate.

*This classic is a good first book to share with a child.*

2. Find books with a multicultural attitude toward society that cultivate appreciation for the individual worth of every person, since children develop attitudes about other cultures based on their perception of their parents, teachers, or caregivers' views. (A good resource to check is *Anti-Bias Curriculum: Tools for Empowering Young Children* by L. Derman-Sparks and the ABC Task Force.)

3. Consider the children's experiences to determine whether the situations and characters are familiar to them. For example, Mercer Mayer's *There's Something in My Attic* is a story about being afraid of nightmares and noises, a situation with which many children will identify.

4. Consider the story and setting from a young child's perspective. Is the story interesting to children? There are books *about* children that are not developmentally appropriate *for* children; these books are sentimental favorites more suited to adults.

5. Locate simple stories with plots, characters, climax, and a satisfying conclusion that help children understand the ways stories work. *Rosie's Walk* by Pat Hutchins has a simple plot: a fox follows a hen around the barnyard and is repeatedly foiled when he tries to catch her. Rosie escapes without ever realizing she was in danger.

## THERE'S SOMETHING IN MY ATTIC

**written and illustrated by MERCER MAYER**

*A nightmare in the attic may look and sound scary, but it's no match for a brave girl with a lasso.*

For lists of touchstone books for children and references for adults to consult, see the special lists at the end of the Recommended Children's Books section in this chapter.

## CLASSROOM ACTIVITIES TO ENHANCE LITERARY EXPERIENCE

Initially, children are attracted to storytelling and story reading because these are social activities that they enjoy with their parents. They respond to the parent's voice and may find it calming. Toddlers are interested in the illustrations and like to point at pictured objects and animals, as well as repeating words and phrases from the story (Yaden et al., 1989). Such interactive behavior leads children to respond with questions and comments that become

more complex over time and demonstrate more sophisticated thinking about printed text. Eventually, children remark on story content, title, setting, characters, and story events (Morrow, 1988; Roser and Martinez, 1985). Activities with literature can build on these responses.

### Oral Reading

Since young children cannot read for themselves, hearing stories read is their primary avenue for accessing literature; therefore read-aloud activities are central to literary experience both at home and in the preschool. Some guidelines for reading aloud to children include:

1. The book can be read at a single sitting not longer than 10 to 15 minutes.
2. All of the children in the group must be able to see and enjoy the pictures.
3. The words are interesting, with distinctive sounds and repetition to captivate the listener.
4. Young children frequently request to have their favorite books read again and again. This is a valuable experience for them. Some children will ask to hear a favorite book 30 or 40 times (not all at once, though!).
5. Introduce each book in the same way that you would a new toy or game. Connect story content to what children already know and to their experiences.
6. Encourage children to ask questions and discuss the book. Respond to their questions. Compare the books to their own experiences and other books they have read.
7. Provide children with browsing time. They should have constant, free access to books. Place books where children can easily pick them up and look at them.
8. Encourage dramatic play. Provide a chest of dress-up clothing, puppets, and art materials for dramatization purposes.
9. Encourage children to retell stories or to read them to others or to their toys or pets.
10. Encourage children to make up their own stories and tell them.
11. Refer to Chapter 10 for ideas regarding oral literature experiences.

## Big Books

At the emergent literacy stage, literature is often integrated through shared book experiences based on big books. These are enlarged books that are placed so the children can see the print as the teacher models reading, pointing to each word while reading aloud. When children become familiar with the story, they can join in by predicting the upcoming words and phrases. The teacher may ask students to point out specific words or phrases. Soon, the children "read" the big books from memory (Slaughter, 1993).

The big books for emergent reading should have simple, highly predictable language. Cumulative tales and stories with repeated phrases, words, and refrains are especially useful in the early stages of literacy. These books give children the foundation for language-related activities that help them grow into literacy. Students who have several opportunities to read *Brown Bear, Brown Bear* by Bill Martin, Jr., can compose their own version of this story with animals of their choice, and these stories can be written on charts for more big book reading. Big book activities lead naturally into choral reading, dramatization, role playing, music, and art.

Big books can be purchased from publishers or made by the class: The teacher prints the text from the children's own stories or favorite books, and the children illustrate it. Big books can be created from predictable books, rhymes, riddles, camp songs, finger plays, jump-rope rhymes, or anything else imaginable. Laminate the big books to preserve them for the classroom literature collection. A list of predictable books that are perfect for big books is shown in the Recommended Children's Books section at the end of the chapter.

## Recordings, Films and Video, and Toys

Technology is growing so rapidly that many sources of stories are now available to young children. Although viewing or listening to electronic media is no substitute for a personal read-aloud, it can expand children's literary repertoire. In addition, toys, puzzles, games, puppets, dramatic play props, chalkboards, paper bags, boxes, and paints are useful materials to encourage children's response to literature. Most public libraries can provide up-to-date information about the latest technology available and have such materials available for check-out. A few examples are listed in the special book lists at the end of this chapter.

UNIT
SUGGESTIONS

## 12.1 The five senses

### Week One—Hearing

1. Introduce the senses unit and identify the senses to be studied.

2. Discuss deafness. Use a model or poster to show the ear. Use disposable ear plugs to simulate deafness. After the children experience deafness, discuss the problems and have them dictate their feelings to create a language experience chart.

3. Take a listening walk and listen for sounds. Have children dictate lists of sounds they heard.

4. Conduct a black box experiment by placing ob-jects such as paper clips, peas, jelly beans, gummy bears, and other small objects in separate boxes, one box for each pair of children. Ask the each pair to shake their box to determine what is in it. After each group has decided and reported what they think is in their box, open the boxes and share the contents.

5. Record each of the children's speaking voices and see if they can recognize their own voices. Use a baby monitor to have children listen to one another from a different room. Compare the sounds on the monitor with the recording. Listen to commercially prepared recordings of music and stories.

6. Provide children with rhythm instruments and have them imitate the sounds they hear. Tap out sounds and rhythms, ring bells, and use rhythm instruments to make interesting sounds. After they understand the concept, let different children lead in creating sounds for the other children to follow in a variation of Follow the Leader.

7. Have the children draw their favorite sound.

8. Use books from the list at the end of this activity.

### Week Two—Seeing

1. Introduce seeing and the eyes. Discuss things the children like to see and have them draw pictures of their favorite things to see.

2. Blindfold half of the children and pair a blindfolded child with a seeing child. The children who can see guide their partners for a while, then switch places. Discuss their feelings about not being able to see and the most difficult aspect of it. Then make a chart of these ideas.

3. Use *Handtalk Alphabet* or *Handtalk School* (Miller and Ancona, 1991) to teach the children to sign some words. Invite a deaf person or a teacher of the deaf to come to the class and demonstrate signing as a form of communication.

4. Play blind man's bluff.

5. Invite a blind person who has a seeing-eye dog to visit the class. Discuss the dog's training. (Find out ahead of time what the rules are regarding touching, feeding, speaking to, or playing with the dog and impress these on the children.)

6. Line up objects on a table. After the children observe the objects, have them close their eyes and take one object away. See who recognizes which object is gone. Repeat the game, taking away two, then three, and so forth. This teaches observation.

7. Sort objects by color (jelly beans, buttons, toys, crayons, blocks).

8. Have the children vote for their favorite color and make a bar graph of everyone's favorite colors.

9. Read books each day from this chapter's bibliography.

### Week Three—Touch

1. Introduce the sense of touch. Gather several objects that can be recognized through texture (satin, velvet, sandpaper), shape (ball, block, toy), or both texture and shape (lemon, orange, apple). Put each object in a separate bag and have the children reach in and touch the items, trying to identify them. Discuss texture and shape and identify the sense that helped them most.

2. Make a collection of objects similar to those above for the children to sort. Let them think about different ways that the objects can be sorted: according to roundness, softness, hardness, and so on.

3. Let the students finger paint. Discuss the paint's texture and using the sense of touch to paint.

4. Use a stamp pad and white paper for each child to make a thumbprint. Then add to the print with crayon to make a thumbprint picture.

5. Choose finger plays from a favorite book, then have children make up one for the sense of touch.

6. Use plaster of Paris and paper plates to make plaster casts of the children's hands.

7. Read books from the list at the end of this activity.

## Week Four—Taste

1. Introduce taste by having the children tell about their favorite taste.

2. Introduce the words *salty, sweet, sour,* and *bitter.* Gather several items with these tastes, such as pickles, lemons, pretzels, potato chips, marshmallows, chocolate kisses, and baking chocolate and let the children taste them. Make a chart of the categories and let children draw pictures of the items that belong in each of the four taste types.

3. Blindfold children and have them taste various foods and identify them. List all of the foods identified.

4. Read Eric Carle's *The Very Hungry Caterpillar,* then have a fruit-tasting party. Each child can bring fruit to taste. After tasting the individual fruits, mix them to make a fruit salad.

5. Make a bulletin board of favorite fruits.

6. Read Lois Ehlert's *Growing Vegetable Soup* and have a vegetable-tasting party. After tasting the vegetables, mix them together and make vegetable soup. (The book has a recipe.)

7. Make posters featuring their favorite vegetables. Exhibit the posters in the corridor.

8. Read books from the list at the end of this activity.

## Week Five—Smell

1. Introduce smell by discussing favorite smells. Use soap, shampoo, bubble bath, popcorn, and other common things to smell.

2. Obtain scratch and sniff stickers for the children to scratch and identify. List the different smells.

3. Put extracts like vanilla, lemon, peppermint, orange, and others on cotton balls and place the cotton balls in plastic containers. The children can smell, identify, and label the different odors.

4. Use boiling sachets on a hot plate (out of reach) to create different odors in the classroom.

5. Have children draw or cut out pictures of their favorite smells. Make a collage using all of the children's pictures.

6. Read books from the following suggested reading list.

## Reading List

- Brown, Ruth. (1985). *The Big Sneeze.* New York: Lothrop, Lee & Shepard.
- Carle, Eric. (1981). *The Very Hungry Caterpillar.* New York: Philomel.
- Dantzer-Rosenthal, Marya. (1986). *Some Things Are Different, Some Things Are the Same.* Morton Grove, IL: Whitman.
- Ehlert, Lois. (1987). *Growing Vegetable Soup.* New York: Harcourt Brace Jovanovich.
- Hoban, Tana. (1971). *Look Again.* New York: Macmillan.
- Hoban, Tana. (1981). *Take Another Look.* New York: Greenwillow.
- Hoban, Tana. (1978). *Is It Red? Is It Yellow? Is It Blue?* New York: Greenwillow.
- Isadora, Rachel. (1985). *I Touch.* New York: Greenwillow.
- Isadora, Rachel. (1985). *I See.* New York: Greenwillow.
- Isadora, Rachel. (1985). *I Hear.* New York: Greenwillow.
- Jeunesse, Gallimard and Pascale De Bourgoing. (1989). *Colors.* New York: Scholastic.
- Martin, Bill Jr. and John Archambault. (1986). *Here Are My Hands.* San Diego: Henry Holt.
- Peek, Merle. (1985). *Mary Wore Her Red Dress and Henry Wore His Green Sneakers.* New York: Clarion.
- Richardson, J. (1986). *What Happens When You Listen?* Riverside, NJ: Four Winds.
- Rockwell, Ann. (1986). *In the Rain.* New York: Crowell.
- Rylant, Cynthia. (1986). *Night in the Country.* New York: Bradbury.
- Stinson, Kathy. (1982) *Red Is Best.* Toronto: Annick.
- Tafuri, Nancy. (1985). *Rabbit's Morning.* New York: Greenwillow.
- Tafuri, Nancy. (1983). *Early Morning in the Barn.* New York: Greenwillow.
- Tafuri, Nancy. (1983). *All Year Long.* New York: Greenwillow.
- Yoshi. (1987). *Who's Hiding Here?* Old Tappan, NJ: Picture Book Studio.

## SUMMARY

Literacy is very important in life. Infants and young children should have many opportunities for literary experiences to develop the knowledge and abilities that will enable them to read and write later. Most young children cannot read and write in their early years, but they should have considerable exposure to print so that their emergent literacy will enable them later to develop these proficiencies. Parents and caretakers should read to children and let children see them using their reading ability in a variety of situations. The environment should include many books that children can handle. Providing children with writing materials encourages them to scribble and eventually to convey their own thoughts in writing.

Literary quality is just as important for young children's first literary experiences as for adults, but available books should be appropriately geared to their stage of development. Simple plots and satisfying conclusions are important to children in developing emergent literacy.

## THOUGHT QUESTIONS

1. What factors should be considered when selecting books for young children?
2. Describe a book (an imaginary one) that would be just right for a toddler.
3. Identify each of the three environments that affect children's development and suggest ways that the contribution of each could be improved to enhance children's development.
4. How do you think emergent literacy is related to the whole language movement?
5. Describe a preschool program that would enhance emergent literacy and fit with beginning reading instruction.

## ENRICHMENT ACTIVITIES

1. Visit a preschool or head-start center and observe the availability of books and writing materials.
2. Interview a preschool teacher or teachers. Ask them how often they read aloud to children and what books they read.
3. Create a literature unit for preschool children.
4. Create a file of books for infants, toddlers, and preschoolers.
5. Arrange to read stories to an infant, a toddler, and a preschooler. What books did they prefer?
6. Create a display or bulletin board related to children's books for use in a preschool or kindergarten.

## RECOMMENDED CHILDREN'S BOOKS

Bang, Molly. (1991). *Yellow Ball*. New York: Morrow. (preschool–2)
   This is the story of the travels of a yellow ball that bounces into the ocean.
Barton, Byron. (1985). *Trucks*. New York: Greenwillow. (preschool–2)
   This picture book is based on pictures of different types of trucks in bold colors.
Brown, Margaret Wise. (1947). *Goodnight Moon*. New York: Harper & Row. (preschool–1)
   A child says goodnight to each object in the bedroom.
Carle, Eric. (1984). *The Very Busy Spider*. New York: Philomel. (K–2)
   A spider spins a web and catches a fly in this picture book.
_____ . (1969). *The Very Hungry Caterpillar*. New York: Philomel. (preschool–1)

A tiny egg hatches into a tiny caterpillar who eats its way through all sorts of foods, such as plums and salami, and grows into a big caterpillar who spins a cocoon and on the last page emerges as a beautiful butterfly.

Carlstrom, Nancy White. (1986). *Jesse Bear What Will You Wear?* Illustrated by Bruce Degen. New York: Macmillan. (K–2)

These verses and illustrations make getting dressed and undressed fun.

Dorros, Arthur. (1991). *Abuela*. New York: Dutton. (K–3)

A little girl and her grandmother have an imaginary flight over New York.

Ehlert, Lois. (1990). *Fish Eyes*. New York: Harcourt Brace Jovanovich. (preschool–1)

This counting book is based on counting brightly colored fish and adding the number of fish to the reader to make one more.

Fleming, Denise. (1991). *In the Tall, Tall Grass*. New York: Holt. (preschool–1)

This picture book is of a caterpillar's view of the world as he crawls through the grass.

————. (1992). *Lunch*. New York: Holt. (K–2)

A young mouse has lunch and gets different colors of juice all over his clothing.

Forman, Michael. (1981). *Michael Forman's Mother Goose*. New York: Harcourt Brace Jovanovich. (preschool–1)

Forman's illustrations of the traditional Mother Goose rhymes decorate this book.

Freeman, Don. (1968). *Corduroy*. New York: Viking. (preschool–K)

This is a well-known story about a stuffed bear who searches for his lost button and finds a friend.

Gag, Wanda. (1928). *Millions of Cats*. New York: Coward McCann. (preschool–2)

The old man and woman in this story could not choose just one cat, so they ended up with hundreds, thousands, millions, billions, and trillions of cats. The cats solved the problem.

Ginsburg, Mirra. (1972). *The Chick and the Duckling*. Illustrated by Jose Aruego and Ariane Dewey. New York: Macmillan. (preschool–1)

The chick discovers that he can do everything the duckling does except swim.

Gray, Nigel. (1988). *A Balloon for Grandad*. Illustrated by Jane Ray. New York: Orchard. (K–2)

Sam is saddened when his red balloon blows away, but his father points out that the balloon is headed toward his grandfather's home.

Henkes, Kevin. (1991). *Chrysanthemum*. New York: Greenwillow. (K–2)

A young mouse is disturbed by her long name when she goes to school, but she learns to appreciate it.

Hill, Eric. (1980). *Where's Spot?* New York: Putnam. (preschool)

Spot the dog is lost. The reader plays peek-a-boo, hunting for Spot by lifting the flaps on each page until Spot is found on the last page.

Hoffman, Mary. (1991). *Amazing Grace*. New York: Dial. (1–4)

A girl named Grace loves pretending and hopes to play the role of Peter Pan, but is told that she cannot because she is a girl and she is black.

Hutchins, Pat. (1968). *Rosie's Walk*. New York: Macmillan. (K–2)

Rosie the hen goes for a walk around the barnyard, followed by a sly fox. The fox gets what he deserves and Rosie never realizes that she was in danger.

Isadora, Rachel. (1991). *At the Crossroads*. New York: Greenwillow. (2–4)

South African children celebrate their fathers' return from working in the mines.

Keats, Ezra Jack. (1962). *The Snowy Day*. New York: Viking. (preschool–2)

Peter plays in the snow. He brings a snowball into the house and cannot find it later.

Kunhardt, Dorothy. (1962). *Pat the Bunny.* Chicago: Golden. (preschool)

This touchable book is a simple, small book for very young children.

Lear, Edward. (1991). *The Owl and the Pussy Cat.* Illustrated by Jan Brett. New York: Putnam. (preschool–2)

This is a newly illustrated version of Lear's well-known lyric poem.

Lindgren, B. (1983). *Sam's Bath.* New York: Morrow. (preschool–1)

A young boy enjoys playing in the bathtub.

Livingston, Myra Cohn. (1989). *Up in the Air.* Illustrated by Leonard Everett Fisher. New York: Holiday. (K–3)

The illustrations show what a young boy sees on his first airplane trip. The text is written in rhyming triplets.

Marshall, James. (1991). *Old Mother Hubbard and Her Wonderful Dog.* New York: Farrar, Straus & Giroux. (K–2)

This is James Marshall's interpretation of the traditional tale.

Martin, Bill. (1990). *Polar Bear, Polar Bear, What Do You Hear?* Illustrated by Eric Carle. New York: Henry Holt. (preschool–1)

This repetitive story, similar to *Brown Bear,* encourages children to listen.

_____ . (1983). *Brown Bear, Brown Bear, What Do You See?* Illustrated by Eric Carle. San Diego: Holt, Rinehart & Winston. (preschool–1)

This repetitive book asks each animal "What do you see?" and the animal says "I see a . . . looking at me," thus identifying another animal. Then that animal is asked the same question.

Mayer, Mercer. (1988). *There's Something in My Attic.* New York: Dial. (preschool–2)

In this story, a big, noisy nightmare lives in the attic. So the heroine goes to the attic to lasso it and rescue her new teddy bear that the nightmare stole.

Numeroff, Laura. (1991). *If You Give a Moose a Muffin.* Illustrated by Felicia Bond. New York: Harper & Row. (K–2)

This circle story is composed of cause-and-effect situations that result from offering one mouse a single cookie.

Oxenbury, Helen. (1981). *Playing.* New York: Simon & Schuster. (preschool–K)

This book shows pictures of a baby playing with toys.

_____ . (1987). *All Fall Down.* New York: Aladdin.

This book shows children at play.

Say, Allen. (1991). *Tree of Cranes.* Boston: Houghton Mifflin. (K–4)

This Japanese story, decorated with origami, centers on paper cranes.

Segal, Lore. (1970). *Tell Me a Mitzi.* New York: Farrar, Straus & Giroux. (K–2)

This collection of three stories tells about a big sister and little brother who explore their city.

Tafuri, Nancy. (1984). *Have You Seen My Duckling?* New York: Greenwillow. (preschool–K)

Mother duck searches for her duckling.

Walsh, Ellen. (1991). *Mouse Count.* New York: Harcourt Brace Jovanovich. (K–1)

This book teaches counting sequences, based on counting mice.

Ward, Cindy. (1988). *Cookie's Week.* New York: Putnam. (K–1)

Cookie is a cat and the reader goes through the days of the week with Cookie's activities.

Wells, Rosemary. (1985). *Max's Breakfast.* New York: Dial. (preschool–2)

Max, a little rabbit, and his big sister Ruby act like real children with funny results. They argue and play just like their readers.

_____ . (1991). *Max's Dragon Shirt*. New York: Dial. (preschool–2)

Max goes shopping with his big sister Ruby. Ruby helps him choose a shirt.

Woods, Audrey. (1989). *Piggies*. New York: Harcourt Brace Jovanovich. (preschool–1)

This new version of the old rhyme about the little piggies is applied to fingers instead of toes.

Zelinsky, Paul. (1990). *The Wheels on the Bus*. New York: Dutton. (preschool–2)

This book illustrates the traditional rhyming song, including text, music, and hand motions.

## Touchstone Books for Young Children

### Infants

Ahlberg, Janet. (1982). *The Baby's Catalogue*. Illustrated by Janet and Allan Ahlberg. Boston: Little, Brown. (board)

Asch, Frank. (1978). *Turtle Tale*. New York: Dial. (board)

Carle, Eric. (1984). *The Very Busy Spider*. New York: Philomel. (book)

Chorao, Kay. (1977). *Freight Train*. New York: Dutton. (book)

Di Fiori, Lawrence. (1983). *My First Book*. New York: Macmillan. (board)

Fleming, Denise. (1985). *This Little Pig Went to Market*. New York: Random House. (board)

Ford, George. (1979). *Baby's First Cloth Book*. New York: Random House, 1979. (cloth)

Greeley, Valerie. (1984). *Zoo Animals*. New York: Bedrick/Blackie. (board)

Hill, Eric. (1984). *Spot's Toys*. New York: Putnam. (washable vinyl)

_____ . (1987). *Where's Spot?* New York: Putnam. (board)

Hoban, Tana. (1983). *What Is It?* New York: Greenwillow. (board)

_____ . (1986). *Red, Blue, Yellow Shoe*. New York: Greenwillow. (board)

Miller, J. P. (1985). *Little Rabbit's Garden*. New York: Random House. (cloth doll/book)

Miller, Margaret. (1989). *In My Room*. New York: Crowell. (board)

_____ . (1989). *Me and My Clothes*. New York: Crowell. (board)

_____ . (1989). *Time to Eat*. New York: Crowell. (board)

_____ . (1989). *At My House*. New York: Crowell. (board)

Oxenbury, Helen. (1987). *Clap Hands*. New York: Macmillan. (board)

_____ . (1987). *Say Goodnight*. New York: Macmillan. (board)

_____ . (1987). *Tickle, Tickle*. New York: Macmillan. (board)

_____ . (1981). *Playing*. New York: Simon & Schuster. (board)

_____ . (1987). *All Fall Down*. New York: Macmillan. (board)

Prelutsky, Jack. (1986). *Read-Aloud Rhymes for the Very Young*. Illustrated by Marc Brown. New York: Knopf. (book)

Ra, Carol. (1987). *Trot, Trot to Boston*. Illustrated by Catherine Stock. New York: Lothrop, Lee & Shephard. (book)

Schlesinger, Alice. (1959). *Baby's Mother Goose*. New York: Platt and Munk. (cloth)

Wik, Lars. (1985). *Baby's First Words*. Photographs by Lars Wik. New York: Random House. (board)

### Nursery rhymes/Mother Goose

Briggs, Raymond. (1980). *Mother Goose Treasury*. New York: Coward McCann (Putnam).

Brown, Marc. (1980). *Finger Rhymes*. New York: Dutton.

dePaola, Tomie. (1985). *Tomie dePaola's Mother Goose*. Illustrated by Tomie dePaola. New York: Putnam.

Fisher, Blanche Wright. (1987). *The Real Mother Goose*. New York: Macmillan Checkerboard Press.
Glazer, Tom. (1973). *Eye Winker, Tom Tinker, Chin Chopper: 50 Musical Finger Plays*. Phoenix, AZ: Zephyr.
Hague, Michael. (1984). *Mother Goose: A Collection of Classic Nursery Rhymes*. New York: Holt.
Hines, Anna. (1983). *Taste the Raindrops*. New York: Greenwillow.
Wildsmith, Brian. (1982). *Brian Wildsmith's Mother Goose*. New York: Oxford University Press.
Wilkin, Eloise. (1981). *Rock-a-Bye Baby: Nursery Songs and Cradle Games*. New York: Random House.

### Counting books

Aruego, Jose and Ariane Dewey. (1984). *One Duck, Another Duck*. New York: Greenwillow.
Bang, Molly. (1983). *Ten, Nine, Eight*. New York: Greenwillow.
Boynton, Sandra. (1984). *Doggies*. New York: Simon & Schuster.
Burningham, John. (1986). *John Burningham's 1 2 3*. Westminister, MD: Crown.
Ehlert, Lois. (1990). *Fish Eyes*. New York: Harcourt Brace Jovanovich.
Hughes, Shirley. (1985). *Noisy*. New York: Lothrop, Lee & Shepard.
Kitchen, Bert. (1984). *Animal Numbers*. New York: Dial.
Tafuri, Nancy. (1986). *Who's Counting?* New York: Greenwillow.

### Toddlers (1–3)

Aliki. *Hush Little Baby*. New York: Prentice Hall.
Blegvad, Lenore. (1986). *This Is Me*. Illustrated by Erik Blegvad. New York: Random House.
Carle, Eric. (1984). *The Very Busy Spider*. New York: Philomel.
Crews, Donald. (1985). *Freight Train*. New York: Greenwillow.
Hoban, Tana. (1976). *Big Ones, Little Ones*. New York: Greenwillow.
———. (1986). *A Children's Zoo*. New York: Greenwillow.
Isadora, Rachel. (1985). *I See*. New York: Greenwillow.
McDonnell, Flora. (1994). *I Love Animals*. Cambridge, MA: Candlewick Press.
Ormerod, Jan. (1985). *Dad's Book*. New York: Lothrop, Lee & Shepard.
Oxenbury, Helen. (1982). *Shopping Trip*. New York: Dial.
Price, Matthew. (1986). *My Daddy*. Illustrated by Jean Claverie. New York: Knopf.
Rockwell, Anne. (1985). *In Our House*. New York: Crowell.
Rounds, Glen. (1989). *Old MacDonald Had a Farm*. New York: Holiday.
Scarry, Richard. (1976). *Color Book*. New York: Random House.
Spanner, Helmut. (1983). *I Am a Little Cat*. Hauppauge, NY: Barrons.
Watanabe, Shiegeo. (1984). *How Do I Put It On?* Illustrated by Yasuo Ohtomo. New York: Philomel.
Watson, Clyde. (1983). *Catch Me and Kiss Me and Say It Again*. Illustrated by Wendy Watson. New York: Philomel.
Wheeler, Cindy. (1983). *Marmalade's Nap*. New York: Knopf.

### Preschoolers (3–5)

The books in this list are categorized by the emergent literacy abilities they address: pattern perception, repetitive patterns, language development, and simple plots. Many of the books listed could fit into more than one classification.

**Pattern Perception**
Bang, Molly. (1991). *Yellow Ball*. New York: Morrow.

Galdone, Paul. (1971). *The Gingerbread Boy*. New York: Seabury (Clarion).

_____ . (1973). *The Three Bears*. New York: Clarion.

Kent, Jack. (1971). *The Fat Cat*. New York: Parents.

Lillegard, Dee. (1989). *Sitting in My Box*. Illustrated by Jon Agee. New York: Dutton.

Martin, Bill Jr. (1991). *Polar Bear, Polar Bear, What Do You Hear?* New York: Henry Holt.

Robart, Rose. (1987). *The Cake that Mack Ate*. New York: Atlantic Monthly Press.

VanLaan, Nancy. (1987). *The Big Fat Worm*. New York: Knopf.

Williams, Linda. (1986). *The Little Old Lady Who Was Not Afraid of Anything*. Illustrated by Megan Lloyd. New York: HarperCollins.

Wood, Audrey. (1984). *The Napping House*. Illustrated by Don Wood. New York: Harcourt Brace Jovanovich.

**Language Development**

Christelow, Eileen. (1989). *Five Little Monkeys Jumping on the Bed*. New York: Clarion.

Duff, Maggi. (1978). *Rum, Pum, Pum*. New York: Macmillan.

Fleming, Denise. (1991). *In the Tall, Tall Grass*. New York: Henry Holt.

Maris, Ron. (1987). *I Wish I Could Fly*. New York: Greenwillow.

Singer, Marilyn. (1991). *Nine O'Clock Lullaby*. Illustrated by Frane Lessac. New York: HarperCollins.

Westcott, Nadine. (1987). *Peanut Butter and Jelly: A Play Rhyme*. New York: Dutton.

_____ . (1989). *Skip to My Lou*. Boston: Little, Brown.

**Simple Plot**

Hewett, Joan. (1987). *Rosalie*. New York: Lothrop, Lee & Shepard.

Hutchins, Pat. (1968). *Rosie's Walk*. New York: Macmillan.

_____ . (1983). *Good-Night Owl!* New York: Macmillan.

Kraus, Robert. (1970). *Whose Mouse Are You?* Illustrated by Jose Aruego and Ariane Dewey. New York: Collier.

_____ . (1986). *Where Are You Going, Little Mouse?* Illustrated by Jose Aruego and Ariane Dewey. New York: Greenwillow.

Lindenbaum, Pija. (1991). *Else-Marie and Her Seven Little Daddies*. New York: Henry Holt.

Piumini, Roberto. (1991). *The Saint and the Circus*. Illustrated by Bary Root. New York: Tambourine.

Ward, Cindy. (1988). *Cookie's Week*. Illustrated by Tomie dePaola. New York: Putnam.

Wildsmith, Brian. (1983). *The Cat on the Mat*. New York: Oxford.

Wood, Audrey. (1986). *King Bidgood's in the Bathtub*. New York: Greenwillow.

## Predictable Books to Use for Big Book Teaching

Asbjornsen, P. C. (1973). *Three Billy Goats Gruff*. Illustrated by Paul Galdone. New York: Seabury. (K–2)

   The traditional story as interpreted by Paul Galdone.

Brown, Ruth. (1981). *A Dark, Dark Tale*. New York: Dial. (preschool–1)

   A mystery for young children who try to figure out who they are searching for in this tale.

Carle, Eric. (1985). *The Very Busy Spider*. New York: Philomel. (preschool–1)

   The story of a spider who is very busy spinning a web.

Ginsburg, Mirra. (1972). *The Chick and the Duckling*. Illustrated by Jose Aruego and Ariane Dewey. New York: Macmillan. (preschool–1)

   The chick tries to do everything the duck does.

Hill, Eric. (1980). *Where's Spot?* New York: Putnam. (preschool)
  Spot the dog hides behind flaps in this book.

Krauss, Robert. (1980). *Whose Mouse Are You?* New York: Collier. (preschool–1)
  A little mouse saves all the members of his family.

Stinson, Kathy. (1984). *Big and Little.* Toronto, CA: Annick Press. (preschool–K)
  A young boy tells about events that make him feel big and those that make him feel little.

———. (1982). *Red Is Best.* Toronto: Firefly Press. (K–2)
  A little girl tells why she thinks red is the best color.

Tolstoy, Aleksei. (1968). *The Great Big Enormous Turnip.* Chicago: Watts. (K–2)
  This cumulative tale tells about a peasant's efforts to pull a huge turnip.

Westcott, Nadine Bernard. (1991). *The House That Jack Built.* New York: Little, Brown (K–2)
  The traditional story with newer illustrations.

## Recordings and Films/Videos

### Recordings

*Birds, Beasts, Bugs and Little Fishes.* Sung by Pete Seeger. Smithsonian Folkways.

*Camels, Cats and Rainbows.* (1983). Sung by Paul Strausman. A Gentle Wind Recording. (ALA Notable Children's Recording)

*Hello Everybody! Playsongs and Rhymes from a Toddler's World.* Sung by Rachael Buchman. A Gentle Wind Recording. (ALA Notable Children's Recording)

Jenkins, Ella. *Can You Feed My Cow?* Sung by Fred Koch and a group of children. Red Rover Records.

*Mainly Mother Goose: Songs and Rhymes for Merry Young Souls.* (1985). Performed by Sharon, Lois & Bram. Elephant Records. (ALA Notable Children's Recording)

Raffi. (1988). *Everything Grows.* Sung by Raffi. MCA. (ALA Notable Children's Recording)

### Films/videos

*Caps for Sale.* Weston, CT: Weston Woods. (5 min)

*Chicken Soup and Rice.* Weston, CT: Weston Woods. (5 min)

*Harold and the Purple Crayon.* Weston, CT: Weston Woods. (7 min)

*Max's Chocolate Chicken.* Weston, CT: Weston Woods. (5 min)

*Reading Rainbow.* Daily series on public television.

*Three Billy Goats Gruff.* Weston, CT: Weston Woods. (6 min)

Review sources for films and videos include *Booklist, School Library Journal, Parent's Choice, Video Librarian,* and *Children's Video Report.*

### Media resources

*Booklist*
American Library Association
50 East Huron Street
Chicago, IL 60611

Children's Video Report
P.O. Box 3228
Princeton, NJ 08543

KIDSNET: A computerized clearinghouse for children's television and radio.
Suite 208
6856 Eastern Ave., NW
Washington, DC 20012

Parents Choice Guide to Videocassettes for Children
Parents Choice Foundation
P.O. Box 185
Newton, MA 02168

*Reading Rainbow: A Guide for Teachers*
P.O. Box 80669
Lincoln, NE 68501

Video Source Book annual
Detroit: Gale Research Company

## OTHER RECOMMENDED BOOKS— REFERENCES FOR SELECTING LITERATURE

Carlson, Anne D. (1991). *The Preschooler and the Library*. Metuchen, NJ: Scarecrow.

Cianciolo, Patricia. (1990). *Picture Books for Children* (3d ed.). Chicago: American Library Association.

Copperman, Paul. (1986). *Taking Books to Heart: How to Develop a Love of Reading in Your Child*. Reading, MA: Addison-Wesley.

Crago, Maureen and Hugh Crago. (1980). *Prelude to Literacy: A Preschool Child's Encounter with Picture and Story*. Carbondale: Southern Illinois University Press.

Jalongo, Mary Renck. (1988). *Young Children and Picture Books*. Washington, DC: National Association for the Education of Young Children.

Lamme, Linda Leonard. (1985). *Growing Up Reading: Sharing with Your Children the Joys of Reading*. New York: Acropolis.

————. (1980). *Raising Readers: A Guide to Sharing Literature with Young Children*. New York: Walker.

Larrick, Nancy. (1982). *A Parent's Guide to Children's Reading* (5th ed.). New York: Doubleday.

Sierra, Judy and Robert Kaminski. (1991). *Multicultural Folktales: Stories to Tell Young Children*. Phoenix, AZ: Oryx.

Thomas, James. (1992). *Play Learn & Grow. (An Annotated Guide to the Best Books and Materials for Very Young Children)*. New Providence, NJ: Bowker.

Trelease, Jim. (1989). *The New Read-Aloud Handbook* (2d. rev. ed.). New York: Penguin.

Winkel, Lois and Sue Kimmel. (1990). *Mother Goose Comes First: An Annotated Guide to the Best Books and Recordings for Your Preschool Child*. New York: Holt.

# Thirteen

## KEY TERMS

diverse background
exceptional students
inclusion
individual differences

individualized education
   plan (IEP)
mainstreaming

## GUIDING QUESTIONS

As you read this chapter, think about the following questions and answer them after you complete the chapter.

1. What principles should be considered when selecting literature that addresses problems that children encounter?

2. How important is literature for and about children with special problems? Why?

3. How is inclusion related to this chapter?

## OVERVIEW

More than any other group in the history of education, contemporary students have **diverse backgrounds,** *varying in physical and emotional development and in the environments they come from* (Pallas, Natriello, and McDill, 1989). The contemporary emphasis on maintaining individuality and cherishing the differences manifested in a diverse population contribute to the variability encountered in classrooms. Educational practices such as mainstreaming and inclusion increase the diversity among students today. In mainstreaming, exceptional students who formerly were taught in separate classes now spend a large part of the school day in regular classrooms. Students in inclusion programs are placed in regular classrooms accompanied by an aide or a teacher assistant who helps them participate in classroom instruction.

Contemporary social attitudes emphasize respect for individual differences, human rights, and quality of life for all people. Some of the major factors that shape individual differences are environment, society, culture, language, socioeconomic status, physical development, and emotional development. This chapter examines diversity from the perspective of **exceptional students**—*those with differences of intellect, communication, senses, behavior, emotions, or physical development.*

As discussed at length in previous chapters, one of the great benefits of literature for children is identifying with the characters portrayed. Literature is therefore an important consideration when addressing student diversity and should include characters representing the same broad range of diversity as the readers dealing with the universal challenges of living that help children understand and empathize with others.

# Real-Life Literature and Children with Challenges

## Introduction

Prior to 1950, most of the literature for children featured secure, loving families that protected children from the harsh realities of life. That is not to say that characters like the Bobbsey twins had no problems, but their problems reflected a simpler society and the morality of the times. Children did not tell lies, and the rare character who failed to conform was punished so that young readers would understand the consequences of misbehavior. Books for children in this period were obviously didactic. Authors wrote to teach children how to behave. Many characters were portrayed as simplistic stereotypes of good or bad behavior, failing to convey the true complexity of children's personalities and their lives.

Through research in child development, the study of sociology, and the popularity of psychology during the second half of the 20th century, authors arrived at a different conceptualization of children's characters. Gradually, these new understandings evolved into a different kind of children's literature that made more of an effort to depict reality, basing stories on complex characters and downplaying any didactic tendencies.

The new writers of children's literature seek to explore the real-life experiences of their readers (Peck, 1983). Real-life literature addresses families with problems, children with problems, children with disabilities, abused children, substance abuse, divorce, and other difficulties. The family image of years past—two middle-class white parents (a stay-at-home mom with an apron and a go-to-work dad with a briefcase), two children, a dog and a cat, and a single-family dwelling with a picket fence—is gone forever. The profile of children and their lives changed in real-life as well as in their books, and as their lives changed, the demographics of the student population in the United States changed.

These changes are continuing and even accelerating. Classrooms today may include students with all types of differences: hearing or sight impairments, impaired mobility, economic disadvantages, cultural differences, giftedness, emotional disabilities, or mental disabilities. These students are no longer segregated because society in general is becoming more sensitive to the special needs of all people and individual differences are respected and encouraged as never before. Current educational institutions encourage each individual to realize his or her full potential.

Sensitivity to the special needs of students escalated when Public Law 94-142 was passed in 1978. This law provides for the education of all children with disabilities and requires that these students be taught in the least restrictive educational environment possible, which often involves mainstreaming. In **mainstreaming,** *exceptional students who formerly were taught in separate classes now spend a large part of the school day in regular classrooms.* Each of these students is provided with an **individualized education plan (IEP)** to *map out the most suitable education for the student with special needs.* Parents are invited to participate in the planning process, and the IEP is not implemented until the student's parents have approved it. Total **inclusion** of exceptional students is a major movement in education today: the goal is to *place these students in classrooms with fewer students and to provide an aide or assistant who will work to help the child participate in the regular classroom.*

................... VIGNETTE

"Good morning Steve." Mary Allison, the principal, walked into Steve Liu's fifth-grade classroom.

"Hi! How are you this fine morning?"

"Good. I'm here because you're getting a new student in a few weeks."

"This is a lot of advance notice," Steve responded.

"You'll probably need it, because this student is legally blind. He can only see the difference between light and dark and will have a tutor. You'll need time to create a good learning environment for everyone," Mary replied.

Steve looked thoughtful. "This should be interesting. I've just started reading Jean Little's autobiography, *Little by Little*. She is virtually blind and lives a full life. The children enjoyed her book *Different Dragons* so much I decided to read her autobiography to them. They have been appalled at the way she was treated by other children."

"Good! Do you think your students could find some other literature and perhaps some films about blind and partially sighted people?" Mary said.

"I'm sure they can. The media specialist will help," he answered.

"Then we can prepare the school. This could be the beginning of a schoolwide study of people with special problems," Mary said. Steve nodded his agreement, then looked up. "Say, I just had a thought! Would it be all right with you if the children dramatized some of the incidents in *Little by Little*?"

## THE VALUE OF REAL-LIFE LITERATURE

Literature, as this book has emphasized many times, can be a powerful influence in children's lives. Many children who had problems as they grew, as adults now write about their childhoods, hoping to help other children who may be experiencing the same kinds of problems. Sandra Wilde (1989) provides an example.

> My reason for telling this story is to celebrate the power of literature in helping us to know who we really are, and the power of the human spirit to recognize and remember that true self despite pain and adversity. . . .
>
> Many years ago, I looked like any other little girl on the outside, but there was something different about me on the inside. My parents were two needy people who didn't know how to love, and I spent much of my childhood being either bullied or casually ignored. My physical self was looked after, but not my emotional needs. To my parents, appearances were very important; what people thought about me took precedence over how I felt and who I was. Growing up in the 1950s suburbia, where each family was shut away in its own little house, where children belonged to their parents and were seen but not heard, where if a family appeared conventional and middle-class everything was assumed to be all right, I had no one to turn to. Fortunately, I had the public library (p. 49).

Children's books enable students to understand and appreciate themselves and others. Literature that includes characters with disabilities gives children who have special needs an opportunity to identify with people who are like themselves. Equally important, such literature can cultivate in other students an understanding, empathy, and appreciation of children with special needs. Protagonists in children's books usually do not have physical, mental, or emotional impairments, so children who have never interacted with a person with disabilities and who have no disabilities themselves have no exposure to or experience with people with disabilities. The way children view these challenges of living is based on their values, usually learned from their families.

Teaching values is a very controversial educational issue, yet today liberals and conservatives

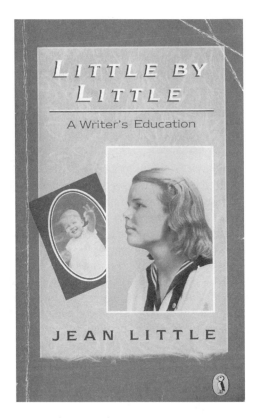

*By the time she was seventeen, Jean Little's poetry had been published in a national magazine.*

alike decry a "moral crisis" among young people. They attribute increased school violence to youngsters who do not know right from wrong. Such influential educators as Thomas Lickona and Nel Noddings have studied these issues. Values clarification is surrounded by contentious issues such as: Can we actually teach values? What values should be taught? When should values be taught? Who should teach values? How should values be taught? While this book cannot resolve these thorny issues, literature can serve as a context for inquiry into values. Books such as Lickona's *Educating for Character* (1991), Noddings's *The Challenge to Care in Schools* (1991), and Andrews's *Teaching Kids to Care* (1994) are helpful resources. For instance, in *Teaching Kids to Care*, Andrews includes units of study and lists of literature for an inquiry approach to values. She includes topics such as appreciation of differences, empathy, compassion, homelessness, consequences of doing right and wrong, gentleness, obedience, self-concept, individuality and independence, honesty, honor, patience, and many others.

## SELECTING AND EVALUATING REAL-LIFE LITERATURE

In selecting appropriate literature, character portrayal, as well as literary quality, should be considered (Sage, 1977). Unfortunately, many traditional stories depict people with physical deformities as villains or use them to frighten and menace other story characters (Rudman, 1976). Teachers and media specialists must analyze literature with great sensitivity to avoid presenting literature that expresses insensitive attitudes and to present literature that addresses the problems many children experience.

However it portrays characters with disabilities, any poem, story, or informational piece must have literary merit, or it will not attract readers. Books that are written to teach or preach rarely capture readers' interest. In *Stay Away from Simon!* Carol Carrick creates an excellent adventure story set on Martha's Vineyard in the 1830s. Lucy and her friend Desire are afraid of Simon, a handicapped boy they see laughing and playing in the schoolyard snow. When a heavy snowfall closes school early, Lucy and her little brother start home together, but wander in the wrong direction when the snow makes the landscape look different. When they hear a deep voice behind them they fear that Simon is following them. It is Simon, and he helps guide them home. This story is an exciting, suspenseful story enhanced with well-drawn characters that include a boy with physical disabilities.

Once the literary quality of the story is ensured, check the portrayal of the disabling condition. This should be accurate, including any physical and emotional aspects, again avoiding didacticism. A good example of a sensitive portrayal of a disability is Barbara Corcoran's *Child of the Morning*, in which Susan suffers a skull fracture in a volleyball game at school. Her dizzy "spells" continue so long that everyone in the small town, including her own sister, considers her strange. Her sister tells their mother to keep Susan away

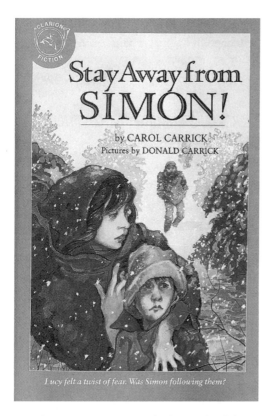

Lucy felt a twist of fear. Was Simon following them?

*This poignant story, which reveals children's fear of those who are disabled, takes an unexpected turn.*

from their place of business because they are losing customers due to her strange behavior. Everyone in town refuses to give her a summer job because they are afraid of what might happen. Finally, she is hired to work in a newly opened summer theater; the people involved do not know about her spells. Susan is allowed to join a dance class and to have a small part in a play, and she is treated with respect rather than pity in these groups. Nevertheless, she worries because she wants to be a dancer and is unsure how her spells will influence her dancing ability. Susan's character is fully developed through her interactions with other characters, her actions, and her thoughts. This book is excellent for making children aware of the emotional aspects of physical disabilities.

As in all quality literature, story characters in real-life literature are portrayed as complex personalities with strengths, flaws, problems, feelings, and responses. Any characters with disabilities are clearly integral to the plot and not an expendable part of the background. Characters with disabilities are capable of helping others and of having loving family relationships and friendships. The characters with disabilities develop through their experiences, just as characters without disabilities do. Quality literature, however, will avoid stereotypical behavior in characters with disabilities and will not portray them as being superhuman—a device often used by authors to make these characters acceptable to other characters in the story (Rudman, 1976). Characters with disabilities must be permitted to have ordinary flaws and to be average, nonspectacular people.

The characters in *Stay Away from Simon!* are portrayed as real people. Simon is a slow individual whose odd expressions, strange behavior, and hulking presence frighten others. Some even think he's dangerous—he is being blamed for a drowning because he was present at the pond when it happened—so the children are told, "Stay away from Simon." Lucy is a very real character who is uncomfortable with Simon because he is different. Even though she is grateful for Simon's help (Simon knows his way through the woods because he works in the mill, so his ability to lead them to safety is plausible), she is still afraid of him until her father explains that Simon actually tried to save the boy who drowned. Her mother explains how proud Simon's mother was when he was born because he was the only one of her children to live. Then Lucy overhears Simon saying the counting rhyme she and her brother were chanting on the way home and realizes that he followed them to learn the counting rhyme. Both the descriptions and pictures of Simon help readers understand Lucy's attitude at the beginning of the story, which changes as a result of her parents' conversation and her own experiences.

Fiction and nonfiction should provide honest, up-to-date, realistic information and advice about any disabling condition. Miracle cures are not possible for all handicapping conditions. Some authors portray a disability as something that positive thinking, prayer, and hard work will overcome. This has the effect of making it seem as if the disability is somehow the person's own fault and that good behavior or wishing can cure the condition

(Rudman, 1976). In *Child of the Morning*, Susan learns that she has epilepsy from her fall. She experiences a wide range of side effects from the various anticonvulsant drugs the physician prescribes: double vision, headache, speech impairment, stomach upsets, and other conditions typical for these drugs. Finally, she reaches the point that she feels the side effects are worse than epilepsy. The names of the drugs and their side effects are skillfully embedded into the story. Realizing that she cannot fulfill her dream of being a dancer because of the epilepsy, her former dance teacher suggests choreography, which gives Susan realistic expectations by the end of the book.

Two volumes by the same name, *Portraying Persons with Disabilities*, are of particular value when choosing books that have characters with disabilities. One volume, by Joan Friedberg, June Mullins, and Adelaide Sukiennik, addresses nonfiction works (1992, 2nd ed., New Providence, NJ: R. R. Bowker), while the other, by Debra Robertson, addresses fiction (1992, New Providence, NJ: R. R. Bowker).

The following discussions of children's books featuring characters with special problems is categorized by the specific problems of the characters, including hearing impairments, visual impairments, health problems, abuse, substance abuse, physical handicaps, emotional handicaps, and mental handicaps. The majority of books with handicapped characters fall into the categories of realistic fiction, historical fiction, and informational books, although this section includes at least some books from each genre.

## Hearing Challenges

Children with hearing impairments exhibit a full range of **individual differences.** *Their experiences, families, interests, intelligence, and motivation are as diverse* as any other children. Their impairments may range from moderate to severe: Some live in a silent world while others may hear a few sounds. Hearing aids may help some people with hearing impairments to perceive as much sound as possible. However, children whose hearing is impaired usually have distorted or incomplete auditory input even with hearing aids and have difficulty producing and understanding speech sounds. *Dan* and *tan* can confuse anyone who does not hear sounds

clearly enough to discriminate between them. Special instruction is therefore necessary for these children to learn language.

*Anna's Silent World* depicts the complex life of a child with a hearing impairment. Bernard Wolf based this informational book on the life of six-year-old Anna, who was born deaf. She has a profound hearing loss but has learned to speak and to understand people around her after four years of therapy with the New York League for the Hard of Hearing. In the therapy, she learned to lip-read and to use hearing aids, which enable her to go to school with boys and girls who have normal hearing. The photographs that illustrate this book allow readers to see Anna in therapy, in school, and with her family and her pets, which helps readers understand the complexity of her life.

One of the issues in educating children who are deaf or hard of hearing is whether they should learn to talk as Anna did or learn the manual alphabet and sign language. Some authorities believe that children who learn to sign before they develop oral language will not learn to talk because signing is easier. In the beautiful picture book *The Handmade Alphabet*, Laura Rankin presents a striking interpretation of the manual alphabet. Her stepson is deaf and he communicated through lipreading for the first 18 years of his life. Then he learned American Sign Language, which allowed him to share ideas fully. Through it he gained understanding and communication. This book is especially useful in introducing the manual alphabet to children who can hear.

Although they are commonly thought of as being only for persons with visual impairments, guide dogs are sometimes trained to interpret sounds for people with hearing impairments as well. Patricia Curtis tells about the training of such a dog in *Cindy, A Hearing Ear Dog*.

## Vision Challenges

Some people with visual impairments cannot see or sense any light at all, but others have at least some vision. Their limited vision may enable them to see only the difference between darkness and light, to perceive distorted images, or to see print held very close to their eyes. People with visual handicaps

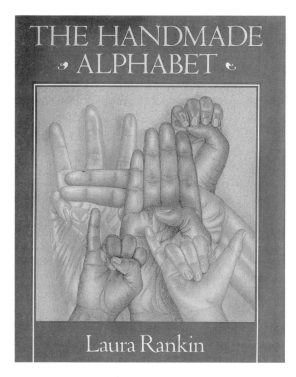

THE HANDMADE
ALPHABET

Laura Rankin

*The author's stepson inspired her to create
this book about the language of signing.*

Some people with visual impairments use guide dogs to achieve greater independence, a skill that requires education for the person as well as the dog. *A Guide Dog Puppy Grows Up* by Caroline Arnold follows Honey, a golden retriever, through her training from puppy to guide dog. Each stage of her training is explained with text and photographs.

A variety of genre include books about children with visual challenges and the ways they have adjusted. These authors sensitize readers to the individual differences among people with this disability, whose lives are as varied as individuals who do not have this disability. In *Through Grandpa's Eyes*, Patricia MacLachlan introduces John, who learns really to see from his grandfather, who is blind. MacLachlan helps readers appreciate the creativity of John's grandfather, who plays the cello, and his grandmother, who is a sculptor. Both grandparents are shown as capable and able to take care of themselves.

Jean Little, who has visual impairments, writes sensitively about this condition. In *From Anna* she tells about Anna, whose family escapes to Canada from Nazi Germany. Anna is awkward and unsure of herself and feels rejected. After her disability is identified, she has opportunities to develop competence and confidence, which enable her to overcome her difficulties in a realistic fashion.

## Mobility Challenges

People who have impaired mobility are sometimes identified as orthopedically disabled. They may have impaired legs, arms, or both, or may even have paralyzed body parts. Mobility impairments may originate at birth, through accident, or through illness. Some children are born with cerebral palsy, which can impair mobility quite seriously or very mildly. Injury to the spinal cord often causes paralysis below the injury. Illnesses such as polio can also paralyze parts of the body.

Mobility for people with physical impairments usually requires special equipment such as wheelchairs, walkers, braces, prostheses, and canes. Of course, using this equipment requires therapy and training. In recent years, ramps have been added to buildings to permit better access by people who have special equipment. Likewise, many public places now have restrooms that offer access to

may have corrective glasses or contact lenses; in some instances they have surgery or corneal transplants to correct their vision.

Children with visual impairments or blindness do not have the visual input necessary to learn about their world, so they need special instruction. They often learn to read Braille and listen to "talking" or recorded books. Fortunately, many more recorded books are available today than ever before. Listening to recorded books extends their experiential background and prepares them to learn to read, either Braille or print if they can see that well. Children with visual impairments need many opportunities to explore concrete objects with their senses of smell, touch, taste, and hearing. Tactile books made from fabric, yarn, buttons, and zippers are excellent learning tools for young children with impaired vision. Pockets in these books can hold cardboard or plastic shapes. Discussion and descriptions of these concrete experiences is essential to building background knowledge and experience.

wheelchairs. In the nonfiction book, *What Do You Do When Your Wheelchair Gets a Flat Tire? Questions and Answers about Disabilities*, Douglas Biklen and Ellen Barnes answer the questions that most children would like to have answered about many different types of disabilities. Black-and-white photographs help explain physical handicaps in *A Look at Physical Handicaps*, by Maria Forrai and Margaret Pursell.

Seeing eye dogs and hearing ear dogs are not the only animals that help people with disabilities. Recently animals have been trained to assist people with impaired mobility as well. Researchers have trained monkeys to prepare food, to feed people, to pick up the telephone when it rings, to pick up things that have been dropped, and even to brush teeth. Suzanne Haldane tells about some of the ways that monkeys assist people in *Helping Hands: How Monkeys Assist People Who Are Disabled*. The photographs in this book help readers understand how useful monkeys can be.

Many excellent books address the topic of mobility for people with disabilities and help children understand and accept differences in themselves and others. Marguerite de Angeli's *The Door in the Wall* is set in medieval times. Robin has physical impairments in his legs and is mistreated by other children. The monks help Robin learn to read, write, whittle, and use crutches, and eventually he shows his mettle and becomes a hero. This book has retained its popularity for many years, probably because Robin overcomes his handicap and becomes a hero in the story. In *Rachel*, Barbara Franshawe emphasizes what a girl in a wheelchair can do. Rachel goes to a regular school and does many things that the other children do. *The Balancing Girl* by Bernice Rabe shows a first grader who adeptly adjusts to her braces, crutches, and wheelchair to do many different things. Maxine Rosenberg's *My Friend Leslie* is a kindergartner with multiple handicaps. This photographic essay shows her classmates' acceptance of her handicaps.

Some parents are so concerned about their children with disabilities that they overprotect them, a topic addressed by Jan Slepian in *The Alfred Summer*. Alfred has an overprotective mother and a father who ignores him, but during a very special summer he is able to make friends. *Wheelchair Champions* focuses on activities for people in wheel-

chairs. Harriet Savitz tells about real people in wheelchairs who excel in various sports. Marie Killilea's *Karen* is about a baby born with cerebral palsy whose family recognizes that she must learn to do things for herself and that she has to struggle to walk with braces. Sally in Jean Little's *Mine for Keeps* has a different problem. She has always attended a special school for children with disabilities, but she leaves the school to attend regular school. The changes in her life frighten her and make her anxious, but she gets a puppy who matures along with her.

## Health Challenges

Children experience many of the same health challenges as adults. Epilepsy, diabetes, childhood arthritis, leukemia, cystic fibrosis, and heart malfunction are only a few of the physical conditions that can affect a child's life. Although medication is helpful for some of these conditions, serious side effects can alter the lives of people who take it. Children who depend upon medication must become responsible for taking medication and monitoring their own reactions to it. For example, Susan in *Child of the Morning* has epileptic seizures from a head injury and develops problems with her medication. In *Edith Herself*, Ellen Howard shows the attitude toward seizures before medication was commonly available. Edith and her family had to accept and adjust to her problem without the aid of modern medicine.

Leukemia often requires extensive medical treatment and can be life threatening. Bone marrow transplants are sometimes used in its treatment, as Diana Amadeo demonstrates in *There's a Little Bit of Me in Jamey*. Brian tells about his concern for his younger brother Jamey, a leukemia victim. He has ambivalent feelings about the situation because he is worried about his brother's terrible illness, yet at the same time he resents the fact that his parents have very little time for him. Then the doctor discovers that Brian's bone marrow is a good match for Jamey, so a transplant is performed. The book is very realistic because Brian observes that the transplant is a hope not a cure.

Many diabetics must take insulin, but they also have to control their diet. In *You Can't Catch Diabetes from a Friend*, Lynn Kipnis and Susan Adler explain diabetes with simple text and photographs. Ron Roy's *Where's Buddy?* approaches diabetes from the point of view of a boy who must become responsible for taking his medication and who must deal with the problem of overprotective parents.

AIDS is a health problem of recent origin, but the numbers of AIDS victims are growing by leaps and bounds. *Ryan White: My Own Story* is a fine, upbeat book in which Ryan White documents his public battle with AIDS. The book is an account of his day-to-day life with AIDS, of the discrimination that he encountered, and of his dying. This book is intended for sixth grade and above, but middle-grade children can appreciate it as a read aloud. *Fighting Back: What Some People Are Doing About AIDS* is also a nonfiction piece. Susan Kuklin tells with candor the facts of living with AIDS. *Children and the AIDS Virus* by Rosmarie Hausherr is a different treatment of this subject. The book is written at two levels, large print for younger children and smaller print for older children, and looks at the ways children can and cannot contract AIDS. Linda Walvoord Girard wrote a fiction story about AIDS: *Alex, the Kid with AIDS*. This superb story is so well written that Alex's illness almost seems incidental to the story. Alex acts very much like any fourth-grade boy—he even speculates about taking advantage of the fact that he has AIDS. When the school nurse explains his illness and the appropriate precautions, she does so without overly dramatizing them.

Allergies are a great problem for many people today. Some physicians believe they are increasing due to the pollution in our atmosphere. Judith Seixas has written an easy-to-read book, *Allergies: What They Are and What They Do*, which discusses the causes of allergic reactions. Doris Buchanan Smith's novel *A Taste of Blackberries* is built around the death of a boy who is allergic to bee stings and his best friend's reaction to the tragedy.

## Emotional Challenges

Emotional dysfunction is an aspect of the human condition that afflicts many people from time to time. Emotional ups and downs are a fact of life with the stresses, fast pace, and high expectations of contemporary life. Many of the challenges that children must cope with have emotional dimensions. Reading about characters with emotional disturbances helps readers empathize with their problems and in some instances with the problems their children and families face because of the character's emotional difficulties. In Cynthia Voigt's *Homecoming* and its sequel *Dicey's Song*, the mother's mental breakdown forces Dicey to take the responsibility for her younger siblings. She eventually seeks assistance from the grandmother she does not know and her mother dies in the mental hospital. In *Notes for Another Life* by Sue Ellen Bridgers, a father is emotionally ill and the mother is unable to cope. The grandparents in this story support Wren and her brother as they cope with these problems.

Some authors address the emotional difficulties of children in their books. In *The Bears' House* by Marilyn Sachs, Fran Ellen is a disturbed child who tries to cope with her mother's problems by seeking safety in her fantasies about the bears' house in her classroom. Another character who chooses to escape problems through fantasy is Junior Brown, who escapes this world by going to a planet where he is safe in Virginia Hamilton's *The Planet of Junior Brown*.

## Learning Challenges

Challenges to learning take many forms, from mild learning disabilities to severe mental retardation. Quality literature that addresses this issue is hopeful, with characters who adjust to their circumstances or make progress through education, therapy, schools, rehabilitation, or determination.

Learning disabilities arise from a number of sources that are often unidentifiable. Children are considered to have a learning disability when a significant discrepancy exists between their estimated intellectual potential and their actual level of achievement. This discrepancy is related to disorders in the learning process (Bateman, 1965) and often prevents these children from experiencing success in school. Doris Buchanan Smith writes about a nine-year-old boy in *Kelly's Creek* who cannot read, write, or draw circles, so he is unsuccessful in school. Kelly experiences success for the first time when studying marsh life in a nearby creek. His success is recognized by peers and adults. In *Just One Friend*, Lynn Hall writes

In this book, Junior and Buddy are
best friends who share a secret hideout.

about a girl with learning disabilities who fears being mainstreamed in a regular classroom. She hopes she will have just one friend.

Some students have learning difficulties because of educational or mental disabilities. These students often have specialized teachers for part of the school day, but they may be mainstreamed into regular classrooms for all or part of the day as well. In Vera Cleaver's *Me Too*, Lydia tries to help her twin Lorna, who has a disability, do simple tasks so that their father will find her more acceptable, but she is not successful. Marlene Fanta Shyer has a similar theme in *Welcome Home, Jelly Bean*. Twelve-year-old Neil's sister returns home from an institution for the retarded, and because of this their father leaves home. He invites Neil to live with him, but Neil discovers that he cannot leave. This author communicates the family torment arising from this problem and helps readers see the love and compassion that Neil feels for his sister.

Harriet Sobol writes a sister's feelings about her retarded brother in *My Brother Steven Is Retarded*. She is honest to say that he embarrasses her sometimes, but that she is very happy when he laughs. Sue Ellen Bridgers uses an adult with mental retardation as a character in *All Together Now*. The major character becomes friends with him, and her grandmother demonstrates understanding for him. *My Friend Jacob* by Lucille Clifton is also about a friendship between two people. Sam is sensitive to the problems of his friend who has Down's syndrome, and they discover that they are able to teach each other different things.

Mags, Karen Hesse's main character in *Wish on a Unicorn*, is like many siblings of disabled children. She must grow up fast because she must take care of her little brother and her sister who has brain damage, while her mother works. This means that she cannot do the things that sixth graders like to do and she cannot make friends because she must constantly attend to the younger children.

## Abused Children

Abuse of children, a painful subject, has been addressed very little until recent times. Abuse takes various forms: some children are physically abused, some are sexually abused, some are emotionally abused, and some are neglected. Giving children opportunities to read or hear books with abused characters is important because abused children usually feel they are to blame. Many abused children react with shame and try to protect their abuser. In Betsy Byars's *The Pinballs*, Harvey, a foster child, lies to protect his father who ran him down with a car while in a drunken rage. Some abused children think they imagined the whole thing. Til, in *The Girl Who Lived on the Ferris Wheel* by Louise Moeri, is not sure that she is being abused or is imagining it until she is almost killed by her mother; she thinks perhaps other children's parents punish their children the same way. It is only after she discusses the situation with a friend that she realizes her mother is not normal. Literature can help youngsters realize they are abused and their friends and relatives can understand their need for help.

Literature about abused children must not blame the victim or excuse the abusers, although it may offer insight about the abuse. Some abusive adults are also substance abusers who hurt children when they are under the influence of alcohol or drugs. In Irene Hunt's *The Lottery Rose*, the mother and her boyfriend beat Georgie when they drink. After a savage beating, Georgie spends time in the hospital and goes to a Catholic school, where he experiences the first kindness in his life. This powerful story ends with hope for Georgie's future, an important aspect of literature about abused children.

Abuse takes many different forms and is a complex issue. Virginia Hamilton's compelling story, *Sweet Whispers, Brother Rush* conveys this concept. Dabney has a congenital illness that impairs his capacity and causes him to die prematurely. Dabney's mother confines him to his bed and leaves his younger sister to care for him. The mother is not a substance abuser nor is she a disturbed character, but she is trying to protect him in her own way. Virginia Hamilton's fine book sensitizes readers to the complex issues surrounding the issue of child abuse.

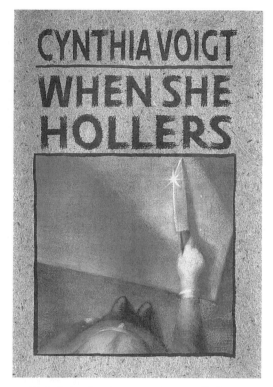

*Tish fights back against her stepfather's abuse in this compelling story.*

Cynthia Voigt takes on the challenge of writing about a difficult subject in *When She Hollers:* sexual abuse by a stepfather and a mother who won't believe it. The protagonist struggles with her problem and tries to talk with a school counselor, and eventually consults with her best friend's father, a lawyer, who cannot give her easy answers. After this she takes control of the situation and makes it clear to her stepfather that he is to leave her alone, and she takes a knife to bed with her. The resolution is not pat or clear, but is realistic.

Some nonfiction books also address abuse. Books help both children and adults recognize children's behaviors that indicate abuse and offer advice about what to do if one is the victim of abuse. Margaret Hyde's *Cry Softly! The Story of Child Abuse* provides lists of organizations that help abused children and their parents. This book helps readers understand the many types of people who abuse children.

Some children are neglected by their parents or caregivers, which is a form of abusive behavior. Ten-year-old Kitty in Vera Cleaver's *Moon Lake Angel* is abandoned by her father, who has a new family; then her mother remarries and Kitty ends up in a boarding house. She spends her time plotting revenge, but when the chance for revenge comes she finds that she has changed. In *Dr. Dredd's Wagon of Wonders* by Bill Brittain, Calvin is in bondage to Dr. Dredd, who took him from an orphanage because of his rain-making talent. Dr. Dredd uses him but does not provide for his basic needs. Calvin escapes Dr. Dredd, but his freedom is in the hands of a community that vacillates about what to do.

Joan Lowery Nixon writes about the lives of children sent west on an orphan train in 1860 in *A Family Apart*. The parents of these children are unable to care for them and believe their children will be better off adopted by others who can provide for them, but the children feel abandoned by their parents. Charlene Talbot also writes about the orphan train in *An Orphan for Nebraska*.

## Substance Abuse

Substance abuse may involve drugs or alcohol, and it is an issue addressed in both fiction and nonfiction literature. Authors of informational books on this subject focus most often on the ways that drugs and alcohol change the brain and the body, as do Catherine O'Neill in *Focus on Alcohol*, Jeffrey Shulman in *Focus on Cocaine and Crack*, and Paula Klevan Zeller in *Focus on Marijuana*. These nonfiction books are part of a series that provides a factual approach to substance abuse.

Walter Dean Myers writes about a gang of friends who join a basketball team at a youth center and unexpectedly become involved with drugs in *Fast Sam, Cool Clyde, and Stuff*. Alice Childress, the author of *A Hero Ain't Nothin' But a Sandwich*, takes a somewhat different approach to this issue by depicting different points of view of the various characters.

## Lifestyle Challenges

Children whose family life is different from the traditional two-parent family are apt to feel that they

Mr. Henshaw's surprising answer to Leigh Bott's letter changes Leigh's life.

are different. They may feel responsible for the changes in their family, and they often feel unloved. These children may be the victims of divorce, they may be in foster care, or they may be adopted.

Many children today experience pain and unhappiness as a result of their parents' separation: Approximately 50 percent of marriages today end in divorce. Some children live with one parent and have no memory of ever living with both; others live with neither parent. Literature can help them and their friends understand their difficulties. Books like Beverly Cleary's *Dear Mr. Henshaw*, Peggy Mann's *My Dad Lives in a Downtown Hotel*, and Jeanette Caines's *Daddy* show characters learning about the realities of living with a single parent and visiting with the other parent. They feel awkward with the situation and wonder if anything will ever be right again. Children like Joey and Lee in *My Dad* feel they are the only ones who have ever lived through this pain, but they eventually adjust to the situation. In *Daddy*, Windy learns that her father plays with her on Saturdays and that her new stepmother will join in the fun. This book shows a loving relationship in a changed family.

Middle-grade children, as well as younger children, experience pain and confusion when their parents separate. In *I, Trissy*, Norma Fox Mazer tells about the problems of a girl caught between her parents in divorce. She manages to show both the humor and the heartbreak in this story. Paula Danziger's *The Divorce Express* depicts an all-too-common situation: children shuttling back and forth between parents. During holiday times, airplanes, trains, and buses are filled with youngsters who must divide their time between parents. Betsy Byars writes about children spending a vacation with their father in *The Animal, the Vegetable & John D. Jones.*

Readers learn that life goes on after divorce in the story *A Girl Called Al* by Constance Greene. Al lives with her divorced mother in this story, which is told by a friend who lives in the same apartment building. In *The Night Swimmers*, Betsy Byars introduces three children who are raising themselves while their father tries to become a country and western singer. Retta attempts to take care of her brothers, but learns that she has to let her brothers grow up. In these stories, readers see situations that are both humorous and poignant in the lives of children growing up without family support.

Learning to get along with stepparents is a fact of modern life. Mavis Jukes has written two books focusing on this situation. In *Like Jake and Me* a young boy is learning to get along with his stepfather and preparing to live with the twins his mother is expecting. *No One Is Going to Nashville* focuses on the relationship of Sonia with her father and stepmother.

Children live with foster parents for a variety of reasons. Some are abandoned, others are waiting to be adopted, and some have suffered abuse and been removed from the abuser's care. Foster children often find their own means of survival in foster care. In Shirley Gordon's *The Boy Who Wanted a Family*, seven-year-old Michael has been in many different foster homes, but he finally finds the mother of his dreams. Chad in C. S. Adler's *The Cat That Was Left Behind*, finds it easier to relate to an old fisherman and a cat than to his foster family.

He learns how to relate to his foster family as a result of understanding the abandoned cat. Gilly in Katherine Paterson's *The Great Gilly Hopkins* has been in many foster homes and has learned not to trust people. She dreams of meeting her mother, but when she does it is not at all like her dreams. Gilly discovers that Trotter, her foster mother, is the one who understands her.

Children who are adopted and their new parents must make many adjustments. Jeanette Caines writes about the loving relationship between Abby and her adopted family in *Abby*. Harriet Sobol writes about adoption in the informational book *We Don't Look Like Our Mom and Dad*, as does Maxine Rosenberg in *Being Adopted*. Both of these books are illustrated with photographs that add to the reality of the information.

Unusual family situations arise from a variety of circumstances. In Doris Buchanan Smith's *Return to Bitter Creek*, Lacey was born out of wedlock. Her independent mother took Lacey away from her disapproving family, so Lacey grows up without family contacts. Finally, her mother takes her live-in boyfriend and Lacey to meet the family. *Mom, the Wolf Man, and Me* (Klein, 1972) is also a story of an unmarried mother. These stories shock some people, but both stories show warmth and love in unconventional situations.

An unconventional lifestyle is the theme of *I Would Rather Be a Turnip* by Vera and Bill Cleaver. Annie's older sister has an illegitimate child who comes to live with the family in a small town. Annie is prepared to hate her nephew, but discovers that she likes him.

## CLASSROOM ACTIVITIES TO ENHANCE REAL-LIFE LITERATURE

A good way to help children who do not have disabilities learn about the difficulties faced by their peers with disabilities is through units that focus on the universal problems they face. These units are also important to students who do have disabilities, as they can identify with the story characters and realize they are not the only people in the world who have encountered problems.

UNIT
SUGGESTIONS

## 13.1 Adjusting for the problems of students with disabilities

### Purpose

The purpose of this unit, designed for grades 1–4, is to introduce the kinds of adjustments that can be made to help classmates who have sensory or physical disabilities. This unit can help students understand the feelings of their peers who have disabilities and learn appropriate ways to be their friends. The outcome of this unit is a discussion of disabilities, the feelings of people about their disabilities, and ways to treat people who have disabilities. Middle-grade students can prepare a written handbook of ways that students can help students with disabilities in their classes and those they meet in other places.

### Introduction

Preceding this unit, the students should have participated in a literature-based unit to acquaint them with physical disabilities.

### Introductory Activities

1.  Ask children to explain the terms *disability, physical disability,* and *sensory disability.* Create a language experience chart about the information they volunteer. In fourth grade, the teacher could ask children to write their own meanings for these words.

2.  Ask the students to make a list of all the physical and sensory disabilities they can think of.

3.  Discuss the things that people who have physical and sensory disabilities need to have or do in order to compensate for their disabilities. For example, ask why some people wear glasses, why some people wear hearing aids, and why others use wheelchairs.

4.  Explain that there are additional adjustments that some people make, such as learning Braille, sign

language, and so forth, and that the class will be studying about these for the next few weeks.

5.  Let the children use some of the equipment used by people who have disabilities so that they can experience the difficulties involved. Bring to class a collection of eye patches, drugstore nonprescription glasses, a wheelchair, walkers, ear plugs, bandages for eyes, arm braces, a boot cast, braces if available, and crutches. Let them attempt to take the wheelchair into the bathroom and through doors, use a walker while their legs are in casts, walk with casts, leave ear plugs in for an hour, cover one eye and then both eyes with patches or bandages, and use any other equipment available.

6.  After using the equipment, have students write about their feelings and experiences. They may choose to write a letter to a friend, parent, or grandparent or to write a journal entry about their feelings. Younger children can dictate rather than write. The students could write and illustrate a class book about their experiences as handicapped people.

7.  Students can learn to communicate through the manual alphabet. They may visit with deaf children and try their new skills in communication. Books such as the following would be helpful in developing this skill.

    -   *Handmade ABC: A Manual Alphabet* by Linda Bourke
    -   *The Handmade Alphabet* by Laura Rankin
    -   *Handtalk School* by Mary Beth Miller and George Ancona
    -   *Handtalk Birthday: A Number and Story Book in Sign Language* by Remy Charlip, Mary Beth Miller, and George Ancona

## SUMMARY

Every classroom is composed of individuals who vary in social and emotional background, language ability, cultural background, physical ability, and intellectual ability. These differences are acknowledged and accepted in contemporary schools more than ever before. The variability in the school population carries with it the responsibility for making appropriate adjustments in the curriculum and materials. Presenting literature that portrays people with disabilities in a well-balanced manner enables students who do not have disabilities to better understand and identify with their peers with disabilities, and helps students who do have disabilities to identify with the characters and understand themselves better.

A wide variety of excellent literature is available for educating students about individual differences. All students are individuals, and those who have disabilities are as varied and individual as students without disabilities. Quality literature will depict this individuality and not stereotype characters. Any characters with disabilities will be integral to the book and not just stuck in to make a point.

## THOUGHT QUESTIONS

1. How has the portrayal of people with disabilities and those facing universal problems changed?

2. Why do you think the portrayal of people with disabilities has changed?

3. What trends do you predict in this kind of literature?

4. This subject has more informational books than any other discussed in this book. Why do you think this is true?

5. What kinds of books should be written about people with disabilities?

6. What kinds of books need to be written about the children who face universal problems?

## ENRICHMENT ACTIVITIES

1. Make a card file of books about people facing universal problems or disabilities. Each book should meet the standards identified earlier in this chapter.

2. Compare the treatment of a child with disabilities in two different books. How are they alike? How are they different?

3. Visit a class that has mainstreamed students and find out how often the teacher introduces literature with characters who have disabilities.

4. Write a short story about a person who has a disability.

# RECOMMENDED CHILDREN'S BOOKS

Adler, C. S. (1981). *The Cat That Was Left Behind.* Boston: Houghton Mifflin. (4–6)

Chad goes to a new foster home where the parents welcome him, but he finds it hard to warm up to them. However, after he makes friends with a cat he is able to accept the foster family.

Amadeo, Diana M. (1989). *There's a Little Bit of Me in Jamey.* Illustrated by Judith Friedman. Morton Grove, IL: Whitman. (3–6)

Brian tells this story about his younger brother Jamey, a leukemia victim. Brian gives his brother a bone marrow transplant, which is Jamey's best chance to live.

Arnold, Caroline. (1991). *A Guide Dog Puppy Grows Up.* Photographs by Richard Hewett. New York: Harcourt Brace Jovanovich. (2–5)

This book follows Honey, a golden retriever, through her training from puppy to guide dog. Each stage of training is explained with text and photographs.

Biklen, Douglas, and Ellen Barnes. (1978). *What Do You Do When Your Wheelchair Gets a Flat Tire? Questions and Answers About Disabilities.* New York: Human Policy Press. (2–5)

This book tells about children with various disabilities and how they feel about their disabilities. It also tells about their likes and dislikes, as well as how they would like to be treated.

Bourke, Linda. (1978). *Handmade ABC: A Manual Alphabet.* New York: Harvey House. (1–5)

This book uses pictures of hands to demonstrate sign language.

Bridgers, Sue Ellen. (1979). *All Together Now.* New York: Knopf. (4–6)

Casey, who is 12, goes to visit her grandmother and discovers a neighbor who is 30 but who has the mind of a 12-year-old. This man spends his days playing baseball. This is a good story with well-rounded characters.

———. (1981). *Notes for Another Life.* New York: Knopf.

Wren's father has an incurable mental illness and her mother is unable to cope with the situation. Fortunately, their grandparents are able to give Wren and her brother emotional support.

Brittain, Bill. (1987). *Dr. Dredd's Wagon of Wonders.* Illustrated by Andrew Glass. New York: Harper & Row. (5–7)

Calvin is in bondage to Dr. Dredd who took him from an orphanage because of his rain-making talent. Calvin escapes Dr. Dredd, but his freedom is in the hands of a community that vacillates about what to do.

Byars, Betsy. (1977). *The Pinballs.* New York: Delacorte. (4–6)

Harvey lies to protect his father, who ran him down with a car in a drunken rage.

———. (1980). *The Night Swimmers.* New York: Delacorte. (4–6)

Retta takes care of her brothers because their father is busy starting his career as a country and western singer. However, she discovers that she has to let the boys grow and become independent of her.

———. (1982). *The Animal, the Vegetable & John D. Jones.* Illustrated by Ruth Sanderson. New York: Delacorte. (4–6)

Clara and her older sister are looking forward to vacationing with their father until they discover that his girlfriend and her son are coming too.

Caines, Jeanette. (1973). *Abby.* Illustrated by Steven Kellogg. New York: Harper & Row. (1–3)

Abby is an adopted child whose parents and brother love her very much.

———. (1977). *Daddy.* Illustrated by Ronald Himler. New York: Harper & Row. (2–4)

Windy's daddy now plays with her only on Saturday because her parents are divorced. But she has fun playing with him and her new stepmother.

Carrick, Carol. (1985). *Stay Away from Simon!* Illustrated by Donald Carrick. New York: Clarion. (3–6)

Lucy is afraid of Simon, who has a mental disability. One snowy day he follows her and her brother after school and helps them find their way home. She is grateful, but still afraid until her parents tell her more about Simon.

Caseley, Judith. (1991). *Harry and Willy and Carrothead.* New York: Greenwillow. (K–2)

Harry was born without a hand. With his parents' guidance he develops a positive attitude. He is not disturbed by his classmates' curiosity about his disability. It is not a problem to him.

Charlip, Remy, Mary Beth Miller, and George Ancona. (1987). *Handtalk Birthday: A Number and Story Book in Sign Language.* New York: Four Winds. (all ages)

At her surprise birthday party, a deaf woman and her guests communicate using sign language. Photographs are used for illustrations.

Childress, Alice. (1973). *A Hero Ain't Nothin' But a Sandwich.* New York: Coward McCann. (5–8)

This novel focuses on drug abuse. Thirteen-year-old Benjie is in the process of becoming a heroin addict. The story is told from his point of view. The book has some humorous moments but it is generally depressing.

Cleary, Beverly. (1983). *Dear Mr. Henshaw.* New York: Morrow. (4–6)

This story is told through letters written between Leigh Botts and the author, Mr. Henshaw. Leigh explains that his parents are divorced and his mother works hard to support him. The reader comes to realize that Leigh loves his father very much.

Cleaver, Vera. (1973). *Me Too.* Philadelphia: Lippincott. (5–7)

Lydia tries to help her twin Lorna, who has a disability, do simple tasks so that their father will find her more acceptable, but she is not successful.

————. (1987). *Moon Lake Angel.* New York: Lothrop, Lee & Shephard. (4–8)

Ten-year-old Kitty is abandoned by her father, who has a new family. Her mother remarries and Kitty is sent to stay in a boarding house. She plots revenge, but cannot carry out her plans.

Cleaver, Vera and Bill. (1971). *I Would Rather Be a Turnip.* Philadelphia: Lippincott. (5–7)

Annie lives in a small town where everyone knows everything about the people who live there. She is angry because her older sister's illegitimate son, Calvin, is coming to live with them.

Clifton, Lucille. (1980). *My Friend Jacob.* Illustrated by Thomas DeGrazia. New York: Dutton. (1–4)

Sam has a friend with Down's syndrome, whose name is Jacob. This story tells how the two friends help each other.

Corcoran, Barbara. (1982). *Child of the Morning.* New York: Atheneum. (4–6)

After a skull fracture, Susan experiences odd "spells" that cause her sister and the townspeople to treat her differently. Then she learns that she has epilepsy and fears for the career in dance that she hoped to have.

Curtis, Patricia. (1981). *Cindy, a Hearing Ear Dog.* Photographs by David Cupp. New York: Dutton. (2–6)

This nonfiction book shows how dogs are trained to interpret sounds for people with hearing impairments. The photographs are appealing and instructive.

Danziger, Paula. (1982). *The Divorce Express.* New York: Delacorte. (5–7)

Phoebe must ride the divorce express every weekend because she lives with her interior decorator mother and visits her painter father each weekend. Phoebe survives the situation and becomes involved in her father's life and in school life.

de Angeli, Marguerite. (1950). *The Door in the Wall.* New York: Doubleday. (4–9)

Robin has physical impairments in his legs and is mistreated by other children. The monks help Robin learn to read, write, whittle, and use crutches. Eventually he shows his mettle and becomes a hero.

Fassler, Joan. (1975). *Howie Helps Himself*. Illustrated by Joe Lasker. Morton Grove, IL: Whitman. (K–3)

Howie is confined to a wheelchair that he cannot manage, so he must rely on others. He eventually learns to make his wheels move and is able to wheel himself to his dad.

Forrai, Maria, and Margaret Pursell. (1976). *A Look at Physical Handicaps*. Illustrated by the authors. Minneapolis: Lerner. (K–3)

This book explains physical disabilities and their causes, and ways of adjusting.

Franshawe, Elizabeth. (1975). *Rachel*. Illustrated by Michael Charlton. New York: Bradbury. (5–8)

Rachel must use a wheelchair, but she attends a regular school and does many of the same things the other children do. The author emphasizes acceptance of those with differences.

Girard, Linda Walvoord. (1991). *Alex, the Kid with AIDS*. Illustrated by Blanche Sims. Morton Grove, IL: Whitman. (3–5)

Alex is the new kid in fourth grade, who also has AIDS. This good story entertains without overdoing the informative aspect of his illness.

Gordon, Shirley. (1980). *The Boy Who Wanted a Family*. New York: Harper & Row. (1–3)

Seven-year-old Michael has been in many foster homes. In this story with a happy ending, he finally finds the mother of his dreams.

Greene, Constance. (1969). *A Girl Called Al*. Illustrated by Byron Barton. New York: Viking. (4–7)

Al lives with her mother because her parents are divorced. She is an independent character who expresses a sophisticated attitude toward life. This story is told by a friend who lives in the same apartment building.

Haldane, Suzanne. (1991). *Helping Hands: How Monkeys Assist People Who Are Disabled*. New York: Dutton. (3–7)

Through this nonfiction book illustrated with photographs, children can learn about the ways that monkeys can help disabled people.

Hall, Lynn. (1985). *Just One Friend*. New York: Macmillan. (4–6)

In this book, a girl with learning disabilities faces her fears of being mainstreamed. Her greatest fear is that she will not have a friend.

Hamilton, Virginia. (1971). *The Planet of Junior Brown*. New York: Macmillan. (6–8)

Junior Brown is a talented musician who weighs nearly 300 pounds and has a very unhappy life. His friend, Buddy, builds a community of homeless children, so Junior moves out of his destructive home into the community of homeless children.

————. (1981). *Sweet Whispers, Brother Rush*. New York: Philomel. (6–8)

This story is about Dabney who is "slow" and "different." He has a rare illness and eventually dies. The mother confines Dabney to bed and his 14-year-old sister must care for him until he dies.

Hausherr, Rosmarie. (1989). *Children and the AIDS Virus*. New York: Clarion. (3–6)

This book looks at AIDS and the ways that children can and cannot get the disease. The book is written at two levels, with big print for young children and small print for older children.

Hesse, Karen. (1991). *Wish on a Unicorn*. San Diego: Holt. (4–6)

Mags must take care of her younger brother and her sister, who has brain damage, while their mother works. She longs to be like other sixth graders.

Howard, Ellen. (1987). *Edith Herself.* New York: Atheneum. (3–7)

Edith is orphaned and goes to live with her older sister. But then she begins to have seizures. This story is set in the 1890s, before there was any help for people with epilepsy.

Hunt, Irene. (1976). *The Lottery Rose.* New York: Scribner's. (4–7)

Georgie has been abused from babyhood by his mother and her boyfriend, who beat him savagely when they drink. Then he is placed in a Catholic school where he is treated better than he was ever treated before.

Hyde, Margaret. (1980). *Cry Softly! The Story of Child Abuse.* Louisville, KY: Westminster Press. (3–6)

This book provides a list of organizations that help abused children and their parents. It also helps concerned people to understand that child abuse is not confined to any particular people or class of people in society.

Jukes, Mavis. (1983). *No One Is Going to Nashville.* Illustrated by Lloyd Bloom. New York: Knopf. (1–3)

This book tells about the relationship between Sonia and her father and stepmother. She is adjusting to the new relationships that resulted from her parents' divorce.

————. (1984). *Like Jake and Me.* Illustrated by Lloyd Bloom. New York: Knopf. (1–3)

This story portrays a young boy who is learning to understand his stepfather. His mother is expecting twins and he obviously has a warm, loving relationship with her.

Killilea, Marie. (1954). *Karen.* New York: Dodd Mead. (2–6)

Karen is born with cerebral palsy. This book addresses her family's adjustment and acceptance of her disability.

Kipnis, Lynn, and Adler, Susan. (1979). *You Can't Catch Diabetes from a Friend.* Illustrated by Richard Benkof. Gainesville, FL: Crestwood House. (2–6)

In simple text and photographs, this book explains diabetes and the daily routines of diabetic children. The children in the book are different ages and from different backgrounds.

Klein, Norma. (1972). *Mom, the Wolf Man, and Me.* New York: Pantheon. (5–7)

Brett is afraid life with her unwed mother will change if her mother marries. She and her mother are involved in a variety of activities together.

Kuklin, Susan. (1989). *Fighting Back: What Some People Are Doing About AIDS.* New York: Putnam. (6–12)

This nonfiction book tells what it is like to live with AIDS. The author writes factual material with candor.

Little, Jean. (1962). *Mine for Keeps.* Illustrated by Lewis Parker. New York: Little, Brown. (4–6)

Sally has always attended a special school for the disabled. Now she is to attend a regular school and she is frightened of the change. A puppy helps her make the adjustment.

————. (1972). *From Anna.* New York: Harper & Row. (4–6)

Anna and her family escape from Nazi Germany. In Canada, her family discovers that her clumsy, awkward behavior is caused by vision difficulties. She overcomes her problems by getting glasses.

————. (1986). *Different Dragons.* Illustrated by Laura Fernandez. New York: Viking. (3–6)

The story of a boy's battle with his fears of darkness, thunderstorms, and dogs. In the process of facing his fears he learns about his brother's and father's fears.

————. (1987). *Little by Little.* New York: Puffin. (3–6)

The autobiography of Jean Little, who has led an extraordinary life. She has been nearly blind from birth, but overcame ridicule, rejection, and bullying to find friends and to write both poetry and stories.

MacLachlan, Patricia. (1979). *Through Grandpa's Eyes*. New York: Harper & Row. (1–3)

John's grandfather is blind, but he learns to see better from his grandfather, who also plays the cello.

Mann, Peggy. (1973). *My Dad Lives in a Downtown Hotel*. Illustrated by Richard Cuffari. New York: Doubleday. (3–5)

Joey learns about life in a divorced family in this book. He finds it awkward and uncomfortable to visit his dad in a hotel.

Mazer, Norma Fox. (1973). *I, Trissy*. New York: Delacorte. (4–6)

Trissy is caught between her divorced parents. This divorce story includes both humor and sadness.

Miller, Mary Beth, and George Ancona. (1991). *Handtalk School*. New York: Four Winds. (1–3)

Colored photographs illustrate this book based on an actual school, teachers, and students.

Moeri, Louise. (1979). *The Girl Who Lived on the Ferris Wheel*. Bergenfield, NJ: Dutton. (5–8)

Til is not sure if she is being abused or is imagining it until she is almost killed by her mother. After she discusses the situation with a friend she realizes her mother is not normal.

Myers, Walter Dean. (1975). *Fast Sam, Cool Clyde, and Stuff*. New York: Viking. (6–12)

Stuff and his friends join a basketball team and inadvertently become involved with drugs.

Nixon, Joan Lowery. (1987). *A Family Apart*. New York: Bantam. (4–6)

This book tells about the lives of a family of children sent west on an orphan train because their families could not care for them. The children struggle with their parents' decision because they feel abandoned.

O'Neill, Catherine. (1990). *Focus on Alcohol*. Illustrated by David Neuhaus. New York: 21st Century Books. (4–6)

This is one of a series of books that examines drugs. This one looks at the impact of alcohol on the brain.

Paterson, Katherine. (1978). *The Great Gilly Hopkins*. New York: Crowell. (4–6)

Gilly has lived in many foster homes and has lost faith in foster parents. She dreams about meeting her mother, but the meeting is nothing like her dreams. She matures and discovers that she loves Trotter, her foster mother.

Rabe, Bernice. (1981). *The Balancing Girl*. Illustrated by Lillian Hoban. New York: Dutton. (K–3)

Margaret, a first grader, is able to balance many things while using braces with crutches. She also gets around easily in a wheelchair.

Rankin, Laura. (1991). *The Handmade Alphabet*. New York: Dial. (1–4)

This is an alphabet picture book that features the manual alphabet used in sign language. The author explains that her stepson is deaf.

Rosenberg, Maxine. (1983). *My Friend Leslie*. Photographs by George Ancona. New York: Lothrop, Lee & Shepard. (K–3)

This book is a photographic essay about Leslie, who has multiple handicaps. The book shows the acceptance of her kindergarten classmates.

————. (1984). *Being Adopted*. Photographs by George Ancona. New York: Lothrop, Lee & Shephard. (3–6)

This informational book, illustrated with photographs, provides straightforward information about adoption.

Roy, Ron. (1982). *Where's Buddy?* Illustrated by Troy Howell. New York: Clarion. (2–5)

Seven-year-old Buddy has diabetes. While his older brother is babysitting, he disappears. He is found in a cave and has not taken his medicine.

Sachs, Marilyn. (1971). *The Bears' House.* Illustrated by Louis Glanzman. New York: Doubleday. (3–6)

Fran Ellen and her siblings try to run the house after their father deserts them and their mother has a nervous breakdown. Readers are left to imagine whether Fran Ellen will survive.

Savitz, Harriet. (1978). *Wheelchair Champions: A History of Wheelchair Sports.* New York: Crowell. (3–6)

This is an informational book about real people in wheelchairs who excel in sports and are involved in wheelchair competition.

Seixas, Judith. (1991). *Allergies: What They Are, What They Do.* Illustrated by Tom Huffman. New York: Greenwillow. (2–4).

This easy-to-read book addresses the causes of allergic reactions. It is illustrated with cartoons.

Shulman, Jeffrey. (1990). *Focus on Cocaine and Crack.* Illustrated by David Neuhaus. New York: 21st Century. (4–6)

This is one of a series of books that examines the impact of drugs on the body and the brain.

Shyer, Marlene Fanta. (1978). *Welcome Home, Jellybean.* New York: Scribner's. (4–6)

Twelve-year-old Neil has a sister who has lived in an institution for people with mental retardation, but when she returns home the family has problems.

Slepian, Jan. (1980). *The Alfred Summer.* New York: Macmillan. (4–6)

Alfred has an overprotective mother and a father who ignores him. He makes two friends during the summer and his independence grows.

Smith, Doris Buchanan. (1973). *A Taste of Blackberries.* Illustrated by Charles Robinson. New York: Crowell. (3–5)

Jamie dies of an allergic reaction to a bee sting. His best friend blames himself for his death. After the funeral, he offers to become Jamie's mother's son.

———. (1975). *Kelly's Creek.* Illustrated by Alan Tiegreen. New York: Crowell. (2–5)

Nine-year-old Kelly knows that he is not like other children. He can't read, write, or even draw circles. He develops an interest in marsh life and becomes successful.

———. (1986). *Return to Bitter Creek.* New York: Viking. (5–8)

Lacey has never known her grandparents and cousins because her mother moved away right after Lacey was born out of wedlock. Lacey's mother, her mother's boyfriend, and Lacey return to meet the family.

Sobol, Harriet. (1977). *My Brother Steven Is Retarded.* Photos by Patricia Agre. New York: Macmillan. (1–4)

This story is told from the point of view of Beth, who has a brother with mental retardation. She expresses her embarrassment in his behavior and her pleasure when he laughs.

———. (1984). *We Don't Look Like Our Mom and Dad.* Photographs by Patricia Agre. New York: Macmillan. (3–6)

This informational book explores the problems of adjustment in an adopted family. It is a candid treatment of multiracial adoption.

Talbot, Charlene. (1979). *An Orphan for Nebraska.* New York: Atheneum. (2–5)

This historical fiction is based on the actual orphan trains that carried children from the East to be adopted by families in the Midwest.

Voigt, Cynthia. (1994). *When She Hollers.* New York: Atheneum. (4–8)

This is a sensitive book about sexual abuse by a stepfather and a mother who won't believe it.

_____ . (1981). *Homecoming*. New York: Atheneum. (3–6)

Dicey's mother experiences a mental breakdown and goes to a mental hospital in this book. Dicey manages to take care of her younger siblings and to get them to their grandmother, who is virtually unknown to all of the children.

_____ . (1983). *Dicey's Song*. New York: Atheneum. (3–6)

In this sequel to *Homecoming*, Dicey and her younger siblings are living with their grandmother while their mother is confined to a mental hospital. Dicey and her grandmother build a relationship, and the children's mother dies.

White, Ryan, and Ann Marie Cunningham. (1991). *Ryan White: My Own Story*. New York: Dial. (6–12)

In this account, co-authored by Ryan White, he tells about his battle with AIDS, the discrimination he suffered, and dying. Nevertheless, this is an upbeat treatment.

Wolf, Bernard. (1974). *Don't Feel Sorry for Paul*. Philadelphia: Lippincott. (1–6)

Paul wears prostheses on his right arm and both legs. Nevertheless, he can write, run, play ball, and do many other things that children without disabilities can do. This book is illustrated with black-and-white photographs.

_____ . (1977). *Anna's Silent World*. Philadelphia: Lippincott. (1–6)

Six-year-old Anna was born deaf. She has a profound hearing loss but has learned to speak and to understand the people around her. The black-and-white photographs in this picture book show Anna's life and help us realize that she is a many-faceted person who thoroughly enjoys life.

Zeller, Paula Klevan. (1990). *Focus on Marijuana*. Illustrated by David Neuhaus. New York: 21st Century. (4–6)

This is one of a series of books that explores the influence of drugs on the body and brain.

# Fourteen

## GUIDING QUESTIONS

1. What factors are important when selecting literature for developing multicultural sensitivity?

2. Think of a holiday or custom that is different from those your family celebrates. How did you first become aware of this tradition? Is this holiday or custom similar to one that you celebrate?

3. How can literature contribute to multicultural education?

## OVERVIEW

Today's educators instruct a more varied student population than did those of any preceding generation, a result of the diversity of the larger society. Asian American, African American, Hispanic American, and Native American students all have widely diverse cultural experiences. Increased numbers of immigrants have come to our shores to escape political, economic, and social ferment throughout the world. Our diverse culture is constituted of many traditions, beliefs, and lifestyles, but we are all human beings who share needs, hopes, and dreams. Parents, teachers, and librarians have a responsibility to present a world view that enables children to respect and value the traditions of people from varied backgrounds.

**Multicultural children's literature** encompasses literature that *represents any distinct cultural group through accurate portrayal and rich detail.* The "cultural information may be so naturally and truthfully woven into the story that it becomes evident that the author and illustrator are intimately familiar with the nuances of a culture" (Yokota, 1993, p. 157). Unless a book is culturally accurate, it cannot be considered a quality piece of multicultural literature.

Harris (1990) argues that quality multicultural literature presents cultural experiences in culturally and historically authentic ways. Culturally conscious books provide exceptional aesthetic experiences. They entertain, educate, and inform; they also engender racial pride (p. 551). An example of such a book is Yoko Kawashima Watkins' *So Far from the Bamboo Grove,* the sensitive story of a young Japanese girl's escape from Korea during World War II.

In addition to cultural consciousness, some authorities believe that multicultural literature should reflect an **inside perspective,** meaning that *a cultural group should be portrayed from the point of view of one who*

# Literature and Multicultural Understanding

is a member of the group (Yokota, 1993). Of course, this is a controversial issue; some authors who are not members of a particular cultural group have written authentic books that have been well received, such as Suzanne Staples's story about Pakistan, *Shabanu: Daughter of the Wind.* Authenticity, however, is an important consideration in selecting multicultural literature, whichever point of view is held.

The foundations of multiculturalism in the United States and the goals of multicultural education are the focus of this chapter. The role of multicultural literature in creating children's awareness and cultural understanding is also explored.

## INTRODUCTION

Young children reflect the culture into which they are born. When children come to school, they bring knowledge of the social world that is unique to their cultural background. Their concepts of family, morality, rules, time, gender roles, dress, safety, and values are part of their cultural heritage. All of these factors play roles in students' adjustment to school and their success. They do, however, continue to acquire knowledge through their school experience. Through encountering children from other cultures and those with different family structures, they learn to value the similarities and differences among people.

Multicultural education seeks to promote pride in belonging to a particular racial, ethnic, cultural, or economic group and to validate the traditions and experiences of minority groups. The curricula and school materials should afford children opportunities to understand themselves and others. No matter what their cultural background, students should have opportunities to point with pride to role models, to have positive group identity, and to cherish their own heritage. The overall goal of multicultural education is to promote understanding and acceptance of self and others (Tway, 1993).

As the opening vignette demonstrates, children can experience others' lives vicariously through literature. Although young children are ethnocentric and unable to "conceptualize another's point of view, they can respond to another's emotional experience" (Ramsey, 1987, p. 13). Children can predict how a person will react to a given situation and communicate this understanding (Borke, 1971). A young child will kiss another child who has fallen down or hand her a favorite toy to make her feel better. A four-year-old showed her ability to empathize when she said to a friend, "Poor Prissy, why do you look so gloomy?" Then she patted her friend.

Children who are from three to seven years old are more accepting of different social conventions than children from eight to nine (Carter and Patterson, 1982). Children aged three to eight are developing group-referenced identities, early perceptions of human differences, and interpersonal skills (Ramsey, 1987). These data suggest that it is important to introduce culturally diverse materials early in the elementary school curriculum.

Angie Clifford saw a copy of Sherley Anne Williams's *Working Cotton* on display at the local children's bookstore and decided to buy it to read to her first-grade class. Her class was clearly multicultural, with a mix of African American, Cambodian, and white children, and she already had exhausted the library's supply of multicultural literature.

The next morning she introduced *Working Cotton*. She held the book up and asked, "How many of you have seen cotton growing?"

Most of the children held up their hands.

"How many of you have picked cotton?"

None of the children had.

Tyrone said, "My daddy picked cotton and he said it was real hard work."

May said, "My mama and daddy both picked cotton and they said it made their hands bleed."

"My daddy topped 'bacca.' Does that count?" Tyree offered.

In a chorus the children said, "Cotton's harder to pick than 'bacca.'"

Ms. Clifford said, "As you listen, think about how the people in this story lived and how their lives are different from your life."

After completing the story, she asked the children, "What do you think of the people in the story?"

Several students said, "They had a hard life."

"I'm glad I don't have to work like that!" another child volunteered.

Then several others said, "Yeah! That's awful."

Ms. Clifford asked the children to think of all the "bad" things about working cotton—the children produced a long list. Then she asked them to think of the good things in the story, and they discovered a number of happy things such as the family feelings and the way they cared for one another. Then she asked them what they would like to do to show their feelings about the story. One of the students suggested they act out the story and the others thought that was a good idea.

The next day, she brought a bag, weighted to simulate a bag full of cotton. She also provided some cotton bolls to give the children an idea of how the bolls hurt the pickers' hands. As they dramatized the story they discovered the bag's weight and the backache that goes with dragging it. The following day they continued this theme by discussing migrant workers and how they lived.

## MULTICULTURALISM IN THE UNITED STATES

The richness and **diversity** of this country is based on the traditions of its *many different racial and ethnic groups* (Dyer, 1978; Stoodt, 1992b). This philosophy of multiculturalism is in direct contrast with the melting pot concept of one nation, one people, a homogenized view of culture inspired by Zangwill's play *Melting Pot*. The Industrial Revolution and its accompanying surge of nationalism created a climate that nurtured the melting-pot concept as a symbol of assimilation, which became a goal of educators and educational institutions (Dyer, 1978). Immigrants were expected to leave their own traditions at the gates of Ellis Island and assume the culture and traditions of American society. In *An Ellis Island Christmas* Maxine Leighton portrays a young Polish girl's arrival on Ellis Island. Her first encounter in this new world was filled with strange words, smells, and foods. Bananas were unknown in Poland so she ate the skin.

Immigrants came to the United States for many different reasons. Some came to find freedom and a better life for their children. The Italian American father in Elisa Bartone's *Peppe the*

*Lamplighter* says, "Did I come to America for my son to light the street lamps?" The literature about European immigrants offers children from the majority culture insight into their own cultural heritages. Many European immigrants faced prejudice and tried to lose the traces of their heritage that made them different from the dominant culture of the time.

African Americans, Mexican Americans, Native Americans, and Asian Americans were also forced to assimilate into this dominant European culture of white, Anglo-Saxon Protestant traditions (Weinberg, 1974). Japanese Americans were hurt and betrayed when they were sent into internment camps in this country during World War II. Jerry Stanley portrays this troubled time in our history in *I Am an American: A True Story of Japanese Internment.* The photographs illustrating this book create a poignant portrait of Japanese American families.

## Defining Multiculturalism

There is little agreement about the meaning of multiculturalism and of multicultural literature. Madigan (1993) interviewed a number of leaders in multicultural education and literature to obtain an understanding of these terms. Harriet Rohmer, the founder and driving force behind Children's Book Press, says that **multicultural literature** is a *literature of inclusion: stories from and stories about all our children* (Madigan, 1993). Elizabeth Martinez, a college teacher and reviewer of children's books, considers multiculturalism a world view. She believes that multicultural literature emphasizes respect for the different historical perspectives and cultures in human society (Madigan, 1993).

Ginny Moore-Kruse, director of the Cooperative Children's Book Center at the University of Wisconsin-Madison library, points out that although many people believe multicultural books are flooding the market, of the 65,000 to 70,000 children's books in print only a small percentage can be classified as multicultural. In reality there is only a gradual increase in the number of these books (Madigan, 1993).

Hazel Rochman (1993), herself an immigrant, is vehement about two essentials of **multiculturalism:**

*(1) multiculturalism means across cultures, against borders, and (2) multiculturalism doesn't mean only people of color.* Although multicultural education is difficult to define, beginning with an understanding of its goals will help. The following objectives reflect some of the areas of common agreement (Stoodt, 1992a; Ramsey, 1987):

1. Cultural studies help children understand the humanity they share with all people and their membership in the larger society. All people can feel love, have fear, experience joy, and have their own values. Realizing that they are like people in other cultures helps children develop the ability to take different perspectives.

2. Children learn to view themselves as members of many different groups rather than seeking an identity based solely on race, gender, or socioeconomic status. For example, an individual may be black and an American, as well as a six-year-old member of a first-grade class and a member of the Methodist Church. Teachers and students alike learn to understand that Chinese Americans are members of a cultural group and they are also Americans; but being a member of a cultural group does not make an individual exactly like other members of that group.

3. Multicultural education increases children's understanding, appreciation, and respect for different cultures and their contributions to the quality of life in the world.

4. Multicultural education encourages open communication between schools and families and demonstrates a genuine concern for the individual.

5. Multicultural education fosters the development of positive group identities and understandings of many lifestyles. This encourages a broad range of social relationships, openness, and interest in others.

Through multicultural education, these goals are integrated throughout the curriculum so that children can internalize and act upon them. Multiculturalism is not a class or a subject; instead, it involves attitudes, sensitivities, and values that are infused throughout the school day in everything that is done. It fosters children's social, emotional, and cognitive development. This helps children to recognize and accept cultural diversity as a part of the society and to understand that these differences can enhance the quality of life.

## MULTICULTURAL EDUCATION

**Culture** is defined as *the shared knowledge a group uses to construct meaning for its members* (Goodenough, 1971; Wurzel, 1988; Costello, 1992). The family culture is the primary socializing agent for young children. Cultural experiences shape world view and influence interaction with others (Wurzel, 1988). Children enter school reflecting the cultural knowledge of their families and immediate environment. Their conceptualization of family, morality, values, rules, sex roles, time, dress, and safety are part of their subculture (Ramsey, 1987). This knowledge guides their understandings and interactions in social contexts and influences their ability to adjust and succeed in school (Goodenough, 1971; Dyer, 1978; Wurzel, 1988; Stoodt, 1992b). Families do not work alone to socialize children, however; schools, churches, neighborhoods, and places of work also function in socializing children and adults.

Traditionally the school has been viewed as an agent of acculturation. Outside the home, the school is the major socializing institution (Banks, 1989; Ramsey, 1987). Schools have their own culture. All teaching occurs in a sociocultural context and all materials and practices reflect social values. Therefore, teachers' attitudes, materials, and practices—particularly as they relate to multicultural education—are very important.

### The Role of Teachers

Teachers have unique and powerful opportunities to influence the experiences and attitudes of their students. With children's literature and classroom activities, they can expand students' knowledge beyond immediate experiences. An ancient Native American proverb says, "Do not judge another man until you have walked in his moccasins for three moons." Reading and exploring literature permit children to "walk in another's moccasins," to identify with others, and to share in their lives.

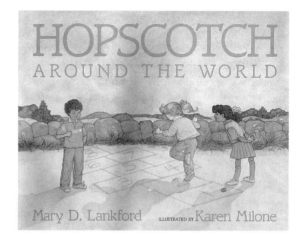

*This book is a collection of nineteen hopscotch games from all over the world.*

When they recognize the humanity that all people have in common no matter what their cultural heritage, they learn that racism, discrimination, and prejudice are unacceptable in a just world.

By making themselves knowledgeable about different cultural styles and traditions, teachers can help children appreciate the diversity within their classrooms and the world. They can learn about games, holidays, music, and literature that distinguish cultural groups. Books such as Mary Lankford's *Hopscotch Around the World* and Jane Yolen's *Street Rhymes Around the World* help them explore the differences and similarities of play around the world. Children will enjoy playing the games, singing the songs, and dancing the street rhymes. Since schools exist all over the world, books such as Edith Baer's *The Way We Go to School* can be a means of amplifying global awareness. Ten well-known artists reveal a day in the lives of children in eight different countries, showing the similarities and differences but emphasizing the commonality of all human beings in Anno's *All in a Day*.

### The Role of Literature

Attitudes toward people who are different are influenced by the images of racial and ethnic groups portrayed in books and in the media. Young children

*Fourteen simple poems celebrate the power of childhood from the perspectives of a rich variety of cultures.*

are especially susceptible to stereotypes, as they do not have critical thinking skills yet and accept information from books, television, and newspapers as factual. Books transmit messages to readers and listeners about minority groups. Unfortunately, these messages frequently encourage children to develop negative attitudes toward individuals who have a different physical appearance from themselves (Gast, 1970; Dieterich, 1972).

Books can also, however, foster feelings of pride in culture and understanding of people who look different. In *My Song Is Beautiful*, Mary Ann Hoberman helps children celebrate childhood from many cultural perspectives. Eloise Greenfield's poems in *Night on Neighborhood Street* realistically describe African American families and their friends. The illustrations, by Jan Spivey Gilchrist, are done is such a way that children see themselves and others realistically. After listening to this story, kindergarten children made comments such as,

"Hey, that baby looks just like me when I was little." An African American mother reading the book became tearful because it reminded her so much of her family growing up and her children when they were babies (Costello, 1992). One white child commented, "My little brother does the same thing," after hearing a poem from the book. Books such as these foster pride in one's own culture and understanding of other cultures. Reading about familiar experiences conveys the message that each person is valuable and important (Rasinski and Padak, 1990).

## The Role of the Curriculum

The use of literature is one way to integrate the goals of a multicultural program into the overall curriculum. Textbooks often provide sanitized descriptions of events, but authors of trade books can write authentic descriptions. Textbooks are usually written from the perspective of the majority population. Trade books can give more than a single point of view, as well as introduce controversy and examine issues. Banks (1989) has proposed a four-level curriculum model for integrating multicultural literature in the classroom. The following levels are adapted from Banks' work:

1. *Contributions approach.* The lowest level of the model is already found in many classrooms. Literature in this category focuses on holiday traditions and biographies of heroes of a particular culture. Such books are used regularly during Black History Month or Native American Week.

2. *Additive approach.* The structure of the curriculum is unchanged, but certain themes incorporating multiculturalism are added. Rasinski and Padak (1990) suggest that the two lower levels of Banks' model are relatively simple to incorporate, but they patronize the cultural groups addressed.

3. *Transformation approach.* This level encourages students to view a problem from more than one perspective, allowing them "to see the interconnectedness of various ethnic groups with the dominant culture" (Rasinski and Padak, 1990, p. 578). A goal of this curriculum model is to help children learn to

experience another person's fate as their own (Chukovsky, 1963).

4. *Decision making and social action.* In thinking at this level, students consider other points of view and "identify social problems and concerns, make decisions and take actions to resolve the problems they have identified" (Banks, 1989, p. 75). Literature enables children to experience a viewpoint different from the majority. Stories can foster in children compassion and humanness, as well as the ability to feel joy about another person's happiness (Chukovsky, 1963).

## THE VALUE OF MULTICULTURAL LITERATURE

Literature is one way of transmitting values to children. Children broaden their experiences and understanding of people and events through quality literature. Vicarious experiences provide readers new lenses with which to view the world. Moreover, literature is an effective means of developing the following three components essential to the understanding of multiculturalism (Bishop, 1987):

1. Literature shows the emotions we share with one another, making us aware of our emotional bonds to humanity.

2. Literature enables us to appreciate our differences and recognize the uniqueness of each cultural group that enriches "the larger society by adding distinctive flavors to the 'salad bowl' of our common nationality" (p. 61).

3. Literature can be a catalyst for social reform.

Carefully selected literature enables children to "walk in another's moccasins," making literature an excellent medium for building respect for and sensitivity to other cultures. Through literature children learn that others have the same expectations, fears, and aspirations as they do. "Books are an effective and powerful way to validate children's unique lifestyles and to expand their awareness beyond their immediate experiences" (Ramsey, 1987, p. 14). Literature is art that is not so concerned with reproducing the world in which we live as with creating a world that we can imagine

(Sloan, 1984). Imagination permits us to see possibilities for living in harmony with one another. *Amazing Grace* by Mary Hoffman illustrates the power of imagination in a young girl's life as she confronts being told what she cannot do because she is female and African American. Grace is beautiful and the exquisite illustrations draw readers into the warm family situation. Multicultural literature enables children to recognize both their similarities and differences with other people.

Fine literature helps children recognize the commonalities they share with others who may be of a different gender, race, or socioeconomic class (Costello, 1991). It also promotes a positive self-identity and pride in cultural heritage. In *Brown Angels: An Album of Pictures and Verse*, Walter Dean Myers has combined superb photographs of African American children with sensitive poetry. The pictures show the pride and love of parents. Elizabeth Fitzgerald Howard's *Aunt Flossie's Hats (and Crab Cakes Later)* develops readers' understanding of the complex nature of African American life. In this story Sarah and Susan enjoy sharing tea, cookies, crab cakes, and stories about hats with their Aunt Flossie; all of the characters are actual people.

Early childhood educators have the opportunity to expand and influence children's social perceptions through selecting quality literature. Children's perceptions of themselves and others are influenced by the stories they see and hear (Cohen, 1972; Miel and Kiesten, 1967). Children learn about different cultural groups through literature such as *Mrs. Katz and Tush* by Patricia Polacco, a picture book that teaches about discrimination against both Jewish people and African Americans.

Literature can increase children's cultural sensitivity and awareness. Reading about people from different cultural backgrounds provides students with contrasting perspectives that ultimately increase their understanding and acceptance of others (Tway, 1989; Stoodt, 1992a; Madigan, 1993). Multicultural literature fosters children's social and emotional development throughout the elementary school. It is, therefore, particularly important to select books that are free of stereotypes and minority misrepresentation (Deane, 1989). Limited availability of quality books with

Larnel, a young black boy, discovers common themes of suffering and triumph with Mrs. Katz, an older Jewish neighbor he befriends.

minority characters can negatively affect children's reading, language development, and self-esteem (Costello, 1991; Meyer-Reimer, 1992).

Literature can provide children with models, heroes and heroines they can emulate. Students of all ages in all cultures need models who have "made it" in the world. Such people are very important in their lives. *Diego* is an example of such a book. Jeanette Winter uses vibrant miniature paintings to tell about Diego Rivera's early years. She shows how his love of painting and of his country made him one of the greatest muralists of Mexico and of the world. Another inspiring book is William Miller's *Zora Hurston and the Chinaberry Tree*, which shows the independent spirit and belief in her own dreams of Zora Neale Hurston, a renowned writer who happens to be African American.

Stories provide a framework for interpretation of reality (Hardy, 1978). Narrative is used to organize and interpret perceptions of the world. Fiction allows children to experience the lives of others. It can reconfirm one's own existence and humanity. Children's culture is affirmed when they find their own life experiences mirrored in books. When literature positively reflects their culture, children are empowered (Rasinski and Padak, 1990). Writing from the perspective of a Chinese girl and her family, Laurence Yep depicts the struggle of Chinese immigrants as they move to West Virginia in the 1920s in the story *Star Fisher*. Many youngsters can identify with their struggles to adjust.

On the other hand, "Children who discover that people like themselves are excluded or denigrated get a different message altogether. They learn that they are not valued members of society and that reading can be a negative or hurtful experience" (Bishop, 1987, p. 61). Some stories that are potentially negative, however, such as Mildred Taylor's historical fiction *The Gold Cadillac*, can help present-day students understand the prejudice with which African Americans have often been treated in this country. Such understanding can be a positive influence on their development.

Students are able to take pride in their ethnic membership when they enjoy stories that have characters who look and feel as they often do (Harris, 1990). In *Tall Boy's Journey* Joanna Kraus describes Kim Moo Yong, who is having difficulty adjusting to his adoptive parents' culture. Not all children have had this exact experience, but many children can empathize with him because they have been in similar confusing situations. Sherry Garland's Japanese story *The Lotus Seed* emphasizes the importance of family and family traditions. *Storm in the Night* by Mary Stolz helps children understand that fear is part of being human and that it is nothing to be ashamed of feeling. In *Sister*, Eloise Greenfield helps older readers understand feelings of isolation and despair when a family member dies. Joyce Hansen's *Yellow Bird and Me* discusses the topic of reading difficulty and helps children gain insights and understandings about the frustrations students experience when they have difficulty reading printed materials.

Honest portrayal of characters in literature permits young readers to recognize themselves in stories and illustrations. Books can prove meaningless if children do not encounter something familiar that triggers their own schemata. *Clean Your Room, Harvey Moon!* by Pat Cummings illustrates the kind of book that children can relate to. They empathize with Harvey Moon, who dislikes cleaning his room just as much as they do. When children's experiences do not relate to a particular book someone has to provide connections that will help them connect with the story.

Multicultural literature also helps children learn the beliefs and values of their own cultures as well as others. Traditional literature is especially valuable for increasing this awareness (Piper, 1986). A number of stories for younger children help them understand the traditions and rituals associated with various groups. The Jewish holiday Passover is the focus of the book *The Four Questions* by Lynn Schwartz. Rachna Gilmore's *Lights for Gita* explains the Hindu celebration of Divali, and *My First Kwanzaa Book* by Deborah Chocolate explains the traditions of this African holiday. These books can be used to show children that people celebrate many different holidays in many different ways and also that many holidays are based on different religious beliefs. But they share similarities too, because light is important in each of these rituals.

## SELECTING AND EVALUATING MULTICULTURAL LITERATURE

Classrooms and libraries should be filled with books that authentically represent many different people, cultures, lifestyles, and points of view. Multicultural literature must be chosen carefully. Books should not be chosen simply because they have a minority character and are available (Dyer, 1978). A collection of multicultural books that lack integrity may do more harm than having no multicultural literature. Literature influences children's attitudes toward reading and books, so literature that contains stereotyped characters will influence them toward believing in those stereotypes (Davis, 1972). High-quality literature is **culturally conscious** with *authentic depictions of cultural groups.*

Literature affects not only how students view children from other cultures, but it also influences how children view themselves and their

own culture. Children's self-concepts are influenced by the images they see portrayed in media (Cohen, 1969; Miel and Kiesten, 1967). These images influence the way they see themselves, as well as the way they view people from different ethnic and cultural groups. Children respond well to stories that reflect situations they can identify within their own communities. Research with middle-school students indicates that these students prefer characters who have high self-concepts and who interact positively in middle-class settings (Johns, 1975).

Clearly minority groups have been underrepresented in children's literature in the past and this discrepancy continues. Although Bishop (1991) finds reason for optimism about multicultural literature, Reimer (1992) finds that popular booklists used to select literature for elementary classrooms and basal readers have very limited multiethnic representation. A limited number of multiethnic titles were included in Trelease's *Read Aloud Handbook* (1989) and in the 1989 International Reading Association Children's Choices List. Reimer also reports a predominance of European American authors writing multicultural literature from an "outside" point of view and a lack of teacher awareness of and attention to other cultures in the classroom. She notes a need for publishers to provide more multicultural literature, and other writers concur (Bishop, 1992; Harris, 1991). There is a particular need for multicultural literature with contemporary settings.

Although there is no consensus regarding the issues involved in selecting multicultural literature, research and discussion suggest a few significant factors to consider in reviewing multicultural literature. As you work with children from different cultures, you may think of additional factors that you believe should be added.

1. The book must be of excellent literary quality. Fiction must tell a good story, information must be interesting, and the poetry excellent. Mary Hoffman's *Amazing Grace* is a wonderful picture book and story that confronts the issues of African Americans and of women.

2. The book is culturally accurate, reflecting the values and beliefs of the culture. Cultural information helps readers develop a "true" sense of the culture. The dialogue and relationships are

*The love between a little girl and her abuela is the subject of this story told in English and spiced with Spanish phrases.*

authentic, with in-depth treatment of any cultural issues (Yokota, 1993). A shining example of such a book is Carmen Garza's *Family Pictures*, an authentic portrayal of Mexican American culture. The family album illustrations in folk art style convey a feeling of the family-centered culture.

3. Cultural details enrich stories, poems, and informational pieces. These should be woven into literature in such a way that readers develop a sense of the culture they are reading about. In *The Girl Who Loved Caterpillars*, Jean Merrill's descriptions and details help readers understand Japan.

4. The dialogue and relationships depicted in the book are authentic. *Abuela* by Arthur Dorros portrays the relationship between a girl and her abuela (grandmother). The dialogue, the relationship between grandparent and grandchild, and the relationships with the extended family are accurately portrayed in this delightful story.

5. Minority group characters are distinct individuals whose lives are rooted in their culture (Yokota, 1993). These individuals should be depicted as three-dimensional characters that children can identify with. Michael Dorris (1993), a member of the Modoc tribe, tells of turning to the Hardy boys rather than to the boring, humorless characters populating Native American literature during his childhood. A more authentic view of Native Americans is portrayed in *Toughboy and Sister*. Kirkpatrick Hill's powerful story has very real characters. The young native Alaskan brother and sister in this story must survive when their father dies in an alcoholic seizure while they are on a fishing trip in the bush.

6. Each culture has many central issues. These issues should be realistically portrayed and explored in depth so that readers can understand them and develop a realistic point of view. A fine example of such a book is Minfong Ho's *The Clay Marble*, which shows the impact of war on people's lives.

## African Americans in Children's Literature

Nancy Larrick documents what minorities already knew in her article "The All-White World of Children's Books" (1965). Her survey dramatically revealed that only 47 of the 349 books published between 1962 and 1964 depicted African Americans in contemporary settings. The few characters depicted were in menial positions. By 1975 the situation had changed somewhat, with 689 of 4,775 books showing at least one African American character in the text or illustrations (Chall, Radwin, French, and Hall, 1985). But the progress halted during the 1980s. There was a dramatic decline in the number of new authors and illustrators publishing. Walter Dean Myers (1985) attributes the changes to lack of money, conservative attitudes, and a loss of interest in politics. However, new publishers like Black Butterfly Press and Just Us Books, specializing in multicultural books by minority authors, soon emerged and the picture brightened somewhat.

Multicultural literature is most often presented during a special period, such as Black History Month, and teachers most often use biographies to focus on multicultural contributions to society. For example, Jean Marzollo's *Happy Birthday, Martin Luther King*, is a skillful description of Dr. King's life and depicts prejudice in ways that young children can understand; this a popular read-aloud for African American theme months. This an appropriate use for a biography, but multicultural literature should be infused in the classroom throughout the school year. Moreover, a variety of multicultural literature is appropriate to help children understand the diversity of the African American culture.

Gloria Pinkney illustrates the diversity among African Americans in *Back Home*, in which Ernestine returns to her North Carolina home after living up North. A "city girl," she is surprised and delighted with farm life. Donald Crews also tells a story of children who live up North, but who look forward to summer at *Bigmama's*. Many African American children identify with trips to visit family in the South. They also identify with the characters and their activities in books such as Shulamith Oppenheim's *Fireflies for Nathan*. The exquisite illustrations show a contemporary setting and a little boy chasing fireflies with his grandparents watching. African American girls take pride in their *Cornrows*, as Camille Yarbrough demonstrates. In this story, Great-Grammaw explains traditions as she braids and creates patterns. Readers learn that in the past, the patterns of the braids told much about family, village, social status, and religion.

Racism, discrimination, and prejudice are discussed openly and honestly in books such as Faith Ringgold's *Tar Beach*, which illustrates how African Americans experience discrimination in the workplace. Patricia and Frederick McKissack, in *A Long Hard Journey*, document the struggle of Pullman porters to form the first union for African Americans. In the powerful story *Scorpions*, Walter Dean Myers reveals the prejudice African American children sometimes encounter in schools, as well as the complexity of their lives. These books are good ones to stimulate discussion.

*The Righteous Revenge of Artemis Bonner*, also by Walter Dean Myers, shows a different type of multicultural literature. This very funny story is set in the Wild West, where Artemis, a tenderfoot from New York, meets all sorts of evildoers as he searches for his uncle's murderer and gold. *Drylongso* is a different and fascinating character created by Virginia Hamilton. He comes into a distressed family farm in time to relieve their desperation during a great drought. In *Masai and I*, Virginia Kroll tells the story of a little girl who learns about East Africa and the Masai in school and imagines what her life might be like if she were Masai.

## Traditional literature

African American traditional literature has many of the same themes that appear in traditional literature rooted in other cultures. *Mufaro's Beautiful Daughters* by John Steptoe has similarities to Cinderella, as does Robert San Souci's *The Talking Eggs: A Folktale of the American South*. Patricia McKissack's *Flossie and the Fox* is a well-loved tale that children like to hear again and again, probably because Flossie outsmarts the fox.

## Biography

Biography gives children heroes, heroines, and role models and includes both males and females. The biography of *Martin Luther King* by Rosemary Bray gives a detailed account of his life and his peaceful crusade to overcome injustice, while Faith Ringgold's *Aunt Harriet's Underground Railroad in the Sky* tells the story of Harriet Tubman in terms that young children can understand. Biography can be combined with other literature to create a fascinating unit. For instance, a book of Langston Hughes's poetry could be taught with Patricia McKissack's biography *Langston Hughes* to educate and interest students.

The majority of African American biographies are of sports figures, such as Lawrence Ritter's *Leagues Apart*, which tells about the lives of African American baseball players. These are only a small segment of the population, however, and children need balanced presentations. There is a wide variety of biographies available to include in the classroom, including *Rosa Parks: My Story* by Rosa

Parks and Jim Haskins, and *Sorrow's Kitchen: The Life and Folklore of Zora Neale Hurston* by Mary Lyons. Virginia Hamilton created the biography *Anthony Burns: The Defeat and Triumph of a Fugitive Slave* for older students, in which she tells how Burns gained his freedom and became a minister. Three African American women, a grandmother, a mother, and a daughter, are the focus of Eloise Greenfield's *Childtimes: A Three-Generation Memoir*, a memoir that shows the struggle of African Americans and the importance of family. Walter Dean Myers's *Now Is Your Time: The African American Struggle for Freedom* provides profiles of slaves, soldiers, inventors, and political leaders. This Coretta Scott King Award winner is important in developing pride and self-concept.

## Asian Americans in Children's Literature

As with other cultural groups, Asian Americans have been omitted from much of contemporary children's literature. The Asian American Project in 1976 revealed that the available books were either traditional literature or overgeneralized fictional books (Asian American Project, p. 76). These stories, mostly using Chinese American characters, stereotyped the physical attributes of Asian Americans. All of the characters tended to have the same straight black hair, slanted eyes, and yellowish tint to their skin coloring. These one-dimensional characters denied their own cultural traditions as part of their assimilation into the dominant culture. Another assumption in these earlier books was that all Asian countries shared the same culture and traditions. This idea is untrue and contributes to unfortunate stereotypes and overgeneralizations. Asian Americans can be funny, lyrical, angry, or wry. They are not in any way a homogenous group, although many are caught in the difficult situation of living between two cultures, the old and the new. The literature selected for developing children's multicultural sensitivity should show the complexity and conflicts faced by people everywhere. Moreover, it should contribute to children's appreciation of their own heritages. Cambodian political refugees bring memories of harrowing war experiences and

The text of this book, written in both English and Korean, will help immigrant children who are trying to adjust to a new culture.

an ancient heritage (Rochman, 1993). This is true of the Vietnamese as well.

Min Paek's *Aekyung's Dream* gives teachers an excellent opportunity to discuss the fact that all people from Asia do not look alike, talk alike, or have the same culture. Aekyung is very frustrated because her classmates call her "Chinese Eyes." She does not like living in America because people tease her. In a dream she learns "to be strong like a tree with deep roots." She uses this advice to keep from giving up as she learns English. Ellen Levine's character Mei Mei comes from Hong Kong, and she does not want to learn English. Her feelings are apparent in *I Hate English*, in which readers learn that language is important to individuals and that one does not have to give up one language in order to learn another.

Much multicultural literature that includes Asian Americans focuses on their immigration or their experiences once they are in America. Many Asian American young people came to this country alone and were thrust into a strange environment without a strong family unit for support. Brent Ashabranner's compelling book, *Into a Strange Land: Unaccompanied Refugee Youth in America*, is based on interviews with young Asian Americans from Vietnam, Cambodia, and other countries. Students from all cultures can empathize with the young people in this book. Ut, a Vietnamese girl, lives in the United States while her mother remains in Vietnam in Michele Maria Surat's *Angel Child, Dragon Child*. She feels isolated in this unfamiliar place. But she is able to express her hurt and angry feelings, which helps others understand and accept her. Some Asian children came to this country alone because they were adopted by American families. A young boy traveling to the United States to live with adoptive parents is Ann Turner's focus in *Through Moon and Stars and Night Skies*. Linda Girard also wrote about an adopted Asian boy in *We Adopted You, Benjamin Koo*. Harriet Sobol addresses the sensitive issue of adopted children's feelings about the rude questions and insensitive comments of the people they encounter in *We Don't Look Like Our Mom and Dad*.

Another major theme in this literature is the experience of war that many Asian Americans bring with them to this country. Courage in the face of the sadness of war is the theme of *Sadako and the Thousand Paper Cranes* by Elaine Coerr. This is the true story of a young girl who develops leukemia as a result of the atom bomb dropped on Hiroshima. This story shows how resilient people can be in the face of disaster and how comforting the traditional Japanese culture and symbols were to Sadako. After learning about the symbolism of the crane and the ancient art of origami, Sadako sets out to make a thousand paper cranes, but she dies before completing them. After her death, her friends honor her by completing the task. A memorial was dedicated to Sadako and others who died as a result of the atom bomb.

The turmoil of the Vietnam War is the theme of Tran-Khanh Tuyet's *The Little Weaver of Thai Yen Village*. Hien lives in a small Vietnamese village until gunfire kills her grandmother and mother. Hien is wounded and sent to the United States for medical treatment. Alone and frightened, she is befriended by a family in the United States. This true story shows how individuals struggle to maintain their culture while living in a new culture. The

oppression that stems from war is the theme of *Year of Impossible Goodbyes*. Sook Nyul Choi tells her own true story of living through Japanese oppression and Russian occupation in Korea. She eventually escaped and now lives in the United States.

### Traditional literature

Traditional literature reflects the culture, values, and beliefs of a cultural or ethnic group. Traditional literature from various Asian cultures illustrates some of the differences and similarities among these groups.

Laurence Yep's Chinese tale, *The Boy Who Swallowed Snakes*, is a story of honesty and how this trait helped the boy become prosperous, while an old man dies because of his greed. In another Chinese folktale, Julie Lawson's *The Dragon's Pearl*, a boy finds a pearl that brings great good fortune until robbers threaten to steal it. He swallows the pearl to save it and becomes a dragon. After that bad luck follows the robbers wherever they go and they learn that nothing good comes to evildoers. In *Little Plum*, Chinese author Ed Young introduces a tiny character who is able to protect the people in his village from robbers. He proves that size is not important in overcoming incredible obstacles. Laurence Yep's *The Rainbow People* is a collection of Chinese American folktales that express values and rules for living. These tales help us understand Chinese American culture.

The Japanese culture is an ancient, multifaceted culture that has often seemed mysterious to Western cultures. However, traditional literature can also help us learn about the Japanese culture. Dianne Snyder's Japanese folktale, *The Boy of the Three-Year Nap*, reveals that laziness and trickery are vices in the Japanese culture just as they are everywhere. The laziest boy in town plots to become the richest, and he does marry a rich wife but still must go to work in the end. The artist's detailed illustrations and use of color convey a feeling for the Japanese setting. Alan Schroeder's *Lily and the Wooden Bowl* is another Japanese folktale that shows the power of a grandmother's love and punishment for evil. The simple and direct language in this tale creates memorable images. These verbal images, combined with spare Japanese paintings that rely on empty space and composition, create a seamless work of art and culture. *The Tale of the Mandarin Ducks* by Katherine Paterson is an original Japanese folktale. In this story, kindly servants are rewarded for helping a mandarin duck escape a cruel lord. The story creates a feeling of compassion and love. In *The Paper Crane*, Molly Bang focuses on the significance of the origami crane in the Japanese culture. In this story, a restaurant owner has good fortune when he is paid with a paper crane instead of money.

Storytellers discovered long ago that certain themes appear in the traditional literature of cultures around the world. One of the most prevalent is the Cinderella story, which appears in many guises. *Yeh-Shen: A Cinderella Story from China* is one of these variants. Ai-Ling Louie, the author, states that Yeh-Shen predated the European versions. *Lon Po Po: A Red Riding Hood Story from China* by Ed Young is another interesting version of a well-known story.

### Historical fiction

Historical fiction is important to our understanding of Chinese Americans and to their appreciation of their own culture. Readers will find it impossible to retain a stereotypical Chinese image in their minds after reading these thrilling books. Laurence Yep portrays the courage and industry of the Chinese Americans in the exquisitely written *Dragonwings*. He pictures San Francisco of the early 20th century, including the earthquake, from an immigrant's point of view. Paul Yee writes about the customs and traditions of family life in Chinatown during the early 1900s in *Roses Sing on New Snow: A Delicious Tale*. The compelling story of the Chinese who built the transcontinental railroad at the time of the American Civil War is told in *Dragon's Gate*, another story by Laurence Yep. Paul Yee writes about the world of Chinese immigrants during the Gold Rush in *Tales from Gold Mountain: Stories of the Chinese in the New World*. These tales, similar in some ways to Chinese traditional literature, tell about the joys, sorrows, successes, and failures of the Chinese in America.

### Contemporary literature

The importance of the paper crane in contemporary Japanese culture is demonstrated in Allen

*In this book a Chinese boy struggles to rebuild his dreams against overwhelming odds.*

Say's book, *Tree of Cranes*. This lovely story combines two cultures. A Japanese boy learns about Christmas when his mother decorates a pine tree with paper cranes.

Yoshiko Uchida helps readers understand the complexity of Japanese Americans in *The Invisible Thread*. She describes growing up in Berkeley, California, as a Nisei, a second-generation Japanese American, and her family's internment in a Utah concentration camp during World War II. She has drawn on her experiences to write about the Japanese internment in several books, including the fiction story *A Jar of Dreams*, in which Rinko, an 11-year-old Japanese girl in Oakland, California, faces prejudice in 1930s California. Racism against Japanese Americans during World War II is seen from the perspective of an American girl in *The Moon Bridge* by Marcia Savin.

*Grandfather's Journey* is the remarkable story of the life journey of Allen Say's grandfather between two places and two worlds. He was born in Japan, but he was fascinated by the diversity of America. Over the course of his life, he traveled back and forth between the two countries, always yearning for the country he had left. This sensitive portrayal helps readers understand that many Japanese Americans, as well as others who come to America, live between two worlds. The story also tells how many people feel about their ancestors who came to this country.

## Hispanic Americans in Children's Literature

The Hispanic culture is rich and varied and includes the ancient traditions of Spanish, Aztec, and Mayan cultures. Hispanic American children's literature includes the cultural traditions of Spain, Cuba, Central America, South America, the Caribbean, Mexico, and Puerto Rico. The differing Hispanic cultures have been treated in much the same way as other cultures—that is, they have been treated as though they were all the same (Schon, 1988). Generalization, stereotypes, and inaccurate information have permeated much of the Hispanic American literature of the past. In 1976, the Council on Interracial Books expressed concern over the apparent lack of understanding and respect extended to Hispanic Americans. For instance, Mexican Americans were often depicted in impoverished settings as characters who did not learn English, which prevented them from participating in the dominant culture. However, the number of excellent Hispanic American children's books is gradually increasing; many of them are bilingual, written in both Spanish and English.

The body of children's literature about Hispanic Americans is increasing, but there is much more traditional literature than contemporary and very little biography. It is to be hoped that this picture will change in the near future.

### Traditional literature

Traditional folktales also develop cultural understanding and appreciation. Angel Vigil (1994) explains that Hispanic *cuentos* (stories) are representative of folklore from the various Hispanic

cultures. Vigil, who was reared in New Mexico, spent a large amount of time at his grandparents' farm, where he was immersed in the oral traditions of folklore. He says, "I was amazed to discover that my living relatives were sources of folklore. Suddenly I recognized the truth that oral tradition is passed from generation to generation and that the passing depends on close contact between the generations" (p. xi). In his collection of stories and legends from the Southwest, *The Corn Woman*, Vigil shares some of the stories he has collected throughout the southwestern part of the United States. He cautions readers that in keeping with oral tradition, he has told the stories in his own voice.

*Cuentos* are stories that share culture with another person. The *cuentos* enable one generation to pass on to another the beauty and richness of traditions. Historically, *cuentos* were a way to share truth and insights with members of the community. Similarly, *dichos* are proverbs that were frequently part of the oral tradition and sometimes written down. "The *dichos* reflect a kind of philosophy and proverbial wisdom" (Vigil, p. xxi). They were used to explain human interaction and relationships. For example, *no hay rosa sin espinas* means that nothing comes easily. Unfortunately, these are becoming a dying art form. Vigil believes that television, urbanization, and lack of extended family have contributed to the shortage of written *cuentos*. When Vigil asked the various people he met while collecting research for his collection of stories about this, he was told that the younger generations were not interested in stories of the past.

Rudolfo Anaya's *Cuentos: Tales from the Hispanic Southwest* includes myths and legends from New Mexico and Colorado. The Aztec myth *All of You Was Singing* by Richard Lewis explains how the wind helped bring music to the earth. *Tigers and Opossums* is a collection of Mexican pourquoi tales by Marcos Kurtycs and Ana Garcia Kobeh. These pourquoi explain why animals have certain characteristics. Verna Aardema's folktales explain animal behaviors and their relationships. *Borreguita and the Coyote* is a humorous tale about a lamb who is pursued by a coyote. The coyote wants to eat the lamb, but she continually outsmarts him by convincing him the moon is a wheel of cheese and that

*In this story, told in both English and Spanish, Uncle Nacho learns a valuable lesson about how to accept change.*

he must hold up a mountain so that it does not fall. *The Woman Who Outshone the Sun/La mujer que brillaba aun mas que el sol* by Alejandro Cruz Martinez is a legend about a beautiful woman with magical powers who punishes a mountain village when she is mistreated. Harriet Rohmer's *Uncle Nacho's Hat/El sombrero del tío Nacho* is a Nicaraguan folktale that explains that it is hard to change the way you do things until you change the way you think. The myth *Pancho's Piñata* (Stefan Czernecki, 1993) explains how the piñata became a tradition at Hispanic celebrations.

## Poetry

Poetry from the Hispanic American culture is rich and lyrical. Lulu Delacre's popular book *Arroz con leche* is a collection of rhythms and rhymes from Latin American countries that includes lullabies and singing games reflecting these cultures. *The Desert Is My Mother/El desierto es mi madre* by Pat Mora describes in verse the richness and fertility of the desert, dispelling the notion that a desert is just hot sand by telling about its many dimensions. Gary Soto, author of *Neighborhood Odes*, chose Fresno, California, as the setting for his poems about the adventures of Hispanic young people growing up.

## Contemporary literature

A prominent theme in Hispanic fiction is the importance of families and the extended family. In many stories, children develop insights and wisdom about the world around them from their grandparents. Arthur Dorros's *Abuela* tells a warm story about the friendship between Rosalba and her abuela (grandmother). Carmen Garza's *Family Pictures* portrays warm family relationships and family holidays. Life in a Mexican American family is also portrayed in *Hello Amigos!* by Patricia Brown. Family tradition is central to Gary Soto's *The Skirt*, which tells about the skirt Miata's mother wore in Mexico and that Miata is to wear for dancing. In Juanita Havill's *Treasure Map*, in which a great-grandmother describes her voyage from

Mexico to the United States and the treasures she brought with her.

Some contemporary fiction addresses the feelings of isolation and frustration that many Hispanic Americans experience because they speak a different language (Fournier, 1993). Children experience alienation because almost everything in their environment is unfamiliar. They often find that no one can pronounce their names and that there are few books written in Spanish. In *Felita*, Nicholasa Mohr tells about the rich Puerto Rican heritage that Felita's family brings with them to America. Unfortunately, their neighbors do not understand their culture. In *Going Home*, Felita travels to Puerto Rico when her grandmother dies, and discovers her heritage, but she also experiences a different form of prejudice.

## Native Americans in Children's Literature

Native Americans are members of cultural groups whose ancestors lived in North America prior to Europeans. Each group of Native Americans had their own rich culture and traditions. There is great diversity among Native Americans—there is as much cultural diversity among their groups as there is with other cultures. The vast majority of children's literature about Native Americans is traditional literature. These fine stories give readers insights regarding their culture, values, and traditions, but they do not permit readers to see themselves in books because they are not contemporary stories.

Roger Welsch (1994) states that Native Americans are present "working in the stock market in three-piece business suits, farming in overalls, dancing with the ballet in tutus, buying groceries in jeans and sweatshirts, or opening a locker next to yours in school. They speak English and drive cars and trucks. Native Americans run for Congress, become boxing champions, write books, teach classes, and run businesses" (p. ix). If children are to internalize Welsch's ideas, teachers must use realistic fiction and carefully selected biographies to help children see Native Americans as an important part of our society.

*A boy fashions a much-wanted pony out of mud, only to have it come to life.*

### Traditional literature

Native American traditional tales include teaching tales that help children learn lessons, pourquoi that tell why things are the way they are, and legends and stories that help children learn traditions and values. *Baby Rattlesnake* by Te Ata is a teaching tale that helps children learn that they have to wait until they are old enough for certain privileges. Howard Norman's *Who-Paddled-Backward-with-Trout* is the story of a Cree boy who searches for a new name. This story shows readers the importance that Native Americans place on names. Caron Cohen's *The Mud Pony: A Traditional Skidi Pawnee Tale* explains the path to greatness and demonstrates the importance of horses to Native Americans. In *Dragonfly's Tale*, Kristina Rodanas warns children about the evils of wasting the good things that are given to them.

Some of the Native American pourquoi include *First Strawberries* by Joseph Bruchac, which explains how strawberries were created to help first man and first woman settle an argument and now represent the sweetness of friendships. Jerrie Oughton's *How the Stars Fell into the Sky* is a Navajo tale that explains the constellations in the night sky. In *Her Seven Brothers*, Paul Goble explains how the Big Dipper came to be.

Horses are important in the lives of many Native Americans and appear in many stories. Jane Yolen's *Sky Dogs* recounts the legend of the horse coming to the Blackfeet. In *The Great Race of the Birds and Animals*, Paul Goble tells the story of a great race between two-legged and four-legged animals to decide who would rule the world. Kristina Rodanas's *Dance of the Sacred Circle* is a Blackfeet legend that explains how the Great Chief created the horse to help them hunt buffalo. Another interesting horse story is told by Betty Boegehold in *A Horse Called Starfire:* a Native American boy and his father encounter a strange new animal, a horse, while on a hunting trip.

Native American traditional stories include trickster tales. The trickster in these stories is often the rabbit or the spider; sometimes, as in Roger Welsch's *Uncle Smoke Stories*, the trickster is the coyote. Valerie Carey's *Quail Song* is a Pueblo tale that tells how Quail outwitted Coyote. Iktomi is a Plains Indian trickster who attempts to defeat a boulder with the help of some bats in *Iktomi and the Boulder: A Plains Indian Story*, recounted by Paul Goble.

## Poetry

Poetry also expands our understanding of the Native American culture. Virginia Driving Hawk Sneve collected poems from the oral tradition of Native Americans in *Dancing Teepees*. Another popular collection of Native American poems and legends is *Thirteen Moons on Turtle's Back: A Native*

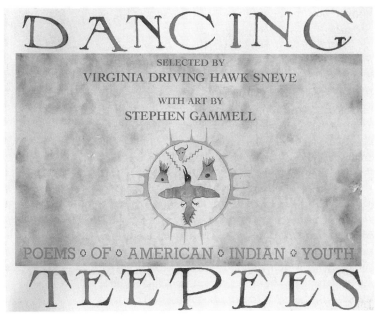

This book contains nineteen poems of American Indian youth.

*American Year of Moons* by Joseph Bruchac and Jonathan London. This collection celebrates the seasons of the year in poems drawn from a number of Native American cultures including Cherokee, Cree, and Sioux.

## Biography

Ben Nighthorse Campbell is an example of a Native American who has been a leader in both the Native American and Anglo American cultures. His biography, *Ben Nighthorse Campbell: Cheyenne Chief and U. S. Senator* by Chris Henry provides interesting reading for members of both cultures. In a partially autobiographical account entitled *Night Flying Woman: An Ojibway Narrative*, Ignatia Broker, an Ojibway, tells about life on the White Earth Reservation and of moving to Minneapolis in the hopes of finding a better life. The Native American artist George Littlechild wrote and illustrated *This Land Is My Land*, in which he tells about the important people and symbols of his own life. The story of an Indian princess and John Smith is recounted by William Accorsi in *My Name Is Pocahontas*. This book shows the complexity of Pocahontas's life as she moves into the white culture.

Teachers will find that Alvin Josephy's biographical series on traditional Native American heroes is thorough, accurate, and emphasizes Native American perspectives. Each tells the story of a great Native American—from Sitting Bull to Sequoyah to Hiawatha. Moreover, the writing is clear and rich with historical detail, explanation, analysis, and narrative excitement. This series is published by Silver Burdett & Ginn.

## Contemporary literature

Much of contemporary Native American literature focuses on family and family feelings, a subject with which all children can identify easily. The relationship between parent and child is featured in Barbara M. Joosse's beautiful book *Mama Do You Love Me?*, which tells about the loving relationship between an Inuit child and her mother. In a similar book, *On My Mother's Lap* by Ann Scott, an Inuit child and her mother express universal feelings of love. Family storytelling is featured in *My Grandmother's Cookie Jar* by Montzalee Miller. A Native American boy struggles with his worries about going to kindergarten in Margaret Garaway's *Ashkii and His Grandfather*. In *Powwow*, June Behrens makes us aware that Native Americans can live and work in today's world while retaining their culture and traditions. Nancy Carlstrom's *Northern Lullaby* is an exquisite picture book that vividly illustrates the beauty of an Alaskan winter evening. In *Dancing with the Indians*, Angela Medearis offers a different perspective, that of an African American family watching and joining in a Seminole celebration.

## Jewish Americans in Children's Literature

Jewish people who came to Ellis Island brought with them stories, language, and memories, as every ethnic group did. The old stories were told and retold, sometimes even altered to fit the new environment and culture. As in other ethnic groups, there are vast differences among American Jews: There are strict Hasidic Jews and secular

The author of Northern Lullaby uses water-color images of an Alaskan winter to create a perfect lullaby.

Jews, Zionists and non-Zionists, Sephardic Jews and Ashkenazi Jews (Rochman, 1993).

Jewish holidays are very interesting to all children and a number of books tell the legends, traditions, and foods associated with these special times. Judith Gross's *Celebrate: A Book of Jewish Holidays* is a nonfiction book for younger children that blends early origins and modern interpretation. In *The Chanukkah Guest*, Eric Kimmel tells about Bubba Brayna, who makes potato latkes to celebrate Hanukkah with the rabbi. Because of her poor eyesight, she entertains a bear, which young children will find hilarious. Hanukkah is also the theme of the 1990 Caldecott honor book *Hershel and the Hanukkah Goblins*, also by Kimmel. The full-color, shadow-filled paintings that illustrate the book enhance the story. Another facet of Hanukkah is presented in Jeanne Modesitt's *Songs of Chanukah*, which includes 14 songs, written in both Hebrew and English, for the eight-day holiday. Games, dances, recipes, and candle lighting are included in this book.

## Traditional literature

Jewish traditional literature is so rich that it is difficult to select only a few that represent this treasure trove. The Russian tale *The Place Where Nobody Stopped* by Jerry Segal appeals to a broad age-range of listeners and readers. Esther Hautzig's *Riches* tells of hard-working shop owners who seek guidance from a rabbi to learn how to please the Almighty. *My Grandmother's Stories: A Collection of Jewish Folk Tales* by Adele Geras tells wonderful tales that are ideally suited for reading aloud or retelling. Julius Lester created a varied and unusual collection of folktales in *How Many Spots Does a Leopard Have? and Other Tales*. He includes both African and Jewish tales, carefully crafted so the stories are more effective for American readers. Isaac B. Singer's *Zlateh the Goat* is a great collection of Yiddish folktales that appeals to young and old.

## Biography and contemporary literature

Esther Hautzig's book *The Endless Steppe* is an autobiography of her early years. This book is such a wonderful read that it should not be missed by children in grades four through seven. Milton Meltzer tells his personal story as a child of Jewish American immigrants in Worcester, Massachusetts, in his book *Starting from Home: A Writer's Beginnings*. Twelve-year-old Rifka tells of her journey to America in 1919 in letters to her cousin back home in Russia in Karen Hesse's *Letters from Rifka*. Kathryn Lasky's *The Night Journey* is the story of a Jewish immigrant family. Another strong immigration story about a Jewish family forced to leave Nazi Germany and make a new life in the United States is *Journey to America* by Sonia Levitin.

# CLASSROOM ACTIVITIES TO ENHANCE MULTICULTURAL LITERATURE

Multicultural literature must become part of everything that is going on in the classroom all year around. Reading multicultural books and encouraging children to read them is only the beginning. After that you can develop children's understanding and response through classroom experiences with literature.

Multicultural literature offers good opportunities for oral literature experiences. Dramatizing stories and scenes from multicultural stories gives students opportunities to identify with story characters, to walk in their shoes. Reader's theater and puppet shows are dramatic experiences that also encourage identification with characters. Children enjoy choral reading of all or parts of traditional stories and poems from different cultures. Review Chapter Eleven for more on oral experiences with literature.

ACTIVITIES

## 14.1 Comparing cultures

A good way to introduce cultural studies is to discuss culture with children. Explain that *culture* includes manners, feelings about self and other people, religion, right and wrong, education, entering adulthood, holidays, foods, clothes, and games—all the things we learned from our parents, grandparents, friends, neighbors, churches, and schools (Stoodt, 1992b).

Ask the children to brainstorm what they have learned from each aspect of their cultures. Make lists of their ideas on the chalkboard or on charts. Organize the material into a chart like the one in Figure 14.1. Older students can create individual charts.

### FIGURE 14.1

Chart of cultural teachings.

WHAT I LEARNED FROM MY ...

| Parents | Grandparents | Teachers | Friends | School | Church |
|---------|--------------|----------|---------|--------|--------|
| To say thank you | To bake cookies | To read | To jump rope | To communicate | To pray |

## 14.2 Contemporary stories

Read aloud a contemporary story from another culture and have the students compare the cultural information with their own lives. A Venn diagram is helpful in making this comparison.

## 14.3 Mapping cultures

Have each student make a map of his or her culture using Figure 14.2 as a model. Culture maps can be the basis for bulletin boards. As students learn about culture, they can create culture maps for characters in stories.

### FIGURE 14.2

Culture map. (Students fill in information about their individual culture in the circles.)

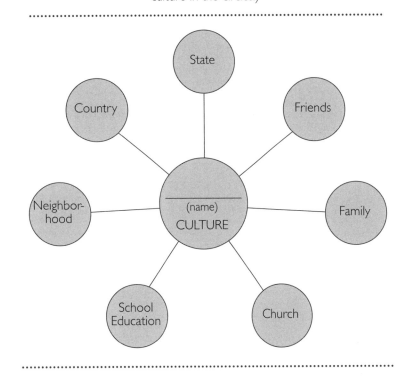

## 14.4 Cultural collages

Discuss special family ways of celebrating holidays and birthdays, favorite colors, favorite foods, places they have lived, family size and composition, family education, religion, and values. Then students can make collages using magazine pictures (or those drawn by students), squares of colored paper, wallpaper, newspaper, cloth, and objects or symbols that are important to the individual to create collages representing their family's culture.

## 14.5 Family trees

Create family trees going as far back into family history as possible. Older students can learn how to research the family genealogy. Studies like these sometimes give students clues about family ways of doing things that they did not realize had cultural implications. For example, this kind of research led one of the authors to Pennsylvania Dutch connections through family foods, names, and the stories her grandfather told.

## 14.6 Comparing folktales

Students can compare the Cinderella story in various cultures such as *Cinderella* (European), *The Rough-Face Girl* (Native American), and *Yeh-Shen* (Chinese). Figure 14.3 illustrates a comparison chart.

## 14.7 Traditional stories

Read aloud or have students read three traditional stories or poems from the same culture and identify the recurrent themes and details in these stories. A chart with headings such as those in Figure 14.3 will help them organize their ideas.

### FIGURE 14.3

Chart for comparing traditional stories.

| Title and Author | Main Character | Setting | Problem | How Solved | Conclusion |
|---|---|---|---|---|---|
| <u>Cinderella</u> Marcia Brown | Cinderella | European house and castle | Mean step-mother and stepsisters | The prince finds her and proposes. | They marry and live happily ever after. |
| <u>The Rough-Face Girl</u>, Rafe Martin | An Algonquin girl with a | Native American | The tribe rejects her scarred face | She can see the Invisible Being. | She marries the Invisible Being. |
| <u>Yeh-Shen: A Cinderella Story from China</u> Ai-Ling Louie | Yeh-Shen | China | Her stepmother kills the fish that is Yeh-Shen's friend and eats it. | The fish's magic resides in its bones. The magic magic provides her with clothing for a festival. | She loses her slipper, and the King searches for her and marries her. |

UNIT
SUGGESTION

## 14.1 Studying Native American culture

Third-grade students often enjoy studying Native American cultures. This unit focuses on the importance of the earth and nature in Native American culture and comparing their attitudes with current movements in the United States to take care of the earth. Native American literature is an excellent resource for this unit because these people honor and respect nature in their stories and poems.

Guiding Question for Unit:

Why do Native Americans have such a deep respect for nature, the earth, and the animals of the earth?

Unit Introduction

Read these books to begin the unit, because each one relates to the theme and the guiding question. Then brainstorm a web of connections among these books including plots, themes, settings, characters, and cultural details.

- *The People Shall Continue* by Samuel Ortiz
- *People of the Breaking Day* by Marcia Sewall
- *Rainbow Crow* by Nancy Van Laan
- *Still Turtle Watched* by Sheila MacGill-Callahan
- *Rising Voices* by Arlene Hirschfelder and Beverly Singer

1. Creating a web of connections gives students opportunities to discuss their response to the books. After they have completed the web or webs, have students categorize their responses. They can identify their own categories or the teacher can guide them. Possible categories include animals, land, sacred things, homes, transportation, foods, important people, and important events.

2. Have students select the book that told them most about a Native American culture.

3. Have the students tell how they felt after reading or listening to the various books. For example, did the book feel like a gentle caring book, a sad book, a funny book? Then have them think of ways to respond to the various books.

4. Have the students decide whether they want to read Native American poetry, traditional literature, nonfiction, or fiction and group the students by their chosen genre. The following list of recommended books can be a starting point for students and they can add books as they find others they like.

- *Corn Is Maize* by Aliki
- *U. S. Kids History of the American Indians* by Marlene Smith-Baranzini and Howard Bovet
- *Where the Buffaloes Begin* by Olaf Baker
- *When Clay Sings; The Desert Is Theirs; Hawk, I'm Your Brother;* and *The Other Way to Listen* by Byrd Baylor
- *A Horse Called Starfire* by Betty Boegehold
- *Native American Stories* by Joseph Bruchac
- *A River Ran Wild* by Lynne Cherry
- *The Mud Pony* by Caron Cohen
- *Ka-ha-si and the Loon, Quillworker,* and *Turquoise Boy* by Terri Cohlene
- *Love Flute* by Paul Goble
- *If You Lived with the Sioux Indians* by Ann McGovern
- *Dancing Teepees* by Virginia Driving Hawk Sneve
- *People of the Breaking Day* by Marcia Sewall
- *A Trickster Tale from the Pacific Northwest* by Gerald McDermott

5. Students can keep a response journal making entries about their reading each day, what they have learned, and how they feel about it.

6. Students can study Native American art in pictures, prints, pottery, blankets, jewelry, and headdresses to identify sacred objects, animals, and symbols.

## SUMMARY

The United States is made up of diverse racial and cultural groups. Educators face the need to provide literary experiences that reflect the many backgrounds from which children come. Multicultural literature can play an important role in filling this need. In the past, minority cultures have been omitted or inaccurately portrayed in many children's books, which has a negative impact on children from all cultural groups. Quality literature permits children to experience others' lives, thus increasing their understanding and appreciation of cultures and people different from themselves. Children from minority cultures need books and characters to identify with because these books foster self-esteem and pride in ethnic heritage. Teaching strategies for multicultural literature help children compare and contrast cultures to understand them better. Most important is encouraging children to recognize that people from different cultures share more likenesses than differences.

## THOUGHT QUESTIONS

1. Develop your own definition of multicultural education and multicultural literature and explain why this definition expresses your thoughts on the subject.

2. Why do so many people believe there is an abundance of multicultural books today when the data show otherwise?

3. What would you recommend to publishing companies regarding publishing multicultural literature?

4. Discuss the pros and cons of using children's literature to develop multicultural understanding.

5. Can someone who is not a member of a particular culture write a book about that culture? Discuss the pros and cons and your reasons for adopting the point of view that you have chosen.

## ENRICHMENT ACTIVITIES

1. Visit a school or public library and analyze the multicultural literature collection. Which cultures are best represented? Which are underrepresented? What books would you recommend they purchase?

2. Examine your own prejudices and stereotypes. How did you form these attitudes? What types of literature could you read to challenge these beliefs?

3. Identify criteria you feel are important when selecting multicultural literature for children.

4. Why are multicultural materials not readily available? Make a list of books you feel should be part of every school's collection.

5. Design a multicultural unit on a general topic such as families, transportation, pets, holidays, or friendships. Identify the books and activities that will help children develop a better understanding of a particular cultural group.

6. Develop a bibliography of excellent children's books for one cultural group based on a careful evaluation of each book. Different students may choose to research books for various cultural groups, so that you can exchange bibliographies.

# RECOMMENDED CHILDREN'S BOOKS

Aardema, Verna. (1991). *Borreguita and the Coyote*. New York: Knopf. (1–4)
   This Mexican folktale tells how a lamb outwits a coyote.

Accorsi, W. (1992). *My Name Is Pocahontas*. New York: Harper & Row.
   This book recounts the story of the Native American princess who met John Smith, married John Rolfe, and traveled to England.

Adler, David. (1992). *A Picture Book of Harriet Tubman*. New York: Holiday House. (1–3)
   This informative picture book tells about the life and work of Harriet Tubman.

Aliki. (1976). *Corn Is Maize: The Gift of the Indians*. New York: Thomas Crowell. (1–3)
   The history of corn is described and illustrated in interesting ways.

Anaya, Rudolfo. (1980). *Cuentos: Tales from the Hispanic Southwest*. Albuquerque, NM: The Museum of New Mexico Press. (2–6)
   This collection of *cuentos* includes myths and legends from New Mexico that pass on rich Hispanic traditions.

Anno, Mitsumasa. (1986). *All in a Day*. New York: Philomel. (1–5)
   This picture book reveals a day in the lives of children in eight different countries, showing the similarities and differences.

Ashabranner, Brent. (1987). *Into a Strange Land: Unaccompanied Refugee Youth in America*. New York: Putnam. (5–12)
   This nonfiction book is based on interviews with young Asian Americans from Vietnam, Cambodia, and other countries.

Ata, Te. (1989). *Baby Rattlesnake*. San Francisco: Children's Book Press. (1–3)
   The baby rattlesnake can't wait to grow up and get his rattles, but he learns about the problems of getting what you want too soon.

Baer, Edith. (1990). *This Is the Way We Go to School*. New York: Scholastic. (1–4)
   This book describes the different ways children around the world travel to school.

Baker, Olaf. (1981). *Where the Buffaloes Begin*. Illustrated by Stephen Gammell. New York: Frederick Warne. (all ages)
   A folktale from the Plains Indians that describes how the buffaloes came from a lake.

Bang, Molly. (1985). *The Paper Crane*. New York: Greenwillow. (2–4)
   This Japanese tale is about a man who is paid with an origami crane instead of money. The paper crane brings him good fortune and happiness.

Bartone, Elisa. (1993). *Peppe, The Lamplighter*. New York: Lothrop, Lee & Shepard. (2–4)
   This is an Italian American story about a boy who lights the street lamps in Little Italy.

Baylor, Byrd. (1972). *When Clay Sings*. Illustrated by Tom Bahti. New York: Scribner's. (2–5)
   When children find pieces of pottery from long ago, they reflect on the lives of early Native Americans.

———. (1975). *The Desert Is Theirs*. Illustrated by Peter Parnall. New York: Scribner's. (2–5)
   This book describes the desert as well as the plant, animal, and human life there.

———. (1976). *Hawk, I'm Your Brother*. Illustrated by Peter Parnall. New York: Scribner's. (2–5)
   A Native American boy captures a hawk that he hopes will help him learn to fly.

———. (1978). *The Other Way to Listen*. Illustrated by Peter Parnall. New York: Scribner's. (4–8)
   When we become quiet, we are able to listen to nature.

Begay, Shonto. (1992). *Ma'ii and Cousin Horned Toad: A Traditional Navajo Story*. New York: Scholastic. (1–4)

This traditional Navajo story was Shonto Begay's childhood favorite. It is the story of how cousin Horned Toad taught Coyote a lesson.

Behrens, June. (1983). *Powwow*. San Francisco: Children's Book Press. (1–4)

This book describes the Native American festival called a Powwow.

Boegehold, Betty. (1990). *A Horse Called Starfire*. New York: Bantam. (1–4)

A Native American boy and his father who are on a hunting trip encounter a strange new creature, a horse.

Bray, Rosemary. (1995). *Martin Luther King*. New York: Greenwillow. (2–5)

The folk art illustrations by Malcah Zeldis help even young readers identify with this biography of Martin Luther King.

Brown, Tricia. (1986). *Hello Amigos!* Photographs by Fran Ortiz. San Diego, CA: Holt, Rinehart and Winston. (1–3)

A Hispanic American boy combines traditions from both cultures to celebrate his birthday.

Bruchac, Joseph. (1992). *First Strawberries*. New York: Philomel. (2–4)

This tale tells how strawberries were invented to resolve an argument and why their sweetness represents friendship.

Bruchac, Joseph, and Jonathan London. (1992). *Thirteen Moons on Turtle's Back: A Native American Year of Moons*. Illustrated by T. Locker. New York: Philomel. (1–5)

This collection of Native American poems and legends celebrates the seasons of the year. Included in the collection are Cherokee, Cree, and Sioux literature.

Bryan, Ashley. (1991). *All Night, All Day: A Child's First Book of African-American Spirituals*. New York: Atheneum. (1–6)

This superb collection of spirituals appeals to children of all ages.

Bunting, Eve. (1988). *How Many Days to America?* New York: Clarion. (1–4)

A Caribbean family experiences fear and danger as they attempt to leave their homeland for America. They arrive on American soil in time to celebrate Thanksgiving Day.

Cameron, Ann. (1988). *The Most Beautiful Place in the World*. New York: Knopf. (2–5)

Juan lives in the small village of San Pablo, with his grandmother. He discovers that his village is the most beautiful place in the world.

Carey, Valerie. (1990). *Quail Song*. Illustrated by Ivan Barnett. New York: Putnam. (2–5)

In this traditional Pueblo tale, Quail outwits Coyote.

Carlstrom, Nancy. (1992). *Northern Lullaby*. New York: Philomel. (1–4)

This beautifully illustrated book depicts an Alaskan winter evening.

Casler, Leigh. (1994). *The Boy Who Dreamed of an Acorn*. New York: Philomel. (1–4)

This is the story of a boy who climbs a mountain in search of his dream. He is given an acorn as a symbol of power and strength.

Cherry, Lynne. (1992). *A River Ran Wild*. New York: Harcourt Brace Jovanovich. (2–5)

This history of the Nashua River emphasizes the respect given to it by Native Americans.

Chocolate, Deborah. (1992). *My First Kwanzaa Book*. New York: Scholastic. (1–3)

The history and customs of the African holiday Kwanzaa are explained and an explanation of vocabulary is provided for the reader.

Choi, Sook Nyul. (1991). *Year of Impossible Goodbyes*. Boston: Houghton Mifflin. (5–9)

This dramatic story is set in war-torn Korea under Japanese oppression, then after 1945 under Russian occupation. Choi escaped and lives in the United States.

Coerr, Eleanor. (1988). *Chang's Paper Pony.* New York: HarperCollins. (2–5)

This story depicts a young boy's loneliness when he comes to America from China during the Gold Rush.

_____ . (1993). *Sadako and the Thousand Paper Cranes.* New York: Putnam. (2–5)

This beautiful story tells of a young girl's battle with leukemia, which she developed as the result of the atomic bomb.

Cohen, Caron. (1988). *The Mud Pony: A Traditional Skidi Pawnee Tale.* New York: Scholastic. (1–4)

A young boy's dream of owning a real pony comes true.

Cohlene, Terri. (1990). *Dancing Drum.* Mahwah, NJ: Watermill. (1–4)

In this Cherokee legend, Dancing Drum tries to make Grandmother Sun smile on the people again.

_____ . (1990). *Quillworker.* Mahwah, NJ: Watermill. (1–4)

This Cheyenne legend explains the origin of the stars.

_____ . (1990). *Turquoise Boy: A Navajo Legend.* Illustrated by Charles Reasoner. Mahwah, NJ: Watermill. (1–4)

In this Navajo legend, Turquoise Boy looks for something that will make the lives of his people easier.

_____ . (1990). *Ka-ha-si and the Loon.* Mahwah, NJ: Watermill. (1–4)

This is the legend of Ka-ha-si, who rescues his people in a time of desperate need.

Crews, Donald. (1991). *Bigmama's.* New York: Greenwillow. (preschool–2)

The author visits Bigmama's house in the country and his relatives. He discovers that the surroundings are the same as the year before.

_____ . (1992). *Shortcut.* New York: Greenwillow. (1–3)

A group of African American children encounter danger when they decide to take a shortcut home by the railroad tracks.

Cruz Martinez, Alejandro. (1991). *The Woman Who Outshone the Sun/La mujer que brillaba aun mas que el sol.* Illustrated by Fernando Olivera. San Francisco: Children's Book Press. (2–4)

This is the legend of a beautiful woman with magical powers.

Cummings, Pat. (1991). *Clean Your Room, Harvey Moon!* New York: Bradbury. (1–3)

Harvey, an African American child, tackles cleaning his room in this story.

Czernecki, Stefan. (1993). *Pancho's Piñata.* New York: Hyperion. (1–4)

This story explains the origins and traditions of the piñata.

De Gerez, Toni. (1981). *My Song Is a Piece of Jade: Poems of Ancient Mexico in English and Spanish.* New York: Little Brown. (4–12)

This is a collection of Mexican poetry.

Delacre, Lulu. (1989). *Arroz con leche: Popular Songs and Rhymes from Latin America.* New York: Scholastic. (all ages)

This is a collection of games, rhymes, and songs from Latin America.

Dooley, Norah. (1991). *Everybody Cooks Rice.* Minneapolis: Carolrhoda. (1–3)

A little girl visits her neighbors and discovers they are all having rice for dinner, although each one is preparing it differently.

Dorros, Arthur. (1991). *Abuela*. New York: Dutton Children's Books. (1–3)

Rosalba tells about an outing with her abuela (grandmother).

Emberley, Rebecca. (1990). *My House: A Book in Two Languages/Mi casa: un libro en dos lenguas*. Boston: Little, Brown.

This book introduces the words for various items in a house in both English and Spanish, which will help children develop a greater understanding of one another's culture.

Garaway, Margaret. (1989). *Ashkii and His Grandfather*. Tucson, AZ: Treasure Chest. (2–5)

A young boy does not want to go to school because he prefers his grandfather's ways.

Garland, Sherry. (1993). *The Lotus Seed*. Illustrated by Tatsuro Keuchi. New York: Harcourt Brace Jovanovich. (1–4)

A Vietnamese family leaves their country because of the war. They carry only one possession to the United States, a lotus seed, the "flower of life and hope."

Garza, Carmen. (1990). *Family Pictures*. San Francisco: Children's Book Press. (1–4)

A collection of folk art pictures portrays the life of a Hispanic family.

Gates, Frieda. (1994). *Owl Eyes*. New York: Lothrop, Lee & Shepard. (1–3)

This Mohawk legend describes Owl's inability to decide between having feathers or fur to cover his body.

Gelaber, Carol. (1993). *Masks Tell Stories*. New York: Millbrook. (2–6)

This nonfiction selection explains the meaning and traditions behind Native American masks.

Geras, Adele. (1990). *My Grandmother's Stories: A Collection of Jewish Folk Tales*. New York: Knopf. (2–5)

This is a collection of wonderful Jewish tales that are ideally suited for reading aloud or retelling.

Gilmore, Rachna. (1994). *Lights for Gita*. Gardiner, MA: Tilbury House. (1–3)

The Hindu celebration Divalia is explained in this beautifully illustrated book.

Giovanni, Nikki. (1985). *Spin a Soft Black Song*. Illustrated by George Martins. New York: Farrar, Straus & Giroux. (1–6)

The poet reflects on the life of an African American child.

Girard, Linda. (1989). *We Adopted You, Benjamin Koo*. Niles, IL: Whitman. (1–4)

This is the story of one child's adjustment after his adoption by parents from the United States.

Goble, Paul. (1978). *The Girl Who Loved Wild Horses*. New York: Bradbury. (2–5)

A young girl's love and understanding for horses enables her to communicate with animals.

———. (1985). *The Great Race of the Birds and Animals*. New York: Bradbury. (2–5)

This story is a Sioux and Cheyenne myth about the great race between buffalo and man.

———. (1988). *Her Seven Brothers*. New York: Bradbury. (2–5)

This is a Cheyenne tale of how the Big Dipper became part of the night sky.

———. (1988). *Iktomi and the Boulder: A Plains Indian Story*. New York: Orchard Books. (2–4)

Iktomi is a trickster who attempts to defeat a boulder with the assistance of some bats. This story explains why the Great Plains are covered with small stones.

Gray, Libba Moore. (1993). *Dear Willie Rudd*. New York: Simon & Schuster. (2–5)

A woman sits on her porch and writes a letter to Willie Rudd, the housekeeper in her childhood home. In the letter, the woman describes and apologizes for the injustices directed toward African Americans when she was growing up.

Greenfield, Eloise. (1974). *Sister*. Illustrated by Moneta Barnett. New York: Crowell. (3–6)

Sister reflects on the journal she has kept, in which she recorded the hard times and the good times of her life.

_____ . (1988). *Grandpa's Face*. New York: Philomel. (2–5)

This beautifully illustrated book is about a grandfather and his love for his granddaughter.

_____ . (1991). *Night on Neighborhood Street*. Illustrated by Jan Spivey Gilcrest. New York: Dial. (K–5)

This collection of poems depicts the lives of African Americans and their families.

_____ . (1993). *Childtimes: A Three-Generation Memoir*. New York: HarperTrophy. (3–6)

This pictorial history of the lives of three women from 1880 to 1950 is told from the various perspectives of a daughter, her mother, and her grandmother.

_____ . (1993). *She Come Bringing Me That Little Baby Girl*. New York: HarperTrophy. (1–3)

This is the story of a young boy's gradual acceptance of his new baby sister.

Gross, Judith. (1992). *Celebrate: A Book of Jewish Holidays*. New York: Platt and Munk (Putnam). (K–3)

This nonfiction book for younger children blends early origins and modern interpretations of Jewish holidays.

Hamilton, Virginia. (1992). *Drylongso*. Illustrated by Jerry Pinkney. New York: Harcourt Brace Jovanovich. (4–8)

A young man called Drylongso relieves a farm family's distress caused by drought.

_____ . (1988). *Anthony Burns: The Defeat and Triumph of a Fugitive Slave*. New York: Knopf. (3–7)

This is the true story of Anthony Burns, who escaped slavery and then was arrested and returned south. Though he was finally able to buy his freedom, he lived only a few years as a free man.

Hansen, Joyce. (1994). *Yellow Bird and Me*. New York: Clarion. (4–6)

This is the story of a girl with reading problems.

Hautzig, Esther. (1967). *The Endless Steppe*. New York: Harper. (4–7)

The dramatic, true story of a Jewish family imprisoned by the Russians in Siberia.

_____ . (1992). *Riches*. New York: HarperCollins. (3–6)

This is the story of Samuel and Chaya-Rivka, who seek a way to please the Almighty. The wise rabbi helps them.

Havill, Juanita. (1992). *Treasure Map*. Boston: Houghton Mifflin. (1–4)

A great-grandmother describes her voyage from Mexico to the United States.

Henry, Charles. (1994). *Ben Nighthorse Campbell: Cheyenne Chief and U. S. Senator*. New York: Little, Brown. (3–6)

This is the story of a Native American who has been a leader in both the Native American and Anglo American cultures.

Hesse, Karen. (1992). *Letters from Rifka*. New York: Holt. (4–7)

Twelve-year-old Rifka tells of her journey to America in 1919 in letters to her cousin back home in Russia.

Hill, Kirkpatrick. (1990). *Toughboy and Sister*. New York: Macmillan. (4–8)

While away on a fishing trip, a young native Alaskan brother and sister learn to survive when their father dies after suffering an alcoholic seizure.

Hoberman, Mary Ann. (1994). *My Song Is Beautiful*. New York: Little, Brown. (1–6)

This book is a collection of multicultural poetry.

Hoffman, Mary. (1991). *Amazing Grace*. Illustrated by Caroline Binch. New York: Dial. (K–3)

Grace loves stories and acting them out. But a friend says that she can't be Peter Pan because she is black and she is a girl.

Ho, Minfong. (1991). *The Clay Marble*. New York: Farrar, Straus & Giroux. (4–7)

This is the story of Cambodian youngsters living in a refugee camp because they had to flee their homes. Their problems are realistically portrayed.

Howard, Elizabeth. (1991). *Aunt Flossie's Hats (and Crab Cakes Later)*. Illustrated by James Ransome. New York: Clarion. (1–3)

Two African American children visit their Aunt Flossie and enjoy tea, cookies, crab cakes, and stories about hats.

Hoyt-Goldsmith, Diane. (1991). *Pueblo Storyteller*. Illustrated by L. Migdale. New York: Holiday House. (4–6)

A Cochiti girl describes her life with her grandparents in the Cochiti pueblo.

Joosse, Barbara M. (1991). *Mama Do You Love Me?* Illustrated by Barbara Lavalle. Chronicle. (K–2)

A young Inuit girl asks the question all children ask: "Do you love me?" Her mother always answers, "Yes."

Keegan, Marcia. (1991). *Pueblo Boy: Growing Up in Two Worlds*. New York: Cobblehill. (2–5)

This is the story of a young boy who is a member of a Pueblo tribe that lives in New Mexico. Photographs are used for illustrations.

Kimmel, Eric. (1989). *Hershel and the Hanukkah Goblins*. Illustrated by Trina Schart Hyman. New York: Holiday House. (all ages)

Hanukkah is the theme of this 1990 Caldecott honor book. The full-color, shadow-filled paintings that illustrate the book enhance the story.

————. (1990). *The Chanukkah Guest*. New York: Holiday House. (all ages)

Bubba Brayna makes potato latkes to celebrate Hanukkah with the rabbi, but due to poor eyesight she entertains a bear.

Klein, Norma. (1974). *Confessions of an Only Child*. Illustrated by Richard Cuffari. New York: Pantheon.

Twelve-year-old Brett tells about her life with her photographer mother who has never been married.

Knight, Margy Burns. (1992). *Talking Walls*. Illustrated by Anne Sibley O'Brien. Gardiner, MA: Tilbury House. (2–5)

The author has depicted walls from around the world in this picture book and uses them to introduce the reader to different cultures.

————. (1993). *Who Belongs Here?* Gardiner, MA: Tilbury House. (1–4)

This is a thought-provoking story about Navy, who came to this country from Cambodia. He and his grandmother overcame many dangerous obstacles in order to get to this country, but they were rejected here.

Kraus, Joanna. (1992). *Tall Boy's Journey*. Illustrated by Karen Ritz. Minneapolis: Carolrhoda. (2–4)

Kim Moo Yong is adopted by American parents, but he is lonely and frightened. Then he meets his father's friend who came to America as a child and he understands the problems of adapting to a new culture.

Kroll, Virginia. (1992). *Masai and I*. Illustrated by Nancy Carpenter. New York: Four Winds. (1–4)

Linda lives in the city, but after she learns about East Africa and the Masai in school, she imagines what her life would be like if she were Masai.

————. (1993). *Africa Brothers and Sisters*. New York: Four Winds. (2–5)

A father helps his son recognize his ties to Africa.

Kurtycz, Marcos, and Ana Garcia Kobeh. (1984). *Tigers and Opossums: Animal Legends.* New York: Little, Brown. (1–8)

This is a collection of animal legends and tales from Mexico.

Lankford, Mary. (1992). *Hopscotch Around the World.* New York: Morrow Junior. (1–5)

The format and rules for hopscotch around the world are explained.

Lasky, Kathryn. (1981). *The Night Journey.* Illustrated by Trina Schart Hyman. New York: Warne. (3–6)

Anti-Semitism forces a Jewish family to flee czarist Russia and the great-grandmother who made the journey shares her experiences with her great-granddaughter.

Lawson, Julie. (1993). *The Dragon's Pearl.* New York: Clarion. (1–4)

Xiao Sheng finds a pearl that brings his family food and fortune until one day robbers try to steal the pearl. Not knowing what to do, the boy swallows the pearl; then he becomes a dragon.

Leighton, Maxine Rhea. (1992). *An Ellis Island Christmas.* New York: Viking. (2–4)

This book describes a girl's emigration from Poland and her first impressions of Ellis Island.

Lester, Julius. (1989). *How Many Spots Does a Leopard Have? and Other Tales.* Illustrated by David Shannon. New York: Scholastic. (all ages)

The author created a varied and unusual collection of folktales including both African and Jewish tales, with careful retellings so the stories are more effective for American readers.

Levine, Ellen. (1989). *I Hate English.* New York: Scholastic. (2–4)

Mei Mei finally recognizes the advantages of understanding two languages, Chinese and English.

Levitin, Sonia. (1970). *Journey to America.* Illustrated by Charles Robinson. New York: Atheneum. (5–8)

This is a strong immigration story about a Jewish family forced to leave Nazi Germany and make a new life in the United States.

Lewis, Richard. (1991). *All of You Was Singing.* New York: Atheneum. (all ages)

This is an Aztec myth that explains how the wind helped bring music to Earth.

Littlechild, George. (1993). *This Land Is My Land.* San Francisco: Children's Book Press. (all ages)

This wonderful book was written and illustrated by the Native American artist George Littlechild. In it he tells about important people, places, and symbols in his life.

Louie, Ai-Ling. (1982). *Yeh-Shen: A Cinderella Story from China.* Illustrated by Ed Young. New York: Philomel. (1–3)

This is a Chinese version of *Cinderella.*

Lyons, Mary E. (1990). *Sorrow's Kitchen: The Life and Folklore of Zora Neale Hurston.* New York: Macmillan. (5–9)

Hurston is a folklorist, writer, and anthropologist who celebrates black pride.

MacGill-Callahan, Sheila. (1991). *And Still the Turtle Watched.* New York: Dial. (3–5)

A turtle carved in a rock by Native Americans observes many changes in humankind throughout the years.

Martin, Rafe. (1992). *The Rough-Face Girl.* Illustrated by David Shannon. New York: Putnam. (2–4)

This is an Algonquin Indian version of the Cinderella story.

Marzollo, Jean. (1993). *Happy Birthday, Martin Luther King.* New York: Dial. (2–5)

This skillful description of Dr. King's life depicts prejudice in ways that young children can understand.

McDermott, Gerald. (1993). *Raven: A Trickster Tale from the Pacific Northwest.* New York: Harcourt.

This Native American myth is about the Raven's search for light.

McGovern, A. (1974). *If You Lived with the Sioux Indians.* New York: Scholastic. (2–5)

This book tells about day-to-day life among the Souix.

McKissack, Patricia. (1986). *Flossie and the Fox.* Illustrated by Rachel Isadora. New York: Dial. (1–5)

In this tale of the South, Flossie outwits the fox.

———. (1988). *Mirandy and Brother Wind.* Illustrated by Jerry Pinkney. New York: Knopf. (1–3)

This picture book tells about Mirandy's wish to win the cakewalk, a traditional African American dance.

———. *Nettie Jo's Friends.* Illustrated by Scott Cook. New York: Knopf. (1–3)

Nettie Jo must find a needle so that she can make her doll a dress to wear to a wedding. While searching for the needle she meets some new animal friends.

———. (1992). *Langston Hughes.* Hillside, NJ: Enslow. (4–7)

This is a detailed biography of the African American poet Langston Hughes.

McKissack, Patricia, and Frederick McKissack. (1989). *A Long Hard Journey: The Story of the Pullman Porter.* New York: Walker and Company. (4–7)

This Coretta Scott King Award book describes the Brotherhood of Sleeping Car Porters and their struggles to unionize in this country.

Medearis, Angela Shelf. (1991). *Dancing with the Indians.* New York: Holiday House. (3–6)

A black family joins a Seminole celebration, participating in the exciting dances of this Native American culture.

Meltzer, Milton. (1988). *Starting from Home: A Writer's Beginnings.* New York: Viking Kestrel. (4–7)

Meltzer tells his personal story as a child of Jewish American immigrants in Worcester, Massachusetts.

Merrill, Jean. (1992). *The Girl Who Loved Caterpillars.* Illustrated by Floyd Cooper. New York: Philomel. (2–4)

A young woman ignores the strict social rules of Japan and is kind to caterpillars and other socially unacceptable creatures.

Miller, William. (1994). *Zora Hurston and the Chinaberry Tree.* Illustrated by Cornelius Van Wright and Ying-Hwa Hu. New York: Lee & Low Books. (1–3)

This picture book tells about the early years of Zora Hurston's life.

Miller, Montzalee. (1987). *My Grandmother's Cookie Jar.* New York: Price Stern Sloan. (2–5)

A cookie jar helps a young girl remember her ancestors' stories.

Modesitt, Jeanne (compiler). (1992). *Songs of Chanukah.* New York: Little, Brown. (1–6)

This book includes 14 songs, written in both Hebrew and English, for the eight-day holiday. Games, dances, recipes, and candle lighting are included.

Mohr, Nicholasa. (1986). *Going Home.* New York: Dial. (4–7)

In this story, Felita goes to Puerto Rico to learn about her family and her heritage.

———. (1990). *Felita.* Illustrated by Ray Cruz. New York: Dial. (2–5)

Felita and her family move from a Puerto Rican neighborhood. In the new neighborhood, they experience prejudice and discrimination.

Mora, Pat. (1994). *The Desert Is My Mother.* Houston, TX: Pinata. (1–5)

This book is told in verse that describes the desert's beauty and fertility.

Myers, Walter Dean. (1993). *Brown Angels: An Album of Pictures and Verse*. New York: HarperCollins.

This is a collection of superb photographs of African American children combined with sensitive poetry. These pictures show the pride and love of parents.

———. (1988). *Scorpions*. New York: Harper & Row. (5–9)

Jamal is trying to survive the inner-city streets. He helps his mother take care of his sister and tries to stay away from gangs. He faces many difficult decisions.

———. (1991). *Now Is Your Time: The African American Struggle for Freedom*. New York: HarperCollins. (5–12)

Sketches of slaves, soldiers, inventors, and political leaders and the path of African Americans in their struggle for freedom fill this book.

———. (1992). *The Righteous Revenge of Artemis Bonner*. New York: HarperCollins. (3–6)

Artemis leaves New York to revenge his uncle's murder. In the process, he meets an interesting array of characters as he seeks revenge and gold.

Norman, Howard. (1987). *Who-Paddled-Backward-with-Trout*. Illustrated by Ed Young. New York: Little, Brown. (1–4)

A Cree boy searches for a new name in this story showing the importance that Native Americans place on names.

Oppenhein, Shulamith Levey. (1994). *Fireflies for Nathan*. New York: Tambourine. (1–3)

Nathan learns to catch fireflies with his grandparents one summer evening. The illustrations are very realistic and capture the human emotion of love.

Ortiz, Samuel. (1977). *The People Shall Continue*. San Francisco: Children's Book Press. (3–5)

The theme of this book is the Native Americans' struggle for survival throughout history. They have struggled with the earth, with one another, and finally with the white people.

Oughton, Jerrie. (1992). *How the Stars Fell into the Sky: A Navajo Legend*. Illustrated by Lisa Desimini. Boston: Houghton Mifflin. (1–6)

This is a Navajo myth about the constellations in the sky.

Paek, Min. (1988). *Aekyung's Dream*. San Francisco: Children's Book Press. (2–5)

Aekyung is taunted by her classmates because of her "Chinese eyes." Through a dream she learns to be strong.

Parks, Rosa, and Jim Haskins. (1992). *Rosa Parks: My Story*. New York: Dial. (5–9)

A straightforward autobiography with many photographs, this book conveys the honesty and dignity of Rosa Parks.

Paterson, Katherine. (1990). *The Tale of the Mandarin Ducks*. Illustrated by Leo and Diane Dillon. Bergenfield, NJ: Lodestar Books. (1–4)

This is an original Japanese folktale. A cruel lord captures a beautiful mandarin duck. Kind servants pity the duck and release it. Their kindness is magically repaid.

Pinkney, Andrea Davis. (1995). *Alvin Ailey*. New York: Hyperion Books for Children. (2–4)

The life of Alvin Ailey, a dancer who recognized the beauty and strength of the blues and gospel music, is described in this book.

Pinkney, Gloria Jean. (1992). *Back Home*. New York: Dial. (2–4)

Ernestine returns to her birthplace, North Carolina, to spend a summer with her relatives. Ernestine loves her time on the farm and learning more about her extended family.

———. (1994). *The Sunday Outing*. New York: Dial. (2–4)

This book tells of the times Ernestine and her aunt Odessa spend at the train station telling stories. Ernestine loves watching the trains.

Polacco, Patricia. (1992). *Mrs. Katz and Tush*. New York: Bantam. (1–4)

Mrs. Katz tells the story of her journey to America from Poland to her new friend Larnel. The traditions of the Jewish faith are depicted in this story.

Ringgold, Faith. (1991). *Tar Beach*. New York: Crown. (1–4)

This is the story of a young girl's flight over New York City and the sights she sees. She describes her life and her dreams.

————. (1992). *Aunt Harriet's Underground Railroad in the Sky*. New York: Crown. (1–4)

This is a fictional account of Harriet Tubman's work to free the slaves. The concept of the Underground Railroad is depicted so that younger readers gain a clearer understanding.

Ritter, Lawrence. (1995). *Leagues Apart*. New York: Morrow. (2–5)

This is a collection of biographies about some of the most famous African American baseball players.

Rodanas, Kristina. (1992). *Dragonfly's Tale*. New York: Clarion. (1–4)

This Zuni legend explains that you should treasure the good things that come to you or they will be taken away.

————. (1994). *Dance of the Sacred Circle*. New York: Little, Brown. (2–5)

A boy sets out to search for the great chief for help in saving his starving tribe.

Rohmer, Harriet. (1989). *Uncle Nacho's Hat*. San Francisco: Children's Book Press. (1–3)

This Nicaraguan tale explains how an old man changes his way of thinking to get rid of his old hat.

Roop, Peter, and Connie Roop. (1992). *Ahyoka and the Talking Leaves*. New York: Greenwillow. (3–6)

Sequoyah and his daughter create a Cherokee alphabet.

San Souci, Robert D. (1989). *The Talking Eggs: A Folktale from the American South*. Illustrated by Jerry Pinkney. New York: Dial. (1–4)

In this traditional story, the thoughtful daughter is rewarded.

Santiago, Carmen. (1992). *Abuelita's Paradise*. Morton Grove, IL: Whitman. (1–4)

Marita recalls her grandmother's Puerto Rican stories.

Savin, Marcia. (1993). *The Moon Bridge*. New York: Scholastic. (5–8)

Ruthie Fox's best friend, Mitsuko Fujimoto, is interned in a camp during World War II. This story is told from the friend's point of view.

Say, Allen. (1991). *Tree of Cranes*. Boston: Houghton Mifflin. (1–4)

A Japanese boy learns about Christmas when his mother decorates a tree with paper cranes.

————. (1993). *Grandfather's Journey*. Boston: Houghton Mifflin. (1–4)

This is the story of how Say's grandfather came to America and explored the wonders of his new country.

Schroeder, Alan. (1989). *Ragtime Tumpie*. New York: Little, Brown. (1–3)

This is the story of Josephine Baker, a ragtime dancer and singer.

————. (1994). *Lily and the Wooden Bowl*. New York: Doubleday. (1–3)

This Japanese folktale is told in simple, exquisite language that complements the illustrations. Lily makes a promise to her grandmother that she keeps in spite of a life of hardship. In the end everyone gets what they deserve.

Schwartz, Lynn Sharon. (1989). *The Four Questions*. New York: Dial. (1–4)

This beautifully illustrated text addresses four questions relating to the Jewish holiday of Passover.

Scott, Ann. (1992). *On Mother's Lap.* New York: Clarion. (K–2)

A mother shows her love by making room on her lap for both her children.

Segal, Jerry. (1991). *The Place Where Nobody Stopped.* New York: Orchard Books. (5–up)

This tale of a Russian baker tells how generous he is. He is a happy man because he could protect his family from soldiers.

Sewall, Marcia. (1990). *People of the Breaking Day.* New York: Atheneum. (2–5)

An informational book that describes the Wampanoag Indians before the English come to Massachusetts. Many aspects of their culture are elaborated.

Singer, Isaac B. (1966). *Zlateh the Goat and Other Stories.* Illustrated by Maurice Sendak. New York: Harper & Row. (1–6)

This great collection of Yiddish folktales appeals to young and old.

Sneve, Virginia Driving Hawk. (1989). *Dancing Teepees: Poems of American Indian Youth.* Illustrated by Stephen Gammell. New York: Holiday House. (1–6)

A collection of Native American poems from the oral tradition of this cultural group fills this book.

Snyder, Dianne. (1988). *The Boy of the Three-Year Nap.* Illustrated by Allen Say. Boston: Houghton Mifflin. (2–4)

A lazy boy plans to marry the rich girl next door so he won't have to work. But his plan fails.

Sobol, Harriet. (1984). *We Don't Look Like Our Mom and Dad.* New York: McCann. (1–4)

This is the story of two Korean boys who are adopted by an American family.

Soto, Gary. (1992). *Neighborhood Odes.* Illustrated by David Diaz. New York: Harcourt Brace Jovanovich. (3–7)

The poems in this collection tell about growing up in a Hispanic neighborhood, highlighting the delights of everyday experiences.

————. (1992). *The Skirt.* Illustrated by Eric Velasquez. New York: Delacorte. (2–5)

Miata is scared because she left a skirt on the bus. This very special skirt belonged to her mother who wore it in Mexico. Miata is supposed to wear the skirt to a dance.

Stanley, Jerry. (1994). *I Am an American: A True Story of Japanese Internment.* New York: Crown. (4–6)

This book tells the story of the removal of all Japanese from the West Coast and their confinement in relocation camps during World War II. It is illustrated with photographs.

Staples, Suzanne Fisher. (1989). *Shabanu: Daughter of the Wind.* New York: Knopf. (4–8)

Eleven-year-old Shabanu is torn between the traditions of her Pakistani culture, which demands she marry a man her father has chosen, and her desire to rebel and choose her own husband.

Steptoe, John. (1987). *Mufaro's Beautiful Daughters: An African Tale.* New York: Lothrop, Lee & Shepard. (all ages)

This African folktale has some Cinderella elements.

Stolz, Mary. (1988). *Storm in the Night.* Illustrated by Pat Cummins. New York: Harper & Row. (1–3)

A grandfather helps his grandson overcome his fear of thunderstorms.

Surat, Michele Maria. (1983). *Angel Child, Dragon Child.* Illustrated by Vo-Dinh Mai. Milwaukee, WI: Carnival/Raintree. (1–4)

Ut, a Vietnamese girl who lives in the United States while her mother remains in Vietnam, feels isolated in this unfamiliar place. But she is able to express her hurt, angry feelings, which helps others understand and accept her.

Taylor, Mildred. (1987). *The Gold Cadillac.* Illustrated by Michael Hays. New York: Dial. (3–5)

A black family travels in a new gold Cadillac to the southern United States and encounters prejudice.

Turner, Ann. (1974). *Nettie's Trip South.* New York: Macmillan. (3–6)

Nettie records her impressions of life in the South during slavery.

———. (1990). *Through Moon and Stars and Night Skies.* New York: HarperCollins. (1–3)

This is the story of a boy's journey to the United States to be adopted.

Tuyet, Tran-Khanh. (1987). *The Little Weaver of Thai Yen Village.* San Francisco: Children's Press. (2–4)

Hien survives gunfire in her Vietnamese village, but she must go to the United States for medical treatment.

Uchida, Yoshiko. (1981). *A Jar of Dreams.* New York: Macmillan. (5–8)

Rinko, an 11-year-old Japanese girl in Oakland, California, faces prejudice in 1930s California.

———. (1991). *The Invisible Thread.* Westwood, NJ: Messner. (4–7)

The author describes growing up in California as a Nisei, a second-generation Japanese American, and her family's internment in a concentration camp during World War II.

Van Lann, Nancy. (1989). *Rainbow Crow.* Illustrated by Beatriz Vidal. New York: Knopf.

This is a traditional Native American story.

Vigil, Angel. (1994). *The Corn Woman.* Englewood, CO: Libraries Unlimited. (2–8)

This collection of stories is from the southwestern United States.

Waters, Kate, and Madeline Slovenz-Low. (1990). *Lion Dancer: Ernie Wan's Chinese New Year.* Photographs by Martha Cooper. New York: Scholastic. (1–4)

This is the story of Ernie Wan, a Chinese American who participates in the Lion Dance for the Chinese New Year.

Watkins, Yoko Kawashima. (1986). *So Far from the Bamboo Grove.* New York: Lothrop, Lee & Shepard. (6–10)

An 11-year-old Japanese girl and her family, who were living in North Korea at the end of World War II, become refugees who are in grave danger.

Welsch, Roger. (1994). *Uncle Smoke Stories.* New York: Knopf. (4–7)

These Native American coyote tales are filled with wisdom and humor.

Williams, Sherley Anne. (1992). *Working Cotton.* Illustrated by Carole Byard. New York: Harcourt Brace Jovanovich. (1–3)

This story depicts the hard life of one migrant family working in the cotton fields.

Winter, Jonah. (1991). *Diego.* Translated by Amy Prince. Illustrated by Jeanette Winter. New York: Knopf. (1–6)

This biography of Diego Rivera's early years shows his patriotism and his strong desire to paint. This book won a Parents' Choice Award and the New York Times Best Illustrated Children's Book Award.

Wolff, Ferida. (1994). *The Emperor's Garden.* New York: Tambourine. (1–3)

The villagers work together to build a beautiful garden in honor of their Emperor, but the garden is ruined by rain.

Yarbrough, Camille. (1979). *Cornrows.* New York: Coward McCann. (1–4)

This book explains the traditions of cornrows and the hardships endured by the African people who were forced to come to the United States as slaves.

Yee, Paul. (1990). *Tales from Gold Mountain: Stories of the Chinese in the New World.* New York: Macmillan. (2–6)

This is a collection of stories about the Chinese immigrant experience in this country.

_____ . (1991). *Roses Sing on New Snow: A Delicious Tale.* Illustrated by Harvey Chan. New York: Macmillan. (4–8)

This story depicts the customs and traditions of family life in Chinatown during the early 1900s.

Yep, Laurence. (1975). *Dragonwings.* New York: HarperCollins. (4–8)

This adventure story portrays early 20th-century San Francisco from the point of view of Chinese immigrants.

_____ . (1989). *Rainbow People.* Illustrated by David Wiesner. New York: Harper & Row. (4–8)

This book is a superb collection of Chinese folktales that disseminate Chinese culture to younger generations.

_____ . (1993). *Dragon's Gate.* New York: HarperCollins. (4–8)

This story is based on the experiences of the Chinese who helped build the transcontinental railroad at the time of the American Civil War.

New York: (1994). *The Boy Who Swallowed Snakes.* New York: Scholastic. (1–4)

A boy swallows the ku snake so that it will not harm the people of his village in this Chinese folktale.

_____ . (1991). *Star Fisher.* New York: Morrow. (5–7)

This story depicts the struggle of Chinese immigrants as they move to West Virginia in the 1920s.

Yolen, Jane. (1990). *Sky Dogs.* Illustrated by Barry Moser. San Diego, CA: Harcourt Brace Jovanovich. (1–3)

This is a legend about the horse coming to the Blackfeet.

_____ . (1992). *Street Rhymes Around the World.* New York: Wordson/Boyds Mill (distributed by St. Martins Press). (1–6)

This book is a collection of rhymes from many different countries that are written in their native language and then translated to English.

Young, Ed. (1989). *Lon Po Po: A Red Riding Hood Story from China.* New York: Philomel. (1–3)

This version of Little Red Riding Hood received the Caldecott Award. In this variation, the mother leaves her three daughters home and goes to visit the grandmother, and the wolf comes to the girls.

_____ . (1994). *Little Plum.* New York: Philomel. (1–4)

A childless couple wishes for a child. Finally they have a tiny son and name him Little Plum. In spite of his small size, he is a hero. This is a Tom Thumb-type story.

Zhensun, Zheng, and Alice Low. (1991). *A Young Painter.* Illustrated by Wang Yani. New York: Scholastic. (2–5)

This book examines the life and works of the young Chinese girl who started painting animals at the age of three. She became the youngest artist to have a one-person show at the Smithsonian.

# Fifteen

## GUIDING QUESTIONS

1. Have you been a student in a classroom or observed in a classroom using literature-based instruction?

2. What do you think are the benefits of literature-based instruction?

3. What problems might a teacher encounter in developing literature-based instruction?

4. How can literature enrich content textbooks?

5. What are the basic components of a literature unit?

## OVERVIEW

Throughout this book, the focus has been on encouraging children's response to literature. Readers construct meaning from literature, meaning for understanding self and for understanding the world. Readers glean knowledge from literature, knowledge of self and of others. The more children read and respond to literature, the better understanding they may have of the world they live in. Readers also respond to the aesthetic nature of literature, finding beauty in the stories, listening to the sounds of words, relating their emotions, their sense of being alive, and what they feel as they read (Rosenblatt, 1993).

The goal of this chapter is to synthesize and organize what has been learned in the study of children's literature from the preceding chapters. Reflecting on this material will enable adults to create experiences that will facilitate childrens' growth into life-long readers. Incorporating literature into children's daily experiences gives them both the power and the desire to read, as well as developing their response to literature.

Reading books aloud to children or having them read books for themselves is only the beginning. Careful planning of literature-based themes and units maximizes children's understanding of and response to literature. It is important to identify the focus, goals, and experiences that will help children achieve these goals and to select carefully the literature, media, magazines, newspapers, reference materials, and textbooks for the thematic unit, integrating these materials into teaching plans (Hughes, 1993).

This text is a resource for identifying books in the various genre that interest children and that address the subject matter or theme. The text is a resource for exploring literature in classrooms, media centers (libraries), and homes, and this chapter includes practical, usable guides and units that classroom teachers

# Unit Studies

## LITERATURE, RESPONSE, AND LEARNING

have developed, used, and refined. These units are organized around a variety of formats, reflecting the different ways teachers think about them.

The literature and materials mentioned throughout this book are recommended books, teaching strategies, and activities to develop literature-based curricula or to add literature experiences to basal textbooks or programs.

## INTRODUCTION

The challenge in elementary education today is to rethink curriculum so that the time devoted to language arts and the other subject areas is better balanced. Since reading, writing, listening, and speaking are vehicles for accessing, exploring, and communicating content knowledge, they are best learned within the context of exploring world knowledge (Walmsley, 1994). As students acquire, extend, and enrich their knowledge of the world, they expand their language abilities.

The opening vignette portrays a third-grade teacher whose classroom incorporated integrated instruction. The students in her classroom have opportunities to find patterns and connections through **inquiry,** or *collaborative research,* that enables them to create meaning from the books they read and respond to. Connections is a key word in integrated learning. Students learn through building connections among books and ideas that facilitate their understanding (Hartman, 1992). As integrated studies unfold, students construct connections among subjects and topics, which occur as they reflect on the subject in relation to their experiences.

in these stories develops comprehension and critical thinking. The teacher reads aloud each day from *Celebrate America in Poetry and Art* to expand their understanding and appreciation.

After language arts, the students have physical education or recess.

### Mathematics

As a part of this unit, the students are exploring the concept of centuries, time, and history. In addition, they are learning about 100s concepts.

### Social Studies/Science

The students are comparing the physical geography and descriptions of the three regions depicted in the books they are reading through photographs, illustrations, and written language. They are also identifying regional foods and recipes for the county fair, which will be the culminating activity for the unit.

### Fine Arts

The students are reading about regional arts in the areas they are studying in *Celebrate America in Poetry and Art.* Exploring the arts in the various regions involves contacting regional and local art museums to order prints and slides for classroom display. Their art focus is primitive painting and the art teacher is exploring the techniques used in primitive paintings so that the students can create their own primitive paintings.

### Closure

At the end of each day, the students discuss their experiences and write in their learning logs.

## UNITS OF STUDY

Literature provides one way of learning about the world and making connections that increases children's understanding and awareness (Peterson, 1991). A unit of study is a collection of lessons that motivates students toward in-depth research

on a topic, issue, person, idea, or theme. These studies give students a chance to become experts on the focus of the study to discover relationships and connections. Moreover, well-developed units encourage students to become active, involved learners.

Units may focus on a single book, an author, or a group of books that address the same topic or theme. Students use reading, writing, talking, listening, and thinking as tools to discover relationships and to link new connections with prior understandings. Every time students use reading, writing, talking, listening, and thinking they are increasing their literacy and learning to construct meaning.

In an integrated program, certain important aspects of two or more subjects are deployed to achieve goals focused on substantial themes such as a specific disaster, racial tension, loneliness, or survival, the solar system, the water cycle, and endangered species. Terry Johnson and Daphne Louis (1990) found they could sensibly and productively integrate some subject areas for some of the time. Language arts, social studies, and science offer numerous opportunities for integration with art and music. The language arts processes of reading, writing, speaking, and listening are best learned in relation to content areas. Learning across the curriculum is a natural outcome of literature-based instruction. Units may be whatever you choose to make them—there is no right or wrong way to conceptualize these studies. The way teachers use literature in their classrooms or media centers may change many times during their professional life.

## Integrating Literature into the Curriculum

Teaching with literature is not a specific method or process based on hard-and-fast rules. Uses of literature can be molded and adapted to fit local curricula and students, creating a personal definition of literature-based teaching. Teachers grow and change in their philosophies of teaching as they experience different schools, children, and educational philosophies. Moreover, professional teachers continue reflecting, evolving, and learning throughout their careers. Literature, however, can be brought into classrooms no matter what the prevailing philosophy, and the goal of this text is exploring ways to do this. This chapter presents a variety of ideas that can be adapted to many different classrooms. Unit teaching, integrated teaching, thematic teaching, and child-centered classrooms coexist with many approaches to education. For example, many elementary teachers modify basal reader lessons by drawing on their students' experiences and interests. Basal readers are often organized in units that facilitate literature connections. These teachers develop concepts and vocabulary that are critical to understanding lessons and ask questions that stimulate higher order thinking. Teachers may offer students a wide range of extension activities.

These guidelines are helpful in developing a literature emphasis in literacy programs:

1. Read aloud to students every day at every grade level. Read fiction, poetry, and nonfiction.

2. Find out about students' interests, what they know and have experienced, and what they need to know. This will help in planning extensions and selecting literature.

3. After completing a unit or lesson in a basal program, develop a unit on the same theme or topic that permits students to read whole books rather than the abridged, edited versions of literature that appear in most basals. For example, after reading a basal unit on dreams, develop a dreams unit. Discuss the basal selections the students have read. They could discuss dreams from many perspectives. What are their dreams about growing up? What do they dream about? What is the importance of dreams?

4. Ask the students to think of questions they would like to have answered about dreams. Write the questions on a chart or chalkboard.

5. Give booktalks for the books selected for the unit and give the children choices about the questions they will research and the books they will read. For four or five groups of five to seven students, seven or eight sets of books is adequate. The children should read their books individually.

6. Have the students participate in literature discussion groups after they have completed the book. Students who are accustomed to reading page by page in the basal, however, may do better at the outset by reading half of the book and participating in discussion, then completing the book and participating in another discussion. Develop the students' reading fluency and confidence so they can read the entire book first, because it is only after reading the entire book that they will have an understanding of plot, characterization, and other story elements.

7. Have the students keep literature logs as they read their books. An alternative is to write a letter to a friend or their teacher about their book.

8. Have the students select extensions that will express their response to the literature they read.

## Making Connections Through Inquiry

Units provide a framework for children's inquiry in the classroom; inquiry is one of the processes through which children learn. Knowledge only gives the illusion of residing in books: In reality, knowledge is a relationship that resides among people in particular times and contexts (Harste, 1993). Learners feed off one another and help one another learn and respond. Learning is social inquiry (Copenhaver, 1993). Talking with others often helps readers make sense of new information; although they can arrive at a meaning alone, they do so more often in collaboration (Barnes, 1995). This is why creating classrooms of inquirers is so important (Harste, 1993).

The beginning or access point for inquiry is what students already know about a topic. A good beginning point for a unit and for inquiry is creating a web that shows what students already know about the topic or theme. Create a group web for a class by putting up a large sheet of paper and writing the topic in the center of the sheet. Students brainstorm what they know about the subject, which is written around the topic. Students can

# FIGURE 15.1

Friends web.

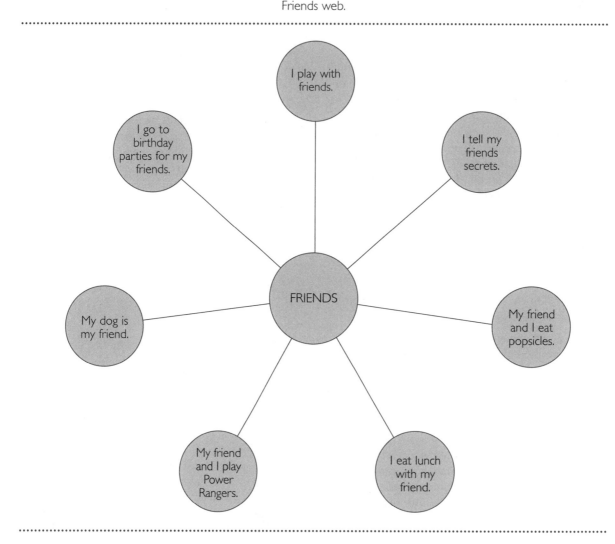

create individual webs of their own prior knowledge. Figure 15.1 shows a web of prior knowledge for the topic of friends that a group of second graders created for a "Being Friends" unit. The teacher of this class chose to begin this inquiry with the subject "things we do with friends" because this was the most frequent response given on the map of knowledge.

Inquiry is an important concept today because it focuses on authentic learning since the questions students research have meaning for them. Moreover, the students are *actively* engaged in learning. They are learning through *doing*. Inquiry is based on students' questions and their investigations to answer their questions. Some teachers ask students to think of questions about curriculum topics that are personally important. Both student-generated questions and teacher-generated questions focus inquiries. Students may spend a week or so thinking of questions, writing them in journals, and explaining why the particular questions are personally powerful questions.

be sufficiently powerful to sustain a period of inquiry (Copenhaver, 1993). The questions need to Inquiry that involves curriculum topics can have personal values for students also.

In order to investigate their questions, students discuss, listen, read, write, view films and television, and consult with people who have special knowledge related to the questions. They may conduct their own experiments, as a group of kindergarten students did when investigating insects. They experimented to find out which insects crawled fastest. All of these approaches to investigation and more can be applied during integrated instruction.

## DEVELOPING THEMES AND UNITS

Defining themes and units is difficult since the applications of this concept are so varied. Some educators use the terms synonymously, while others differentiate them (Walmsley, 1994). This book uses **theme** to identify *the meaning, focus, or central idea of a unit of study,* such as "ocean life" or "courage." A **unit** is *the organizing framework for a thematic study.* A unit for ocean life identifies the goals, experiences, activities, and materials the teacher plans to develop through the theme. In addition to theme units, teachers can devise structural units. The boxes on pages 428 and 429 show a theme unit that identifies the focus and the framework of a given topic.

In theme unit learning, students and teachers investigate topics, themes, and concepts in various ways. Students who are independent readers can read books, magazines, and reference books, while emergent readers hear stories and information read aloud. Discussion plays an important role in examining a topic, as does writing about it. Many teachers encourage students to maintain learning logs about their units. Students do individual or group activities and projects related to the topic. Frequently the arts (music, drama, visual art) are incorporated into the unit. In many instances, science, math, and social studies are relevant to the unit. These connections offer opportunities for both direct and indirect teaching of the skills and strategies that students are expected to accomplish.

A theme unit is an intensive learning experience for students and teachers. Teachers can initiate theme units or they can involve students in selecting theme units. Some educators call *student-generated units* **theme cycles** (Altwerger and Flores, 1994). Some teachers choose to include both teacher-generated units and student-generated units in their curricula. The suggested theme topics in the box on page 430 can be used at many different grade levels because they can be approached in a variety of ways and at several different levels.

Students use their language arts abilities as they learn through theme units. Jean Dickinson (1995) reports that her fifth- and sixth-grade students, using picture books, novels, and textbooks to explore World War II, developed these reading strategies:

1. to visualize while reading
2. to use prior knowledge
3. to reread interesting and exciting parts and parts with especially interesting language
4. to ask questions about what they read
5. to make predictions
6. to discuss books with friends
7. to find ideas for writing
8. to look beyond the cover
9. to relate books to other books they have read and to books by the same author
10. to put themselves in the story
11. to know when they don't understand something in the book
12. to read the rest of a paragraph to figure out a word meaning

### Shared Book Experiences

There are at least five general ways to manage book sharing for a unit. The approach depends on the age and maturity of the students and the availability of materials. No matter which system of managing book sharing is used, give the students time to discuss and share their ideas about the books they read.

1. Read the book or books aloud, with the students responding through discussion. Read books more than once: Children's responses increase and deepen with each rereading of a book (Jacque, 1993).

## Theme Unit

Focus:        Time Fantasy for Upper Elementary

Objectives:   To develop students' concepts of fantasy and the rules of well-written fantasy

To develop students' concepts of time and space as they are related to time fantasy

To develop students' ability to compare and contrast

## Part I. Teacher-Planned Whole-Class Reading and Viewing

Teacher Read-aloud:   *Wrinkle in Time* by Madeleine L'Engle

Group or Partner Reading:   *Tom's Midnight Garden* by Philippa Pearce

*Playing Beatie Bow* by Ruth Park

*The Root Cellar* by Joyce Lunn

"Flying Saucers" nonfiction magazine article

Music:   appropriate to the past or future

Art:   art of the period

## Part II. Overview of Literature Presentation

Introduce the unit with a discussion of time travel. Ask the students questions like these:

1. Do you think people can travel through time?
2. If you could travel through time where would you go and to what time period would you choose to go?
3. What do you think the advantages are to time travel?
4. What do you think the disadvantages of time travel are?

In addition to discussion have students write their thoughts about these questions. Then have them think of questions they would like to have answered. Create time capsules with paper towel rollers or some similar container. Seal the containers and store them until the unit is complete.

The teacher will read *Wrinkle in Time* aloud over a three-week period. When the book is finished, have students read in small groups or in pairs one of the titles listed for group or partner reading in Part I. Additional related reading is listed at the end of this unit.

The beginning point when devising a literature unit is to determine the focus of the project. Next, locate and sequence relevant material and develop appropriate experiences. Choosing the focus may be the most difficult aspect of the process because it demands a fairly broad familiarity with the world of children's literature and an understanding of the structure of the discipline. Units can be formulated around topic, form, structure, or theme (Johnson and Louis, 1990).

Have students work in small groups or pairs and assign a novel to be read by a specified date. Ask each group or pair of students to prepare analyses of their novels to share with the rest of the class. All students should be prepared to contribute to the comparison chart on page 429.

## Related Readings

- Conrad, Pam *Stonewords*
- Dickinson, Peter *Eva*
- L'Engle, Madeleine *A Swiftly Tilting Planet*
- Utley, Alison *A Traveler in Time*

## Curricular Connections

Math.  Have students discuss the role of math in space travel and how math relevant to space relates to their current math instruction.

Social studies.  Describe the lifestyle and values of the people in the various stories. Have the students identify what kinds of things they need to consider when describing a society and its values.

Writing.  Instruct students to keep reading journals in which each writes a response to a novel he or she has read.

Students also may use art and/or music to express their responses to the novels.

## COMPARISON CHART

| Novel | *Stonewords* | *Wrinkle in Time* | *Playing Beatie Bow* | |
|---|---|---|---|---|
| Main character | | | | |
| Age | | | | |
| Sex | | | | |
| Friend or companion | | | | |
| Setting 1 | | | | |
| Setting 2 | | | | |
| Theme | | | | |
| Historical connections | | | | |
| Climax | | | | |
| Plot resolution | | | | |

## THE NOVEL ANALYSIS

1. Plot      Is the plot interesting? _____

            Does the plot explain time travel in a logical fashion? _____

            How does the author convince you this story could have happened? _____

            _____

2. Characters    Are the characters convincing? _____

            Do you care about the characters? _____

            What made them seem like real people? _____

3. Setting      How does the author convince readers that the setting is a real place? _____

            _____

            How does the author convince readers the time setting is real? _____

            _____

# Theme topics for units

## Holidays Across Cultures

| | |
|---|---|
| New Year's | Flag Day |
| Christmas | Memorial Day |
| Kwanzaa | Arbor Day |
| Hanukkah | |

## Concepts

| | |
|---|---|
| being a friend/having friends | journeys around the world |
| what do your senses tell you? | journeys around our state |
| how many kinds of courage are there? | journeys around our country |
| heroes | what makes you laugh? |
| superheroes | what is a family? |
| space | conservation |
| communities | growing |

## Artists and Writers

| | |
|---|---|
| Steven Kellogg | Trina Schart Hyman |
| Avi | Lois Ehlert |
| Pam Conrad | Katherine Paterson |
| Marc Brown | Tomie dePaola |

## Current Events

| | |
|---|---|
| disasters | hurricanes |
| floods | blizzards |
| earthquakes | random acts of kindness |
| senseless acts of beauty | |

## Curriculum Topics

(consult your own curriculum)

| | |
|---|---|
| addition | multiplication |
| great sentences from literature | great paragraphs from literature |
| water cycle—where has all the rain gone? | nutrition—you are what you eat |
| interpreting maps—where in the world are you going? | rain forests—what do rain forests have to do with me? |
| weather—it's raining cats and dogs | genre (traditional literature, poetry, biography, etc.) |

2. Read each book aloud and have the students respond in a response journal, literature log, or interactive journal.

3. Obtain a class set of one title and have all the students read that book independently. This is probably the least-favored approach because it easily leads to reading and analyzing the book in the same way that a basal reader selection is analyzed. This fragmentation interferes with the benefits of integrating literature in the reading program.

4. Divide the class into four cooperative groups and have each group read a different book. Booktalk the books in advance to help children choose a book that appeals to their interests.

5. Have various groups or individuals read a book and retell the high points of the parts they read.

## Planning Units

There are a number of factors to consider in choosing the unifying theme or focus of each unit. Curriculum goals and objectives are central to the units. For instance, first-grade teachers are usually accountable for emergent reading and writing and for developing concepts of family, friends, and holidays, among others. These concepts can be developed through units that focus on many different topics or themes.

Once the curriculum goals and objectives are accounted for, consider what the students already know and what they need to know about the selected topic. In addition to prior knowledge, teachers usually consider the students' interests when planning units, as they will be more motivated and have a greater sense of ownership when pursuing their own interests. Other considerations regarding choice of topic include the students' learning needs, developmental levels, and previous experiences. Teachers and librarians need to build background experiences with students who lack them.

The available resources are an important consideration when planning units. A good supply of well-written books is essential. The books must, of course, address the unit topic or theme, but they also must match the students' range of reading levels. Both print and nonprint media develop children's knowledge base and understanding. Videos, films, pictures, and computer programs are useful in developing units. Human resources, such as guest speakers or people who can demonstrate skills or materials, add interest to unit studies. For example, a study of Britain is more lively when someone from that country visits the classroom. Students could also take field trips to look for products imported from England.

In planning units, remember to include opportunities for students to respond to the literature they read. Opportunities for response such as art, music, writing, and similar experiences enable readers to develop, refine, and personalize their understandings (Weston, 1993). The box on p. 432 shows some of the possibilities for response experiences with literature-based units. The box on p. 433 provides a form that can be used to summarize the unit plan.

## Assessing Unit Experiences

Assessment is an aspect of teaching because teachers need information about what students have learned. Gathering information regarding students' reading achievement is an integral part of instruction, and one means of gathering such information is through the use of tests. Teachers need assessment to determine whether students have learned what they were trying to teach. Students may need additional practice and experience, or teachers may need to reteach concepts, skills, and processes. Moreover, teachers are responsible for knowing students' progress and reporting their progress to the school and parents.

Literature-based reading programs usually do not have standardized tests to evaluate student achievement. The portfolio method of assessment (discussed below) is one means of effectively evaluating many different areas of students' reading achievement. Some school systems have adopted reading assessments or reading inventories to gather additional information, which can be combined with portfolio assessment. Other sources of information regarding student progress include work samples, journal entries, projects and displays, individual conferences, oral presentations, and student assessment forms. Teachers' observations and documentation are viable alternatives to testing, especially when combined with work samples. Since the goal is to develop readers who understand and respond to literature, as well as to accomplish content goals and objectives, the best way to find out whether we are meeting our goals is to hand a child a book and listen to them read and discuss the text. Then both teacher and child will know whether they are meeting their goals.

When using informal observations, the teacher creates anecdotal records of children's reading and literature experiences, observing and recording competency in skills. Teachers often use informal checklists to guide their observations. These checklists identify the skills and abilities that are a part of the adopted curriculum. For instance a reading competence checklist might include items such as *reads left to right, shows the front of a book, turns pages of the book correctly, follows the sequence of events in a story, understands and follows plot, and chooses to read for pleasure.*

For informal evaluation teachers also collect writing samples, record data on miscue analysis in oral reading passages, list trade books used for instruction, and collect special projects or creative writing entries for the assessment folder. These varied materials give the teacher a more complete picture of children's abilities and enable the teacher to plan instruction that meets the needs of individual students. This information also gives the student more control over the learning process.

### Portfolio assessment

Portfolio assessment is a continuous process in which student and teacher gather information about each student's academic progress. Student input is a critical component in this type of assessment.

# Response experiences for literature-based units

## Language Arts

### Listening

- Listening exercises using passages with outstanding language
- Visualize scenes from the book
- Listen for sensory images
- Identify book's structures
- Retell a story
- Speakers on special subjects

### Speaking

- Discuss the book in a group
- Discuss the book using student-generated questions
- Tell the story as a news report
- Tell a student-composed story

### Reading

- Use reader's theater for all or part of a story or poem
- Read cultural variations of a traditional story
- Read and compare to other books

### Writing

- Write an original story with the same pattern
- Write the story as a play
- Write more about a character or add a new character
- Write song lyrics based on the story

- Keep a journal of feelings, ideas, parallels evoked as a result of story reading or listening

### Science

- Study the habitat of the story
- Create an experiment to solve a story problem or mystery
- Think about how science is related to the book
- Relate scientific method to book

### Social Studies

- Research the country, people, geography, history, anthropology of the setting
- Study the descriptions of places

### Physical Education

- Create a dance of a scene in a story or a poem

### Math

- Discuss the math concepts that appear in the story

### Fine Arts

- Create a mural depicting scenes from the story
- Draw a picture story map
- Make puppets
- Dramatize one character

---

Although portfolios can be whatever the teacher wants them to be, there are three common types of portfolio assessment (Meinbach, Rothlein, and Fredericks, 1995):

1. *Showcase portfolios.* The student selects the work samples to be placed in the portfolio. Some teachers have the student explain the context of the work and why the work is exemplary from the student's perspective.

2. *Descriptive portfolios.* The teacher assigns projects and selects completed work to place in the portfolio.

3. *Evaluative portfolios.* Qualitative materials, such as tests, are placed in the portfolio.

The important aspect of portfolio assessment is obtaining the data that permits teachers to assess students' progress (Kimeldorf, 1994). Data can be gathered from anecdotal records, check-

# Unit Plan

Unit topic, theme, concept
Concepts (goals, objectives—include adopted curriculum, student interests, and student needs)
Science:
Social Studies:
Math:
Language Arts:
Others: art, music, physical education, dance, etc.

Response experiences:
Literature and textbooks used:

Resources used: (experts, references, film, experiments, field trips, media center)

Describe processes used:
    inquiry:
    discussion:
    cooperative groups:
    paired activities:
    writing:
    observation:
    models:
    whole group:

Response activities:
    storytelling
    writing
    art
    music
    dance
    drama
    response journal
    other

Evaluation:
    portfolios
    booklist
    products
    checklists
    journals

lists, samples of students' work, comments written by students, teacher reflection notes, photographs of student projects, videos or audiocassettes, thematic logs, standardized tests, writing samples, and cooperative group assignments.

Portfolio assessments give the student, teacher and parent a more complete picture of an individual's strengths and weaknesses. Through careful planning, teachers can help students identify goals for the next area of study. The student also has input into the planning process. Portfolio assessment is a reflective process in which both the student and the teacher collaboratively review what has been taught and learned and plan for the future.

## CLASSROOM UNIT SUGGESTIONS TO ENHANCE LITERARY EXPERIENCE

This section of the chapter includes actual units that classroom teachers have developed, used, and refined. These units are organized around a variety of formats, some narrative and others outlined, reflecting the different ways teachers think about them. Experienced teachers, beginning teachers, and those in the middle of their careers may approach units and literature-based teaching differently.

UNIT SUGGESTIONS

## 15.1 Day and night (kindergarten)

When planning a thematic unit, I usually consider the students' interests and the activities they have previously enjoyed. I also consult the Standard Course of Study for our grade level and identify specific curricular goals and objectives from each of the content areas that correspond to the unit I plan to teach. Often the units selected come from the area of social studies or science. It is very important when using an integrated approach that materials selected teach skills in reading/language arts, mathematics, social studies, science, fine arts, and physical education.

When planning this type of unit, I first identify my goals related directly to the content area in which the unit was selected. In this particular unit on day and night I want the students to be able to explain both verbally and nonverbally why we have day and night. Many other skills can be developed during this time. I plan to introduce the concept of telling time to the hour and half-hour, review counting and number identification 0–12, and review seasons, months of the year, and days of the week. Children will experience using a sundial for the first time and will create a crude form of a sundial for themselves. Children will have fun discovering shadows and measuring their own shadows during different times of day. These are the goals I identified.

Topic: Day and Night

### Goals

1. To help children understand that day and night are caused by the rotation of the earth.
2. To introduce the concepts of the sun, moon, stars, and the planet Earth.
3. To introduce the concept of telling time using various instruments (sundial, clock, calendar).

### Skills to Develop

*Mathematics*

- counting 0–12 (review)
- number identification 0–12 (review)
- telling time—compare/contrast a clock, calendar, and sundial
- telling time to the hour and half-hour (introduction)

*Reading*

- sequencing (story events)
- letter identification: Mm, Ss, Dd, Nn
- rhyming words (continued)
- phonemic awareness: m, s, d, n

*Writing*

Stories for dictation. Children dictate stories to their teacher based on their responses to these books: *Sounds in the Night*; *Night in the City*; *Me and My Shadow*; and *Things We Do During the Day*.

*Literature*

- journals
- logs
- shared writing

*Science*

- day/night
- constellations
- earth, sun, stars, moon
- rotation or turning
- shadows
- seasons with respect to day/night

*Social Studies*

- things we do during the day/night
- days of the week
- birthdays
- careers that require working at night
- months of the year
- culture

*Fine Arts*

- tracing shadows
- nighttime pictures using black wash paint
- daytime pictures
- constellation patterns

*Physical Education*

- focus on circle games that move clockwise (Duck, Duck, Goose; With Stars; Farmer in the Dell; London Bridge)

## Introduction

### Thought Question

Why do we have day and night? Record student responses on chart paper.

### Circle Time

Use the book *I Have a Friend* by Keiko Narahashi to introduce the concept of shadows. After reading, have children go out and find their shadows. With a friend, they can use a nonstandard unit of measurement (jump ropes or blocks) to measure one another's shadows. Compare the height of the shadow with the child's actual height. Repeat this activity at another time of day. Discuss concepts of taller and shorter. Ask the children why they have shadows and record responses.

### Small-Group Activities

Read the story *Bear Shadow* by Frank Asch.

### Discussion questions:

- Why did the bear want to lose his shadow?
- What things did he do to lose his shadow?
- How would you lose your shadow?
- Draw a picture of where you might go so your shadow would not find you.

### Activities:

- Have children dictate a story about losing their shadow.
- Trace children's shadows on butcher paper outside. Have the children come inside and paint their shadows to show the clothing they are wearing.
- Have children write a story about something they and their shadow like to do together.
- Share the poem *My Shadow* by Robert Louis Stevenson and ask students to compare the poem with the activities they and their shadow like to do together.
- Using paper clocks, show the children the time they went outside to trace their shadows.
- Play the recording "Paper Clocks" by Hap Palmer.
- Discuss the events of a school day. Using the clock, show the time children get up in the morning, eat breakfast, start school, have circle time, go outside to play, and so forth. Let children experiment with clocks to show when they do certain things at home. *The Very Grouchy Ladybug* by Eric Carle may

be read in a small group and then placed in the mathematics or exploration center with clocks for the children to use.

## Learning About Daytime

### Circle Time

Discuss why we are able to see our shadows. Ask the children if they think they would see their shadows if it were cloudy or raining outside. Encourage the children to deduce that we see our shadows because of the sun. Discuss that the sun is a star, that we live on a planet called Earth, and why we are able to see the sun part of the day. Discuss why we have day and night.

Read *Rooster Crows* by Ragnhild Scamell. Discuss why the rooster couldn't get the sun to come up at the stroke of midnight, and show this time on the clock. Explain that we have day and night because the earth rotates or turns. When the earth turns, part of it is exposed to the sun and the other part is not. Using a globe, help the children locate your state and mark it with a sticker. Gently turn the globe so that the children can see the earth rotate or turn. Let the children practice rotating the globe. Have one child hold a flashlight on the part of the globe with the students' state. Explain that the sun is a star and it does not move.

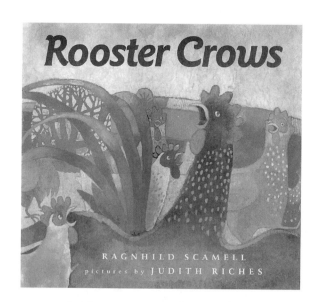

*In this story, a proud rooster bets that he can crow the sun up into the sky at midnight.*

Rather the earth slowly rotates or turns. As it turns the sun is no longer pointing directly at the state, it is becoming afternoon. As the earth turns we no longer face the sun and it is nighttime. The other part of the world is facing the sun and therefore having daytime. As the earth continues to turn, the part that is far away from the sun gets closer, creating dawn, then morning. Let children take turns holding the flashlight (the sun) and turning the globe (Earth).

## Circle Time

Share *The Napping House* by Don and Audrey Wood with the students. After several readings students will enjoy predicting what is coming next. The children can dramatize the story with puppets. Read *Grandfather Twilight* by Barbara Berger to the students. Discuss what the pearl in the story represents (the moon). This will lead into the study of night.

Writing. Have the children do a shared writing activity. For example, the children can write to their parents explaining their experiences and what they learned.

## Learning About Nighttime

## Circle Time

Have the children observe the night sky. Ask them to record everything they see. They can do this for several evenings. During circle time have the children tell what they saw and record their information. Categorize and count the different things. Discuss what the moon looked like. Introduce the phases of the moon with Frank Asch's book *Moon Bear.* Have children compare the moon they saw with the one in the story. Have children draw the different phases of the moon on the calendar as they observe them in the night sky.

## Small-Group Activities

Share picture books of constellations. Show the children that the constellations make patterns in the sky. Tell them how long ago people used these patterns to help find their way. Help children recreate the pattern of the Big Dipper and Little Dipper. Place glue-backed stars on black paper as they appear in the night sky (copy pattern from constellation book). Use chalk to connect the stars so that children can see the pattern. Repeat using other stars.

Have children cut out pictures of activities that are done during the day and others that are done at night, then sort and paste the pictures onto poster board. Record words and phrases that are dictated about the pictures. (One half of the poster board can be yellow and the other half black to simplify the sorting process for students. It also helps to have some pictures already available for cutting for children who are unable to locate any pictures in magazines.)

Introduce /Ss/ for stars. Have children look for /s/ on stars. Use sand trays to trace the letter /s/. Discuss the /s/ sound. Help children identify words beginning with the /s/ sound. Use a dictionary to help children associate pictures with the letter and sound. (Repeat this activity with other letters when appropriate.)

## Circle Time

Introduce *Goodnight Moon* by Margaret Wise Brown. Read the story several times. Begin leaving out the final word in the second sentence and have children supply it. Pull out pairs of rhyming words and illustrate each on an index card. Have children practice putting the pairs of words together.

## Small-Group Activities

Read *Time For Bed* by Mem Fox. Study the end papers. Listen for pairs of rhyming words. Help the children find the rhyming words. Create a book of rhyming words with things associated with day and night. Encourage the students to make end papers for their books. Make nighttime pictures using crayons. Use a tempera paint wash to cover the pictures. Have children dictate sentences about things they like to do at night.

Read *Happy Birthday Moon* by Frank Asch. Help the children learn their birthdays. Discuss the book, asking what kind of present the children would give the moon. Discuss the idea of an echo, which is introduced in this story. Then have children make a birthday board with their birthdays and the birthdays of family members.

## Circle Time

Read Cynthia Rylant's *Night in the Country*. Have the children listen and record the night sounds of the city. Share these during circle time. Compare the night sounds of the city and the night sounds of the country.

## Small-Group Activities

Share *Goodnight Owl* by Pat Hutchins. Have the animals that keep the owl awake cut out to use on the flannel board. Have the children practice retelling the story using the flannel board animals to sequence the retelling.

Other Books to Use in Unit

- *Ladybird First Facts About Space* by Caroline Arnold
- *What the Moon Is Like* by Franklin M. Branley
- *While I Sleep* by Mary Calhoun
- *Turtle Day* by Douglas Florian

- *Star, Little Star* by Lonnie George
- *The Moon and You* by E. C. Krupp
- *Under the Moon* by Joanne Ryder
- *Nine O'Clock Lullaby* by Marilyn Singer

......................................

## 15.2 Recycling (first or second grade)

The students in this classroom had already had experiences with big books prior to this unit. They had many experiences with *Raffi Songs to Read* and had listened to Raffi tapes. They had big book experiences with books like Ruth Krauss's *The Happy Day*, which has a simple, repetitive text that children enjoy. They dramatized some of these stories and thoroughly enjoyed reading and rereading or singing their big books. See Chapter Twelve for more information on big books.

The unit described here was planned in response to the schoolwide recycling project suggested by the principal. After my initial panic at the thought of first graders and recycling, I remembered a new book I had seen at my favorite children's bookstore and ran to the phone to put a hold on *Round and Round Again* by Nancy Van Laan. On the way home from school, I picked up the book and started planning.

Topic: Recycling

Objectives:

- to learn the meaning of recycling
- to identify things that can be recycled
- to identify language repetition and predict it
- to identify rhyming words

*Reading Selections:*

- *Round and Round Again* by Nancy Van Laan. This is a predictable book.
- *Mother Earth's Counting Book* by Andrew Clements

Background Information for the Teacher:

Recycling means reusing. The mother recycles everything in Van Laan's story. The refrain in the book is: "Round and round and round again, over yonder and back again." The story is told in couplets and the rhymes will be easy for first graders to find.

The key points are:

1. the meaning of recycling
2. the materials that are usually recycled
3. the recycling symbol
4. local recycling and how the children can help
5. yard sales are a form of recycling and so is giving your clothes to a little brother or sister

Materials:

- recycling decal
- recycling bin
- picture of the recycling truck
- student journals
- chart paper

Language Arts

Read the story aloud twice and ask the children to join in on the repeated parts. After the second reading, ask the children to chant the refrain and show them it in print on the chart.

Ask these questions to start discussion:

1. Why do you think the title of this book is *Round and Round Again?* (Relate to recycle and reuse).
2. What was your favorite of all the things that mother made in this story?
3. What were the funniest things that mother recycled?
4. How do you recycle things at your home?
5. (Show them the recycling symbol.) Why do you think it looks like this? Can you think of any ways this symbol is related to the book we just read?
6. Think of some questions you would like to ask about the story or about recycling. Then we will discuss your questions.

Science

Discuss the fact that Styrofoam is permanent garbage. Think of things made of Styrofoam and materials that could be used instead.

*Mama is the most creative recycler in town.*
*This story told in rhyme is about discovering*
*the potential in all things.*

*Science Experiment*

Have the children bring in paper, glass, and similar items and bury them in soil in an inflatable child's pool. Check each week to see how long it takes for the garbage to decay. Write up the experiment on a chart and add each week's observations.

Social Studies

Discuss the reasons that recycling is important. The students will develop the understanding that they are taking care of the earth for their own future.

Imagine some funny ways to recycle things and write about them in your journal or draw a picture of what you imagine.

Math

Count the number of things that mother recycled in this book.

Extension Activities

- Find the rhyming words in the story.

- Have the children compose their own recycling story. Begin by thinking of a good refrain. Then they can use their ideas about funny things to recycle. Let them brainstorm ideas and write them on the chalkboard. Check their ideas and try to rhyme couplets as in the story. Once they have revised and edited, create a chart for them to illustrate and make a bulletin board or door poster with their composition and art.

Other Books to Use in Unit

- *Dinosaurs to the Rescue! A Guide to Protecting Our Planet* by Laurie Krasny Brown and Marc Brown

- *Regards to the Man in the Moon* by Ezra Jack Keats

- *Recycle! A Handbook for Kids* by Gail Gibbons

## 15.3 Counting (second, third, or fourth grade)

This unit, which focuses on various ways of counting, is presented in a unit map.

Questions:
- What do you want or need to count?
- What is the best way to count that thing?

*Math*
- Why do we need to count things?
- What kinds of things need to be counted?
- One to one correspondence

*Writing*
- Think of a new way to count and write it down.

*Art*
- Make illustrations and art to go with the project.

*Social Studies*
- Why is it important to count people?
- What do we call it when we count people?
- What is a poll?
- Why do we conduct polls?

*Reading*
- *The King's Commissioners* by Ann Friedman
- *The Search for Delicious* by Natalie Babbit

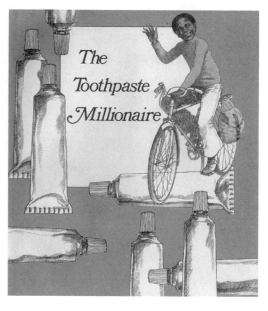

*Rufus was a millionaire by the sixth grade.*

- *Only One* by Marc Harshman
- *The Librarian Who Measured the Earth* by Kathryn Lasky
- *The Toothpaste Millionaire* by Jean Merrill
- *Counting Jenny* by Helena Pittman
- *Chestnut Cove* by Terry Egan
- *Turtle Time* by Sandol Stoddard

........................................

## 15.4 Native American folktales (third grade)

Topic:  Native American Folktales

Objectives:
- to learn the characteristics of the folktale genre
- to identify Native American values through their folktales.
- to develop vocabulary related to the Native American culture

Background Information:
Originally folktales were told around campfires, which is why their structure differs from other genre. Folktales were told by people who did not read or write. They were used to entertain, to teach lessons, and to teach listeners about their culture. Folktales were very important

in transmitting culture. These tales help us know how Native Americans lived and what is important to them.

Reading Selections:
- *Baby Rattlesnake* by Te Ata. This teaching tale is written at an independent reading level for third grade.
- *Iktomi and the Berries: A Plains Indian Story* by Paul Goble. Read aloud to introduce Native American storytelling. Trickster tales like this one appear in the traditional literature of all cultures.
- *The Great Buffalo Race: A Seneca Tale* retold by Barbara Juster Esbensen. This pourquoi tale explains how the buffalo got its hump. It is a good read-aloud.
- *Sky Dogs* by Jane Yolen. This read-aloud explains why Native Americans first thought horses were dogs.

- *Ma'ii and Cousin Horned Toad* by Shonto Begay. The author, a Navajo, tells his own favorite childhood tale in this book.
- *The Mud Pony: A Traditional Skidi Pawnee Tale* by Caron Cohen. This story shows the importance of horses in the Native American culture. Children can read this one.
- *The Legend of the Bluebonnet* by Tomie dePaola. This picture book is one children can read for themselves.
- *Rainbow Crow: A Lenape Tale* by Nancy Van Laan. A read-aloud.
- *The Rough-Face Girl* by Rafe Martin. This is a tale from both the Algonquin and Comanche. It is a Native American version of *Cinderella*. Good for oral reading, discussion, and comparison with other Cinderella versions.
- *Navajo: Visions and Voices Across the Mesa* by Shonto Begay. The talented Navajo artist combines his art with his prose and poetry in this book.

## Before the Unit:

Have the students make a web of words they associate with Native Americans.

## Vocabulary:

The students can make an illustrated dictionary of words from the books they read or listen to. They may choose words from the web and the stories they read. These words can be done on cards, charts, or notebooks.

## Discussion Questions:

*Prereading*

- What do you think a "teaching tale" is?

- Have your parents ever told you a teaching tale? What about?
- As you read one of these stories, think about who is teaching something and who is supposed to learn something.

*Postreading*

- What lesson do you think the characters were supposed to learn?
- What did you notice in these stories?
- Did any of the stories remind you of other books you have read or television shows you have seen?
- What questions would you like to ask the characters in these stories?

## Extensions for Response:

- Summarize one of the stories orally or in writing.
- Describe the setting of one of the stories.
- Tell what you learned about Native Americans from these tales. Tell or write what makes you think this.
- Look at the Seneca page borders in *The Great Buffalo Race* and create the borders you would like if you were a Native American.
- Have the children draw numbers and participate in small-group sharing according to the number they drew. In the small groups, ask them to:
  1. Retell a favorite part of the story.
  2. Identify the words that describe the main character.
  3. Tell two new things learned from one story.
  4. Summarize the story.
  5. Complete the following chart for each story.

Title and author: _____

Problem: _____

Resolution: _____

Main character: _____

What was the reward? _____

Who received the reward? _____

What did you learn about Native Americans? _____

_____

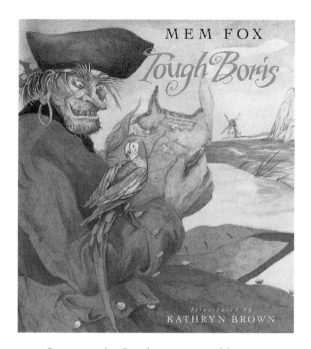

*Boris von der Borch is a mean old pirate,*
*tough as nails—or is he?*

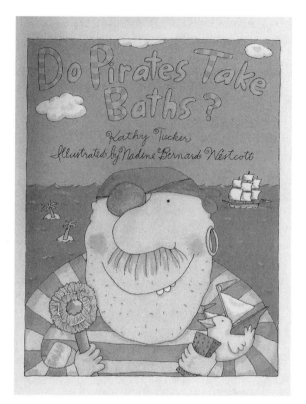

*In this book, pirates take baths in the*
*ocean, with lathers of sea foam.*

## 15.5 Pirates (third or fourth grade)

Topic: Pirates

Goals:

- to study oceans through pirate routes
- to study the difference between salt water and fresh water
- to learn about the importance of vitamin C and how sailors got vitamin C
- to learn how pirates needed math to figure out where they were and to plot their route
- to learn pirate songs
- to learn pirate words and language

Questions:

1. Why did they live on ships? Did they always live on ships? Can you be a pirate if you don't live on a ship?
2. Why do pirates wear funny clothes?
3. How did they get their treasure?
4. Did they help other people?
5. How do you get to be a pirate?
6. Why do they use funny words?
7. Did all the pirates live long ago? Are there pirates today?
8. Why did people become pirates?
9. Can girls be pirates?

References:

- *Tough Boris* by Mem Fox
- *Pirates: Robbers of the High Seas* by Gail Gibbons
- *One-Eyed Jake* by Pat Hutchins
- *Do Pirates Take Baths?* by Kathy Tucker
- *The Ballad of the Pirate Queens* by Jane Yolen

# 15.6 Inventors (fourth or fifth grade)

Topic: Inventors

Questions

- What is the best invention in the world?
- What is an invention that changed the world?
- What is creativity?

Math

- measurement
- computers
- probability

Art

- make drawings of inventions
- make a model of your favorite invention

Thinking

- classify inventions

Science

- identify important scientific inventions

Writing

- write to the U. S. Patent Office to get information about obtaining patents
- write about a needed invention that would improve your life

Social Studies

- how did these inventions change American life: automobile, telephone, computers, computer chips

Reading

- biographies of famous inventors and some not so famous—what made them creative?

Literature

- *100 Inventions That Shaped World History* by Bill Yenne
- *The Wright Brothers: How They Invented the Airplane* by Russell Freedman
- *Walt Disney* by Barbara Ford
- *Outward Dreams: Black Inventors and Their Inventions* by Jim Haskins
- *The Many Lives of Benjamin Franklin* by Mary Osborne
- *Pinkerton: America's First Private Eye* by Richard Wormser
- *Mistakes That Worked: 40 Familiar Inventions and How They Came To Be* by Charlotte Foltz Jones
- *The Toothpaste Millionaire* by Jean Merrill

## 15.7 Courage (fifth grade)

Topic: Courage

Objectives:

- to develop students' concept of courage
- to develop students' understanding of the ways authors develop historical setting
- to develop students' understanding of the kinds of conflict that lead to exceptional expressions of courage
- to develop a time line that shows the time period of the wars in this unit
- to relate the time periods studied to the music of those periods

Background:

The students will read books set in the Civil War, World War II, the 1950s in Montgomery, Alabama, and in the present day. The goal is to develop their understanding of courage and to recognize different kinds of courage.

Materials:

- journals
- Star Wars video
- Tape recorders and tapes
- Tapes or records of music for the various eras
- Other materials will be needed as students develop ways to express their response to the books they read.

Books:

- Mountain Valor by Gloria Houston
- Rosa Parks: My Story by Rosa Parks, with Jim Haskins
- Shades of Gray by Carolyn Reeder
- Letters from a Slave Girl: The Story of Harriet Jacobs by Mary Lyons
- Number the Stars by Lois Lowry
- Waiting for Anya by Michael Morpurgo
- Hatchet by Gary Paulsen

Beginning:

Ask the students to write a definition of courage in their journals and date it. Explain that they will write in their journals after each reading session. Their journal entries will focus on their response to the books they are reading.

Guiding Questions:

1. What kind of courage is expressed in this book?
2. Did you notice any symbols of courage in this book? If so, what were they?
3. What kinds of conflict appeared in the book that caused a character to demonstrate courage?
4. How did the author build tension in the book you read?
5. How did the author create a historical setting in your book?
6. How did the events in the book change the lives of the characters, particularly the main character?

Extensions:

1. Write a new definition of courage in your journal and date it.
2. Collect newspaper stories about people who demonstrate courage.
3. Listen to the music of this time period and compare it to the ideas expressed in the book you read. What similarities and differences can you identify?
4. Create a time line for the story you have read.
5. Prepare interview questions that you would like to ask the main character in your book.
6. Read another book from the list and compare it with the first one you read.

## SUMMARY

This chapter guides readers' synthesis of their learning about children's literature. The chapter focus is planning literature-based reading instruction using integrated curriculum, inquiry learning, units, and assessment. Units are intensive learning experiences that help students make connections as they learn. **Integrated units** *develop language skills within a context that may involve social studies, math, science, art, music, and physical education.* Inquiry learning focuses on students' questions as powerful stimulators for learning. Units may focus on curriculum topics, themes, authors/illustrators, current events, concepts, or student-generated ideas.

A unit includes these components: goals or objectives, resources, science, social studies, math, language arts, art, music, physical education, literature, and textbooks. A unit plan serves as a road map for teachers, which may be revised as it is used.

## THOUGHT QUESTIONS

1. What kinds of factors should be considered in developing units? Can you think of any additional considerations?

2. Explain what a unit is in your own words.

3. How do teachers use portfolios to assess literature-based instruction?

4. How is standardized testing related to literature-based approaches to instruction?

## ENRICHMENT ACTIVITIES

1. Prepare a complete integrated unit for a grade level of your choice. Teach your unit if possible.

2. Prepare a unit that could be integrated with a specific unit in a basal reader of your choice.

3. Make a list of unit topics or themes appropriate for the grade level you teach or hope to teach.

4. Read a unit ideas book and decide which units you would be interested in using and why you would use these.

5. Write a narrative plan for inquiry instruction and getting children to raise important questions.

6. What items do you think should be included in a portfolio for your class or the class you plan to teach? Explain why you would choose these items.

## RECOMMENDED CHILDREN'S BOOKS

Arnold, Caroline. (1990). *Ladybird First Facts About Space.* New York: Ladybird. (1–3)
Space concepts are developed for young children.

Asch, Frank. (1985). *Bear Shadow.* Englewood Cliffs, NJ: Prentice Hall. (preschool–1)
Little Bear sees his shadow and he is fascinated.

————. (1985). *Happy Birthday Moon.* New York: Simon & Schuster. (preschool–1)
A birthday celebration leads to discussion of moons.

————. (1978). *Moon Bear.* New York: Scribner's. (preschool–1)
Bear thinks he sees a bear in the moon.

Ata, Te. (1989). *Baby Rattlesnake.* Adapted by Lynn Moroney. San Francisco: Children's Book Press. (1–2)
This is a Native American teaching tale.

Babbit, Natalie. (1987). *The Search for Delicious.* New York: Farrar, Straus & Giroux. (3–6)
The king searches for the meaning of "delicious."

Begay, Shonto. (1992). *Ma'ii and Cousin Horned Toad.* New York: Scholastic. (1–3)
This is a traditional Navajo story about the coyote trickster.

————. (1994). *Visions and Voices Across the Mesa.* New York: Scholastic. (2–6)
Shonto Begay combines his art with his prose and poetry in this book.

Berger, Barbara. (1986). *Grandfather Twilight.* New York: Putnam. (2–4)
Grandfather Twilight is a gentle person, a storyteller children enjoy.

Branley, Franklin M. (1986). *What the Moon Is Like.* New York: Harper & Row. (1–3)
This is a simple, informational book.

Brown, Laurie Krasny, and Marc Brown. (1992). *Dinosaurs to the Rescue! A Guide to Protecting Our Planet.* New York: Little, Brown. (2–6)
This informational book is a guide to conservation.

Brown, Margaret Wise. (1947). *Goodnight Moon.* Illustrated by Clement Hurd. New York: Harper & Row. (preschool–1)
A young child wishes goodnight to everything in his room and to the moon.

Carle, Eric. (1977). *The Very Grouchy Ladybug.* New York: Thomas Crowell. (K–2)
The grouchy ladybug tries to fight with everyone she meets but makes a friend.

Clements, Andrew. (1992). *Celebrate America in Poetry and Art.* New York: Picture Book Studio. (1–3)
Mother Earth counts plants, animals, lakes, oceans, and continents.

Cohen, Caron. (1988). *The Mud Pony: A Traditional Skidi Pawnee Tale.* New York: Scholastic. (1–3)
A Pawnee boy makes a pony from mud, which comes to life.

Cooney, Barbara. (1990). *Hattie and the Wild Waves: A Story from Brooklyn.* New York: Viking. (K–3)
Hattie, the daughter of German immigrants, tells about growing up in Brooklyn at the turn of the century.

dePaola, Tomie. (1983). *The Legend of the Bluebonnet.* New York: Putnam. (all ages)
A Comanche tale in which selfishness is punished and unselfishness is rewarded.

Dorros, Arthur. (1990). *Me and My Shadow.* New York: Scholastic. (1–3)

The author explores the concept of shadows.

Emberley, Ed. (1987). *Sounds*. New York: Little, Brown. (preschool)

This book is all about sounds and noises.

Esbensen, Barbara Juster. (1994). *The Great Buffalo Race: A Seneca Tale*. New York: Little, Brown.

This pourquoi tale explains how the buffalo got its hump.

Florian, Douglas. (1989). *Turtle Day*. New York: Thomas Crowell. (1–3)

This book helps children learn about turtles and reptiles.

Ford, Barbara. (1989). *Walt Disney*. New York: Walker. (4–8)

A biography of Disney that provides children with insight.

Fox, Mem. (1994). *Time for Bed*. New York: Harcourt Brace Jovanovich. (preschool–1)

All of the animals are ready for bed in this book.

_____ . (1994). *Tough Boris*. New York: Harcourt Brace Jovanovich. (2–4)

Boris is a pirate who is not so tough.

_____ . (1989). *Night Noises*. Illustrated by Terry Denton. New York: Harcourt Brace Jovanovich. (K–2)

This story is about the sounds of animals at night.

Freedman, Russell. (1991). *The Wright Brothers: How They Invented the Airplane*. New York: Holiday House. (all ages)

A description of the contest and the Wright brothers' quest to fly. Photographs from the time add realism to the presentation.

Friedman, Ann. (1994). *The King's Commissioners*. New York: Scholastic. (2–5)

Commissioners of the king find a mathematical solution to their problems.

George, Lonnie. (1991). *Star, Little Star*. East Rutherford, NJ: Grosset and Dunlap. (K–2)

This is a book of poetry about night and sleeping.

Gibbons, Gail. (1992). *Recycle! A Handbook for Kids*. New York: Little, Brown. (2–5)

This book suggests specific recycling projects.

_____ . (1993). *Pirates: Robbers of the High Seas*. New York: Little, Brown. (2–5)

Facts are presented about pirates in this descriptive book.

Goble, Paul. (1989). *Iktomi and the Boulder*. New York: Watts. (K–6)

A trickster story from the Lakota Sioux.

Harshman, Marc. (1993). *Only One*. New York: Cobblehill. (K–2)

This counting book is different in that it focuses on counting multiples like one hive of bees.

Harvey, Brett. (1990). *My Prairie Christmas*. New York: Holiday House. (K–3)

The Plaisted family is snowed in on their first prairie Christmas, but Papa finally arrives with a "goodie fill" barrel from Maine.

Haskins, Jim. (1991). *Outward Dreams: Black Inventors and Their Inventions*. New York: Walker. (5–8)

Significant accomplishments of African Americans that have been omitted from history books fill this book.

Hendershot, Judy. (1987). *Coal Country*. New York: Knopf. (2–4)

A girl tells about growing up in a miner's family in Ohio during the 1930s.

Houston, Gloria. (1990). *Littlejim*. New York: Philomel. (3–5)

*Littlejim* is a Civil War story about one of the author's ancestors.

———. (1994). *Mountain Valor*. New York: Philomel. (5–7)

Twelve-year-old Valor dresses like a boy to help her family during the Civil War.

———. (1988). *The Year of the Perfect Christmas Tree: An Appalachian Story*. Illustrated by Barbara Cooney. New York: Dial. (1–4)

This is the story of a family during World War I.

Hutchins, Pat. (1979). *One-Eyed Jake*. New York: Mulberry. (1–3)

One-eyed Jake is a mean-looking pirate.

———. (1972). *Good-Night Owl*. New York: Macmillan. (K–2)

A cumulative tale about night and going to sleep.

Jones, Charlotte Foltz. (1991). *Mistakes That Worked: 40 Familiar Inventions and How They Came To Be*. New York: Doubleday. (4–8)

This book presents the stories behind 40 things that were invented or named by accident.

Keats, Ezra Jack, (1981). *Regards to the Man in the Moon*. New York: Four Winds. (1–3)

Two children build a spaceship from junk and use their imaginations to blast off.

Krauss, Ruth. (1950). *The Happy Day*. Illustrated by Marc Simont. New York: Harper. (preschool–1)

The forest animals find a spring flower.

Krulik, N. (1991). *My Picture Book of the Planets*. New York: Scholastic. (1–3)

This book introduces the planets to young children.

Krupp, E. C. (1993). *The Moon and You*. New York: Macmillan. (1–3)

Lasky, Kathryn. (1995). *The Librarian Who Measured the Earth*. Illustrated by Kevin Hawkes. New York: Little, Brown. (1–4)

This story tells about an actual person who was a librarian, and he measured the earth before we had modern technology.

Lowry, Lois. (1989). *Number the Stars*. Boston: Houghton Mifflin. (4–7)

A Jewish girl is "adopted" by her neighbors who hide her from the Nazis.

Lyons, Mary E. (1992). *Letters from a Slave Girl: The Story of Harriet Jacobs*. New York: Scribner's. (4-7)

Martin, Bill, Jr. (1970). *Brown Bear, Brown Bear, What Do You See?* New York: Holt Rinehart & Winston. (preschool–1)

This predictable story about large colorful animals is good for the youngest readers.

Martin, Rafe. (1992). *The Rough-Face Girl*. New York: Putnam. (all ages)

This tale, from both the Algonquin and Comanche Indians, is the Native American version of *Cinderella*.

Merrill, Jean. (1972). *The Toothpaste Millionaire*. Boston: Houghton Mifflin. (4–7)

A homemade toothpaste project becomes very profitable.

Morpurgo, Michael. (1991). *Waiting for Anya*. New York: Viking. (4–7)

Jewish children are taken to an isolated farm and then across the border to escape from the Germans during World War II.

Narahashi, Keiko. (1987). *I Have a Friend*. New York: Macmillan. (preschool–3)

Some children have dolls or pets or toys as friends; this boy has a shadow as a friend.

Osborne, Mary. (1990). *The Many Lives of Benjamin Franklin*. New York: Dial. (4–8)

The author focuses on Franklin as a scientist, statesman, diplomat, and inventor.

Parks, Rosa, and Jim Haskins. (1992). *Rosa Parks: My Story*. New York: Dial. (6–up)

Rosa Parks tells her story of defying Jim Crow laws in Montgomery, Alabama.

Pittman, Virginia. (1994). *Counting Jenny*. New York: Knopf. (1–3)

In this picture book, Jenny counts everything she sees.

Raffi. *Raffi Songs to Read*. New York: Crown. (preschool)

This is a cassette tape containing songs to help children learn the rhythm of language. Printed text for the tape is available.

Reeder, Carolyn. (1989). *Shades of Gray*. New York: Macmillan. (4–7)

Ryder, Joanne. (1989). *Under the Moon*. New York: Random House. (preschool–K)

Mama mouse teaches her child special things such as how to use his nose.

Rylant, Cynthia. (1986). *Night in the Country*. New York: Bradbury. (1–3)

This is a beautifully illustrated exploration of night.

Scamell, Ragnhild. (1994). *Rooster Crows*. New York: Morrow. (1–3)

A placid rooster bets he can crow the sun up.

Singer, Marilyn. (1989). *Nine O'Clock Lullaby*. New York: HarperCollins. (preschool–1 and up)

A poetic lullaby for young children.

Stoddard, Sandol. (1995). *Turtle Time*. Boston: Houghton Mifflin. (preschool–up)

When climbing into bed a young child is reminded of her pet turtle.

Tucker, Kathy. (1994). *Do Pirates Take Baths?* Morton Grove, IL: Albert Whitman. (1–3)

In this humorous story, children learn that even pirates take baths.

Van Laan, Nancy. (1989). *Rainbow Crow: A Lenape Tale*. New York: Knopf/Borzoi. (1–3)

A traditional tale about a smart crow.

_____ . (1994). *Round and Round Again*. Illustrated by Nadine Bernard Westcott. New York: Hyperion (1–3)

This delightful story of an unusual mother who cannot waste anything is told in couplets with a refrain that children will immediately join in with.

Wood, Audrey, and Don Wood. (1984). *The Napping House*. New York: Harcourt Brace Jovanovich. (K–2)

A child and a number of animals go to sleep in Granny's bed.

Wormser, Richard. (1990). *Pinkerton: America's First Private Eye*. New York: Walker. (5–8)

This book begins with Pinkerton growing up in the slums of Glasgow.

Yenne, Bill. (1994). *100 Inventions That Shaped World History*. San Francisco: Bluewood Books. (4–up)

Yolen, Jane. (1990). *Sky Dogs*. Illustrated by Barry Moser. New York: Harcourt Brace Jovanovich. (all ages)

The story is about how the Blackfoot Indians got horses.

_____ . (1994). *The Ballad of the Pirate Queens*. New York: Harcourt Brace Jovanovich. (3–8)

This picture book is about two women pirates and their exploits.

_____ . (1992). *Letting Swift River Go*. Illustrated by Barbara Cooney. New York: Little, Brown. (2–4)

This book tells about changing the course of a river by flooding a town.

## OTHER RECOMMENDED BOOKS— REFERENCES FOR LITERATURE-BASED TEACHING

Laughlin, M., and C. Swisher. (1990). *Literature-Based Reading.* Phoenix, AZ: Oryx Press.

Walmsley, Sean. (1994). *Children Exploring Their World.* Portsmouth, NH: Heinemann.

Weaver, C., J. Chaston, and S. Peterson. (1993). *Theme Exploration.* Portsmouth, NH: Heinemann.

# Appendix

## BOOK AWARDS

## THE UNITED STATES

### The Caldecott Medal

This award, sponsored by the Association for Library Service to Children, division of the American Library Association, is given to the illustrator of the most distinguished picture book for children published in the United States during the preceding year. Only U.S. residents or citizens are eligible for this award.

1995 *Smoky Night* by Eve Bunting. Illustrated by David Diaz. Harcourt Brace and Co.

1994 *Grandfather's Journey* by Allen Say. Houghton Mifflin.

1993 *Mirette on the High Wire* by Emioly Arnold McCully. G. P. Putnam.

1992 *Tuesday* by David Wiesner. Clarion Books.

1991 *Black and White* by David Macaulay. Houghton.

1990 *Lon Po Po: A Red-Riding Hood Story from China.* Translated and illustrated by Ed Young. Philomel.

1989 *Song and Dance Man* by Karen Ackerman. Illustrated by Stephen Gammell. Knopf.

1988 *Owl Moon* by Jane Yolen. Illustrated by John Schoenherr. Philomel.

1987 *Hey, Al* by Arthur Yorinks. Illustrated by Richard Egielski. Farrar.

1986 *The Polar Express* by Chris Van Allsburg. Houghton.

1985 *Saint George and the Dragon*, retold by Margaret Hodges. Illustrated by Trina Schart Hyman. Little, Brown.

1984 *The Glorious Flight: Across the Channel with Louis Blériot* by Alice and Martin Provensen. Viking.

1983 *Shadow* by Blaise Cendrars. Translated and illustrated by Marcia Brown. Scribner's.

1982 *Jumanji* by Chris Van Allsburg. Houghton.

1981 *Fables* by Arnold Lobel. Harper.

1980 *Ox-Cart Man* by Donald Hall. Illustrated by Barbara Cooney. Viking.

1979 *The Girl Who Loved Wild Horses* by Paul Goble. Bradbury.

1978 *Noah's Ark* by Peter Spier. Doubleday.

1977 *Ashanti to Zulu: African Traditions* by Margaret Musgrove. Illustrated by Leo and Diane Dillon. Dial.

1976 *Why Mosquitoes Buzz in People's Ears* retold by Verna Aardema. Illustrated by Leo and Diane Dillon. Dial.

1975 *Arrow to the Sun* adapted and illustrated by Gerald McDermott. Viking.

### The Newbery Award

This award, sponsored by the Association for Library Service to Children, division of the American Library Association, is given to the author of the most distinguished contribution to children's literature published during the preceding year. Only U.S. citizens or residents are eligible for this award.

1995 *Walk Two Moons* by Sharon Creech. Houghton Mifflin.

1994 *The Giver* by Lois Lowry. Houghton Mifflin.

1993 *Missing May* by Cynthia Rylant. Jackson-Orchard.

1992 *Shiloh* by Phyllis Reynolds Naylor. Atheneum.

1991 *Maniac Magee* by Jerry Spinelli. Little, Brown.

1990 *Number the Stars* by Lois Lowry. Houghton.

1989 *Joyful Noise: Poems for Two Voices* by Paul Fleischman. Harper.

1988 *Lincoln: A Photobiography* by Russell Freedman. Clarion.

1987 *The Whipping Boy* by Sid Fleischman. Greenwillow.

1986 *Sarah Plain and Tall* by Patricia MacLachlan. Harper.

1985 *The Hero and the Crown* by Robin McKinley. Greenwillow.

1984 *Dear Mr. Henshaw* by Beverly Cleary. Morrow.

1983 *Dicey's Song* by Cynthia Voigt. Atheneum.

1982 *A Visit to William Blake's Inn: Poems for Innocent and Experienced Travelers* by Nancy Willard. Illustrated by Alice and Martin Provensen. Harcourt.

1981 *Jacob Have I Loved* by Katherine Paterson. Crowell.

1980 *A Gathering of Days: A New England Girl's Journal, 1830–1832* by Joan Blos. Scribner's.

1979 *The Westing Game* by Ellen Raskin. Dutton.

1978 *Bridge to Terabithia* by Katherine Paterson. Crowell.

1977 *Roll of Thunder, Hear My Cry* by Mildred D. Taylor. Dial.

1976 *The Grey King* by Susan Cooper. McElderry/Atheneum.

1975 *M. C. Higgins, the Great* by Virginia Hamilton. Macmillan.

## Coretta Scott King Awards

These awards, founded to commemorate Dr. Martin Luther King, Jr., and his wife, Coretta Scott King, for their work in promoting peace and world brotherhood, are given to an African American author and since 1974, an African American illustrator whose children's books, published during the preceding year, made outstanding inspirational and educational contributions to literature for children and young people. The awards are sponsored by the Social Responsibilities Round Table of the American Library Association.

1995 Author: *Christmas in the Big House, Christmas in the Quarters* by Frederick L. McKissack. Illustrated by John Thompson. Scholastic.

Illustrator: *The Creation* by James Weldon Johnson. Illustrated by James E. Ransome. Delacorte.

1994 Author: *Toning the Sweep* by Angela Johnson. Orchard.

Illustrator: *Soul Looks Back in Wonder* by Tom Feelings. Dial.

1993 Illustrator: *The Dark-Things: Southern Tales of the Supernatural* by Patricia McKissack.

*The Origins of Life on Earth: An African Creation Myth* by Kathleen Atkins Wilson. Illustrated by David Anderson.

1992 Author: *Now Is Your Time! The African-American Struggle for Freedom* by Walter Dean Myers. HarperCollins.

Illustrator: *Tar Beach* by Faith Ringgold. Crown.

1991 Author: *Road to Memphis* by Mildred D. Taylor. Dial.

Illustrator: *Aïda*, retold by Leontyne Price. Illustrated by Leo and Diane Dillon. Harcourt.

1990 Author: *A Long Hard Journey* by Patricia and Frederick McKissack. Walker.

Illustrator: *Nathaniel Talking* by Eloise Greenfield. Illustrated by Jan Spivey Gilchrist. Black Butterfly Press.

1989 Author: *Fallen Angels* by Walter Dean Myers. Scholastic.

Illustrator: *Mirandy and Brother Wind* by Patricia McKissack. Illustrated by Jerry Pinkney. Knopf.

1988 Author: *The Friendship* by Mildred D. Taylor. Illustrated by Max Ginsburg. Dial.

Illustrator: *Mufaro's Beautiful Daughters: An African Tale* retold and illustrated by John Steptoe. Lothrop.

1987 Author: *Justin and the Best Biscuits in the World* by Mildred Pitts Walter. Lothrop.

Illustrator: *Half Moon and One Whole Star* by Crescent Dragonwagon. Illustrated by Jerry Pinkney. Macmillan.

1986    Author: *The People Could Fly: American Black Folktales* by Virginia Hamilton. Knopf.

Illustrator: *Patchwork Quilt* by Valerie Flourmoy. Illustrated by Jerry Pinkney.

1985    Author: *Motown and Didi* by Walter Dean Myers. Viking.

Illustrator: No award

1984    Author: *Everett Anderson's Good-Bye* by Lucille Clifton. Holt.

Illustrator: *My Mama Needs Me* by Mildren Pitts Walter. Illustrated by Pat Cummings. Lothrop.

1983    Author: *Sweet Whispers, Brother Rush* by Virginia Hamilton. Philomel.

1982    Author: *Let the Circle Be Unbroken* by Mildred Taylor. Dial.

Illustrator: *Mother Crocodile: An Uncle Amadou Tale from Senegal*, adapted by Rosa Guy. Illustrated by John Steptoe. Delacorte.

1981    Author: *This Life* by Sidney Poitier. Knopf.

Illustrator: *Beat the Story-Drum, Pum-Pum* by Ashley Bryan. Atheneum.

1980    Author: *The Young Landlords* by Walter Dean Myers. Viking.

Illustrator: *Cornrows* by Camille Yarbrough. Illustrated by Carole Bayard. Coward.

1979    Author: *Escape to Freedom* by Ossie Davis. Viking.

Illustrator: *Something on My Mind* by Nikki Grimes. Illustrated by Tom Feelings. Dial.

1978    Author: *Africa Dream* by Eloise Greenfield. Day/Crowell.

Illustrator: *Africa Dream*. Illustrated by Carole Bayard.

1977    Author: *The Story of Stevie Wonder* by James Haskins. Lothrop.

Illustrator: No award

1976    Author: *Duey's Tale* by Pearl Bailey. Harcourt.

Illustrator: No award

1975    Author: *The Legend of Africana* by Dorothy Robinson. Johnson.

Illustrator: *The Legend of Africana*. Illustrated by Herbert Temple.

## Nonfiction Awards: Orbis Pictus Award

The Orbis Pictus Award for Outstanding Nonfiction for Children was established by the National Council of Teachers of English (NCTE) in 1990. The award was established to promote and recognize excellence in the field of nonfiction writing.

1995    *Safari Beneath the Sea* by Diane Sezanson. Sierra Club Books.

*Wildlife Rescue* by Jennifer Dewey. Boyds Mills.

*Kids at Work* by Russell Freedman. Clarion.

1994    *Across America on an Immigrant Train* by Jim Murphy.

*To the Top of the World: Adventures with Artic Wolves* by Jim Brandenberg.

1991    *Franklin Delano Roosevelt* by Russell Freedman. Clarion.

1990    *The Great Little Madison* by Jean Fritz. Putnam.

Other nonfiction awards not listed are: the Boston Globe-Horn Book Award; the Carter B. Woodson Book Award; the Children's Book Guild Nonfiction Award; the Christopher Awards; and the Eva L. Gordon Award for Children's Science Literature.

## GREAT BRITIAN

### Kate Greenaway Medal

This award, sponsored by the British Library Association, is given to the illustrator of the most distinguished work in illustration in a children's book first published in the United Kingdom during the preceding year.

1991    *The Whale's Song* by Dyan Sheldon. Illustrated by Gary Blythe. Dial.

1990    *War Boy: A Country Childhood* by Michael Foreman. Arcade.

1989 *Can't You Sleep, Little Bear?* by Martin Waddell. Illustrated by Barbara Firth. Walker.

1988 *Crafty Chameleon* by Mwenye Hadithi. Illustrated by Adrienne Kennaway. Hodder & Stoughton.

1987 *Snow White in New York* by Fiona French. Oxford.

1986 *Sir Gwain and the Loathly Lady* by Selina Hastings. Illustrated by Juan Wijngaard. Walker.

1985 *Hiawatha's Childhood* by Errol LeCain. Faber.

1984 *Gorilla* by Anthony Browne. Julia McRae Books.

1983 *Long Neck and Thunder Foot.* Kestrel; and *Sleeping Beauty and Other Favorite Fairy Tales.* Both illustrated by Michael Foreman. Gollancz.

1982 *The Highwayman* by Alfred Noyes. Illustrated by Charles Keeping. Oxford.

1981 *Mr. Magnolia* by Quentin Blake. Jonathan Cape.

1980 *The Haunted House* by Jan Pienkowski. Heinemann.

1979 *Each Peach Pear Plum* by Janet and Allan Ahlberg. Kestrel.

1978 *Dogger* by Shirley Hughes. Bodley Head.

1977 *The Post Office Cat* by Gail E. Haley. Bodley Head.

1976 *Horse in Battle* by Victor Ambrus. Oxford. *Mishka* by Victor Ambrus. Oxford.

1975 *The Wind Blew* by Pat Hutchins. Bodley Head.

## Carnegie Medal

This award is sponsored by the British Library Association and is given to the author of the most outstanding children's book first published in English in the United Kingdom during the preceding year.

1991 *Wolf* by Gillian Cross. Oxford.

1990 *My War with Goggle-Eyes* by Anne Fine. Joy Street.

1989 *Pack of Lies* by Geraldine McCaughrean. Oxford.

1988 *The Ghost Drum* by Susan Price. Faber.

1987 *Granny Was a Buffer Girl* by Berlie Doherty. Methuen.

1986 *Storm* by Kevin Crossley-Holland. Heinemann.

1985 *The Changeover* by Margaret Mahy. Dent.

1984 *Handles* by Jan Mark. Kestrel.

1983 *The Haunting* by Margaret Mahy. Dent.

1982 *The Scarecrows* by Robert Westall. Chatto and Windus.

1981 *City of Gold* by Peter Dickinson. Dutton.

1980 *Tulku* by Peter Dickinson. Dutton.

1979 *The Exeter Blitz* by David Rees. Hamish Hamilton.

1978 *The Turbulent Term of Tyke Tiller* by Gene Kemp. Faber.

1977 *Thunder and Lightnings* by Jan Mark. Kestrel.

1976 *The Machine-Gunners* by Robert Westall. Macmillan.

1975 *The Stronghold* by Mollie Hunter. Hamilton.

## CANADA

### Amelia Frances Howard-Gibbon Medal

This award, sponsored by the Canadian Library Association, is given to the illustrator of the most distinguished work in illustration in a children's book first published in Canada during the preceding year. Only Canadian citizens are eligible for this award.

1991 *The Orphan Boy* by Tololwa M. Mollel. Illustrated by Paul Morin. Oxford.

1990 *Til All the Stars Have Fallen: Canadian Poems for Children* selected by David Booth. Illustrated by Kady MacDonald Denton. Kids Can Press.

1989 *Amos' Sweater* by Janet Lunn. Illustrated by Kim LaFave. Douglas & McIntyre.

1988 *Rainy Day Magic* by Marie-Louise Gay. Hodder & Stoughton.

1987 *Moonbeam on a Cat's Ear* by Marie-Louise Gay. Stoddard.

1986 *Zoom Away* by Tim Wynne-Jones. Illustrated by Ken Nutt. Douglas & McIntyre.

1985 *Chin Chiang and the Dragon's Dance* by Ian Wallace. Groundwood.

1984 *Zoom at Sea* by Tim Wynne-Jones. Illustrated by Ken Nutt. Douglas & McIntyre.

1983 *Chester's Barn* by Lindee Climo. Tundra.

1982 *Ytek and the Artic Orchid: An Inuit Legend* by Garnet Hewitt. Illustrated by Heather Woodall. Douglas & McIntyre.

1981 *The Trouble with Princesses* by Christie Harris. Illustrated by Douglas Tait. McClelland & Stewart.

## Canadian Children's Book of the Year Award

This award, sponsored by the Canadian Library Association, is given to the author of a children's book of outstanding literary merit. Since 1954, an equivalent award has been presented to the author of a children's book published in French. Only Canadian citizens are eligible for these awards.

1992 *Eating Between the Line* by Kevin Major. Doubleday Canada.

1991 *Redwork* by Michael Bedard. Dennys.

1990 *The Sky Is Falling* by Kit Pearson. Penguin.

1989 *Easy Avenue* by Brian Doyle. Groundwood.

1988 *A Handful of Time* by Kit Pearson. Penguin.

1987 *Shadow in Hawthorn Bay* by Janet Lunn. Dennys.

1986 *Julie* by Cora Taylor. Western.

1985 *Mama's Going to Buy You a Mockingbird* by Jean Little. Penguin.

1984 *Sweetgrass* by Jan Hudson. Tree Frog Press.

1983 *Up to Low* by Brian Doyle. Douglas & McIntyre.

1982 *The Root Cellar* by Janet Lunn. Dennys.

1981 *The Violin Maker's Gift* by Donn Kushner. Macmillan.

1980 *River Runners: A Tale of Hardship and Bravery* by James Houston. McClelland & Stewart.

1979 *Hold Fast* by Kevin Major. Clarke, Irwin.

1978 *Garbage Delight* by Dennis Lee. Macmillan.

1977 *Mouse Woman and the Vanished Princesses* by Christie Harris. McClelland & Stewart.

1976 *Jacob Two-Two Meets the Hooded Fang* by Mordecai Richler. McClelland & Stewart.

1975 *Alligator Pie* by Dennis Lee. Macmillan.

# AUSTRALIA

## Australian Children's Books of the Year Awards

The Australian Children's Book Council sponsors three awards for excellence in children's books: The Picture Book of the Year Award; The Children's Book of the Year for Younger Readers (for books that bridge the gap between picture books and longer novels); and The Children's Book of the Year for Older Readers.

## Australian Picture Book of the Year Award

1994 *V Is for Vanishing: Alphabet of Endangered Animals* by Patricia Mullins. Margaret Hamilton Books.

*Rowan of Rin* by Emily Rodda. Greenwillow.

1992 *Window* by Jeannie Baker. MacRae.

1991 *Greetings from Sandy Beach* by Bob Graham. Lothian.

1990 *The Very Best of Friends* by Margaret Wild. Illustrated by Mem Fox. Margaret Hamilton.

1989 *Drac and the Grenlins* by Allan Baillie. Illustrated by Jane Tanner. Viking/Kestrel.

*The Eleventh Hour* by Graeme Base. Viking/Kestrel.

1988 *Crusher Is Coming!* by Bob Graham. Lothian.

1987 *Kojuro and the Bears,* adapted by Helen Smith. Illustrated by Junko Morimoto. Collins.

1986    *Felix and Alexander*, written and illustrated by Terry Denton. Oxford.

1985    No award

## Australian Children's Book of the Year for Younger Readers Award

1994    *Angel's Gate* by Gary Crew. Heinemann of Australia.

1992    *The Magnificent Nose and Other Marvels* by Anna Fienberg and Kim Gamble. Allen & Unwin.

1991    *Finders Keepers* by Emily Rodda. Omnibus.

1990    *Pigs and Honey* by Jeanie Adams. Omnibus.

1989    *The Best-Kept Secret* by Emily Rodda. Angus & Robertson.

1988    *My Place* by Nadia Wheatley and Donna Rawlins. Collins Dove.

1987    *Pigs Might Fly* by Emily Rodda. Illustrated by Noela Young. Angus & Robertson.

1986    *Arkwright* by Mary Steele. Hyland House.

1985    *Something Special* by Emily Rodda. Illustrated by Noela Young. Angus & Robertson.

## Australian Children's Book of the Year for Older Readers Award

1994    *First Light* by Gary Crew. Heinemann of Australia.

        *The Gathering* by Isobelle Carmody. Dial.

1992    *The House Guest* by Eleanor Nilson. Viking.

1991    *Strange Objects* by Gary Crew. Heinemann.

1990    *Came Back To Show You I Could Fly* by Robin Klein. Viking/Kestrel.

1989    *Beyond the Labyrinth* by Gilliam Rubinstein. Hyland House.

1988    *So Much To Tell You* by John Marsden. Walter McVitty Books.

1987    *All We Know* by Simon French. Angus & Robertson.

1986    *The Green Wind* by Thurley Fowler. Rigby.

1985    *The True Story of Lilli Stubeck* by James Aldridge. Hyland House.

1984    *A Little Fear* by Patricia Wrightson. Hutchinson.

1983    *Master of the Grove* by Victor Kelleher. Penguin.

1982    *The Valley Between* by Colin Thiele. Rigby.

1981    *Playing Beatie Bow* by Ruth Park. Nelson.

1980    *Displaced Person* by Lee Harding. Hyland House.

1979    *The Plum-Rain Scroll* by Ruth Manley. Hodder & Stoughton.

1978    *The Ice Is Coming* by Patricia Wrightson. Hutchinson.

1977    *The October Child* by Eleanor Spence. Oxford.

1976    *Fly West* by Ivan Southall. Angus & Robertson.

1975    No award.

# NEW ZEALAND

## Russell Clark Award for Illustrations

This award is given to an illustrator for the most distinguished illustrations for a children's book published in New Zealand the previous year. Only citizens or residents of New Zealand are eligible for this award.

1992    *One Lonely Kakapo* by Sandra Morris. Hodder & Stoughton.

1991    *Arthur and the Dragon* by David Elliot. Steck-Vaughn.

1990    *A Walk to the Beach* by Chris Gaskin.

1989    *Joseph's Boat* by Caroline Macdonald. Illustrated by Chris Gaskin. Hodder & Stoughton.

1988    *The Magpies* by Denis Glover. Illustrated by Dick Frizzell.

1987    *Taniwha* by Patricia Grace. Illustrated by Robyn Kahukiwa. Viking Kestrel.

1986    *A Lion in the Night* by Pamela Allen. Hamilton.

1985    *The Duck in the Gun* by Joy Cowley. Illustrated by Robyn Belton. Shortland.

1984    *The Tree Witches* by Gwenda Turner. Penguin.

1983    No award

1982    *Mrs. McGinty and the Bizarre Plant* by Gavin Bishop. Oxford.

1981    No award

1980    No award

1979    *Kim* by Bruce Treloar. Collins.

1978    *The House of the People* by Ron L. Bacon. Illustrated by Robert F. Jahnke. Collins.

## Esther Glen Award

This award is given to an author for the most distinguished contribution to New Zealand children's literature during the previous year. Only New Zealand citizens or residents are eligible.

1993    *Underrunners* by Margaret Mahy.
        *Lily and the Present* by Christine Ross.
        *Albatross Adventure* by Kim Westerkous (for nonfiction).

1992    *Allesandra: Alex in Rome* by Tessa Duder. Oxford.

1991    *Agnes the Sheep* by William Taylor. Scholastic.

1990    *Alex in Winter* by Tessa Duder. Oxford.

1989    *The Mangrove Summer* by Jack Lazenby. Oxford.

1988    *Alex* by Tessa Duder. Oxford.

1987    No award

1986    *Motherstone* by Maurice Gee. Oxford.

1985    *The Changeover* by Margaret Mahy. Dent.

1984    *Elephant Rock* by Caroline Macdonald. Hodder.

1983    *Jacky Nobody* by Anne de Roo. Methuen.

1982    *The Haunting* by Margaret Mahy. Dent.

1981    *The Year of the Yelvertons* by Katherine O'Brien. Oxford.

1980    No award

1979    *Take the Long Path* by Joan de Hamel. Lutterworth.

1978    *The Lighthouse Keeper's Lunch* by Ronda Armitage. Deutsch.

1977    No award

1976    No award

1975    *My Cat Likes To Hide in Boxes* by Eve Sutton and Lynley Dodd. Hamish Hamilton.

# Glossary

**Aesthetic reading**  pleasurable, interesting reading, done for its own sake.

**Antagonist**  a character in a story who is in conflict with the main character or protagonist.

**Authentic activities**  activities that have meaning for the students engaged in them.

**Author**  the title given to the person who writes the text in books.

**Autobiography**  a category of biography written by the subject of the book.

**Ballads**  rhymes and rhythms set to music, centering on a single character in a dramatic situation.

**Benchmark**  a term describing an exemplary book that is used as a standard of quality for comparing other similar books.

**Biography**  tells the story of a particular person's life. In biography, authors conduct careful research in order to explore and record the lives and significant acts and accomplishments of a person. Three styles of biography are typical. For children: (1) authentic biography is based on documented words, speeches, and writing of the subject; (2) the biographical fiction style of biography permits the author to create conversations and portray the everyday life of the subject, but these details are based on thorough historical research into the subject's character and life as well as the time in which the person lived; (3) when writing fictionalized biography, the author takes greater latitude in creating a story around the actual life of a subject.

**Board books**  books for young children that are printed on cardboard.

**Booktalking**  the act of telling or reading highlights of a book without revealing its entire plot. The purpose of booktalking is to motivate others to read a book.

**Caldecott Medal**  This award is presented by the American Library Association to the creator of an outstanding picture book each year.

**Censorship**  the act of controlling what literature is available to be read in any given setting. Censors may attempt to remove books from library shelves because they believe the works in question violate particular values, religious beliefs, or good taste.

**Character frames**  A strategy for developing students' understanding of character development in a story.

**Characters**  the people in a story, comparable to actors in movies or on stage. Their actions, thoughts, and conversations tell the story.

**Choral reading**  an oral literary activity in which a selection from literature is read by several persons in unison with the direction of a leader. The most common types of choral reading are: (1) refrain, in which the teacher reads most of the lines and the children read the refrain; (2) line-a-child choral reading, in which individual students read specific lines, while the entire group reads the beginning and ending of the selection; (3) antiphonal or dialogue choral reading, based on boys and girls (sometimes in groups) varying their voices to speak different parts of a selection.

**Classroom sets**  multiple copies of trade books for classroom use.

**Community of response**  This term denotes shared understandings within a group of readers who discuss ideas about the same books.

**Concrete poetry**  poetry written in the shape of the topic; a poem about a boat, for example, would be written in the shape of a boat.

**Concept books**  These books explore the various facets of a particular concept and in the process develop a reader's understanding of it. Geometric shapes, nature, and maps are some of the subjects of concept books.

**Conflict** the result of difficulties or opposing views between characters in a story. Conflict gives a story the tension that makes it interesting. There are a number of types of conflict, such as conflict within an individual, between individuals, or between an individual and nature.

**Connections** the process of identifying ways that books are related to one another and to the experiences of the reader.

**Connotative meaning** inferred meaning as opposed to literal meaning. It is meaning deduced from "reading between the lines."

**Contemporary** describes events and settings that readers recognize as being in the present.

**Core literature** literature that is the focus of a unit study.

**Creative drama** informal drama created by the participants in the drama. It is improvisational and process-centered: the players create the dialogue and there are no written scripts to follow.

**Culture** the context in which children develop. Culture is comprised of the values and customs that form an identifiable heritage.

**Culturally conscious literature** recognizes the importance of culture and shows respect for people of all cultures and races.

**Cumulative stories** refers to stories that accumulate. Events build on events and phrases build on phrases, leading to a climax at which point the accumulation falls apart.

**Developmentally appropriate** a phrase describing instruction that is compatible with the learner's stage of development.

**Didacticism** consists of obvious moral messages or values that some authors believe should be taught directly.

**Diversity variation.** The student population of today's schools is more varied than in the past. Diversity arises from many sources, including ethnicity and emotional and physical development.

**Early literacy experiences** experiences with literature that are had through listening to stories and handling books and writing materials.

**Efferent reading** has a narrow focus and depends upon the reader's purpose; for example, efferent reading may be done to seek specific information, such as directions.

**Elements of literature** the structural elements of fiction that include plot, characterization, setting, style, and theme.

**Emergent literacy** refers to the beginning stages of learning to read and write.

**Emotional disability** a state in which feelings interfere with learning.

**Engaging with literature** describes readers' response to reading in which readers' minds, interests, and feelings connect with the ideas in a text. It connotes an understanding and an emotional response to what is read.

**Envisionment** the unique meaning each reader creates when reading; each reader has slight to significant differences in interpretation.

**Epic** a story of a person's life and death told in poetic form.

**Episode** the name given to a small plot within a larger one. It usually occurs in a single chapter within a book. In some books, each chapter is an episode.

**Exceptional** a descriptive word for individual differences that fall outside the average, or bell curve. Exceptional students need adjustments in their instruction in order to achieve their potential.

**Experiencing literature** reading with pleasure and with understanding.

**Fable** a story about an animal that teaches a lesson.

**Fact frames** a strategy for organizing the facts that one acquires from reading.

**Family literacy** reading and writing that occur in the home.

**Fantastic element** an impossible element in a story, something that could not really happen such as a person or animal that does not really exist, or an aberration of some other aspect of the laws of the real world.

**Fantasy** a genre of literature that is based on make-believe elements; it may include such factors as characters, place, events, and time.

**Figurative language** has a nonliteral meaning; it may include similes, metaphors, hyperbole, and personification.

**Folktales**   pieces of literature that mirror the mores and values of a culture; they are passed down from generation to generation and have no identifiable author.

**Free verse**   poetry that does not follow a traditional form in that it does not have a regular rhythm or meter, nor does it usually rhyme.

**Genre**   classifications of literature that share the same basic characteristics. The genre of children's literature includes picture books, poetry, fantasy, traditional literature, historical fiction, realistic (contemporary) fiction, biography, and nonfiction.

**Great books**   those books that have lived through several generations, usually because they express universal truths; people in different situations and circumstances can relate to the way these truths are expressed.

**Haiku**   a poetic form which originated in Japan and refers to nature and the seasons; it is patterned poetry of 17 syllables in which the first line contains 5 syllables, the second contains 7, and the third contains 5.

**Historical fiction**   found in books in which the setting is in the past. Events and characters are realistic, and setting and background are true to a particular time period, but descriptions, and sometimes characters, are made up. Characters behave and react the way one would expect of people in the time period in which the story is set.

**Illustrated books**   books in which illustrations are used to supplement the text.

**Illustrators**   artists who create the illustrations for books. These artists create pictures that interpret the text; sometimes illustrations tell the whole story, as in wordless picture books.

**Imagery**   images that are created in the mind through the use of language; imagery appeals to the senses of sight, sound, touch, and smell.

**Inclusion**   a plan for teaching educationally handicapped students in the regular classroom rather than segregating them in special education classrooms.

**Individual differences**   variations from one individual to another.

**Individualized education plan (IEP)**   the plan developed by teachers, administrators, parents, and special educators to guide the education of students.

**Infants**   children in the first year of life.

**Inferencing**   interpretation of literature based on meanings that are not directly stated in a text; readers must "fill in the empty spaces."

**Informational books**   books that explain, impart knowledge, or describe persons, places, things, or events.

**Inquiry**   the process of searching for information, ideas, and truth about questions the student has raised.

**Inside perspective**   a perspective of a culture from a member inside that culture.

**Integrated units**   address various subjects and literacy processes included in the elementary curriculum.

**Interests**   topics and experiences toward which individuals gravitate because they are motivated. Interests are usually developed and cultivated through experience.

**Intertextuality**   the process of interpreting one text by connecting the ideas in it with the ideas in all other texts previously read.

**Legends**   stories that are often based on an actual historical figure whose deeds and exploits have been embellished.

**Literary quality**   describes well-written literature that has well-developed plots, themes, characterization, setting, and style. Nonfiction has literary quality when it is accurate, well-written, and interesting. It presents main ideas and supporting details, differentiates theories from facts, and has illustrations that are appropriate to the subject.

**Literate environment**   a place where reading and writing are used for authentic purposes; many kinds of reading and materials are available in such a place.

**Literature**   a body of written works, an art form in which language is used in creative, artistic ways.

**Mainstreaming**   a practice that places exceptional students in the regular classroom.

**Modern fantasy**   stories that take for granted not only the realities of the world that we see and feel, but also the supernatural aspects that lead to all sorts of possibilities; fantasies have identifiable authors.

**Multicultural literature**   portrays the diversity of the population.

**Multiculturalism**   the process of developing sensitivity to the various cultures comprising a community, state, country, and world.

**Myths**   stories that explain the origin of the world and natural phenomena.

**Narrative poetry**   tells a story; it includes the story elements of plot, character, setting, and theme.

**Newbery**   the name given to a medal that is awarded annually by the American Library Association to an outstanding children's book.

**Nonfiction books**   those in which all the information presented is true, such as a biography. No fictional elements are included in nonfiction.

**Nonsense poetry**   composed in lyric or narrative form, it is playful and does not conform to what is expected; it pokes fun at what is usually taken seriously.

**Partial biographies**   focus on a particular part of a person's life. For example, a partial biography focuses on a subject's childhood or adult life.

**Physical disability**   refers to the condition of an individual who has learning challenges because of physical exceptionalities.

**Picture books**   tell stories by integrating language and pictures. Some picture books, however, are wordless.

**Plot**   the plan and structure of the story. Plots usually consist of introductory material, a gradual building of suspense, a climax, the falling of action, and the culmination.

**Plot frames**   strategies that help readers understand the plot line of a story.

**Poetry**   literature in its most intense, imaginative, and rhythmic form, which expresses and interprets the essence of experience through language; it is not the same as "verse."

**Popular literature**   in vogue at a particular time, it is usually characterized as a fad that enjoys a period of popularity and then disappears. Popular literature is produced very quickly and lacks the literary quality that would inspire readers to read and reread it.

**Pourquoi**   a story that explains why things are the way they are.

**Preschool children**   are those from ages three to four years. Preschool programs are usually designed for this age group.

**Problem resolution**   refers to the way conflicts and story problems are resolved.

**Racial and ethnic stereotyping**   based on the assumption that all members of a racial or ethnic group have the same characteristics. The characteristics assumed in stereotypes are usually negative views of people. Stereotyping interferes with the ability to see individuals as human beings.

**Readability**   the level at which a person can read a book (or other printed text) with comprehension.

**Realistic fiction**   fiction that is written true to the physical and factual details of a particular time period. The problems that characters encounter are related to the realities of life during that time.

**Reader's theater**   an oral presentation of literature—the oral delivery of stories, poetry, biography, or information by two or more readers who characterize and narrate clearly and expressively.

**Response**   what readers take to a text, what happens during reading, how they feel about what they have read, how it becomes alive and personal, and the ways these feelings are displayed.

**Setting**   the time and place of the story.

**Sexual stereotyping**   assumes that all men or all women behave in certain ways (for example, that all women are weak and all men are strong). Sexual stereotyping functions in a negative way and interferes with the ability to appreciate individuals as human beings.

**Skills-based themes**   those that focus on skills development; they are often the subject of unit studies. They may concentrate on literary skills such as the development of characters, sensory imagery, alliteration, and so forth.

**Social studies**   one of the primary content areas studied in schools; some of the subjects within this discipline are history, geography, and anthropology.

**Stance**   the purpose or purposes a reader has for reading. It gives form to the literacy experience as well as the mode for expressing a response.

**Story frames**   strategy for developing students' understanding of story structure.

**Story grammar**   refers to story structure.

**Story telling**   the act of telling stories. Many storytellers tell traditional stories that they have heard from other storytellers, and they often read and memorize stories and retell them.

**Student-generated themes**   those that students identify or suggest.

**Survey nonfiction**   a form of nonfiction that gives readers a broad overview of a topic rather than in-depth information.

**Style**   the way an author uses language and symbols to express ideas.

**Teacher-generated themes**   those that teachers identify or suggest.

**Theme**   the universal meaning (big idea) that the author expresses through a literary work.

**Theme cycle**   a term some educators use to identify student-generated units.

**Theme immersion instruction**   that focuses on thematic units.

**Theme unit**   a unit of study that focuses on a specific theme.

**Toddler**   a term for a child who is in the second year of life. A toddler is usually walking or crawling, and is able to explore the world to a greater extent than an infant.

**Traditional literature**   based on oral tradition. "Little Red Riding Hood" is an example of a traditional story.

**Transaction**   the interaction between a text and a reader in which both are modified and changed.

**Unit**   an organizing framework for children's inquiry and study.

**USSR (Uninterrupted Sustained Silent Reading)**   sometimes called DEAR (Drop Everything and Read) and is a specific period set aside for reading. Everyone in the class reads, including the teacher. In some schools, this is a school-wide reading time.

**Visual art**   evokes both cognitive and aesthetic understanding and response.

**Visual literacy**   a major avenue of communication in which understanding is gained visually by interpreting information presented on billboards, signs, television, pictures, and photographs.

**Wordless picture book**   describes a book in which the story is told entirely through the use of illustrations.

**Young child**   a term used to refer to children younger than age six. Some authors describe young children as those in the primary grades.

# References

Aaron, I. (1987). "Enriching the Basal Reading Program with Literature." In Ira Aaron (Ed.), *Children's Literature in the Reading Program* (pp. 126–137). Newark, DE: International Reading Association.

Abramson, R. (1980). "An Analysis of Children's Favorite Picture Storybooks." *Reading Teacher* 34, pp. 167–170.

Adams, M. J. (1990). *Thinking and Learning About Print.* Cambridge, MA: MIT.

Adams, M., and Collins, A. (1986). "A Schema-Theoretic View of Reading." In H. Singer and R. Ruddell (Eds.), *Theoretical Models and Processes of Reading* (pp. 404–425). Newark, DE: International Reading Association.

Alexander, L. (1965). "The Flat-Heeled Muse." *The Hornbook*, 14(2), pp. 143–144.

———. (1981). "The Grammar of Story." In B. Hearne and M. Kaye (Eds.), *Celebrating Children's Books* (pp. 3–13). New York: Lothrop, Lee & Shepard.

Altwerger, B., and Flores, B. (1994, January). "Theme Cycles: Creating Communities of Learners." *Primary Voices*, 2(1), pp. 2–6.

Altwerger, B., Edelsky, C. and Flores, B. (1987). "Whole Language: What's New?" *The Reading Teacher*, 41, 144–154.

Anderson, G., Higgins, D., and Wurster, S. R. (1985). "Differences in the Free-reading Books Selected by High, Average, and Low Achievers." *Reading Teacher*, 39, pp. 326–330.

Anderson, R., and Pearson, P. D. (1984). "A Schema-Theoretic View of the Reading Processes in Reading Comprehension." In P. D. Pearson (Ed.), *Handbook of Reading Research* (pp. 255–291). New York: Longman.

Anderson, R. C., Hiebert, E. H., Scott, J. A., and Wilkinson, I. A. (1985). *Becoming a Nation of Readers: The Report of the Commission on Reading.* Urbana, IL: The Center for the Study of Reading.

Andronik, J. (1991) "An Interview with James Howe." *Language Arts* 70(6), pp. 450–453.

Anzul, M. (1988). "Exploring Literature for Children Within a Transactional Framework." Unpublished doctoral dissertation. New York University.

Applebee, A. (1978). *The Child's Concept of Story.* Chicago: University of Chicago.

Arbuthnot, M. H. (1964). *Children and Books.* Glenview, IL: Scott Foresman.

Ardizonne, Edward. (1980). "Creation of a Picture Book." In S. Egoffe, G. Stubbs, and L. Ashley (Eds.), *Only Connect* (pp. 289–298). New York: Oxford University Press.

Asher, S., and Markell, R. (1974). "Sex Differences in Comprehension of High- and Low-Interest Reading Material." *Journal of Educational Psychology*, 61, pp. 680–687.

Auden, W. H. (1956). As quoted by Robert B. Heilman in "Literature and Growing Up." *English Journal*, 45(1), p. 307.

Avi. (1990). *About the Author.* New York: Avon.

Bagert, B. (1992). "Act It Out: Making Poetry Come Alive." In B. Cullinan (Ed.), *Invitation to Read: More Children's Literature in the Reading Program.* Newark, DE: International Reading Association.

Baghban, M. J. M. (1984). *Our Daughter Learns to Read and Write: A Case Study from Birth to Age Three.* Newark, DE: International Reading Association.

Ballantyne, M. M. (1993). "The Effects of Narrative and Expository Discourse on the Reading Comprehension of Middle School-aged Good and Poor Readers" (University Microfilms No. 94-06, 749). *Dissertation Abstracts International* 54, 4046.

Banks, J. A. (1989). "Integrating the Curriculum with Ethnic Content: Approaches and Guidelines." In J. A. Banks and C. A. McGee (Eds.), *Multicultural Education: Issues and Perspectives*, pp. 189–207.

Barnes, D. (1995, January). "Talking and Learning in Classrooms: An Introduction." *Primary Voices K–6*, 3(1), pp. 2–7.

Barone, D. (1990). "The Written Responses of Young Children: Beyond Comprehension to Story Understanding." *The New Advocate*, 3, pp. 49–56.

Barthes, R. (1975). *The Pleasure of the Text*. London: Jonathan Cape.

Barton, B. (1986). *Tell Me Another*. Portsmouth, NH: Heinemann.

Bateman, B. (1965). "An Educator's View of a Diagnostic Approach to Learning Disorders." *Learning Disorders*, 1(2).

Bauer, C. J., and Sanborn, L. (1981). "The Best of Both Worlds: Children's Books Acclaimed by Adults and Young Readers." *Top of the News*, 38, pp. 53–56.

Bauso, J. A. (1988). "Incorporating Reading Logs into the Literature Course." *Teaching English in the Two-Year College*, 15, pp. 255–261.

Bernstein, J. E. (1989). "Bibliotherapy: How Books Can Help Young Children Cope." *Books to Help Children Cope with Separation and Loss* (pp. 166–178). Second edition. New York: R. R. Bowker.

Bettelheim, B. (1975, December 8). "The Uses of Enchantment." *New Yorker*, p. 5.

Bishop, R. S. (1987). "Extending Multicultural Understanding Through Children's Books." In B. Cullinan (Ed.), *Children's Literature in the Reading Program* Newark, DE: International Reading Association.

———. (1990, December). "Profile: Walter Dean Myers." *Language Arts*, 67, pp. 862–866.

———. (1991). "African-American Literature for Children: Anchor, Compass and Sail." *Perspectives*, 7(3), pp. ix–xii.

Bissex, J. (1980). *Gnys at Wrk: A Child Learns to Write and Read*. Cambridge, MA: Harvard University Press.

Black, J. B., and Wilensky, R. (1979). "An Evaluation of Story Grammars." *Cognitive Science*, 3, pp. 213–230.

Blatt, G., and Cunningham, J. (1981). *It's Your Move: Expressive Movement Activities in the Classroom*. New York: Teachers College Press.

Bleich, D. (1978). *The Subjective Paradigm. Subjective Criticism*. Baltimore: Johns Hopkins University.

Bloome, D., and Bailey, F. M. (1992). "Studying Language and Literature Through Events, Particularity, and Intertextuality." In R. Beach (Ed.), *Multidisciplinary Perspectives on Literacy Research* (pp. 181–210). Urbana, IL: National Conference on Research in English.

Bond, N. (1984, June). "Conflict in Children's Fiction." *The Horn Book*, 49(4), pp. 297–306.

Borders, S., and Naylor, A. (1993). *Children Talking About Books*. Phoenix: Oryx.

Borke, H. (1971). "Interpersonal Perception of Young Children: Egocentrism or Empathy?" *Developmental Psychology*, 5, pp. 263–269.

Bosma, B. (1987, March). "Profile: Byrd Baylor." *Language Arts*, 64, pp. 315–318.

Bowker, R. R. (1991). *Children's Reference Plus*. New Providence, NJ: Reed Reference Publishing.

Brett, B., and Huck, C. (1982). "Children's Literature: The Search for Excellence." *Language Arts*, 59(8), pp. 877–883.

Bridge, E. (1966). "Using Children's Choices and Reactions to Poetry as Determinants in Enriching Literary Experience in the Middle Grades" (University Microfilm No. 67–6246). Philadelphia: Temple University.

Britton, J. (1969, March). "Language and Understanding." Lecture presented at the Ohio State University Reading Conference, Columbus, Ohio.

———. (1970). *Language and Learning*. London: Penguin.

———. (1977). "The Role of Fantasy." In M. Meek, A. Worlow, and G. Barton (Eds.), *The Cool Web: The Pattern of Children's Reading*. London: Bodley Head.

Bronfenbrenner, U. (1986). "Ecology of the Family as a Context for Human Development." *Developmental Psychology*, 22, pp. 723–742.

Brown, A. (1975). "Recognition, Reconstruction and Recall of Narrative Sequences of Preoperational Children." *Child Development*, 46, pp. 155–166.

Brown, C. L. (1971). "A Study of Procedures for Determining Fifth Grade Children's Book Choices." Unpublished doctoral dissertation. Columbus: Ohio State University.

Bruner, J. (1986). *Actual Minds Possible Worlds*. Cambridge, MA: Harvard University Press.

Bugeja, M. (1992, March). "Why We Stop Reading Poetry." *English Journal*, 81(3), pp. 32–42.

Burch, R. (1973). "The New Realism." In V. Haviland (Ed.), *Children and Literature: Views and Reviews*. Glenview, IL: Scott Foresman.

Burgess, S. A. (1985). "Reading But Not Literate: The ChildRead Survey." *School Library Journal*, 31, pp. 27–30.

Burton, H. (1973). "The Writing of Historical Novels." In V. Haviland (Ed.), *Children and Literature: Views and Reviews*. Glenview, IL: Scott Foresman.

Busching, B. (1981, March). "Readers Theater: An Education for Language and Life." *Language Arts*, 58, pp. 330–338.

Butler, D. (1989, September). "Saying It Louder." *School Library Journal*, 35, pp. 155–159.

Byars, B. (1989). *Introducing Betsy Byars*. New York: Viking Penguin.

———. (1993, October). "Writing for Children." *Speech*. Durham, NC: Southeastern Children's Writers Association.

Cairney, T. (1990, March). "Intertextuality: Infectious Echoes from the Past." *The Reading Teacher*, 43, pp. 478–484.

Calkins, L. (1986). *The Art of Teaching Writing*. Portsmouth, NH: Heinemann.

Cambourne, B. (1987). "Language, Learning, and Literacy." In A. Butler and J. Turbill (Eds.), *Towards a Reading–Writing Classroom* (pp. 5–9). Portsmouth, NH: Heinemann.

Cameron, E. (1969). *The Green and Burning Tree*. Boston: Little, Brown.

———. (1983, February). "The Inmost Secret." *The Horn Book* 48(1), pp. 23–24.

Campbell, R. (1990). *Reading Together*. London: Open University.

Canavan, Dianel, and Sanborn, LaVonne. (1992). *Using Children's Books in Reading/Language Arts Programs*. New York: Neal-Schman.

Cappa, D. (1958). "Kindergarten Children's Spontaneous Responses to Story Books Read by Teachers." *Journal of Educational Research*, 52, p. 75.

Carlsen, G. R., and Sherrill, A. (1988). *Voices of Readers: How We Come to Love Books*. Urbana, IL: National Council of Teachers of English.

Carlson, A. D. (1991). *The Preschooler and the Library*. Metuchen, NJ: Scarecrow.

Carr, J. (1982). "What Do We Do About Bad Biographies?" In *Beyond Fact: Nonfiction for Children and Young People*. Chicago: American Library Association.

Carroll, L. (1946). *Through the Looking Glass and What Alice Found There*. New York: Random House.

Carter, D. B., and Patterson, C. J. (1982). "Sex Roles as Social Conventions: The Development of Children's Conception of Sex-Role Stereotypes." *Developmental Psychology*, 18, pp. 812–824.

Castro, E. (1994, January). "Implementing Theme Cycle: One Teacher's Way." *Primary Voices*, 2(1), pp. 7–14.

Chall, J. S. (1980). "The Great Debate: Ten Years Later, with a Model Proposal for Reading Stages." In L. Resnick and P. A. Weaver (Eds.), *Theory and Practice of Early Reading*. Hillsdale, NJ: Lawrence Erlbaum.

———. (1983). *Stages of Reading Development*. New York: McGraw-Hill.

Chall, J. S., Radwin, E., French, V., and Hall, C. (1985). "Blacks in the World of Children's Books." In D. MacCann and G. Woodward (Eds.), *The Black American in Books for Children: Readings in Racism* (pp. 211–221). Metuchen, NJ: Scarecrow.

Chambers, A. (1978). "Three Fallacies About Children's Books." *The Horn Book*, 54(4), pp. 556–561.

———. (1983). *Introducing Books to Children*. Boston: The Horn Book.

Children's Book Council. (1994). *75 Years of Children's Book Week Posters*. New York: Knopf.

Chukovsky, K. (1963). *From Two to Five*. Los Angeles: University of California Press.

Cianciolo, P. (1990). *Picture Books for Children*. 3d edition. Chicago: American Library Association.

Clark, M. (1976). *Young Fluent Readers*. London: Heinemann Educational Books.

———. (1984). "Literacy at Home and at School: Insight from a Study of Young Fluent Readers." In H. Goelman, A. Oberg, and F. Smith (Eds.), *Awakening to Literacy* (pp. 122–130). Portsmouth, NH: Heinemann.

Clay, M. (1967). "The Reading Behavior of Five-Year-Old Children: A Research Report." *New Zealand Journal of Reading Studies*, 2, pp. 11–31.

Cockburn, V. (1991). "The Uses of Folk Music and Songwriting in the Classroom." *Harvard Educational Review* 61(1), pp. 55–66.

Cohen, D. (1968). "The Effect of Literature on Vocabulary and Reading Achievement." *Elementary English*, 45(2), pp. 209–213, 217.

Cohen, S. (1972). "Minority Stereotypes in Children's Literature: The Bobbsey Twins 1904–1968." *The Education Forum*, 34, pp. 119–125.

Commire, A. (Ed.). (1983). *Something About the Author* (Vol. 33) (pp. 236–237). Detroit, MI: Gale Research Company.

Conrad, J. (1922). "Preface to a Career." In *The Nigger of the Narcissus* (p. x). New York: Doubleday.

Consuelo, M. (1967). "What Do First Graders Like to Read?" *Catholic School Journal*, 67, pp. 42–43.

Cook, E. (1969). *The Ordinary and the Fabulous.* Cambridge, England: Cambridge University Press.

Coolidge, O. (1974). *The Apprenticeship of Abraham Lincoln.* New York: Scribner's.

Cooney, B. (1990). *Author Information Brochure.* New York: Viking Penguin Children's Books.

Cooper, P., and Collins, R. (1992). *Look What Happened to Frog.* Scottsdale, AZ: Gorsuch Scarisbrick, Publishers.

Cooper, S. (1981). "Some Thoughts on Imagination in Children's Literature." In Z. Sutherland, B. Hearn, and M. Kaye (Eds.), *Celebrating Children's Books.* New York: Lee, Lothrop, & Shepard.

Copenhaver, J. (1993). "Instances of Inquiry." *Primary Voices K–6*, pp. 6–12. National Council of Teachers of English.

Costello, J. H. (1992). "An Inquiry into the Attitudes of a Selected Group of African Americans Towards the Portrayal of African Americans in Contemporary Children's Literature." Unpublished doctoral dissertation. Greensboro: University of North Carolina at Greensboro.

Council on Interracial Books for Children. (1976). *Human (and Anti-Human) Values in Books for Children.* New York: Racism and Sexism Resource Center for Educators.

Cox, C., and Many, J. (1989, March). "Worlds of Possibilities in Response to Literature, Film, and Life." *Language Arts*, 66, pp. 287–295.

Crabtree, C., et al. (1992). "Lessons from History: Essential Understandings and Historical Perspectives Students Should Acquire. Los Angeles: University of California.

Crisp, S. (1991). "Children's Poetry in the United States: The Best of the 1980s." *Children's Literature in Education*, 22(3), pp. 143–160.

Cross, D. E., Baker, G., Stiles, L. (1977). *Teaching in a Multicultural Society: Perspectives and Professional Strategies.* New York: Free Press.

Culler, J. (1975). *Structuralist Poetics: Structuralism, Linguistics and the Study of Literature.* London: Routledge and Kegan Paul Ltd.

Cullinan, B. (1971). *Literature: Its Discipline and Content.* Dubuque, IA: Brown.

———. (1989). *Literature and the Child* (2d ed.). New York: Harcourt Brace Jovanovich.

———. (1992). "Leading with Literature." In B. Cullinan (Ed.), *Invitation to Read: More Children's*

*Literature in the Reading Program.* Newark, DE: International Reading Association.

Cullinan, B., and Galda, L. (1994). *Literature and the Child* (3d ed.). Fort Worth, TX: Harcourt Brace.

Cullinan, B., Greene, E., and Jaggar, A. (1990, November). "Books, Babies, and Libraries: The Librarian's Role in Literacy Development." *Language Arts*, 67, pp. 750–755.

Cullinan, B. E., Harwood, K. T., and Galda, L. (1983, Spring). "The Reader and the Story: Comprehension and Response." *Journal of Research and Development in Education*, 16(3), pp. 29–38.

Cullinan, B., Jaggar, A., and Strickland, D. (1974). "Language Expansion for Black Children in the Primary Grades: A Research Report." *Young Children*, 29(1), pp. 98–112.

Cummings, P. (1992). *Talking with Artists.* New York: Bradbury.

Davis, M. W. (1972). "Black Images in Children's Literature: Revised Editions Needed." *Library Journal*, 97(1), pp. 261–263.

Davison, A., Lutz, R., and Roalef, A. (Eds.). (1981). "Text Readability: Proceedings of the March 1980 Conference" (Technical Report No. 213). Urbana: University of Illinois Center for the Study of Reading; Cambridge, MA: Bolt, Beranek, and Newman.

Deane, P. C. (1989). "Black Characters in Children's Fiction Series Since 1968." *Journal of Negro Education*, 58(2), pp. 153–263.

De Beaugrande, R. (1980). *Text Discourse and Process.* Norwood, NJ: Ablex.

Debes, J., and Williams, C. (1974). "The Power of Visuals." *Instructor*, 84, pp. 32–38.

DeFord, D. (1981). "Literacy: Reading, Writing, and Other Essentials." *Language Arts*, 58(7), pp. 652–658.

Dias, P. (1987). *Making Sense of Poetry.* Ottawa, Canada: The Canadian Council of Teachers of English.

Dickinson, J. (1995, January) "Talk and Picture Books in Intermediate Classrooms." *Primary Voices K–6*, 3(1), 8–14.

Didion, J. (1968). *Slouching Toward Bethlehem.* New York: Delta-Dell.

Dieterich, D. J. (1972). "Books that Lie and Lullabye." *ERIC/RCS Report, Elementary English*, 49(7), pp. 1000–1009.

Dillon, Leo, and Dillon, Diane. (1992). "Leo's Story." In Pat Cummings (Ed.), *Talking With Artists.* New York: Bradbury Press, pp. 22–23.

————. (1992b) "Diane's Story." In Pat Cummings (Ed.), *Talking With Artists*. New York: Bradbury Press, pp. 24–25.

Dorros, M. (1993). "The Way We Weren't." In H. Rochman (Ed.), *Against Borders* (pp. 219–235). Chicago: American Library Association.

Dowen, T. W. (1971). "Personal Reading Interests as Expressed by Children in Grades Three, Four and Five." Unpublished doctoral dissertation, Florida State University.

Downing, J., and Leong, C. K. (1982). *Psychology of Reading*. New York: Macmillan.

Doyle, R. P. (1994). *Banned Books 1994 Resource Guide*. Chicago: American Library Association.

Dundes, A. (1965). *The Study of Folklore*. Englewood Cliffs, NJ: Prentice-Hall.

Durkin, D. (1966). *Children Who Read Early*. New York: Teacher's College Press.

————. (1974–75). "A Six-Year Study of Children Who Learned to Read in School at the Age of Four." *Reading Research Quarterly*, 10, pp. 9–61.

Duthie, C. (1994). "Nonfiction: A Genre Study for the Primary Classroom." *Language Arts*, 71, pp. 588–595.

Dyer, E. R. (1978). "Children's Media for a Culturally Pluralistic Society." In Esther Dyer, compiler, *Cultural Pluralism and Children's Media*. Chicago: American Association of School Libraries, pp. vii–ix.

Eckhoff, B. (1983, May). "How Reading Affects Children's Writing." *Language Arts* 60 (pp. 607–616).

Educational Testing Service. (1987). *Bookwhiz*. Princeton, NJ: Author.

Egielski, R. (1992). In Pat Cummings.(Ed.), *Talking with Artists*. (pp. 30–35). New York: Bradbury.

Egoff, S. (1981). "Picture Books." In S. Egoff (Ed.), *Thursday's Child* (pp. 247–274). Chicago: American Library Association.

Ehlert, L. (1991). Video of Lois Ehlert. New York: Harcourt, Brace Jovanovich.

"Elementary School Burnout." *Young Children*, 39(8), pp. 19–21.

Elkind, D. (1978, January). "Language Arts and the Young Child." *Language Arts*, 55(1), pp. 2–3.

————. (1987). *Miseducation: Preschoolers at Risk*. New York: Knopf.

Elleman, B. (1991, September). "Paula Fox's *The Village by the Sea*." *Book Links*, pp. 48–50.

Elliott, D. L. "Textbooks and the Curriculum in the Postwar Era: 1950–1980." In D. Elliott and A.

Woodward (Eds.), *Textbooks and Schooling in the United States: NSSE Yearbook*, (pp. 42–45). Chicago: National Society for the Study of Education.

Emans, R. (1968). "What Do Children in the Inner City Like to Read?" *Elementary School Journal*, 69, pp. 118–122.

England, C., and Fasick, A. (1987). *Child View*. Littleton, CO: Libraries Unlimited.

Ennis, R. (1989, April). "Critical Thinking and Subject Specificity: Clarification and Needed Research." *Educational Researcher*, 18(4), pp. 4–10.

Esmond, M. P. (1984). "Children's Science Fiction." In P. Donely (Comp.), *The First Steps: Best of the Early CHLA Quarterly* (pp. 45–49). Purdue University: Children's Literature Association.

Estes, C. P. (1992). *Women Who Run with the Wolves*. New York: Ballantine.

Farjeon, E. (1960). *Eleanor Farjeon's Poems for Children*. New York: Walck.

Farris, P. and Fuhler, C. (1994). "Developing Social Studies Concepts Through Picture Books." *The Reading Teacher*, 47(5):380–387.

Favat, A. (1977). *Child and Tale: The Origins of Interest*. Urbana, IL: National Council of Teachers of English.

Feeley, J. T. (1981). "What Do Our Children Like to Read?" New Jersey Education Association Review, 54(8), pp. 26–27.

————. (1982). "Content Interests and Media Preferences of Middle Graders: Differences in a Decade." *Reading World*, 22, pp. 11–16.

Feitelson, D., Kita, B., and Goldstein, Z. (1986). "Effects of Listening to Series Stories on First Graders' Comprehension and Use of Language." *Research in the Teaching of English*, 20, pp. 339–356.

Feminists on Children's Media. (1972). *Little Miss Muffet Fights Back* (rev. ed.). Whitestone, NY: Feminist Book Mart.

Fielding, L. G., Wilson, P., and Anderson, R. (1986). "A New Focus on Free Reading: The Role of Trade Books in Reading Instruction." In T. Raphael (Ed.), *The Contexts of School-Based Literacy*, (pp. 149–160). New York: Random House.

Fisher, C., and Natarella, M. (1982). "Young Children's Preferences in Poetry: A National Survey of First, Second, and Third Graders." *Research in the Teaching of English*, 16(4), pp. 339–354.

Fisher, L. E. (1988). "The Artist at Work: Creating Nonfiction." *The Horn Book*, 64(3), pp. 315–323.

Fisher, M. (1972). *Matters of Fact: Aspects of Non-fiction for Children.* New York: Crowell.

Fisher, P. (1988). "The Reading Preferences of Third, Fourth, and Fifth Graders." *Reading Horizons,* 29(1), pp. 62–70.

Fitzgerald, J., and Spiegel, D. (1983). "Enhancing Children's Reading Comprehension Through Instruction in Narrative Structure." *Journal of Reading Behavior,* 15, pp. 1–17.

Fleischman, P. (1986). "Sound and Sense." *The Horn Book* 62(50), pp. 551–555.

Flitterman-King, S. (1988). "The Role of the Response Journal in Active Reading." *The Quarterly of the National Writing Project and the Center for the Study of Writing,* 10, pp. 4–11.

Flood, J., Jensen, J., Lapp, D., and Squire, J. (Eds.). (1991). *The Teaching of the English Language Arts.* New York: Macmillan.

Ford, E. A. (1991, January–June). *CBC Features.* New York: Children's Book Council.

Fournier, J. (1993). "Seeing with New Eyes: Becoming a Better Teacher of Bilingual Children." *Language Arts,* 70(3), pp. 177–181.

Fox, P. (1991, September). "Writing *The Village by the Sea.*" *Book Links,* 1(1), pp. 48–50.

———. (1991, September/October). "To Write Simply." *The Horn Book,* pp. 552–555.

Fox, R. (Ed.). (1994). *Images in Language, Media, and Mind.* Urbana, IL: National Council of Teachers of English.

Fractor, J. S., Woodruff, M. C., Martinez, M. G., and Teale, W. H. (1993). "Let's Not Miss Opportunities to Promote Voluntary Reading: Classroom Libraries in the Elementary School." *The Reading Teacher* 46(7), pp. 476–484.

Fredericks, A. (1991). *Social Studies Through Children's Literature.* Englewood, CO: Teachers Ideas Press.

Freedman, R. (1988). Newbery Acceptance Speech. *Journal of Youth Services in Libraries,* 1(4), pp. 421–427.

Fritz, J. (1982). *Homesick: My Own Story.* New York: Putnam.

———. (1990). "The Teller and the Tale." In W. Zinsser (Ed.), *Worlds of Childhood: The Art and Craft of Writing for Children* (pp. 21–46). Boston: Houghton Mifflin.

Frye, N. (1964). *The Educated Imagination.* Bloomington, IN: Indiana University.

Frye, N., Baker, S., and Perkins, G. (1985). *The Harper Handbook of Literature.* New York: Harper & Row.

Galda, L. (1980). "Three Children Reading Stories: A Developmental Approach to Literature for Preadolescents." Unpublished doctoral dissertation. New York University.

———. (1988a). "A Response-Based View of Literature in the Classroom." *The New Advocate,* 1(2), pp. 92–102.

———. (1988b, Spring). "Readers, Texts and Contexts: A Response-Based View of Literature in the Classroom." *The New Advocate,* 1, pp. 92–102.

Galda, L., and Pillar, A. (1983). "For Dreamers, Wishers, and Magic Bean Buyers Only: Encouraging Children's Responses to Literature." In N. Roser and M. Frith (Eds.), *Children's Choices: Teaching with Books Children Like* (pp. 39–47). Newark, DE: International Reading Association.

Gallo, D. R. (1977). "Teaching Writing: Advice from the Professionals." *Connecticut English Journal,* 8(3), pp. 45–50.

Gardner, H. (1993). *Multiple Intelligences: The Theory in Practice.* New York: HarperCollins.

Gast, D. K. (1970). "The Dawning of the Age of Aquarius for Multiethnic Children's Literature." *Elementary English,* 47, pp. 661–665.

Giblin, J. (1990). *Writing Books for Young People.* Boston: The Writer.

Giblin, J. C. (1987). "A Publisher's Perspective." *The Horn Book,* 63(1), pp. 104–107.

Gillespie, J. T. (1991). *Best Books for Junior High Readers.* New Providence, NJ: R. R. Bowker.

Glazer, J. I. (1985). "Profile: Lilian Moore." *Language Arts,* 63(6), pp. 647–652.

———. (1991). *Literature for Young Children* (3d ed.). New York: Merrill.

Golden, J. M. (1984, March). "Children's Concept of Story in Reading and Writing." *The Reading Teacher,* 37, pp. 578–584.

Goldstone, B. (1989). "Visual Interpretation of Children's Books. *The Reading Teacher* 42(8), 592–595.

Goodenough, W. (1971). *Cultural Languages and Society.* Reading, MA: Addison-Wesley.

Goodman, K. (1988). "Look What They've Done to Judy Blume! The Basalization of Children's Literature." *The New Advocate,* 1(1), pp. 29–41.

Goodman, Y. (1986). "Children Coming to Know Literacy." In W. H. Teale and E. Sulzby (Eds.), *Emergent Literacy: Writing and Reading* (pp. 1–14). Norwood, NJ: Ablex.

Gordon, C. (1957). *How to Read a Novel.* New York: Viking.

Graves, D. (1983). *Writing Teachers and Children at Work.* Exeter, NH: Heinemann.

Graves, S. B. (1987, Fall). "Developmentally Appropriate Educational Experiences for Preschoolers." *Reading Horizons,* 24, pp. 206–208.

Greene, E. (1991). *Books Babies and Libraries.* Chicago: American Library Association.

Greene, M. (1992). "Texts and Margins." In Merryl Goldberg and Ann Phillips (Eds.), *Arts as Education.* Cambridge, MA: Harvard Educational Review. Reprint Series No. 24., 1–18.

Greenlaw, M. J. (1983). "Reading Interest Research and Children's Choices." In N. Roser and M. Frith (Eds.), *Children's Choices: Teaching with Books Children Like.* Newark, DE: International Reading Association.

Greenlaw, M. J., and Wielan, O. P. (1979). "Reading Interests Revisited." *Language Arts,* 56, pp. 432–434.

Gregory, L. B. (1987). *Pass the Poetry Please.* New York: Harper & Row.

Gunn, J. (1975). *Alternate Worlds: The Illustrated History of Science Fiction.* Englewood Cliffs, NJ: Prentice-Hall, A. and W. Visual Library.

Guthrie, J. H. (1981, May). "Reading Interests." *Reading Teacher,* 34, pp. 984–986.

Hamilton, V. (1992). "Planting Seeds." *The Horn Book Magazine* 68(6), 674–680.

———. (1981, December). "Ah, Sweet Rememory!" *The Horn Book,* 57(8), pp. 638.

———. (1991, May). "The House of Dies Drear." *Book Links,* pp. 56.

Hammond, D. (1991). "Prediction Chart." In J. Macon, D. Bewell, and M. Vogt (Eds.), *Responses to Literature.* Newark, DE: International Reading Association.

Hancock, Jolie. (1991). *Teaching with Picture Books.* Portsmouth, NH: Heinemann.

Hancock, J., and Hill, S. (1988). *Literature-based Reading Programs at Work.* Portsmouth, NH: Heinemann.

Handy, A. E. (1991, May/June). "An Interview with Gary Paulsen." *The Book Report,* pp. 111–114.

Hanjian, L. (1985). "Are the Interests of Third-Grade Students the Same as the Topics Found in Their Classroom Basal Readers?" Master's thesis, ED 255 890. Kean College of New Jersey.

Hansen, J. (1991, Spring). "I Wonder What Kind of Person He'll Be." *The New Advocate,* pp. 89–100.

Harding, D. W. (1963). "Response to Literature: The Report of the Study Group." In J. Squire (Ed.), *Response to Literature* (pp. 11–30). Champaign, IL: National Council of Teachers of English.

———. (1977). "The Author as Creator of Social Relation." In M. Meek, A. Warlow, and G. Barton (Eds.), *The Cool Web* (pp. 135–141). London: Bodley Head.

Hardy, B. (1977). "Narrative as a Primary Act of Mind." In M. Meek, A. Warlow, and G. Barton (Eds.), *The Cool Web: The Pattern of Children's Reading* (pp. 12–23). London: Bodley Head.

Harms, J. M. (1972). "Children's Responses to Fantasy in Relation to Their Stages of Intellectual Development." Unpublished doctoral dissertation. Ohio State University.

Harris, V. J. (1990). "African American Children's Literature: The First One Hundred Years." *Journal of Negro Education,* 59, pp. 540–555.

———. (1992). *Teaching Multicultural Literature in Grades K–8.* Norwood, MA: Christopher Gordon.

Harste, J. (1993, April). "Inquiry-Based Instruction." *Primary Voices K–6,* pp. 2–5.

Harste, J. C., Burke, C. A., and Woodward, B. (1982). "Children's Language and World: Initial Encounters with Print." In J. A. Langer and M. T. Smith-Burke (Eds.), *Reader Meets Author/Bridging the Gap: A Psycholinguistic and Sociolinguistic Perspective.* Newark, DE: International Reading Association, 105–131.

Harste, J., Woodward, V., and Burke, C. (1984). *Language Stories and Literacy Lessons.* Portsmouth, NH: Heinemann.

Hartman, D. K. (1992). "Eight Readers Reading: The Intertextual Links of Able Readers Using Multiple Passages." *Reading Research Quarterly,* pp. 122–123.

Hawkins, S. (1984). "Reading Interests of Gifted Children." *Reading Horizons,* 24(1), pp. 18–22.

Haynes, C. (1988). "Explanatory Power of Content for Identifying Children's Literature Preferences." *Dissertation Abstracts International,* 49–12A, p. 3617. University Microfilms No. DEW8900468.

Hazen, B. (1979). *Tight Times.* Illustrated by Trina Schart Hyman. New York: Viking.

Healy, J. M. (1991). *Endangered Minds.* New York: Simon & Schuster.

Hearne, B. (1990). *Choosing Books for Children: A Commonsense Approach.* New York: Delacorte.

Heath, S. B. (1982). "What No Bedtime Story Means: Narrative Skills at Home and School." *Language in Society,* 11(1), pp. 49–76.

———. (1983). *Ways with Words: Language, Life and Work in Communities and Classrooms.* Cambridge, England: Cambridge University.

Heathcote, D. (1983, September). "Learning, Knowing, and Languaging in Drama: An Interview with Dorothy Heathcote." *Language Arts,* 60, pp. 695–701.

Hennings, D. (1994). *Language Arts.* Boston: Houghton Mifflin.

Hentoff, N. (1969). "Among the Wild Things." In G. T. Stubbs and L. F. Ashley (Eds.), *Only Connect* (pp. 207–241). New York: Oxford University.

Hepler, S. (1991). "Talking Our Way to Literacy in the Classroom Community." *The New Advocate,* 4(3), pp. 179–192.

Hepler, S., and Hickman, J. (1982). "The Book Was Okay. I Love You." *Social Aspects of Responses to Literature. Theory into Practice,* 21, pp. 278–283.

Herman, G. (1980). "Footprints on the Sands of Time: Biography for Children." *Children's Literature in Education,* 9(2), pp. 85–94.

Hickman, J. (1986). "Children's Response to Literature." *Language Arts,* 63(2), pp. 122–125.

Hickman, J., and Cullinan B. (1989). "A Point of View on Literature and Learning." In J. Hickman and B. Cullinan (Eds.), *Children's Literature in the Classroom: Weaving Charlotte's Web* (pp. 47–55). Needham Heights, MA: Christopher-Gordon.

Hiebert, E. H. (1980). "The Relationship of Logical Reasoning Ability, Oral Language Comprehension, and Home Experiences to Preschool Children's Print Awareness." *Journal of Reading Behavior,* 12(4), pp. 313–324.

———. (1981). "Developmental Patterns and Interrelationships of Preschool Children's Print Awareness." *Reading Research Quarterly,* 16, pp. 236–260.

———. (1988). "The Role of Literacy Experiences in Early Childhood Programs." *The Elementary School Journal,* pp. 161–171.

Hiebert, E., Mervar, K. and Person, D. (1990). "Children's Selection of Trade Books in Libraries and Classrooms." *Language Arts,* 67(7), pp. 758–763.

Hill, M. (1989). *Home—Where Reading and Writing Begin.* Portsmouth, NH: Heinemann.

Hill, S. (1986). "What Are Children Reading?" *Australian Journal of Reading,* 7(4), pp. 196–198.

Hill, S., and Hancock, J. (1994). *Reading and Writing Communities: Co-operative Literacy Learning in the Classroom.* Portsmouth, NH: Heinemann.

Hillerich, R. (1987). "Those Content Areas." *Teaching K–8,* 17, pp. 31–33.

Hoffman, J. (1992, February). "Critical Reading/ Thinking Across the Curriculum: Using I–Charts to Support Learning." *Language Arts,* 69, pp. 121–127.

Holdaway, D. (1979). *The Foundations of Literacy.* Exeter, NH: Heinemann.

Holland, K., Hungerford, R., and Ernst, S. (1993). *Journeying: Children Responding to Literature.* Portsmouth, NH: Heinemann.

Holland, N. (1975). *Five Readers Reading.* New Haven, CT: Yale University.

Holman, C. H., and Harmon, W. (1986). *A Handbook to Literature* (4th ed.). New York: Macmillan.

Holmes, B. C., and Ammon, R. I. (1985). "Teaching Content with Trade Books." *Childhood Education,* 61(5), pp. 166–170.

Hopkins, L. B. (1986, September). "Profile in Memoriam: E. B. White." *Language Arts,* 63, pp. 491–494.

———. (1987). *Pass the Poetry Please!* New York: Harper.

———. (1992). *Let Them Be Themselves* (3d ed.). New York: Harper Trophy.

Huck, C. (1979). "No Wider Than the Heart Is Wide." In J. Shapiro (Ed.), *Using Literature and Poetry Effectively* (pp. 29–36). Newark, DE.: International Reading Association.

Huck, C., Hepler, S. and Hickman, J. (1987). *Children's Literature in the Elementary School* (4th ed.). New York: Holt, Rinehart and Winston.

———. Huck, C., Hepler, S., and Hickman, J. (1993). *Children's Literature in the Elementary School* (5th ed.). Dubuque, IA: William C. Brown.

Hughes, S. (1993, September). "The Impact of Whole Language on Four Elementary School Libraries." *Language Arts,* pp. 521–530.

Hunter, M. (1975). *Talent Is Not Enough.* New York: Harper & Row.

Huus, H. (1964). "Interpreting Research in Children's Literature." In M. Dawson (Ed.), *Children's Books and Reading* (pp. 31–35). Urbana, IL: National Council of Teachers of English.

Hymes, J. L. (1987, January). "Public School for 4-Year-Olds." *Young Children,* 42, pp. 51–52.

Ingham, R. (1980). "The Poetry Preferences of Fourth and Fifth-Grade Students in a Suburban Setting in 1980." Unpublished doctoral dissertation. University of Houston.

Iser, W. (1978). *The Act of Reading: The Study of Aesthetic Response*. Baltimore: Johns Hopkins University.

Jacobs, L. (1955). "Children's Experiences in Literature." In V. Hewitt and L. B. Jacobs (Eds.), *Children and the Language Arts* (pp. 193–217). Englewood Cliffs, NJ: Prentice-Hall.

Jacque, D. (1993). "The Judge Comes to Kindergarten." In K. Holland, R. Hungerford, and S. Ernst (Eds.), *Journeying: Children Responding to Literature* (pp. 43–53). Portsmouth, NH: Heinemann.

Jaggar, A. M. (1985). "On Observing the Language Learner: Introduction and Overview." In A. M. Jaggar and M. T. Smith-Burke (Eds.), *Observing the Language Learner* (pp. 1–7). Newark, DE: International Reading Association.

Jalongo, M. R. (1988). *Young Children and Picture Books*. Washington D.C.: National Association for the Education of Young Children.

Janezcko, P. (1990). *The Place My Words Are Looking For*. New York: Bradbury.

Johns, J. L. (1975). "Reading Preferences of Urban Students in Grades Four Through Six." *Journal of Educational Research*, 68(8), pp. 306–309.

Jones, L. (1986, February). "Profile: Elaine Konigsburg." *Language Arts*, 63, pp. 177–184.

Jones, M. G. (1983). "The Reading Attitudes and Interests of Fifth Graders." Master's thesis, ED 228–626. Kean College of New Jersey.

Kalkoff, A. (1973). "Innocent Children or Innocent Librarians." In A. Kalkoff (Ed.), *Issues in Children's Book Selection* (pp. 11–19). New York: Bowker.

Kantor, R., Anderson, T., and Armbruster, B. (1983). "How Inconsiderate Are Children's Textbooks?" *Journal of Curriculum Studies*, 15, pp. 61–72.

Kellogg, S. (1990). *Author Brochure*. New York: Dial.

Kelly, P. R. (1990). "Guiding Young Students' Responses to Literature." *Reading Teacher's Journal*, 43, pp. 464–470.

Kennedy, D., and Spangler, S. S. (1986, December). "Story Structure 3: The How or Why Story." *The Reading Teacher*, p. 365.

———. (1986, October). "Helping Your Students Write Stories." *The Reading Teacher*, pp. 118–119.

———. (1987, February). "Story Structure 5: The Fable." *The Reading Teacher*, p. 575.

———. (1987, January). "Story Structure 4: The Accumulative Story." *The Reading Teacher*, p. 477.

———. (1987, May). "Story Structure 6: The Journey Story." *The Reading Teacher*, p. 923.

Kennemer, P. K. (1993). *Using Literature to Teach Middle Grades About War*. Phoenix: Oryx.

Kiefer, B. (1983). "The Responses of Children in a Combination First/Second Grade Classroom to Picture Books in a Variety of Artistic Styles." *Journal of Research and Development in Education*, 16, pp. 14–20.

———. (1984). "Thinking Language and Reading: Children's Responses to Picture Books." Paper presented at the International Reading Association, Atlanta [ED 253 869].

———. (1986). "The Child and the Picture Book: Creating Live Circuits." *Children's Literature Association Quarterly*, 11, pp. 63–68.

———. (1988, March). "Picture Books as Contexts for Literacy, Aesthetic, and Real-World Understandings." *Language Arts*, 65(3), pp. 272–278.

———. (1995). *The Potential of Picturebooks*. Englewood Cliffs, NJ: Merrill.

Kimeldorf, M. (1994). *A Teacher's Guide to Creating Portfolios*. Minneapolis, MN: Free Spirit.

King, E. (1967). "Critical Appraisal of Research on Children's Interests, Preferences, and Habits." *Canadian Education and Research Digest*, 7, pp. 312–326.

Kingsbury, M. (1984). "Perspectives on Criticism." *The Horn Book*, 60(10), pp. 17–23.

Knapp, M., and Knapp, H. (1976). *One Potato, Two Potato: The Secret Education of American Children*. New York: Norton.

Krementz, J. (1991). "Listening to Children." In W. Zinsser (Ed.), *The Art and Craft of Writing for Children* (pp. 71–96). Boston: Houghton Mifflin.

Kristeva, J. (1980). *Desire in Language: A Semiotic Approach to Literature and Art*. (T. Gora, A. Jardine, and L. S. Roudiez, Trans.) New York: Columbia University.

Kropp, J. J., and Halverson. C. (1983). "Preschool Children's Preferences and Recall for Stereotyped Versus Non-Stereotyped Stories." *Sex Roles*, 9(2), pp. 261–272.

Kulleseid, E. R., and Strickland. D. S. (1989). *Literature, Literacy and Learning: Classroom Teachers, Library Media Specialists, and the Literature-Based Curriculum*. Chicago: American Library Association.

Kuskin, K. (1975). *Near the Window Tree*. New York: Harper.

Lacey, L. E. (1986). *Art and Design in Children's Picture Books.* Chicago: American Library Association.

Lacey, L. (1980). "A Newbery Honor Book Collection for Elementary Readers." *Top of the News,* 37(3), pp. 297–301.

Lamme, L. "Exploring the World of Music Through Picture Books." *Reading Teacher,* 44(4), pp. 294–300.

Lamme, L. L., Cox, V., Matanzo, J., and Olson, M. (1980). *Raising Readers: A Guide to Sharing Literature with Young Children.* New York: Walker.

Lanes, S. G. (1987). *The Art of Maurice Sendak.* New York: Abradale Press (Harry N. Abrams.)

Langer, J. (1992a). "A New Look at Literature Instruction." *ERIC Digest.* Bloomington, IN: Indiana University Clearinghouse on Reading and Communication Skills.

———. (1992b). "Rethinking Literature Instruction." In J. Langer (Ed.), *Literature Instruction: A Focus on Student Response* (pp. 35–53). Urbana, IL: National Council of Teachers of English.

Langer, J. A. (1995, Spring). "Literature and Learning to Think." *Journal of Curriculum and Supervision,* 10(3), pp. 207–226.

Langer, J., and Applebee, A. (1987). *How Writing Shapes Thinking.* Urbana, IL: National Council of Teachers of English.

Langton, J. (1977). "The Weak Place in the Cloth: A Study of Fantasy for Children." In P. Heins (Ed.), *Crosscurrents of Criticism: Hornbook Essays 1968–1977* (pp. 143–150). Boston: The Horn Book.

Largent, M. (1986). "Response to Literature: Moving Towards an Aesthetic Transaction." Unpublished manuscript. Berkeley: University of California.

Larrick, N. (1965). "The All-White World of Children's Books." *Saturday Review,* pp. 63–65.

———. (1991a, Spring). "Give Us Books!…But Also …Give Us Wings!" *The New Advocate,* pp. 77–84.

———. (1991b). *Let's Do a Poem!* New York: Delacorte.

Latrobe, K. H. (1994). *Exploring the Great Lakes States Through Literature.* Phoenix: Oryx.

Laughlin, M. K., and C. L. Swisher. (1990). *Literature Based Reading.* Phoenix: Oryx.

Laurence, F. (1956). "Facts About the Newbery Books." *Library Journal,* 72, pp. 942–943.

Leavitt, J. and Sohn, D. (1964). *Stop, Look, and Write!* New York: Bantam.

Lees, S. (1987). "Feet on the Ground: The Problem Novel." In M. Saxby and G. Winch (Eds.), *Give Them Wings: The Experience of Children's Literature* (pp. 000–000). South Melbourne, Australia: Macmillan of Australia

Le Guin, U. K. (1979). National Book Award Acceptance Speech. In S. Wood (Ed.), *The Language of the Night: Essays on Fantasy and Science Fiction* (pp. 60–61). New York: Putnam.

———. (1991, October). "Recreating Reality: Making It Happen for Your Reader." *The Writer,* 104(10), pp. 11–13.

Lehman, B. A. (1991). "Children's Choice and Critical Acclaim: A United Perspective for Children's Literature." *Reading Research and Instruction,* 30(3), pp. 1–20.

Lehr, S. (1991). "The Child's Developing Sense of Theme." New York: Teachers College.

Lester, J. (1969). *Black Folktales.* New York: Pantheon.

———. (1988, Summer). "The Storyteller's Voice: Reflections on the Rewriting of Uncle Remus." *The New Advocate,* 1, pp. 143–147.

Lewis, C. S. (1961). *An Experiment in Criticism.* Cambridge, England: Cambridge University.

———. (1980). "On Three Ways of Writing for Children." In S. Egoff, G. T. Stubbs, and L. F. Ashley (Eds.), *Only Connect.* New York: Oxford University.

Liebowicz, J. (1983). "Children's Reading Interests." *Reading Teacher,* 37(2), pp. 184–187.

Lima, C., and Lima, J. (1993). *A to Zoo Subject Access to Children's Picture Books.* New Providence, NJ: R. R. Bowker.

Livingston, M. C. (1976). "But Is It Poetry?" *The Horn Book,* 52(4), pp. 24–31.

———. (1981). "Nonsense Verse: The Complete Escape." In B. Hearne and M. Kaye (Eds.), *Celebrating Children's Books* (pp. 122–142). New York: Lothrop, Lee, & Shepard.

———. (1988). "Children's Literature Today: Perils and Prospects." *The New Advocate,* 1(1), pp. 18–28.

———. (1990). *Climb into the Bell Tower: Essays on Poetry.* New York: Harper & Row.

———. (1991). *Poem-Making: Ways to Begin Writing Poetry.* New York: HarperCollins.

Livingston, M. C. (Ed.). (1968). "Editor's note." In *A Tune Beyond Us.* New York: Harcourt, Brace and World.

Livo, N. J., and Rietz, S. A. (1986). *Storytelling Process and Practice.* Littleton, CO: Libraries Unlimited.

———. (1987). *Storytelling Activities*. Littleton, CO: Libraries Unlimited.

Lobel, A. (1981). "A Good Picture Book Should…" In B. Hearne and M. Kaye (Eds.), *Celebrating Children's Books* (pp. 73–80). New York: Lothrop, Lee & Shepard.

Lukens, R. (1986). *A Critical Handbook of Children's Literature* (3rd ed.). Glenview, IL: Scott, Foresman.

Lundsteen, S. W. (1986, October 3). "Developmental Aspects of Composition (or Think Young)." Address presented at the Meeting of Colorado Educators, Denver.

Macaulay, D. (1991, July/August). Caldecott Medal Acceptance. *The Horn Book*, pp. 410–421.

McAuley, K. and Wilson, R. H. (1987) *The United States Past to Present*. Lexington, MA: D. C. Heath.

MacCann, D., and Richard, O. (1991). "Picture Books About Blacks: An Interview with Opal Moore." *Wilson Library Bulletin*, 65, pp. 24–28.

Mackey, M. (1990). "Filling the Gaps: The Baby-sitters Club, The Series Book, and the Learning Reader." *Language Arts*, 67(5), pp. 484–489.

MacNeil, R. (1989). *Wordstruck*. New York: Viking.

Macon, J. M., Bewell, D., and Vogt, M. E. (1991). *Responses to Literature*. Newark, DE: International Reading Association.

Madigan, D. (1993). "The Politics of Multicultural Literature for Children and Adolescents: Combining Perspectives and Conversations." *Language Arts*, 70(3), pp. 168–176.

Mandler, J., and Johnson, N. (1977). "Remembrance of Things Past: Story Structure and Recall." *Cognitive Psychology*, 9, pp. 111–151.

Manna, A. L. (1984). "Making Language Come Alive Through Reading Plays." *The Reading Teacher*, 37, pp. 713–717.

Mansfield, R. S., and Busse, T. V. (1981). *The Psychology of Creativity and Discovery*. Chicago: Nelson-Hall.

Marantz, K. (1978). "On the Mysteries of Reading and Art: The Picturebook as Art Object." *Reading, the Arts and the Creation of Meaning*. Reston, VA: NAEA.

Martinez, M., and Nash, M. F. (1991, February). "Bookalogues: Talking About Children's Books." *Language Arts*, 68, pp. 140–147.

Martinez, M. G., and Roser, N. L. (1991). "Children's Responses to Literature." In J. Flood, J. M. Jensen, D. Lapp, and J. R. Squire (Eds.). *Handbook of Research on Teaching the English Language Arts*. New York: Macmillan.

Mason, J. (1984). "Early Reading from a Developmental Perspective." In P. D. Pearson (Ed.), *Handbook of Reading Research* (pp. 346–405). New York: Longman.

McCaslin, N. (1990). *Creative Drama in the Classroom* (5th ed.). New York: Longman.

McCracken, R., and McCracken. M. (1983). "Chants, Charts and 'Chievement." In J. Cowen (Ed.), *Teaching Through the Arts* (pp. 44–50). Newark, DE: International Reading Association.

McKay, M. A. (1971). "The Expressed Reading Interests of Intermediate Grade Students from Selected Schools in the Metropolitan Pittsburgh Area." Unpublished doctoral dissertation. University of Pittsburgh.

Meek, M. (1977). "Introduction." In M. Meek, A. Warlow, and G. Barton (Eds.), *The Cool Web: The Pattern of Children's Reading* (pp. 7–11). London: Bodley Head.

———. (1982). *Learning to Read*. Portsmouth, NH: Heinemann.

Meek, M., Warlow, A. and Barton, G. (1977). *The Cool Web: The Pattern of Children's Reading*. London: Bodley Head.

Meinback, A., Rothlein, L. and Fredericks, A. (1995). *The Complete Guide to Thematic Units: Creating the Integrated Curriculum*. Norwood, MA: Christopher-Gordon.

Meisel, S., and Glass, G. G. (1970). "Voluntary Reading Interests and the Interest Content of Basal Readers." *The Reading Teacher*, 23(7), pp. 655–659.

Meltzer, M. (1981). "Beyond the Span of a Single Life." In B. Hearne and M. Kaye (Eds.), *Celebrating Children's Books* (pp. 87–96). New York: Lothrop, Lee & Shepard.

———. (1987). "The Reader and the Writer." In C. Bauer (Ed.), *The Best of the Bulletin* (pp. 13–16). Urbana, IL: National Council of Teachers of English.

———. (1994). *Non-Fiction for the Classroom*. New York: Teacher's College.

Mendoza, A. (1985). "Reading to Children: Their Preferences." *The Reading Teacher*, 38, pp. 522–527.

Metzer, L. (1987). *Contemporary Authors: New Revision Series* (Vol. 12). Detroit, MI: Gale.

Meyer, B., and Rice, G. E. (1984). "The Structure of Text." In P. D. Pearson (Ed.), *Handbook of Reading Research* (pp. 319–352). New York: Longman.

Miccinati, J. (1985, November). "Using Prosodic Cues to Teach Oral Reading Fluency." *The Reading Teacher*, 39, pp. 206–212.

Miccinati, J., and Phelps, S. (1980, December). "Classroom Drama from Children's Reading: From the Page to the Stage." *The Reading Teacher*, 34, pp. 269–272.

Miel, A., and Kiesten, E. (1967). *The Shortchanged Children of Suburbia: What Schools Don't Teach About Human Differences and What Can Be Done About It.* New York: Institute of Human Relations Press, American Jewish Committee.

Mohr, C., Nixon, D., and Vickers, S. (1991). *Books That Heal: A Whole-Language Approach.* Englewood, CO: Teacher Ideas Press.

Moon, C., and Wells, C. G. (1979). "The Influence of the Home on Learning to Read." *Journal of Research in Reading*, 2, pp. 53–62.

Morner, K., and Rausch, R. (1991). *NTC's Dictionary of Literary Terms.* Lincolnwood, IL: National Textbook.

Morrow, L. M. (1979). *Super Tips for Story Telling.* New York: Scholastic.

———. (1982). "Relationships Between Literature Programs, Library Corner Designs and Children's Use of Literature." *Journal of Educational Research*, 75, pp. 339–344.

———. (1983). "Home and School Correlates of Early Interest in Literature." *Journal of Educational Research*, 76(4), pp. 221–230.

———. (1985). "Retelling Stories to Young Children: Effects of Story Structure and Traditional Questioning Strategies on Comprehension." *Journal of Reading Behavior*, 16, pp. 273–288.

———. (1987). "Promoting Voluntary Reading: The Effects of an Inner-City Program in Summer Day Care Centers." *The Reading Teacher*, 41, pp. 266–274.

———. (1988). "Young Children's Responses to One-to-One Story Readings in School Settings." *Reading Research Quarterly*, 23(1), pp. 89–107.

———. (1989, November 21). Research Report. Baltimore, MD. Annual Meeting of the National Council of Teachers of English.

Morrow, L. M., and Weinstein, C. S. (1982). "Increasing Children's Use of Literature Through a Literature Program on Children's Use of Library Centers." *Elementary School Journal*, 83, pp. 131–137.

———. (1986). "Encouraging Voluntary Reading: The Impact of a Literature Program on Children's Use of Library Centers." *Reading Research Quarterly*, 21, pp. 330–346.

Moss, J. (1977). "Learning to Write by Listening to Literature." *Language Arts*, 54(5), pp. 537–542.

Meyers, W. D. (1985). "The Black Experience in Children's Books: One Step Forward, Two Steps Back." In D. MacCann and G. Woodward (Eds.), *Black Americans in Books for Children: Readings in Racism.* Metuchen, NJ: Scarecrow Press, pp. 222–226.

———. (1992, January). "Walter Dean Myers' *Now Is Your Time!*" *Book Links*, pp. 22–23.

Myers-Reimer, K. (1992). Multiethnic Literature: Holding Fast to Dreams (Technical Report No. 551). Urbana: University of Illinois at Urbana-Champaign.

National Council of the Social Studies and National Center for History in the Schools. (1994). "Social Studies Standards." Los Angeles: University of California.

Nelson, O. (1989). "Storytelling: Language Experience for Meaning Making." *The Reading Teacher* 42(6), pp. 386–390.

Nodelman, P. (1984). "Some Presumptuous Generalizations About Fantasy." In P. Donley (Comp.), *The First Steps: Best of the Early CHLA Quarterly* (pp. 15–16). Purdue University, Children's Literature Association.

———. (1988). *Words About Pictures. The Narrative Art of Children's Picture Books.* Athens: University of Georgia.

Norton, D. (1991). *Through the Eyes of a Child.* Columbus, OH: Merrill.

———. (1995). *Through the Eyes of a Child.* Second edition. Columbus, OH: Merrill.

Ocvirk, O., Bone, C., Stinson, O., Wigg, R., and Wigg, P. (1991). *Art Fundamentals: Theory and Practice* (6th ed.). Dubuque, IA: Brown & Benchmark.

Ohanian, S. (1990). "How to Create a Generation of Aliterates." In K. Goodman, L. Bird, and Y. Goodman (Eds.), *Whole Language Catalog* (p. 76). New York: American School.

O'Neil, J. M. (1988). "Early Childhood Education: Advocates Square Off Over Goals." *Association for Supervision and Curriculum Development*, 30, pp. 1–6,

Opie, I., and Opie. P. (1974). *The Classic Fairy Tales.* London: Oxford University.

Oppenheim, J., Brenner, B., and Boegehold, B. (1985). *Choosing Books for Kids.* New York: Ballantine.

Pahl, M., and R. Monson. (1992, April). "In Search of Whole Language: Transforming Curriculum and Instruction." *Journal of Reading*, 35(7), pp. 518–524.

Painter, H. (1970). *Poetry for Children.* Newark, DE: International Reading Association.

Palmer, P. A., and Palmer, B. C. (1983). "Reading Interests of Middle-School Black and White Students." *Reading Improvement*, 20, pp. 151–155.

Papalia, D., and Olds, S. W. (1986). *A Child's World: Infancy Through Adolescence*. New York: McGraw-Hill.

Pappas, C. C., and Brown, E. (1987). "Learning to Read by Reading: Learning How to Extend the Functional Potential of Language." *Research in the Teaching of English*, 21, pp. 160–184.

Pappas, C. C., Kiefer, B., and Levstik, L. (1990). *An Integrated Language Perspective in the Elementary School*. White Plains, NY: Longman.

Parsons, L. (1992). *Poetry Themes and Activities*. Portsmouth, NH: Heinemann.

Paterson, K. (1980, December)." Creativity Limited." *The Writer*.

———. (1981a). *The Gates of Excellence: On Reading and Writing Books for Children*. New York: Dutton.

———. (1981b, August). Newbery Medal Acceptance. *The Horn Book*, pp. 545–551.

———. (1989). *The Spying Heart*. New York: Dutton.

———. (1992). "Tell All the Truth but Tell It Slant." In *The Zena Sutherland Lectures 1983–1992*. Ed. by Betsy Hearne, New York: Clarion Books. p. 44–70.

Pearson, D., and Johnson, D. (1977). *Teaching Reading Comprehension*. New York: Holt, Rinehart and Winston.

Peck, P. (1979). "Poetry: A Turn-on to Reading." In J. Shapiro (Ed.), *Using Literature and Poetry Affectively* (pp. 92–105). Newark, DE: International Reading Association.

———. (1983, Winter). "The Invention of Adolescence and Other Thoughts on Youth." *Top of the News*, 39(2), pp. 45–47.

Pellegrini, A., and Galda, L. (1982). "The Effects of Thematic Fantasy Play Training on the Development of Children's Story Comprehension." *American Educational Research Journal*, 19, pp. 443–452.

Pellowski, A. (1977). *The World of Storytelling*. New York: Bowker.

Perez-Stable, M. A., and Cordier, M. H. (1994). *Understanding American History Through Children's Literature*. Phoenix: Oryx.

Perkins, D. (1986). "Where Is Creativity?" In R. M. Caplan (Ed.), *Exploring the Concept of Mind* (pp. 101–119). Iowa City: University of Iowa Press.

Perrine, L. (1969). *Sound and Sense: An Introduction to Poetry* (3d ed.). New York: Harcourt Brace Jovanovich.

Peterson, B. (1991). "Selecting Books for Beginning Readers." In D. E. Deford, C. A. Lyons, and G. S. Pinnell (Eds.), *Bridges to Literacy: Learning from Reading Recovery*. Portsmouth, NH: Heinemann.

Peterson, L., and Solt, M. (1982). *Newbery and Caldecott Medal and Honor Books*. Boston: Hall.

Peterson, M. (1982). "Mexican-American Children: What Do They Prefer to Read?" *Reading World*, 22(2), pp. 129–131.

Peterson, R., and Peterson, M. (Eds.). *Grand Conversations: Literature Groups in Action*. Scholastic-Tab, Ltd.

Petrosky, A. (1977, Spring). "Genetic Epistemology and Psychoanalytic Ego Psychology: Clinical Support for the Study of Response to Literature." *Research in the Teaching of English*, 11, pp. 28–38.

Piaget, J. (1969). *Judgment and Reasoning in the Child*. M. Warden (Trans.). Totowa, NJ: Littlefield, Adams.

Piaget, J., and Inhelder, B. (1969). *The Psychology of the Child*. (H. Weaver, Trans.) New York: Basic.

Pieronek, F. T. (1980). "Do Basal Readers Reflect the Interests of Intermediate Students?" *Reading Teacher*, 33(4), pp. 408–412.

Piper, P. (1986). "Language Growth in the Multiethnic Classroom." *Language Arts*, 63, pp. 23–36.

Pitcher, E., and Prelinger, E. (1963). *Children Tell Stories: An Analysis of Fantasy*. New York: International Universities.

Poole, Roger. (1986). "The Books Teachers Use." *Children's Literature in Education*, 17(3), pp. 159–180.

Porter, J. D. (1971). *Black Child, White Child: The Development of Racial Attitudes*. Cambridge: Harvard University Press.

Prelutsky, J. (1991). "In Search of the Addle-Pated Paddlepuss." In W. Zinsser (Ed.), *The Art and Craft of Writing for Children* (pp. 99–120). Boston: Houghton Mifflin.

Presseisen, B. (1986). *Thinking Skills: Research and Practice*. Washington D.C.: National Education Association.

Probst, R. (1992). "Five Kinds of Literary Knowing." In J. Langer (Ed.), *Literature Instruction: A Focus on Student Response* (pp. 54–77). Urbana, IL: National Council of Teachers of English.

Purcell-Gates, V. (1988). "Lexical Syntactic Knowledge of Written Narrative Held by Well-Read-To Kindergartners and Second Graders." *Research in Teaching English*, 22, pp. 128–160.

———. (1991). "Ability of Well-Read-to Kindergartners to Decontextualize/Recontextalize Experience into a Written-Narrative Register." *Language and Education*, 5, pp. 177–188.

Purves, A., and Beach, R. (1972). *Literature and the Reader: Research in Response to Literature, Reading Interests, and the Teaching of Literature*. Urbana, IL: National Council of Teachers of English.

Purves, A., and Monson, D. (1984). *Experiencing Children's Literature*. Glenview, IL: Scott, Foresman.

Purves, A., and Rippere, A. (1968). *Elements of Writing about a Literary Work: A Study of Response to Literature*. Urbana, IL: National Council of Teachers of English.

Rachlin, J. (1988, August 1). "Timeless Tales = Big Sales." *U. S. News and World Report*, pp. 50–51.

Rampersad, A. (1983). "Biography, Autobiography, and Afro-American Culture." *The Yale Review*, 73(1), pp. 1–17.

Ramsey, P. (1987). *Teaching and Learning in a Diverse World: Multicultural Education for Young Children*. New York: Teachers College.

Rasinski, T. V., and Padak, N. (1990). "Multicultural Learning Through Children's Literature." *Language Arts*, 67, pp. 576–580.

Raymond, C. (1991). "Pioneering Research Challenges Accepted Notions Concerning the Cognitive Abilities of Infants." *Chronicle of Higher Education*, 37(10), pp. A5–A7.

Reed, A. (1994). *Reaching Adolescents: The Young Adult Book and the Schools*. New York: Merrill.

Reimer, K. (1992). "Multiethnic Literature: Holding Fast to Dreams." *Language Arts*, 69, 14–21.

Richards, L. (1902). *Tirra-Lirra, Rhymes Old and New*. Boston: Little, Brown.

Ripple, R. E., and Rockcastle, V. N. (Eds.). (1964). *Piaget Rediscovered: A Report of the Conference and Curriculum Studies*. Ithaca: Cornell University.

Robbins, P. (Ed.). (1982, November 22). "National Geographic Books for World Explorers." Presentation to Children's Literature Association, Washington, D.C.

Rochman, H. (1989, January/February). "Booktalking: Going Global." *The Horn Book*, 58(1), pp. 30–35.

———. (1989). "The Booklist Interview: Cynthia Voigt." *Booklist*, April 15, 1989. Chicago: American Library Association.

———. (1993). *Against Borders: Promoting Books for a Multicultural World*. Chicago: American Library Association.

Roney, R. C. (1989, March). "Back to the Basics with Storytelling." *The Reading Teacher*, 42, pp. 520–523.

Rosen, B. (1986). *And None of It Was Nonsense: The Power of Storytelling in School*. Portsmouth, NH: Heinemann.

Rosenblatt, L. M. (1983). *Literature As Exploration*. New York: Noble and Noble.

———. (1978). *The Reader, The Text, The Poem: The Transactional Theory of the Literary Work*. Edwardsville: Southern Illinois University.

———. (1982, Spring). "The Literary Transaction: Evocation and Response." *Theory into Practice*, XXI, pp. 268–277.

———. (1993). "The Literary Transaction: Evocation and Response." In K. Holland, R. Hungerford, and S. Ernst (Eds.). *Journeying: Children Responding to Literature* (pp. 6–24). Portsmouth, NH: Heinemann.

Rosenthal, A. (1973). "An Ecological Study of the Free Play in a Nursery School." Unpublished doctoral dissertation. Wayne State University, Detroit.

Roser, N. L. (1987, January). "Research Currents Relinking Literature and Literacy." *Language Arts*, 64, pp. 90–97.

Roser, N. L., and Hoffman, J. V., with Labbo, L. and Farest, C. (1991, January). "Language Charts: A Record of Story Time Talk." *Language Arts*, 69, pp. 44–52.

Roser, N., and Martinez, M. (1985). "Roles Adults Play in Preschool Responses to Literature." *Language Arts*, 62, pp. 485–490.

Ross, R. R. (1972). *Storyteller*. Columbus, OH: Merrill.

Rothman, R. (1990, February 21). "Experts Warn of Attempts to Censor Classic Texts." *Education Week*, p. 5.

———. (1991). *Invitations: Changing as Teachers and Learners*. Portsmouth, NH: Heinemann.

Rudman, M. K. (1976). *Children's Literature: An Issues Approach* (2d ed.). New York: Longman.

Rudman, M. K. (Ed.). (1993). *Children's Literature: Resource for the Classroom*. Norwood, MA: Christopher-Gordon.

Rumelhart, D. E. (1975). "Notes on a Schema for Stories." In D. G. Bobrow and A. M. Collins (Eds.), *Representation and Understanding* (pp. 573–603). New York: Academic Press.

———. (1981). "Schemata: The Building Blocks of Cognition." In *Comprehension and Teaching: Research Reviews*. Newark, DE: International Reading Association, pp. 3–26.

Rumelhart, D. E., and Ortony, A. (1977). "Representation of Knowledge." In R. C. Anderson, R. J. Spiro, and W. E. Montague (Eds.), *Schooling and the Acquisition of Knowledge* (pp. 99–135). Hillsdale, NJ: Erlbaum.

Russell, D. (1961). *Children Learn to Read*. Boston: Ginn.

———. (1994). *Children's Literature: A Short Introduction*. New York: Longman.

Russell, D. H. (1949). *48th Yearbook of the NSSE, Part II—Reading in the Elementary School*. Chicago: University of Chicago.

Russell, D. L. (1991). *Literature for Children: A Short Introduction*. White Plains, NY: Longman.

Sage, M. (1977). "A Study of the Handicapped in Children's Literature." In A. S. MacLeod (Ed.), *Children's Literature: Selected Essays and Bibliographies*. College Park: University of Maryland College of Library and Informational Service.

Saint-Exupéry, A. de. (1943). *The Little Prince*. New York: Harcourt Brace Jovanovich.

Saul, W. (1994). "Introduction." In *Nonfiction for the Classroom* (pp. vii–viii). New York: Teachers College.

Sawyer, R. (1962). *The Way of the Storyteller*. New York: Viking.

Saxby, M. (1987). "The Gift of Wings: The Value of Literature to Children." In M. Saxby and G. Winch (Eds.), *Give Them Wings: The Experience of Children's Literature* (pp. 3–19). South Melbourne, Australia: Macmillan.

Saxby, M., and Winch, G. (1987). *Give Them Wings: The Experience of Children's Literature*. South Melbourne, Australia: Macmillan.

Sayers, F. C. (1965). *Summoned by Books*. New York: Viking.

Schallert, D. L., and. Tierney, R. J. (1981). "The Nature of High Textbooks and Learners: Overview and Update." Paper presented at the annual meeting of the National Reading Conference, Dallas.

Schlager, N. (1978). "Predicting Children's Choices in Literature: A Developmental Approach." *Children's Literature in Education*, 9(3), pp. 136–142.

Schmitt, B., and Buckley, M. (1991). "Plot Relationships Chart." In J. Macon, D. Bewell, and M. Vogt (Eds.), *Responses to Literature*. Newark, DE: International Reading Association.

Scholes, R., and Kellog, R. (1966). *The Nature of Narrative*. New York: Oxford University Press.

Schon, I. (1988). *A Hispanic Heritage: A Guide to Juvenile Books About Hispanic People and Culture* (3d ed.). Metuchen, NJ: Scarecrow.

Schulte, E. S. (1969). "Independent Reading Interests of Children in Grades Four, Five, and Six." In J. A. Figurel (Ed.), *Reading and Realism* (pp. 728–732). Newark, DE: International Reading Association.

Schwarcz, J. H., and Schwarcz, C. (1991). *The Picture Book Comes of Age*. Chicago: American Library Association.

Schwartz, A. (1977). "Children, Humor, and Folklore." In P. Heins (Ed.), *Crosscurrents of Criticism: Horn Book Essays 1968–1977* (pp. 214–215). Boston: The Horn Book.

Scott-Mitchell, C. (1987). "Further Flight: The Picture Book." In M. Saxby and G. Winch (Eds.), *Give Them Wings: The Experience of Children's Literature* (pp. 61–75). South Melbourne, Australia: Macmillan.

Sebesta, S. (1990). "Visitors from My Boyhood." In W. Zinsser (Ed.), *The Art and Craft of Writing for Children* (pp. 47–70). Boston: Houghton Mifflin.

———. (1983). "Choosing Poetry." In N. Roser and M. Frith (Eds.), *Children's Choices: Teaching with Books Children Like* (pp. 56–70). Newark, DE: International Reading Association.

———. (1979). "What Do Young People Think About the Literature They Read?" *Reading Newsletter No. 8* (p. 3). Rockleigh, NJ: Allyn & Bacon.

Sebesta, S. L., and Iverson, W. J. (1975). *Literature for Thursday's Child*. Chicago: Science Research Associates.

Sendak, M. (1988). *Caldecott & Co.: Notes on Books and Pictures*. New York: Farrar, Straus & Giroux.

Service, P. (1985). Dust Jacket. *Winter of Magic's Return*. New York: Macmillan.

Shafer, P. J. (1976, May). "The Readability of the Newbery Medal Books." *Language Arts*, 53, pp. 557–559.

Shanahan, T. (1992). "Nine Good Reasons for Using Children's Literature Across the Curriculum." In T. Shanahan (Ed.), *Distant Shores: Teacher's Resource Package Level N* (pp. 19–22). New York: McGraw Hill School Division.

Shanahan, T., and Hogan, V. (1983). "Parent Reading Style and Print Awareness." In J. A. Niles and L. A. Harris (Eds.), *Searches for Meaning in Reading/Language Processing and Instruction* (pp. 212–217). Rochester, NY: National Reading Conference.

Sharp, S. (1992). "Why Didacticism Endures." *The Horn Book*, 68,(6), pp. 694–696.

Short, K. (1993). "Making Connections Across Literature and Life." In K. Holland, R. Hungerford, and S. Ernst (Eds.), *Journeying: Children Responding to Literature* (pp. 284–301). Portsmouth, NH: Heinemann.

Shulevitz, U. (1985). *Writing with Pictures: How to Write and Illustrate Children's Books.* New York: Watson-Guptill.

Shure, M. B. (1963). "Psychological Ecology of a Nursery School." *Child Development*, 34, pp. 979–992.

Sierra, J., and Kaminski, R. (1991). *The Preschooler and the Library.* Metuchen, NJ: Scarecrow.

Siks, G. B. (1983). *Drama with Children* (2d ed.). New York: Harper & Row.

Silvern, S. B. (1988). "Continuity/Discontinuity Between Home and Early Childhood Education Environments." *The Elementary School Journal*, 89, pp. 147–157.

Silvey, A. (1988). "The Goats." *The Horn Book*, 54(1), p. 23.

Simmons, M. (1980). "Intermediate-Grade Children's Preferences in Poetry." Unpublished doctoral dissertation. Birmingham: University of Alabama.

Sims, R. (1982). *Shadow and Substance: The Afro-American Experience in Contemporary Children's Literature.* Urbana, IL: National Council of Teachers of English.

Slaughter, J. P. (1993). *Beyond Storybooks: Young Children and the Shared Book Experience.* Newark, DE: International Reading Association.

Sloan, G. D. (1984). *The Child as Critic* (2d ed.). New York: Teachers College.

Smith, C. B. (1988). "Emergent Literacy—An Environmental Concept." *The Reading Teacher*, 42, p. 528.

Smith, D. B. (1990). "A Profile." In an unpaged author brochure from Viking Publishing Co., New York.

Smith, F. (1982). *Writing and the Writer.* New York: Holt, Rinehart and Winston.

———. (1985). *Reading Without Nonsense* (2d ed.). New York: Teachers College.

———. (1988). *Joining the Literacy Club: Further Essays into Education.* Portsmouth, NH: Heinemann.

Smith, G. (1987). "Inner Reality: The Nature of Fantasy." In M. Saxby and G. Winch (Eds.), *Give Them Wings: The Experience of Children's Literature* (pp. 259–276). South Melbourne, Australia: Macmillan.

Smith, L. H. (1991). *The Unreluctant Years.* New York: Viking.

Solsken, J. W. (1985). "Authors of Their Own Learning." *Language Arts*, 62, pp. 491–499.

Spangler, K. (1981). "Chicano and Anglo Children's Reactions to Anglo-Authored Children's Books."

Unpublished doctoral dissertation. University of Washington, Seattle.

Spinelli, J. (1991, July/August). Newbery Medal Acceptance. *The Horn Book*, 67(4), pp. 426–432.

Spiro, R. J. (1977). "Remembering Information from Text: The State of Schema Approach." In R. C. Anderson, R. J. Spiro, and W. E. Montague (Eds.), *School and the Acquisition of Knowledge* (pp. 137–165). Hillsdale, NJ: Erlbaum.

Stanchfield, J. M. (1962). "Boys' Reading Interests as Revealed Through Personal Conferences." *The Reading Teacher*, 16(2), pp. 41–44.

Stanchfield, J. M., and Fraim, S. (1979). "A Follow-Up Study on the Reading Interests of Boys." *The Reading Teacher*, 39(3), p. 326.

Stanley, D. (1988). "Picture Book History." *The New Advocate*, 1(1), pp. 209–220.

Steele, M. (1973). "Realism, Truth and Honesty". In V. Haviland (Ed.) *Children and Literature: News and Reviews.*

Steffel, N., and Zetzl, M. (1991, May). "Start Your Day with Kellogg's." *Book Links*, pp. 59–61.

Steffensen, M., Joag-Dev, C., and Anderson, R. C. (1979). "A Cross-Cultural Perspective on Reading Comprehension." *Reading Research Quarterly*, 15(1), pp. 1–29.

Stein, N. L., and Glenn, C. G. (1979). "An Analysis of Story Comprehension in Elementary School Children." In R. O. Freedle (Ed.), *New Directions in Discourse Processing* (pp. 53–101). Norwood, NJ: Ablex.

Stephens, J. W. (1981). *A Practical Guide in the Use and Implementation of Bibliotherapy.* Great Neck, NY: Todd and Honeywell.

Stewig, J. (1972, December). "Children's Preferences in Picture Book Illustration." *Educational Leadership*, 30, pp. 276–277.

———. (1988). *Children and Literature* (2d ed.). Boston: Houghton Mifflin.

———. (1989). "Book Illustration: Key to Visual and Oral Literacy." In J. Stewig and S. Sebesta (Eds.), *Using Literature in the Elementary Classroom.* Urbana, IL: National Council of Teachers of English.

———. (1992, Winter). "Reading Pictures, Reading Text." *The New Advocate*, 5(1), pp. 11–22.

Stodart, E. (1987). "Wings of Fact: Non-Fiction for Children." In G. Saxby and M. Winch (Eds.), *Give Them Wings: The Experience of Children's Literature* (pp. 247–257). South Melbourne, Australia: Macmillan.

Stoodt, B. (1988). *Teaching Language Arts.* New York: Harper & Row.

———. (1989). *Reading Instruction* (2d ed.). New York: Harper & Row.

———. (1993). "Children's Literature Awards." Unpublished paper. University of North Carolina, Greensboro.

———. (1995). "Preschool Children's Preferences for Picturebook Illustrators." Unpublished research. Northern Kentucky University, Highland Heights, KY.

———. (1992a). *Exploring Cultures Through Literature.* Greensboro, NC: Carson-Dellosa.

———. (1992b). "Multicultural Children's Literature." A paper presented at the World Congress on Reading, Maui, HI.

Stoodt, B., and Amspaugh, L. (1994, May). "Children's Response to Nonfiction." A paper presented to the Annual Meeting of The International Reading Association, Toronto, Canada.

Stotsky, S. (1984). "Research on Reading/Writing Relationships: A Synthesis and Suggested Directions." In J. Jensen (Ed.), *Composing and Comprehending* (pp. 7–22). Urbana, IL: ERIC Clearinghouse on Reading and Communication Skills and NCRE.

Strickland, D., and Morrow, L. (1990, March). "Family Literacy: Sharing Good Books." *The Reading Teacher,* 43(7), pp. 518–519.

Sulzby, E. (1985). "Children's Emergent Reading of Favorite Storybooks: A Developmental Study." *Reading Research Quarterly,* 20, pp. 458–481.

———. (1991). "The Development of the Young Child and the Emergence of Literacy." In *Handbook of Research on Teaching the English Language Arts.* James Flood, et al. (Eds.). New York: Macmillan.

Sulzby, E., and Teale, W. H. (1985). "Writing Development in Early Childhood." *Educational Horizons,* 64, pp. 8–12.

Sutcliff, R. (1973). "History Is People." In V. Haviland, *Children and Literature: Views and Reviews.* New York: T. H. Cromwell.

Sutherland, Z., and Arbuthnot, M. H. (1991). *Children and Books.* (8th ed.). Chicago: Scott Foresman.

Sutherland, Z., and Livingston, M. C. (1984). *The Scott/Foresman Anthology of Children's Literature.* Chicago: Scott Foresman.

Sutherland, Z., and Hearne, B. (1984). "In Search of the Perfect Picture Book Definition." In P. Barron and J. Burley (Eds.), *Jump Over the Moon: Selected Professional Readings.* New York: Holt, Rinehart and Winston.

Sutton, R. (1994). Editorial. In *The Bulletin of the Center for Children's Books* 47(1), p. 3.

Swanton, S. (1984, March). "Minds Alive! What and Why Gifted Students Read for Pleasure." *School Library Journal,* 30, pp. 99–102.

Swinger, A. K. (1987, November). "Profile: Mitsumasa Anno's Journey." *Language Arts,* 64, pp. 762–766.

Taxel, J. (1994). "Political Correctness, Cultural Politics and Writing for Young People." *The New Advocate,* 1(2), pp. 93–107.

Taylor, D. (1983). *Family Literacy: Young Children Learning to Read and Write.* Exeter, NH: Heinemann.

Teale, W. (1981). "Parents Reading to Their Children: What We Know and Need to Know." *Language Arts,* 58, pp. 902–911.

Teale, W., and Martinez, G. (1987). "Connecting Writing: Fostering Emergent Literacy in Kindergarten Children." Technical Report No. 412. San Antonio TX: University of Texas at San Antonio.

Teale, W. H., and Sulzby, E. (1983). "Emergent Literacy: A Perspective for Examining How Young Children Become Writers and Readers." In W. Teale and E. Sulzby (Eds.), *Emergent Literacy: Writing and Reading* Norwood, NJ: Ablex.

———. (1989). "Emergent Literacy: New Perspectives." In D. Strickland and L. Morrow (Eds.), *Emerging Literacy: Young Children Learn to Read and Write* Newark, DE: International Reading Association.

Terry, A. (1974). *Children's Poetry Preferences: A National Survey of Upper Elementary Grades.* Urbana, IL.: National Council of Teachers of English.

Thomas, J. A. (1983). "Nonfiction Illustration: Some Considerations." In J. May (Ed.), *Children and Their Literature: A Readings Book* (pp. 47–53). West Lafayette, IN: CHLA.

Thompson, S. (1951). *The Folktale.* New York: Holt, Rinehart and Winston.

Tobin, A. W. (1981). "A Multiple Discriminant Cross-Validation for the Factors Associated with the Development of Precocious Reading Achievement." Unpublished doctoral dissertation. Newark, DE: University of Delaware.

Toth, M. (1990). Character Map. In J. Macon, D. Bewell, and Mary Ellen Vogt (Eds.), *Responses to Literature K–8.* Newark, DE: International Reading Association.

Townsend, J. R. (1990). *Written for Children.* New York: HarperTrophy.

Travers, P. L. (1978, July 2). "I Never Wrote for Children." *New York Times Magazine.*

Trelease, J. (1989). *The New Read-Aloud Handbook.* New York: Penguin.

Tunnell, M., and Ammon, R. (Eds.). (1993). *The Story of Ourselves: Teaching History Through Children's Literature.* Portsmouth, NH: Heinemann.

Tway, E. (1993). "Dimensions of Multicultural Literature for Children." In M. K. Rudman (Ed.), *Children's Literature: Resource for the Classroom* (pp. 109–138). Norwood, MA: Christopher-Gordon.

Van Vliet, L. (1992). *Approaches to Literature Through Genre.* Phoenix: Oryx.

Veltze, L. (Ed.). (1994). *Exploring the Southeast States Through Literature.* Phoenix: Oryx.

Viguers, R. H. (1964). *Part of the Pattern.* Boston: Little, Brown.

Viorst, J. (1990). *Author Information Packet.* New York: Atheneum.

Vigil, A. (1994). *The Corn Woman.* Eglewood, CO: Libraries Unlimited.

Voss, M. (1988, October). "Make Way for Applesauce: The Literate World of a ThreeYear-Old." *Language Arts,* 65, pp. 272–278.

Vygotsky, L. (1978). *Mind in Society.* Cambridge, MA: Harvard University Press.

Waldo, B. (1991). "Story Pyramid." In J. Macon, D. Bewell, and M. Vogt, (Eds.). *Responses to Literature.* Newark, DE: International Reading Association.

Walmsley, S. (1993). "Reflections on the State of Elementary Literature Instruction." *Language Arts,* 69, pp. 508–514.

Walmsley, S. A. (1994). *Children Exploring Their World: Theme Teaching in Elementary School.* Portsmouth, NH: Heinemann.

Walmsley, S. A., and Walp, T. P. (1989). *Teaching Literature in Elementary School.* Albany: SUNY Center for the Learning and Teaching of Literature.

Walsh, J. P. (1979). *The Lords of Time.* Whittall Lecture, Library of Congress, published in the *Library of Congress Quarterly.*

Walt, L. S., and Street, T. P. (1994). *Developing Learning Skills Through Children's Literature.* Phoenix: Oryx.

Walter, V. A. (1993). *War and Peace: Literature for Young Children.* Phoenix: Oryx.

Watson, M. (1985). "Differences in Book Choices for Reading Pleasure Between Second Through Fifth Grade Boys and Girls." In ERIC Document No. Ed 259304.

Weaver, C. (1994). *Reading Process and Practice.* Portsmouth, NH: Heinemann.

Weinberg, M. (1974). "A Historical Framework for Multicultural Education." In D. C. Cross, G. C. Baker, and L. J. Stiles (Eds.), *Teaching in a Multicultural Society.* New York: Free Press.

Weiss, M. J. (1979). *From Writers to Students: The Pleasures and Pains of Writing.* Newark, DE: International Reading Association.

———. (1989). "International Reading Association Stands Out Against Censorship." *Reading Today,* 6(4), p. 6.

Wells, G. (1986). *The Meaning Makers: Children Learning Language and Using Language to Learn.* Portsmouth, NH: Heinemann.

Weston, L. (1993). "The Evolution of Response Through Discussion, Drama, Writing, and Art in a Fourth Grade." In K. Holland, R. Hungerford, and S. Ernst (Eds.), *Journeying: Children Responding to Literature* (pp. 137–150). Portsmouth, NH: Heinemann.

Whalen-Levitt, P. (1984). "Making Picture Books Real: Reflections on a Child's-Eye View." In P. Dooley (Comp.), *The First Steps: Best of the Early CHLA Quarterly.* Lafayette, IN: Purdue University, Children's Literature Association.

White, B. (1988). *Educating the Infant and Toddler.* Lexington, MA: Lexington Books.

White, E. B. (1970, September). Laura Ingalls Wilder Award Acceptance Speech. *The Horn Book,* 56(2), pp. 540–547.

———. (1976). *Letters of E. B. White.* New York: Harper & Row.

Wildberger, M. E. (1993). *Approaches to Literature Through Authors.* Phoenix: Oryx.

Wilde, S. (1989, Winter). "The Power of Literature: Notes from a Survivor." *The New Advocate,* 2, pp. 49–52.

Williams, C. (1989, November)." A Study of the Reading Interests, Habits, and Attitudes of Third, Fourth, and Fifth Graders: A Class Action Research Project." Paper presented at the Annual Meeting of the Mid-South Educational Research Association, Little Rock, AR.

Wilms, D. (1978, September). "An Evaluation of Biography." *Booklist,* 75(2), pp. 218–220.

———. (1985, October 2) "Cracker Jackson." *Booklist*, 3, pp. 275–280).

Wilson, L., Malmgren, D., Ramage, S., and Schulz, L. (1993). *An Integrated Approach to Learning*. Portsmouth, NH: Heinemann.

Wilson, P., and Abrahamson, R. (1988). "What Children's Literature Classics Do Children Really Enjoy?" *The Reading Teacher*, 41(5), pp. 406–411.

Wilt, M. E. (1967, February). "Grouping for Reading or for Reading Instruction." *Educational Leadership*, 24, p. 445.

Witty, P. (1960). "Studies of Children's Interests: A Brief Summary." *Elementary English*, 37, pp. 469–475.

Witucke, V. (1981, Winter). "Trends in Juvenile Biography." *Top of the News*, Vol. 37, Winter 1981, p. 163.

Wolfson, B. J. (1960). "What Do Children Say Their Reading Interests Are?" *The Reading Teacher*, 14, pp. 81–82.

Wolfson, B., Manning, G., and Manning, M. (1984). "Revisiting What Children Say Their Reading Interests Are." *The Reading World*, 24(2), pp. 4–11.

Wood, A. (1990). "Author Discussion." During a question and answer period in Greensboro, NC.

Wood, Don, and Wood, Audrey. (1986). "The Artist at Work: Where Ideas Come From." *The Horn Book*, 60(5), Sept.–Oct. 1986, pp. 556–565.

Wurzel, J. S. (1988). "Multiculturalism and Multicultural Education." In J. S. Wurzel (Ed.), *Toward Multiculturalism: A Reader in Multicultural Education* (pp. 1–10). Yarmouth, ME: Intercultural.

Wyndham, L., and Madison, A. (1988). *Writing for Children and Teenagers*. Cincinnati, OH: Writer's Digest Books.

Yaden, D., Smolkin, L., and Conlon, A. (1989). "Preschoolers' Questions About Pictures, Print Conventions, and Story Text During Reading Aloud at Home." *Reading Research Quarterly*, XXIV(2), pp. 188–214.

Yokota, J. (1993). "Issues in Selecting Multicultural Children's Literature." *Language Arts*, 70(3), pp. 156–167.

Yolen, J. (1973). *Writing Books for Children*. Boston: The Writer.

———. (1981). *Touch Magic*. New York: Philomel.

Young, E. (1990). Caldecott Acceptance Speech. *The Horn Book*, 66(4), pp. 452–456.

Zarnowski, M. (1990). *Learning About Biographies*. Urbana, IL: National Council of Teachers of English.

Zimet, S. (1966). "Children's Interests and Story Preferences." *Elementary School Journal*, 67(3), pp. 123–130.

Zinsser, W. (Ed.). (1990). "Introduction." In *The Art and Craft of Writing for Children* (pp. 1–21). Boston: Houghton Mifflin.

# Credits

*117* Jacket illustration from *The Tale of the Mandarin Ducks* by Katherine Paterson, illustrated by Leo and Diane Dillon. By permission of Penguin USA and Victor Gollancz Limited.

*118 and 119* Illustrations from *The Napping House* by Audrey Wood, illustrated by Don Wood. Text copyright © 1984 by Audrey Wood. Illustrations copyright © 1984 by Don Wood. By permission of Harcourt Brace & Co.

*120* Jacket illustration from *Owl Moon* by Jane Yolen, illustrated by John Schoenherr. Copyright © 1988. Used by permission of Philomel Books, a division of The Putnam Publishing Group.

*122* Jacket illustration from *The Happy Day* by Ruth Krauss, copyright © 1949. Copyright renewed 1977. Illustrations copyright © 1949 by Marc Simont. Copyrights © renewed 1977 by Marc Simont. Used by permission of HarperCollins Publishers, New York.

*123* Jacket front cover from *City Noise* by Karla Kuskin, illustrated by Renee Flower. Jacket art copyright © 1994 by Renee Flower. Used by permission of Harper-Collins Publishers, New York.

*124* Illustration from *One Frog Too Many* by Mercer and Marianna Mayer. Copyright © 1975 by Mercer and Marianna Meyer. A Pied Piper Book, a registered trademark of Dial Books for Young Readers, a division of Penguin Books USA. Used by permission.

*125* Cover illustration from *A Boy, A Dog and a Frog* by Mercer Mayer. Copyright © 1967 by Mercer Mayer. A Pied Piper Book, a registered trademark of Dial Books for Young Readers, a division of E. P. Dutton. Used by permission of Penguin USA.

*127* Interior illustration from *Little Red Riding Hood* by Trina Schart Hyman. Copyright © 1983 by Trina Schart Hyman. All rights reserved. Reprinted by permission of Holiday House, Inc.

*127* Interior illustration from *Red Riding Hood*, retold in verse by Beatrice Schenk de Regniers. Illustrations copyright © 1972 by Edward Gorey. Reprinted by permission of Simon & Schuster, New York.

*134* First interior illustration from *Chicken Little*, by Steven Kellogg. Copyright © 1985 by Steven Kellogg. By permission of Morrow Junior Books, a division of William Morrow & Co., Inc.

*144* "Where Have You Been, Dear?" from Karla Kuskin, *Dogs & Dragons Trees & Dreams: A Collection of Poems.* Copyright © 1980 by Karla Kuskin. Used by permission of HarperCollins, New York.

*145* Jacket illlustration of *Still as a Star* by Lee Bennett Hopkins, illustrated by Karen Milone. By permission of Little, Brown and Co.

*146* "Poem to Mud" from *Today Is Saturday by Zilpha Keatley Snyder;* illustrated by John Arms, and published by Atheneum, New York, 1969, is reproduced by permission of the author.

*147* "Galoshes" from *Stories to Begin On* by Rhoda W. Bacmeister. Copyright © 1940. Published by E. P. Dutton, New York. By permission of Penguin USA.

*148* "Bananas and Cream" is from *Far and Few* by David McCord. Copyright © 1961, 1962 by David McCord. By permission of Little, Brown and Co.

*149* "Eletelephony" is from *Tirra Libra* by Laura Richards. Copyright © 1930, 1932 by Laura E. Richards. Copyright © renewed 1960 by Hamilton Richards. By permission of Little, Brown and Co.

*150* "Dreams" appeared in a collection of poems by Langston Hughes, *The Dream Keeper and Other Poems.* Published by Alfred A. Knopf, 1932. Reprinted by permission of Harold Ober Associates and Alfred A. Knopf.

*150* "A Bug Sat in a Silver Flower" from Karla Kuskin, *Dogs & Dragons Trees & Dreams*, published in 1980. Used by permission of HarperCollins, New York.

*151* Jacket illustration from *There Was an Old Man* by Edward Lear. Illustrated by Michele Lemieux. Jacket copyright © 1994 by Michele Lemieux. By permission of Morrow Junior Books, a division of William Morrow & Co., Inc.

*153* Text only of "Brachiosaurus" from *Tyrannosaurus Was a Beast*, by Jack Prelutsky. Text copyright © 1988 by Jack Prelutsky. By permission of Greenwillow Books, a division of William Morrow & Co., Inc.

*153* "Dinosaur Dances" by Jane Yolen is reprinted by permission of Philomel Books, *Dinosaur Dances;* text copyright © 1990 by Jane Yolen. Reprinted also by permission of Curtis Brown Ltd.

*154* Jacket illustration from *Dinosaur Dances* by Jane Yolen, illustrated by Bruce Degen. Copyright © 1990 by Jane Yolen. Illustrations copyright © 1990 by Bruce Degen. By permission of G. P. Putnam, New York.

*155* Jacket illustration from *Poem Stew*, poems selected by William Cole, pictures by Karen Ann Weinhaus. Illustrations copyright © 1981 by Karen Weinhaus. Used by permission of HarperCollins Publishers, New York.

*156* Jacket illustration from *Animal, Vegetable, Mineral: Poems About Small Things*, selected by Myra Cohn Livingston. Jacket art by Vincent Nasta. Jacket copyright © 1994 by HarperCollins Publishers. Used by permission.

*158* Cover from *Tyrannosaurus Was a Beast* by Jack Prelutsky. Illustrated by Arnold Lobel. Ill. copyright © 1988, by Arnold Lobel. By permission of Greenwillow Books, a division of William Morrow & Co.,Inc.

*161* "Bedtime" is from *8 A.M. Shadows* by Patricia Hubbell. Copyright © 1965 by Patricia Hubbell. Copyright renewed 1993 by Patricia Hubbell. Reprinted by permission of Marian Reiner for the author.

*162* Jacket illustration from *Joyful Noise: Poems for Two Voices* by Paul Fleischman, illustrated by Eric Beddows. Jacket art copyright © 1988 by Eric Beddows. Used by permission of HarperCollins Publishers, New York.

*164* Illustration copyright © 1989 by Leonard Everett Fisher. All rights reserved. Reprinted from *Up in the Air* by Myra Cohn Livingston by permission of Holiday House, Inc.

*181* From *The Boy Who Dreamed of an Acorn* by Leigh Casler, illustrated by Shonto Begay. Jacket art copyright © 1994 by Shonto Begay. Reprinted by permission of The Putnam & Grosset Group.

*187* Cover of *The Fables of Aesop* retold by Frances Barnes-Murphy. Illustrated by Rowan Barnes-Murphy. Copyright © 1994 by Rowan Barnes-Murphy. By permission of Lothrop, Lee & Shepard Books, a division of William Morrow & Co., Inc.

*189* From *Martin's Mice* by Dick King-Smith, illustrated by Jez Alborough. Illustration copyright © 1988 by Jez Alborough. Reprinted by permission of Crown Publishers, Inc.

*190* Jacket illustration from *Charlotte's Web* by E. B. White Pictures by Garth Williams. Copyright © 1952 by E. B. White. Used by permission of Bantam Books, a division of Bantam Doubleday Dell Publishing Group, Inc.

# Subject Index

# Index of Authors, Book Titles, and Illustrators